Big Data Analytics with Applications in Insider Threat Detection

Big Data Analytics with Applications in Insider Threat Detection

Bhavani Thuraisingham
Mohammad Mehedy Masud
Pallabi Parveen
Latifur Khan

CRC Press
Taylor & Francis Group
Boca Raton London New York

CRC Press is an imprint of the
Taylor & Francis Group, an **informa** business
AN AUERBACH BOOK

CRC Press
Taylor & Francis Group
6000 Broken Sound Parkway NW, Suite 300
Boca Raton, FL 33487-2742

First issued in paperback 2020

© 2018 by Taylor & Francis Group, LLC
CRC Press is an imprint of Taylor & Francis Group, an Informa business

No claim to original U.S. Government works

ISBN-13: 978-1-4987-0547-9 (hbk)
ISBN-13: 978-0-367-65742-0 (pbk)

This book contains information obtained from authentic and highly regarded sources. Reasonable efforts have been made to publish reliable data and information, but the author and publisher cannot assume responsibility for the validity of all materials or the consequences of their use. The authors and publishers have attempted to trace the copyright holders of all material reproduced in this publication and apologize to copyright holders if permission to publish in this form has not been obtained. If any copyright material has not been acknowledged please write and let us know so we may rectify in any future reprint.

Except as permitted under U.S. Copyright Law, no part of this book may be reprinted, reproduced, transmitted, or utilized in any form by any electronic, mechanical, or other means, now known or hereafter invented, including photocopying, microfilming, and recording, or in any information storage or retrieval system, without written permission from the publishers.

For permission to photocopy or use material electronically from this work, please access www.copyright.com (http://www.copyright.com/) or contact the Copyright Clearance Center, Inc. (CCC), 222 Rosewood Drive, Danvers, MA 01923, 978-750-8400. CCC is a not-for-profit organization that provides licenses and registration for a variety of users. For organizations that have been granted a photocopy license by the CCC, a separate system of payment has been arranged.

Trademark Notice: Product or corporate names may be trademarks or registered trademarks, and are used only for identification and explanation without intent to infringe.

Library of Congress Cataloging-in-Publication Data

Names: Parveen, Pallabi, author.
Title: Big data analytics with applications in insider threat detection /
Pallabi Parveen, Bhavani Thuraisingham, Mohammad Mehedy Masud, Latifur Khan.
Description: Boca Raton : Taylor & Francis, CRC Press, 2017. | Includes bibliographical references.
Identifiers: LCCN 2017037808 | ISBN 9781498705479 (hb : alk. paper)
Subjects: LCSH: Computer security--Data processing. | Malware (Computer software) | Big data. | Computer crimes--Investigation. | Computer networks--Access control.
Classification: LCC QA76.9.A25 P384 2017 | DDC 005.8--dc23
LC record available at https://lccn.loc.gov/2017037808

Visit the Taylor & Francis Web site at
http://www.taylorandfrancis.com

and the CRC Press Web site at
http://www.crcpress.com

We dedicate this book to

Professor Elisa Bertino
Purdue University

Professor Hsinchun Chen
University of Arizona

Professor Jiawei Han
University of Illinois at Urbana-Champaign

And All Others

For Collaborating and Supporting Our Work in
Cyber Security, Security Informatics, and
Stream Data Analytics

Contents

PART II Stream Data Analytics

PART III Stream Data Analytics for Insider Threat Detection

PART IV Experimental BDMA and BDSP Systems

PART V Next Steps for BDMA and BDSP

Preface

BACKGROUND

Recent developments in information systems technologies have resulted in computerizing many applications in various business areas. Data has become a critical resource in many organizations, and therefore, efficient access to data, sharing the data, extracting information from the data, and making use of the information has become an urgent need. As a result, there have been many efforts on not only integrating the various data sources scattered across several sites, but extracting information from these databases in the form of patterns and trends and carrying out data analytics has also become important. These data sources may be databases managed by database management systems, or they could be data warehoused in a repository from multiple data sources.

The advent of the World Wide Web in the mid-1990s has resulted in even greater demand for managing data, information, and knowledge effectively. During this period, the services paradigm was conceived which has now evolved into providing computing infrastructures, software, databases, and applications as services. Such capabilities have resulted in the notion of cloud computing. Over the past 5 years, developments in cloud computing have exploded and we now have several companies providing infrastructure software and application computing platforms as services.

As the demand for data and information management increases, there is also a critical need for maintaining the security of the databases, applications, and information systems. Data, information, applications, the web, and the cloud have to be protected from unauthorized access as well as from malicious corruption. The approaches to secure such systems have come to be known as cyber security.

The significant developments in data management and analytics, web services, cloud computing, and cyber security have evolved into an area called big data management and analytics (BDMA) as well as big data security and privacy (BDSP). The U.S. Bureau of Labor and Statistics defines *big data* as a collection of large datasets that cannot be analyzed with normal statistical methods. The datasets can represent numerical, textual, and multimedia data. Big data is popularly defined in terms of five Vs: *volume, velocity, variety, veracity*, and *value*. BDMA requires handling huge volumes of data, both structured and unstructured, arriving at high velocity. By harnessing big data, we can achieve breakthroughs in several key areas such as cyber security and healthcare, resulting in increased productivity and profitability. Not only do the big data systems have to be secure, the big data analytics have to be applied for cyber security applications such as insider threat detection.

This book will review the developments in topics both BDMA and BDSP and discuss the issues and challenges in securing big data as well as applying big data techniques to solve problems. We will focus on a specific big data analytics technique called stream data mining as well as approaches to applying this technique to insider threat detection. We will also discuss several experimental systems, infrastructures and education programs we have developed at The University of Texas at Dallas on both BDMA and BDSP.

We have written two series of books for CRC Press on data management/data mining and data security. The first series consist of 10 books. Book #1 (*Data Management Systems Evolution and Interoperation*) focused on general aspects of data management and also addressed interoperability and migration. Book #2 (*Data Mining: Technologies, Techniques, Tools, and Trends*) discussed data mining. It essentially elaborated on Chapter 9 of Book #1. Book #3 (*Web Data Management and Electronic Commerce*) discussed web database technologies and discussed e-commerce as an application area. It essentially elaborated on Chapter 10 of Book #1. Book #4 (*Managing and Mining Multimedia Databases*) addressed both multimedia database management and multimedia data mining. It elaborated on both Chapter 6 of Book #1 (for multimedia database management) and Chapter 11 of Book #2 (for multimedia data mining). Book #5 (*XML, Databases and the Semantic Web*) described XML technologies related to data management. It elaborated on Chapter 11 of Book #3. Book #6 (*Web Data Mining and Applications in Business Intelligence and Counter-terrorism*) elaborated on Chapter 9 of Book #3. Book #7 (*Database and Applications Security*) examined security for technologies discussed in each of our previous books. It focuses on the technological developments in database and applications security. It is essentially the integration of Information Security and Database Technologies. Book #8 (*Building Trustworthy Semantic Webs*) applies security to semantic web technologies and elaborates on Chapter 25 of Book #7. Book #9 (*Secure Semantic Service-Oriented Systems*) is an elaboration of Chapter 16 of Book #8. Book #10 (*Developing and Securing the Cloud*) is an elaboration of Chapters 5 and 25 of Book #9.

Our second series of books at present consists of four books. Book #1 is *Design and Implementation of Data Mining Tools*. Book #2 is *Data Mining Tools for Malware Detection*. Book #3 is *Secure Data Provenance and Inference Control with Semantic Web*. Book #4 is *Analyzing and Securing Social Networks*. Book #5, which is the current book, is *Big Data Analytics with Applications in Insider Threat Detection*. For this series, we are converting some of the practical aspects of our work with students into books. The relationships between our texts will be illustrated in Appendix A.

ORGANIZATION OF THIS BOOK

This book is divided into five parts, each describing some aspect of the technology that is relevant to BDMA and BSDP. The major focus of this book will be on stream data analytics and its applications in insider threat detection. In addition, we will also discuss some of the experimental systems we have developed and provide some of the challenges involved.

Part I, consisting of six chapters, will describe supporting technologies for BDMA and BDSP including data security and privacy, data mining, cloud computing and semantic web. Part II, consisting of six chapters, provides a detailed overview of the techniques we have developed for stream data analytics. In particular, we will describe our techniques on novel class detection for data streams. Part III, consisting of nine chapters, will discuss the applications of stream analytics for insider threat detection. Part IV, consisting of six chapters, will discuss some of the experimental systems we have developed based on BDMA and BDSP. These include secure query processing for big data as well as social media analysis. Part V, consisting of seven chapters, discusses some of the challenges for BDMA and BDSP. In particular, securing the Internet of Things as well as our plans for developing experimental infrastructures for BDMA and BDSP are also discussed.

DATA, INFORMATION, AND KNOWLEDGE

In general, data management includes managing the databases, interoperability, migration, warehousing, and mining. For example, the data on the web has to be managed and mined to extract information and patterns and trends. Data could be in files, relational databases, or other types of databases such as multimedia databases. Data may be structured or unstructured. We repeatedly use the terms data, data management, and database systems and database management systems in this book. We elaborate on these terms in the appendix. We define data management systems to be systems that manage the data, extract meaningful information from the data, and make use of the information extracted. Therefore, data management systems include database systems, data warehouses, and data mining systems. Data could be structured data such as those found in relational databases, or it could be unstructured such as text, voice, imagery, and video.

There have been numerous discussions in the past to distinguish between data, information, and knowledge. In some of our previous books on data management and mining, we did not attempt to clarify these terms. We simply stated that, data could be just bits and bytes or it could convey some meaningful information to the user. However, with the web and also with increasing interest in data, information and knowledge management as separate areas, in this book we take a different approach to data, information, and knowledge by differentiating between these terms as much as possible. For us data is usually some value like numbers, integers, and strings. Information is obtained when some meaning or semantics is associated with the data such as John's salary is 20K. Knowledge is something that you acquire through reading and learning, and as a result understand the data and information and take actions. That is, data and information can be transferred into knowledge when uncertainty about the data and information is removed from someone's mind. It should be noted that it is rather difficult to give strict definitions of data, information, and knowledge. Sometimes we will use these terms interchangeably also. Our framework for data management discussed in the appendix helps clarify some of the differences. To be consistent with the terminology in our previous books, we will also distinguish between database systems and database management systems. A database management system is that component which manages the database containing persistent data. A database system consists of both the database and the database management system.

FINAL THOUGHTS

The goal of this book is to explore big data analytics techniques and apply them for cyber security including insider threat detection. We will discuss various concepts, technologies, issues, and challenges for both BDMA and BDSP. In addition, we also present several of the experimental systems in cloud computing and secure cloud computing that we have designed and developed at The University of Texas at Dallas. We have used some of the material in this book together with the numerous references listed in each chapter for graduate level courses at The University of Texas at Dallas on "Big Data Analytics" as well on "Developing and Securing the Cloud." We have also provided several experimental systems developed by our graduate students.

It should be noted that the field is expanding very rapidly with several open source tools and commercial products for managing and analyzing big data. Therefore, it is important for the reader to keep up with the developments of the various big data systems. However, security cannot be an afterthought. Therefore, while the technologies for big data are being developed, it is important to include security at the onset.

Acknowledgments

We thank the administration at the Erik Jonsson School of Engineering and Computer Science at The University of Texas at Dallas for giving us the opportunity to conduct our research. We also thank Ms. Rhonda Walls, our project coordinator, for proofreading and editing the chapters. Without her hard work this book would not have been possible. We thank many additional people who have supported our work or collaborated with us.

- Dr. Robert Herklotz (retired) from the Air Force Office of Scientific Research for funding our research on insider threat detection as well as several of our experimental systems.
- Dr. Victor Piotrowski from the National Science Foundation for funding our capacity building work on assured cloud computing and secure mobile computing.
- Dr. Ashok Agrawal, formerly of National Aeronautics and Space Administration, for funding our research on stream data mining.
- Professor Jiawei Han and his team from the University of Illinois at Urbana Champaign as well as Dr. Charu Agrawal from IBM Research for collaborating with us on stream data mining.
- Our colleagues Dr. Murat Kantarcioglu, Dr. Kevin Hamlen, Dr. Zhiqiang Lin, Dr. Kamil Sarac and Dr. Alvaro Cardenas at The University of Texas at Dallas for discussions on our work.
- Our collaborators on Assured Information Sharing at Kings College, University of London (Dr. Maribel Fernandez and the late Dr. Steve Barker), the University of Insubria, Italy (Dr. Elena Ferrari and Dr. Barbara Carminati), Purdue University (Dr. Elisa Bertino), and the University of Maryland, Baltimore County (Dr. Tim Finin and Dr. Anupam Joshi).
- The following people for their technical contributions: Dr. Murat Kantarciogu for his contributions to Chapters 25, 26, 28, 31, and 34; Mr Ramkumar Paranthaman from Amazon for his contributions to Chapter 7; Dr. Tyrone Cadenhead from Blue Cross Blue Shield for his contributions to Chapter 28 (part of his PhD thesis); Dr. Farhan Husain and Dr. Arindam Khaled, both from Amazon, for their contributions to Chapter 23 (part of Husain's PhD thesis); Dr. Satyen Abrol, Dr. Vaibhav Khadilkar, and Mr Gunasekar Rajasekar for their contributions to Chapter 24; Dr. Vaibhav Khadilkar and Dr. Jyothsna Rachapalli for their contributions to Chapter 25; Mr Pranav Parikh from Yahoo for his contributions to Chapter 26 (part of his MS thesis); Dr. David Lary and Dr. Vibhav Gogate, both from The University of Texas at Dallas, for their contributions to Chapter 33; Dr. Alvaro Cardenas for his contributions to Chapter 31; Dr. Zhiqiang Lin for his contributions to Chapters 32 and 34.

Permissions

Chapter 8: Challenges for Stream Data Classification

A practical approach to classify evolving data streams: Training with limited amount of labeled data. M. M. Masud, J. Gao, L. Khan, J. Han, and B. M. Thuraisingham. In: *ICDM '08: Proceedings of the 2008 International Conference on Data Mining*, pp. 929–934, Pisa, Italy, Dec. 15–19, 2008. Copyright 2008 IEEE. Reprinted with permission from IEEE Proceedings.

Integrating novel class detection with classification for concept-drifting data streams. M. M. Masud, J. Gao, L. Khan, J. Han, and B. M. Thuraisingham. In: Buntine, W., Grobelnik, M., Mladenić, D., Shawe-Taylor, J. (eds). *Machine Learning and Knowledge Discovery in Databases.* ECML PKDD 2009. *Lecture Notes in Computer Science*, Vol. 5782. Springer, Berlin. Copyright 2009, with permission of Springer.

A multi-partition multi-chunk ensemble technique to classify concept-drifting data streams. M. M. Masud, J. Gao, L. Khan, J. Han, and B. M. Thuraisingham. In: *PAKDD09: Proceedings of the 13th Pacific-Asia Conference on Knowledge Discovery and Data Mining*, pp. 363–375, Bangkok, Thailand, Apr. 27–30, 2009. Springer-Verlag. Also *Advances in Knowledge Discovery and Data Mining.* Copyright 2009, with permission of Springer.

Classification and novel class detection in concept-drifting data streams under time constraints. M. M. Masud, J. Gao, L. Khan, J. Han, and B. M. Thuraisingham. In: *IEEE Transactions on Knowledge and Data Engineering*, Vol. 23, no. 6, pp. 859–874, June 2011. Copyright 2011 IEEE. Reprinted with permission from IEEE.

Chapter 9: Survey of Stream Data Classification

A practical approach to classify evolving data streams: Training with limited amount of labeled data. M. M. Masud, J. Gao, L. Khan, J. Han, and B. M. Thuraisingham. In: *ICDM '08: Proceedings of the 2008 International Conference on Data Mining*, pp. 929–934, Pisa, Italy, Dec. 15–19, 2008. Copyright 2008 IEEE. Reprinted with permission from IEEE Proceedings.

Facing the reality of data stream classification: Coping with scarcity of labeled data. M M. Masud, C. Woolam, J. Gao, L. Khan, J. Han, K. Hamlen, and B. M. Thuraisingham. *Journal of Knowledge and Information Systems*, Vol. 1, no. 33, pp. 213–244. 2012. Copyright 2012, with permission of Springer.

Integrating novel class detection with classification for concept-drifting data streams. M. M. Masud, J. Gao, L. Khan, J. Han, and B. M. Thuraisingham. In: Buntine, W., Grobelnik, M., Mladenić, D., Shawe-Taylor, J. (eds). *Machine Learning and Knowledge Discovery in Databases.* ECML PKDD 2009. *Lecture Notes in Computer Science*, Vol. 5782. Springer, Berlin. Copyright 2009, with permission of Springer.

A multi-partition multi-chunk ensemble technique to classify concept-drifting data streams. M. M. Masud, J. Gao, L. Khan, J. Han, and B. M. Thuraisingham. In: *PAKDD09: Proceedings of the 13th Pacific-Asia Conference on Knowledge Discovery and Data Mining*, pp. 363–375, Bangkok, Thailand, April 27–30, 2009. Springer-Verlag. Also *Advances in Knowledge Discovery and Data Mining*). Copyright 2009, with permission of Springer.

Chapter 10: A Multi-Partition, Multi-Chunk Ensemble for Classifying Concept-Drifting Data Streams

A multi-partition multi-chunk ensemble technique to classify concept-drifting data streams. M. M. Masud, J. Gao, L. Khan, J. Han, and B. M. Thuraisingham. In: *PAKDD09: Proceedings of the 13th Pacific-Asia Conference on Knowledge Discovery and Data Mining*, pp. 363–375, Bangkok, Thailand, Apr. 27–30, 2009. Springer-Verlag. Also *Advances in Knowledge Discovery and Data Mining.* Copyright 2009, with permission of Springer.

Chapter 11: Classification and Novel Class Detection in Concept-Drifting Data Streams

A practical approach to classify evolving data streams: Training with limited amount of labeled data. M. M. Masud, J. Gao, L. Khan, J. Han, and B. M. Thuraisingham. In: *ICDM '08: Proceedings of the 2008 International Conference on Data Mining*, pp. 929–934, Pisa, Italy, December 15–19, 2008. Copyright 2008 IEEE. Reprinted with permission from IEEE Proceedings.

Integrating novel class detection with classification for concept-drifting data streams. M. M. Masud, J. Gao, L. Khan, J. Han, and B. M. Thuraisingham. In: Buntine, W., Grobelnik, M., Mladenić, D., Shawe-Taylor, J. (eds). *Machine Learning and Knowledge Discovery in Databases.* ECML PKDD 2009. *Lecture Notes in Computer Science*, Vol. 5782. Springer, Berlin. Copyright 2009, with permission of Springer.

A multi-partition multi-chunk ensemble technique to classify concept-drifting data streams. M. M. Masud, J. Gao, L. Khan, J. Han, and B. M. Thuraisingham. In: *PAKDD09: Proceedings of the 13th Pacific-Asia Conference on Knowledge Discovery and Data Mining*, pp. 363–375, Bangkok, Thailand, April 27–30, 2009. Springer-Verlag. Also *Advances in Knowledge Discovery and Data Mining.* Copyright 2009, with permission of Springer.

Classification and novel class detection in concept-drifting data streams under time constraints. M. M. Masud, J. Gao, L. Khan, J. Han, and B. M. Thuraisingham. In: *IEEE Transactions on Knowledge and Data Engineering,* Vol. 23, no. 6, pp. 859–874, June 2011. doi: 10.1109/TKDE.2010.61. Copyright 2011 IEEE. Reprinted with permission from IEEE.

Chapter 12: Data Stream Classification with Limited Labeled Training Data

Facing the reality of data stream classification: Coping with scarcity of labeled data. M M. Masud, C. Woolam, J. Gao, L. Khan, J. Han, K. Hamlen, and B. M. Thuraisingham. *Journal of Knowledge and Information Systems,* Vol. 1, no. 33, pp. 213–244. 2012. Copyright 2012, with permission of Springer.

A practical approach to classify evolving data streams: Training with limited amount of labeled data. M. M. Masud, J. Gao, L. Khan, J. Han, and B. M. Thuraisingham. In: *ICDM '08: Proceedings of the 2008 International Conference on Data Mining*, pp. 929–934, Pisa, Italy, December 15–19, 2008. Copyright 2008 IEEE. Reprinted with permission from IEEE Proceedings.

A multi-partition multi-chunk ensemble technique to classify concept-drifting data streams. M. M. Masud, J. Gao, L. Khan, J. Han, and B. M. Thuraisingham. In: *PAKDD09: Proceedings of the 13th Pacific-Asia Conference on Knowledge Discovery and Data Mining*, pp. 363–375, Bangkok, Thailand, April 27–30, 2009. Springer-Verlag. Also *Advances in Knowledge Discovery and Data Mining.* Copyright 2009, with permission of Springer.

Chapter 13: Directions in Data Stream Classification

A practical approach to classify evolving data streams: Training with limited amount of labeled data. M. M. Masud, J. Gao, L. Khan, J. Han, and B. M. Thuraisingham. In: *ICDM '08: Proceedings of the 2008 International Conference on Data Mining*, pp. 929–934, Pisa, Italy, December 15–19, 2008. Copyright 2008 IEEE. Reprinted with permission from IEEE Proceedings.

Integrating novel class detection with classification for concept-drifting data streams. M. M. Masud, J. Gao, L. Khan, J. Han, B. M. Thuraisingham. In: Buntine, W., Grobelnik, M., Mladenić, D., Shawe-Taylor, J. (eds). *Machine Learning and Knowledge Discovery in Databases.* ECML PKDD 2009. *Lecture Notes in Computer Science*, Vol. 5782. Springer, Berlin. Copyright 2009, with permission of Springer.

A multi-partition multi-chunk ensemble technique to classify concept-drifting data streams. M. M. Masud, J. Gao, L. Khan, J. Han, and B. M. Thuraisingham. In: *PAKDD09: Proceedings of the 13th Pacific-Asia Conference on Knowledge Discovery and Data Mining*, pp. 363–375, Bangkok, Thailand, April 27–30, 2009. Springer-Verlag. Also *Advances in Knowledge Discovery and Data Mining.* Copyright 2009, with permission of Springer.

Chapter 16: Ensemble-Based Insider Threat Detection

Insider threat detection using stream mining and graph mining. P. Parveen, J. Evans, B. M. Thuraisingham, K. W. Hamlen, L. Khan. In *2011 IEEE Third International Conference on Privacy, Security, Risk and Trust and 2011 IEEE Third International Conference on Social Computing*, pp. 1102–1110. Copyright 2011 IEEE. Reprinted with permission from IEEE Proceedings.

Evolving insider threat detection stream mining. P. Parveen, N. McDaniel, Z. Weger, J. Evans, B. M. Thuraisingham, K. W. Hamlen, L. Khan. Copyright 2013. Republished with permission of World Scientific Publishing/Imperial College Press, from *International Journal on Artificial Intelligence Tools*, Vol. 22, no. 5, 1360013, 24 pp., 2013. DOI: 10.1142/S0218213013600130, permission conveyed through Copyright Clearance Center, Inc. Perspective.

Supervised learning for insider threat detection using stream mining. P. Parveen, Z. R. Weger, B. M. Thuraisingham, K. W. Hamlen, L. Khan. In: *2011 IEEE 23rd International Conference on Tools with Artificial Intelligence*, pp. 1032–1039. Copyright 2011 IEEE. Reprinted with permission from IEEE Proceedings.

Chapter 17: Details of Learning Classes

Evolving insider threat detection stream mining. P. Parveen, N. McDaniel, Z. Weger, J. Evans, B. M. Thuraisingham, K. W. Hamlen, L. Khan. Copyright 2013. Republished with permission of World Scientific Publishing/Imperial College Press, from *International Journal on Artificial Intelligence Tools*, Vol. 22, no. 5, 1360013, 24 pp., 2013. DOI: 10.1142/S0218213013600130, permission conveyed through Copyright Clearance Center, Inc. Perspective.

Chapter 18: Experiments and Results for Nonsequence Data

Evolving insider threat detection stream mining. P. Parveen, N. McDaniel, Z. Weger, J. Evans, B. M. Thuraisingham, K. W. Hamlen, L. Khan. Copyright 2013. Republished with permission of World Scientific Publishing/Imperial College Press, from *International Journal on Artificial Intelligence Tools*, Vol. 22, no. 5, 1360013, 24 pp., 2013. DOI: 10.1142/S0218213013600130, permission conveyed through Copyright Clearance Center, Inc. Perspective.

Chapter 19: Insider Threat Detection for Sequence Data

Unsupervised incremental sequence learning for insider threat detection. P. Parveen, B. M. Thuraisingham. In: *2012 IEEE International Conference on Intelligence and Security Informatics*, pp. 141–143. Copyright 2012 IEEE. Reprinted with permission from *IEEE Proceedings.*

Unsupervised ensemble based learning for insider threat detection. P. Parveen, N. McDaniel, V. S. Hariharan, B. M. Thuraisingham, L. Khan. In: *2012 International Conference on Privacy, Security, Risk and Trust and 2012 International Conference on Social Computing*, pp. 718–727. Copyright 2012 IEEE. Reprinted with permission from *IEEE Proceedings.*

Evolving insider threat detection stream mining. P. Parveen, N. McDaniel, Z. Weger, J. Evans, B. M. Thuraisingham, K. W. Hamlen, L. Khan. Copyright 2013. Republished with permission of World Scientific Publishing/Imperial College Press, from *International Journal on Artificial Intelligence Tools*, Vol. 22, no. 5, 1360013, 24 pp., 2013. DOI: 10.1142/S0218213013600130, permission conveyed through Copyright Clearance Center, Inc. Perspective.

Chapter 20: Experiments and Results for Sequence Data

Unsupervised ensemble based learning for insider threat detection. P. Parveen, N. McDaniel, V. S. Hariharan, B. M. Thuraisingham, L. Khan. In: *SocialCom/PASSAT*, 2012, pp. 718–727. Copyright 2012 IEEE. Reprinted with permission from *IEEE Proceedings.*

Chapter 23: Cloud Query Processing System for Big Data Management

Heuristics-based query processing for large RDF graphs using cloud computing. M. F. Husain, J. P. McGlothlin, M. M. Masud, L. R. Khan, *IEEE Transactions on Knowledge and Data Engineering*,

Vol. 23, no. 9, pp. 1312–1327, 2011. Copyright 2011 IEEE. Reprinted with permission from *IEEE Transactions on Knowledge and Data Engineering*.

A token-based access control system for RDF data in the clouds. A. Khaled, M. F. Husain, L. Khan, K. W. Hamlen. In: *The 2010 IEEE Second International Conference on Cloud Computing Technology and Science (CloudCom)*, pp. 104–111, 2010. Copyright 2010 IEEE. Reprinted with permission from IEEE Proceedings.

Chapter 25: Big Data Management and Cloud for Assured Information Sharing

Cloud-centric assured information sharing. V. Khadilkar, J. Rachapalli, T. Cadenhead, M. Kantarcioglu, K. W. Hamlen, L. Khan, M. F. Husain. *Lecture Notes in Computer Science* 7299, 2012, pp. 1–26. *Proceedings of Intelligence and Security Informatics—Pacific Asia Workshop, PAISI 2012*, Kuala Lumpur, Malaysia, May 29, 2012. Springer-Verlag, Berlin, 2012. Copyright 2012, with permission from Springer. DOI 10.1007/978-3-642-30428-6_1, Print ISBN 978-3-642-30427-9.

Chapter 29: Confidentiality, Privacy, and Trust for Big Data Systems

Administering the semantic web: Confidentiality, privacy and trust management. B. M. Thuraisingham, N. Tsybulnik, A. Alam, *International Journal of Information Security and Privacy*, Vol. 1, no. 1, pp. 18–34. Copyright 2007, with permission from IGI Global.

Authors

Dr. Bhavani Thuraisingham is the Louis A. Beecherl, Jr. Distinguished Professor in the Erik Jonsson School of Engineering and Computer Science at The University of Texas, Dallas (UTD) and the executive director of UTD's Cyber Security Research and Education Institute. Her current research is on integrating cyber security, cloud computing, and data science. Prior to joining UTD, she worked at the MITRE Corporation for 16 years including a 3-year stint as a program director at the NSF. She initiated the Data and Applications Security program at NSF and was part of the Cyber Trust theme. Prior to MITRE, she worked for the commercial industry for 6 years including at Honeywell. She is the recipient of numerous awards including the IEEE Computer Society 1997 Technical Achievement Award, the ACM SIGSAC 2010 Outstanding Contributions Award, 2012 SDPS Transformative Achievement Gold Medal, 2013 IBM Faculty Award, 2017 ACM CODASPY Research Award, and 2017 IEEE Computer Society Services Computing Technical Committee Research Innovation Award. She is a 2003 Fellow of the IEEE and the AAAS and a 2005 Fellow of the British Computer Society. She has published over 120 journal articles, 250 conference papers, 15 books, has delivered over 130 keynote addresses, and is the inventor of five patents. She has chaired conferences and workshops for women in her field including Women in Cyber Security, Women in Data Science, and Women in Services Computing/Cloud and has delivered featured addresses at SWE, WITI, and CRA-W.

Dr. Mohammad Mehedy Masud is currently an associate professor at the College of Information Technology (CIT) at United Arab Emirates University (UAEU). Prior to joining UAEU in January 2012, Dr. Masud worked at The University of Texas at Dallas as a research associate for 2 years. He earned his PhD in computer science from The University of Texas at Dallas, USA, in December 2009. Dr. Masud's research interests include big data mining, data stream mining, machine learning, healthcare data analytics, and e-health. His research also contributes to cyber security (network security, intrusion detection, and malware detection) using machine learning and data mining. He has published more than 50 research articles in high impact factor journals including *IEEE Transactions on Knowledge and Data Engineering* (TKDE), *Journal of Knowledge and Information Systems* (KAIS), and top tier conferences including *IEEE International Conference on Data Mining* (ICDM). He is the lead author of the book *Data Mining Tools for Malware Detection* and is also the principal inventor of a U.S. patent. He is the principal investigator of several prestigious research grants funded by government and private funding organizations.

Dr. Pallabi Parveen is a principal big data engineer at AT&T since 2017 where she is conducting research, design, and development activities on big data analytics for various applications. Prior to her work at AT&T, she was a senior software engineer at VCE/EMC2 for 4 years where she was involved in the research and prototyping efforts on big data systems. She completed her PhD at UT Dallas in 2013 on Big Data Analytics with Applications for Insider Threat Detection. She has also conducted research on facial recognition systems. Prior to her PhD, she worked for Texas Instruments in embedded software systems. She has published her research in top tier journals and conferences. She is an expert on big data management and analytics technologies and has published her research in top tier journals and conferences.

Dr. Latifur Khan is a professor of computer science and director of data analytics at The University of Texas at Dallas (UTD) where he has been teaching and conducting research in data management and data analytics since September 2000. He earned his PhD in computer science from the University of Southern California in August of 2000. Dr. Khan is an ACM Distinguished Scientist and has received prestigious awards including the IEEE Technical Achievement Award for Intelligence and Security Informatics. Dr. Khan has published over 250 papers in prestigious journals, and in peer-reviewed top tier conference proceedings. He is also the author of four books and has delivered keynote addresses at various conferences and workshops. He is the inventor of a number of patents and is involved in technology transfer activities. His research focuses on big data management and analytics, machine learning for cyber security, complex data management including geospatial data and multimedia data management. He has served as the program chair for multiple conferences.

1 Introduction

1.1 OVERVIEW

The U.S. Bureau of Labor and Statistics (BLS) defines *big data* as a collection of large datasets that cannot be analyzed with normal statistical methods. The datasets can represent numerical, textual, and multimedia data. Big data is popularly defined in terms of five Vs: *volume, velocity, variety, veracity*, and *value*. Big data management and analytics (BDMA) requires handling huge volumes of data, both structured and unstructured, arriving at high velocity. By harnessing big data, we can achieve breakthroughs in several key areas such as cyber security and healthcare, resulting in increased productivity and profitability. Big data spans several important fields: business, e-commerce, finance, government, healthcare, social networking, and telecommunications, as well as several scientific fields such as atmospheric and biological sciences. BDMA is evolving into a field called data science that not only includes BDMA, but also machine learning, statistical methods, high-performance computing, and data management.

Data scientists aggregate, process, analyze, and visualize big data in order to derive useful insights. BLS projected both computer programmers and statisticians to have high employment growth during 2012–2022. Other sources have reported that by 2018, the United States alone could face a shortage of 140,000–190,000 skilled data scientists. The demand for data science experts is on the rise as the roles and responsibilities of a data scientist are steadily taking shape. Currently, there is no debate on the fact that data science skillsets are not developing proportionately with high industry demands. Therefore, it is imperative to bring data science research, development, and education efforts into the mainstream of computer science. Data are being collected by every organization regardless of whether it is industry, academia, or government. Organizations want to analyze this data to give them a competitive edge. Therefore, the demand for data scientists including those with expertise in BDMA techniques is growing by several folds every year.

While BDMA is evolving into data science with significant progress over the past 5 years, big data security and privacy (BDSP) is becoming a critical need. With the recent emergence of the *quantified self* (QS) movement, personal data collected by wearable devices and smartphone apps are being analyzed to guide users in improving their health or personal life habits. This data are also being shared with other service providers (e.g., retailers) using cloud-based services, offering potential benefits to users (e.g., information about health products). But such data collection and sharing are often being carried out without the users' knowledge, bringing grave danger that the personal data may be used for improper purposes. Privacy violations could easily get out of control if data collectors could aggregate financial and health-related data with tweets, Facebook activity, and purchase patterns. In addition, access to the massive amounts of data collected has to be stored. Yet few tools and techniques exist for privacy protection in QS applications or controlling access to the data.

While securing big data and ensuring the privacy of individuals are crucial tasks, BDMA techniques can be used to solve security problems. For example, an organization can outsource activities such as identity management, email filtering, and intrusion detection to the cloud. This is because massive amounts of data are being collected for such applications and this data has to be analyzed. Cloud data management is just one example of big data management. The question is: how can the developments in BDMA be used to solve cyber security problems? These problems include malware detection, insider threat detection, intrusion detection, and spam filtering.

We have written this book to elaborate on some of the challenges in BDMA and BDSP as well as to provide some details of our ongoing efforts on big data analytics and its applications in cyber security. The specific BDMA techniques we will focus on include stream data analytics. Also, the specific cyber security applications we will discuss include insider threat detection. We will also describe some of the experimental systems we have designed relating to BDMA and BDSP as well as provide some of our views on the next steps including developing infrastructures for BDMA and BDSP to support education and experimentation.

This chapter details the organization of this book. The organization of this chapter is as follows. Supporting technologies for BDMA and BDSP will be discussed in Section 1.2. Our research and experimental work in stream data analytics including processing of massive data streams is discussed in Section 1.3. Application of stream data analytics to insider threat detection is discussed in Section 1.4. Some of the experimental systems we have designed and developed in topics related to BDMA and BDSP will be discussed in Section 1.5. The next steps, including developing education and experimental programs in BDMA and BDSP as well as some emerging topics such as Internet of things (IoT) security as it relates to BDMA and BDSP are discussed in Section 1.6. Organization of this book will be given in Section 1.7. We conclude this chapter with useful resources in Section 1.8. It should be noted that the contents of Sections 1.2 through 1.5 will be elaborated in Parts I through V of this book. Figure 1.1 illustrates the contents covered in this chapter.

1.2 SUPPORTING TECHNOLOGIES

We will discuss several supporting technologies for BDMA and BDSP. These include data security and privacy, data mining, data mining for security applications, cloud computing and semantic web, data mining and insider threat detection, and BDMA technologies. Figure 1.2 illustrates the supporting technologies discussed in this book.

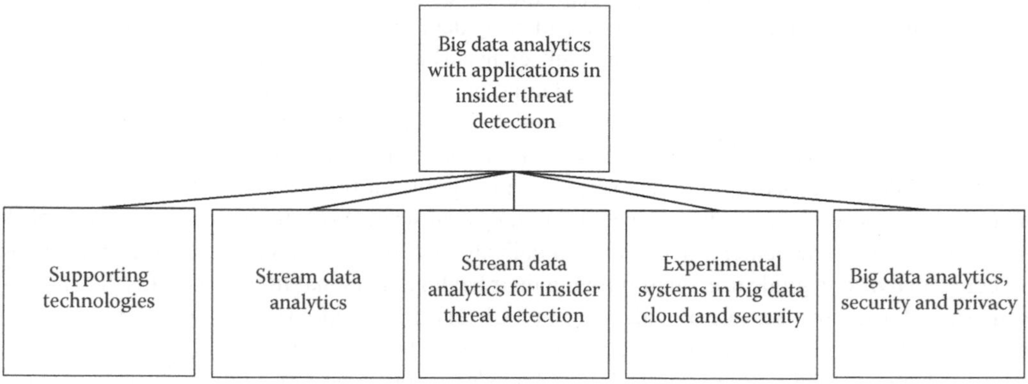

FIGURE 1.1 Concepts of this chapter.

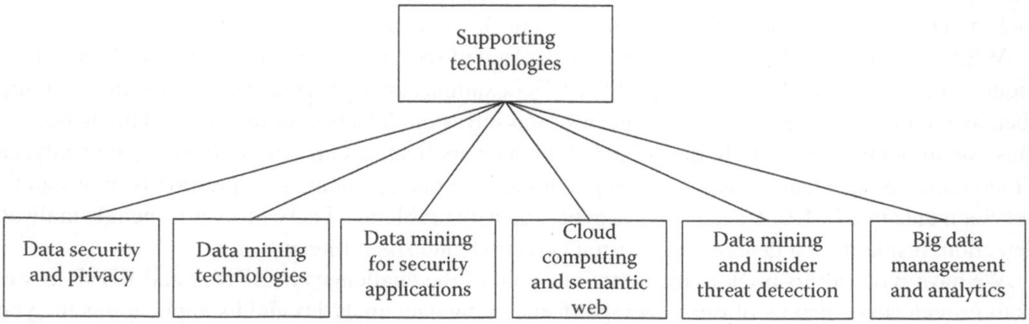

FIGURE 1.2 Supporting technologies.

With respect to data security and privacy, we will describe database security issues, security policy enforcement, access control, and authorization models for database systems, as well as data privacy issues. With respect to data mining, which we will also refer to as data analytics, we will introduce the concept and provide an overview of the various data mining techniques to lay the foundations for some of the techniques to be discussed in Parts II through V. With respect to data mining applications in security, we will provide an overview of how some of the data mining techniques discussed may be applied for cyber security applications. With respect to cloud computing and semantic web, we will provide some of the key points including cloud data management and technologies such as *resource description framework* for representing and managing large amounts of data. With respect to data mining and insider threat detection, we will discuss some of our work on applying data mining for insider threat detection that will provide the foundations for the concepts to be discussed in Parts II and III. Finally, with respect to BDMA technologies, we will discuss infrastructures and frameworks, data management, and data analytics systems that will be applied throughout the various sections in this book.

1.3 STREAM DATA ANALYTICS

Data streams are continuous flows of data being generated from various computing machines such as clients and servers in networks, sensors, call centers, and so on. Analyzing these data streams has become critical for many applications including for network data, financial data, and sensor data. However, mining these ever-growing data is a big challenge to the data mining community. First, data streams are assumed to have *infinite length*. It is impractical to store and use all the historical data for learning, as it would require an infinite amount of storage and learning time. Therefore, traditional classification algorithms that require several passes over the training data are not directly applicable to data streams. Second, data streams observe *concept drift* which occurs when the underlying concept of the data changes over time.

Our discussion of stream data analytics will focus on a particular technique we have designed and developed called *novel class detection*. Usually data mining algorithms determine whether an entity belongs to a predefined class. However, our technique will identify a new class if an entity does not belong to an existing class. This technique with several variations has been shown to have applications in many domains. In Part II of this book, we will discuss novel class detection and also address the challenges of analyzing massive data streams. Figure 1.3 illustrates our discussions in stream data analytics.

1.4 APPLICATIONS OF STREAM DATA ANALYTICS FOR INSIDER THREAT DETECTION

Malicious insiders, both people and processes, are considered to be the most dangerous threats to both cyber security and national security. For example, employees of a company may steal highly

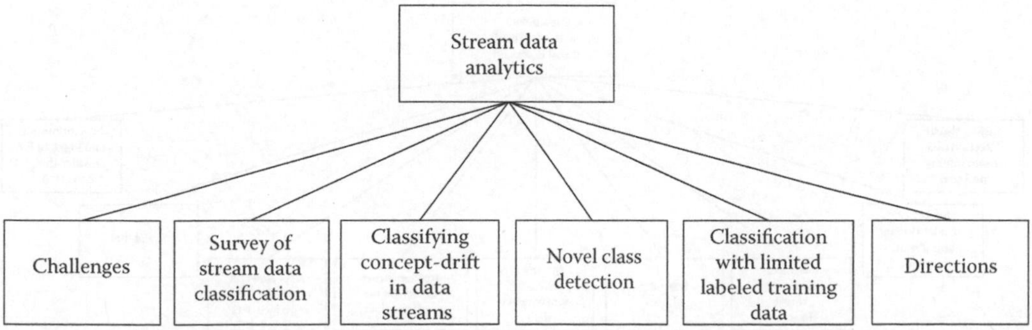

FIGURE 1.3 Stream data analytics.

sensitive product designs and sell them to the competitors. This could be achieved manually or often via cyber espionage. The malicious processes in the system can also carry out such covert operations.

Data mining techniques have been applied for cyber security problems including insider threat detection. Techniques such as support vector machines and supervised learning methods have been applied. Unfortunately, the training process for supervised learning methods tends to be time-consuming and expensive and generally requires large amounts of well-balanced training data to be effective. Also, traditional training methods do not scale well for massive amounts of insider threat data. Therefore, we have applied BDMA techniques for insider threat detection.

We have designed and developed several BDMA techniques for detecting malicious insiders. In particular, we have adapted our stream data analytics techniques to handle massive amounts of data and detect malicious insiders in Part III of this book. The concepts addressed in Part III are illustrated in Figure 1.4.

1.5 EXPERIMENTAL BDMA AND BDSP SYSTEMS

As the popularity of cloud computing and BDMA grows, service providers face ever increasing challenges. They have to maintain large quantities of heterogeneous data while providing efficient information retrieval. Thus, the key emphases for cloud computing solutions are scalability and query efficiency. With funding from the Air Force Office of Scientific Research to explore security for cloud computing and social media as well as from the National Science Foundation to build infrastructure as well as an educational program in cloud computing and big data management, we have developed a number of BDMA and BDSP experimental systems.

Part IV will discuss the experimental systems that we have developed based on cloud computing and big data technologies. We will discuss the cloud query processing systems that we have developed utilizing the Hadoop/MapReduce framework. Our system processes massive amounts of semantic web data. In particular, we have designed and developed a query optimizer for the SPARQL query processor that functions in the cloud. We have developed cloud systems that host social networking applications. We have also designed an assured information sharing system in the cloud. In addition, cloud systems for malware detection are also discussed. Finally, we discuss inference control for big data systems. Figure 1.5 illustrates some of the experimental cloud systems that we have developed.

1.6 NEXT STEPS IN BDMA AND BDSP

Through the experimental systems, we have designed and developed both BDMA and BDSP, we now have an understanding of the research challenges involved for both BDMA and BDSP. We organized a workshop on this topic funded by the National Science Foundation (NSF) in late 2014 and presented the results to the government interagency working group in cyber security in 2015. Following this

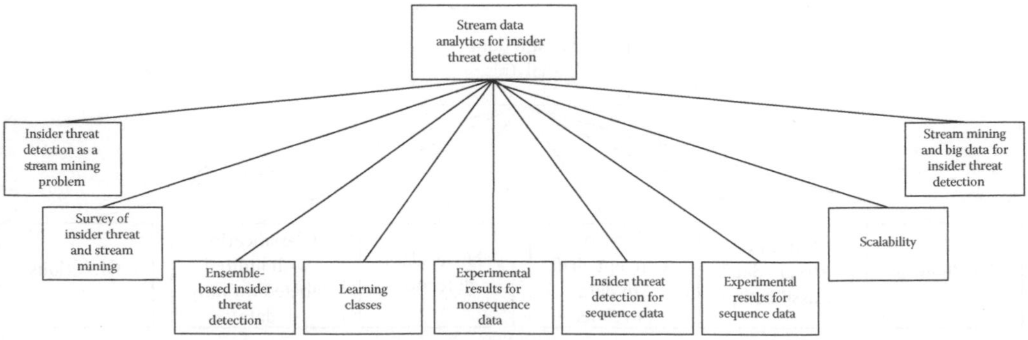

FIGURE 1.4 Stream data analytics for insider threat detection.

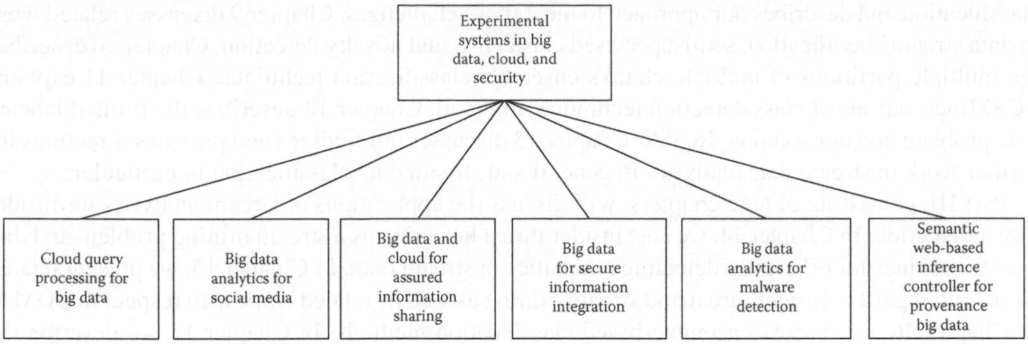

FIGURE 1.5 Experimental systems in big data, cloud, and security.

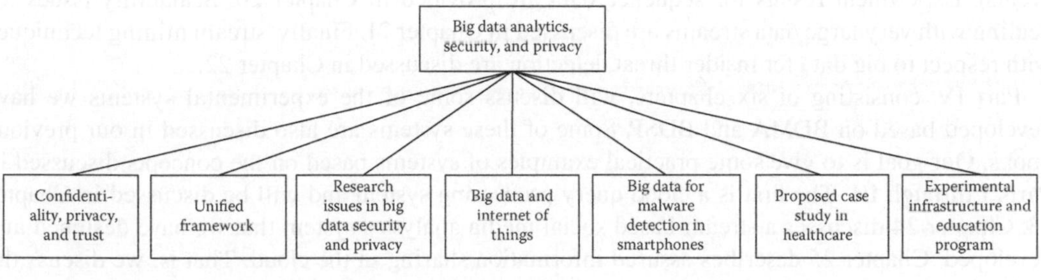

FIGURE 1.6 Big data analytics, security, and privacy.

we have also begun developing both experimental and educational infrastructures for both BDMA and BDSP.

The chapters in Part V will discuss the research, infrastructures, and educational challenges in BDMA and BDSP. In particular, we will discuss the integration of confidentiality, privacy, and trust in big data systems. We will also discuss big data challenges for securing IoT systems. We will discuss our work in smartphone security as an example of an IoT system. We will also describe a proposed case study for applying big data analytics techniques as well as discuss the experimental infrastructure and education programs we have developed for both BDMA and BDSP. Finally, we will discuss the research issues in BDSP. The topics to be covered in Part V are illustrated in Figure 1.6.

1.7 ORGANIZATION OF THIS BOOK

This book is divided into five parts, each describing some aspect of the technology that is relevant to BDMA and BDSP. The major focus of this book will be on stream data analytics and its applications in insider threat detection. In addition, we will also discuss some of the experimental systems we have developed and provide some of the challenges involved.

Part I, consisting of six chapters, will describe supporting technologies for BDMA and BDSP. In Chapter 2, data security and privacy issues are discussed. In Chapter 3, an overview of various data mining techniques is provided. Applying data mining for security applications is discussed in Chapter 4. Cloud computing and semantic web technologies are discussed in Chapter 5. Data mining and its applications for insider threat detection are discussed in Chapter 6. Finally, some of the emerging technologies in BDMA are discussed in Chapter 7. These supporting technologies provide the background information for both BDMA and BDSP.

Part II, consisting of six chapters, provides a detailed overview of the techniques we have developed for stream data analytics. In particular, we will describe our techniques on novel class detection for data streams. Chapter 8 focuses on various challenges associated with data stream classification and describes our approach to meet those challenges. Chapter 9 discusses related work in data stream classification, semisupervised clustering, and novelty detection. Chapter 10 describes the multiple partitions of multiple chunks ensemble classification technique. Chapter 11 explains ECSMiner, our novel class detection technique, in detail. Chapter 12 describes the limited labeled data problem and our solution, ReaSC. Chapter 13 discusses our findings and provides directions for further work in stream data analytics in general and stream data classification in particular.

Part III, consisting of nine chapters, will discuss the applications of stream analytics for insider threat detection. In Chapter 14, we cast insider threat detection as a stream mining problem and discuss techniques for efficiently detecting anomalies in stream data. In Chapter 15, we present related work with regard to insider threat and stream mining as well as related work with respect to BDMA. In Chapter 16, we discuss ensemble-based classification methods. In Chapter 17, we describe the different classes of learning techniques for nonsequence data. In Chapter 18, we discuss our testing methodology and experimental results for the techniques discussed in Chapters 16 and 17. In Chapter 19, we describe insider threat detection for sequence data, an ordered list of objects (or events). Experiment results for sequence data are provided in Chapter 20. Scalability issues for dealing with very large data streams are discussed in Chapter 21. Finally, stream mining techniques with respect to big data for insider threat detection are discussed in Chapter 22.

Part IV, consisting of six chapters, will discuss some of the experimental systems we have developed based on BDMA and BDSP. Some of these systems are also discussed in our previous books. Our goal is to give some practical examples of systems based on the concepts discussed in Parts I through III. The first is a cloud query processing system and will be discussed in Chapter 23. Chapter 24 discusses a stream-based social media analytics system that we have designed and developed. Chapter 25 describes assured information sharing in the cloud. That is, we discuss the policy-based information sharing system we have developed that operates in a cloud. Chapter 26 describes how information can be integrated in the cloud. Chapter 27 shows how some other cyber security applications such as malware detection could be improved by implementing the data analytics techniques in the cloud. Finally, in Chapter 28, we describe the inference controller we have developed for controlling unauthorized inference with provenance data and the use of big data techniques to improve the performance.

Part V, consisting of seven chapters, discusses some of the challenges for BDMA and BDSP. In particular, Chapter 29 describes how the notions of security, privacy, and trust management can be incorporated into big data management systems. Chapter 30 describes a framework for BDMA and BDSP systems. In particular, the design of a global inference controller automated with reasoning engines, policy enforcement systems, and data management systems is discussed. Chapter 31 describes secure IoT systems with respect to BDMA and BDSP. An example of secure IoT system, which is essentially a collection of connected smartphones, is discussed in Chapter 32. Chapter 33 describes a proposed case study for BDMA and BDSP based on scientific applications. In Chapter 34, we discuss our planned experimental infrastructure and educational program for BDMA and BDSP. Finally, Chapter 35 presents the results of the NSF workshop on BDSP and the research directions discussed at this workshop.

Each part begins with an introduction and ends with a conclusion. Furthermore, each of the Chapters 2 through 35 starts with an overview and ends with a summary and references. Chapter 36 summarizes this book and discusses future directions. We have included Appendix A that provides an overview of data management and discusses the relationship between the texts we have written. This has been the standard practice with all of our books. In Appendix B, we discuss database systems management. Much of the work discussed in this book has evolved from the technologies discussed in Appendix B.

We have essentially developed a five-layer framework to explain the concepts in this book. This framework is illustrated in Figure 1.7. Layer 1 is the *supporting technologies* layer and covers the chapters in Part I of this book. Layer 2 is the *stream data analytics* layer and covers the chapters in Part II. Layer 3 is the *stream data analytics* for *insider threat applications* layer and covers the

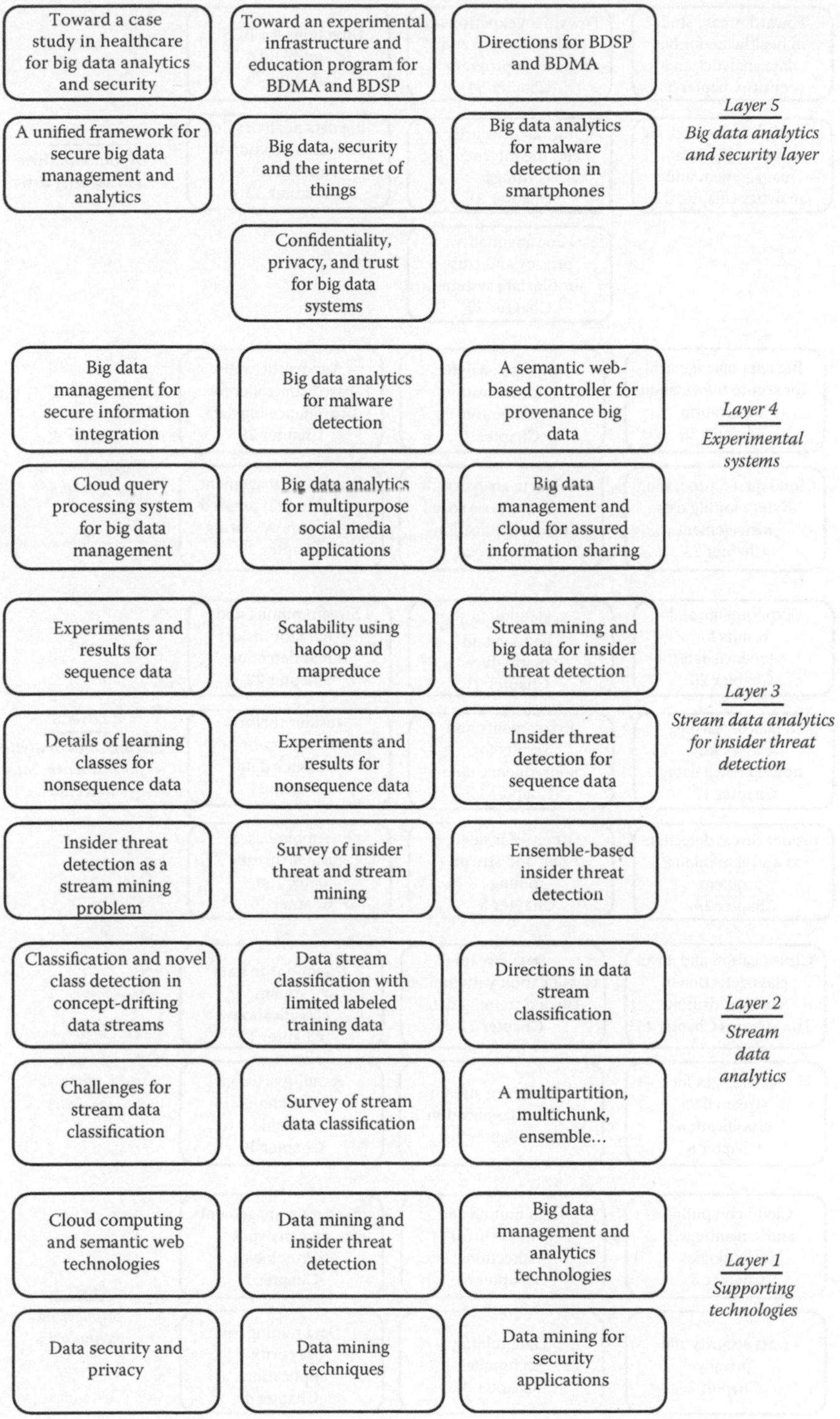

FIGURE 1.7 Five layer framework for this book.

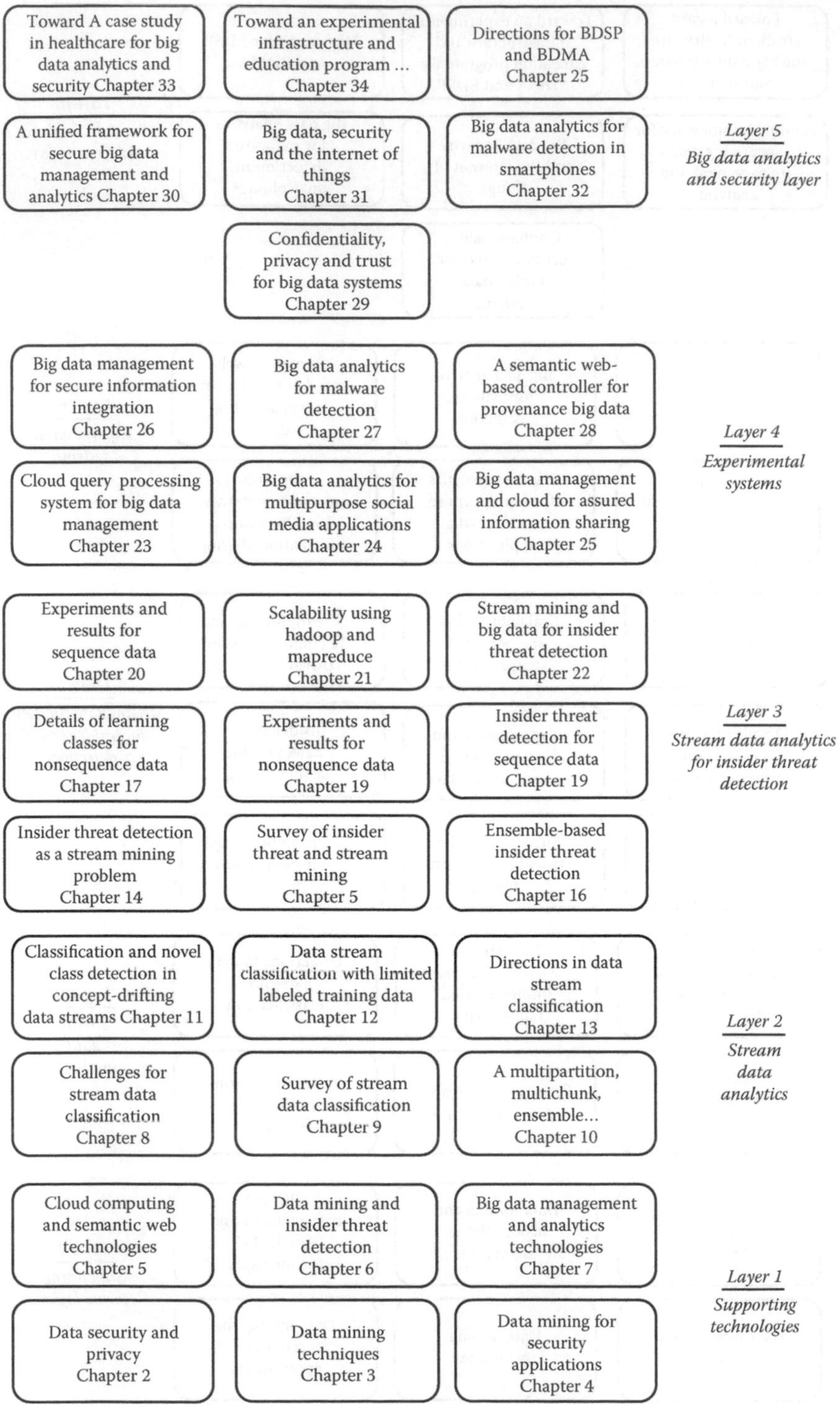

FIGURE 1.8 Contents of this book with respect to the framework.

chapters in Part III. Layer 4 is the *experimental systems* layer and covers the chapters in Part IV. Layer 5 is the *big data analytics and security* layer consisting of the chapters in Part V. The relationship between the various parts of this book is given in Figure 1.8.

1.8 NEXT STEPS

This chapter has provided an introduction to this book. We first provided a brief overview of the supporting technologies for BDMA and BDSP. Next, we discussed stream data analytics with a focus on BDMA. This was followed by a discussion of the applications of stream analytics for insider threat detection. Then a discussion of several experimental systems related to BDMA and BDSP is provided. Finally, we provided an overview of the next steps for BDMA and BDSP. One of the main contributions of this book is raising the awareness of the importance of both BDMA and BDSP through the discussions of experimental systems and tools. We have also given numerous references throughout this book.

Several new cloud computing and big data conferences have emerged in recent years. These include IEEE Computer Society's Cloud Computing Conference held in conjunction with the Services Computing Conference as well as CloudCom. In addition, the IEEE Computer Society has launched a conference on Big Data in addition to the Big Data Congress supported by the Services Computing Society. Also, traditional database management, data mining, and machine learning conferences have focused on BDMA while the cyber security conferences now have a major focus on BDSP including the applications of BDMA (and machine learning) to cyber security. We strongly believe that the future of computing is with cloud computing and the future of data is with BDMA. Services and components will be developed by multiple vendors from all over the world. The challenge is to put these services and components together and build secure cloud computing systems as well as BDMA tools. In addition, secure systems that manage massive amounts of data securely while ensuring the privacy of individuals will become one of the major challenges we will be faced with for the next several decades.

Part I

Supporting Technologies for BDMA and BDSP

Introduction to Part I

Before we discuss the big data management and analytics (BDMA) and big data security and privacy (BDSP) systems that we have designed and developed in Parts II through IV, we need to provide some of the technologies that are needed for an understanding of our systems. Part I will provide an overview of such technologies.

Part I, consisting of six chapters, will describe supporting technologies for BDMA and BDSP. Chapter 2 will describe security technologies. In particular, we will discuss various aspects of data security and privacy. In Chapter 3, we provide some background information about general data mining techniques so that the reader can have an understanding of the field. In Chapter 4, we will discuss ways of applying data mining for cyber security. In particular, we will discuss the threats to computers and networks and describe the applications of data mining to detect such threats and attacks. In Chapter 5, we will provide an overview of cloud computing and semantic web technologies. This is because several of our experimental systems discussed in Part IV utilized cloud and semantic web technologies. In Chapter 6, we will discuss how data mining technologies could be applied for insider threat detection in the cloud. First, we will discuss how semantic web technologies may be used to represent the communication between insiders and then discuss our approach to insider threat detection. Finally, in Chapter 7, we will discuss some of the BDMA technologies we have used in the experimental systems we have designed and developed.

It should be noted that the big data systems supporting technologies that we have discussed have evolved from database systems technology. Therefore, a basic knowledge of database systems technology is essential for an understanding of big data systems. An overview of database systems is discussed in Appendix B of this book.

2 Data Security and Privacy

2.1 OVERVIEW

As we have stated in Chapter 1, secure big data technologies integrate big data technologies with security technologies. In this chapter, we will discuss security technologies. In particular, we will discuss various aspects of data security and privacy. Big data technologies will be discussed in Chapter 7 after we provide an overview of some related technologies such as data mining and cloud computing.

Since much of the discussion in this book is on big data analytics and security, we will provide a fairly comprehensive overview of access control in data management systems. In particular, we will discuss security policies as well as enforcing the policies in database systems. Our focus will be on discretionary security policies. We will also discuss data privacy aspects. More details on secure data management can be found in [FERR00] and [THUR05a].

The most popular discretionary security policy is the access control policy. Access control policies were studied for operating systems back in the 1960s and then for database systems in the 1970s. The two prominent database systems, System R and INGRES, were the first to investigate access control for database systems (see [GRIF76] and [STON74]). Since then several variations of access control policies have been reported including role-based access control (RBAC) and attribute-based access control [NIST]. Other discretionary policies include administration policies. We also discuss identification and authentication under discretionary policies. Note that much of the discussion in this chapter will focus on discretionary security in relational database systems. Many of the principles are applicable to other systems such as object database systems, distributed database systems, and cloud data management systems (see e.g., [THUR94]).

Before one designs a secure system, the first question that must be answered is what is the security policy to be enforced by the system? Security policy is essentially a set of rules that enforce security. Security policies include mandatory security policies and discretionary security policies. Mandatory security policies are the policies that are "mandatory" in nature and enforced by the systems. Discretionary security policies are policies that are specified by the administrator or the owner of the data.

By policy enforcement, we mean the mechanisms to enforce the policies. For example, back in the 1970s, the relational database system products such as System R and INGRES developed techniques such as the query modification mechanisms for policy enforcement (see e.g., [GRIF76] and [STON74]). The query language Structured Query Language (SQL) has been extended to specify security policies and access control rules. More recently languages such as eXtensible Markup Language (XML) and resource description framework (RDF) have been extended to specify security policies (see e.g., [BERT02] and [CARM04]).

The organization of this chapter is as follows. In Section 2.2, we introduce discretionary security including access control and authorization models for database systems. We also discuss RBAC systems. In Section 2.3, we discuss ways of enforcing discretionary security including a discussion of query modification. We also provide an overview of the various commercial products. This chapter is summarized in Section 2.4. Figure 2.1 illustrates the concepts discussed in this chapter. We assume that the reader has some knowledge of data management. For more details on this topic we refer the reader to some texts such as [DATE90] and [THUR97]. We also provide an overview of database systems in Appendix B.

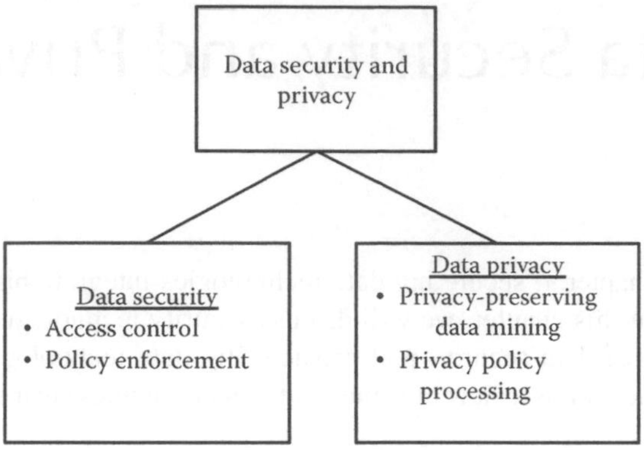

FIGURE 2.1 Data security and privacy.

2.2 SECURITY POLICIES

The organization of this section is as follows. In Section 2.2.1, we will provide an overview of access control policies. Administration policies will be discussed in Section 2.2.2. Issues in identification and authentication will be discussed in Section 2.2.3. Auditing a database management system will be discussed in Section 2.2.4. Views as security objects will be discussed in Section 2.2.5. Figure 2.2 illustrates various components of discretionary security policies discussed in this section.

2.2.1 Access Control Policies

Access control policies were first examined for operating systems. The essential point here is that can a process be granted access to a file? Access could be read access or write access. Write access could include access to modify, append, or delete. These principles were transferred to database systems such as INGRES and System R. Since then various forms of access control policies have been studied. Notable among those are the RBAC policies which are now implemented in several commercial systems. Note that access control policies also include mandatory policies. Figure 2.3 illustrates the various types of access control policies.

2.2.1.1 Authorization-Based Access Control Policies

Many of the access control policies are based on authorization policies. Essentially what this means is that users are granted access to data based on authorization rules. In this section, we will discuss various types of authorization rules. Note that in the book chapter by Ferrari and Thuraisingham [FERR00], a detailed discussion of authorization policies is provided.

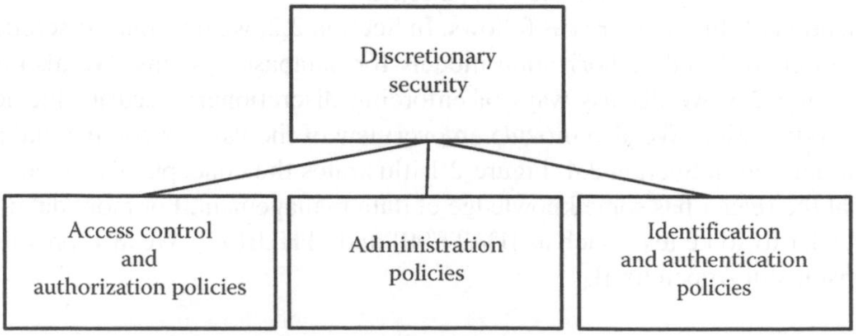

FIGURE 2.2 Discretionary security policies.

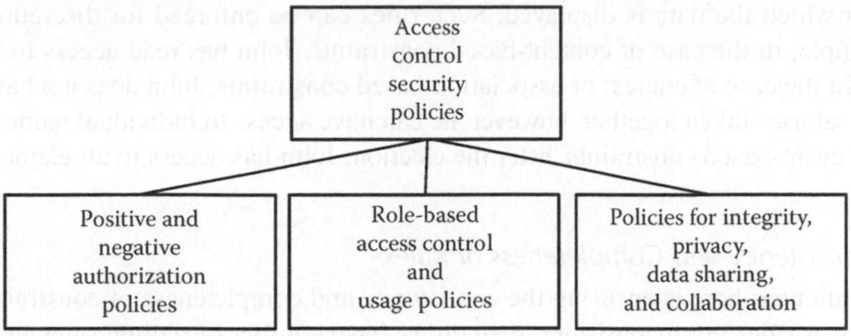

FIGURE 2.3 Access control security policies.

2.2.1.1.1 Positive Authorization

Early systems focused on what is now called positive authorization rules. Here user John is granted access to relation EMP or user Jane is granted access to relation DEPT. These are access control rules on relations. One can also grant access to other entities such as attributes and tuples. For example, John has read access to attribute salary and write access to attribute name in relation EMP. Write access could include append, modify, or delete access.

2.2.1.1.2 Negative Authorization

The question is if John's access to an object is not specified, does this mean John does not have access to that object? In some systems, any authorization rule that is not specified is implicitly taken to be a negative authorization, while in other systems negative authorizations are explicitly specified. For example, we could enforce rules such as John does not have access to relation EMP or Jane does not have access to relation DEPT.

2.2.1.1.3 Conflict Resolution

When we have rules that are conflicting then how do we resolve the conflicts? For example, we could have a rule that grants John read access to relation EMP. However, we can also have a rule that does not grant John read access to the salary attribute in EMP. This is a conflict. Usually a system enforces the least privilege rule in which case John has access to EMP except for the salary values.

2.2.1.1.4 Strong and Weak Authorization

Systems also enforce strong and weak authorizations. In the case of strong authorization, the rule holds regardless of conflicts. In the case of weak authorization, the rule does not hold in case of conflict. For example, if John is granted access to EMP and it is a strong authorization rule and the rule where John is not granted access to salary attribute is a weak authorization, there is a conflict. This means the strong authorization will hold.

2.2.1.1.5 Propagation of Authorization Rules

The question here is how do the rules get propagated? For example, if John has read access to relation EMP, then does it automatically mean that John has read access to every element in EMP? Usually this is the case unless we have a rule that prohibits automatic propagation of an authorization rule. If we have a rule prohibiting the automatic propagation of an authorization rule, then we must explicitly enforce authorization rules that specify the objects that John has access to.

2.2.1.1.6 Special Rules

In our work on mandatory policies, we have explored extensively the enforcement of content and context-based constraints. Note that security constraints are essentially the security rules. Content and context-based rules are those where access is granted depending on the content of the data or the context in which the data is displayed. Such rules can be enforced for discretionary security also. For example, in the case of content-based constraints, John has read access to tuples only in DEPT D100. In the case of context or association-based constraints, John does not have read access to names and salaries taken together, however, he can have access to individual names and salaries. In the case of event-based constraints, after the election, John has access to all elements in relation EMP.

2.2.1.1.7 Consistency and Completeness of Rules

One of the challenges here is ensuring the consistency and completeness of constraints. That is, if the constraints or rules are inconsistent, then do we have conflict resolution rules that will resolve the conflicts? How can we ensure that all of the entities (such as attributes, relations, elements, etc.) are specified in access control rules for a user? Essentially what this means is, are the rules complete? If not, what assumptions do we make about entities that do not have either positive or negative authorizations specified on them for a particular user or a class of users?

We have discussed some essential points with respect to authorization rules. Some examples are given in Figure 2.4. Next, we will discuss some popular access control models and they are RBAC, which is now implemented in commercial systems and attribute-based access control implemented in web-based systems.

2.2.1.2 Role-Based Access Control

RBAC has become one of the most popular access control methods (see [SAND96]). This method has been implemented in commercial systems including Trusted Oracle. The idea here is to grant access to users depending on their roles and functions.

The essential idea behind RBAC is as follows. Users need access to data depending on their roles. For example, a president may have access to information about his/her vice presidents and the members of the board, while the chief financial officer may have access to the financial information and information on those who report to him. A director may have access to information about those working in his division, while the human resources director will have information on personal data about the employees of the corporation. Essentially, RBAC is a type of authorization policy which depends on the user role and the activities that go with the role.

Various research efforts on role hierarchies have been discussed in the literature. There is also a conference series called Symposium on Access Control Models and Technologies that evolved from RBAC research efforts. For example, how does access get propagated? Can one role subsume another? Consider the role hierarchy illustrated in Figure 2.5. This means if we grant access to a node in the hierarchy, does the access propagate upward? That is, if a department manager has access to certain project information, does that access get propagated to the parent node, which is a director node? If a section leader has access to employee information in his/her section, does the access propagate to the department manager who is the parent in the

Authorization rules:

- John has read access to employee relation
- John does not have write access to department relation
- Jane has read access to name values in employee relation
- Jane does not have read access to department relation

FIGURE 2.4 Authorization rules.

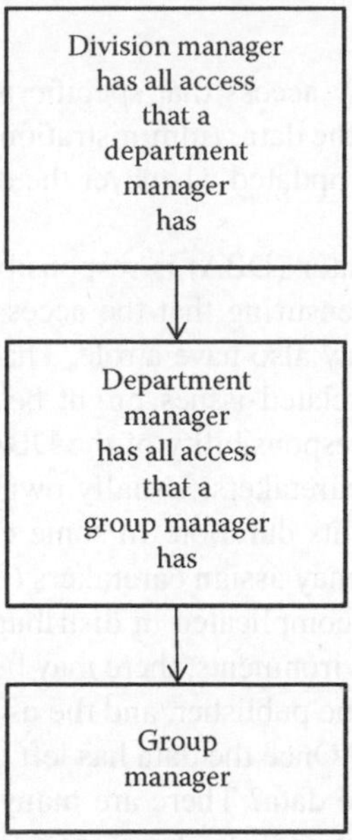

FIGURE 2.5 Role hierarchy.

role hierarchy? What happens to the child nodes? That is, does access propagate downward? For example, if a department manager has access to certain information, then do his subordinates have access to that information? Are there cases where the subordinates have access to data that the department manager does not have? What happens if an employee has to report to two supervisors, one his department manager and the other his project manager? What happens when the department manager is working on a project and has to report to his project leader who also works for him?

RBAC has been examined for relational systems, object systems, distributed systems, and now some of the emerging technologies such as data warehouses, knowledge management systems, semantic web, e-commerce systems, and digital libraries. Furthermore, object models have been used to represent roles and activities (see e.g., Proceedings of the IFIP Database Security Conference series and more recently the Proceedings of the ACM Conference series on Data and Applications Security and Privacy).

2.2.1.3 Usage Control

More recently Sandhu et al. [SAND96] have developed yet another access control-like model that is the usage control (UCON) model (see e.g., the work reported in [PARK04]). The UCON model attempts to incorporate some additional featured into RBAC including attribute mutability and obligations.

2.2.1.4 Attribute-Based Access Control

Due to the fact that roles are not uniform across organization, it was felt that RBAC was not sufficient in web-based systems. Around the same time, web services and service-oriented architectures gained popularity and are not widely used. Therefore, am access control model based on claims was developed for such an environment. This model is attribute-based access control. Here, a user makes certain claims about him or herself. These claims are then verified by the organization that wants to give the user access to the resources. If the user's claims are valid, then the policies are checked as to whether such a user has access to the resources. Attribute-based access control has become extremely popular in the last decade.

2.2.2 Administration Policies

While access control policies specify access that specific users have to the data, administration policies specify who is to administer the data. Administration duties would include keeping the data current, making sure the metadata is updated whenever the data is updated, and ensuring recovery from failures and related activities.

Typically, the database administrator (DBA) is responsible for updating say the metadata, the index and access methods and also ensuring that the access control rules are properly enforced. The system security officer (SSO) may also have a role. That is, the DBA and SSO may share the duties between them. The security-related issues might be the responsibility of the SSO, while the data-related issues might be the responsibility of the DBA. Some other administration policies being considered include assigning caretakers. Usually owners have control of the data that they create and may manage the data for its duration. In some cases, owners may not be available to manage the data, in which case they may assign caretakers (i.e., custodians).

Administration policies get more complicated in distributed environments, especially in a web environment. For example, in web environments, there may be multiple parties involved in distributing documents including the owner, the publisher, and the users requesting the data. Who owns the data? Is it the owner or the publisher? Once the data has left the owner and arrived at the publisher, does the publisher take control of the data? There are many interesting questions that need to be answered as we migrate from a relational database environment to a distributed and perhaps a web environment. These also include managing copyright issues, data quality, data provenance, and governance. Many interesting papers have appeared in recent conferences on administration policies. Figure 2.6 illustrates various administration policies.

2.2.3 Identification and Authentication

For the sake of completion, we discuss identification and authentication as part of our discussion on discretionary security. By identification we mean users must identify themselves with their user ID and password. Authentication means the system must then match the user ID with the password to ensure that this is indeed the person he or she is purporting to be. A user may also have multiple identities depending on his/her roles. Identity management has received a lot of attention especially with the advent of web services (see [BERT06]).

Numerous problems have been reported with the password-based scheme. One is that hackers can break into the system and get the passwords of users and then masquerade as the user. In a centralized system, the problems are not as complicated as in a distributed environment. Now, with the World Wide Web and e-commerce applications, financial organizations are losing billions of dollars when hackers masquerade as legitimate users.

More recently biometrics techniques are being applied for identification and authentication. These include face recognition, fingerprint recognition, and voice recognition techniques to authenticate

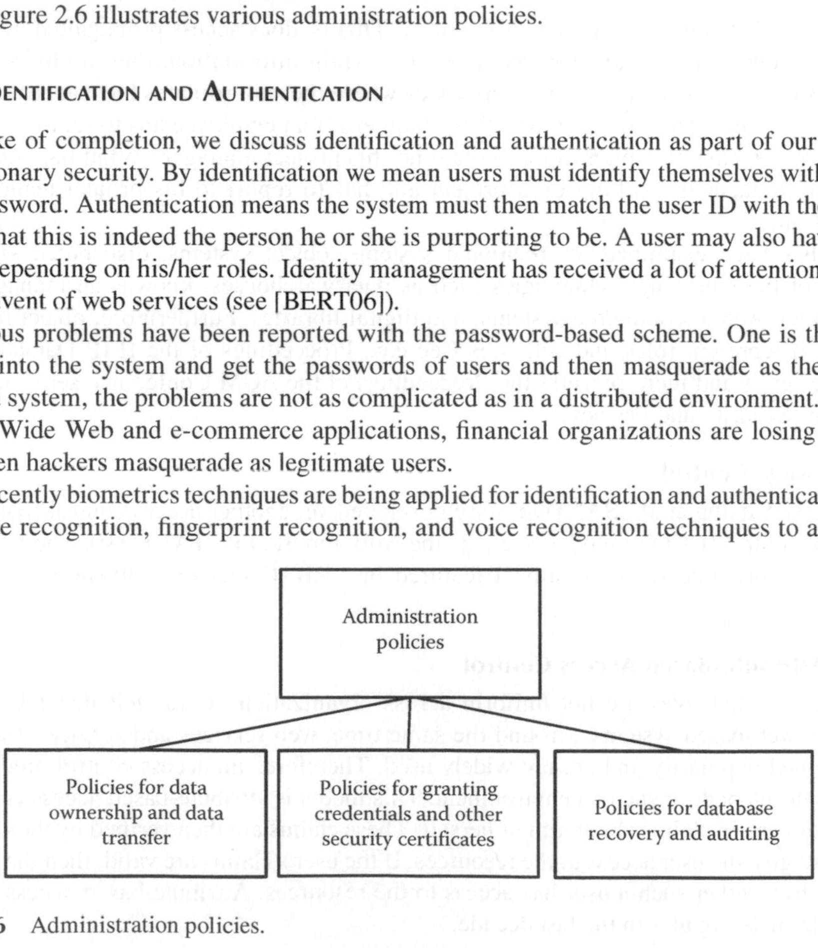

FIGURE 2.6 Administration policies.

the user. These techniques are showing a lot of promise and are already being used. We can expect widespread use of biometric techniques as face recognition technologies advance.

2.2.4 AUDITING: A DATABASE SYSTEM

Databases are audited for multiple purposes. For example, they may be audited to keep track of the number of queries posed, the number of updates made, the number of transactions executed, and the number of times the secondary storage is accessed so that the system can be designed more efficiently. Databases can also be audited for security purposes. For example, have any of the access control rules been bypassed by releasing information to the users? Has the inference problem occurred? Has privacy been violated? Have there been unauthorized intrusions?

Audits create a trail and the audit data may be stored in a database. This database may be mined to detect any abnormal patterns or behaviors. There has been a lot of work in using data mining for auditing and intrusion detection. Audit trail analysis is especially important these days with e-commerce transactions on the web. An organization should have the capability to conduct an analysis and determine problems like credit card fraud and identity theft.

2.2.5 VIEWS FOR SECURITY

Views as a mechanism for security has been studied a great deal both for discretionary security and mandatory security. For example, one may not want to grant access to an entire relation especially if it has, say, 25 attributes such as healthcare records, salary, travel information, personal data, and so on. Therefore, the DBA could define views and grant users access to the views. Similarly, in the case of mandatory security, views could be assigned security levels.

Views have problems associated with them including the view update problem (see [DATE90]). That is, if the view is updated, then we need to ensure that the base relations are updated. Therefore, if a view is updated by John and John does not have access to the base relation, then can the base relation still be updated? That is, do we create different views for different users and then the DBA merges the updates on views as updates on base relations? Figure 2.7 illustrates views for security.

2.3 POLICY ENFORCEMENT AND RELATED ISSUES

The organization of this section is as follows. SQL extensions for security are discussed in Section 2.3.1. In Section 2.3.2, we discuss query modification. Impact of discretionary security on other database functions will be discussed in Section 2.3.3. Note that we will focus on relational database

EMP

SS#	Ename	Salary	D#
1	John	20K	10
2	Paul	30K	20
3	Mary	40K	20
4	Jane	20K	20
5	Bill	20K	10
6	Larry	20K	10
1	Michelle	30K	20

V1. VIEW EMP (D#=20)

SS#	Ename	Salary
2	Paul	30K
3	Mary	40K
4	Jane	20K
1	Michelle	30K

V2. VIEW EMP (D#=10)

SS#	Ename	Salary
1	John	20K
5	Bill	20K
6	Larry	20K

Rules:

John has Read access to V1
John has Write access to V2

FIGURE 2.7 Views for security.

Policy Enforcement Mechanisms:

Query modification algorithm

Rule processing to enforce the access control rules

Theorem proving techniques to determine if policies are violated

Consistency and completeness checking of policies

FIGURE 2.8 Policy enforcement.

systems. Figure 2.8 illustrates the various aspects involved in enforcing security policies. These include specification, implementation, and visualization (where visualization tools are being used for the visualization of the policies).

2.3.1 SQL Extensions for Security

This section discusses policy specification. While much of the focus will be on SQL extensions for security policy specification, we will also briefly discuss some of the emerging languages. Note that SQL was developed for data definition and data manipulation for relational systems. Various versions of SQL have been developed including SQL for objects, for multimedia, and for the web. That is, SQL has influenced data manipulation and data definition a great deal over the past 30 years (see [SQL3]).

As we have stated, SQL is a data definition and data manipulation language. Security policies could be specified during data definition. SQL has GRANT and REVOKE constructs for specifying grant and revoke access to users. That is, if a user John has read access to relation EMP, then one could use SQL and specify something like "GRANT JOHN EMP READ" and if the access is to be revoked, then we need something like "REVOKE JOHN EMP READ." SQL has also been extended with more complex constraints such as granting John read access to a tuple in a relation and granting Jane write access to an element in a relation.

In [THUR89], we specified SQL extensions for security assertions. These assertions were for multilevel security. We could use similar reasoning for specifying discretionary security policies. For example, consider the situation where John does not have read access to names and salaries in EMP taken together, but he can read names and salaries separately. One could specify this in SQL-like language as follows.

```
GRANT JOHN READ
EMP.SALARY
GRANT JOHN READ
EMP.NAME
NOT GRANT JOHN READ
Together (EMP.NAME, EMP.SALARY).
```

If we are to grant John read access to the employees who earn <30K, then this assertion is specified as follows.

```
GRANT JOHN READ
EMP
Where EMP.SALARY <30K
```

Note that the assertions we have specified have been incorporated into any standards. These are some of our ideas. We need to explore ways of incorporating these assertions into the standards.

Policy Specification:

SQL extensions to specify security policies

Rule-based languages to specify policies

Logic programming languages such as Prolog to specify policies

FIGURE 2.9 Policy specification.

SQL extensions have also been proposed for RBAC. In fact, products such as Oracle's Trusted database product enforce RBAC. The access control rules are specified in an SQL-like language.

Note that there are many other specification languages that have been developed. These include XML, RDF, and related languages for the web and the semantic web. Semantic web is essentially an intelligent web. SQL-like languages have been specified for XML and RDF. For example, XML-QL was developed for XML which then evolved into a language called XQuery. SPARQL is now the query language for RDF (see [THUR07]). We will use such languages in our systems to be discussed in Part IV. Figure 2.9 illustrates specification aspects for security policies.

2.3.2 Query Modification

Query modification was first proposed in the INGRES project at the University of California at Berkeley (see [STON74]). The idea is to modify the query based on the constraints. We have successfully designed and implemented query modification for mandatory security (see [DWYE87], [THUR87], and [THUR93]). However, much of the discussion in this section will be on query modification based on discretionary security constraints. We illustrate the essential points with some examples.

Consider a query by John to retrieve all tuples from EMP. Suppose that John only has read access to all the tuples where the salary is <30K and the employee is not in the Security department. Then the query

```
Select * from EMP
Will be modified to
Select * from EMP
Where salary <30K
And Dept is not Security
```

Where we assume that the attributes of EMP are say name, salary, age, and department.

Essentially what happens is that the "where" clause of the query has all the constraints associated with the relation. We can also have constraints that span across multiple relations. For example, we could have two relations EMP and DEPT joined by Dept #. Then the query is modified as follows:

```
Select * from EMP
Where EMP.Salary < 30K
And EMP.D# = DEPT.D#
And DEPT.Name is not Security
```

We have used some simple examples for query modification. The detailed algorithms can be found in [DWYE87] and [STON74]. The high level algorithm is illustrated in Figure 2.10.

2.3.3 Discretionary Security and Database Functions

In Section 2.3.2, we discussed query modification which is essentially processing security constraints during the query operation. Query optimization will also be impacted by security constraints.

Query Modification Algorithm:

Input: Query, security constraints
Output: Modified query

For constraints that are relevant to the query, modify the where clause of the query via a negation

For example: If salary should not be released to Jane and if Jane requests information from employee, then modify the query to retrieve information from employee where attribute is not salary

Repeat the process until all relevant constraints are processed

The end result is the modified query

FIGURE 2.10 Query modification algorithm.

That is, once the query is modified, then the query tree has to be built. The idea is to push selections and projections down in the query tree and carry out the join operation later.

Other functions are also impacted by security constraints. Let us consider transaction management. Bertino and Musto have developed algorithms for integrity constraint processing for transactions management (see [BERT89]). We have examined their techniques for mandatory security constraint processing during transaction management. The techniques may be adapted for discretionary security constraints. The idea is to ensure that the constraints are not violated during transaction execution.

Constraints may be enforced on the metadata. For example, one could grant and revoke access to users to the metadata relations. Discretionary security constraints for metadata could be handled in the same way they are handled for data. Other database functions include storage management. The issues in storage management include developing appropriate access methods and index strategies. One needs to examine the impact of the security constraints on the storage management functions. That is, can one partition the relations based on the constraints and store them in such a way so that the relations can be accessed efficiently? We need to develop secure indexing technologies for database systems. Some work on secure indexing for geospatial information systems is reported in [ATLU04]. Databases are audited to determine whether any security violation has occurred. Furthermore, views have been used to grant access to individuals for security purposes. We need efficient techniques for auditing as well as for view management.

In this section, we have examined the impact of security on some of the database functions including query management, transaction processing, metadata management, and storage management. We need to also investigate the impact of security on other functions such as integrity constraint processing and fault-tolerant computing. Figure 2.11 illustrates the impact of security on the database functions. It should be noted that some of the discussions in this section have been extended for big data management. This will be our focus especially in Parts IV and V of this book.

2.4 DATA PRIVACY

Data privacy is about protecting sensitive information of individuals. While different definitions of privacy have been proposed, the most common definition is that a person decides what information is to be released about him or her. While data privacy has been studied for decades, especially with statistical databases, with the advent of the World Wide Web and the efforts on applying data

Secure Database Functions:

Query processing: Enforce access control rules during query processing; inference control; consider security constraints for query optimization

Transaction management: Check whether security constraints are satisfied during transaction execution

Storage management: Develop special access methods and index strategies that take into consideration the security constraints

Metadata management: Enforce access control on metadata; ensure that data is not released to unauthorized individuals by releasing the metadata

Integrity management: Ensure that integrity of the data is maintained while enforcing security

FIGURE 2.11 Security impact on database functions.

mining for counter-terrorism applications, there has been an increasing interest in this topic over the past 15 years. Much research has been reported on balancing the need between privacy and security. The first effort on privacy-preserving data mining was reported in [AGRA00]. Several other efforts on this topic followed since the early 2000s [KANT04]. In addition, treating the privacy problem as a variation of the inference problem was studied in [THUR05b].

With the developments in big data technologies, there is significant interest in data privacy. For example, a National Science Foundation workshop on Big Data Security and Privacy was held in September 2014 and the results have been reported in [NSF14]. We will discuss some of the findings at this workshop in Part V. With advancements in technology such as data analytics and the interest in data privacy among the policy makers, lawyers, social scientists, and computer scientists, we can expect significant developments in protecting the privacy of individuals as well as ensuring their security. More details on big data security and privacy will be provided in Part V of this book.

2.5 SUMMARY AND DIRECTIONS

In this chapter, we have provided an overview of discretionary security policies in database systems. We started with a discussion of access control policies including authorization policies and RBAC. Then we discussed administration policies. We briefly discussed identification and authentication. We also discussed auditing issues as well as views for security. Next, we discussed policy enforcement. We also discussed SQL extensions for specifying policies as well as provided an overview of query modification.

There is still a lot of work to be done. For example, much work is still needed on RBAC and attribute-based access control for emerging technologies such as digital libraries and the semantic web. We need administration policies to manage multiparty transactions in a web environment. We also need biometric technologies for authenticating users. Digital identity is becoming an important research area especially with cloud systems.

Security policy enforcement is a topic that will continue to evolve as new technologies emerge. We have advanced from relational to object to multimedia to web-based to cloud-based data management systems. Each system has some unique features that are incorporated into the security policies. Enforcing policies for the various systems will continue to be a major focus. We also need to carry out research on the consistency and completeness of policies. Policy visualization may help toward achieving this.

Policy management in the cloud and big data is an active area of research. Our work includes access control as well as policy-based information sharing in the cloud. The experimental systems we have developed on security policy enforcement in the cloud are discussed in Part IV.

REFERENCES

[AGRA00]. R. Agrawal and R. Srikant, "Privacy-Preserving Data Mining," *SIGMOD Conference*, pp. 439–450, 2000.

[ATLU04]. V. Atluri and S. Chun, "An Authorization Model for Geospatial Data," *IEEE Transaction on Dependable and Secure Computing*, 1 (4), 238–254, 2004.

[BERT89]. E. Bertino and D. Musto, "Integrity Constraint Processing During Transaction Processing," *Acta Informatica*, 26 (1–2), 25–57, 1988.

[BERT02]. E. Bertino et al., "Access Control for XML Documents," *Data and Knowledge Engineering*, 43 (3), 2002.

[BERT06]. E. Bertino, "Digital Identity Management and Protection," *Proceedings of the 2006 International Conference on Privacy*, Security and Trust, Ontario, Canada, 2006.

[CARM04]. B. Carminati et al., "Security for RDF," *Proceedings of the DEXA Conference Workshop on Web Semantics*, Zaragoza, Spain, August, 2004.

[DATE90]. C. Date, *An Introduction to Database Systems*, Addison-Wesley, Reading, MA, 1990.

[DWYE87]. P. Dwyer et al., "Multilevel Security for Relational Database Systems," *Computers and Security*, 6 (3), 252–260, 1987.

[FERR00]. E. Ferrari and B. Thuraisingham, "Secure Database Systems," In *Advances in Database Management*, M. Piatini and O. Diaz, editors, Artech House, UK, 2000.

[GRIF76]. P. Griffiths and B. Wade, "An Authorization Mechanism for a Relational Database System," *ACM Transactions on Database Systems*, 1 (3), 242–255, 1976.

[KANT04]. M. Kantarcioglu and C. Clifton, "Privacy-Preserving Distributed Mining of Association Rules on Horizontally Partitioned Data," *IEEE Transactions on Knowledge and Data Engineering*, 16 (9), 1026–1037, 2004.

[NIST]. Guide to Attribute-Based Access Control (ABAC) Definition and Considerations, NIST Special Publication 800-162, 2014.

[NSF14]. National Science Foundation Workshop, http://csi.utdallas.edu/events/NSF/NSF-workhop-Big-Data-SP-Feb9-2015_FINAL.pdf

[PARK04]. J. Park and R. Sandhu, "The UCON Usage Control Model," *ACM Transactions on Information and Systems Security*, 7 (#1), 128–174, 2004.

[SAND96]. R. Sandhu et al., "Role-Based Access Control Models," *IEEE Computer*, 29 (2), 38–47, 1996.

[SQL3]. en.wikipedia.org/wiki/SQL, American National Standards Institute, Draft, Maynard, MN, 1992.

[STON74]. M. Stonebraker and E. Wong, "Access Control in a Relational Database Management System by Query Modification," *Proceedings of the ACM Annual Conference*, ACM Press, NY, 1974.

[THUR87]. B. Thuraisingham "Security Checking in Relational Database Management Systems Augmented with Inference Engines," *Computers and Security*, 6 (6), 479–492, 1987.

[THUR89]. B. Thuraisingham and P. Stachour, "SQL Extensions for Security Assertions," *Computer Standards and Interface Journal*, 11 (1), 5–14, 1989.

[THUR93]. B. Thuraisingham, W. Ford, and M. Collins, "Design and Implementation of a Database Inference Controller," *Data and Knowledge Engineering*, 11 (3), 5–14, 1993.

[THUR94]. B. Thuraisingham, "Security Issues for Federated Database Systems," *Computers and Security*, 13 (6), 509–525, 1994.

[THUR97]. B. Thuraisingham, *Data Management Systems: Evolution and Interoperation*, CRC Press, Boca Raton, FL, 1997.

[THUR05a]. B. Thuraisingham, *Database Security, Integrating Database Systems and Information Security*, CRC Press, Boca Raton, FL, 2005.

[THUR05b]. B. M. Thuraisingham, "Privacy Constraint Processing in a Privacy-Enhanced Database Management System," *Data and Knowledge Engineering*, 55 (2), 159–188, 2005.

[THUR07]. B. Thuraisingham, *Building Trustworthy Semantic Webs*, CRC Press, Boca Raton, FL, 2007.

3 Data Mining Techniques

3.1 INTRODUCTION

We have used data mining and analytics techniques in several of our efforts for various applications such as social media systems and intrusion detection systems. For example, in our previous book [THUR16], we discussed algorithms for location-based data mining that will extract the locations of the various social media (e.g., Twitter) users. These algorithms can be extended to extract other demographics data. Our prior research has also developed data mining tools for sentiment analysis as well as for cyber security applications. In Parts II and III, we will discuss scalability aspects of stream data mining and will apply the techniques for cyber security applications (e.g., insider threat detection). In this chapter, we provide some background information about general data mining techniques so that the reader can have an understanding of the field. Cyber security applications of data mining will be discussed in Chapter 4.

Data mining outcomes (also called tasks) include classification, clustering, forming associations, as well as detecting anomalies. Our tools have mainly focused on classification as the outcome, and we have developed classification tools. The classification problem is also referred to as supervised learning in which a set of labeled examples is learned by a model, and then a new example with unknown labels is presented to the model for prediction.

There are many prediction models that have been used such as the Markov model, decision trees, artificial neural networks (ANNs), support vector machines (SVMs), association rule mining (ARM), among others. Each of these models has its strengths and weaknesses. However, there is a common weakness among all of these techniques, which is the inability to suit all applications. The reason that there is no such ideal or perfect classifier is that each of these techniques was initially designed to solve specific problems under certain assumptions.

In this chapter, we discuss the data mining techniques that have been commonly used. Specifically, we present the Markov model, SVM, ANN, ARM, the problem of multiclassification, as well as image classification, which are the aspects of image mining. In our research and development, we have designed hybrid models to improve the prediction accuracy of data mining algorithms in various applications, namely, intrusion detection, social media analytics, WWW prediction, and image classification [AWAD09].

The organization of this chapter is as follows. In Section 3.2, we provide an overview of various data mining tasks and techniques. The techniques that we have used in our work are discussed in Sections 3.3 through 3.8. In particular, neural networks, SVM, Markov models, and ARM, as well as some other classification techniques will be described. This chapter is summarized in Section 3.9. It should be noted that a breakthrough data mining technique we have designed, called novel class detection, to be discussed in Part III has evolved from the experiences we have gained from using techniques such as SVM, ANN, and ARM. It should be noted that we have used the term data mining and data analytics interchangeably throughout this book.

3.2 OVERVIEW OF DATA MINING TASKS AND TECHNIQUES

Before we discuss data mining techniques, we provide an overview of some of the data mining tasks (also known as data mining outcomes). Then we will discuss the techniques. In general, data mining tasks can be grouped into two categories: predictive and descriptive. Predictive tasks essentially predict whether an item belongs to a class or not. Descriptive tasks in general extract patterns from the examples. One of the most prominent predictive tasks is classification. In some cases, other tasks such as anomaly detection can be reduced to a predictive task such as whether a particular situation

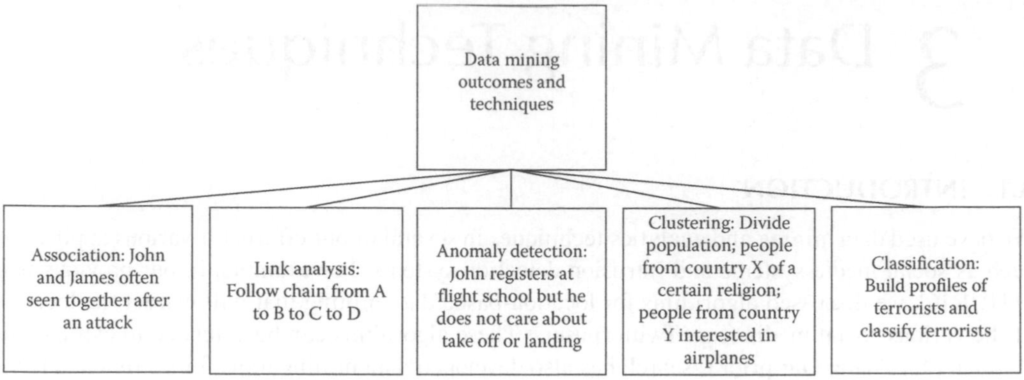

FIGURE 3.1 Data mining tasks.

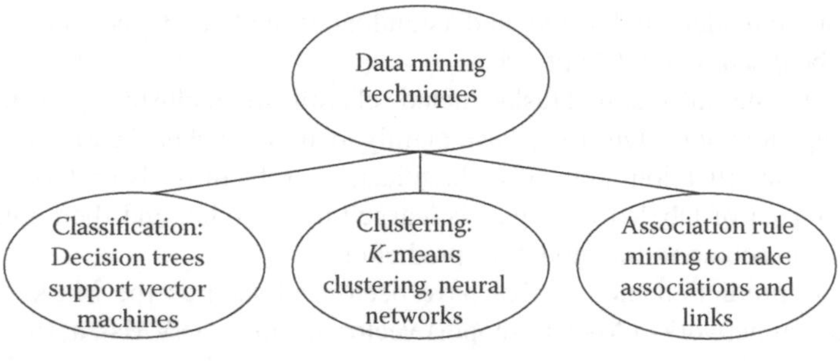

FIGURE 3.2 Data mining techniques.

is an anomaly or not. Descriptive tasks in general include making associations and forming clusters. Therefore, classification, anomaly detection, making associations and forming clusters are also thought to be data mining tasks.

Next, the data mining techniques can either be predictive or descriptive or both. For example, neural networks can perform classification as well as clustering techniques. Classification techniques include decisions trees, SVM, as well as memory-based reasoning. ARM techniques are used in general to make associations. Link analysis that analyzes links can also make associations between links and predict new links. Clustering techniques include *K*-means clustering. An overview of the data mining tasks (i.e., the outcomes of data mining) is illustrated in Figure 3.1. The techniques (e.g., neural networks, SVMs) are illustrated in Figure 3.2.

3.3 ARTIFICIAL NEURAL NETWORKS

ANN is a very well known, powerful and robust classification technique that has been used to approximate real-, discrete-, and vector-valued functions, for example [MITC97] ANNs have been used in many areas such as interpreting visual scenes, speech recognition, and learning robot control strategies. An ANN simulates the biological nervous system in the human brain. The nervous system is composed of a large number of highly interconnected processing units (neurons) working together to produce our feelings and reactions. ANNs, like people, learn by example. The learning process in the human brain involves adjustments to the synaptic connections between neurons. Similarly, the learning process of ANN involves adjustments to the node weights. Figure 3.3 presents a simple neuron unit, which is called a perceptron. The perceptron input, x, is a vector or real-valued inputs. w is the weight vector, in which its value is determined after training. The perceptron computes a linear combination of an input vector x as follows:

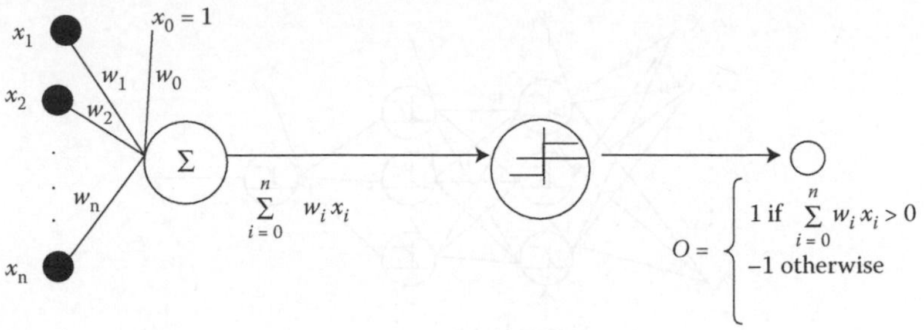

FIGURE 3.3 The perceptron.

$$o(x_1, \ldots, x_n) = \begin{cases} 1 \text{ if } w_0 + w_1 x_1 + \cdots + w_n x_n > 0 \\ -1 \text{ otherwise} \end{cases} \tag{3.1}$$

Notice that w_i corresponds to the contribution of the input vector component x_i of the perceptron output. Also, in order for the perceptron to output a 1, the weighted combination of the inputs $\left(\sum_{i=1}^{n} w_i x_i\right)$ must be greater than the threshold w_0.

Learning the perceptron involves choosing values for the weights $w_0 + w_1 x_1 + \ldots + w_n x_n$. Initially, random weight values are given to the perceptron. Then the perceptron is applied to each training example updating the weights of the perceptron whenever an example is misclassified. This process is repeated many times until all training examples are correctly classified. The weights are updated according to the following rule:

$$\begin{cases} w_i = w_i + \delta w_i \\ \delta w_i = \eta(t - o)x_i \end{cases} \tag{3.2}$$

where η is a learning constant, o is the output computed by the perceptron, and t is the target output for the current training example.

The computation power of a single perceptron is limited to linear decisions. However, the perceptron can be used as a building block to compose powerful multilayer networks. In this case, a more complicated updating rule is needed to train the network weights. In this work, we employ an ANN of two layers and each layer is composed of three building blocks (see Figure 3.4). We use the back-propagation algorithm for learning the weights. The back-propagation algorithm attempts to minimize the squared error function.

A typical training example in WWW prediction is $\langle [k_{t-\tau+1}, \ldots, k_{t-1}, k_t]^T, d \rangle$, where $[k_{t-\tau+1}, \ldots, k_{t-1}, k_t]^T$ is the input to the ANN and d is the target web page. Notice that the input units of the ANN in Figure 3.5 are τ previous pages that the user has recently visited, where k is a web page ID. The output of the network is a Boolean value, not a probability. We will see later how to approximate the probability of the output by fitting a sigmoid function after ANN output. The approximated probabilistic output

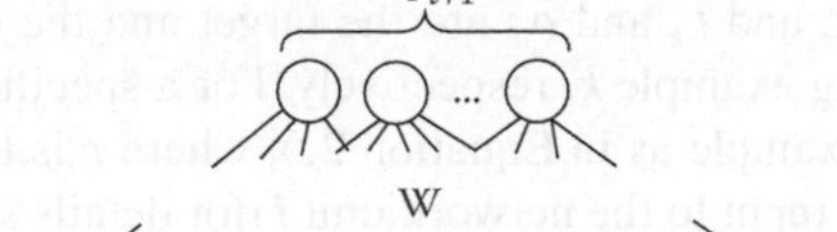

FIGURE 3.4 Artificial neural network.

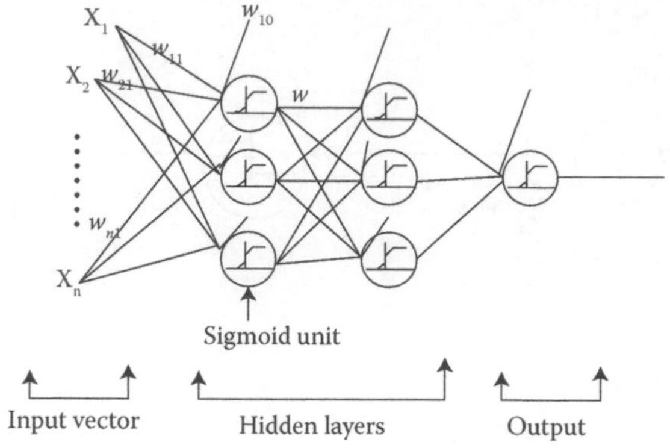

FIGURE 3.5 The design of the ANN used in our implementation.

becomes $o' = f(o(I)) = p_{t+1}$, where I is an input session and $p_{t+1} = p(d|k_{t-\tau+1}, \ldots, k_t)$. We choose the sigmoid function (2.3) as a transfer function so as the ANN can handle nonlinearly separable datasets [MITC97]. Notice that in our ANN design (Figure 3.5), we use a sigmoid transfer function (2.3), in each building block. In Equation 2.3, I is the input to the network, O is the output of the network, W is the matrix of weights, and σ is the sigmoid function:

$$\begin{cases} o = \sigma(w \,.\, I) \\ \sigma(y) = \dfrac{1}{1+e^{-y}} \end{cases} \tag{3.3}$$

$$E(W) = \frac{1}{2}\sum_{k \in D}\sum_{i \in \text{ouputs}} (t_{ik} - o_{ik})^2 \tag{3.4}$$

$$\begin{cases} w_{ji} = w_{ji} + \delta w_{ji} \\ \delta w_{ji} = -\eta \dfrac{\partial E_d}{\partial w_{ji}} \end{cases} \tag{3.5}$$

$$\delta w_{ji}(n) = -\eta \frac{\partial E_d}{\partial w_{ji}} + \alpha \delta w_{ji}(n-1) \tag{3.6}$$

We implement the back-propagation algorithm for training the weights. The back-propagation algorithm employs gradient descent to attempt to minimize the squared error between the network output values and the target values of these outputs. The sum of the error over all of the network output units is defined in Equation 3.3. In Equation 3.4, the *outputs* is the set of output units in the network, D is the training set, and t_{ik} and o_{ik} are the target and the output values associated with the ith output unit and training example k, respectively. For a specific weight w_{ji} in the network, it is updated for each training example as in Equation 2.5, where η is the learning rate and w_{ji} is the weight associated with the ith input to the network unit j (for details see [MITC97]). As we can see from Equation 3.5, the search direction δw is computed using the gradient descent that guarantees convergence toward a local minimum. In order to mitigate that, we add a momentum to the weight update rule such that the weight update direction $\delta w_{ji}(n)$ depends partially on the update direction in the previous iteration $\delta w_{ji}(n - 1)$. The new weight update direction is shown in Equation 3.6, where n is the current iterations and α is the momentum constant. Notice that in Equation 3.6, the step size is slightly larger than that in Equation 3.5. This contributes to a smooth convergence of the search in regions where the gradient is unchanging [MITC97].

In our implementation, we set the step size η dynamically based on the distribution of the classes in the dataset. Specifically, we set the step size to large values when updating the training examples that belong to low-distribution classes and vice versa. This is because when the distribution of the classes in the dataset varies widely (e.g., a dataset might have 5% positive examples and 95% negative examples), the network weights converge toward the examples from the class of the larger distribution, which causes a slow convergence. Furthermore, we adjust the learning rates slightly by applying the momentum constant (3.6) to speed up the convergence of the network [MITC97].

3.4 SUPPORT VECTOR MACHINES

SVM are learning systems that use a hypothesis space of linear functions in a high-dimensional feature space, trained with a learning algorithm from optimization theory. This learning strategy introduced by Vapnik et al. ([VAPN95], [VAPN98], [VAPN95], [CRIS00]) is a very powerful method that has been applied in a wide variety of applications. The basic concept in SVM is the hyper-plane classifier or linear separability. In order to achieve linear separability, SVM applies two basic ideas—margin maximization and kernels, that is, mapping input space to a higher dimension space, feature space.

For binary classification, the SVM problem can be formalized as in Equation 3.7. Suppose we have N training data points $\{(x_1, y_1), (x_2, y_2), \ldots, (x_N, y_N)\}$, where $x_i \in R^d$ and $y_i \in \{+1, -1\}$. We would like to find a linear separating hyper-plane classifier as in Equation 3.8. Furthermore, we want this hyper-plane to have the maximum separating margin with respect to the two classes (see Figure 3.6). The functional margin, or the margin for short, is defined geometrically as the Euclidean distance of the closest point from the decision boundary to the input space. Figure 3.7 gives an intuitive explanation of why margin maximization gives the best solution of separation. In Figure 3.7a, we can find an infinite number of separators for a specific dataset. There is no specific or clear reason to favor one separator over another. In Figure 3.7b, we see that maximizing the margin provides only one thick separator. Such a solution proves to achieve the best generalization accuracy, that is, prediction for the unseen ([VAPN95], [VAPN98], [VAPN99]):

$$\begin{cases} \text{minimize}_{(w,b)} \dfrac{1}{2} w^T w \\ \text{subject to } y_i(w \cdot x_i - b) \geq 1 \end{cases} \tag{3.7}$$

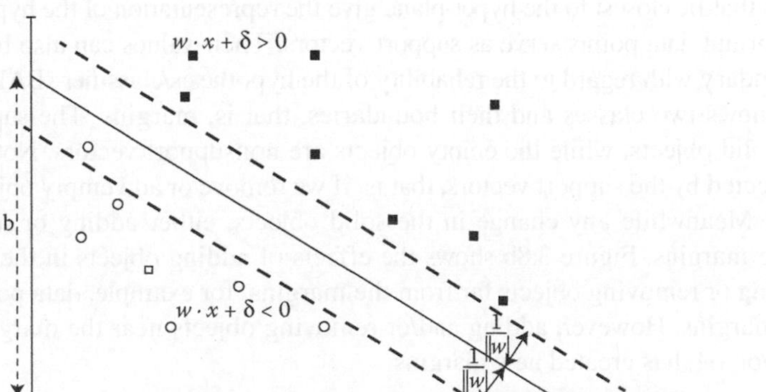

FIGURE 3.6 Linear separation in the SVM.

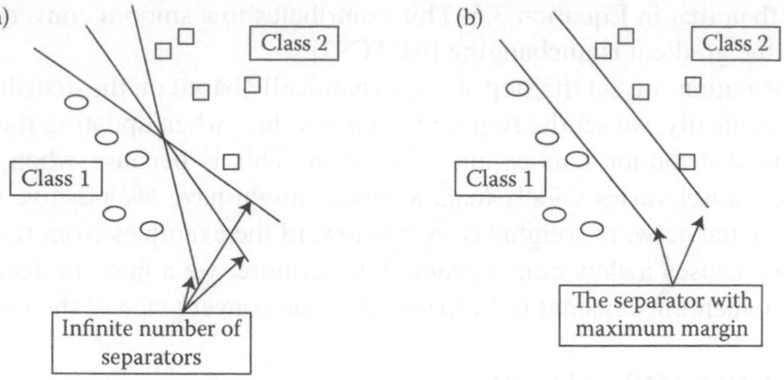

FIGURE 3.7 The SVM separator that causes the maximum margin.

$$f(x) = \text{sign}(w \cdot x - b) \tag{3.8}$$

$$\text{maximize } L(w, b, \alpha) = \frac{1}{2} w^T w - \sum_{i=1}^{N} \alpha_i y_i (w \cdot x_i - b) + \sum_{i=1}^{N} \alpha_i \tag{3.9}$$

$$f(x) = \text{sign}(wx - b) = \text{sign}\left(\sum_{i=1}^{N} \alpha_i y_i (x \cdot x_i - b) \right) \tag{3.10}$$

Notice that Equation 3.8 computes the sign of the functional margin of point x in addition to the prediction label of x, that is, the functional margin of x equals $wx - b$.

The SVM optimization problem is a convex quadratic programming problem (in w, b) in a convex set (Equation 3.7). We can solve the Wolfe dual instead (as in Equation 3.9) with respect to α, subject to the constraints that the gradient of $L(w, b, \alpha)$ with respect to the primal variables w and b vanish and $\alpha_i \geq 0$. The primal variables are eliminated from $L(w, b, \alpha)$ (see [CRIS00] for more details). When we solve α_i, we can obtain $w = \sum_{i=1}^{N} \alpha_i y_i x_i$, and we can classify a new object x using Equation 3.10. Note that the training vectors occur only in the form of the dot product and that there is a Lagrangian multiplier α_i for each training point, which reflects the importance of the data point. When the maximal margin hyper-plane is found, only points that lie closest to the hyper-plane will have $\alpha_i > 0$, and these points are called *support vectors*. All other points will have $\alpha_i = 0$ (see Figure 3.8a). This means that only those points that lie closest to the hyper-plane give the representation of the hypothesis/classifier. These most important data points serve as support vectors. Their values can also be used to give an independent boundary with regard to the reliability of the hypothesis/classifier [BART99].

Figure 3.8a shows two classes and their boundaries, that is, margins. The support vectors are represented by solid objects, while the empty objects are nonsupport vectors. Notice that the margins are only affected by the support vectors, that is, if we remove or add empty objects, the margins will not change. Meanwhile any change in the solid objects, either adding or removing objects, could change the margins. Figure 3.8b shows the effects of adding objects in the margin area. As we can see, adding or removing objects far from the margins, for example, data point 1 or −2, does not change the margins. However, adding and/or removing objects near the margins, for example, data point 2 and/or −1, has created new margins.

3.5 MARKOV MODEL

Some recent and advanced predictive methods for web surfing are developed using Markov models ([YANG01], [PIRO96]). For these predictive models, the sequences of web pages visited by surfers are

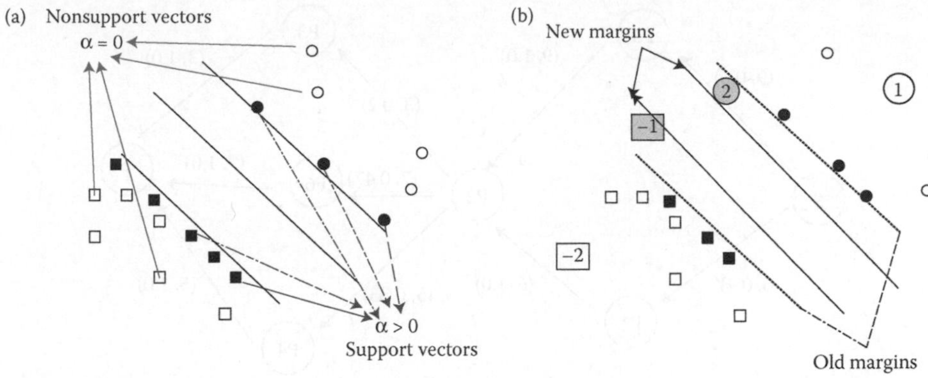

FIGURE 3.8 (a) The values of for support vectors and nonsupport vectors. (b) The effect of adding new data points on the margins.

typically considered as Markov chains that are then fed as input. The basic concept of the Markov model is that it predicts the next action depending on the result of previous action or actions. Actions can mean different things for different applications. For the purpose of illustration, we will consider actions specific for the WWW prediction application. In WWW prediction, the next action corresponds to the prediction of the next page to be traversed. The previous actions correspond to the previous web pages to be considered. Based on the number of previous actions considered, Markov models can have different orders:

$$\mathrm{pr}(P_k) = \mathrm{pr}(S_k) \tag{3.11}$$

$$\mathrm{pr}(P_2 \mid P_1) = \mathrm{pr}(S_2 = P_2 \mid S_1 = P_1) \tag{3.12}$$

$$\mathrm{pr}(P_N \mid P_{N-1}, \ldots, P_{N-k}) = \mathrm{pr}(S_N = P_N \mid S_{N-1} = P_{N-1}, \ldots, S_{N-k} = P_{N-k}) \tag{3.13}$$

The 0th-order Markov model is the unconditional probability of the state (or web page) (Equation 3.11). In Equation 3.11, P_k is a web page and S_k is the corresponding state. The first-order Markov model, Equation 3.12, can be computed by taking page-to-page transitional probabilities or the n-gram probabilities of $\{P_1, P_2\}, \{P_2, P_3\}, \ldots, \{P_{k-1}, P_k\}$.

In the following, we present an illustrative example of different orders of the Markov model and how it can predict.

EXAMPLE:

Imagine a website of six web pages: P1, P2, P3, P4, P5, and P6. Suppose we have user sessions as given in Table 3.1. This table depicts the navigation of many users of that website. Figure 3.9 shows the *first-order Markov model,* where the next action is predicted based on only the last action

TABLE 3.1
Collection of User Sessions and Their Frequencies

Session	Frequency
P1, P2, P4	5
P1, P2, P6	1
P5, P2, P6	6
P5, P2, P3	3

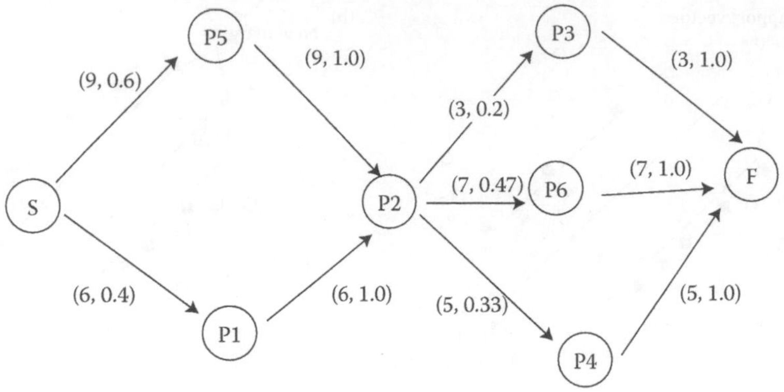

FIGURE 3.9 First-order Markov model.

performed, that is, the last page traversed by the user. States S and F correspond to the initial and final states, respectively. The probability of each transition is estimated by the ratio of the number of times the sequence of states was traversed and the number of times the anchor state was visited. Next, to each arch in Figure 3.8, the first number is the frequency of that transition, and the second number is the transition probability. For example, the transition probability of the transition (P2 to P3) is 0.2 because the number of times users traverse from page 2 to page 3 is 3 and the number of times page 2 is visited is 15 (i.e., 0.2 = 3/15).

Notice that the transition probability is used to resolve prediction. For example, given that a user has already visited P2, the most probable page he or she visits next is P6. That is because the transition probability from P2 to P6 is the highest.

Notice that the transition probability might not be available for some pages. For example, the transition probability from P2 to P5 is not available because no user has visited P5 after P2. Hence, these transition probabilities are set to zeros. Similarly, the *K*th-order Markov model is where the prediction is computed after considering the last *K*th action performed by the users (Equation 3.13). In WWW prediction, the *K*th-order Markov model is the probability of user visits to P_Kth page given its previous $k - 1$ page visits.

Figure 3.10 shows the second-order Markov model that corresponds to Table 3.1. In the second-order model, we consider the last two pages. The transition probability is computed in a similar fashion. For example, the transition probability of the transition (P1, P2) to (P2, P6) is $0.16 = 1 \times 1/6$ because the number of times users traverse from state (P1, P2) to state (P2, P6) is 1 and the number of times pages (P1, P2) is visited is 6 (i.e., 0.16 = 1/6). The transition probability is used for prediction. For example,

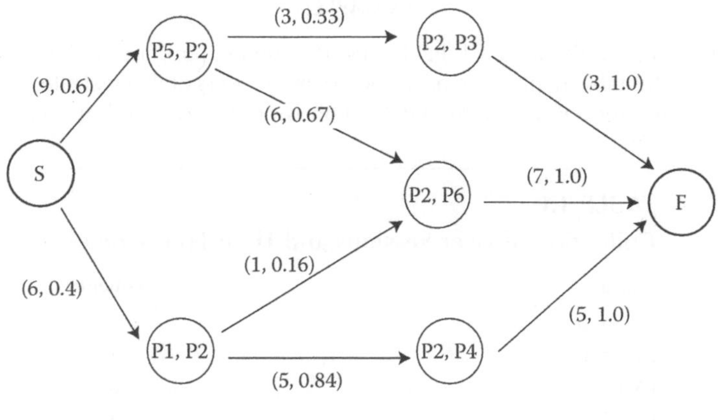

FIGURE 3.10 Second-order Markov model.

given that a user has visited P1 and P2, he or she most probably visits P4 because the transition probability from state (P1, P2) to state (P2, P4) is greater than that from state (P1, P2) to state (P2, P6).

The order of the Markov model is related to the sliding window. The Kth-order Markov model corresponds to a sliding window of size $K - 1$.

Notice that there is another concept that is similar to the sliding window concept, which is the *number of hops*. In this appendix, we use the *number of hops* and the sliding window interchangeably.

In WWW prediction, Markov models are built based on the concept of n-gram. The n-gram can be represented as a tuple of the form $\langle x_1, x_2, \ldots, x_n \rangle$ to depict sequences of page clicks by a population of users surfing a website. Each component of the n-gram takes a specific page ID value that reflects the surfing path of a specific user surfing a webpage. For example, the n-gram $\langle P_{10}, P_{21}, P_4, P_{12} \rangle$ for some user U states that the user U has visited the pages 10, 21, 4, and finally 12 in a sequence.

3.6 ASSOCIATION RULE MINING (ARM)

Association rule mining is a data mining technique that has been applied successfully to discover related transactions. ARM finds the relationships among itemsets based on their co-occurrence in the transactions. Specifically, ARM discovers the frequent patterns (regularities) among those itemsets. For example, what are the items purchased together in a super store? In the following, we briefly introduce ARM. For more details, see [AGRA93] and [AGRA94].

Assume that we have m items in our database; then, define $I = \{i_1, i_2, \ldots, i_m\}$ as the set of all items. A transaction T is a set of items such that $T \subseteq I$. Let D be the set of all transactions in the database. A transaction T contains X if $X \subseteq T$ and $X \subseteq I$. An association rule is an implication of the form $X \rightarrow Y$, where, $X \subset I$, $Y \subset I$, and $X \cap Y = \varphi$. There are two parameters to consider a rule: confidence and support. A rule $R = X \rightarrow Y$ holds with confidence c if $c\%$ of the transactions of D that contain X also contain Y (i.e., $c = \text{pr}(Y|X)$). The rule R holds with support s if $s\%$ of the transactions in D contain X and Y (i.e., $s = \text{pr}(X, Y)$). The problem of mining association rules is defined as follows. Given a set of transactions D, we would like to generate all rules that satisfy a confidence and a support greater than a minimum confidence (σ), *minconf*, and minimum support (ϑ), *minsup*. There are several efficient algorithms proposed to find association rules such as AIS algorithm ([AGRA93], [AGRA94]), SETM algorithm [HOUT95], and AprioriTid [LIU99].

In the case of web transactions, we use association rules to discover navigational patterns among users. This would help to cache a page in advance and reduce the loading time of a page. Also, discovering a pattern of navigation helps in personalization. Transactions are captured from the clickstream data captured in web server logs.

In many applications, there is one main problem in using ARM, that is, using global minimum support (*minsup*). This is because rare hits, that is, web pages that are rarely visited, will not be included in the frequent sets because it will not achieve enough support. One solution to this problem is to have a very small support threshold; however, we will end up with very large frequent itemsets, which is computationally hard to handle. Liu et al. [LIU99] proposed a mining technique that uses different support thresholds for different items. Specifying multiple thresholds allow rare transactions that might be very important to be included in the frequent itemsets. Other issues might arise depending on the application itself. For example, in the case of WWW prediction, a session is recorded for each user. The session might have tens of clickstreams (and sometimes hundreds depending on the duration of the session). Using each session as a transaction will not work because it is rare to find two sessions that are frequently repeated (i.e., identical); hence, it will not achieve even a very high support threshold, *minsup*. There is a need to break each session into many subsequences. One common method for this is to use a sliding window of size w. For example, suppose we use a sliding window $w = 3$ to break the session $S = \langle A, B, C, D, E, E, F \rangle$; then, we will end up with having the subsequences $S' = \{\langle A, B, C \rangle, \langle B, C, D \rangle, \langle C, D, E \rangle, \langle D, E, F \rangle\}$. The total number of subsequences of a session S using window w is length(S)-w. To predict the next page in an active user session, we use a sliding window of the active session and ignore the previous pages. For example, if the current session is ⟨*A*, *B*, *C*⟩, and the user refer to page *D*, then the new active session becomes ⟨*B*, *C*, *D*⟩, using a sliding window 3. Notice that page *A* is dropped, and ⟨*B*, *C*, *D*⟩ will be used for prediction. The rationale behind this is because most users go back and forth while surfing the web trying to find the desired information, and it may be most appropriate to use the recent portions of the user history to generate recommendations/predictions [MOBA01].

Mobasher et al. [MOBA01] proposed a recommendation engine that matches an active user session with the frequent itemsets in the database and predicts the next page the user most probably visits. The engine works as follows. Given an active session of size w, the engine finds all the frequent itemsets of length $w + 1$, satisfying some minimum support *minsup* and containing the current active session. Prediction for the active session A is based on the confidence (ψ) of the corresponding association rule. The confidence (ψ) of an association rule $X \rightarrow z$ is defined as $\psi(X \rightarrow z) = \sigma(X \cup z)/\sigma(X)$, where the length of z is 1, page p is recommended/predicted for an active session A, iff

$$\begin{aligned}
&\forall V, R \text{ in the frequent itemsets,}\\
&\text{length}\,(R) = \text{length}\,(V) = \text{length}(A) + 1 \wedge\\
&R = A \cup \{p\} \wedge\\
&V = A \cup \{q\} \wedge\\
&\psi(A \rightarrow p) > \psi(A \rightarrow q)
\end{aligned}$$

The engine uses a cyclic graph called the frequent itemset graph. The graph is an extension of the lexicographic tree used in the tree projection algorithm of Agrawal et al. [AGRA01]. The graph is organized in levels. The nodes in level l has itemsets of size of l. For example, the sizes of the nodes (i.e., the size of the itemsets corresponding to these nodes) in levels 1 and 2 are 1 and 2, respectively. The root of the graph, level 0, is an empty node corresponding to an empty itemset. A node X in level l is linked to a node Y in level $l + 1$ if $X \subset Y$. To further explain the process, suppose we have the following sample web transactions involving pages 1, 2, 3, 4, and 5 as given in Table 3.2. The Apriori algorithm produces the itemsets as given in Table 3.3, using a *minsup* = 0.49. The frequent itemset graph is shown in Figure 3.11.

Suppose we are using a sliding window of size 2, and the current active session $A = \langle 2,3 \rangle$. To predict/recommend the next page, in the frequent itemset graph, we first start at level 2 and extract all the itemsets at level 3 linked to A. From Figure 3.11, the node {2, 3} is linked to {1, 2, 3} and {2, 3, 5} nodes with confidence:

$$\psi(\{2,3\} \rightarrow 1) = \sigma(\{1,2,3\} / \sigma(\{2,3\}) = 5/5 = 1.0$$
$$\psi(\{2,3\} \rightarrow 5) = \sigma(\{2,3,5\} / \sigma(\{2,3\}) = 4/5 = 0.8$$

TABLE 3.2
Sample Web Transaction

Transaction ID	Items
T1	1, 2, 4, 5
T2	1, 2, 5, 3, 4
T3	1, 2, 5, 3
T4	2, 5, 2, 1, 3
T5	4, 1, 2, 5, 3
T6	1, 2, 3, 4
T7	4, 5
T8	4, 5, 3, 1

TABLE 3.3
Frequent Itemsets Generated by the Apriori Algorithm

Size 1	Size 2	Size 3	Size 4
{2}(6)	{2, 3}(5)	{2, 3, 1}(5)	{2, 3, 1, 5}(4)
{3}(6)	{2, 4}(4)	{2, 3, 5}(4)	
{4}(6)	{2, 1}(6)	{2, 4, 1}(4)	
{1}(7)	{2, 5}(5)	{2, 1, 5}(5)	
{5}(7)	{3, 4}(4)	{3, 4, 1}(4)	
	{3, 1}(6)	{3, 1, 5}(5)	
	{3, 5}(5)	{4, 1, 5}(4)	
	{4, 1}(5)		
	{4, 5}(5)		
	{1, 5}(6)		

The recommended page is 1 because its confidence is larger. Notice that, in recommendation engines, the order of the clickstream is not considered, that is, there is no distinction between the sessions ⟨1, 2, 4⟩ and ⟨1, 4, 2⟩. This is a disadvantage of such systems because the order of pages visited might bear important information about the navigation patterns of users.

3.7 MULTICLASS PROBLEM

Most classification techniques solve the binary classification problem. Binary classifiers are accumulated to generalize for the multiclass problem. There are two basic schemes for this generalization, namely, one-VS-one and one-VS-all. To avoid redundancy, we will present this generalization only for SVM.

One-VS-one: The one-VS-one approach creates a classifier for each pair of classes. The training set for each pair classifier (i, j) includes only those instances that belong to either class i or j. A new instance x belongs to the class upon which most pair classifiers agree. The prediction decision is quoted from the majority vote technique. There are $n(n-1)/2$ classifiers to be computed, where n is the number of classes in the dataset. It is evident that the disadvantage of this scheme is that we need to generate a large number of classifiers, especially if there are a large number of classes in the training set. For example, if we have a training set of 1000 classes, we need 499,500 classifiers.

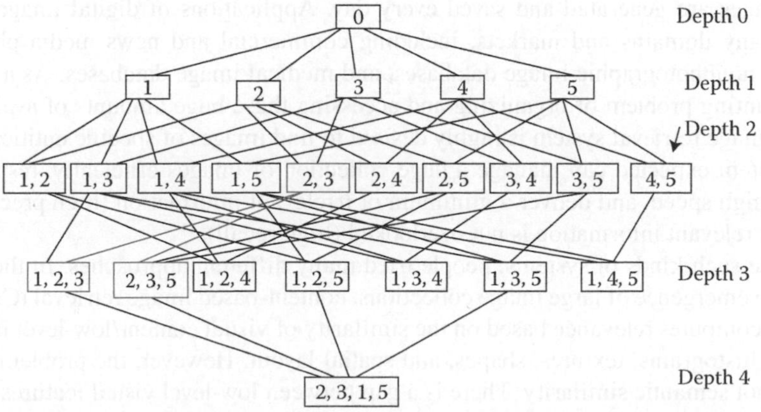

FIGURE 3.11 Frequent itemset graph.

On the other hand, the size of the training set for each classifier is small because we exclude all instances that do not belong to that pair of classes.

One-VS-all: The one-VS-all approach creates a classifier for each class in the dataset. The training set is preprocessed such that for a classifier j instances that belong to class j are marked as class (+1) and instances that do not belong to class j are marked as class (−1). In the one-VS-all scheme, we compute n classifiers, where n is the number of pages that users have visited (at the end of each session). A new instance x is predicted by assigning it to the class that its classifier outputs the largest positive value (i.e., maximal marginal) as in Equation 3.15. We can compute the margin of point x as in Equation 3.13. Notice that the recommended/predicted page is the sign of the margin value of that page (see Equation 3.10):

$$f(x) = wx - b = \sum_{i}^{N} \alpha_i y_i (x.x_i - b) \tag{3.14}$$

$$\text{prediction}(x) = \arg\max_{1 \leq c \leq M} f_c(x) \tag{3.15}$$

In Equation 3.15, M is the number of classes, $x = \langle x_1, x_2, \ldots, x_n \rangle$ is the user session, and f_i is the classifier that separates class i from the rest of the classes. The prediction decision in Equation 3.15 resolves to the classifier f_c that is the most distant from the testing example x. This might be explained as f_c has the most separating power, among all other classifiers, of separating x from the rest of the classes.

The advantage of this scheme (one-VS-all) compared to the one-VS-one scheme is that it has fewer classifiers. On the other hand, the size of the training set is larger for a one-VS-all scheme than that for a one-VS-one scheme because we use the whole original training set to compute each classifier.

3.8 IMAGE MINING

3.8.1 Overview

While image mining is not directly applicable to the work discussed in this book, we expect big data to include large images and video data. This will also include geospatial data. Therefore, an understanding of image mining is useful so that one can adapt the techniques for image-based big data. More details of our work on image mining including geospatial data can be found in [AWAD09] and [LI07].

Along with the development of digital images and computer storage technologies, a huge amount of digital images are generated and saved every day. Applications of digital image have rapidly penetrated many domains and markets, including commercial and news media photo libraries, scientific and nonphotographic image databases, and medical image databases. As a consequence, we face a daunting problem of organizing and accessing these huge amounts of available images. An efficient image retrieval system is highly desired to find images of specific entities from a database. The system expected can manage a huge collection of images efficiently, respond to users' queries with high speed, and deliver a minimum of irrelevant information (high precision), as well as ensure that relevant information is not overlooked (high recall).

To generate such kinds of systems, people tried many different approaches. In the early 1990s, because of the emergence of large image collections, content-based image retrieval (CBIR) was proposed. CBIR computes relevance based on the similarity of visual content/low-level image features such as color histograms, textures, shapes, and spatial layout. However, the problem is that visual similarity is not semantic similarity. There is a gap between low-level visual features and semantic meanings. The so-called semantic gap is the major problem that needs to be solved for most CBIR approaches. For example, a CBIR system may answer a query request for a "red ball" with an image of a "red rose." If we undertake the annotation of images with keywords, a typical way to publish an image data repository is to create a keyword-based query interface addressed to an image database. If all images came with a detailed and accurate description, image retrieval would be convenient based on current powerful pure text search techniques. These search techniques would retrieve the images if their descriptions/annotations contained some combination of the keywords specified by the user. However, the major problem is that most of images are not annotated. It is a laborious, error-prone, and subjective process to manually annotate a large collection of images. Many images contain the desired semantic information, even though they do not contain the user-specified keywords. Furthermore, keyword-based search is useful especially to a user who knows what keywords are used to index the images and who can therefore easily formulate queries. This approach is problematic; however, when the user does not have a clear goal in mind, does not know what is in the database, and does not know what kinds of semantic concepts are involved in the domain.

Image mining is a more challenging research problem than retrieving relevant images in CBIR systems. The goal of image mining is to find an image pattern that is significant for a given set of images and helpful to understand the relationships between high-level semantic concepts/descriptions and low-level visual features. Our focus is on aspects such as feature selection and image classification. It should be noted that image mining and analytics are important for social media as the members of postnumerous images. These images could be used to embed messages that could penetrate into computing systems. Images in social media could also be analyzed to extract various demographics such as location.

3.8.2 Feature Selection

Usually, data saved in databases with well-defined semantics is structured data such as numbers or structured data entries. In comparison, data with ill-defined semantics is unstructured data. Images, audio, and video are data with ill-defined semantics. In the domain of image processing, images are represented by derived data or features such as color, texture, and shape. Many of these features have multi values (e.g., color histogram, moment description) When people generate these derived data or features, they generally generate as many features as possible, since they are not aware which feature is more relevant. Therefore, the dimensionality of derived image data is usually very high. Actually, some of the selected features might be duplicated or may not even be relevant to the problem. Including irrelevant or duplicated information is referred to as noise. Such problems are referred to as the "curse of dimensionality." Feature selection is the research topic for finding an optimal subset of features. In this chapter, we will discuss this curse and feature selection in detail.

We developed a wrapper-based simultaneous feature weighing and clustering algorithm. Clustering algorithm will bundle similar image segments together and generate a finite set of visual symbols (i.e., blob-token). Based on histogram analysis and chi-square value, we assign features of image segments different weights instead of removing some of them. Feature weight evaluation is wrapped in a clustering algorithm. In each iteration of the algorithm, feature weights of image segments are re-evaluated based on the clustering result. The re-evaluated feature weights will affect the clustering results in the next iteration.

3.8.3 Automatic Image Annotation

Automatic image annotation is research concerned with object recognition, where the effort is concerned with trying to recognize objects in an image and generate descriptions for the image according to semantics of the objects. If it is possible to produce accurate and complete semantic descriptions for an image, we can store descriptions in an image database. Based on a textual description, more functionality (e.g., browse, search, and query) of an image database system could be easily and efficiently implemented by applying many existing text-based search techniques.

Unfortunately, the automatic image annotation problem has not been solved in general, and perhaps this problem is impossible to solve.

However, in certain subdomains, it is still possible to obtain some interesting results. Many statistical models have been published for image annotation. Some of these models took feature dimensionality into account and applied singular value decomposition (SVD) or principle component analysis (PCA) to reduce dimension. But none of them considered feature selection or feature weight. We proposed a new framework for image annotation based on a translation model (TM). In our approach, we applied our weighted feature selection algorithm and embedded it in an image annotation framework. Our weighted feature selection algorithm improves the quality of visual tokens and generates better image annotations.

3.8.4 Image Classification

Image classification is an important area, especially in the medical domain because it helps manage large medical image databases and has great potential on diagnostic aid in a real-world clinical setting. We describe our experiments for the image CLEF medical image retrieval task. Sizes of classes of CLEF medical image dataset are not balanced, which is really a serious problem for all classification algorithms. To solve this problem, we resample data by generating subwindows. *K* nearest neighbor (KNN) algorithm, distance weighted KNN, fuzzy KNN, nearest prototype classifier, and evidence theory-based KNN are implemented and studied. Results show that evidence-based KNN has the best performance based on classification accuracy.

3.9 SUMMARY

In this chapter, we first provided an overview of the various data mining tasks and techniques, and then discussed some of the techniques that we have used in our work. These include neural networks, SVM, and ARM. We have utilized a combination of these techniques together with some other techniques in the literature as well as our own techniques to develop data analytics techniques for very large databases. Some of these techniques are discussed in Parts II through V.

Numerous data mining techniques have been designed and developed, and many of them are being utilized in commercial tools. Several of these techniques are variations of some of the basic classification, clustering, and ARM techniques. One of the major challenges today is to determine the appropriate technique for various applications. We still need more benchmarks and performance studies. In addition, the techniques should result in fewer false positives and negatives. While there is still much to be done, the progress over the last decade has been extremely promising. Our challenge is to develop data mining techniques for big data systems.

REFERENCES

[AGRA93]. R. Agrawal, T. Imielinski, A. Swami, "Mining Association Rules between Sets of Items in Large Database," *Proceedings of the ACM SIGMOD Conference on Management of Data*, Washington, D.C., May, pp. 207–216, 1993.

[AGRA94]. R. Agrawal and R. Srikant, "Fast Algorithms for Mining Association Rules in Large Database," *Proceedings of the 20th International Conference on Very Large Data Bases*, San Francisco, CA, pp. 487–499, 1994.

[AGRA01]. R. Agrawal, C. Aggarawal, V. Prasad, "A Tree Projection Algorithm for Generation of Frequent Itemsets," *Journal of Parallel and Distributed Computing Archive* 61 (3), 350–371, 2001.

[AWAD09]. M. Awad, L. Khan, B. Thuraisingham, L. Wang, *Design and Implementation of Data Mining Tools*. CRC Press, Boca Raton, FL, 2009.

[BART99]. P. Bartlett and J. Shawe-Taylor, "Generalization Performance of Support Vector Machines and Other Pattern Classifiers," *Advances in Kernel Methods—Support Vector Learning*, B. Schölkopf, C. J. C. Burges, A. J. Smola (eds.), MIT Press, Cambridge, MA, pp. 43–53, 1999.

[CRIS00]. N. Cristianini and J. Shawe-Taylor, *Introduction to Support Vector Machines*, 1st ed. Cambridge University Press, Cambridge, pp. 93–122, 2000.

[HOUT95]. M. Houtsma and A. Swanu, "Set-Oriented Mining of Association Rules in Relational Databases," *Proceedings of the 11th International Conference on Data Engineering*, Washington, D.C., pp. 25–33, 1995.

[LI07]. C. Li, L. Khan, B. M. Thuraisingham, M. Husain, S. Chen, F. Qiu, "Geospatial Data Mining for National Security: Land Cover Classification and Semantic Grouping," *In ISI'07: Proceedings of the IEEE Conference on Intelligence and Security Informatics*, May 23–24, New Brunswick, NJ, 2007.

[LIU99]. B. Liu, W. Hsu, Y. Ma, "Mining Association Rules with Multiple Minimum Supports," *Proceedings of the 5th ACM SIGKDD International Conference on Knowledge Discovery and Data Mining*, San Diego, CA, pp. 337–341, 1999.

[MITC97]. T. M. Mitchell, *Machine Learning*. McGraw Hill, New York, NY, Chapter 3, 1997.

[MOBA01]. B. Mobasher, H. Dai, T. Luo, M. Nakagawa, "Effective Personalization Based on Association Rule Discovery from Web Usage Data," In *WIDM01: Proceedings of the ACM Workshop on Web Information and Data Management*, pp. 9–15, 2001.

[PIRO96]. P. Pirolli, J. Pitkow, R. Rao, "Silk from a Sow's Ear: Extracting Usable Structures from the Web," In *CHI-96: Proceedings of the 1996 Conference on Human Factors in Computing Systems*, Vancouver, British Columbia, Canada, pp. 118–125, 1996.

[THUR16]. B. Thuraisingham, S. Abrol, R. Heatherly, M. Kantarcioglu, V. Khadilkar, L. Khan, *Analyzing and Securing Social Networks*. CRC Press, Boca Raton, FL, 2016.

[VAPN95]. V. N. Vapnik, *The Nature of Statistical Learning Theory*. Springer, New York, NY, 1995.

[VAPN98]. V. N. Vapnik, *Statistical Learning Theory*. Wiley, New York, 1998.

[VAPN99]. V. N. Vapnik, *The Nature of Statistical Learning Theory*. Springer-Verlag, Berlin, 1999.

[YANG01]. Q. Yang, H. Zhang, T. Li, "Mining Web Logs for Prediction Models in WWW Caching and Prefetching," *The 7th ACM SIGKDD International Conference on Knowledge Discovery and Data Mining*, Aug. 26–29, pp. 473–478, 2001.

4 Data Mining for Security Applications

4.1 OVERVIEW

Data mining has many applications in security including in national security (e.g., surveillance) as well as in cyber security (e.g., virus detection). The threats to national security include attacking buildings and destroying critical infrastructures such as power grids and telecommunication systems [BOLZ05]. Data mining techniques are being investigated to find out who the suspicious people are and who is capable of carrying out terrorist activities [THUR03]. Cyber security is involved with protecting the computer and network systems against corruption due to Trojan horses and viruses. Data mining is also being applied to provide solutions such as intrusion and malware detection and auditing [MASU11]. In this chapter, we will focus mainly on data mining for cyber security applications.

To understand the mechanisms to be applied to safeguard the nation and the computers and networks, we need to understand the types of threats. In [THUR03] we described real-time threats, as well as non real-time threats. A real-time threat is a threat that must be acted upon within a certain time to prevent some catastrophic situation. Note that a nonreal-time threat could become a real-time threat over time. For example, one could suspect that a group of terrorists will eventually perform some act of terrorism. However, when we set time bounds such as a threat that will likely occur say before July 1, 2018, then it becomes a real-time threat and we have to take actions immediately. If the time bounds are tighter such as "a threat will occur within 2 days," then we cannot afford to make any mistakes in our response.

There has been a lot of work on applying data mining for both national security and cyber security and our previous books have focused on both aspects (e.g., [THUR03] and [MASU11]). Our focus in this chapter will be mainly on applying data mining for cyber security. In Section 4.2, we will discuss data mining for cyber security applications. In particular, we will discuss the threats to computers and networks and describe the applications of data mining to detect such threats and attacks. Some of the data mining tools for security applications developed at The University of Texas at Dallas will be discussed in Section 4.3. We are reimplementing some of our tools to analyze massive amounts of data. That is, we are developing big data analytics tools for cyber security applications and some of our current work will be discussed later in this book. This chapter is summarized in Section 4.4. Figure 4.1 illustrates data mining applications in security.

4.2 DATA MINING FOR CYBER SECURITY

4.2.1 Cyber Security Threats

This section discusses the various cyber threats including cyber terrorism, insider threats, and external attacks. Figure 4.2 illustrates the various types of cyber-security threats.

4.2.1.1 Cyber Terrorism, Insider Threats, and External Attacks

Cyber terrorism is one of the major terrorist threats posed to our nation today. As we have mentioned earlier, there is now so much of information available electronically and on the web. Attack on our

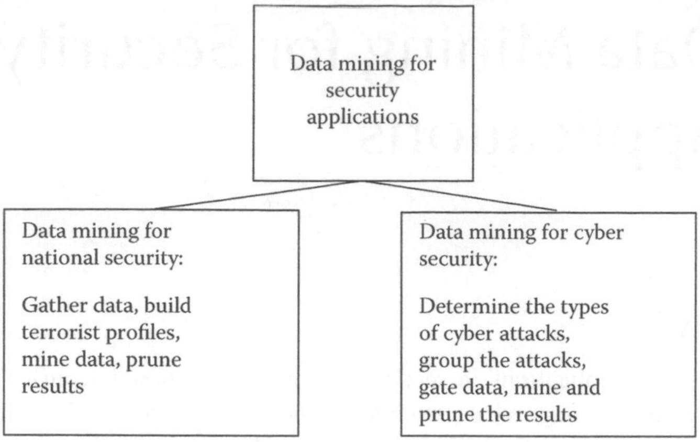

FIGURE 4.1 Data mining applications in security.

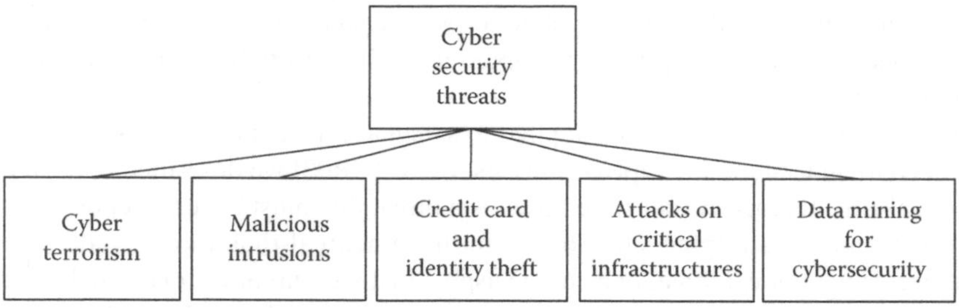

FIGURE 4.2 Cyber security threats.

computers as well as networks, databases, and the Internet could be devastating to businesses. We are hearing almost daily about the cyber attacks to businesses. It is estimated that cyber terrorism could cost billions of dollars to businesses. For example, consider a banking information system. If terrorists attack such a system and deplete accounts of the funds, then the bank could lose millions and perhaps billions of dollars. By crippling the computer system, millions of hours of productivity could be lost and that equates to money in the end. Even a simple power outage at work through some accident could cause several hours of productivity loss and as a result a major financial loss. Therefore, it is critical that our information systems be secure. We discuss various types of cyber terrorist attacks. One is spreading malware that can wipe away files and other important documents and another is intruding the computer networks.

Note that threats can occur from outside or from the inside of an organization. Outside attacks are attacks on computers from someone outside the organization. We hear of hackers breaking into computer systems and causing havoc within an organization. These hackers infect the computers with malware that can not only cause great damage to the files stored in the systems but also spread to other systems via the networks. But a more sinister problem is the insider threat problem. People inside an organization who have studied the business practices develop schemes to cripple the organization's information assets. These people could be regular employees or even those working at computer centers and contractors. The problem is quite serious as someone may be masquerading as someone else and causing all kinds of damage. Malicious processes in the system can also masquerade as benign processes and cause damage. Data mining techniques have been applied to detect the various attacks. We discuss some of these attacks next. Part III will elaborate on applying data mining for the insider threat problem.

4.2.1.2 Malicious Intrusions

Malicious intrusions may include intruding the systems, the networks, the web clients and servers, and the databases and applications. Many of the cyber terrorism attacks are due to malicious intrusions. We hear much about network intrusions. What happens here is that intruders try to tap into the networks and get the information that is being transmitted. These intruders may be human intruders or malicious processes. Intrusions could also happen on files. For example, a malicious individual can masquerade as an employee and log into the corporation's computer systems and network and access the files. Intrusions can also occur on databases. Intruders pretending to be legitimate users can pose queries such as Structured Query Language queries and access the data that they are not authorized to know.

Essentially cyber terrorism includes malicious intrusions as well as sabotage through malicious intrusions or otherwise. Cyber security consists of security mechanisms that attempt to provide solutions to cyber attacks or cyber terrorism. When we discuss malicious intrusions or cyber attacks, it would be useful to think about the noncyber world and then translate those attacks to attacks on computers and networks. For example, a thief could enter a building through a trap door. In the same way, a computer intruder could enter the computer or network through some sort of a trap door that has been intentionally built by a malicious insider and left unattended through perhaps careless design. Another example is a thief entering the bank with a mask and stealing the money. The analogy here is an intruder masquerading as a legitimate user takes control of the information assets. Money in the real world would translate to information assets in the cyber world. More recently, we are hearing about ransomware where hackers are not only stealing the data, but also holding the data to ransom by encrypting the data. Then the owner of the data has to pay a ransom, usually in the form of bit coins, and then retrieve his/her data. That is, there are many parallels between what happens in the real world and the cyber world.

4.2.1.3 Credit Card Fraud and Identity Theft

Credit card fraud and identity theft are common security problems. In the case of credit card fraud, others get hold of a person's credit card numbers though electronic means (e.g., when swiping the card at gas stations) or otherwise and make all kinds of purchases; by the time the owner of the card finds out, it may be too late. A more serious problem is identity theft. Here one assumes the identity of another person, say by getting hold of the social security number and essentially carries out all the transactions under the other person's name. This could even be selling houses and depositing the income in a fraudulent bank account. By the time the owner finds out, it will be far too late. It is very likely that the owner may have lost millions of dollars due to the identity theft.

We need to explore the use of data mining both for credit card fraud detection as well as for identity theft. There have been some efforts on detecting credit card fraud [CHAN99]. However, detecting identity theft still remains a challenge.

4.2.1.4 Attacks on Critical Infrastructures

Attacks on critical infrastructures could cripple a nation and its economy. Infrastructure attacks include attacking the telecommunication lines, the power grid, gas pipelines, reservoirs and water and food supplies, and other basic entities that are critical for the operation of a nation.

Attacks on critical infrastructures could occur during due to malware or by physical means such as bombs. For example, one could attack the software that runs the telecommunication systems and close down all the telecommunications lines. Similarly, software that runs the power grid could be attacked. Infrastructures could also be attacked by natural disaster such as hurricanes and earthquakes. Our main interest here is the attacks on infrastructures through malicious attacks. While some progress has been made on developing solutions to such attacks, much remains to be done. One of the directions we are pursuing is to examine the use of data mining to detect such infrastructure attacks. Figure 4.3 illustrates attacks on critical infrastructures.

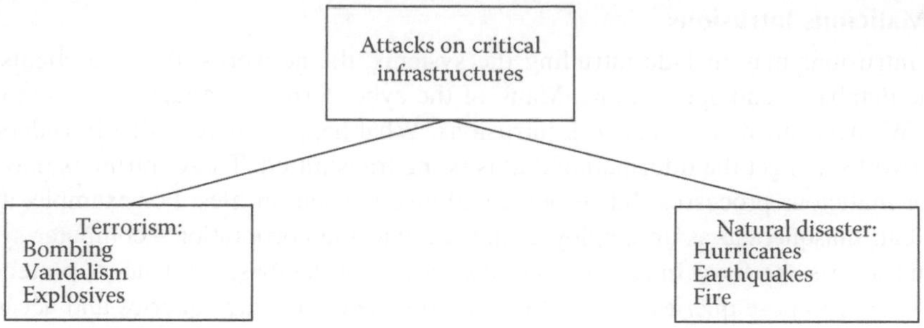

FIGURE 4.3 Attacks on critical infrastructures.

4.2.2 Data Mining for Cyber Security

Data mining is being applied for problems such as intrusion and malware detection and auditing. For example, anomaly detection techniques could be used to detect unusual patterns and behaviors. Link analysis may be used to trace the viruses to the perpetrators. Classification may be used to group various cyber attacks and then use the profiles to detect an attack when it occurs. Prediction may be used to determine potential future attacks depending in a way on information learned about terrorists through email and phone conversations. Also, for some threats, nonreal-time data mining may suffice while for certain other threats such as for network intrusions, we may need real-time data mining. Many researchers are investigating the use of data mining for intrusion detection [AWAD09]. While we need some form of real-time data mining where the results have to be generated in real time, we also need to build models in real time. For example, credit card fraud detection is a form of real-time processing. However, here, models are usually built ahead of time. Building models in real time remains a challenge. Data mining can also be used for analyzing web logs as well as the audit trails. Based on the results of the data mining tool, one can then determine whether any unauthorized intrusions have occurred and/or whether any unauthorized queries have been posed [MASU11].

Other applications of data mining for cyber security include analyzing the audit data. One could build a repository or a warehouse containing the audit data and then conduct an analysis using various data mining tools to see if there are potential anomalies. For example, there could be a situation where a certain user group may access the database between 3 and 5 a.m. in the morning. It could be that this group is working the night shift, in which case there may be a valid explanation. However, if this group is working between say 9 a.m. and 5 p.m., then this may be an unusual occurrence. Another example is when a person accesses the databases always between 1 and 2 p.m., but for the last 2 days he/she has been accessing the database between 1 and 2 a.m. This could then be flagged as an unusual pattern that would need further investigation.

Insider threat analysis is also a problem both from a national security and from a cyber security perspective. That is, those working in a corporation who are considered to be trusted could commit espionage. Similarly, those with proper access to the computer system could insert malicious code that behaves like benign code until an opportunity arrives to steal the data. Catching such terrorists is far more difficult than catching terrorists outside of an organization. One may need to monitor the access patterns of all the individuals of a corporation even if they are system administrators, to see whether they are carrying out cyber terrorism activities. However, this could result in privacy violations. Our approach to applying data mining for insider threat detection is discussed in Part III.

While data mining can be used to detect and possibly prevent cyber attacks, data mining also exacerbates some security problems such as the inference and privacy problems. With data mining techniques, one could infer sensitive associations from the legitimate responses. Figure 4.4 illustrates data mining services for cyber security. For more details on a high-level overview we refer to [THUR04] and [THUR05].

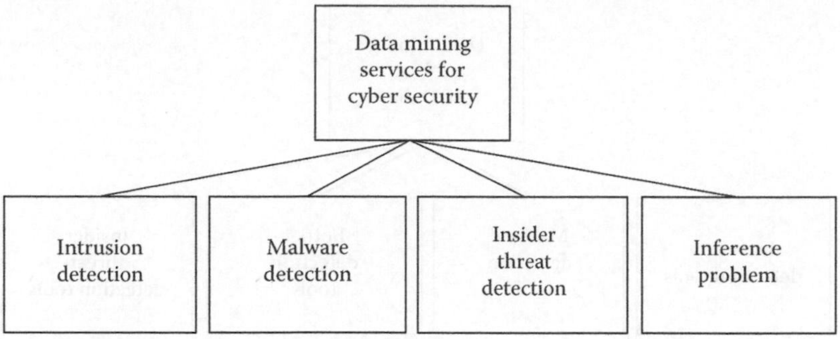

FIGURE 4.4 Data mining services for cyber security.

4.3 DATA MINING TOOLS

Over the past decade, we have developed a number of data mining for cyber security applications at The University of Texas at Dallas. In one of our previous books, we discussed one such tool for intrusion detection [AWAD09]. In another book, we discussed a number of data mining tools for malware detection [MASU11]. In this section, we discuss the tools and provide an overview for the discussion.

An intrusion can be defined as any set of actions that attempts to compromise the integrity, confidentiality, or availability of a resource. As systems become more complex, there are always exploitable weaknesses due to design and programming errors, or through the use of various "socially engineered" penetration techniques. Computer attacks are split into two categories, host-based attacks and network-based attacks. Host-based attacks target a machine and try to gain access to privileged services or resources on that machine. Host-based detection usually uses routines that obtain system call data from an audit process which tracks all system calls made on behalf of each user.

Network-based attacks make it difficult for legitimate users to access various network services by purposely occupying or sabotaging network resources and services. This can be done by sending large amounts of network traffic, exploiting well-known faults in networking services, overloading network hosts, and so on. Network-based attack detection uses network traffic data (i.e., tcpdump) to look at traffic addressed to the machines being monitored. Intrusion detection systems are split into two groups: anomaly detection systems and misuse detection systems.

Anomaly detection is the attempt to identify malicious traffic based on deviations from established normal network traffic patterns. Misuse detection is the ability to identify intrusions based on a known pattern for the malicious activity. These known patterns are referred to as signatures. Anomaly detection is capable of catching new attacks. However, new legitimate behavior can also be falsely identified as an attack, resulting in a false positive. The focus with the current state-of-the-art technology is to reduce false negative and false positive rate. We discussed in detail an innovative data mining technique called DGSOT for intrusion detection. We have shown through experimentation that DGSOT performs much better and gives more accurate results than other tools in the literature at that time.

Following DGSOT, we designed a number of data mining tools for malware detection and this work is presented in [MASU11]. These include tools for email worm detection, malicious code detection, buffer overflow detection, and botnet detection, as well as analyzing firewall policy rules. Figure 4.5 illustrates the various tools we have developed. For example, for email worm detection, we examine emails and extract features such as "number of attachments" and then train data mining tools with techniques such as support vector machine (SVM) or Naïve Bayesian classifiers and develop a model. Then, we test the model and determine whether the email has a virus/worm or not. We use training and testing datasets posted on various web sites. Similarly, for malicious code

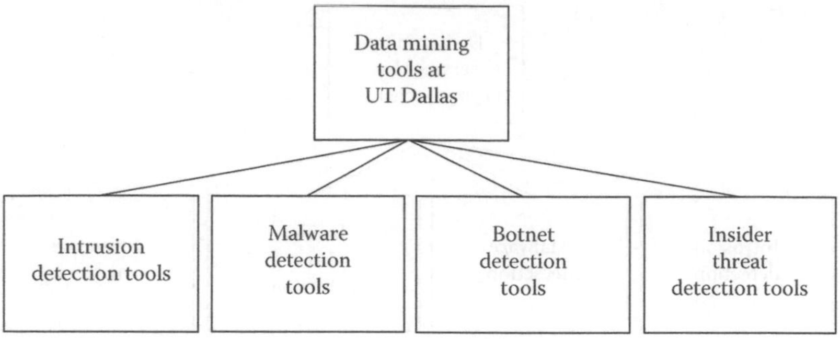

FIGURE 4.5 Data mining tools at the University of Texas, Dallas.

detection, we extract n-gram features both with assembly code and binary code. We first train the data mining tool using the SVM technique and then test the model. The classifier will determine whether the code is malicious or not. For buffer overflow detection, we assume that malicious messages contain code while normal messages contain data. We train SVM and then test to see if the message contains code or data.

We have also reimplemented some of our data mining tools to operate in a cloud. Essentially, we have applied big data analytics techniques for malware detection and showed the significant improvement we can get by using big data analytics versus data mining. This is the approach we have taken for the insider threat detection problems discussed in this book. That is, we discuss stream analytics techniques that we have developed and show how they can be implemented in the cloud for detecting insider threats. We believe that due to the very large amounts of malware data that are dynamic and heterogeneous in nature, we need big data mining tools to analyze such data to detect for security violations.

4.4 SUMMARY AND DIRECTIONS

In this chapter, we provided an overview of data mining for cyber security applications. In particular, we discussed the threats to computers and networks and described the applications of data mining to detect such threats and attacks. Some of the data mining tools for security applications developed at The University of Texas at Dallas were also discussed.

Data mining for national security as well as for cyber security is a very active research area. Various data mining techniques including link analysis and association rule mining are being explored to detect abnormal patterns. Because of data mining, users can now make all kinds of correlations. In addition, in the past 5 years massive amounts of data have been collected. We need big data analytics techniques to detect potential security violations. This also raises privacy concerns. More details on privacy can be obtained from [THUR02]. Much of the contents in this book are on big data management and analytics techniques for cyber security applications.

REFERENCES

[AWAD09]. M. Awad, L. Khan, B. Thuraisingham, L. Wang, *Design and Implementation of Data Mining Tools*, CRC Press, Boca Raton, FL, 2009.

[BOLZ05]. F. Bolz, K. Dudonis, D. Schulz, *The Counterterrorism Handbook: Tactics, Procedures, and Techniques, Third Edition Practical Aspects of Criminal & Forensic Investigations*, CRC Press, Boca Raton, FL, 2005.

[CHAN99]. P. Chan, W. Fan, A. Prodromidis, S. Stolfo, "Distributed Data Mining in Credit Card Fraud Detection," *IEEE Intelligent Systems*, 14, #6, 67–74, 1999.

[MASU11]. M. Masud, L. Khan, B. Thuraisingham, *Data Mining Tools for Malware Detection*, CRC Press, Boca Raton, FL, 2011.

[THUR02]. B. Thuraisingham, *Data Mining, National Security, Privacy and Civil Liberties*, SIGKDD Explorations, Vol. 4, #2, New York, NY, December 2002.

[THUR03]. B. Thuraisingham, *Web Data Mining Technologies and Their Applications in Business Intelligence and Counter-Terrorism*, CRC Press, Boca Raton, FL, 2003.

[THUR04]. B. Thuraisingham, Data mining for security applications. *Managing Threats to Web Databases and Cyber Systems, Issues, Solutions and Challenges*, V. Kumar, J. Srivastava, Al. Lazarevic, editors, Kluwer, MA, 2004.

[THUR05]. B. Thuraisingham, *Database and Applications Security*, CRC Press, Boca Raton, FL, 2005.

5 Cloud Computing and Semantic Web Technologies

5.1 INTRODUCTION

Chapters 2 through 4 have discussed concepts in data security and privacy, data mining, and data mining for cyber security. These three supporting technologies are part of the foundational technologies for the concepts discussed in this book. For example, Section II describes stream data analytics for large datasets. In particular, we discuss an innovative technique called "novel class detection" where we integrate data mining with stream data management technologies. Section III describes our approach to applying the techniques for stream mining discussing Section II for insider threat detection. We utilize the cloud platform for managing and analyzing large datasets. We will see throughout this book that cloud computing is at the heart of managing large datasets. In addition, for some of our experimental systems, to be discussed in Section IV, we have utilized semantic web technologies. Therefore, in this chapter, we discuss two additional technologies that we have used in several of the chapters in this book. They are cloud computing and semantic web technologies.

Cloud computing has emerged as a powerful computing paradigm for service-oriented computing. Many of the computing services are being outsourced to the cloud. Such cloud-based services can be used to host the various cyber security applications such as insider threat detection and identity management. Another concept that is being used for a variety of applications is the notion of the semantic web. A semantic web is essentially a collection of technologies to produce machine-understandable web pages. These technologies can also be used to represent any type of data including schema for big data and malware data. We have based some of our analytics and security investigation for data represented using semantic web technologies.

The organization of this chapter is as follows. Section 5.2 discusses cloud computing concepts. Concepts in semantic web are discussed in Section 5.3. Semantic web and security concepts are discussed in Section 5.4. Cloud computing frameworks based on semantic web are discussed in Section 5.5. This chapter is concluded in Section 5.6. Figure 5.1 illustrates the concepts discussed in this chapter.

5.2 CLOUD COMPUTING

5.2.1 Overview

The emerging cloud computing model attempts to address the growth of web-connected devices and handle massive amounts of data. Google has now introduced the MapReduce framework for processing large amounts of data on commodity hardware. Apache's Hadoop Distributed File System (HDFS) is emerging as a superior software component for cloud computing, combined with integrated parts such as MapReduce ([HDFS], [DEAN04]). Clouds such as HP's Open Cirrus Testbed are utilizing HDFS. This in turn has resulted in numerous social networking sites with massive amounts of data to be shared and managed. For example, we may want to analyze multiple years of stock market data statistically to reveal a pattern or to build a reliable weather model based on several years of weather and related data. To handle such massive amounts of data distributed at many sites (i.e., nodes), scalable hardware and software components are needed. The cloud computing model

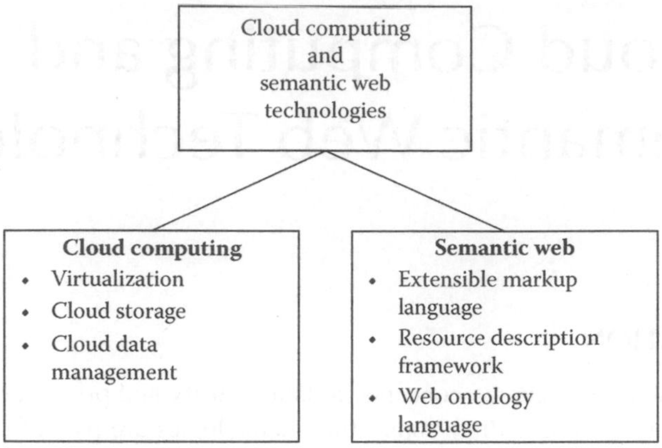

FIGURE 5.1 Cloud computing and semantic web technologies.

has emerged to address the explosive growth of web-connected devices and handle massive amounts of data. It is defined and characterized by massive scalability and new Internet-driven economics.

In this chapter, we will discuss some preliminaries in cloud computing and semantic web. We will first introduce what is meant by cloud computing. While various definitions have been proposed, we will adopt the definition provided by the National Institute of Standards and Technology (NIST). This will be followed by a service-based paradigm for cloud computing. Next, we will discuss the various key concepts including virtualization and data storage in the cloud. We will also discuss some of the technologies such as Hadoop and MapReduce.

The organization of this chapter is as follows. Cloud computing preliminaries will be discussed in Section 5.2.2. Virtualization will be discussed in Section 5.2.3. Cloud storage and data management issues will be discussed in Section 5.2.4. Cloud computing tools will be discussed in Section 5.2.5. Figure 5.2 illustrates the components addressed in this section.

5.2.2 Preliminaries

As stated in [CLOUD], cloud computing delivers computing as a service, while in traditional computing, it is provided in the form of a product. Therefore, users pay for the services based on a pay-as-you-go model. The services provided by a cloud may include hardware services, systems services, data services, and storage services. Users of the cloud need not know where the software and data are located; that is, the software and data services provided by the cloud are transparent to the user. NIST has defined cloud computing to be the following [NIST]:

> Cloud computing is a model for enabling ubiquitous, convenient, on-demand network access to a shared pool of configurable computing resources (e.g., networks, servers, storage, applications, and services) that can be rapidly provisioned and released with minimal management effort or service provider interaction.

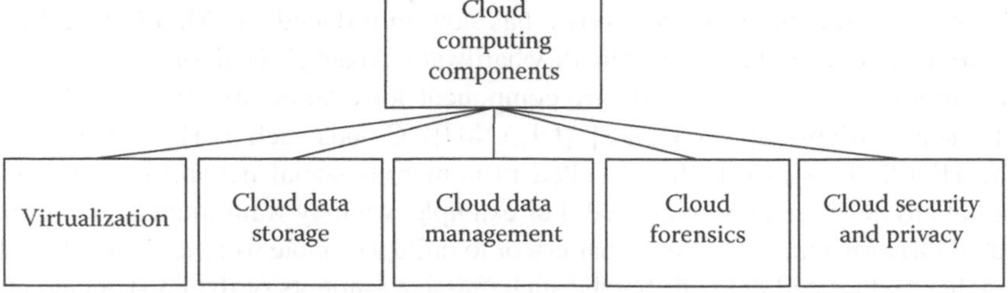

FIGURE 5.2 Cloud computing components.

The cloud model is composed of multiple deployment models and service models. These models are described next.

5.2.2.1 Cloud Deployment Models

There are multiple deployment models for cloud computing. These include the public cloud, community cloud, hybrid cloud, and the private cloud. In a public cloud, the service provider typically provides the services over the World Wide Web that can be accessed by the general public. Such a cloud may provide free services or pay-as-you-go services. In a community cloud, a group of organizations get together and develop a cloud. These organizations may have a common objective to provide features such as security and fault tolerance. The cost is shared among the organizations. Furthermore, the cloud may be hosted by the organizations or by a third party. A private cloud is a cloud infrastructure developed specifically for an organization. This could be hosted by the organization or by a third party. A hybrid cloud consists of a combination of public and private clouds. This way in a hybrid cloud, an organization may use the private cloud for highly sensitive services, while it may use the public cloud for less sensitive services and take advantage of what the World Wide Web has to offer. Kantarcioglu and his colleagues have stated that the hybrid cloud is deployment model of the future [KHAD12a]. Figure 5.3 illustrates the cloud deployment models.

5.2.2.2 Service Models

As stated earlier, cloud computing provides a variety of services. These include Infrastructure as a Service (IaaS), Platform as a Service (PaaS), Software as a Service (SaaS), and Data as a Service (DaaS). In IaaS, the cloud provides a collection of hardware and networks for use by the general public or organizations. The users install operations systems and software to run the applications. The users will be billed according to the resources they utilize for their computing. In PaaS, the cloud provider will provide to their users the systems software such as operating systems (OS) and execution environments. The users will load their applications and run them on the hardware and software infrastructures provided by the cloud. In SaaS, the cloud provider will provide the applications for the users to run. These applications could be say billing applications, tax computing applications, and sales tools. The cloud users access the applications through cloud clients. In the case of DaaS, the cloud provides data to the cloud users. Data may be stored in data centers that are accessed by the cloud users. Note that while DaaS used to denote Desktop as a Service, more recently it denotes Data as a Service. Figure 5.4 illustrates the services models.

5.2.3 Virtualization

Virtualization essentially means creating something virtual and not actual. It could be hardware, software, memory, and data. The notion of virtualization has existed for decades with respect to computing. Back in the 1960s, the concept of virtual memory was introduced. This virtual memory

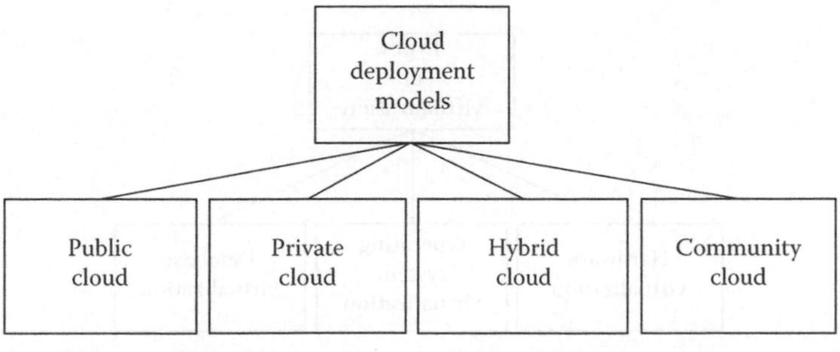

FIGURE 5.3 Cloud deployment models.

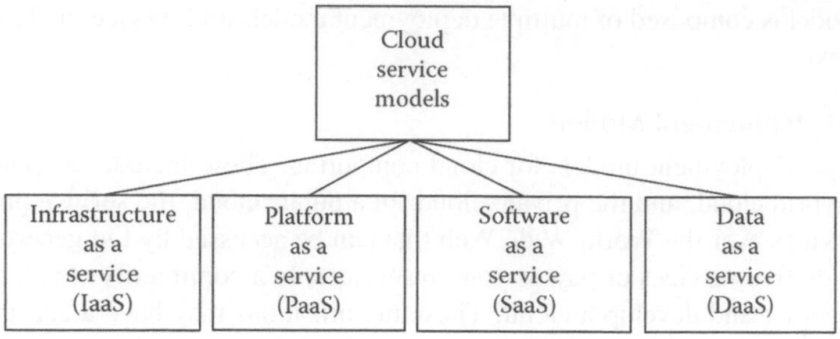

FIGURE 5.4 Cloud service models.

gives the application program the illusion that it has contiguous working memory. Mapping is developed to map the virtual memory to the actual physical memory.

Hardware virtualization is a basic notion in cloud computing. This essentially creates virtual machines hosted on a real computer with an OS. This means while the actual machine may be running a Windows OS, through virtualization it may provide a Linux machine to the users. The actual machine is called the host machine while the virtual machine is called the guest machine. The term virtual machine monitor, also known as the hypervisor, is the software that runs the virtual machine on the host computer.

Other types of virtualization include OS level virtualization, storage virtualization, data virtualization, and database virtualization. In OS level virtualization, multiple virtual environments are created within a single OS. In storage virtualization, the logical storage is abstracted from the physical storage. In data virtualization, the data is abstracted from the underlying databases. In network virtualization, a virtual network is created. Figure 5.5 illustrates the various types of virtualizations.

As we have stated earlier, at the heart of cloud computing is the notion of hypervisor or the virtual machine monitor. Hardware virtualization techniques allow multiple OSs (called guests) to run concurrently on a host computer. These multiple OSs share virtualized hardware resources. Hypervisor is not a new term; it was first used in the mid 1960s in the IBM 360/65 machines. There are different types of hypervisors; in one type the hypervisor runs on the host hardware and manages the guest OSs. Both VMware and XEN which are popular virtual machines are based on this model. In another model, the hypervisor runs within a conventional OS environment. Virtual machines are also incorporated into embedded systems and mobile phones. Embedded hypervisors have real-time processing capability. Some details of virtualization are provided in [VIRT].

5.2.4 Cloud Storage and Data Management

In a cloud storage model, the service providers store massive amounts of data for customers in data centers. Those who require storage space will lease the storage from the service providers who are

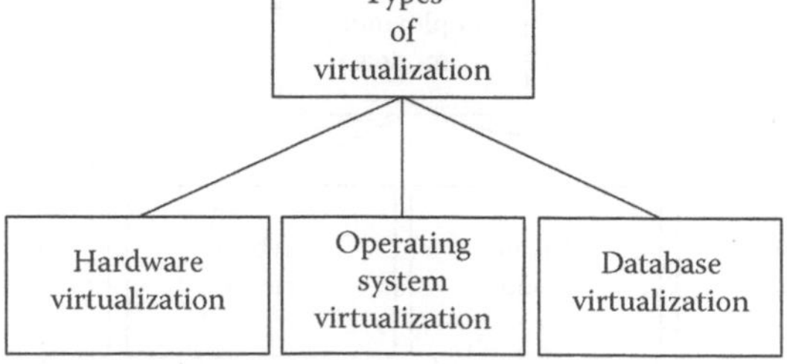

FIGURE 5.5 Types of virtualization.

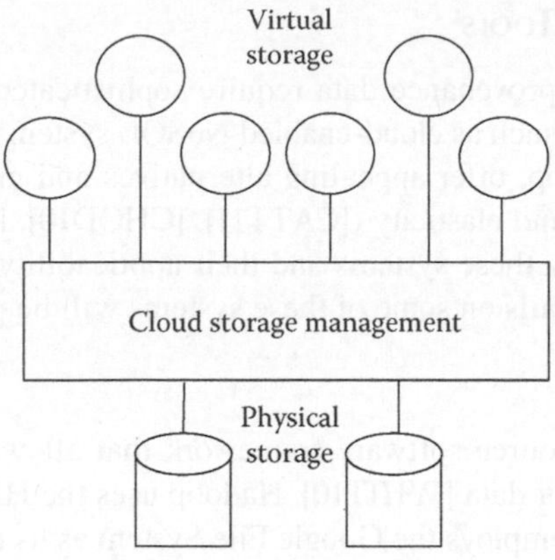

FIGURE 5.6 Cloud storage management.

the hosting companies. The actual location of the data is transparent to the users. What is presented to the users is virtualized storage; the storage managers will map the virtual storage with the actual storage and manage the data resources for the customers. A single object (e.g., the entire video database of a customer) may be stored in multiple locations. Each location may store objects for multiple customers. Figure 5.6 illustrates cloud storage management.

Virtualizing cloud storage has many advantages. Users need not purchase expensive storage devices. Data could be placed anywhere in the cloud. Maintenance such as backup and recovery are provided by the cloud. The goal is for users to have rapid access to the cloud. However, due to the fact that the owner of the data does not have complete control of his data, there are serious security concerns with respect to storing data in the cloud.

A database that runs on the cloud is a cloud database manager. There are multiple ways to utilize a cloud database manager. In the first model, for users to run databases on the cloud, a *virtual machine image* must be purchased. The database is then run on the virtual machines. The second model is the database as a service model; the service provider will maintain the databases. The users will make use of the database services and pay for the service. An example is the Amazon relational database service which is a Structured Query Language (SQL) database service and has a MySQL interface [AMAZ]. A third model is the cloud provider which hosts a database on behalf of the user. Users can either utilize the database service maintained by the cloud or they can run their databases on the cloud. A cloud database must optimize its query, storage, and transaction processing to take full advantage of the services provided by the cloud. Figure 5.7 illustrates cloud data management.

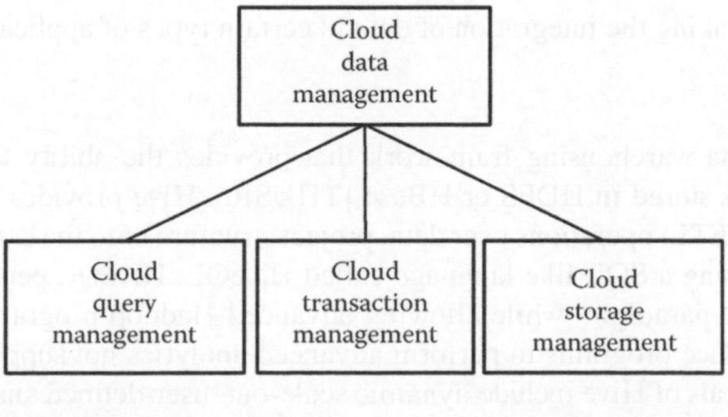

FIGURE 5.7 Cloud data management.

5.2.5 Cloud Computing Tools

Processing large volumes of provenance data require sophisticated methods and tools. In recent years, cloud computing tools, such as cloud-enabled NoSQL systems, MongoDB, CouchDB as well as frameworks such as Hadoop, offer appealing alternatives and great promises for systems with high availability, scalability, and elasticity ([CATT11], [CHOD10], [ANDE10], [WHIT10]). In this section, we will briefly survey these systems and their applicability and usefulness for processing large-scale datasets. More details on some of these systems will be provided in Chapter 7.

5.2.5.1 Apache Hadoop

Apache Hadoop is an open source software framework that allows batch processing tasks to be performed on vast quantities of data [WHIT10]. Hadoop uses the HDFS, a Java-based open source distributed file system which employs the Google File System as its underlying storage mechanism. HDFS provides several advantages such as data replication and fault tolerance [GHEM03]. HDFS uses a master/slave architecture that consists of a single namenode process (running on the master node) and several datanode processes (usually one per slave node).

5.2.5.2 MapReduce

A MapReduce job consists of three phases: (1) A "map" phase in which each slave node performs some computation on the data blocks of the input that it has stored. The output of this phase is a key–value pair based on the computation that is performed. (2) An intermediate "sort" phase in which the output of the map phase is sorted based on keys. (3) A "reduce" phase in which a reducer aggregates various values for a shared key and then further processes them before producing the desired result.

5.2.5.3 CouchDB

Apache CouchDB is a distributed, document-oriented database which can be queried and indexed in a MapReduce fashion [ANDE10]. Data is managed as a collection of JSON documents [CROC06]. Users can access the documents with a web browser, via HTTP as well as querying, combining, and transforming documents with JavaScript.

5.2.5.4 HBase

Apache HBase is a distributed, versioned, column-oriented store modeled after Google's Bigtable, written in Java. Organizations such as Mendeley, Facebook, and Adobe are using HBase [GEOR11].

5.2.5.5 MongoDB

It is an open source, schema-free, (JSON) document-oriented database written in C++ [CHOD10]. It is developed and supported by 10gen and is part of the NoSQL family of database systems. MongoDB stores structured data as JSON-like documents with dynamic schemas (MongoDB calls the format BSON), making the integration of data in certain types of applications easier and faster.

5.2.5.6 Hive

Apache Hive is a data warehousing framework that provides the ability to manage, query, and analyze large datasets stored in HDFS or HBase [THUS10]. Hive provides basic tools to perform extract-transfer-load (ETL) operations over data, project structure onto the extracted data, and query the structured data using a SQL-like language called HiveQL. HiveQL performs query execution using the MapReduce paradigm, while allowing advanced Hadoop programmers to plug in their custom-built MapReduce programs to perform advanced analytics not supported by the language. Some of the design goals of Hive include dynamic scale-out, user-defined analytics, fault-tolerance, and loose coupling with input formats.

5.2.5.7 Apache Cassandra

Apache Cassandra is an open source distributed database management system [HEWI10]. Apache Cassandra is a fault tolerant, distributed data store which offers linear scalability allowing it to be a storage platform for large high-volume websites. Cassandra is designed to handle big data workloads across multiple nodes with no single point of failure. Its architecture is based on the understanding that system and hardware failures can and do occur.

5.3 SEMANTIC WEB

As we have mentioned earlier in this chapter, some of our experimental big data systems we have developed have utilized cloud and semantic web technologies. While cloud computing was the subject of Section 5.2, in this section we will provide an overview of semantic web technologies.

While the current web technologies facilitate the integration of information from a syntactic point of view, there is still a lot to be done to handle the different semantics of various systems and applications. That is, current web technologies depend a lot on the "human-in-the-loop" for information management and integration. Tim Berners Lee, the father of the World Wide Web, realized the inadequacies of current web technologies and subsequently strived to make the web more intelligent. His goal was to have a web that would essentially alleviate humans from the burden of having to integrate disparate information sources as well as to carry out extensive searches. He then came to the conclusion that one needs machine-understandable web pages and the use of ontologies for information integration. This resulted in the notion of the semantic web [LEE01]. The web services that take advantage of semantic web technologies are semantic web services.

A semantic web can be thought of as a web that is highly intelligent and sophisticated so that one needs little or no human intervention to carry out tasks such as scheduling appointments, coordinating activities, searching for complex documents, as well as integrating disparate databases and information systems. While much progress has been made toward developing such an intelligent web, there is still a lot to be done. For example, technologies such as ontology matching, intelligent agents, and markup languages are contributing a lot toward developing the semantic web. Nevertheless, one still needs the human to make decisions and take actions. Since the 2000s, there have been many developments on the semantic web. The World Wide Web consortium (W3C) is specifying standards for the semantic web [W3C]. These standards include specifications for XML (eXtensible Markup Language), RDF (resource description framework), and interoperability.

Figure 5.8 illustrates the layered technology stack for the semantic web. This is the stack that was developed by Tim Berners Lee. Essentially the semantic web consists of layers where each layer takes

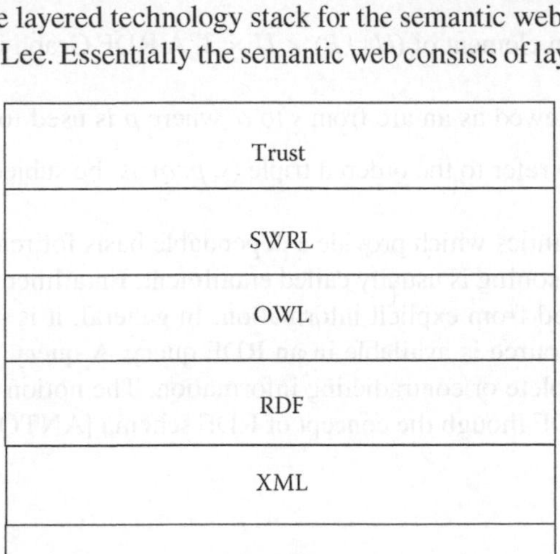

FIGURE 5.8 Technology stack for the semantic web.

advantage of the technologies of the previous layer. The lowest layer is the protocol layer and this is usually not included in the discussion of the semantic technologies. The next layer is the XML layer. XML is a document representation language. While XML is sufficient to specify syntax, semantics such as "the creator of document D is John" is hard to specify in XML. Therefore, the W3C developed RDF which uses XML syntax. The semantic web community then went further and came up with a specification of ontologies in languages such as Web Ontology Language (OWL). Note that OWL addresses the inadequacies of RDF. In order to reason about various policies, the semantic web community has come up with web rules language such as Semantic Web Rules Language (SWRL). Next, we will describe the various technologies that constitute the semantic web.

5.3.1 XML

XML is needed due to the limitations of hypertext markup language and complexities of standard generalized markup language. XML is an extensible markup language specified by the W3C and designed to make the interchange of structured documents over the Internet easier. An important aspect of XML used to be Document Type Definitions which define the role of each element of text in a formal model. XML schemas have now become critical to specify the structure of data. XML schemas are also XML documents [BRAY97].

5.3.2 RDF

The RDF is a standard for describing resources on the semantic web. It provides a common framework for expressing this information so it can be exchanged between applications without loss of meaning. RDF is based on the idea of identifying things using web identifiers (called uniform resource identifiers (URIs)), and describing resources in terms of simple properties and property values [KLYN04].

The RDF terminology T is the union of three pairwise disjoint infinite sets of terms: the set U of URI references, the set L of literals (itself partitioned into two sets, the set L_p of plain literals and the set L_t of typed literals), and the set B of blanks. The set $U \cup L$ of names is called the vocabulary.

Definition 5.1 (RDF Triple)

A RDF Triple (s, p, o) is an element of $(U \cup B) \times U \times T$. A RDF Graph is a finite set of triples.

A RDF triple can be viewed as an arc from s to o, where p is used to label the arc. This is represented as $s \xrightarrow{p} o$. We also refer to the ordered triple (s, p, o) as the subject, predicate, and object of a triple.

RDF has a formal semantics which provide a dependable basis for reasoning about the meaning of an RDF graph. This reasoning is usually called entailment. Entailment rules state which implicit information can be inferred from explicit information. In general, it is not assumed that complete information about any resource is available in an RDF query. A query language should be aware of this and tolerate incomplete or contradicting information. The notion of class and operations on classes are specified in RDF though the concept of RDF schema [ANTO08].

5.3.3 SPARQL

SPARQL (Simple Protocol and RDF Query Language) [PRUD06] is a powerful query language. It is a key semantic web technology and was standardized by the RDF Data Access Working Group of the W3C. SPARQL syntax is similar to SQL, but it has the advantage whereby it enables queries to span multiple disparate data sources that consist of heterogeneous and semistructured data. SPARQL is based around graph pattern matching [PRUD06].

Definition 5.2 (Graph Pattern)

A SPARQL graph pattern expression is defined recursively as follows:

1. A triple pattern is a graph pattern.
2. If *P*1 and *P*2 are graph patterns, then expressions (*P*1 AND *P*2), (*P*1 OPT *P*2), and (*P*1 *UNION P*2) are graph patterns.
3. If *P* is a graph pattern, *V* a set of variables, and $X \in U \cup V$, then (*XGRAPH P*) is a graph pattern.
4. If *P* is a graph pattern and *R* is a built in SPARQL condition, then the expression (*P* FILTER *R*) is a graph pattern.

5.3.4 OWL

The OWL [MCGU04] is an ontology language that has more expressive power and reasoning capabilities than RDF and RDF schema (RDF-S). It has additional vocabulary along with a formal semantics. OWL has three increasingly expressive sublanguages: OWL Lite, OWL DL, and OWL Full. These are designed for use by specific communities of implementers and users. The formal semantics in OWL is based on description logics (DL), which is a decidable fragment of first-order logics.

5.3.5 Description Logics

DL is a family of knowledge representation (KR) formalisms that represent the knowledge of an application domain [BAAD03]. It defines the concepts of the domain (i.e., its terminology) as sets of objects called classes, and it uses these concepts to specify properties of objects and individuals occurring in the domain. A DL is characterized by a set of constructors that allow one to build complex concepts and roles from atomic ones.

$\mathcal{ALCQ}$**:** A DL language $\mathcal{ALCQ}$ consists of a countable set of individuals *Ind*, a countable set of atomic concepts *CS*, a countable set of roles *RS* and the concepts built on *CS* and *RS* as follows:

$$C,D := A \mid \neg A \mid C \sqcap D \mid C \sqcup D \mid \exists R \cdot C \mid \forall R \cdot C \mid (\leq nR \cdot C) \mid (\geq nR \cdot C)$$

where $A \in CS$, $R \in RS$, *C*, and *D* are concepts and *n* is a natural number. Also, individuals are denoted by *a*, *b*, *c*, … (e.g., lower case letters of the alphabet).

This language includes only concepts in negation normal form. The complement of a concept $\neg(C)$ is inductively defined, as usual, by using the law of double negation, de Morgan laws and the dualities for quantifiers. Moreover, the constants $\top$ and $\bot$ abbreviate $A \sqcup \neg A$ and $A \sqcap \neg A$, respectively, for some $A \in CS$.

An interpretation *I* consists of a nonempty domain, Δ^I, and a mapping, a^I, that assigns

- To each individual $a \in Ind$ an element $a^I \in \Delta^I$
- To each atomic concept $A \in CS$ a set $A^I \subseteq \Delta^I$
- To each role $R \in RS$ a relation $R^I \subseteq \Delta^I \times \Delta^I$

The interpretation extends then on concepts as follows:

$$\neg A^{I} = \Delta^{I} \setminus A^{I}$$
$$(C \sqcup D)^{I} = C^{I} \cup D^{I}$$
$$(C \sqcap D)^{I} = C^{I} \cap D^{I}$$
$$(\exists R \cdot C)^{I} = \{x \in \Delta^{I} \mid \exists y((x,y) \in R^{I} \wedge y \in C^{I})\}$$
$$(\forall R \cdot C)^{I} = \{x \in \Delta^{I} \mid \forall y((x,y) \in R^{I} \Rightarrow y \in C^{I})\}$$
$$(\leq R \cdot C)^{I} = \{x \in \Delta^{I} \mid \#\{y \mid ((x,y) \in R^{I} \wedge y \in C^{I})\} \leq n\}$$
$$(\geq R \cdot C)^{I} = \{x \in \Delta^{I} \mid \#\{y \mid ((x,y) \in R^{I} \wedge y \in C^{I})\} \geq n\}$$

We can define the notion of a knowledge base and its models. An $\mathcal{ALCQ}$ knowledge base is the union of the following.

1. A finite terminological set (TBox) of inclusion axioms that have the form $T \sqsubseteq C$, where C is called inclusion concept.
2. A finite assertional set (ABox) of assertions of the form $a{:}C$ (concept assertion) or $(a, b){:}R$ (role assertion) where R is called assertional role, and C is called assertional concept.

We denote the set of individuals that appear in *KB* by *Ind*(*KB*). An interpretation I is a model of

- An inclusion axiom $T \sqsubseteq C(\, I \models \sqsubseteq T \sqsubseteq C)$ if $C^{I} = \Delta^{I}$
- A concept assertion a: $C(I \models a{:}C)$ if $a^{I} \in C^{I}$
- A role assertion a, b: $(I \models (a, b){:}\, R)$ if $(a^{I}, b^{I}) \in R^{I}$

Let K be the $\mathcal{ALCQ}$-knowledge base of a TBox, T, and an ABox $\mathcal{A}$. An interpretation I is a model of K if $I \sqsubseteq \phi$, for every $\phi \in T \cup \mathcal{A}$. A knowledge base K is consistent if it has a model. Moreover, for φ an inclusion axiom or an assertion, we say that $K \sqsubseteq \varphi$ (in words, K entails φ) if for every model I of K, $I \models \varphi$ also holds.

The consistency problem for $\mathcal{ALCQ}$ is ExpTime-complete. The entailment problem is reducible to the consistency problem as follows:

Let K be an $\mathcal{ALCQ}$ knowledge base and d be an individual not belonging to *Ind*(K). Then,

- $K \models T \sqsubseteq C$ iff $K \cup \{d{:}\, \neg C\}$ is inconsistent.
- $K \models a{:}\, C$ iff $K \cup \{a{:}\, \neg C\}$ is inconsistent.

This shows that an entailment can be decided in ExpTime. Moreover, the inconsistency problem is reducible to the entailment problem and so deciding an entailment is an ExpTime-complete problem too.

5.3.6 Inferencing

The basic inference problem for DL is checking a knowledge base consistency. A knowledge base K is consistent if it has a model. The additional inference problems are

- *Concept Satisfiability*. A concept C is satisfiable relative to K if there is a model I of K such that $C^{I} \neq \varnothing$.
- *Concept Subsumption*. A concept C is subsumed by concept D relative to K if, for every model I of K, $C^{I} \sqsubseteq D^{I}$.
- *Concept Instantiation*. An individual a is an instance of concept C relative to K if, for every model I of K, $a^{I} \in C^{I}$.

All these reasoning problems can be reduced to KB consistency. For example, concept *C* is satisfiable with regard to the knowledge base *K* if $K \cup C(a)$ is consistent where *a* is an individual not occurring in *K*.

5.3.7 SWRL

The SWRL extends the set of OWL axioms to include horn-like rules, and it extends the Horn-like rules to be combined with an OWL knowledge base [HORR04].

Definition 5.3 (Horn Clause)

A Horn Clause *C* is an expression of the form.

$D_0 \leftarrow D_1 \cap \ldots \cap D_n$, where each D_i is an atom. The atom D_0 is called the head and the set $D_1 \cap \ldots \cap D_n$ is called the body. Variables that occur in the body at most once and do not occur in the head are called unbound variables; all other variables are called bound variables.

The proposed rules are of the form of an implication between an antecedent (body) and a consequent (head). The intended meaning can be read as: whenever the conditions specified in the antecedent hold, the conditions specified in the consequent must also hold. Both the antecedent (body) and consequent (head) consist of zero or more atoms. An empty antecedent is treated as trivially true (i.e., satisfied by every interpretation), so the consequent must also be satisfied by every interpretation. An empty consequent is treated as trivially false (i.e., not satisfied by any interpretation), so the antecedent must not be satisfied by any interpretation.

Multiple atoms are treated as a conjunction, and both the head and body can contain conjunction Wof such atoms. Note that rules with conjunctive consequents could easily be transformed (via Lloyd-Topor transformations) into multiple rules each with an atomic consequent. Atoms in these rules can be of the form *C*(*x*), *P*(*x*, *y*), *SameAs*(*x*, *y*) or *DifferentFrom*(*x*, *y*) where *C* is an OWL description, *P* is an OWL property, and *x*, *y* are either variables, OWL individuals, or OWL data values.

5.4 SEMANTIC WEB AND SECURITY

We first provide an overview of security issues for the semantic web and then discuss some details on XML security, RDF security, and secure information integration which are components of the secure semantic web. As more progress is made on investigating these various issues, we hope that appropriate standards would be developed for securing the semantic web. Security cannot be considered in isolation. Security cuts across all layers.

For example, consider the lowest layer. One needs secure TCP/IP, secure sockets, and secure HTTP. There are now security protocols for these various lower layer protocols. One needs end-to-end security. That is, one cannot just have secure TCP/IP built on untrusted communication layers, we need network security. The next layer is XML and XML schemas. One needs secure XML. That is, access must be controlled to various portions of the document for reading, browsing, and modifications. There is research on securing XML and XML schemas. The next step is securing RDF. Now with RDF not only do we need secure XML, but we also need security for the interpretations and semantics. For example, under certain contexts, portions of the document may be *unclassified*, while under certain other contexts the document may be *classified*.

Once XML and RDF have been secured, the next step is to examine security for ontologies and interoperation. That is, ontologies may have security levels attached to them. Certain parts of the ontologies could be *secret* while certain other parts may be *unclassified*. The challenge is how does one use these ontologies for secure information integration? Researchers have done some work on the secure interoperability of databases. We need to revisit this research and then determine what else needs to be done so that the information on the web can be managed, integrated, and exchanged securely. Logic, proof, and trust are at the highest layers of the semantic web. That is, how can we trust the information that the web gives us? Next we will discuss the various security issues for XML, RDF, ontologies, and rules.

5.4.1 XML Security

Various research efforts have been reported on XML security (see e.g., [BERT02]. We briefly discuss some of the key points. The main challenge is whether to give access to all the XML documents or to parts of the documents. Bertino and Ferrari have developed authorization models for XML. They have focused on access control policies as well as on dissemination policies. They also considered push and pull architectures. They specified the policies in XML. The policy specification contains information about which users can access which portions of the documents. In [BERT02], algorithms for access control as well as computing views of the results are presented. In addition, architectures for securing XML documents are also discussed. In [BERT04] and [BHAT04], the authors go further and describe how XML documents may be published on the web. The idea is for owners to publish documents, subjects request access to the documents, and untrusted publishers give the subjects the views of the documents they are authorized to see. W3C is specifying standards for XML security. The XML security project is focusing on providing the implementation of security standards for XML. The focus is on XML-Signature Syntax and Processing, XML-Encryption Syntax and Processing, and XML Key Management. While the standards are focusing on what can be implemented in the near term, much research is needed on securing XML documents (see also [SHE09]).

5.4.2 RDF Security

RDF is the foundation of the semantic web. While XML is limited in providing machine understandable documents, RDF handles this limitation. As a result, RDF provides better support for interoperability as well as searching and cataloging. It also describes contents of documents as well as relationships between various entities in the document. While XML provides syntax and notations, RDF supplements this by providing semantic information in a standardized way [ANTO08].

The basic RDF model has three components: they are resources, properties, and statements. Resource is anything described by RDF expressions. It could be a web page or a collection of pages. Property is a specific attribute used to describe a resource. RDF statements are resources together with a named property plus the value of the property. Statement components are subject, predicate, and object. So, for example, if we have a sentence of the form "John is the creator of xxx," then xxx is the subject or resource, property, or predicate is "creator" and object or literal is "John." There are RDF diagrams very much like, say, the entity relationship diagrams or object diagrams to represent statements. It is important that the intended interpretation be used for RDF sentences. This is accomplished by RDF-S. Schema is sort of a dictionary and has interpretations of various terms used in sentences.

More advanced concepts in RDF include the container model and statements about statements. The container model has three types of container objects and they are bag, sequence, and alternative. A bag is an unordered list of resources or literals. It is used to mean that a property has multiple values but the order is not important. A sequence is a list of ordered resources. Here the order is important. Alternative is a list of resources that represent alternatives for the value of a property. Various tutorials in RDF describe the syntax of containers in more detail. RDF also provides support for making statements about other statements. For example, with this facility, one can make statements of the form "The statement A is false," where A is the statement "John is the creator of X." Again, one can use object-like diagrams to represent containers and statements about statements. RDF also has a formal model associated with it. This formal model has a formal grammar. The query language to access RDF document is SPARQL. For further information on RDF, we refer to the excellent discussion in the book by Antoniou and van Harmelen [ANTO08].

Now to make the semantic web secure, we need to ensure that RDF documents are secure. This would involve securing XML from a syntactic point of view. However, with RDF, we also need to ensure that security is preserved at the semantic level. The issues include the security implications of the concepts resource, properties, and statements. That is, how is access control ensured? How can statements and properties about statements be protected? How can one provide access control at a finer grain of granularity? What are the security properties of the container model? How can bags, lists, and alternatives be protected? Can we specify security policies in RDF? How can we resolve semantic inconsistencies for the policies? What are the security implications of statements about statements? How can we protect RDF-S? These are difficult questions and we need to start research to provide answers. XML security is just the beginning. Securing RDF is much more challenging (see also [CARM04]).

5.4.3 Security and Ontologies

Ontologies are essentially representations of various concepts in order to avoid ambiguity. Numerous ontologies have been developed. These ontologies have been used by agents to understand the web pages and conduct operations such as the integration of databases. Furthermore, ontologies can be represented in languages such as RDF or special languages such as OWL. Now, ontologies have to be secure. That is, access to the ontologies has to be controlled. This means that different users may have access to different parts of the ontology. On the other hand, ontologies may be used to specify security policies just as XML and RDF have been used to specify the policies. That is, we will describe how ontologies may be secured as well as how ontologies may be used to specify the various policies.

5.4.4 Secure Query and Rules Processing

The layer above the secure RDF layer is the secure query and rule processing layer. While RDF can be used to specify security policies (see e.g., [CARM04]), the web rules language developed by W3C is more powerful to specify complex policies. Furthermore, inference engines were developed to process and reason about the rules (e.g., the Pellet engine developed at the University of Maryland). One could integrate ideas from the database inference controller that we have developed (see [THUR93]) with web rules processing to develop an inference or privacy controller for the semantic web. The query processing module is responsible for accessing the heterogeneous data and information sources on the semantic web. Researchers are examining ways to integrate techniques from web query processing with semantic web technologies to locate, query, and integrate the heterogeneous data and information sources.

5.5 CLOUD COMPUTING FRAMEWORKS BASED ON SEMANTIC WEB TECHNOLOGIES

In this section, we introduce a cloud computing framework that we have utilized in the implementation of our systems for malware detection as well as social media applications, some of which are discussed in this book. In particular, we will discuss our framework for RDF integration and provenance data integration.

5.5.1 RDF Integration

We have developed an RDF-based policy engine for use in the cloud for various applications including social media and information sharing applications. The reasons for using RDF as our data model are as follows: (1) RDF allows us to achieve data interoperability between the seemingly disparate sources of information that are cataloged by each agency/organization separately. (2) The use of RDF allows participating agencies to create data-centric applications that make use of the integrated data that is now available to them. (3) Since RDF does not require the use of an explicit schema for data generation, it can be easily adapted to ever-changing user requirements. The policy engine's flexibility is based on its accepting high-level policies and executing them as rules/constraints over a directed RDF graph representation of the provenance and its associated data. The strength of our policy engine is that it can handle any type of policy that could be represented using RDF technologies, horn logic rules (e.g., SWRL), and OWL constraints. The power of these semantic web technologies can be successfully harnessed in a cloud computing environment to provide the user with capability to efficiently store and retrieve data for data intensive applications. Storing RDF data in the cloud brings a number of new features such as: scalability and on-demand services, resources and services for users on demand, ability to pay for services and capacity as needed, location independence, guarantee quality of service for users in terms of hardware/CPU performance, bandwidth, and memory capacity. We have examined the following efforts in developing our framework for RDF integration.

In [SUN10], the authors adopted the idea of Hexastore and considered both RDF data model and HBase capability. They stored RDF triples into six HBase tables (S_PO, P_SO, O_SP, PS_O, SO_P and PO_S), which covered all combinations of RDF triple patterns. They indexed the triples with HBase-provided index structure on row key. They also proposed a MapReduce strategy for SPARQL basic graph pattern (BGP) processing, which is suitable for their storage schema. This strategy uses multiple MapReduce jobs to process a typical BGP. In each job, it uses a greedy method to select join key and eliminates multiple triple patterns. Their evaluation result indicated that their approach worked well against large RDF datasets. In [HUSA09], the authors described a framework that uses Hadoop to store and retrieve large numbers of RDF triples. They described a schema to store RDF data in the HDFS. They also presented algorithms to answer SPARQL queries. This made use of Hadoop's MapReduce framework to actually answer the queries. In [HUAN11], the authors introduced a scalable RDF data management system. They introduced techniques for (1) leveraging state-of-the-art single node RDF-store technology and (2) partitioning the data across nodes in a manner that helps accelerate query processing through locality optimizations. In [PAPA12], the authors presented H2RDF, which is a fully distributed RDF store that combines the MapReduce processing framework with a NoSQL distributed data store. Their system features unique characteristics that enable efficient processing of both simple and multijoin SPARQL queries on virtually unlimited number of triples. These include join algorithms that execute joins according to query selectivity to reduce processing, and include adaptive choice among centralized and distributed (MapReduce-based) join execution for fast query responses. They claim that their system can efficiently answer both simple joins and complex multivariate queries, as well as scale up to 3 billion triples using a small cluster consisting of nine worker nodes. In [KHAD12b], the authors designed a Jena-HBase framework. Their HBase-backed triple store can be used with the Jena framework. Jena-HBase provides end users with a scalable storage and querying solution that supports all features from the RDF specification.

5.5.2 Provenance Integration

While our approach for assured information sharing in the cloud for social networking applications is general enough for any type of data including cyber security data, we have utilized provenance data as an example. We will discuss the various approaches that we have examined in our work on provenance data integration. More detailed of our work can be found in [THUR15].

In [IKED11], the authors considered a class of workflows which they call generalized map and reduce workflows. The input datasets are processed by an acyclic graph of map and reduce functions to produce output results. They also showed how data provenance (lineage) can be captured for map and reduce functions transparently. In [CHEB13], the authors explored and addressed the challenge of efficient and scalable storage and querying of large collections of provenance graphs serialized as RDF graphs in an Apache HBase database. In [PARK11], they proposed reduce and map provenance (RAMP) as an extension to Hadoop that supports provenance capture and tracing for workflows of MapReduce jobs. The work discussed in [ABRA10] proposed a system to show how HBase Bigtable-like capabilities can be leveraged for distributed storage and querying of provenance data represented in RDF. In particular, their ProvBase system incorporates an HBase/Hadoop backend, a storage schema to hold provenance triples, and a querying algorithm to evaluate SPARQL queries in their system. In [AKOU13], the authors' research introduced HadoopProv, a modified version of Hadoop that implements provenance capture and analysis in MapReduce jobs. Their system is designed to minimize provenance capture overheads by (i) treating provenance tracking in Map and Reduce phases separately and (ii) deferring construction of the provenance graph to the query stage. The provenance graphs are later joined on matching intermediate keys of the RAMP files.

5.6 SUMMARY AND DIRECTIONS

This chapter has introduced the notions of the cloud and semantic web technologies. We first discussed concepts in cloud computing including aspects of virtualization. We also discussed the various service models and deployment models for the cloud and provided a brief overview of cloud functions such as storage management and data management. In addition, some of the cloud products, especially that relate to big data technologies, were also discussed. Next, we discussed technologies for the semantic web including XML, RDF, Ontologies, and OWL. This was followed by a discussion of security issues for the semantic web. Finally, we discussed cloud computing frameworks based on semantic web technologies. More details on cloud computing and semantic web can be found in [THUR07] and [THUR14].

Our discussion of cloud computing and semantic web will be useful in understanding some of the experimental systems discussed in Section IV of this book. For example, we have discussed experimental very large data processing systems that function in a cloud. We have also discussed access control for big data systems represented using semantic web technologies. These topics will be discussed in Section IV of this book.

REFERENCES

[ABRA10]. J. Abraham, P. Brazier, A. Chebotko, J. Navarro, A. Piazza, "Distributed Storage and Querying Techniques for a Semantic Web of Scientific Workflow Provenance," In *Proceedings Services Computing (SCC), 2010 IEEE International Conference on Services Computing*, Miami, FL, 2010.

[AKOU13]. A. Sherif, R. Sohan, H. Andy, "HadoopProv: Towards Provenance as a First Class Citizen in MapReduce," In *Proceedings of the 5th USENIX Workshop on the Theory and Practice of Provenance*, Lombard, IL, 2013.

[AMAZ]. Amazon Relational Database Service, http://aws.amazon.com/rds/

[ANDE10]. A. Chris, J. Lehnardt, N. Slater, *CouchDB: The Definitive Guide*, The Definitive Guide, O'Reilly Media, Sebastopol, CA, 2010.

[ANTO08]. A. Grigoris and V. Harmelen, Frank, *Semantic Web Primer*, MIT Press, Cambridge, MA, 2008.

[BAAD03]. F. Baader, The description logic handbook: Theory, implementation, and applications, 2003.

[BERT02]. E. Bertino and E. Ferrari, "Secure and Selective Dissemination of XML Documents," *ACM Transactions on Information and System Security (TISSEC)*, 5, (3), 290–331, 2002.

[BERT04]. E. Bertino, and G. Giovanna, M. Marco, "A matching Algorithm for Measuring the Structural Similarity between an XML Document and a DTD and its Applications," *Information Systems*, 29 (1), 23–46, 2004.

[BHAT04]. B. Rafae, E. Bertino, G. Arif, J. James, "XML-Based Specification for Web Services Document Security," *Computer*, 37 (4), 41–49, 2004.

[BRAY97]. B. Tim, P. Jean, S. McQueen, C. Michael, M. Eve, Y. Francois, "Extensible Markup Language (XML)," *World Wide Web Journal*, 2 (4), 1997.

[CARM04]. B. Carminati, E. Ferrari, B.M. Thuraisingham, "Using RDF for Policy Specification and Enforcement," *DEXA Workshops*, Zaragoza, Spain, 2004.

[CATT11]. C. Rick, "Scalable SQL and NoSQL Data Stores," *ACM SIGMOD Record*, 39, (4), 12–27, 2011.

[CHEB13]. C. Artem, J. Abraham, P. Brazier, A. Piazza, A. Kashlev, S. Lu, "Storing, Indexing and Querying Large Provenance Data Sets as RDF Graphs in Apache HBase," *IEEE International Workshop on Scientific Workflows*, 2013, Santa Clara, CA.

[CHOD10]. C. Kristina and M. Dirolf, *MongoDB: The Definitive Guide*, O'Reilly Media, Sebastopol, CA, 2010.

[CLOUD]. Cloud Computing, http://en.wikipedia.org/wiki/Cloud_computing

[CROC06]. C. Douglas, The Application/Json Media Type for Javascript Object Notation (JSON), 2006. https://tools.ietf.org/html/rfc4627

[DEAN04]. J. Dean and S. Ghemawat, "MapReduce: Simplified Data Processing on Large Clusters," http://research.google.com/archive/mapreduce.html

[GEOR11]. G. Lars, *HBase: The Definitive Guide*, O'Reilly Media, Sebastopol, CA, 2011.

[GHEM03]. G. Sanjay, G. Howard, L. Shun-Tak, "The Google File System," *ACM SIGOPS Operating Systems Review*, 37, (5), 29–43, 2003.

[HDFS]. Apache Hadoop, http://hadoop.apache.org/

[HEWI10]. H. Eben, *Cassandra: The Definitive Guide*, O'Reilly Media, Sebastopol, CA, 2010.

[HORR04]. I. Horrocks, P.E. Patel-Schneider, H. Boley, S. Tabet, B. Grosof, M. Dean, "SWRL: A semantic web rule language combining OWL and RuleML," W3C Member Submission, 2004.

[HUAN11]. H. Jiewen, D.J. Abadi, R. Kun, "Scalable SPARQL Querying of Large RDF Graphs," *Proceedings of the VLDB Endowment*, 4, (11), 1123–1134, 2011.

[HUSA09]. H.M. Farhan, D. Pankil, K. Latifur, T. Bhavani, "Storage and Retrieval of Large RDF Graph using Hadoop and MapReduce," *Cloud Computing*, 680–686, 2009.

[IKED11]. I. Robert, P. Hyunjung, W. Jennifer, "Provenance for Generalized Map and Reduce Workflows," *5th Biennial Conference on Innovative Data Systems Research (CIDR '11)*, January 9–12, 2011, Asilomar, CA, 2011.

[KHAD12a]. V. Khadilkar, K.Y. Octay, M. Kantarcioglu, S. Mehrotra, "Secure Data Processing over Hybrid Clouds," *IEEE Data Engineering Bulletin*, 35 (4), 46–54, 2012.

[KHAD12b]. V. Khadilkar, K. Murat, P. Castagna, B. Thuraisingham, "Jena-HBase: A Distributed," *Scalable and Efficient RDF Triple Store*, 2012, Technical report: http://www.utdallas.edu/~vvk072000/Research/Jena-HBase-Ext/tech-report.Pdf

[KLYN04]. G. Klyne, J.J. Carroll, B. McBride, Resource description framework (RDF): Concepts and abstract syntax, W3C Recommendation 10, 2004.

[LEE01]. T.B. Lee, J. Hendler, O. Lasilla, "The Semantic Web," *Scientific American*, May 2001.

[MCGU04]. D.L. McGuinness and F. Van Harmelen, "OWL Web Ontology Language Overview," W3C Recommendation, 2004.

[NIST]. Definition of Cloud Computing, National Institute of Standards and Technology, http://csrc.nist.gov/publications/nistpubs/800-145/SP800-145.pdf

[PAPA12]. P. Nikolaos, K. Ioannis, T. Dimitrios, K. Nectarios, "H2RDF: Adaptive Query Processing on RDF Data in the Cloud," In *Proceedings of the 21st International Conference Companion on World Wide Web*, Lyon, France, 2012.

[PARK11]. P. Hyunjung, I. Robert, W. Jennifer, "Ramp: A System for Capturing and Tracing Provenance in Mapreduce Workflows," In *37th International Conference on Very Large Data Bases (VLDB), Stanford InfoLab*, Seattle, WA, 2011.

[PRUD06]. E. Prud'hommeaux and A. Seaborne, "SPARQL Query Language for RDF," W3C Working Draft, 2006.

[SHE09]. W. She, I.L. Yen, B. Thuraisingham, E. Bertino, "The SCIFC Model for Information Flow Control in Web Service Composition," *Web Services, 2009. ICWS* 2009. *IEEE International Conference*, 1–8, Los Angeles, CA.

[SUN10]., S. Jianling and J. Qiang, "Scalable RDF Store Based on Hbase and Mapreduce," In *Proceedings Advanced Computer Theory and Engineering (ICACTE), 2010 3rd International Conference*, 1, pp. V1–633, Chengdu, China, 2010.

[THUR93]. B. Thuraisingham, W. Ford, M. Collins, J. O'Keeffe, "Design and Implementation of a Database Inference Controller," *Data and Knowledge Engineering Journal*, 11 (3), 271–297, 1993.

[THUR07]. B. Thuraisingham, *Building Trustworthy Semantic Webs*, CRC Press, Boca Raton, FL, 2007.

[THUR14]. B. Thuraisingham, *Developing and Securing the Cloud*, CRC Press, Boca Raton, FL, 2014.

[THUR15]. B. Thuraisingham, *Secure Data Provenance and Inference Control with Semantic Web*, CRC Press, Boca Raton, FL, 2015.

[THUS10]. T. Ashish, S. Joydeep Sen, J. Namit, S. Zheng, C. Prasad, Z. Ning, A. Suresh, L. Hao, M. Raghotham, "Hive-A Petabyte Scale Data Warehouse using Hadoop," In *Proceedings Data Engineering (ICDE), 2010 IEEE 26th International Conference on Data Engineering (ICDE)*, Long Beach, CA, 2010.

[VIRT]. Virtualization and Cloud Management, http://www.vmware.com/solutions/virtualization-management/index.html

[W3C]. World Wide Web Consortium, www.w3c.org

[WHIT10]. W. Tom, "*Hadoop: The Definitive Guide*," O'Reilly Media, Inc., Sebastopol, CA, 2010.

6 Data Mining and Insider Threat Detection

6.1 INTRODUCTION

The discussions in Chapters 2 through 5 provide the background for applying data mining for insider threat detection. Effective detection of insider threats requires monitoring mechanisms that are far more fine-grained than for external threat detection. These monitors must be efficiently and reliably deployable in the software environments where actions endemic to malicious insider missions are caught in a timely manner. Such environments typically include user-level applications, such as word processors, email clients, and web browsers for which reliable monitoring of internal events by conventional means is difficult.

To monitor the activities of the insiders, tools are needed to capture the communications and relationships between the insiders, store the captured relationships, query the stored relationships, and ultimately analyze the relationships so that patterns can be extracted that would give the analyst better insights into the potential threats. Over time, the number of communications and relationships between the insiders could be in the billions. Using the tools developed under our project, the billions of relationships between the insiders can be captured, stored, queried, and analyzed to detect malicious insiders.

In this chapter, we will discuss how data mining technologies could be applied for insider threat detection in the cloud. First, we will discuss how semantic web technologies may be used to represent the communication between insiders. Next, we will discuss our approach to insider threat detection. Finally, we will provide an overview of our framework for insider threat detection that also incorporated some other techniques.

The organization of this chapter is as follows. In Section 6.2, we provide an overview of insider threat detection. In Section 6.3, we will discuss the challenges, related work, and our approach to this problem. Our approach will be discussed in detail in Section 6.4. Our framework will be discussed in Section 6.5. This chapter is concluded in Section 6.6. Figure 6.1 illustrates the contents of this chapter. It should be noted that while the discussion in this chapter provides our overall approach to insider threat detection using data mining, more details of the big data analytics tools we have designed and developed for insider threat detection will be the subject of Section 6.3. Therefore, this chapter is essentially a snapshot of the contents to be described in Section 6.3.

6.2 INSIDER THREAT DETECTION

There is a growing consensus among various government and commercial organizations that malicious insiders are perhaps the most potent threats to information assurance in many or most organizations ([BRAC04], [HAMP99], [MATZ04], [SALE11]). Just like their human counterparts, the malicious insider processes try their best to conceal their behavior and carry out surveillance and reconnaissance of their targets. When there is an opportunity, they will exploit the vulnerabilities and steal highly classified proprietary information.

The U.S. Homeland Security has defined insider threat as follows [DHS14]. "*An insider threat is generally defined as a current or former employee, contractor, or other business partner who has or had authorized access to an organization's network, system, or data and intentionally misused that access to negatively affect the confidentiality, integrity, or availability of the organization's information or information systems. Insider threats, to include sabotage, theft, espionage, fraud,*

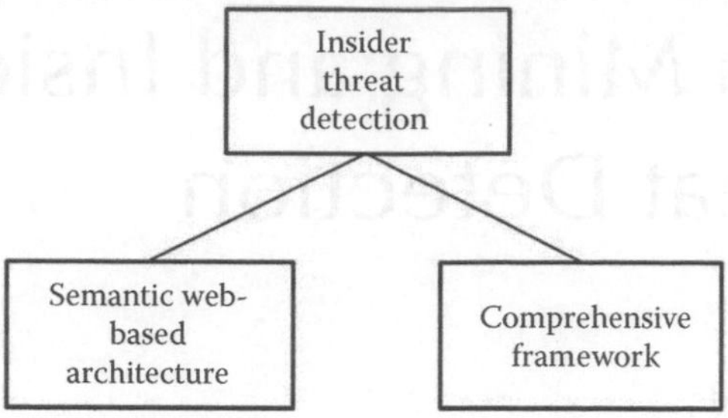

FIGURE 6.1 Data mining and insider threat detection.

and competitive advantage are often carried out through abusing access rights, theft of materials, and mishandling physical devices. Insiders do not always act alone and may not be aware they are aiding a threat actor (i.e., the unintentional insider threat). It is vital that organizations understand normal employee baseline behaviors and also ensure employees understand how they may be used as a conduit for others to obtain information."

The activities carried out by the malicious insiders could generate massive volumes of data over time. Our challenge is to analyze this data and detect whether the activities are malicious or not. One traditional approach to the *insider threat* detection problem is *supervised learning* which builds data classification models from training data. Unfortunately, the training process for supervised learning methods tends to be time-consuming and expensive, and generally requires large amounts of well-balanced training data to be effective. In our experiments, we observe that <3% of the data in realistic datasets for this problem is associated with insider threats (the minority class); over 97% of the data is associated with nonthreats (the majority class). Hence, traditional support vector machines (SVM) ([CHAN11], [MANE02]) trained from such imbalanced data are likely to perform poorly on test datasets.

After an extensive investigation of the various data mining techniques for insider threat detection, we believe that the best way to handle the insider threat problem is to conceptualize it as a stream mining problem that applies to continuous data streams. Whether using a supervised or unsupervised learning algorithm, the method chosen must be highly adaptive to correctly deal with concept drifts under these conditions. In Section III of this book, we describe the various big data analytics techniques for data streams that we have developed for insider threat detection. In this chapter, we will discuss our preliminary investigation of modeling the activities of the insider as a collection of graphs and discuss our approach to mining the graphs to extract the patterns of the insiders.

6.3 THE CHALLENGES, RELATED WORK, AND OUR APPROACH

The insiders and the relationships between the insiders will be presented as nodes and links in a graph. Therefore, the challenge is to represent the information in graphs, develop efficient storage strategies, develop queries processing techniques for the graphs, and subsequently develop data mining and analysis techniques to extract information from the graphs. In particular, there are three major challenges.

1. Storing these large graphs in an expressive and unified manner in a secondary storage.
2. Devising scalable solutions for querying the large graphs to find relevant data.
3. Identifying relevant features for the complex graphs and subsequently detecting insider threats in a dynamic environment that changes over time.

The motivation behind our approach is to address these challenges. We have developed solutions based on cloud computing to (i) characterize graphs containing up to billions of nodes and edges between nodes representing activities (e.g., credit card transactions), e-mail, or text messages. Since the graphs will be massive, we have developed technologies for efficient and persistent storage. (ii) In order to facilitate novel anomaly detection, we require an efficient interface to fetch relevant data in a timely manner from this persistent storage. Therefore, we have developed efficient query techniques on the stored graphs. (iii) The fetched relevant data can then be used for further analysis to detect anomalies. In order to do this, first we have to identify relevant features from the complex graphs and subsequently develop techniques for mining large graphs to extract the nuggets.

Insider threat detection is a difficult problem to solve. The problem becomes increasingly complex with more data originating from heterogeneous sources and sensors. Recently, there are some that focus on anomaly-based insider threat detection from graphs [EBER09]. This method is based on the *minimum description length* principle. The solution proposed by [EBER09] has some limitations. First, with their approach, scalability is an issue. In other words, they have not discussed any issue related to large graphs. Second, the heterogeneity issue has not been addressed. Finally, it is unclear how their algorithm will deal with a dynamic environment which changes over time.

There are also several graph mining techniques that have been developed especially for social network analysis ([COOK06], [TONG09], [CARM09], [THUR09]). The scalability of these techniques is still an issue. There is some work from the mathematics research community to apply linear programming techniques for graph analysis [BERR07]. Whether these techniques will work in a real-world setting is not clear.

For a solution to be viable, it must be highly scalable and support multiple heterogeneous data sources. Current state-of-the-art solutions do not scale well or preserve accuracy. By leveraging Hadoop technology, our solution will be highly scalable. Furthermore, by utilizing the flexible semantic web RDF data model, we are able to easily integrate and align heterogeneous data. Thus, our approach will create a scalable solution in a dynamic environment. No existing threat detection tools offer this level of scalability and interoperability. We have combined these technologies with novel data mining techniques to create a complete insider threat detection solution.

We have exploited the cloud computing framework based on Hadoop/MapReduce technologies. The insiders and their relationships are represented by nodes and links in the form of graphs. In particular, in our approach, the billions of nodes and links will be presented as resource description framework (RDF) graphs. By exploiting RDF representation, we have addressed heterogeneity. We have developed mechanisms to efficiently store the RDF graphs, query the graphs using SPARQL technologies, and mine the graphs to extract patterns within the cloud computing framework.

6.4 DATA MINING FOR INSIDER THREAT DETECTION

6.4.1 Our Solution Architecture

Figure 6.2 shows the architectural view of our solution. Our solution will pull data from multiple sources and then extract and select features. After feature reduction, the data will be stored in our Hadoop repository. Data will be stored in the RDF format, so a format conversion may be required if the data is in any other format. RDF is the data format for the semantic web and is very able to represent graph data. The anomaly prediction component will submit SPARQL protocol and RDF Query Language (SPARQL) to the repository to select data. It will then output any detected insider threats. SPARQL is the query language for RDF data. It is similar to Structured Query Language (SQL) in syntax. The details of each of the components are given in the following sections. For choosing RDF representation for graphs over relational data models, we will address heterogeneity issue effectively (semistructured data model). For querying, we exploit standard query language, SPARQL, instead of starting from scratch. Furthermore, in our proposed framework inference will be provided.

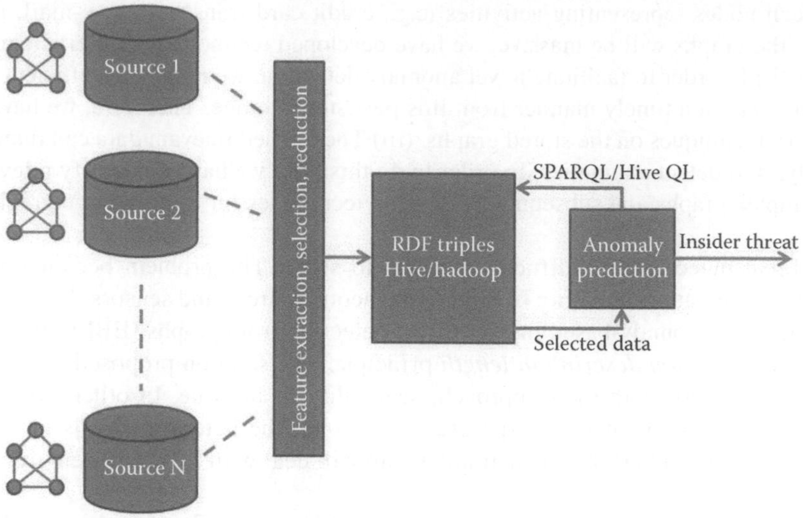

FIGURE 6.2 Solution architecture.

We are assuming that the large graphs already exist. To facilitate persistent storage and efficient retrieval of this data, we use a distributed framework based on the cloud computing framework Hadoop [HADO]. By leveraging the Hadoop technology, our framework is readily fault-tolerant and scalable. To support large amounts of data, we can simply add more nodes to the Hadoop cluster. All the nodes of a cluster are commodity class machines; there is no need to buy expensive server machines. To handle large complex graphs, we exploit the Hadoop Distributed File System (HDFS) and MapReduce framework. The former is the storage layer which stores data in multiple nodes with replication. The latter is the execution layer where MapReduce jobs can be run. We use HDFS to store RDF data and the MapReduce framework to answer queries.

6.4.2 Feature Extraction and Compact Representation

In traditional graph analysis, an edge represents a simple number which represents strength. However, we may face additional challenges in representing link values due to the unstructured nature of the content of text and email messages. One possible approach is to keep the whole content as a part of link values which we call explicit content (EC). EC will not scale well, even for a moderate size graph. This is because content representing a link between two nodes will require a lot of main memory space to process the graph in the memory. We propose a vector representation of the content (VRC) for each message. In RDF triple representation, this will simply be represented as a unique predicate. We keep track of the feature vector along with physical location or URL of the original raw message in a dictionary encoded table.

6.4.2.1 Vector Representation of the Content

During the preprocessing step for each message, we extract keywords and phrases (n-grams) as features. Then if we want to generate vectors for these features, the dimensionality of these vectors will be very high. Here, we observe the curse of dimensionality (i.e., sparseness and processing time will increase). Therefore, we can apply feature reduction (PCA, SVD, NMF) as well as feature selection. Since feature reduction maps high-dimensional feature spaces to a space of fewer dimensions, and new feature dimension may be the linear combination of old dimensions that may be difficult to interpret, we exploit feature selection.

With regard to feature selection, we need to use a class label for supervised data. Here, for the message we may not have a class label; however, we know the source/sender and the destination/recipient of a message. Now, we would like to use this knowledge to construct an artificial label. The sender and destination pair will form a unique class label and all messages sent from this sender to the recipient will serve as data points. Hence, our goal is to find appropriate features that will have discriminating power across all these class labels based on these messages. There are several methods for feature selection that are widely used in the area of machine learning, such as information gain (IG) ([MITC97], [MASU10a], [MASU10b]), Gini index, chi-square statistics, subspace clustering [AHME09], and so on. Here, we present IG, which is very popular and for the text domain, we can use subspace clustering for feature selection.

IG can be defined as a measure of the effectiveness of a feature in classifying the training data [MITC97]. If we split the training data on these attribute values, then IG provides the measurement of the expected reduction in entropy after the split. The more an attribute can reduce entropy in the training data, the better the attribute in classifying the data. IG of an attribute A on a collection of examples S is given by

$$\text{Gain}(S,A) \equiv \text{Entropy}(S) - \sum_{V \in \text{Values}(A)} \frac{|S_v|}{|S|} \text{Entropy}(S_v) \tag{6.1}$$

where Values(A) is the set of all possible values for attribute A, and S_v is the subset of S for which attribute A has value v. Entropy of S is computed using the following equation:

$$\text{Entropy}(S) = -\sum_{i=1}^{n} p_i(S) \log_2 p_i(S) \tag{6.2}$$

where $p_i(S)$ is the prior probability of class i in the set S.

6.4.2.2 Subspace Clustering

Subspace clustering can be used for feature selection. Subspace clustering is appropriate when the clusters corresponding to a dataset form a subset of the original dimensions. Based on how these subsets are formed, a subspace clustering algorithm can be referred to as soft or hard subspace clustering. In the case of soft subspace clustering, the features are assigned weights according to the contribution each feature/dimension plays during the clustering process for each cluster. In the case of hard subspace clustering, however, a specific subset of features is selected for each cluster and the rest of the features are discarded for that cluster. Therefore, subspace clustering can be utilized for selecting which features are important (and discarding some features if their weights are very small for all clusters). One such soft subspace clustering approach is semisupervised impurity-based subspace clustering [AHME09]. The following objective function is used in that subspace clustering algorithm. An E-M formulation is used for the clustering. In every iteration, the feature weights are updated for each cluster and by selecting the features that have higher weights in each cluster, we can select a set of important features for the corresponding dataset

$$F(W,Z,\Lambda) = \sum_{l=1}^{k}\sum_{j=1}^{n}\sum_{i=1}^{m} w_{lj}^{f} \lambda_{li}^{q} D_{lij} * (1+\text{Imp}_l) + \gamma \sum_{l=1}^{k}\sum_{i=1}^{m} \lambda_{li}^{q} \chi_{li}^{2}$$

Where

$$D_{lij} = (z_{li} - x_{ji})^2$$

Subject to

$$\sum_{jl=1}^{k} w_{lj} = 1, \quad 1 \le j \le n, 1 \le l \le k, 0 \le w_{lj} \le 1$$

$$\sum_{i=1}^{m} \lambda_{li} = 1, \quad 1 \le i \le m, 1 \le l \le k, 0 \le \lambda_{li} \le 1$$

In this objective function, W, Z, and Λ represent the cluster membership, cluster centroid, and dimension weight matrices, respectively. Also, the parameter f controls the fuzziness of the membership of each data point, q further modifies the weight of each dimension of each cluster (λ_{li}), and finally, γ controls the strength of the incentive given to the *Chi Square* component and dimension weights. It is also assumed that there are n documents in the training dataset, m features for each of the data points and k subspace clusters are generated during the clustering process. Imp_l indicates the cluster impurity, whereas χ^2 indicates the *chi square statistic*. Details about these notations and how the clustering is done can be found in our prior work, funded by NASA [AHME09]. It should be noted that feature selection using subspace clustering can be considered as an unsupervised approach toward feature selection as no label information is required during an unsupervised clustering process.

Once we select features, a message between two nodes will be represented as a vector using these features. Each vector's individual value can be binary or weighted. Hence, this will be a compact representation of the original message and it can be loaded into main memory along with graph structure. In addition, the location or URL of the original message will be kept in the main memory data structure. If needed, we fetch the message. Over time, the feature vector may be changed due to dynamic nature content [MASU10a], and hence, the feature set may evolve. Based on our prior work for evolving streams with dynamic feature sets [MASU10b], we investigate alternative options.

6.4.3 RDF Repository Architecture

RDF is the data format for semantic web. However, it can be used to represent any linked data in the world. RDF data is actually a collection of triples. Triples consist of three parts: subject, predicate, and object. In RDF, almost everything is a resource and hence the name of the format. Subject and predicate are always resources. Objects may be either a resource or a literal. Here, RDF data can be viewed as a directed graph where predicates are edges which flow from subjects to objects. Therefore, in our proposed research to model any graph, we exploit RDF triple format. Here, an edge from the source node to destination node in graph dataset will be represented as predicate, subject, and object of an RDF triple, respectively. To reduce storage size of RDF triples, we exploit dictionary encoding, that is, replace each unique string with a unique number and store the RDF data in binary format. Hence, RDF triples will have subject, predicate, and object in an encoded form. We maintain a separate table/file for keeping track of dictionary encoding information. To address the dynamic nature of the data, we extend RDF triple to quad by adding a timestamp along with subject, predicate, and object representing information in the network.

Figure 6.3 shows our repository architecture which consists of two components. The upper part of the figure depicts the data preprocessing component, and the lower part shows the component which answers a query. We have three subcomponents for data generation and preprocessing. If the data is not in N-Triples, we convert it to N-Triples serialization format using the N-Triples converter component. The predicate split component takes the N-Triples data and splits it into predicate files. The predicate-based files then will be fed into the predicate object split component which would split the predicate files into smaller files based on the type of objects.

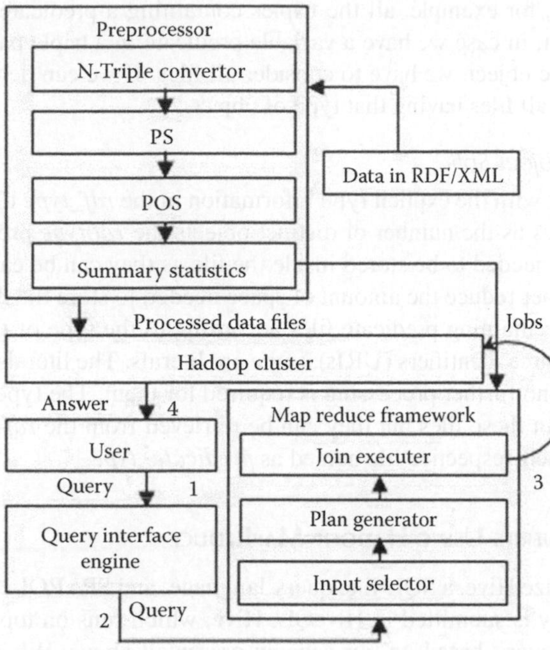

FIGURE 6.3 RDF repository architecture.

Our MapReduce framework has three subcomponents in it. It takes the SPARQL query from the user and passes it to the input selector and plan generator. This component will select the input files and decide how many MapReduce jobs are needed and pass the information to the Join Executer component which runs the jobs using MapReduce framework. It will then relay the query answer from Hadoop to the user.

6.4.4 Data Storage

We store the data in the N-Triples format because in this format we have a complete RDF triple (subject, predicate and object) in one line of a file, which is very convenient to use with MapReduce jobs. The data is dictionary encoded for increased efficiency. Dictionary encoding means replacing text strings with a unique binary number. This not only reduces disk space required for storage but also query answering will be fast because handling primitive data type is much faster than string matching. The processing steps to get the data in our intended format are described below.

6.4.4.1 File Organization

We do not store the data in a single file because, in a Hadoop and MapReduce framework, a file is the smallest unit of input to a MapReduce job and, in the absence of caching, a file is always read from the disk. If we have all the data in one file, the whole file will be input to jobs for each query. Instead, we divide the data into multiple smaller files. The splitting will be done in two steps which we discuss in the following sections.

6.4.4.1.1 Predicate Split

In the first step, we divide the data according to the predicates. In real world RDF datasets, the number of distinct predicates is no >100. This division will immediately enable us to cut down the search space for any SPARQL query which does not have a variable predicate. For such a query, we can just pick a file for each predicate and run the query on those files only. For simplicity, we name the files with predicates, for example, all the triples containing a predicate *p1:pred* go into a file named *p1-pred*. However, in case we have a variable predicate in a triple pattern and if we cannot determine the type of the object, we have to consider all files. If we can determine the type of the object, then we consider all files having that type of object.

6.4.4.1.2 Predicate Object Split

In the next step, we work with the explicit type information in the *rdf_type* file. The file will be first divided into as many files as the number of distinct objects the *rdf:type* predicate has. The object values will no longer be needed to be stored inside the file as they can be easily retrieved from the file name. This will further reduce the amount of space needed to store the data.

Then, we divide the remaining predicate files according to the type of the objects. Not all the objects are uniform resource identifiers (URIs), some are literals. The literals will remain in the file named by the predicate; no further processing is required for them. The type information of a URI object is not mentioned in these files but they can be retrieved from the *rdf-type_** files. The URI objects will move into their respective file named as *predicate_type*.

6.4.5 Answering Queries Using Hadoop MapReduce

For querying we can utilize Hive, a SQL-like query language, and SPARQL, the query language for RDF data. When a query is submitted in HiveQL, Hive, which runs on top of the Hadoop installation, can answer that query based on our schema presented above. When a SPARQL query is submitted to retrieve relevant data from graph, first, we generate a query plan having the minimum number of Hadoop jobs possible.

Next, we run the jobs and answer the query. Finally, we convert the numbers used to encode the strings back to the strings when we present the query results to the user. We focus on minimizing the number of jobs because, in our observation, we have found that setting up Hadoop jobs is very costly and the dominant factor (time-wise) in query answering. The search space for finding the minimum number of jobs is exponential, so we try to find a greedy-based solution or, generally speaking, an approximation solution. Our proposed approach will be capable of handling queries involving inference. We can infer on the fly and if needed we can materialize the inferred data.

6.4.6 Data Mining Applications

To detect anomaly/insider threat, machine learning and domain knowledge-guided techniques are proposed. Our goal is to create a comparison baseline to assess the effectiveness of chaotic attractors. As a part of this task, rather than modeling normal behavior and detecting changes as anomaly, we apply a holistic approach based on a semi-supervised model. In particular, first, in our machine learning technique, we apply a sequence of activities or dimensions as features. Second, domain knowledge (e.g., adversarial behavior) will be a part of semi-supervised learning and will be used for identifying correct features. Finally, our techniques will be able to identify an entirely brand new anomaly. Over time, activities/dimensions may change or deviate. Hence, our classification model needs to be adaptive and identify new types or brand new anomalies. We have developed adaptive and novel class detection techniques so that our insider threat detection can cope with changes and identify or isolate new anomalies from existing ones.

We apply a classification technique to detect insider threat/anomaly. Each distinct insider mission will be treated as class and dimension and/or activities will be treated as features. Since classification is a supervised task, we require a training set. Given a training set, feature extraction will be a challenge. We apply N-gram analysis to extract features or generate a number of sequences based on temporal property. Once a new test case comes, first, we test it against our classification model. For classification model, we can apply support vector machine, K-NN, and Markovian model.

From a machine learning perspective, it is customary to classify behavior as either anomalous or benign. However, behavior of a malevolent insider (i.e., insider threat) may not be immediately identified as malicious, and it should also have subtle differences from benign behavior. A traditional machine learning-based classification model is likely to classify the behavior of a malevolent insider as benign. It will be interesting to see whether a machine learning-based novel class detection technique [MASU10a] can detect the insider threat as a novel class, and therefore trigger a warning.

The novel class detection technique can be applied on the huge data that is being generated from user activities. Since this data has temporal properties and is produced continuously, it is usually referred to as data streams. The novel class detection model will be updated incrementally with the incoming data. This will allow us to keep the memory requirement within a constant limit, since the raw data will be discarded, but the characteristic/pattern of the behaviors will be summarized in the model. Besides, this incremental learning will also reduce the training time since the model need not be built from the scratch with the new incoming data. Therefore, this incremental learning technique will be useful in achieving scalability.

We examine the techniques that we have developed as well as other relevant techniques to modeling and anomaly detection. In particular, we propose to develop:

- Tools that will analyze and model benign and anomalous mission.
- Techniques to identify right dimensions and activities and apply pruning to discard irrelevant dimensions.
- Techniques to cope with changes and novel class/anomaly detection.

In a typical data stream classification task, it is assumed that the total number of classes is fixed. This assumption may not be valid in insider threat detection cases, where new classes may evolve. Traditional data stream classification techniques are not capable of recognizing novel class instances until the appearance of the novel class is manually identified, and labeled instances of that class are presented to the learning algorithm for training. The problem becomes more challenging in the presence of concept drift, when the underlying data distribution changes over time. We have proposed a novel and efficient technique that can automatically detect the emergence of a novel class (i.e., brand new anomaly) by quantifying cohesion among unlabeled test instances, and separating the test instances from training instances. Our goal is to use the available data and build this model.

One interesting aspect of this model is that it should capture the dynamic nature of dimensions of the mission, as well as filter out the noisy behaviors. The dimensions (both benign and anomalous) have dynamic nature because they tend to change over time, which we denote as concept drift. A major challenge of the novel class detection is to differentiate the novel class from concept drift and noisy data. We are exploring this challenge in our current work.

6.5 COMPREHENSIVE FRAMEWORK

As we have stated earlier, insider threat detection is an extremely challenging problem. In the previous section, we discussed our approach to handling this problem. Insider threat does not occur only at the application level, it happens at all levels including the operating system, database system and the application. Furthermore, due to the fact that the insider will be continually changing patterns, it will be impossible to detect all types of malicious behavior using a purely static algorithm; a dynamic learning approach is required. Essentially, we need a comprehensive solution to the insider threat problem. However, to provide a more comprehensive solution, we need a more comprehensive framework. Therefore, we are developing a framework for insider threat detection. Our framework will implement a number of inter-related solutions to detect malicious insiders. Figure 6.4 illustrates such a framework. We propose four approaches to this problem. At

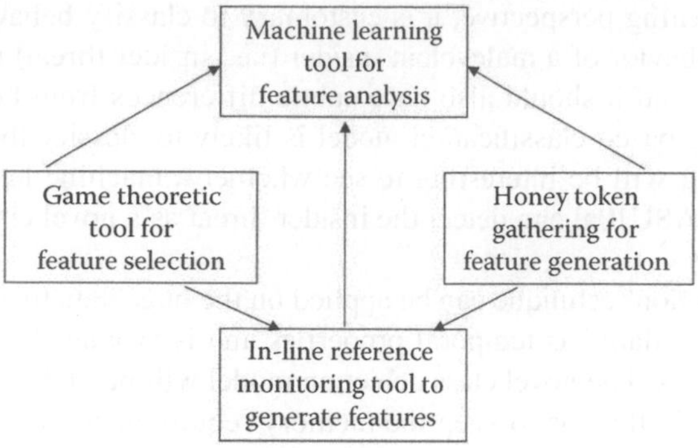

FIGURE 6.4 Framework for insider threat detection.

the heart of our framework is the module that implements in-line reference monitor (IRM)-based techniques for feature collection. This feature collection process will be aided by two modules: one uses game theory approach and the other uses the natural language-based approach to determine which features could be collected. The fourth module implements machine learning techniques to analyze the collected features. In summary, the relationship between the four approaches can be characterized as follows:

- IRMs perform covert, fine-grained feature collection.
- Game theoretic techniques will identify which features should be collected by the IRMs.
- Natural language processing techniques in general and honey token generation in particular, will take an active approach to introducing additional useful features (i.e., honey token accesses) that can be collected.
- Machine learning techniques will use the collected features to infer and classify the objectives of malicious insiders.

Details of our framework are provided in [HAML11]. We assume that the IRM tool, game theoretic tool, and honey token generation tool will select and refine the features we need. Our data mining tools will analyze the features and determine whether there is a potential for insider threat.

We have started implementing parts of the framework. In particular, we have developed a number of data and stream mining techniques for insider threat detection, some of which will be discussed in Section III. Evidence of malicious insider activity is often buried within large data streams such as system logs accumulated over months or years. Ensemble-based stream mining leverages multiple classification models to achieve highly accurate anomaly detection in such streams even when the stream is unbounded, evolving, and unlabeled. This makes the approach effective for identifying insider threats who attempt to conceal their activities by varying their behaviors over time. Our approach applies ensemble-based stream mining, unsupervised learning, supervised learning, and graph-based anomaly detection to the problem of insider threat detection, demonstrating that the ensemble-based approach is significantly more effective than traditional single-model methods. We further investigate suitability of various learning strategies for evolving insider threat data. We also developed unsupervised machine learning algorithms for insider threat detection. Our implementation is being hosted on the cloud. More information can also be found in [PALL12]. For more information on ensemble-based stream mining applications, we also refer to the chapters in Sections 6.2 and 6.3. Details of our algorithms are presented in [MASU10a].

6.6 SUMMARY AND DIRECTIONS

In this chapter, we have discussed the problem of insider threat and our approach to insider threat detection. We represent the insiders and their communication as RDF graphs and then query and mine the graphs to extract the nuggets. We also provided a comprehensive framework for insider threat detection.

The insider threat problem is a challenging one. The problem is that the insider may change his/her patterns and behaviors. Therefore, we need tools that can be adaptive. For example, our stream mining tools discussed in Section II may be used for detecting such threats as they detect novel classes. Because of the massive amounts of data to be analyzed, cloud-based data mining would be a suitable approach for insider threat detection. Our approach is essentially for insider threat detection to be offered as a security-as-a-service solution. As discussed earlier, while the discussion in this chapter provides our overall approach to insider threat detection using data mining, more details of our work and the use of big data analytics for insider threat detection will be the subject of Section III.

REFERENCES

[AHME09]. M.S. Ahmed and L. Khan, "SISC: A Text Classification Approach Using Semi supervised Subspace Clustering," *DDDM '09: The 3rd International Workshop on Domain Driven Data Mining in Conjunction with ICDM 2009*, Dec. 6, Miami, FL, pp. 1–6, 2009.

[BERR07]. M.W. Berry, M. Browne, A. Langville, V.P. Pauca, and R.J. Plemmons, "Algorithms and Applications for Approximate Nonnegative Matrix Factorization," *Computational Statistics and Data Analysis,* 52 (1), 155–173, 2007.

[BRAC04]. R.C. Brackney and R.H. Anderson, editors, *Understanding the Insider Threat*. RAND Corporation, Arlington, VA, 2004.

[CARM09]. B. Carminati, E. Ferrari, R. Heatherly, M. Kantarcioglu, B. Thuraisingham, "A Semantic Web Based Framework for Social Network Access Control" *SACMAT 2009*, Stresa, Italy, pp. 177–186, 2009.

[CHAN11]. C.-C. Chang and C.-J. Lin, "LIBSVM: A library for support vector machines," *ACM Transactions on Intelligent Systems and Technology*, 2, 27:1–27:27, 2011. Software available at http://www.csie.ntu.edu.tw/ cjlin/libsvm.

[COOK06]. D. Cook and L. Holder, *Mining Graph Data*, Wiley Interscience, NY, 2006.

[DHS14]. Department of Homeland Security, Combating Insider Threat, National Cyber Security and Communications Integraiob Center, Department of Homeland Security, May 2014.

[EBER09]. W. Eberle and L. Holder, "Applying Graph-Based Anomaly Detection Approaches to the Discovery of Insider Threats," *IEEE International Conference on Intelligence and Security Informatics (ISI)*, Dallas, TX, June, pp. 206–208, 2009.

[HADO]. Apache Hadoop http://hadoop.apache.org/

[HAML11]. K. Hamlen, L. Khan, M. Kantarcioglu, V. Ng, and B. Thuraisingham. *Insider Threat Detection*, UTD Technical Report, April 2011.

[HAMP99]. M.P. Hampton and M. Levi, "Fast Spinning into Oblivion? Recent Developments in Money-Laundering Policies and Offshore Finance Centres," *Third World Quarterly*, 20 (3), 645–656, 1999.

[MANE02]. L.M. Manevitz and M. Yousef. "One-Class SVMs for Document Classification," *The Journal of Machine Learning Research*, 2, 139–154, 2002.

[MASU10a]. M. Masud, J. Gao, L. Khan, J. Han, B. Thuraisingham, "Classification and Novel Class Detection in Concept-Drifting Data Streams under Time Constraints," *IEEE Transactions on Knowledge and Data Engineering (TKDE)*, April 2010, IEEE Computer Society, 2010.

[MASU10b]. M. Masud, Q. Chen, J. Gao, L. Khan, J. Han, B. Thuraisingham, "Classification and Novel Class Detection of Data Streams in a Dynamic Feature Space," *Proceedings of European Conference on Machine Learning and Knowledge Discovery in Databases, ECML PKDD 2010*, Barcelona, Spain, Sept. 20–24, 2010, Springer 2010, ISBN 978-3-642-15882-7, pp. 337–352, 2010.

[MATZ04]. S. Matzner and T. Hetherington, "Detecting Early Indications of a Malicious Insider," *IA Newsletter*, 7 (2), 42–45, 2004.

[MITC97]. T. Mitchell, *Machine Learning*. McGraw Hill, New York, NY, 1997.

[PALL12]. P. Parveen, N. McDaniel, V.S. Hariharan, B.M. Thuraisingham, L. Khan. "Unsupervised Ensemble Based Learning for Insider Threat Detection," *SocialCom/PASSAT 2012*, pp. 718–727, 2012.

[SALE11]. M.B. Salem and S.J. Stolfo. "Modeling User Search Behavior for Masquerade Detection," *Proceedings of Recent Advances in Intrusion Detection (RAID)*, Menlo Park, CA, pp. 101–200, 2011.

[THUR09]. B. Thuraisingham, M. Kantarcioglu, and L. Khan, "Building a Geosocial Semantic Web for Military Stabilization and Reconstruction Operations," *PAISI 2009*, 1, 2009.

[TONG09]. H. Tong, *Fast Algorithms for Querying and Mining Large Graphs*, CMU Report, ML-09-112, September 2009.

7 Big Data Management and Analytics Technologies

7.1 INTRODUCTION

Over the past 10 years or so, numerous big data management and analytics systems have emerged. In addition, various cloud service providers have also implemented big data solutions. In addition, infrastructures/platforms for big data systems have also been developed. Notable among the big data systems include MongoDB, Google's BigQuery, and Apache HIVE. The big data solutions are being developed by cloud providers including Amazon, IBM, Google, and Microsoft. In addition, infrastructures/platforms based on products such as Apache's Hadoop, Spark, and Storm have been developed.

Selecting the products to discuss is a difficult task. This is because almost every database vendor as well as cloud computing vendors together with analytics tools vendors are now marketing products as big data management and analytics (BDMA) solutions. When we combine the products offered by all vendors as well as include the open-source products, then there are hundreds of products to discuss. Therefore, we have selected the products that we are most familiar with by discussing these products in the courses we teach and/or using them in our experimentation. In other words, we have only selected the service providers, products, and frameworks that we are most familiar with and those that we have examined in our work. Describing all of the service providers, products, and frameworks is beyond the scope of this book. Furthermore, we are not endorsing any product in this book.

The organization of this chapter is as follows. In Section 7.2, we will describe the various infrastructure products that host big data systems. Examples of big data systems are discussed in Section 7.3. Section 7.4 discusses the big data solutions provided by some cloud service providers. This chapter is summarized in Section 7.5. Figure 7.1 illustrates the concepts discussed in this chapter.

7.2 INFRASTRUCTURE TOOLS TO HOST BDMA SYSTEMS

In this section, we will discuss various infrastructure products that host BDMA systems. These are Apache's Hadoop, Spark, Storm, Flink, Kafka, and the MapReduce programming model.

Apache Hadoop: Hadoop is an open-source distributed framework for processing large amounts of data. It uses the MapReduce programming model that we will discuss next. Its storage system is called the Hadoop Distributed File System (HDFS). It is hosted on clusters of machines. A file consists of multiple blocks and the blocks of a file are replicated for availability. It supports the parallel processing of the data for performance. JobTracker is a part of Hadoop that tracks the MapReduce jobs. These jobs are submitted by the client application. Most of the big data systems as well as the cloud applications are hosted on Hadoop. More details of Hadoop can be found in [HADO].

MapReduce: MapReduce is a programming model and an associated implementation that takes the client requests and transforms them into MapReduce jobs. These jobs are then executed by Hadoop. The main feature of the programming model is the generation of the jobs. The MapReduce model has two components: (i) map and (ii) reduce. As stated in [MAPR], "a MapReduce job usually splits the input dataset into independent chunks which are processed by the map tasks in a completely parallel manner. The framework sorts the outputs of the maps, which are then input to the reduce tasks. Typically, both the input and the output of the job are stored in a file system.

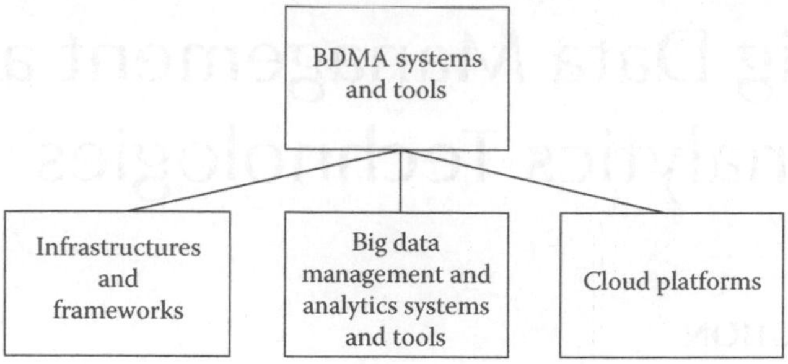

FIGURE 7.1 Big data management and analytics systems and tools.

The framework takes care of scheduling tasks, monitoring them, and re-executes the failed tasks." More details of the MapReduce model are given in [MAPR].

Apache Spark: Apache Spark is an open-source distributed computing framework for processing massive amounts of data. The application programmers use Spark through an interface that consists of a data structure called the resilient distributed dataset (RDD). Spark was developed to overcome the limitations in the MapReduce programming model. The RDD data structure of Spark provides the support for distributed shared memory. Due to the in-memory processing capabilities, Spark offers good performance. Spark has interfaces with various NoSQL-based big data systems such as Cassandra and Amazon's cloud platform. Spark supports SQL capabilities with Spark SQL. More details on Spark can be found in [SPAR].

Apache Pig: Apache Pig is a scripting platform for analyzing and processing large datasets. Apache Pig enables Hadoop users to write complex MapReduce transformations using simple scripting language called Pig Latin. Pig converts Pig Latin script to a MapReduce job. The MapReduce jobs are then executed by Hadoop for the data stored in HDFS. Pig Latin programming is similar to specifying a query execution plan. That is, the Pig Latin scripts can be regarded to be an execution plan. This makes it simpler for the programmers to carry out their tasks. More details on Pig can be found in [PIG].

Apache Storm: Apache Storm is an open-source distributed real-time computation system for processing massive amounts of data. Storm is essentially a real-time framework for processing streaming data and real-time analytics. It can be integrated with the HDFS. It provides features like scalability, reliability, and fault tolerance. The latest version of Storm supports streaming SQL, predictive modeling, and integration with systems such as Kafka. In summary, Storm is for real-time processing and Hadoop is for batch processing. More details on Storm can be found in [STOR].

Apache Flink: Flink is an open-source scalable stream processing framework. As stated in [FLIN], Flink consists of the following features: (i) provides results that are accurate, even in the case of out-of-order or late-arriving data, (ii) is stateful and fault tolerant and can seamlessly recover from failures while maintaining exactly once application state, and (iii) performs at large scale, running on thousands of nodes with very good throughput and latency characteristics. Flink is essentially a distributed data flow engine implemented in Scala and Java. It executes programs both in parallel and pipelined modes. It supports Java, Python, and SQL programming environments. While it does not have its own data storage, it integrates with systems such as HDFS, Kafka, and Cassandra.

Apache Kafka: Kafka was initially developed by LinkedIn and then further developed as an open-source Apache project. It is also implemented in Scala and Java and is a distributed stream processing system. It is highly scalable and handles massive amounts of streaming data. Its storage layer is based on a pub/sub messaging queue architecture. The design is essentially based on distributed transaction logs. Transaction logs are used in database systems to recover from the failure of the transactions. More details on Kafka can be found in [KAFK].

7.3 BDMA SYSTEMS AND TOOLS

In this section, we will discuss the various BDMA systems and tools. We first provide big data systems that are based on SQL. These are Apache Hive and Google BigQuery. Then we discuss NoSQL (non-SQL) databases in general. This is followed by a discussion of examples of NoSQL systems such as Google BigTable, HBase, MongoDB, Cassandra, CouchDB, and the Oracle NoSQL Database. This will be followed by a discussion of two data mining/machine learning systems for big data and they are Weka and Apache Mahout.

7.3.1 Apache Hive

Apache Hive is an open-source SQL-like database/data warehouse that is implemented on top of the Hadoop/MapReduce platform. It was initially developed by Facebook to store the information related to Facebook data. However, later it became an open-source project and a trademark of Apache. Hive manages very large datasets and functions on top of the Hadoop/MapReduce storage model. It provides an SQL-like query language which is called HiveQL. That is, SQL-like queries are supported by Hive. However, since Hadoop is implemented in Java, the queries are also implemented in Java. This way, there is no need to have a low-level Java application programming interface (API) to implement the queries. The Hive engine essentially converts the SQL queries into MapReduce jobs that are then executed by Hadoop. More details on Apache Hive can be found in [HIVE].

7.3.2 Google BigQuery

BigQuery is essentially a data warehouse that manages petabyte scale data. It runs on Google's infrastructure and can process SQL queries or carry out analytics extremely fast. For example, terabyte data can be accessed in seconds, while petabyte data can be accessed in minutes. The BigQuery data is stored in different types of tables: native tables store the BigQuery data, Views store the virtual tables, and External tables store the external data. BigQuery can be accessed in many ways such as command line tools, RESTful interface or a web user interface, and client libraries (e.g., Java,.NET, and Python). More details on BigQuery can be found in [BIGQ].

7.3.3 NoSQL Database

NoSQL database is a generic term for essentially a nonrelational database design or scalability for the web. It is known as a nonrelational high performance database. The data models for NoSQL databases may include graphs, document structures, and key–value pairs. It can be argued that the databases that were developed in the 1960s such as IBM's information management system (IMS) and those based on the network data model are NoSQL databases. However, other object-oriented data models that were developed in the 1990s led the way to develop NoSQL databases in the 2000s. What is different from the NoSQL databases and the older hierarchical, network, and object databases is that the NoSQL databases have been designed with the web in mind. That is, the goal is to access massive amounts of data on the web rapidly.

The most popular NoSQL database model is the key–value pair. While relational databases consist of a collection of relations where each relation has a collection or attributes, these attributes are labeled and included in the schema. NoSQL databases have tables that have two columns: key and value. Key could be anything such as a person's name or the index of a stock. However, the value could be a collection of attributes such as the name of the stock, the value of the stock and other information such as whether to buy the stock and if so the quantity recommended. Therefore, all the information pertaining to a stock can be retrieved without having to perform many joins. Some of the popular NoSQL databases will be discussed in this section (e.g., MongoDB and HBase). For a detailed discussion of NoSQL databases, we refer the reader to [NOSQ].

7.3.4 Google BigTable

BigTable is one of the early NoSQL databases running on top of the Google file system (GFS). It is now provided as a service in the cloud. BigTable maps the row key and the column together with a time stamp into a byte array. That is, it is essentially a NoSQL database that is based on the key value pair model. It was designed to handle petabyte-sized data. It uses compression algorithms when the data gets too large. Each table in BigTable has many dimensions and may be divided into what is called tablets to work with GFS. BigTable is used by many applications including Google's YouTube, Google Maps, Google Earth, and Gmail. More details on BigTable can be found in [BIGT].

7.3.5 Apache HBase

HBase is an open-source nonrelational distributed database that was the first table developed for the Hadoop/MapReduce platform. That is, HBase is a NoSQL database that is based on a column-oriented key value data store model. It is implemented in Java. The queries are executed as MapReduce jobs. It is somewhat similar to Google's Big Table and uses compression for in-memory storage. HBase is scalable and handles billions of rows with millions of columns. It also integrates multiple data stores in different formats as well as facilitates the storage of sparse data. More details on HBase can be found in [HBAS].

7.3.6 MongoDB

MongoDB is a NoSQL database. It is a cross-platform open-source distributed database. It has been used to store and manage documents. That is, it is mainly a document-oriented database. The documents are stored in a JSON-like format. It supports both field and range queries and regular expression-based searches. It supports data replication and load balancing which occurs through horizontal scaling. The batch processing of data as well as aggregation operations can be carried out through MapReduce. More details of MongoDB can be found at [MONG].

7.3.7 Apache Cassandra

Cassandra is a NoSQL distributed database. It was first developed at Facebook to power the Facebook applications and then became an Apache foundation open software initiative. It was designed with no single point of failure in mind. It supports clusters which span multiple data centers. All the nodes in a cluster perform the same function. As a result, there is virtually no single point of failure. It supports replication and is highly scalable. It is also fault tolerant and is integrated with Hadoop with support for MapReduce. The query language supported by Cassandra is Cassandra Query Language which is an alternative to SQL. It can also be accessed from programs such as Java, C++, and Python. More details of Cassandra can be found at [CASS].

7.3.8 Apache CouchDB

As stated in [COUC], CouchDB enables one to access data by implementing the Couch replication protocol. This protocol has been implemented by numerous platforms from clusters to the web to mobile phones. It is a NoSQL database and implemented in a concurrent language called Erlang. It uses JSON to store the data and JavaScript for the query language. More details on CouchDB can be found in [COUC].

7.3.9 Oracle NoSQL Database

Oracle is one of the premier relational database vendors and has marketed relational database products since the late 1970s. It offered object-relational database products in the 1990s and more recently the NoSQL database. The NoSQL database is based on the key value paid model. Each row has a unique key and has a value that is of arbitrary length and interpreted by the applicant. Oracle NoSQL database is a shared nothing system and is distributed across what are called multiple shards in a cluster. The data is replicated in the storage nodes within a shard for availability. The data can be accessed via programs such as those written in Java, C, Python as well as RESTful web services. More details on the Oracle NoSQL database can be found at [ORAC].

7.3.10 Weka

Weka is an open-source software product that implements a collection of data mining techniques from association rule mining to classification to clustering. It has been designed, developed, and maintained by Mankato University in New Zealand. Weka 3, a version of Weka, operated on big datasets. While earlier versions of Weka required the entire datasets to be loaded into memory to carry out say classification, the big data version carried out incremental loading and classification. Weka 3 also supports distributed data mining with map and reduce tasks. It also provides wrappers for Hadoop and Spark. More details on Weka can be found in [WEKA].

7.3.11 Apache Mahout

The Apache Mahout provides an environment to implement a collection of machine learning systems. These systems arc scalable and implemented on top of Hadoop. The machine learning algorithms include classification and clustering. The instructions of the machine learning algorithms are transformed into MapReduce jobs and executed on Hadoop. Mahout provides Java libraries to implement the mathematics and statistical techniques involved in machine learning algorithms. The goal is for the machine learning algorithms to operate on very large datasets. In summary, as stated in [MAHO], Mahout provides the following three features: (i) a simple and extensible programming environment and framework for building scalable algorithms; (ii) a wide variety of premade algorithms for Scala + Apache Spark, H2O, and Apache Flink; and (iii) Samsara, a vector math experimentation environment with R-like syntax which works at scale. More details on Mahout can be found at [MAHO].

7.4 CLOUD PLATFORMS

In this section, we will discuss how some cloud service providers are supporting big data management. In particular, we discuss Amazon's DynamoDB and Microsoft's Cosmos DB. Then we discuss the cloud-based big data solutions provided by IBM and Google.

7.4.1 Amazon Web Services' DynamoDB

Dynamo is a NoSQL database which is part of Amazon Web Services (AWS) product portfolio. It supports both document and the key-value store models. High performance and high throughput are the goals of DynamoDB. With respect to storage, DynamoDB can expand and shrink as needed by the applications. It also has an in-memory cache called Amazon DynamoDB Accelerator that can provide millisecond responses for millions of requests per second. More details on DynamoDB can be found at [DYNA].

7.4.2 Microsoft Azure's Cosmos DB

Cosmos DB is a database that runs on Microsoft's cloud platform, Azure. It was developed with scalability and high performance in mind. It has a distributed model with replication of availability. Its scalable architecture enables the support for multiple data models and programming languages.

As stated in [COSM], "the core type system of Azure Cosmos DB's database engine is atom-record-sequence based. Atoms consist of a small set of primitive types, for example, string, Boolean, number, and so on. Records are structs and sequences are arrays consisting of atoms, records, or sequences." Developers use the Cosmos DB by provisioning a database account. The notion of a container is used to store the stored procedures, triggers, and user-defined functions. The entities under that database account include the containers as well as the databases and permissions. These entities are called resources. Data in containers is horizontally partitioned. More details of the Cosmos DB can be found in [COSM].

7.4.3 IBM's Cloud-Based Big Data Solutions

IBM is a leader in cloud computing including managing big data in the cloud. It has developed an architecture using a collection of hardware and software that can host a number of big data systems. IBM offers database as a service and provides support for data management as well as data analytics. For example, Cloudant is a NoSQL data layer. The dashDB system is a cloud-based data analytics system that carries out analytics. ElephantSQL is an open-source database running in the cloud. In addition, the IBM cloud also provides support for a number of data management capabilities including for stream computing and content management. More details on IBM's cloud big data solutions can be found in [IBM].

7.4.4 Google's Cloud-Based Big Data Solutions

The Google cloud platform is a comprehensive collection of hardware and software that enables the users to obtain various services from Google. The cloud supports both the Hadoop/MapReduce as well as the Spark platforms. In addition to the users accessing the data in BigTable and BigQuery, Google also provide solutions for carrying out analytics as well as accessing systems such as YouTube. More details on Google's cloud platform can be found in [GOOG].

7.5 SUMMARY AND DIRECTIONS

In this chapter, we have discussed three types of big data systems. First, we discussed what we call infrastructures (which we also call frameworks). These are essentially massive data processing platforms such as the Apache Hadoop, Spark, Storm, and Flink. Then we discussed various big data management systems. These included SQL- and NoSQL-based systems. This was followed by a discussion of big data analytics systems. Finally, we discussed cloud platforms that provide capability for management of massive amounts of data.

As we have mentioned, we have experimented with several of these systems. They include Apache Hadoop, Storm, MapReduce, Hive, MongoDB, Weka, and Amazon AWS. Some of the experimental systems we have developed will be discussed in Part IV of this book. We have also developed lectures on all of the products discussed in this chapter for our course on Big Data Analytics.

We believe that BDMA technologies have exploded over the past decade. Many of the systems we have discussed in this chapter did not exist 15 years ago. We expect the technologies to continue to explode. Therefore, it is important for us to not only keep up with the literature, but also experiment with the big data technologies. As progress is made, we will have a better idea as to what system to use when, where, why, and how.

REFERENCES

[HADO]. http://hadoop.apache.org/
[SPAR]. http://spark.apache.org/
[PIG]. https://pig.apache.org/

[HIVE]. https://hive.apache.org/
[STOR]. http://storm.apache.org/
[MONG]. https://www.mongodb.com/
[CASS]. http://cassandra.apache.org/
[BIGT]. https://cloud.google.com/bigtable/
[BIGQ]. https://cloud.google.com/bigquery/
[WEKA]. http://www.cs.waikato.ac.nz/ml/weka/bigdata.html
[ORAC]. https://www.oracle.com/big-data/index.html
[IBM]. https://www-01.ibm.com/software/data/bigdata/
[GOOG]. https://cloud.google.com/solutions/big-data/
[COSM]. https://azure.microsoft.com/en-us/blog/a-technical-overview-of-azure-cosmos-db/
[DYNA]. https://aws.amazon.com/dynamodb/
[KAFK]. http://kafka.apache.org/
[FLIN]. https://flink.apache.org/
[MAHO]. http://mahout.apache.org/
[NOSQ]. http://nosql-database.org/
[COUC]. http://couchdb.apache.org/
[MAPR]. https://hadoop.apache.org/docs/r1.2.1/mapred_tutorial.html
[HBAS]. https://hbase.apache.org/

Conclusion to Part I

Part I, consisting of six chapters, described supporting technologies for BDMA and BDSP. In Chapter 2, we provided an overview of discretionary security policies in database systems. We started with a discussion of access control policies including authorization policies and role-based access control policies. Then we discussed administration policies. We briefly discussed identification and authentication. We also discussed auditing issues as well as views for security. Next, we discussed policy enforcement as well as Structured Query Language (SQL) extensions for specifying policies as well as provided an overview of query modification. Finally, we provided a brief overview of data privacy aspects. In Chapter 4, we provided an overview of data mining for cyber security applications. In particular, we discussed the threats to computers and networks and described the applications of data mining to detect such threats and attacks. Some of the data mining tools for security applications developed at The University of Texas at Dallas were also discussed. Chapter 5 introduced the notions of the cloud and semantic web technologies. This is because some of the experimental systems discussed in Part IV utilize these technologies. We first discussed concepts in cloud computing including aspects of virtualization, deployment models, and cloud functions. We also discussed technologies for the semantic web including eXtensible Markup Language (XML), resource description framework (RDF), Ontologies, and OWL. In Chapter 6, we discussed the problem of insider threat and our approach to insider threat detection. We represented the insiders and their communication as RDF graphs and then queried and mined the graphs to extract the nuggets. We also provided a comprehensive framework for insider threat detection. In Chapter 7, we discussed three types of big data systems. First, we discussed what we call infrastructures (which we also call frameworks). These are essentially massive data processing platforms such as Apache Hadoop, Spark, Storm, and Flink. Then we discussed various big data management systems. These included SQL-based systems and NoSQL-based systems. This was followed by a discussion of big data analytics systems. Finally, we discussed cloud platforms that provide the capability for management of massive amounts of data.

The chapters in Part I lay the foundations of the discussions in Parts II through V. Stream data mining, which is essentially data mining for streaming data, will be discussed in Part II. Applying stream data mining for insider threat detection will be discussed in Part III. Some of the experimental big data systems we have developed will be discussed in Part IV. Finally, the next steps in big data management and analytics and big data security and privacy will be discussed in Part V.

Part II

Stream Data Analytics

Introduction to Part II

Now that we have provided an overview of the various supporting technologies including data mining and cloud computing in Part I, the chapters in Part II will describe various stream data mining techniques that we have designed and developed. Note that we use the term data mining and data analytics interchangeably.

Part II, consisting of six chapters, provides a detailed overview of the novel class detection techniques for data streams. These techniques are part of stream data mining.

Chapter 8 focuses on the various challenges associated with data stream classification and describes our approach to meet those challenges. Data stream classification mainly consists of two steps. Building (or learning) a classification model using historical labeled data and classifying (or predicting the class of) future instances using the model. The focus in Chapter 8 will mainly be on the challenges involved in data stream classification. Chapter 9 discusses related work in data stream classification, semisupervised clustering, and novelty detection. First, we discuss various data stream classification techniques that solve the infinite length and concept-drift problems. Also, we describe how our proposed multiple partition and multiple chunk (MPC) ensemble technique is different from the existing techniques. Second, we discuss various novelty/anomaly detection techniques and their differences from our ECSMiner approach. Finally, we describe different semisupervised clustering techniques and the advantages of our ReaSC approach over them. Chapter 10 describes the MPC ensemble classification technique. First, we present an overview of the approach. Then we establish theoretical justification for using this approach over other approaches. Finally, we show the experimental results on real and synthetic data. Chapter 11 explains ECSMiner, our novel class detection technique, in detail. First, we provide a basic idea about the concept-evolution problem and give an outline of our solution. Then, we discuss the algorithm in detail and show how to efficiently detect a novel class within given time constraints and limited memory. Next, we analyze the algorithm's efficiency in correctly detecting the novel classes. Finally, we present experimental results on different benchmark datasets. Chapter 12 describes the limited labeled data problem, and our solution, ReaSC. First, we give an overview of the data stream classification problem, and a top level description of ReaSC. Then, we describe the semisupervised clustering technique to efficiently learn a classification model from scarcely labeled training data. Next, we discuss various issues related to stream evolution. Last, we provide experimental results on a number of datasets. Finally, Chapter 13 discusses our findings and provides directions for further work in stream data analytics, in general, and stream data classification, in particular. In addition, we will discuss stream data analytics for handling massive amounts of data.

8 Challenges for Stream Data Classification

8.1 INTRODUCTION

Data streams are continuous flows of data being generated from various computing machines such as clients and servers in networks, sensors, call centers, and so on. Analyzing these data streams has become critical for many applications including for network data, financial data, and sensor data. However, mining these ever growing data is a big challenge to the data mining community ([CAI04], [CHEN02], [FAN04a], [GABE05], [GANT01]). Data stream classification ([CHI05], [DING02], [DOMI00], [GANT02], [GEHR99], [HULT01], [JIN03], [KUNC08], [LAST02], [MASU09a], [SCHO05], [WANG03], [WANG06], [WANG07] is one major aspect of data stream mining. Data stream classification mainly consists of two steps. Building (or learning) a classification model using historical labeled data and classifying (or predicting the class of) future instances using the model. Building a classification model from a data stream is more challenging than building a model from static data because of several unique properties of data streams. In this chapter, we will discuss the challenges involved in analyzing such streams.

The organization of this chapter is as follows. Section 8.2 provides an overview of the challenges. The notions of infinite length and concept drift in streaming data are discussed in Section 8.3. The notion of concept evolution is discussed in Section 8.4. Aspects of limited labeled data are discussed in Section 8.5. The experiments we have carried out are discussed in Section 8.6. Our contributions to the field are discussed in Section 8.7. This chapter is summarized in Section 8.8.

8.2 CHALLENGES

First, data streams are assumed to have *infinite length*. It is impractical to store and use all the historical data for learning, since it would require an infinite amount of storage and learning time. Therefore, traditional classification algorithms that require several passes over the training data are not directly applicable to data streams.

Second, data streams observe *concept drift*, which occurs when the underlying concept of the data changes over time. For example, consider the problem of credit card fraud detection. Here our goal is to detect whether a particular transaction is *authentic* or *fraud*. Since the behavior of authentic users as well as the techniques of forgery change over time, what is considered authentic now may appear to be fraud in the next year, and vice versa. In other words, the characteristics/patterns of these two classes of data (i.e., fraud/authentic) change over time. Therefore, the underlying concept (i.e., class characteristics) of the data is dynamic. Traditional classification techniques that assume static concept of the data are not applicable to data streams. In order to address concept drift, a classification model must continuously adapt itself to the most recent concept.

Third, data streams also observe *concept evolution* which occurs when a novel class appears in the stream. For example, consider an intrusion detection problem, where network traffic is analyzed to determine whether it is benign, or it contains some kind of intrusion. It is possible that a completely new kind of intrusion occurs in the network. In that case, traditional classification techniques, which assume that the total number of classes in the data is fixed, would misclassify the new intrusion either as benign, or as a known intrusion. In order to cope with concept evolution, a classification model must be able to automatically detect novel classes when they appear, before being trained with the labeled instances of the novel class.

TABLE 8.1
Data Stream Classification Problems and Proposed Solutions

Proposed Technique	Infinite Length	Concept Drift	Concept Evolution	Limited Labeled Data
MPC ensemble (Chapter 10)	√	√	√	√
ECSMiner (Chapter 11)	√	√		
ReaSC (Chapter 12)	√	√		

Finally, high-speed data streams suffer from *insufficient labeled data*. This is because manual labeling is both costly and time-consuming. Therefore, the speed at which data points are labeled lags far behind the speed at which data points arrive in the stream. As a result, most of the data points in the stream would be left as unlabeled. Most classification algorithms apply a supervised learning technique, which require *completely labeled* training data. By completely labeled we mean that all instances in the training data are labeled. Therefore, supervised classification techniques suffer from the scarcity of labeled data for learning, resulting in a poorly built classifier. In order to deal with this scarcity of labeled data, we need a learning algorithm that is capable of producing a good classification model even if it is supplied with *partially labeled* data for training. By partially labeled, we mean that only $P\%$ ($P < 100$) instances in the training data are labeled.

Most data stream classification techniques concentrate only on the first two issues, namely, infinite length, and concept drift. Our goal is to address all the four issues, providing a more realistic solution than the state of the art.

We propose three different techniques that address two or more of these problems. This is shown in a tabular form in Table 8.1. For example, ECSMiner, the novel class detection technique proposed in Chapter 11, solves the infinite length, concept-drift and concept-evolution problems.

8.3 INFINITE LENGTH AND CONCEPT DRIFT

Traditional data stream classification techniques solve the infinite length problem by providing a *one-pass learning* paradigm using one of the two approaches: *single model* ([DOMI00], [GEHR99], [HULT01]) or *ensemble* ([GAO07], [KOLT03], [KOLT05], [SCHO05], [STRE01], [WANG03]) classification. Single model approaches incrementally update their classification model with the progression of the data stream. As opposed to the *batch learning* algorithms, which require multiple passes over the training data, incremental learning algorithms require a single pass. However, some of the single model classification techniques (e.g., [DOMI00]) consider a stationary data distribution. Therefore, they are not applicable to concept-drifting data streams. Ensemble approaches maintain an ensemble of classification models, which is also updated incrementally. Many ensemble approaches such as [MASU09a], [SCHO05], and [WANG03] follow a hybrid batch-incremental technique. In this technique, the data stream is divided into equally sized *chunks*, and one classifier is trained with one data chunk using a batch-learning algorithm. Whenever a new classifier is trained, the existing ensemble of classifiers is updated by replacing an older classifier in the ensemble with the newest classifier based on a particular replacement strategy (e.g., accuracy of each classifier on the latest training chunk). Therefore, the ensemble itself is updated incrementally, keeping it up to date with the stream evolution. Ensemble approaches require relatively simpler operations to update the model than their single model counterparts. Besides, ensemble techniques can efficiently handle concept drift. In Chapter 10, we describe our proposed novel ensemble technique [MASU09a] called the multipartition and multichunk (MPC) ensemble approach. MPC ensemble addresses both the infinite length and concept-drift problems, and offers a lower classification error than other existing ensemble approaches.

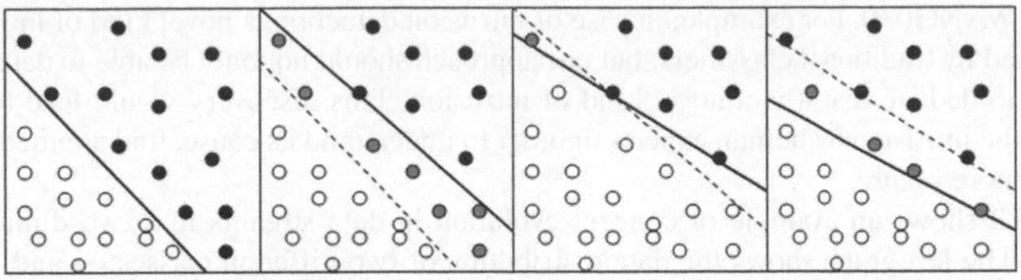

FIGURE 8.1 Illustrating concept drift in a two-class data.

As discussed earlier, we assume that data stream is divided into equally sized chunks. The chunk size is chosen so that all the data in a chunk may fit into the main memory. Each chunk, when labeled, is used to train classifiers. In our approach, there are three parameters that control the MPC ensemble: v, r, and L. The parameter v determines the number of partitions ($v = 1$ means single-partition ensemble), the parameter r determines the number of chunks ($r = 1$ means single-chunk ensemble), and the parameter L controls the ensemble size. The MPC ensemble consists of Lv classifiers. This ensemble is updated whenever a new data chunk is labeled. We take the most recent *labeled* r consecutive data chunks and train v classifiers using v-fold partitioning of these chunks. We then update the ensemble by choosing the best (based on accuracy) Lv classifiers among the newly trained v classifiers and the existing Lv classifiers. Thus, the total number of classifiers in the ensemble is always kept constant.

Figure 8.1 illustrates concept drift in a two-dimensional data stream. Each box represents a chunk in the data stream. The white circles represent the negative class, and the black circles represent the positive class. The dark straight line (analogous to a hyperplane) inside each box separates the data classes, and defines the current concept. The dotted straight line represents the concept corresponding to the previous chunk. As a result of concept drift, some data points have different class labels in the current concept than in the previous concept. Blue circles represent the data points that are negative (positive) according to the current concept but positive (negative) according to the previous concept.

It should be noted that when a new data point appears in the stream, it may not be labeled immediately. We defer the ensemble updating process until the data points in the latest data chunk have been labeled, but we keep classifying new unlabeled data using the current ensemble. For example, consider the online credit card fraud detection problem. When a new credit card transaction takes place, its class ({fraud,authentic}) is predicted using the current ensemble. Suppose a fraudulent transaction has been misclassified as authentic. When the customer receives the bank statement, he will identify this error and report to the authority. In this way, the actual labels of the data points will be obtained, and the ensemble will be updated accordingly.

8.4 CONCEPT EVOLUTION

Concept evolution occurs in data streams when *novel classes* emerge. It is important to detect concept evolution in data streams, because if a novel class appears in the stream, traditional stream classification techniques would misclassify the instances of the novel class, reducing the accuracy and reliability of the classifier. To the best of our knowledge, no data stream classification technique to date addresses the concept-evolution problem. Our approach *ECSMiner*, presented in Chapter 11, is an extension to the approach described in [MASU09a].

ECSMiner solves the concept-evolution problem by automatically detecting novel classes in a data stream. Novel class detection should be an integral part of any realistic data stream classification technique because of the evolving nature of streams. It can be useful in various domains, such as network intrusion detection ([KHAN07], [MASU08ab]), fault detection [CRUP04], malware detection ([MASU06], [MASU07a], [MASU07b], [MASU07d], [MASU08a]), and credit card fraud detection ([WANG03]). For example, in case of intrusion detection, a novel kind of intrusion might go undetected by traditional classifiers, but our approach should not only be able to detect the intrusion, but also deduce that it is a novel kind of intrusion. This discovery would lead to an intense analysis of the intrusion by human experts in order to understand its cause, find a remedy, and make the system more secure.

Figure 8.2 shows an example of concept evolution in data streams in a two-dimensional feature space. The left graph shows the data distribution of two different classes (+ and −) in a data chunk. A rule-based learner learns two rules (shown in the figure) from this data chunk. The right graph shows the data distribution in the next chunk, where a novel class (denoted by x) has evolved. Instances of this class would be misclassified by the rules learned in the previous chunk since class x was not present when the rules were learned. In fact, no traditional classification model can detect the novel class. ECSMiner provides a solution to the concept-evolution problem by enriching each classifier in the ensemble with a novel class detector. If the arrival of a novel class is discovered, potential novel class instances are separated and classified as novel class. Thus, a novel class can be automatically identified without manual intervention.

The novel class detection technique proposed in ECSMiner is different from traditional *one-class* novelty detection techniques ([MARK03], [ROBE00], [YAMA01]) that can only distinguish between the normal and anomalous data. That is, the traditional novelty detection techniques assume that there is only one *normal* class and any instance that does not belong to the normal class is an anomaly/novel class instance. Therefore, they are unable to distinguish among different types of anomaly. But ECSMiner offers a *multiclass* framework for the novelty detection problem that can distinguish between different classes of data and discover the emergence of a completely novel class. Furthermore, traditional novelty detection techniques simply identify data points as outliers/anomalies that deviate from the normal class. On the other hand, ECSMiner not only detects whether a single data point deviates from the existing classes, but also discovers whether a group of such outliers possesses the potential of forming a novel class by showing strong cohesion among themselves. Therefore, ECSMiner is a synergy of a multiclass classification model and a novel class detection model.

Traditional data stream classification techniques also make impractical assumptions about the availability of labeled data. Most techniques ([CHEN08], [HULT01], [YANG05]) assume that the true label of a data point can be accessed as soon as it has been classified by the classification model. Thus, according to their assumption, the existing model can be updated immediately using

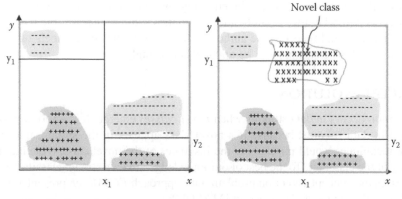

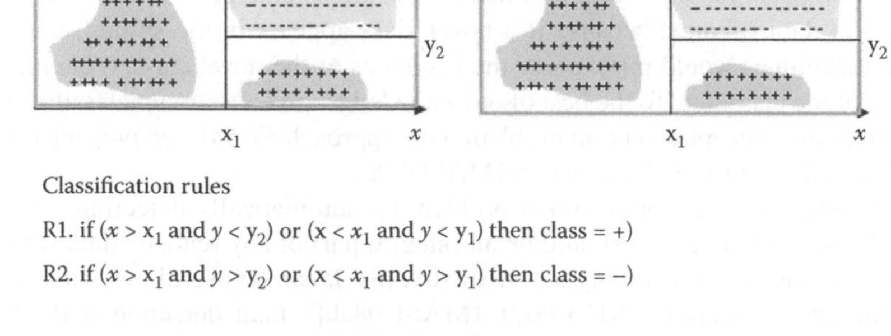

Classification rules

R1. if ($x > x_1$ and $y < y_2$) or ($x < x_1$ and $y < y_1$) then class = +)

R2. if ($x > x_1$ and $y > y_2$) or ($x < x_1$ and $y > y_1$) then class = −)

FIGURE 8.2 Illustrating concept evolution in a two-dimensional feature space.

the labeled instance. In reality, we would not be so lucky in obtaining the label of a data instance immediately, since manual labeling of data is time consuming and costly. For example, in a credit card fraud detection problem, the actual labels (i.e., authentic/fraud) of the credit card transactions by a customer usually become available in the next billing cycle after the customer reviews all his transactions in the last statement and reports fraud transactions to the credit card company. Thus, a more realistic assumption would be to have a data point labeled after *Tl* time units of its arrival. For simplicity, we assume that the *i*th instance in the stream arrives at *i*th time unit. Thus, *Tl* can be considered as a time constraint imposed on the data labeling process. Note that traditional stream classification techniques assume *Tl* = 0. Finally, we impose another time constraint, *Tc*, on classification decision. That is, an instance must be classified by the classification model within *Tc* time units of its arrival. If it assumed that there is no concept-evolution, it is customary to have *Tc* = 0, that is, an instance should be classified as soon as it arrives. However, when novel concepts evolve, classification decisions may have to be postponed until enough instances are seen by the model to gain confidence in deciding whether a novel class has emerged or not. *Tc* is the maximum allowable time up to which the classification decision can be postponed for any instance. Note that *Tc* < *Tl* must be maintained in any practical classification model. Otherwise, we would not need the classifier at all, we could just wait for the labels to arrive. We will discuss this issue in detail in Chapter 10.

Figure 8.3 illustrates the significance of *Tl* and *Tc* with an example. Here *xk* is the last instance that has arrived in the stream. Let *xj* be the instance that arrived *Tc* time units earlier, and *xi* be the instance that arrived *Tl* time units earlier. Then *xi* and all instances that arrived before *xi* (shown with dark-shaded area) are labeled, since all of them are at least *Tl* time units old. Similarly, *xj* and all instances that arrived before *xj* (both the light-shaded and dark-shaded areas) are classified by the classifier since they are at least T_c time units old. However, the instances inside the light-shaded area are unlabeled. Instances that arrived after x_j (age less than T_c) are unlabeled, and may or may not be classified (shown with the unshaded area).

Integrating classification with novel class detection is a nontrivial task, especially in the presence of concept drift, and under time constraints. We assume an important property of each class: the data points belonging to the same class should be closer to each other (cohesion) and should be far apart from the data points belonging to other classes (separation). If a test instance is *well separated from* the training data, it is identified as a *Raw outlier*. Raw outliers that possibly appear as a result of concept drift or noise are filtered out. An outlier that passes the filter (called *F outlier*) has potential to be a novel class instance. However, we must wait to see whether more such *F outliers* appear in the stream that observes strong cohesion among themselves. If a sufficient number of such strongly cohesive *F outliers* are observed, a novel class is assumed to have appeared, and the *F outliers* are classified as novel class instances. However, we can defer the classification decision of a test instance at most *Tc* time units after its arrival, which makes the problem more challenging. Furthermore, we must keep detecting novel class instances in this 'un-supervised' fashion for at least *Tl* time units from the arrival of the first novel class instance, since labeled training data of the novel class(es) would not be available before that.

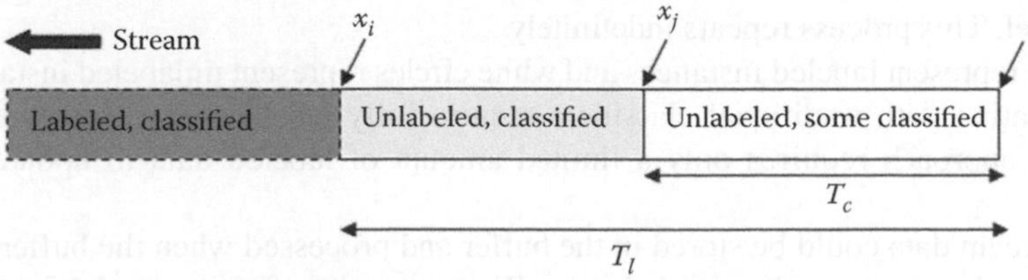

FIGURE 8.3 Illustration of time constraints T_l and T_c.

8.5 LIMITED LABELED DATA

Almost all of the existing data stream classification techniques ([AGGA06], [CHEN08], [FAN04b], [GAO07], [HULT01], [KOLT05], [SCHO05], [WANG03], [YANG05]) are based on an impractical assumption that the true label of a data point becomes available immediately after it is tested by the classifier. In other words, the data stream is assumed to be completely labeled, meaning, the true labels of all historical data are known. This assumption is impractical because manual labeling of data is usually costly and time-consuming. So, in a streaming environment, where data appear at a high speed, it is not possible to manually label all the data as soon as they arrive. If it were possible, we would not need a classifier to begin with. Thus, in practice, only a small fraction of the stream can be labeled by human experts. So, the traditional stream classification algorithms would have very few instances to update their model, leading to a poorly built classifier. But a realistic data stream classification model should demonstrate satisfactory performance even if it is trained with insufficient labeled training data. In Chapter 11, we propose *ReaSC* which is capable of building efficient classification models with a partially labeled data stream, compared to other stream classification techniques that require completely labeled stream.

As an example, suppose an organization receives flight reports as text documents from all over the world, at the rate of a thousand reports per day, and categorizes the reports into different classes: *normal*, *minor mechanical problem*, *minor weather problem*, *major mechanical problem*, and so on. Based on the categories, warning messages are sent to the corresponding airlines and aviation authorities for proper action. Important decision-making actions such as flight planning, resource allocation, and personnel assignment are affected by these warnings. Therefore, timely delivery of these warnings is necessary to avoid both financial loss, and customer dissatisfaction. Without loss of generality, suppose only 200 of the reports can be labeled manually by human experts each day. So, an automated stream document classification system is employed so that all the 1000 documents can be classified each day. If a traditional stream classification technique is used, it will have to deal with a trade-off when updating the classifier. Either the classifier will have to be updated with only 200 labeled data per day, or it will have to wait 5 days to be updated with all the 1000 labeled data that arrived today. None of the trade-offs are acceptable since the former will lead to a poor classifier, and the latter will lead to an outdated classifier. In order to completely avoid these problems, the organization must increase its manpower (and cost) five times and classify all the 1000 instances manually.

Considering these difficulties, we propose our technique (ReaSC) that updates the existing classification model utilizing the available 200 labeled and 800 unlabeled instances, while achieving the same or better classification accuracy than a classification model that is updated using 1000 labeled instances. Thus, ReaSC offers a practical data stream classifier that not only views the data stream classification problem from a real perspective, but also provides a cost-effective solution. Figure 8.4 shows the basic idea of a data stream classification using traditional approach and limited labeled data. Traditional approach (Figure 8.4a) requires a completely labeled data chunk to update the existing model. Whereas ReaSC requires a partially labeled (*P%* labeled) data chunk to update the existing classification model. After updating the existing model, the latest data chunk, which is entirely unlabeled, is classified using the model. Eventually, when the *i*+ 2nd data chunk arrives, *P%* instances of the *i*+ 1st data chunk are assumed to have been labeled and that chunk is used to update the model. This process repeats indefinitely.

Black circles represent labeled instances and white circles represent unlabeled instances. (a) Data stream classification with traditional classifiers require fully labeled data to update the existing model. (b) Our approach requires only a limited amount of labeled data to update the existing model.

Naturally, stream data could be stored in the buffer and processed when the buffer is full, so we divide the stream data into equally sized chunks. We train a classification model from each chunk. We propose a semisupervised clustering algorithm to create *K* clusters from the partially labeled

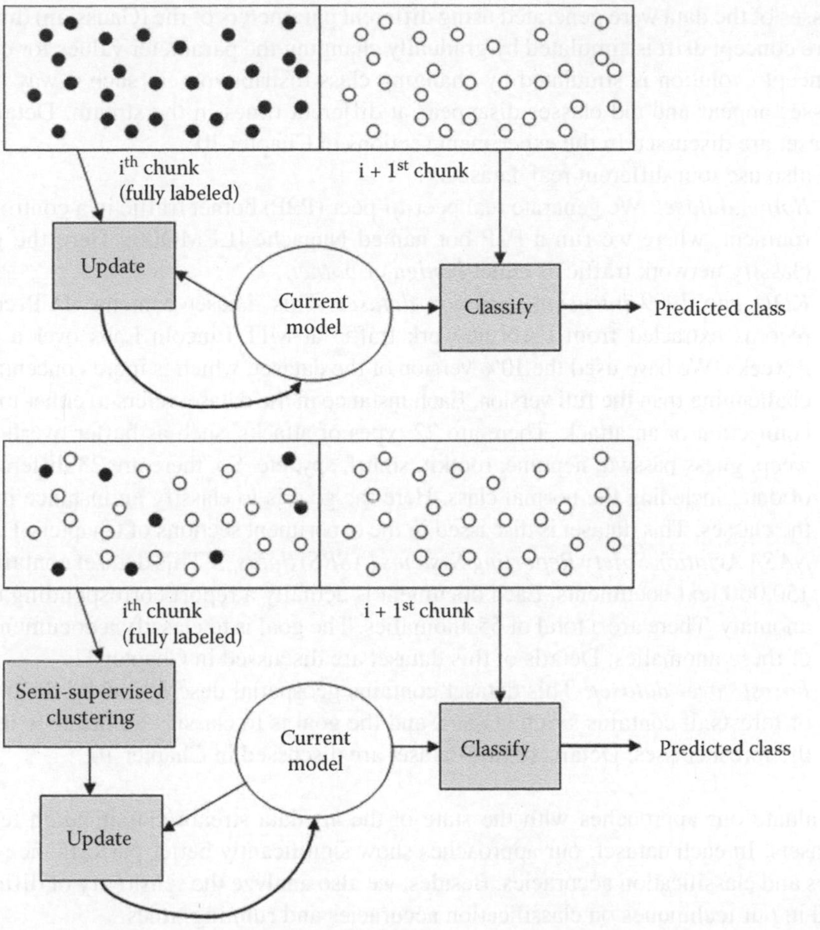

FIGURE 8.4 Illustrating the limited labeled data problem in data streams.

training data ([MASU08b], [WOOL09]). A summary of the statistics of the instances belonging to each cluster is saved as a *microcluster*. The microclusters created from each chunk serve as a classification model for the nearest neighbor algorithm. In order to cope with concept drift, we keep an ensemble of L models. Whenever a new model is built from a new data chunk, we update the ensemble by choosing the best L models from the $L + 1$ models (previous L models and the new model), based on their individual accuracies on the labeled training data of the new data chunk. Besides, we refine the existing models in the ensemble whenever a novel class of data evolves in the stream.

8.6 EXPERIMENTS

We evaluate our approaches on several synthetic and real datasets. We use two kinds of synthetic datasets:

- *Synthetic data with only concept drift:* This synthetic data was generated with a moving hyperplane. It contains 10 real-valued attributes and two classes. The hyperplane is moved gradually to simulate concept drift in the data. Details of this dataset are discussed in the experiment sections in Chapters 10 through 12.
- *Synthetic data with concept drift and concept evolution:* This synthetic data was generated with Gaussian distribution. It contains 20 real-valued attributes and 10 classes. Different

classes of the data were generated using different parameters of the (Gaussian) distribution. Here concept drift is simulated by gradually changing the parameter values for each class. Concept evolution is simulated by changing class distributions in such a way that novel classes appear and old classes disappear at different times in the stream. Details of this dataset are discussed in the experiment sections in Chapter 10.

- We also use four different real datasets:
    - *Botnet dataset:* We generate real peer-to-peer (P2P) botnet traffic in a controlled environment, where we run a P2P bot named Nugache [LEMO06]. Here the goal is to classify network traffic as either *benign* or *botnet*.
    - *KDD cup 1999 intrusion detection dataset:* This dataset contains TCP connection records extracted from LAN network traffic at MIT Lincoln Labs over a period of 2 weeks. We have used the 10% version of the dataset, which is more concentrated, and challenging than the full version. Each instance in the dataset refers to either to a normal connection or an attack. There are 22 types of attacks, such as buffer overflow, portsweep, guess-passwd, neptune, rootkit, smurf, spy, etc. So, there are 23 different classes of data, including the normal class. Here the goal is to classify an instance into one of the classes. This dataset is discussed in the experiment sections of Chapters 11 and 12.
    - *NASA Aviation Safety Reporting Systems (ASRS) dataset:* This dataset contains around 150,000 text documents. Each document is actually a report corresponding to a flight anomaly. There are a total of 55 anomalies. The goal is to classify a document into one of these anomalies. Details of this dataset are discussed in Chapter 11.
    - *Forest cover dataset:* This dataset contains geospatial descriptions of different types of forests. It contains seven classes, and the goal is to classify an instance into one of the forest classes. Details of this dataset are discussed in Chapter 10.

We evaluate our approaches with the state-of-the-art data stream classification techniques on these datasets. In each dataset, our approaches show significantly better performance both in running times and classification accuracies. Besides, we also analyze the sensitivity of different parameters used in our techniques on classification accuracies and running times.

8.7 OUR CONTRIBUTIONS

In this book, we propose solutions to different data stream classification problems, namely, concept drift, concept evolution, and limited labeled data.

An *MPC ensemble for classifying concept-drifting data streams*

- We propose a generalized MPC ensemble technique that significantly reduces the expected classification error over the existing single-partition, single-chunk ensemble methods. The MPC ensemble technique addresses both infinite length and concept drift.
- We have theoretically justified the effectiveness of the MPC ensemble approach.
- We apply the MPC ensemble on synthetically generated data as well as on real botnet traffic, and achieve better detection accuracies than other stream data classification techniques.

Classification and novel class detection in concept-drifting data streams (ECSMiner)

- To the best of our knowledge, no other data stream classification technique addresses the concept-evolution problem. This is a major problem with data streams that must be dealt with. In this light, ECSMiner offers a more realistic solution to data stream classification. ECSMiner also addresses infinite length and concept-drift problems.
- ECSMiner offers a more practical framework for stream classification by introducing time constraints for delayed data labeling and making classification decision.

- ECSMiner enriches a traditional classification model with a novel class detection mechanism.
- We apply ECSMiner on both synthetic and real-world data and obtain much better results than the state-of-the-art stream classification algorithms.

Data stream classification with scarcely labeled training data (ReaSC)

- We provide a solution to the more practical situation of data stream classification when labeled data are scarce. We show ReaSC, using only 20% labeled training data, achieves better classification accuracy in real-life datasets than other stream classification approaches that use 100% labeled training data. ReaSC addresses infinite length, concept drift and limited labeled data problems.
- ReaSC applies semisupervised clustering to build classification models. To the best of our knowledge, no other stream data classification algorithms apply semisupervised clustering.
- We propose an efficient semisupervised clustering algorithm based on a cluster-impurity measure.

We believe that the proposed methods provide promising, powerful, and practical techniques to the stream classification problem in general.

8.8 SUMMARY AND DIRECTIONS

This chapter has stressed the need for mining data streams and discussed the challenges. The challenges include infinite length, concept drift, concept evolution and limited labeled data. We also provided an overview of our approach to mining data streams. Specifically, our approach determines whether an item belongs to a pre-existing class or whether it is a novel class.

Our work has applications in numerous fields. In the real world, it could very well be the case that an item does not belong to a specific class. For example, it does not have to be either black or white. We could create a new color called "BLITE" which could have properties of both black and white. Our approaches will be elaborated in Chapters 9 through 13.

REFERENCES

[AGGA06]. C.C. Aggarwal, J. Han, J. Wang, P.S. Yu. "A Framework for On-Demand Classification of Evolving Data Streams," *IEEE Transactions on Knowledge and Data Engineering*, 18 (5), 577–589, 2006.

[CAI04]. Y.D. Cai, D. Clutter, G. Pape, J. Han, M. Welge, L. Auvil, "Maids: Mining Alarming Incidents from Data Streams," In *23rd ACM SIGMOD International Conference on Management of Data*, Paris, France, June 13–18, ACM, 2004.

[CHEN08]. S. Chen, H. Wang, S. Zhou, P.S. Yu, "Stop Chasing Trends: Discovering High Order Models in Evolving Data," In *ICDE '08: Proceedings of the 24th International Conference on Data Engineering*, Cancun, Mexico, April 7–12, pp. 923–932, IEEE Computer Society, 2008.

[CHEN02]. Y. Chen, G. Dong, J. Han, B.W. Wah, J. Wang, "Multi-Dimensional Regression Analysis of Time-Series Data Streams," In *VLDB '02: Proceedings of the 28th International Conference on Very Large Data Bases*, Hong Kong, China, August 20–23, pp. 323–334, VLDB Endowment, 2002.

[CHI05]. Y. Chi, P.S. Yu, H. Wang, R.R. Muntz, "Loadstar: A Load Shedding Scheme for Classifying Data Streams," In *SDM '05: Proceedings of the 2005 SIAM International Conference on Data Mining*, Newport Beach, CA, USA, April 21–23, p. 3, SIAM, 2005.

[CRUP04]. V. Crupi, E. Guglielmino, G. Milazzo, "Neural-Network-Based System for Novel Fault Detection in Rotating Machinery," *Journal of Vibration and Control*, 10(8):1137–1150, 2004.

[DING02]. Q. Ding, Q. Ding, W. Perrizo, "Decision Tree Classification of Spatial Data Streams Using Peano Count Trees," In *SAC '02: Proceedings of the 2002 ACM symposium on Applied Computing*, Madrid, Spain, March 10–14, pp. 413–417, ACM, 2002.

[DOMI00]. P. Domingos and G. Hulten, "Mining High-Speed Data Streams," In *KDD '00: Proceedings of the 2000 ACM SIGKDD International Conference on Knowledge Discovery and Data Mining*, August 20–23, Boston, MA, USA, pp. 71–80, ACM, 2000.

[FAN04a]. W. Fan, Y. an Huang, H. Wang, P. S. Yu, "Active Mining of Data Streams" In *SDM '04: Proceedings of the 2004 SIAM International Conference on Data Mining*, April 22–24, Lake Buena Vista, Florida, USA, pp. 457–461, SIAM, 2004.

[FAN04b]. W. Fan, "Systematic Data Selection to Mine Concept-Drifting Data Streams," In *KDD '04: Proceedings of the Tenth ACM SIGKDD International Conference on Knowledge Discovery and Data Mining*, August 22–25, Seattle, WA, USA, pp. 128–137, ACM, 2004.

[GABE05]. M.M. Gaber, A. Zaslavsky, S. Krishnaswamy, "Mining Data Streams: A Review," *ACM SIGMOD Record*, 34 (2), 18–26, June 2005.

[GANT01]. V. Ganti, J. Gehrke, R. Ramakrishnan, "Demon: Mining and Monitoring Evolving Data," *IEEE Transactions on Knowledge and Data Engineering*, 13 (1), 50–63, 2001.

[GANT02]. V. Ganti, J. Gehrke, R. Ramakrishnan, "Mining Data Streams Under Block Evolution," *ACM SIGKDD Explorations Newsletter*, 3 (2), 1–10, 2002.

[GAO07]. J. Gao, W. Fan, J. Han. "On Appropriate Assumptions to Mine Data Streams," In *ICDM '07: Proceedings of the 2007 International Conference on Data Mining*, October 28–31, Omaha, NE, USA, pp. 143–152, IEEE Computer Society, 2007.

[GEHR99]. J. Gehrke, V. Ganti, R. Ramakrishnan, W.-Y. Loh, "Boat-Optimistic Decision Tree Construction," In *SIGMOD '99: Proceedings of the 1999 ACM SIGMOD International Conference on Management of Data*, Jun. 1–3, Philadelphia, PA, USA, pp. 169–180, ACM, 1999.

[HULT01]. G. Hulten, L. Spencer, P. Domingos, "Mining Time-Changing Data Streams," In *KDD '01: Proceedings of the Seventh ACM SIGKDD International Conference on Knowledge Discovery and Data Mining*, August 26–29, San Francisco, CA, USA, pp. 97–106, ACM, 2001.

[JIN03]. R. Jin and G. Agrawal, "Efficient Decision Tree Construction on Streaming Data," In *KDD '03: Proceedings of the Ninth ACM SIGKDD International Conference on Knowledge Discovery and Data Mining*, August 24–27, Washington, DC, pp. 571–576, ACM, 2003.

[KHAN07]. L. Khan, M. Awad, B.M. Thuraisingham, "A New Intrusion Detection System Using Support Vector Machines and Hierarchical Clustering," *VLDB Journal*, 16 (4), 507–521, 2007.

[KOLT03]. J.Z. Kolter and M.A. Maloof, "Dynamic Weighted Majority: A New Ensemble Method for Tracking Concept Drift," In *ICDM '03: Proceedings of the Third IEEE International Conference on Data Mining*, Nov. 19–22, Melbourne, FL, USA, IEEE Computer Society, pp. 123–130, 2003.

[KOLT05]. J.Z. Kolter and M.A. Maloof, "Using Additive Expert Ensembles to Cope with Concept Drift," In *ICML '02: Proceedings of the Twenty-Second International Conference on Machine Learning*, August 7–11, Morgan Kaufmann, Bonn, Germany, pp. 449–456, 2005.

[KUNC08]. L.I. Kuncheva and J. Salvador Śanchez, "Nearest Neighbour Classifiers for Streaming Data with Delayed Labelling," In *ICDM '08: Proceedings of the 2008 Eighth IEEE International Conference on Data Mining*, December 15–19, Pisa, Italy, pp. 869–874, IEEE Computer Society, 2008.

[LAST02]. M. Last, "Online Classification of Nonstationary Data Streams," *Intelligent Data Analysis*, 6(2), 129–147, 2002.

[LEMO06]. R. Lemos, Bot software looks to improve peerage, http://www.securityfocus.com/news/11390, 2006.

[MARK03a]. M. Markou and S. Singh, "Novelty Detection: A Review—Part 2: Neural Network Based Approaches," *Signal Processing*, 83(12), 2499–2521, 2003.

[MASU07a]. M.M. Masud, L. Khan, B.M. Thuraisingham, "E-mail Worm Detection Using Data Mining," *International Journal of Information Security and Privacy*, 1 (4), 47–61, 2007.

[MASU07b]. M.M. Masud, L. Khan, B.M. Thuraisingham, "Feature Based Techniques for Auto-Detection of Novel Email Worms," In *PAKDD '07: Proceedings of the 11th Pacific-Asia Conference on Knowledge Discovery and Data Mining*, May 22–25, Springer-Verlag, Nanjing, China, pp. 205–216, 2007.

[MASU06]. M.M. Masud, L. Khan, E. Al-Shaer, "Email Worm Detection Using Näıve Bayes and Support Vector Machine," In *ISI '06: Proceedings of the 2006 IEEE Intelligence and Security Informatics Conference*, May 23–24, San Diego, CA, USA, pp. 733–734, IEEE Computer Society, 2006.

[MASU07c]. M.M. Masud, L. Khan, B.M. Thuraisingham, "A Hybrid Model to Detect Malicious Executables," In *ICC '07: Proceedings of the 2007 IEEE International Conference on Communications*, June 24–28, Glasgow, Scotland, pp. 1443–1448, IEEE Computer Society, 2007.

[MASU08a]. M.M. Masud, J. Gao, L. Khan, J. Han, B.M. Thuraisingham, "A Practical Approach to Classify Evolving Data Streams: Training with Limited Amount of Labeled Data," In *ICDM '08: Proceedings of the 2008International Conference on Data Mining*, December 15–19, Pisa, Italy, pp. 929–934, IEEE Computer Society, 2008.

[MASU08b]. M.M. Masud, L. Khan, B.M. Thuraisingham, "A Scal- Able Multi-Level Feature Extraction Technique to Detect Malicious Executables," *Information Systems Frontiers*, 10 (1), 33–45, 2008.

[MASU09a]. M.M. Masud, J. Gao, L. Khan, J. Han, B. M. Thuraisingham, "A Multi-Partition Multi-Chunk Ensemble Technique to Classify Concept-Drifting Data Streams," In *PAKDD09: Proceedings of The 13th Pacific- Asia Conference on Knowledge Discovery and Data Mining*, April 27–30, Springer-Verlag, Bangkok, Thailand, pp. 363–375, 2009. (also Advances in Knowledge Discovery and Data Mining).

[MASU09b]. M.M. Masud, J. Gao, L. Khan, J. Han, B.M. Thuraisingham, "Integrating Novel Class Detection with Classification for Concept- Drifting Data Streams," In *ECML PKDD '09: Proceedings of the 2009 European Conference on Machine Learning and Principles and Practice in Knowledge Discovery in Databases*, volume II, Springer-Verlag, Bled, Slovenia, September 7–11, pp. 79–94, 2009.

[ROBE00]. S.J. Roberts, "Extreme Value Statistics for Novelty Detection in Biomedical Signal Processing," In *Proceedings of the First International Conference on Advances in Medical Signal and Information Processing*, Bristol, UK, pp. 166–172, 2000.

[SCHO05]. M. Scholz and R. Klinkenberg, "An Ensemble Classifier for Drifting Concepts," In *IWKDDS '05: Proceedings of the Second International Workshop on Knowledge Discovery in Data Streams*, Porto, Portugal, Oct. 3–7, pp. 53–64, 2005.

[WANG03]. H. Wang, W. Fan, P. S. Yu, J. Han, "Mining Concept-Drifting Data Streams Using Ensemble Classifiers," In *KDD '03: Proceedings of the Ninth ACM SIGKDD International Conference on Knowledge Discovery and Data Mining*, Washington, DC, USA, August 24–27 pp. 226–235, ACM, 2003.

[WANG06]. H. Wang, J. Yin, J. Pei, P.S. Yu, J.X. Yu, "Suppressing Model Overfitting in Mining Concept-Drifting Data Streams," In *KDD '06: Proceedings of the 12th ACM SIGKDD International Conference on Knowledge Discovery and Data Mining*, New York, NY, USA, August 20–23, pp. 736–741, ACM, 2006.

[WANG07]. P. Wang, H. Wang, X. Wu, W. Wang, B. Shi, "A Low- Granularity Classifier for Data Streams with Concept Drifts and Biased Class Distri bution," *IEEE Transactions on Knowledge and Data Engineering*, 19 (9), 1202–1213, 2007.

[WOOL09]. C. Woolam, M.M. Masud, L. Khan, "Lacking Labels in the Stream: Classifying Evolving Stream Data with Few Labels," In *ISMIS '09: Proceedings of the 18th International Symposium on Methodologies for Intelligent Systems*, Springer, Prague, Czech Republic, September 14–17, pp. 552–562, 2009.

[YAMA01]. K. Yamanishi and J. ichi Takeuchi, "Discovering Outlier Filtering Rules from Unlabeled Data: Combining a Supervised Learner with An Uunsupervised Learner," In *KDD '01: Proceedings of the Seventh ACM SIGKDD International Conference on Knowledge Discovery and Data Mining*, San Francisco, CA, USA, 26–29 August pp. 389–394, ACM, 2001.

[YANG05]. Y. Yang, X. Wu, X. Zhu, "Combining Proactive and Reactive Predictions for Data Streams," In *KDD '05: Proceedings of the Eleventh ACM SIGKDD International Conference on Knowledge Discovery in Data Mining*, Chicago, IL, USA, August 21–24, pp. 710–715, ACM, 2005.

9 Survey of Stream Data Classification

9.1 INTRODUCTION

Data streams are continuously arriving data in applications such as finance, networks, and sensors. These data streams have to be analyzed so that nuggets can be extracted to determine network intrusions, financial stock market price, and suspicious event detection. As discussed in Chapter 8, there are many challenges that need to be addressed for analyzing data streams. These include infinite length, concept drift, concept evolution, and limited labeled data. In Chapters 10 through 12, we will discuss our approach to data stream analytics. Our approach has been built upon several of the previous works. Therefore, in this chapter we review the previous works in data stream classification and novelty detection. Also, we discuss related works in semisupervised clustering which is an important component of our data stream classification technique with limited labeled data.

The organization of this chapter is as follows. General approach to data stream classification is discussed in Section 9.2. Single model classification is discussed in Section 9.3. Ensemble classification is discussed in Section 9.4. Novel class detection is discussed in Section 9.5. Data stream classification with limited labeled data is discussed in Section 9.6. Summary and directions are provided in Section 9.7.

9.2 APPROACH TO DATA STREAM CLASSIFICATION

Data stream classification is a challenging task because of several important properties of a data stream: infinite length, concept drift, concept evolution, and limited labeled data. The main goal of data stream classification is to predict the class of future instances from the knowledge gained from the past instances. Figure 9.1 shows a possible implementation and application of data stream classification. A classification model is first built using the available initial data. The goal of this classification model is to distinguish *attack* traffic from normal, *benign* traffic. This model is installed in a firewall that monitors all incoming and outgoing traffic to a local network. If any incoming traffic is classified as attack traffic, it is blocked and quarantined for further study. All other traffic is considered as benign and passed to the server. The quarantined data and data passed to the server are periodically checked by experts to detect any possible misclassification, and also to label the data. These labeled data are used to update the classification model using data mining techniques. In this way, the model is kept up-to-date with the stream. In a nonstreaming environment, ensemble classifiers like Boosting [FREU96] are popular alternatives to single model classifiers. But these are not directly applicable to stream mining. However, several ensemble techniques for data stream mining have been proposed ([FAN04], [GAO07], [KOLT05], [SCHO05], [WANG03]). These ensemble approaches have the advantage that they can be more efficiently built than updating a single model and they observe higher accuracy than their single-model counterparts [TUME96].

Among these approaches, our MPC ensemble approach (Chapter 10) is related to that of Wang et al. [WANG03]. Wang et al. [WANG03] keep an ensemble of the L best classifiers. Each time a new data chunk appears, a classifier is trained from that chunk. If this classifier shows better accuracy than any of the L classifiers in the ensemble, then the new classifier replaces the old one. When classifying an instance, weighted voting among the classifiers in the ensemble is taken, where the weight of a classifier is inversely proportional to its error. Figure 9.2 illustrates the basic principle of

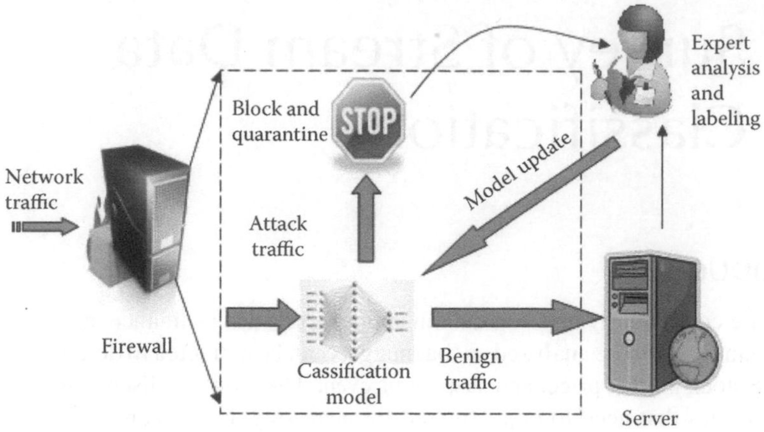

FIGURE 9.1 Network intrusion detection using data stream classification.

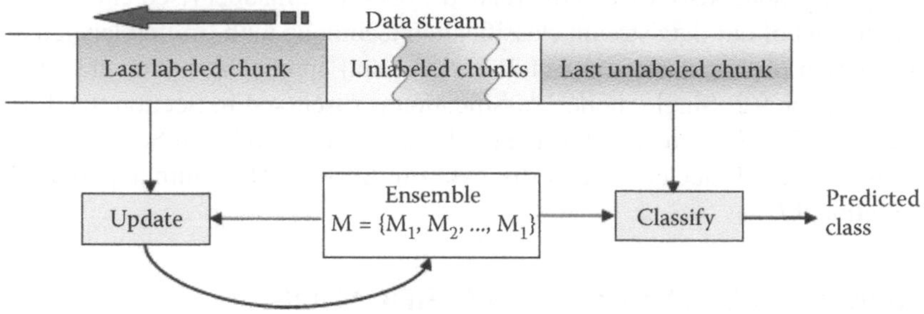

FIGURE 9.2 Illustrating the basic principle of data stream classification using the ensemble approach.

the ensemble approaches. Here the last labeled chunk is used to update the existing ensemble. Then the ensemble is used to classify the last data chunk, which is unlabeled.

There have been many works in stream data classification. Their main difference lies in the way the existing classification model is updated. There are two main approaches—single-model classification and ensemble classification.

9.3 SINGLE-MODEL CLASSIFICATION

These techniques incrementally update their model with new data to cope with the evolution of stream ([DOMI00], [GEHR99], [HULT01], [UTGO89]). These *incremental learning* techniques, such as the very fast decision tree learner (VFDT) [DOMI00] and bootstrapped optimistic decision tree (BOAT) [GEHR99] try to ensure that the incrementally built model be the same as the model built using *batch learning* techniques, given the same amount of training data. In doing so, these techniques usually require complex operations to modify the internal structure of the model. Although these techniques solve the infinite length problem using incremental learning, they assume static concept, that is, assume that there is no concept drift. Although the concept-adapting very fast decision tree learner (CVFDT) [HULT01] addresses concept drift, in this algorithm, only the most recent data is used to update the current model. Thus, contributions of historical data are forgotten at a constant rate even if some of the historical data are consistent with the current concept.

In a nonstreaming environment, ensemble classifiers like Boosting [FREU96] are popular alternatives to single model classifiers. But these are not directly applicable to stream mining. However, several ensemble techniques for data stream mining have been proposed ([FAN04], [GAO07],

[KOLT05], [SCHO05], [WANG03]). These ensemble approaches have the advantage that they can be more efficiently built than updating a single model and they observe higher accuracy than their single model counterparts [TUME96].

Among these approaches, our MPC ensemble approach (Chapter 10) is related to that of Wang et al. [WANG03]. Wang et al. [WANG03] keep an ensemble of the *L* best classifiers. Each time a new data chunk appears, a classifier is trained from that chunk. If this classifier shows better accuracy than any of the *L* classifiers in the ensemble, then the new classifier replaces the old one. When classifying an instance, weighted voting among the classifiers in the ensemble is taken, where the weight of a classifier is inversely proportional to its error. Figure 9.2 illustrates the basic principle of the ensemble approaches. Here the last labeled chunk is used to update the existing ensemble. Then the ensemble is used to classify the last data chunk, which is unlabeled.

9.4 ENSEMBLE CLASSIFICATION AND BASELINE APPROACH

Figure 9.3 illustrates the ensemble updating process of Wang et al. [WANG03]. The ensemble *M* consists of *L* models = {*M*1, … , *ML*}. In this example, *L* = 3. In Figure 9.3a, we see that the initial ensemble of models {*M*1, *M*2, *M*3} is built from the first three chunks {*D*1, *D*2, *D*3} of the stream. The ensemble is used to predict the class labels of the instances in *D*4, which is the latest data chunk. In Figure 9.3b, a new data chunk *D*5 appears in the stream. In the meantime, chunk *D*4 has been labeled. It is used to train a new model *M*4. Now, we choose the best three models from *M*1, … , *M*4 based on their classification accuracies on *D*4. In this example, *M*2 is found to be the worst model.

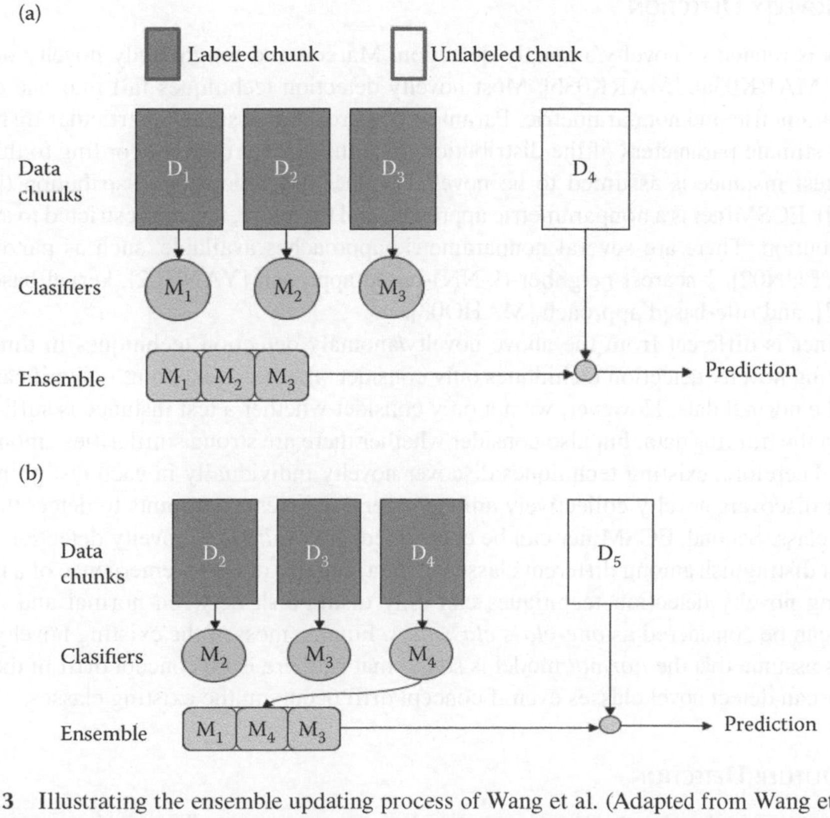

FIGURE 9.3 Illustrating the ensemble updating process of Wang et al. (Adapted from Wang et al. Mining Concept-Drifting Data Streams Using Ensemble Classifiers. In *KDD '03: Proceedings of the 9th ACM SIGKDD International Conference on Knowledge Discovery and Data Mining*, pp. 226–235, Washington, DC, August 24–27, ACM, 2003.)

Therefore, it is replaced by the new model *M*4, and the ensemble is updated. This new ensemble is used to classify the instances in the latest data chunk *D*5. This process continues indefinitely.

There are several differences between the MPC ensemble approach and the approach of Wang et al. First, we apply multipartitioning of the training data to build multiple (i.e., *v*) classifiers from that training data. Second, we train each classifier from *r* consecutive data chunks, rather than from a single chunk. Third, when we update the ensemble, the *v* classifiers that are removed may come from different chunks; thus, although some classifiers from a chunk may have been removed, other classifiers from that chunk may still remain in the ensemble. Whereas, in the approach of Wang et al. removal of a classifier means total removal of the knowledge obtained from one whole chunk. Finally, we use simple voting, rather than weighted voting. Thus, our MPC ensemble approach is a generalized form of the approach of Wang et al. and users have more freedom to optimize performance by choosing the appropriate values of these two parameters (i.e., *r* and *v*).

9.5 NOVEL CLASS DETECTION

Our proposed novel class detection technique ECSMiner is related to both data stream classification and novelty detection. ECSMiner also applies the ensemble classification technique. However, ECSMiner is different from all other stream classification techniques in two different aspects. First, none of the existing techniques can detect novel classes, but ECSMiner can. Second, ECSMiner is based on a more practical assumption about the time delay in data labeling, which is not considered in most of the existing algorithms.

9.5.1 Novelty Detection

ECSMiner is related to novelty/anomaly detection. Markou and Singh study novelty detection in details in [MARK03a], [MARK03b]. Most novelty detection techniques fall into one of two categories: parametric and nonparametric. Parametric approaches assume a particular distribution of data, and estimate parameters of the distribution from the normal data. According to this assumption, any test instance is assumed to be novel if it does not follow the distribution ([NAIR97], [ROBE00]). ECSMiner is a nonparametric approach, and therefore, it is not restricted to any specific data distribution. There are several nonparametric approaches available, such as parzen window method [YEUN02], *k*-nearest neighbor (k-NN)-based approach [YANG02], kernel-based method [AHME07], and rule-based approach [MAHO03].

ECSMiner is different from the above novelty/anomaly detection techniques in three aspects. First, existing novelty detection techniques only consider whether a test point is significantly different from the normal data. However, we not only consider whether a test instance is sufficiently different from the training data, but also consider whether there are strong similarities among such test instances. Therefore, existing techniques discover novelty individually in each test point, whereas ECSMiner discovers novelty collectively among several coherent test points to detect the presence of a novel class. Second, ECSMiner can be considered as a *multiclass* novelty detection technique, since it can distinguish among different classes of data and also discover emergence of a novel class. But existing novelty detection techniques can only distinguish between normal and novel, and, therefore, can be considered as *one-class classifiers*. Finally, most of the existing novelty detection techniques assume that the *normal* model is static, that is, there is no concept drift in the data. But ECSMiner can detect novel classes even if concept drift occurs in the existing classes.

9.5.2 Outlier Detection

Novelty detection is also closely related to outlier detection techniques. There are many outlier detection techniques available, such as [AGAR05], [BAY03], [BREU00], [LAZA05], and [YAMA01]. Some of them are also applicable to data streams ([SUBR06], [TAND07]). However, the main difference with these outlier detection techniques from the outlier detection technique in ECSMiner is that the primary objective of ECSMiner is novel class detection, not outlier detection. Outliers are the byproduct of intermediate computation steps in ECSMiner algorithm. Thus, the precision of our outlier detection technique is not too critical to the overall performance of ECSMiner.

9.5.3 Baseline Approach

Spinosa et al. [SPIN08] propose a cluster-based novel concept detection technique that is applicable to data streams. However, this is also a one-class novelty detection technique, where authors assume that there is only one normal class and all other classes are novel. Thus, it is not directly applicable to a multiclass environment where more than one class is considered as normal or *non-novel*. But ECSMiner can handle any number of existing classes, and also detect a novel class that does not belong to any of the existing classes. Therefore, ECSMiner offers a more practical solution to the novel class detection problem, which has been proved empirically.

ECSMiner extends our previous work [MASU09c], in which we proposed a novel class detection technique. However, in the previous work, we did not consider the time constraints *Tl* and *Tc*. Therefore, ECSMiner addresses a more practical problem than the previous one. These time constraints impose several restrictions on the classification algorithm, making classification more challenging [MASU09a]. We encounter these challenges and provide efficient solutions.

9.6 DATA STREAM CLASSIFICATION WITH LIMITED LABELED DATA

Our proposed work for data stream classification with limited labeled data, ReaSC, applies semisupervised clustering. Here we discuss related semisupervised clustering techniques.

9.6.1 Semisupervised Clustering

Semisupervised clustering techniques utilize a small amount of knowledge available in the form of *pairwise* constraints (*must-link, cannot-link*), or class labels of the data points. According to [BASU06], semisupervised clustering techniques can be subdivided into two categories: *constraint-based* and *distance-based*. Constraint-based approaches, such as [BASU02], [DEMI99], and [WAGS01] try to cluster the data points without violating the given constraints. Distance-based techniques use a specific distance metric or similarity measure (e.g., Euclidean distance), but the distance metric is parameterized so that it can be adjusted to satisfy the given constraints. Examples of the distance-based techniques are [COHN03], [HALK05], [KLEI02], and [XING03]. Some recent approaches for semisupervised clustering integrated the search-based and constraint-based techniques into a unified framework, by applying pairwise constraints on top of the unsupervised *K*-means clustering technique and formulating a constrained *K*-means clustering problem ([BASU04], [BASU06], [BILE04]). These approaches usually apply the expectation-maximization (E-M) [DEMP77] technique to solve the constrained clustering problem.

ReaSC follows the constraint-based technique, but it is different from other constraint-based approaches. Most constraint-based approaches use pairwise constraints (e.g., [BILE04]), whereas we utilize a *cluster-impurity* measure based on the limited labeled data contained in each cluster [MASU08]. If pairwise constraints are used, the running time per E-M step becomes quadratic in the total number of labeled points, whereas the running time becomes linear if the impurity measures are used. So, the impurity measures are more realistic in classifying a high-speed stream data. Although Basu et al. [BASU02] did not use any pairwise constraints, they did not use any cluster-impurity measure either. However, cluster-impurity measure was used by Demiriz et al. [DEMI99]. But they applied expensive *genetic algorithms*, and had to adjust weights given to different components of the clustering objective function to obtain good clusters. On the contrary, we apply E-M, and we do not need to tune parameters to get a better objective function. Furthermore, we use a *compound impurity-measure* rather than the simple impurity measures used in [DEMI99]. Besides, to the best of our knowledge, no other work applies a semisupervised clustering technique to classify stream data.

9.6.2 Baseline Approach

In ReaSC, we follow an ensemble classification approach, but it is different from other ensemble approaches in two aspects. First, previous ensemble-based techniques use the underlying learning algorithm (such as decision tree, Naive Bayes, etc.) as a black-box and concentrate only on optimizing the ensemble. But we concentrate mainly on building efficient classification models in an evolving scenario. In this light, ReaSC is more closely related with the work of Aggarwal et al. [AGGA06]. Secondly, previous techniques including [AGGA06] require *completely labeled* training data. But in practice, a very limited amount of labeled data may be available in the stream, leading to poorly trained classification models. We show that high classification accuracy can be achieved even with limited amount of labeled data.

Aggarwal et al. [AGGA06] apply a supervised *microclustering* technique along with horizon-fitting to classify evolving data streams. They have achieved higher accuracy than other approaches that use fixed horizon or the entire dataset for training. We also apply a microclustering technique. But there are two major differences between ReaSC and this approach. First, we do not use horizon-fitting for classification. Rather, we use a fixed-sized ensemble of classifiers. So, we do not need to store historical snapshots which allows us to save memory. Second, we apply semisupervised clustering, rather than supervised. Thus, we need only a fraction of training data to be labeled, compared to a completely labeled data that is required for the approach of Aggarwal et al. [AGGA06]. Thus, ReaSC not only saves more memory, but also it is more applicable to a realistic scenario where labeled data are scarce.

ReaSC extends our previous work [MASU08]. In the previous work, it was assumed that there were two parallel, disjoint streams: a training stream and a test stream. The training stream contained the labeled instances and was used to train the models. The test stream contained the unlabeled instances and was used for testing. However, this assumption was not so realistic since in a real-world scenario, labeled data may not be immediately available in the stream, and therefore, it may not be possible to construct a separate training stream. So, ReaSC makes a more realistic assumption that there is a single continuous stream. Each data chunk in the stream is first tested by the existing ensemble, and then the same chunk is used for training, assuming that the instances in the chunk have been labeled. Thus, all the instances in the stream are eventually tested by the ensemble. Besides, in this book we have described our technique more elaborately and provided detailed understanding and proof of the proposed framework. Finally, we have enriched the experimental results by adding three more datasets, run more rigorous experiments, and reported in-depth analysis of the results [MASU09b].

9.7 SUMMARY AND DIRECTIONS

In this chapter, we have discussed several prior approaches as well as our approach on stream analytics that have influenced the work discussed in this book. For example, in the single model classification approach incremental learning techniques are used. The ensemble-based techniques are more efficiently built than the single model approach. Our novel class detection approach integrates both data stream classification and novelty detection. Our data stream classification technique with limited labeled data uses a semisupervised technique.

As stated earlier, data stream classification is a critical area in big data analytics. Large amounts of data streams are being generated. These streams may have evolving concepts. Therefore, we need techniques to address the challenges and produce meaningful results. Our techniques will be elaborated in Chapters 10 through 12.

REFERENCES

[AGAR05]. D Agarwal, "An Empirical Bayes Approach to Detect Anomalies in Dynamic Multidimensional Arrays," In *ICDM '05: Proceedings of the 5th IEEE International Conference on Data Mining*, Nov. 27–30, Houston, TX, pp. 26–33, IEEE Computer Society, 2005.

[AGGA06]. C.C. Aggarwal, J. Han, J Wang, P.S. Yu, "A Framework for On-Demand Classification of Evolving Data Streams," *IEEE Transactions on Knowledge and Data Engineering*, 18(5):577–589, 2006.

[AHME07]. T. Ahmed, M. Coates, A. Lakhina, "Multivariate Online Anomaly Detection Using Kernel Recursive Least squares," In *INFOCOM '07: Proceedings of the 26th Annual IEEE Conference on Computer Communications*, May 6–12, Anchorage, Alaska, pp. 625–633, IEEE Computer Society, 2007.

[BASU02]. S Basu, A Banerjee, R.J. Mooney, "Semi-Supervised Clustering by Seeding." In *ICML '02: Proceedings of the 19th International Conference on Machine Learning*," July 8–12, Sydney, Australia, pp. 27–34, Morgan Kaufmann, 2002.

[BASU04]. S Basu, A Banerjee, R.J. Mooney, "Active Semi-Supervision for Pairwise Constrained Clustering," In *SDM '04: Proceedings of the 2004 SIAM International Conference on Data Mining*, April 22–24, Lake Buena Vista, FL, pp. 333–344, SIAM, 2004.

[BASU06]. S Basu, M Bilenko, A Banerjee, R.J. Mooney. Probabilistic Semi-Supervised Clustering with Constraints. *Semi-Supervised Learning*, O. Chapelle, B. Schoelkopf, A. Zien, editors, MIT Press, Cambridge, MA, pp. 73–102, 2006.

[BAY03]. S.D. Bay and M. Schwabacher, "Mining Distance-Based Outliers in Near Linear Time with Randomization and a Simple Pruning Rule," In *KDD '03: Proceedings of the 9th ACM SIGKDD International Conference on Knowledge Discovery and Data Mining*, August 24–27, Washington, DC, pp. 29–38, ACM, 2003.

[BILE04]. M. Bilenko, S Basu, and R.J. Mooney, "Integrating Constraints and Metric Learning in Semi-Supervised Clustering," In *ICML '04: Proceedings of the 21st International Conference on Machine Learning*, July 4–8, Banff, Canada, Morgan pp. 81–88, Kaufmann, 2004.

[BREU00]. M.M. Breunig, H-P. Kriegel, R.T. Ng, J. Sander, "LOF: Identifying Density-Based Local Outliers," *ACM SIGMOD Record*, 29(2):93–104, June 2000.

[COHN03]. D. Cohn, R. Caruana, A. McCallum. *Semi-Supervised Clustering with User Feedback*. Technical Report TR2003-1892, Cornell University, 2003.

[DEMI99]. A. Demiriz, K.P. Bennett, M.J. Embrechts, "Semi-Supervised Clustering Using Genetic Algorithms," In *ANNIE '99: Proceedings of the 1999 International Conference on Artificial Neural Networks in Engineering*, Nov. 7–10, St. Louis, MO, pp. 809–814, ASME Press, 1999.

[DEMP77]. A.P. Dempster, N.M. Laird, D.B. Rubin, "Maximum Likelihood from Incomplete Data via the EM Algorithm," *Journal of the Royal Statistical Society B*, 39:1–38, 1977.

[DOMI00]. P. Domingos and G. Hulten, "Mining High-Speed Data Streams," In *KDD '00: Proceedings of the 2000 ACM SIGKDD International Conference on Knowledge Discovery and Data Mining*, August 20–23, Boston, MA, pp. 71–80, ACM, 2000.

[FAN04]. W. Fan, "Systematic Data Selection to Mine Concept-Drifting Data Streams," In *KDD '04: Proceedings of the 10th ACM SIGKDD International Conference on Knowledge Discovery and Data Mining*, August 22–25, Seattle, WA, pp. 128–137, ACM, 2004.

[FREU96]. Y. Freund and R.E. Schapire, "Experiments with a New Boosting Algorithm," In *ICML '96: Proceedings of the 13th International Conference on Machine Learning*, Jul. 3–6, Bari, Italy, pp. 148–156, Morgan Kaufmann, 1996.

[GAO07]. J. Gao, W. Fan, J. Han, "On appropriate Assumptions to Mine Data Streams," In *ICDM '07: Proceedings of the 2007 International Conference on Data Mining*, October 28–31, Omaha, NE, pp. 143–152, IEEE Computer Society, 2007.

[GEHR99]. J. Gehrke, V. Ganti, R. Ramakrishnan, W-Y. Loh, "Boat-Optimistic Decision Tree Construction," In *SIGMOD '99: Proceedings of the 1999 ACM SIGMOD International Conference on Management of Data*, Jun. 1–3, Philadelphia, PA, pp. 169–180, ACM, 1999.

[HALK05]. M. Halkidi, D. Gunopulos, N. Kumar, M. Vazirgiannis, C. Domeniconi, "A Framework for Semi-Supervised Learning Based on Subjective and Objective Clustering Criteria," In *ICDM '05: Proceedings of the 5th IEEE International Conference on Data Mining*, November 27–30, Houston, TX, pages 637–640, IEEE Computer Society, 2005.

[HULT01]. G. Hulten, L. Spencer, P. Domingos, "Mining Time-Changing Data Streams," In *KDD '01: Proceedings of the 7th ACM SIGKDD International Conference on Knowledge Discovery and Data Mining*, August 26–29, San Francisco, CA, pp. 97–106, CA, ACM, 2001.

[KLEI02]. D. Klein, S.D. Kamvar, C.D. Manning, "From Instance- Level Constraints to Space-Level Constraints: Making the Most of Prior Knowledge in Data Clustering," In *ICML '02: Proceedings of the 19th International Conference on Machine Learning*, July 8–12, Sydney, Australia, pp. 307–314, Morgan Kaufmann, 2002.

[KOLT05]. J.Z. Kolter and M.A. Maloof, "Using Additive Expert Ensembles to Cope with Concept Drift," In *ICML '02: Proceedings of the 22nd International Conference on Machine Learning*, August 7–11, Bonn, Germany, pp. 449–456, Morgan Kaufmann, 2005.

[LAZA05]. A. Lazarevic and V. Kumar, "Feature Bagging for Outlier Detection," In *KDD '05: Proceedings of the 11th ACM SIGKDD International Conference on Knowledge Discovery in Data Mining*, August 21-24, Chicago, IL, pp. 157-166, ACM, 2005.

[MAHO03]. M.V. Mahoney and P.K. Chan, "Learning Rules for Anomaly Detection of Hostile Network Traffic," In *ICDM '03: Proceedings of the 3rd International Conference on Data Mining*, November 19–22, Melbourne, Florida, pp. 601–604, IEEE Computer Society, 2003.

[MARK03a]. M. Markou and S. Singh, "Novelty Detection: A Review—Part 2: Neural Network-Based Approaches," *Signal Processing*, 83(12):2499–2521, 2003.

[MARK03b]. M. Markou and S. Singh, "Novelty detection: A Review—Part 1: Statistical Approaches," *Signal Processing*, 83(12):2481–2497, 2003.

[MASU08]. M.M. Masud, J. Gao, L. Khan, J. Han, B.M. Thuraisingham, "A Practical Approach to Classify Evolving Data Streams: Training with Limited Amount of Labeled Data," In *ICDM '08: Proceedings of the 2008 International Conference on Data Mining*, Dec. 15–19, Pisa, Italy, pp. 929–934, IEEE Computer Society, 2008.

[MASU09a]. M.M. Masud, J. Gao, L. Khan, J. Han, B.M. Thuraisingham, "Classification and Novel Class Detection in Concept-Drifting Data Streams under Time Constraints," *IEEE Transactions on Knowledge and Data Engineering*, 23(6):859–874, 2011.

[MASU09b]. M.M. Masud, C. Woolam, J. Gao, L. Khan, J. Han, K. Hamlen, B.M. Thuraisingham, "Facing the Reality of Data Stream Classification: Coping with Scarcity of Labeled Data," *Journal of Knowledge and Information Systems*, 1(33):213–244. 2012.

[MASU09c]. M.M. Masud, J. Gao, L. Khan, J. Han, B.M. Thuraisingham, "Integrating Novel Class Detection with Classification for Concept-Drifting Data Streams," In *ECML PKDD '09: Proceedings of the 2009 European Conference on Machine Learning and Principles and Practice in Knowledge Discovery in Databases, Volume II*, Sep 7–11, Bled, Slovenia, pp. 79–94, Springer-Verlag, 2009.

[NAIR97]. A. Nairac, T.A. Corbett-Clark, R. Ripley, N.W. Townsend, L. Tarassenko, "Choosing an Appropriate Model for Novelty Detection," In *ICANN '97: Proceedings of the 7th International Conference on Artificial Neural Networks*, pp. 117–122, Lausanne, Switzerland, October 8–10, Springer, 1997.

[ROBE00]. S.J. Roberts, "Extreme Value Statistics for Novelty Detection in Biomedical Signal Processing," In *Proceedings of the 1st International Conference on Advances in Medical Signal and Information Processing*, pp. 166–172, 2000.

[SCHO05]. M. Scholz and R. Klinkenberg, "An Ensemble Classifier for Drifting Concepts," In *IWKDDS '05: Proceedings of the 2nd International Workshop on Knowledge Discovery in Data Streams*, October 3–7, Porto, Portugal, pp. 53–64, 2005.

[SPIN08]. E.J. Spinosa, A.P. de Leon F. de Carvalho, J. Gama, "Cluster-Based Novel Concept Detection in Data Streams Applied to Intrusion Detection in Computer Networks," In *SAC '08: Proceedings of the 23rd ACM symposium on Applied Computing*, March 16–20, Ceara, Brazil, pp. 976–980, ACM, 2008.

[SUBR06]. S. Subramaniam, T. Palpanas, D. Papadopoulos, V. Kalogeraki, D. Gunopulos, "Online Outlier Detection in Sensor Data Using Non-Parametric Models," In *VLDB '06: Proceedings of the 32nd International Conference on Very Large Data Bases*, September 12–15, Seoul, Korea, pp. 187–198, VLDB Endowment, 2006.

[TAND07]. G. Tandon and P.K. Chan, "Weighting versus Pruning in Rule Validation for Detecting Network and Host Anomalies," In *KDD '07: Proceedings of the 13th ACM SIGKDD International Conference on Knowledge Discovery and Data Mining*, August 12–15, San Jose, CA, pp. 697–706, ACM, 2007.

[TUME96]. K. Tumer and J. Ghosh, "Error Correlation and Error Reduction in Ensemble Classifiers," *Connection Science,* 8(304):385–403, 1996.

[UTGO89]. P.E. Utgoff, "Incremental Induction of Decision Trees," *Machine Learning*, 4:161–186, 1989.

[WAGS01]. K. Wagsta, C. Cardie, S. Schroedl, "Constrained K-Means Clustering with Background Knowledge," In *ICML '01: Proceedings of the 18th International Conf. on Machine Learning*, June 28–July 1, Williamstown, MA, pp. 577–584, Morgan Kaufmann, 2001.

[WANG03]. H. Wang, W. Fan, P.S. Yu, J. Han, "Mining Concept-Drifting Data Streams Using Ensemble Classifiers," In *KDD '03: Proceedings of the 9th ACM SIGKDD International Conference on Knowledge Discovery and Data Mining*, August 24–27, Washington, DC, pp. 226–235, ACM, 2003.

[XING03]. E.P. Xing, A.Y. Ng, M.I. Jordan, S. Russell, "Distance Metric Learning, with Application to Clustering with Side-Information," *Advances in Neural Information Processing Systems 15*, 15:505–512, 2003.

[YAMA01]. K. Yamanishi and J. Takeuchi, "Discovering Outlier Filtering Rules from Unlabeled Data: Combining a Supervised Learner with an Unsupervised Learner," In *KDD '01: Proceedings of the 7th ACM SIGKDD International Conference on Knowledge Discovery and Data Mining*, August 26–29, San Francisco, CA, pp. 389–394, ACM, 2001.

[YANG02]. Y. Yang, J. Zhang, J. Carbonell, C. Jin, "Topic-Conditioned Novelty Detection," *In KDD '02: Proceedings of the Eighth ACM SIGKDD International Conference on Knowledge Discovery in Data Mining*, July, 23–26, Alberta, Canada, pp. 688–693, ACM, 2002.

[YEUN02]. D-Y. Yeung and C. Chow, "Parzen-Window Network Intrusion Detectors," In *ICPR '02: Proceedings of the 16th International Conference on Pattern Recognition*, August 11–15, Quebec City, Canada, pp. 385–388, 2002.

10 A Multi-Partition, Multi-Chunk Ensemble for Classifying Concept-Drifting Data Streams

10.1 INTRODUCTION

While the challenges and prior work for stream data classification were discussed in Chapters 8 and 9, in this chapter, we describe our innovative technique for classifying concept-drifting data streams using a novel ensemble classifier originally discussed in [MASU09]. It is a multiple partition of multiple chunk (MPC) ensemble classifier-based data mining technique to classify concept-drifting data streams. Existing ensemble techniques in classifying concept-drifting data streams follow a single-partition, single-chunk (SPC) approach, in which a single data chunk is used to train one classifier. In our approach, we train a collection of *v* classifiers from *r* consecutive data chunks using *v*-fold partitioning of the data, and build an ensemble of such classifiers. By introducing this MPC ensemble technique, we significantly reduce classification error compared to the SPC ensemble approaches. We have theoretically justified the usefulness of our algorithm, and empirically proved its effectiveness over other state-of-the-art stream classification techniques on synthetic data and real botnet traffic.

The organization of this chapter is as follows. Ensemble development will be discussed in Section 10.2. Our experiments are discussed in Section 10.3. This chapter is summarized in Section 10.4. We have developed several variations of the technique presented in this chapter and some of them are discussed in Chapters 11 through 13. We have also applied a variation of the techniques discussed in Chapters 10 through 12 for insider threat detection and these techniques are discussed in Section III.

10.2 ENSEMBLE DEVELOPMENT

10.2.1 Multiple Partitions of Multiple Chunks

10.2.1.1 An Ensemble Built on MPC

We keep an ensemble $M = \{M1, M2, \ldots, MLv\}$ of the most recent best Lv classifiers. Each time a new data chunk Dn arrives, we test the data chunk with the ensemble M. We update the ensemble when Dn is labeled. This ensemble training process is illustrated in Figure 10.1 and explained in Section 10.2. The ensemble classification process uses simple majority voting. Section 10.2.1 explains how MPC ensemble reduces classification error over other approaches.

10.2.1.2 MPC Ensemble Updating Algorithm

The ensemble training and updating process is illustrated in Algorithm 10.1.

10.2.1.2.1 Description of the Algorithm (Algorithm 10.1)

Let Dn be the most recent data chunk that has been labeled. In lines 1–3 of the algorithm, we compute the error of each classifier $Mi \in M$ on Dn. Let $D = \{Dn-r+1, \ldots, Dn\}$, that is, the most recently labeled *r* data chunks including Dn. In line 5, we randomly divide D into *v* equal parts $= \{d1, \ldots, dv\}$, such that roughly, all the parts have the same class distributions. In lines 6–9, we train a new batch of *v* classifiers, where each classifier M'_j is trained with the dataset $D - \{dj\}$.

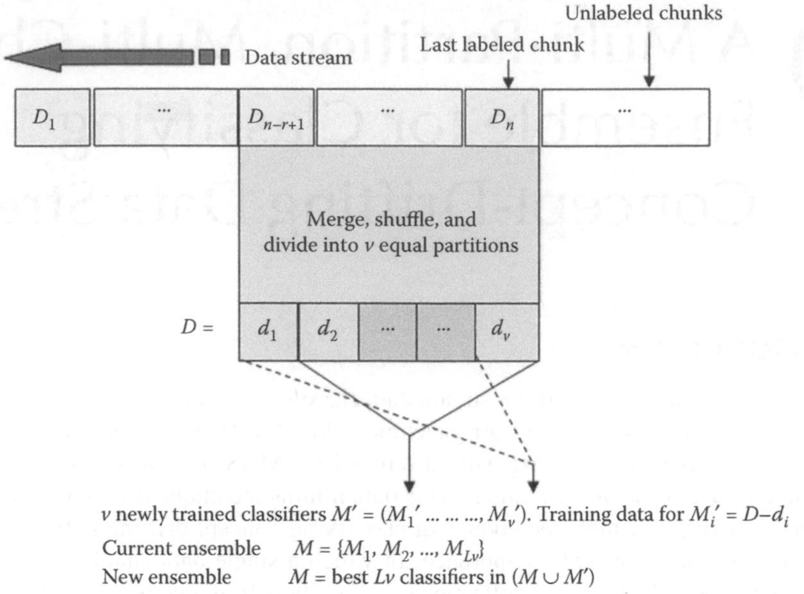

FIGURE 10.1 Illustration: How data chunks are used to build an ensemble with MPC.

We compute the expected error of each classifier M_j' on its corresponding test data *dj*. Finally, on line 10, we select the best *Lv* classifiers from the $Lv + v$ classifiers $M' \cup M$. Note that any subset of the *n*th batch of *v* classifiers may take place in the new ensemble.

10.2.2 Error Reduction Using MPC Training

As explained in Algorithm 10.1, we build an ensemble of *Lv classifiers M*. A test instance *x* is classified using a majority voting of the classifiers in the ensemble. We use simple majority voting, as opposed to weighted majority voting used in [WANG03], since simple majority voting is theoretically proven to be the optimal choice [GAO07]. Besides, in our experiments, we also obtain better results with simple voting. In the next few paragraphs, we show that MPC can significantly reduce the expected error in classifying concept-drifting data streams compared to other approaches that use only one data chunk for training a single classifier (i.e., $r = 1$, $v = 1$), which will be referred to henceforth as "single-partition single-chunk (SPC)" ensemble approach.

Algorithm 10.1 MPC Ensemble

Input: $\{Dn - r + 1, \dots, Dn\}$: most recently labeled *r* data chunks
  M : Current ensemble of best *Lv* classifiers
Output: Updated ensemble *M*
1: **for** each classifier $Mi \in M$ **do**
2:   Test *Mi* on *Dn* and compute its expected error
3: **end for**
4: Let $D = \{Dn - r + 1 \cup Dn\}$
5: Divide *D* into *v* equal disjoint partitions $\{d1, d2, \dots, dv\}$
6: **for** j = 1 to *v* **do**
7:   $M_j' \leftarrow$ Train a classifier with training data $D - dj$

8: Test M'_j on its test data *dj* and compute its expected error
9: **end for**
10: $M \leftarrow$ best *Lv* classifiers from $M' \cup M$ based on expected error

Given an instance *x*, the posterior probability distribution of class *a* is $p(a|x)$. For a two-class classification problem, $a = +$ or $-$. According to Tumer and Ghosh [TUME96], a classifier is trained to learn a function $f^a(.)$ that approximates this posterior probability:

$$f^a(.) = p(a\|x) + \eta a(x) \tag{10.1}$$

where $\eta a(x)$ is the error of $f^a(.)$ relative to $p(a\|x)$. This is the error in addition to Bayes error and usually referred to as the "added error." This error occurs either due to the bias of the learning algorithm, and/or the variance of the learned model. According to [TUME96], the expected added error can be obtained from the following formula:

$$Error = \frac{\sigma^2_{\eta^a(x)}}{s}$$

where $\sigma^2_{\eta^a(x)}$ is the variance of $\eta a(x)$ and *s* is the difference between the derivatives of $p(+|x)$ and $p(-|x)$, which is independent of the learned classifier.

Let $C = \{C_1, \ldots, C_L\}$ be an ensemble of *L* classifiers, where each classifier C_i is trained from a single data chunk (i.e., *C* is an SPC ensemble). If we average the outputs of the classifiers in an *L*-classifier ensemble, then according to [TUME96], the ensemble output would be

$$f_C^a = \frac{1}{L}\sum_{i=i}^{L} f_{C_i}^a(x) = p(a|x) + \eta_C^a(x) \tag{10.2}$$

where f_C^a is the output of the ensemble *C*, $f_{C_i}^a(x)$ is the output of the *i* classifier C_i, and $\eta_C^a(x)$ is the average error of all classifiers, given by

$$\eta_C^a(x) = \frac{1}{L}\sum_{i=1}^{L} \eta_{C_i}^a(x) \tag{10.3}$$

where $\eta_{C_i}^a(x)$ is the added error of the *i*th classifier in the ensemble. Assuming the error variances are independent, the variance of $\eta_C^a(x)$ is given by

$$\sigma^2_{\eta_C^a(x)} = \frac{1}{L^2}\sum_{i=1}^{L} \sigma^2_{\eta_{C_i}^a(x)} = \frac{1}{L}\bar{\sigma}^2_{\eta_C^a(x)} \tag{10.4}$$

where $\sigma^2_{\eta_{C_i}^a(x)}$ is the variance of $\eta_{C_i}^a(x)$, and $\bar{\sigma}^2_{\eta_C^a(x)}$ is the common variance. In order to simplify the notation, we would denote $\sigma^2_{\eta_{C_i}^a(x)}$ with $\sigma^2_{C_i}$.

Let *M* be the ensemble of *Lv* classifiers $M_1, M_2, \ldots, M_{Lv}$, M_i is a classifier trained using *r* consecutive data chunks (i.e., the MPC approach). The following lemma proves that MPC reduces error over SPC by a factor of *rv* when the outputs of the classifiers in the ensemble are independent.

Lemma 10.1

Let σ_C^2 *be the error variance of SPC. If there is no concept drift, and the errors of the classifiers in the ensemble M are independent, then the error variance of MPC is* 1/*rv times of that of SPC,* that is,

$$\sigma_M^2 = \frac{1}{rv}\sigma_C^2$$

Proof: Each classifier $M_i \in M$ is trained on r consecutive data chunks. If there is no concept drift, then a classifier trained on r consecutive data chunks may reduce the error of the single classifiers trained on a single data chunk by a factor of r [WANG03]. So, it follows that

$$\sigma_{M_i}^2 = \frac{1}{r^2}\sum_{j=i}^{r+i-1}\sigma_{C_j}^2 \tag{10.5}$$

where $\sigma_{M_i}^2$ is the error variance of classifier M_i, trained using data chunks $\{D_i \cup D_{i+1} \ldots \cup D_{i+r-1}\}$ and $\sigma_{C_j}^2$ is the error variance of C_j, trained using a single data chunk D_j. Combining Equations 10.4 and 10.5 and simplifying, we get

$$\begin{aligned}
\sigma_M^2 &= \frac{1}{L^2v^2}\sum_{i=1}^{Lv}\sigma_{M_i}^2 \quad \text{(using Equation 9.4)}\\
&= \frac{1}{L^2v^2}\sum_{i=1}^{Lv}\frac{1}{r^2}\sum_{j=i}^{r+i-1}\sigma_{C_j}^2 \quad \text{(using Equation 9.5)}\\
&= \frac{1}{L^2v^2r^2}\sum_{i=1}^{Lv}\sum_{j=i}^{r+i-1}\sigma_{C_j}^2 = \frac{1}{L^2v^2r}\sum_{i=1}^{Lv}\left(\frac{1}{r}\sum_{j=i}^{r+i-1}\sigma_{C_j}^2\right)\\
&= \frac{1}{L^2v^2r}\sum_{i=1}^{Lv}\bar{\sigma}_{C_i}^2 \quad (\bar{\sigma}_{C_i}^2 \text{ is common variance of } \sigma_{C_j}^2,\ j=i,\ldots,i+r-1)\\
&= \frac{1}{Lrv}\left(\frac{1}{Lv}\sum_{i=1}^{Lv}\bar{\sigma}_{C_i}^2\right) = \frac{1}{Lrv}\bar{\sigma}_C^2 \quad (\bar{\sigma}_C^2 \text{ is the common variance of } \bar{\sigma}_{C_i}^2,\ i=1,\ldots,Lv)\\
&= \frac{1}{rv}\left(\frac{1}{L}\bar{\sigma}_C^2\right) = \frac{1}{rv}\sigma_C^2 \quad \text{(using Equation 9.4)} \ \square
\end{aligned} \tag{10.6}$$

However, since we train v classifiers from each r consecutive data chunks, the independence assumption given above may not be valid since each pair of these v classifiers has overlapping training data. We need to consider correlation among the classifiers to compute the expected error reduction. The following lemma shows the error reduction considering error correlation. ■

Lemma 10.2

Let σ_C^2 *be the error variance of SPC. If there is no concept drift, then the error variance of MPC is at most* (v – 1)/*rv times of that of SPC,* that is,

$$\sigma_M^2 \le \frac{v-1}{rv}\sigma_C^2, \quad v > 1$$

Proof: According to [TUME96], the error variance of the ensemble M, given some amount of correlation among the classifiers is as follows:

$$\sigma_M^2 = \left(\frac{1+\delta(Lv-1)}{Lv} \right) \bar{\sigma}_M^2 \tag{10.7}$$

where $\bar{\sigma}_M^2$ is the common variance of $\sigma_{M_i}^2$ and δ is the mean correlation of error among the classifiers in the ensemble, given by

$$\delta = \frac{1}{(Lv)(Lv-1)} \sum_{m=1}^{Lv} \sum_{m \neq l} corr(\eta_m, \eta_l) \tag{10.8}$$

where $corr(\eta_m,\eta_l)$ is the correlation between the errors of classifiers M_m and M_l.

To simplify the computation of error correlation between M_m and M_l, we assume that if they are trained with the identical training data, then $corr(\eta_m,\eta_l) = 1$, and if they are trained with completely disjoint training data, then $corr(\eta_m, \eta_l) = 0$. Given this assumption, the correlation between M_m and M_l can be computed as follows:

$$corr(\eta_m, \eta_l) = \begin{cases} \dfrac{v-2}{v-1} & \text{if } \{M_m, M_l\} \in M^i \\ 0 & \text{otherwise} \end{cases} \tag{10.9}$$

The first case of Equation 10.9 says that the error correlation between M_m and M_l is $(v-2)/(v-1)$ if they are in the same batch of classifiers M^i. In this case, each pair of classifiers have $v-2$ partitions of common training data, and each one has a total of $v-1$ partitions of training data. In the worst case, all the v classifiers of the ith batch will remain in the ensemble M. However, this may not the case most of the time, because, according to the ensemble updating algorithm, it is possible that some classifiers of the ith batch will be replaced and some of them will remain in the ensemble.

Therefore, in the worst case, the ensemble is updated each time by a replacement of a whole batch of v classifiers by a new batch of v classifiers. In this case, each classifier will be correlated with $v-1$ classifiers. So, the mean correlation becomes

$$\delta \leq \frac{1}{(Lv)(Lv-1)} Lv(v-1) \frac{v-2}{v-1} = \frac{v-2}{Lv-1}$$

Substituting this value of δ in Equation 10.7, and following lemma, we obtain

$$\sigma_M^2 \leq \left(\frac{1+\frac{v-2}{Lv-1}(Lv-1)}{Lv} \right) \sigma_M^2 \quad \text{(using Equation 10.7)}$$

$$= \frac{v-1}{Lv} \bar{\sigma}_M^2 = \frac{v-1}{Lv} \frac{1}{Lv} \sum_{i=1}^{Lv} \sigma_{M_i}^2 = \frac{v-1}{Lv} \frac{1}{Lv} \sum_{i=1}^{Lv} \frac{1}{r^2} \sum_{j=i}^{r+i-1} \sigma_{C_j}^2 \quad \text{(using Equation 10.5)}$$

$$= \frac{v-1}{Lv} \frac{1}{Lv} \sum_{i=1}^{Lv} \frac{1}{r} \left(\frac{1}{r} \sum_{j=i}^{r+j-1} \sigma_{C_j}^2 \right) = \frac{v-1}{Lv} \frac{1}{Lv} \sum_{i=1}^{Lv} \frac{1}{r} \bar{\sigma}_{C_i}^2$$

$$= \frac{v-1}{Lv} \frac{1}{r} \left(\frac{1}{Lv} \sum_{i=1}^{Lv} \bar{\sigma}_{C_i}^2 \right) = \frac{v-1}{Lv} \frac{1}{r} \bar{\sigma}_C^2 = \frac{v-1}{rv} \left(\frac{1}{L} \bar{\sigma}_C^2 \right) = \frac{v-1}{rv} \sigma_C^2 \quad \text{(using Equation 10.4)}$$

For example, if v, and $r = 2$ then at least we have an error reduction by a factor of 4. If $v = 5$, and $r = 2$, we have at least a reduction by a factor of 2.5. However, if there is concept drift, then the assumption in Equation 10.5 may not be valid. In order to analyze error in the presence of concept drift, we introduce a new term "Magnitude of drift" or ρ_d. ■

Definition 10.1

Magnitude of drift or ρ_d is the maximum error introduced to a classifier due to concept drift. That is, every time a new data chunk appears, the error variance of a classifier is incremented ρ_d times due to concept drift.

For example, let D_j, $j \in \{i, i+1, \ldots, i+r-1\}$ be a data chunk in a window of r consecutive chunks $\{D_i, \ldots, D_{i+r-1}\}$ and C_j be the classifier trained with D_j. Let the actual error variance of C_j in the presence of concept drift is $\hat{\sigma}^2_{C_j}$, and the error variance of C_j in the absence of concept drift is $\sigma^2_{C_j}$. Then we have:

$$\hat{\sigma}^2_{C_j} = (1+\rho_d)^{(i+r-1)-j}\sigma^2_{C_j} \tag{10.10}$$

In other words, $\hat{\sigma}^2_{C_j}$ is the actual error variance of the j classifier C_j in the presence of concept drift, when the last data chunk in the window, D_{i+r-1} appears. Our next lemma deals with error reduction in the presence of concept drift. ■

Lemma 10.3

Let $\hat{\sigma}^2_M$ be the error variance of MPC in the presence of concept drift, σ^2_C be the error variance of SPC, and ρd be the drifting magnitude defined by definition. Then $\hat{\sigma}^2_M$ is bounded by

$$\hat{\sigma}^2_M \le \frac{(v-1)(1+\rho_d)^{r-1}}{rv}\sigma^2_C$$

Proof: Replacing $\sigma^2_{C_j}$ with $\hat{\sigma}^2_{C_j}$ in Equation 10.6 and following lemma, we get

$$\begin{aligned}
\hat{\sigma}^2_M &\le \frac{v-1}{L^2v^2}\sum_{i=1}^{Lv}\frac{1}{r^2}\sum_{j=i}^{r+i-1}\hat{\sigma}^2_{C_j} \\
&= \frac{v-1}{L^2r^2v^2}\sum_{i=1}^{Lv}\sum_{j=i}^{r+i-1}(1+\rho_d)^{(i+r-1)-j}\sigma^2_{C_j} \quad \text{(using Equation 10.10)} \\
&\le \frac{v-1}{L^2r^2v^2}\sum_{i=1}^{Lv}(1+\rho_d)^{r-1}\sum_{j=i}^{r+i-1}\sigma^2_{C_j} \\
&= \frac{(v-1)(1+\rho_d)^{r-1}}{L^2r^2v^2}\sum_{i=1}^{Lv}\sum_{j=i}^{r+i-1}\sigma^2_{C_j} \\
&= \frac{(v-1)(1+\rho_d)^{r-1}}{Lrv}\bar{\sigma}^2_C \\
&= \frac{(v-1)(1+\rho_d)^{r-1}}{rv}\sigma^2_C, r > 0 \quad \square
\end{aligned}$$

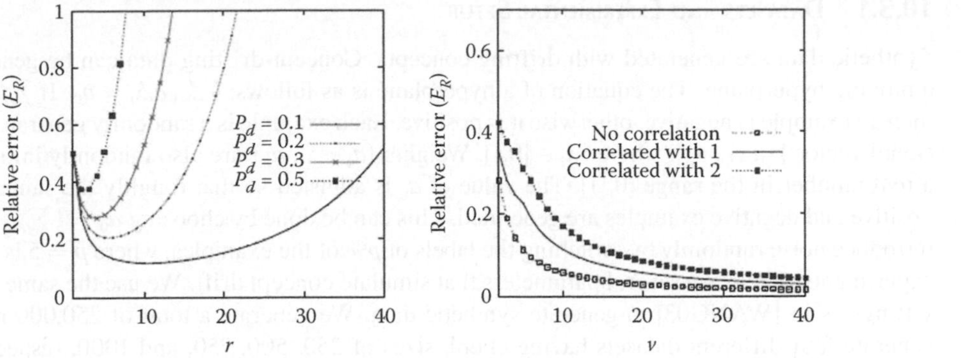

FIGURE 10.2 Error reduction by increasing (a) r and (b) v.

Therefore, we would achieve a reduction of error provided that

$$\frac{(v-1)(1+\rho_d)^{r-1}}{rv} \leq 1 \quad \text{or,} \quad E_R \leq 1 \tag{10.11}$$

where E_R is the ratio of MPC error to SPC error in the presence of concept drift. As we increase r and v, the relative error keeps decreasing up to a certain point. After that, it becomes flat or starts increasing. Next, we analyze the effect of parameters r and v on error reduction, in the presence of concept drift.

For a given value of v, r can only be increased up to a certain value. After that, increasing r actually hurts the performance of our algorithm, because inequality (10.11) is violated. Figure 10.2a shows the relative error ER for $v = 2$, and different values of ρd, for increasing r. It is clear from the graph that for lower values of ρd, increasing r reduces the relative error by a greater margin. However, in any case, after a certain value of r, ER becomes >1. Although it may not possible to know the actual value of ρd from the data, we can determine the optimal value of r experimentally. In our experiments, we found that for smaller chunk sizes, higher values of r work better, and vice versa. However, the best performance-cost trade-off is found for $r = 2$ or 3. We have used $r = 2$ in our experiments. Figure 10.2b shows the relative error ER for $r = 2$, $\rho d = 0.3$, and three cases of correlation (no correlation, a classifier is correlated with one other classifier on average, and a classifier is correlated with two other classifiers on average) for increasing v. We see that in all three cases, relative error keeps decreasing as we increase v. This is true for any value of ρd. However, after certain value of v, the rate of improvement gradually diminishes. From our experiments, we obtained the best performance-cost trade-off for $v = 5$. ■

10.2.2.1 Time Complexity of MPC

Let m be the size of the data stream and n be the total number of data chunks. Then our time complexity is $O(Lvm + nvf(rm/n))$, where $f(z)$ is the time to build a classifier on a training data of size z. Since v is constant, the complexity becomes $O(Lm + nf(rm/n)) = O(n.(Ls + f(rs))$, where s is the size of one data chunk. It should be mentioned here that the time complexity of the approach by Wang et al. [WANG03] is $O(n.(Ls + f(s))$. Thus, the actual running time of MPC would be at most a constant factor (rv times) higher than that of Wang et al. [WANG03]. But at the same time, we also achieve significant error reduction.

10.3 EXPERIMENTS

We evaluate our proposed method on both synthetic data and botnet traffic generated in a controlled environment, and compare with several baseline methods.

10.3.1 Datasets and Experimental Setup

Synthetic data are generated with drifting concepts. Concept-drifting data can be generated with a moving hyperplane. The equation of a hyperplane is as follows: $\sum_{i=1}^{d} a_i x_i = a_0$. If $\sum_{i=1}^{d} a_i x_i \leq a_0$, then an example is negative, otherwise it is positive. Each example is a randomly generated d-dimensional vector $\{x_1, \ldots, x_d\}$, where $\$x_i \in [0,1]$. Weights $\{a_1, \ldots, a_d\}$ are also randomly initialized with a real number in the range [0, 1]. The value of a_0 is adjusted so that roughly the same number of positive and negative examples are generated. This can be done by choosing $a_0 = \frac{1}{2}\sum_{i=1}^{d} a_i$. We also introduce noise randomly by switching the labels of $p\%$ of the examples, where $p = 5$ is used in our experiments. There are several parameters that simulate concept drift. We use the same parameters settings as in [WANG03] to generate synthetic data. We generate a total of 250,000 records and generate four different datasets having chunk sizes of 250, 500, 750, and 1000, respectively. The class distribution of these datasets is 50% positive and 50% negative.

10.3.1.1 Real (Botnet) Dataset

Botnet is a network of compromised hosts or *bots*, under the control of a human attacker known as the *botmaster* ([BARF06], [MASU08]). The botmaster can issue commands to the bots to perform malicious actions, such as launching DDoS attacks, spamming, spying, and so on. Thus, botnets have appeared as enormous threat to the internet community. Peer-to-Peer (P2P) is the new emerging technology of botnets. These botnets are distributed and small, so they are hard to detect and destroy. Examples of P2P bots are Nugache [LEMO06], Sinit [LURH04], and Trojan.Peacomm [GRIZ07].

Botnet traffic can be considered as a data stream having both properties: infinite length and concept drift. So, we apply our stream classification technique to detect P2P botnet traffic. We generate real P2P botnet traffic in a controlled environment, where we run a P2P bot named Nugache [LEMO06]. There are 81 continuous attributes in total. The whole dataset consists of 30,000 records, representing 1 week's worth of network traffic. We generate four different datasets having chunk sizes of 30, 60, 90, and 120 minutes, respectively. The class distribution of these datasets is 25% positive (botnet traffic) and 75% negative (benign traffic).

10.3.1.2 Baseline Methods

For classification, we use the "Weka" machine learning open source package, available at http://www.cs.waikato.ac.nz/ml/weka/. We apply three different classifiers—J48 decision tree, Ripper, and Bayes Net. In order to compare with other techniques, we implement the following:

MPC: This is our MPC ensemble algorithm.

BestL: This is a SPC ensemble approach where an ensemble of the best L classifiers is used. Here L is the ensemble size. This ensemble is created by storing all the classifiers seen so far, and selecting the best L of them based on expected error. An instance is tested using simple voting.

Last: In this case, we only keep the last trained classifier, trained on a single data chunk. It can be considered a SPC approach with $L = 1$.

Wang: This is an SPC method implemented by Wang et al. [WANG03].

All: This is also an SPC approach. In this case, we create an ensemble of all the classifiers seen so far, and the new data chunk is tested with this ensemble by simple voting among the classifiers.

10.3.2 Performance Study

In this section, we compare the results of all the five techniques, *MPC*, *Wang*, *BestL*, *All,* and *Last*. As soon as a new data chunk appears, we test each of these ensembles/classifiers on the new data, and update its accuracy, false positive, and false negative rates. In all the results shown here, we fix the parameter values of $v = 5$, and $r = 2$, unless mentioned otherwise.

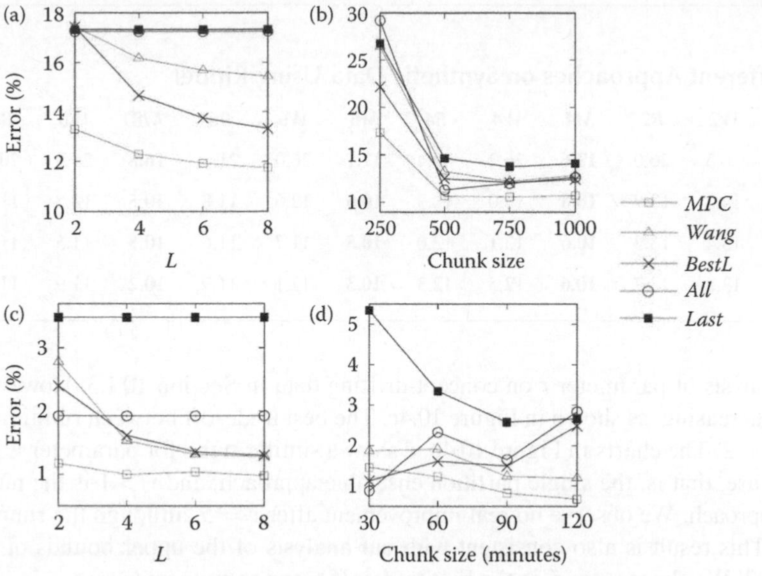

FIGURE 10.3 Error vs L and chunk size on synthetic data (a, b) and botnet data (c, d).

Figure 10.3a shows the error rates for different values of L of each method, averaged over four different chunk sizes on synthetic data, and Figure 10.3c shows the same for botnet data. Here decision tree is used as the base learner. It is evident that MPC has the lowest error among all approaches. Besides, we observe that the error of MPC is lower for higher values of L. This is desired because higher values of L means larger ensemble, and more error reduction. However, accuracy does not improve much after $L = 8$. *Wang* and *BestL* also show similar characteristic. *All* and *Last* do not depend on L, so their error remains the same for any L. Figure 10.3b shows the error rates for four different chunk sizes of each method (also using decision tree) averaged over different values of L (2, 4, 6, 8) on synthetic data, and Figure 10.3d shows the same for botnet data. Again, MPC has the lowest error of all. Besides, the error of MPC is lower for larger chunk sizes. This is desired because larger chunk size means more training data for a classifier.

Tables 10.1 and 10.2 report the error of decision tree and Ripper learning algorithms, respectively, on synthetic data, for different values of L and chunk sizes. The columns denoted by $M2$, $W2$, and $B2$ represent *MPC*, *Wang*, and *BestL*, respectively, for $L = 2$. Other columns have similar interpretations. In all the tables, we see that MPC has the lowest error for all values of L (shown in bold).

Figure 10.4 shows the sensitivity of r and v on error and running times on synthetic data for MPC. Figure 10.4a shows the errors for different values of r for a fixed value of v (=5) and L (=8). The highest reduction in error occurs when r is increased from 1 to 2. Note that $r = 1$ means single chunk training. We observe no significant reduction in error for higher values of r, which follows

TABLE 10.1
Error of Different Approaches on Synthetic Data Using Decision Tree

S	*M2*	*W2*	*B2*	*M4*	*W4*	*B4*	*M6*	*W6*	*B6*	*M8*	*W8*	*B8*	*All*	*Last*
250	**19.3**	26.8	26.9	**17.3**	26.5	22.1	**16.6**	26.3	20.4	**16.2**	26.1	19.5	29.2	26.8
500	**11.4**	14.8	14.7	**10.6**	13.2	12.4	**10.3**	12.7	11.6	**10.2**	12.4	11.3	11.3	14.7
750	**11.1**	13.9	13.9	**10.6**	12.1	11.9	**10.3**	11.5	11.4	**10.3**	11.3	11.2	15.8	13.8
1000	**11.4**	14.3	14.3	**10.7**	12.8	12.2	**10.5**	12.2	11.7	**10.3**	11.9	11.4	12.6	14.1

TABLE 10.2
Error of Different Approaches on Synthetic Data Using Ripper

S	*M2*	*W2*	*B2*	*M4*	*W4*	*B4*	*M6*	*W6*	*B6*	*M8*	*W8*	*B8*	*All*	*Last*
250	**19.2**	26.5	26.0	**17.6**	26.2	22.4	**17.1**	26.0	21.3	**16.8**	25.9	20.9	30.4	26.3
500	**11.5**	14.2	13.9	**10.8**	13.0	12.3	**10.6**	12.6	11.8	**10.5**	12.5	11.5	11.6	14.1
750	**11.0**	13.4	13.3	**10.6**	12.1	12.0	**10.5**	11.7	11.6	**10.5**	11.5	11.5	15.7	13.3
1000	**11.1**	13.8	13.7	**10.6**	12.5	12.3	**10.3**	12.1	11.9	**10.2**	11.9	11.8	12.6	13.6

from our analysis of parameter r on concept-drifting data in Section 10.1.3. However, the running time keeps increasing, as shown in Figure 10.4c. The best trade-off between running time and error occurs for $r = 2$. The charts in Figure 10.4b, d show a similar trend for parameter v. Note that $v = 1$ is the base case, that is, the single partition ensemble approach, and $v > 1$ is the multiple partition ensemble approach. We observe no real improvement after $v = 5$, although the running time keeps increasing. This result is also consistent with our analysis of the upper bounds of v, explained in Section 10.1.3. We choose $v = 5$ as the best trade-off between time and error.

Figure 10.5a shows the total running times of different methods on synthetic data for $L = 8$, $v = 5$ and $r = 2$. Note that the running time of *MPC* is within five times of that of *Wang*. This also supports our complexity analysis that the running time of *MPC* would be at most rv times the running time of *Wang*. The running times of *MPC* on botnet data shown in Figure 10.5b also have similar characteristics. The running times shown in Figure 10.5 include both training and testing time. Although the total training time of *MPC* is higher than that of *Wang*, the total testing times are almost the same in both techniques. Considering that training can be done offline, we may conclude that both these techniques have the same runtime performances in classifying data streams. Besides, users have the flexibility to choose either better performance or shorter training time just by changing the parameters r and v.

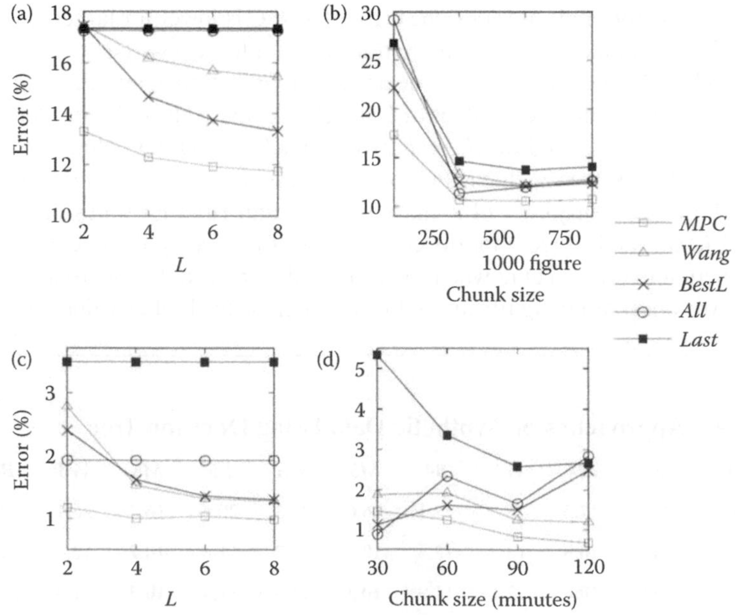

FIGURE 10.4 Sensitivity of parameters r and v on error (a, b) and running time (c, d).

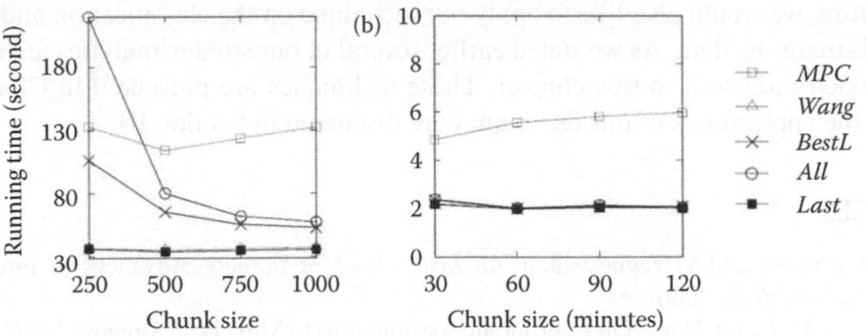

FIGURE 10.5 Chunk size versus running times on (a) synthetic data and (b) real data.

TABLE 10.3
Error Comparison with the Same Number of Classifiers in the Ensemble

Chunk Size	*M*2(J48)	*W*10(J48)	*M*2(Ripper)	*W*10(Ripper)
250	**19.9**	26.1	**21.0**	26.1
500	**11.7**	12.5	**12.2**	12.6
1000	**11.4**	12.5	**11.8**	13.0

We also report the results of using equal number of classifiers in *MPC* and *Wang* by setting $L = 10$ in *Wang*, and $L = 2$, $v = 5$, and $r = 1$ in MPC, which is shown in Table 10.3. We observe that error of *MPC* is lower than that of *Wang* in all chunk sizes. The columns *M*2(J48) and *W*10(J48) show the error of *MPC* ($L = 2$, $v = 5$, $r = 1$) and *Wang* ($L = 10$), respectively, for decision tree algorithm. The columns *M*2(Ripper) and *W*10(Ripper) show the same for Ripper algorithm. For example, for chunk size 250, and decision tree algorithm, *MPC* error is 19.9%, whereas *Wang* error is 26.1%. We can draw two important conclusions from this result. First, if the ensemble size of *Wang* is simply increased v times (i.e., made equal to Lv), its error does not become as low as *MPC*. Second, even if we use the same training set size in both these methods (i.e., $r = 1$), the error of *Wang* still remains higher than that of *MPC*. There are two possible reasons behind this performance. First, when a classifier is removed during ensemble updating in *Wang*, all information obtained from the corresponding chunk is forgotten, but in *MPC*, one or more classifiers from a chunk may survive. Thus, the ensemble updating approach in *MPC* tends to retain more information than that of *Wang*, leading to a better ensemble. Second, *Wang* requires at least Lv data chunks, whereas *MPC* requires at least $L + r - 1$ data chunks to obtain Lv classifiers. Thus, *Wang* tends to keep much older classifiers in the ensemble than *MPC*, leading to some outdated classifiers that can put a negative effect on the ensemble outcome.

10.4 SUMMARY AND DIRECTIONS

In this chapter, we have introduced a MPC ensemble method for classifying concept-drifting data streams. Our ensemble approach keeps the best $K * v$ classifiers, where a batch of v classifiers are trained with v overlapping partitions of r consecutive data chunks. It is a generalization over previous ensemble approaches that train a single classifier from a single data chunk. By introducing this MPC ensemble, we have reduced error significantly over the SPC approach. We have proved our claims theoretically, tested our approach on both synthetic data and real botnet data, and obtained better classification accuracies compared to other approaches.

In the future, we would also like to apply our technique on the classification and model evolution of other real streaming data. As we stated earlier several of our stream analytics techniques are based on the approach discussed in this chapter. These techniques are presented in Chapters 11 and 12. In addition, the applications of our techniques are discussed in Section III.

REFERENCES

[BARF06]. P. Barford and V. Yegneswaran, *An Inside Look at Botnets.* Advances in Information Security. Springer, New York, 2006.

[GAO07]. J. Gao, W. Fan, J. Han, "On Appropriate Assumptions to Mine Data Streams," *ICDM'07:Proceedings of the 2007 International Conference on Data Mining*, Oct. 28–31, Omaha, NE, pp. 143–152, IEEE Computer Society, 2007.

[GRIZ07]. J. B. Grizzard, V. Sharma, C. Nunnery, B. B. Kang, D. Dagon, "Peer-to-Peer Botnets: Overview and Case Study," *Hot- Bots '07: Proceedings of the 1st Workshop on Hot Topics in Understanding Botnets*, April 10, Cambridge, MA, pp. 1, 2007.

[LURH04]. LURHQ Threat Intelligence Group, Sinit p2p trojan analysis. 2004. http://www.lurhq.com/sinit.html.

[LEMO06]. R. Lemos, Bot software looks to improve peerage. 2006, http://www.securityfocus.com/news/11390.

[MASU08]. M. M. Masud, T. Al-khateeb, L. Khan, B. M. Thuraisingham, K. W. Hamlen, "Flow-Based Identification of Botnet Traffic by Mining Multiple Log Files," *DFMA '08: Proceedings of the 2008 International Conference on Distributed Frameworks and Applications*, Oct. 21–22, Penang, Malaysia, pp. 200–206, 2008.

[MASU09]. M. M. Masud, J. Gao, L. Khan, J. Han, B. M. Thuraisingham, "A Multi-Partition Multi-Chunk Ensemble Technique to Classify Concept-Drifting Data Streams," *PAKDD09: Proceedings of the 13th Pacific–Asia Conference on Knowledge Discovery and Data Mining*, Apr. 27–30, Bangkok, Thailand, pp. 363–375, Springer-Verlag, 2009.

[TUME96]. K. Tumer and J. Ghosh, "Error correlation and error reduction in ensemble classifiers," *Connection Science*, 8(304), 385–403, 1996.

[WANG03]. H. Wang, W. Fan, P. S. Yu, J. Han, "Mining Concept-Drifting Data Streams Using Ensemble Classifiers," *KDD '03: Proceedings of the 9th ACM SIGKDD International Conference on Knowledge Discovery and Data Mining*, Aug. 24–27, Washington, DC, pp. 226–235, ACM, 2003.

11 Classification and Novel Class Detection in Concept-Drifting Data Streams

11.1 INTRODUCTION

As discussed in [MASU09], in a typical data stream classification task, it is assumed that the total number of classes are fixed. This assumption may not be valid in a real streaming environment, where new classes may evolve. Traditional data stream classification techniques are not capable of recognizing novel class instances until the appearance of the novel class is manually identified, and labeled instances of that class are presented to the learning algorithm for training. The problem becomes more challenging in the presence of concept drift, when the underlying data distribution changes over time. We propose a novel and efficient technique that can automatically detect the emergence of a novel class in the presence of concept drift by quantifying cohesion among unlabeled test instances and separation of the test instances from training instances.

Our approach is nonparametric, meaning it does not assume any underlying distributions of data. A comparison with the state-of-the-art stream classification techniques proves the superiority of our approach. In this chapter, we discuss our proposed framework for classifying data streams with automatic novel class detection mechanism. It is based on our previous work [MASU09].

The organization of this chapter is as follows. Our ECS Miner algorithm is discussed in Section 11.2. Classification with novel class detection is discussed in Section 11.3. Experiments are discussed in Section 11.4. This chapter is summarized in Section 11.5.

11.2 ECSMINER

11.2.1 Overview

ECSMiner (pronounced like ExMiner), stands for Enhanced Classifier for Data Streams with novel class Miner. Before describing ECSMiner, we mathematically formulate the data stream classification problem (Figure 11.1).

- The data stream is a continuous sequence of data points: $\{x_1, \ldots, x_{now}\}$, where each x_i is a d-dimensional feature vector, x_1 is the very first data point in the stream, and x_{now} is the latest data point that has just arrived.
- Each data point x_i is associated with two attributes: y_i, and t_i, being its class label and time of arrival, respectively.
- For simplicity, we assume that $t_{i+1} = t_i + 1$ and $t_1 = 1$.
- The latest T_l instances in the stream: $\{x_{now-T_l+1}, \cdots, x_{now}\}$ are unlabeled, meaning their corresponding class labels are unknown. But the class labels of all other data points are known.
- We are to predict the class label of x_{now} before the time $t_{now} + T_c$, that is, before the data point x_{now+T_c} arrives, and $T_c < T_l$.

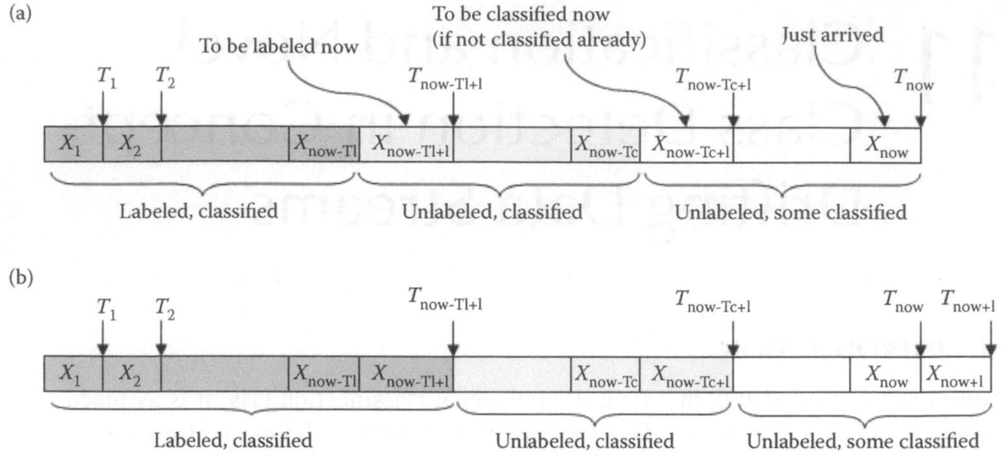

FIGURE 11.1 Illustrating the mathematical formulation of data stream classification problem under time constraints.

11.2.2 High Level Algorithm

Algorithm 11.1 ECSMiner

1:*M*←Build-initial-ensemble()
2:*buf*←empty//temporary buffer
3:*U*←empty//unlabeled data buffer
4:*L*←empty//labeled data buffer –+62393+*(training data)
5:**while true do**
6: ***xj***←the latest data point in the stream
7: **Classify**(*M*,***xj***,buf)//(Algorithm 11.2, Section 11.2)
8: *U*⇐*xj*//enqueue
9: **if** |*U*|>*Tl* **then**//time to label the oldest instance
10: *xk* ⇐*U*//dequeue the instance
11: *L*⇐<*xk*,*yk*>//label it and save in training buffer
12: **if** |*L*|=*S* **then**//training buffer is full
13: *M′*←**Train-and-save-decision-boundary** (*L*) (Section 11.1.5)
14: *M*←Update(*M*, *M′*, *L*)
15: *L*←empty
16: **endif**
17: **endif**
18:**endwhile**

Algorithm 11.1 outlines the top level overview of our approach. The algorithm starts with building the initial ensemble of models $M = \{M_1, \ldots, M_L\}$ with the first *L* labeled data chunks. The algorithm maintains three buffers: buffer *buf* keeps potential novel class instances, buffer *U* keeps unlabeled data points until they are labeled, and buffer *L* keeps labeled instances until they are used to train a new classifier. After initialization, the while loop begins from line 5, which continues indefinitely. At each iteration of the loop, the latest data point in the stream, *xj* is classified (line 7) using *Classify*() (Algorithm 11.2). The novel class detection mechanism is implemented inside Algorithm 11.2. If the class label of *xj* cannot be predicted immediately, it is stored in *buf* for future processing. Details of

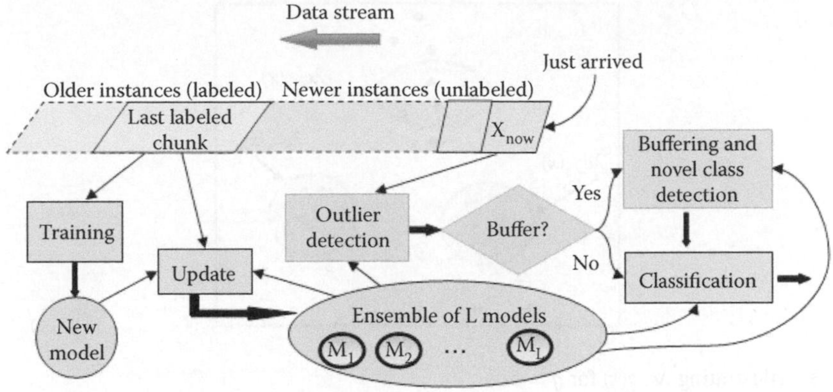

FIGURE 11.2 Overview of the ECS Miner algorithm.

this step will be discussed in Section 11.3. *xj* is then pushed into the unlabeled data buffer *U* (line 8). If the buffer size exceeds *Tl*, the oldest element *xk* is dequeued and labeled (line 9), since *Tl* units of time has elapsed since *xk* arrived in the stream (so it is time to label *xk*). The pair ⟨*xk*, *yk*⟩ is pushed into the labeled data buffer *L* (line 9). When we have *S* instances in *L*, where *S* is the chunk size, a new classifier *M′* is trained using the chunk (line 13). Then the existing ensemble is updated (line 14) by choosing the best *L* classifiers from the $L + 1$ classifiers $M \cup \{M'\}$ based on their accuracies on *L*, and the buffer *L* is emptied to receive the next chunk of training data (line 15).

Figure 11.2 illustrates the overview of our approach. A classification model is trained from the last labeled data chunk. This model is used to update the existing ensemble. The latest data point in the stream is tested by the ensemble. If it is found to be an outlier, it is temporarily stored in a buffer. Otherwise, it is classified immediately using the current ensemble. The temporary buffer is processed periodically to detect whether the instances in the buffer belong to a novel class.

Our algorithm will be mentioned henceforth as "ECSMiner" (pronounced like ExMiner), which stands for Enhanced Classifier for Data Streams with novel class Miner. We believe that any base learner can be enhanced with the proposed novel class detector, and used in ECSMiner. The only operation that needs to be treated specially for a particular base learner is *Train-and-save-decision-boundary*. We illustrate this operation for two base learners in this section.

11.2.3 Nearest Neighborhood Rule

We assume that the instances belonging to a class *c* is generated by an underlying generative model *θc*, and the instances in each class are independently identically distributed. With this assumption, one can reasonably argue that the instances which are close together under some distance metric are supposed to be generated by the same model, that is, belong to the same class. This is the basic assumption for nearest-neighbor classifications [COVE67]. Besides, this assumption is used in numerous semisupervised learning techniques, such as [PANG04], and in many other semisupervised learning works [ZHU08]. We generalize this assumption by introducing the concept of "nearest neighborhood."

Definition 11.1 (*λc*, *q*-Neighborhood)

λc, *q*-neighborhood, or *λc*, *q (x)* of any instance *x* is the set of *q* nearest neighbors of *x* within class *c*.

For example, let there be three classes *c*+, and *c*−, and *c*0, denoted by the symbols "+," "−," and black dots, respectively (Figure 11.3). Also, let $q = 5$, then *λc* +, *q (x)* of any arbitrary instance *x* is the set of 5 nearest neighbors of *x* in class *c*+, and so on.

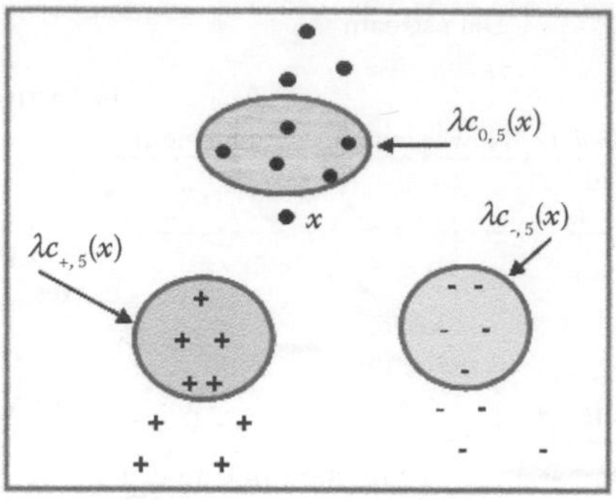

FIGURE 11.3 Illustrating $\lambda c, q(x)$ for $q = 5$.

Let $\bar{D}_{c,q(x)}$ be the mean distance from x to $\lambda_{c,q}(x)$, that is,

$$\bar{D}_{c,q}(x) = \frac{1}{q} \sum_{x_i \in \lambda_{c,q}(x)} D(x, x_i) \tag{11.1}$$

where $D(x_i,x_j)$ is the distance between the data points x_i and x_j in some appropriate metric.

Let $c_{\min}$ be the class label such that $\bar{D}_{c_{\min},q(x)}$ is the minimum among all $\bar{D}_{c,q(x)}$, that is, $\lambda_{c_{min},q(x)}$ is the nearest $\lambda_{c,q}(x)$ neighborhood (or q-nearest neighborhood or q-NH) of x. For example, in Figure 11.3, $c_{\min} = c_0$, that is, $\lambda_{c0,q(x)}$ is the q-NH of x.

Definition 11.2 (q-NH rule)

Let *cmin* be the class label of the instances in *q-NH* of *x*. According to the *q-NH* rule, the predicted class label of x is $c_{\min}$.

In the example of Figure 11.3, $c_{\min} = c_0$, therefore, the predicted class label of x is $c0$. Our novel class detection technique is based on the assumption that any class of data follows the q-NH rule. In this section, we discuss the similarity of this rule with k-NN rule and highlight its significance.

11.2.4 Novel Class and Its Properties

Definition 11.3 (Existing Class and Novel Class)

Let M be the current ensemble of classification models. A class c is an existing class if at least one of the models $Mi \in M$ has been trained with the instances of class c. Otherwise, c is a novel class.

Therefore, if a novel class c appears in the stream, none of the classification models in the ensemble will be able to correctly classify the instances of c. An important property of the novel class follows from the q-NH rule.

Property 1 *Let x be an instance belonging to a novel class c, and let c′ be an existing class. Then according to q-NH rule,* $\bar{D}_{c,q}(x)$*, that is, the average distance from x to* $\lambda_{c,q}(x)$ *is* $<\bar{D}_{c',q}(x)$*, the average distance from x to* $\lambda_{c',q}(x)$*, for any existing class c′. In other words, x is closer to the neighborhood of its own class (cohesion), and farther from the neighborhood of any existing classes (separation).*

Figure 11.4 shows a hypothetical example of a decision tree and the appearance of a novel class. A decision tree and its corresponding feature vector partitioning by its leaf nodes are shown in the

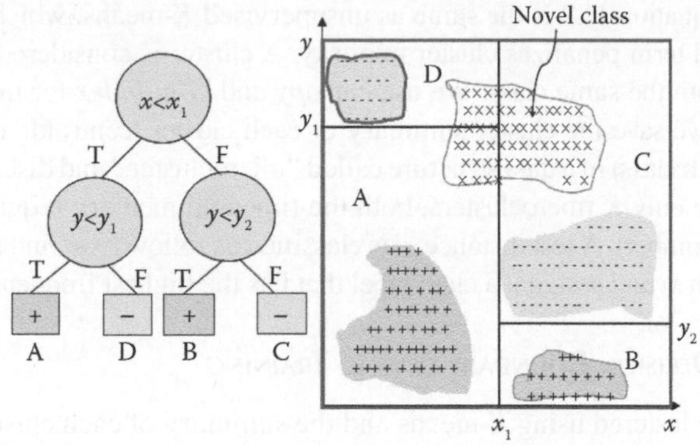

FIGURE 11.4 A decision tree and corresponding feature space partitioning.

figure. The shaded portions of the feature space represent the training data. After the decision tree is built, a novel class appears in the stream (shown with "x" symbol). The decision tree model misclassifies all the instances in the novel class as existing class instance since the model is unaware of the novel class. Our goal is to detect the novel class without having to train the model with that class. Note that instances in the novel class follow property 1, since the novel-class neighborhood of any novel-class instance is much closer to the instance than the neighborhoods of any other classes. If we observe this property in a collection of unlabeled test instances, we can detect the novel class. This is not a trivial task, since we must decide when to classify an instance immediately, and when to postpone the classification decision, and wait for more test instances so that property 1 can be revealed among those instances. Because in order to discover property 1 (cohesion), we need to deal with a collection of test instances simultaneously. Besides, we cannot defer the decision $>Tc$ time units after the arrival of a test instance.

Therefore, the *main challenges* in novel class detection are as follows:

- Saving the training data efficiently without using much memory.
- Knowing when to classify a test instance immediately, and when to postpone the classification decision.
- Classifying the deferred instances within *Tc* time unit.
- Predicting the presence of a novel class quickly and correctly.

11.2.5 Base Learners

We apply our technique on two different classifiers: decision tree, and *k*-nearest neighbor (*k*-NN). When decision tree is used as a classifier, each training data chunk is used to build a decision tree. When *k*-NN is used, each chunk is used to build a *k*-NN classification model. The simplest way to build such a model is to just store all the data points of the training chunk in memory. But this strategy would lead to an inefficient classification model, both in terms of memory and running time. In order to make the model more efficient, we build *K* clusters with the training data [MASU08]. Note that we use small *k* as the parameter for *k*-NN and capital *K* to denote the number of clusters. We apply a semisupervised clustering technique using expectation maximization (E-M) that tries to minimize both intracluster dispersion (same objective as unsupervised *K*-means) and cluster impurity

$$\mathcal{O}bj = \sum_{i=1}^{K}\left(\sum_{x\in\mathcal{X}_i} \| x-u_i \|^2 + \sum_{x\in\mathcal{X}_i} \| x-u_i \|^2 * Imp_i\right) \quad (11.2)$$

The first term in Equation 11.2 is the same as unsupervised *K*-means, which penalizes intracluster dispersion. The second term penalizes cluster impurity. A cluster is considered pure if all data points in the cluster come from the same class. We use *entropy* and *Gini index* for impurity measure. After building the clusters, we save the cluster summary of each cluster (centroid, and frequencies of data points belonging to each class) in a data structure called "microcluster," and discard the raw data points. Since we store and use only *K* microclusters, both the time and memory requirements become functions of *K* (a constant number). A test instance *xj* is classified as follows: we find the microcluster whose centroid is nearest from *xj* and assign it a class label that has the highest frequency in that microcluster.

11.2.6 Creating Decision Boundary during Training

The training data are clustered using *K*-means and the summary of each cluster are saved as "pseudopoint." Then the raw training data are discarded. These pseudopoints form a decision boundary for the training data.

Clustering: *K* clusters are built per chunk from the training data. This clustering step is specific to each base learner. For example, for *k*-NN, existing clusters are used that were created using the approach discussed in Section 11.2.4. For decision tree, clustering is done at each leaf node of the tree, since we need to create decision boundaries in each leaf node separately. This is done as follows. Suppose *S* is the chunk size. During decision tree training, when a leaf node *li* is reached, *ki* = (*ti/S*) ∗*K* clusters are built in that leaf, where *ti* denotes the number of training instances belonging to leaf node *li*. Therefore, the number of clusters built in each leaf node is proportional to the number of training instances that belong to the leaf node. If a leaf node is not empty (has one or more instances), then at least one cluster is built in that node. Figure 11.5 illustrates how the decision boundaries are created for a decision tree.

On the left, clusters are built at each leaf node. On the right, raw data are discarded and pseudopoints are saved at the leaf nodes. These pseudopoints define the decision boundary for the tree.

Storing the cluster summary information: For each cluster, we store the following summary information in a data structure called pseudopoint:

Weight, *w*: Total number of points in the cluster, that is,

$$w = |\mathcal{X}|$$

where $\mathcal{X}$ is the set of points belonging to the cluster.

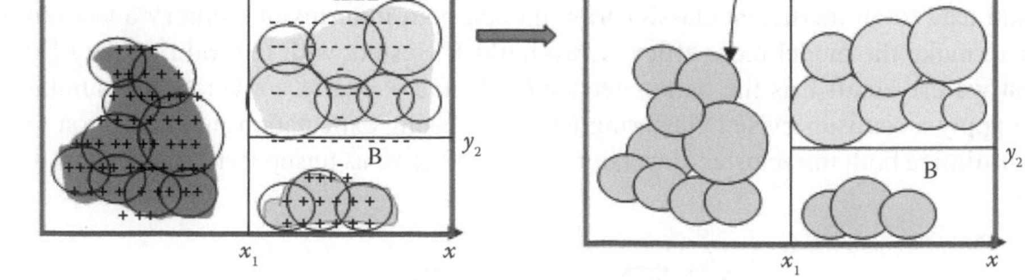

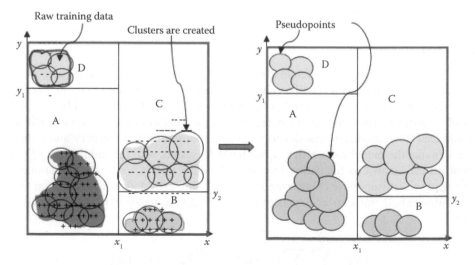

FIGURE 11.5 Creating decision boundary for the decision tree of Figure 11.4.

- *Centroid*, μ, that is,

$$\mu = \frac{\sum_{x \in \mathcal{X}} x}{w}$$

- *Radius*, R: Distance between the centroid and the farthest data point in the cluster, that is,

$$\mathcal{R} = \max_{x \in \mathcal{X}}(dist(\mu, x))$$

where *dist*(*x*, *y*) is the distance between two data points *x* and *y* in some appropriate metric.

- *Mean distance*, μd: The mean distance from each point to the cluster centroid, that is,

$$\mu d = \frac{\sum_{x \in \mathcal{X}} dist(\mu, x)}{w}$$

So, *w*(*h*) denotes the "weight" value of a pseudopoint *h*, and so on. After computing the cluster summaries, the raw data are discarded and only the pseudopoints are stored in memory. Any pseudopoint having too few (less than three) instances is considered as noise and is also discarded. Thus, the memory requirement for storing the training data becomes constant, that is, *O*(*K*).

Each pseudopoint *h* corresponds to a hypersphere in the feature space having center $\mu(h)$ and radius *R*(*h*). Let us denote the portion of feature space covered by a pseudopoint *h* as the "region" of *h* or *RE*(*h*). Therefore, *RE*(*Mi*) denotes the union of the regions of all pseudopoints *h* in the classifier *Mi*, that is,

$$RE(M_i) \bigcup_{h \in M_i} RE(h)$$

RE(*Mi*) forms a decision boundary for the training data of classifier *Mi*.

11.3 CLASSIFICATION WITH NOVEL CLASS DETECTION

11.3.1 High-Level Algorithm

The algorithm consists of two main parts: classification (lines 1–5) and novel class detection Algorithm 11.2 (Classify) sketches the classification and novel class detection technique (lines 6–14). Details of the steps of this algorithm will be explained in the following subsections.

Algorithm 11.2 Classify(*M,xj,buf*)

Input: *M* : Current ensemble of best *L* classifiers
xj : test instance
buf : buffer holding temporarily deferred instances
Output: Immediate or deferred class prediction of *xj*
1: fout ← **true**
2: **if** F outlier(*M,xj*) = **false then**
3: *y!* ← majority-voting(*M,xj*) //classify immediately
4: fout ← **false**

5: **end if**
6: Filter(*buf*)
7: **if** fout = **true then**
8: *buf* ⇐ *xj* //enqueue
9: **if** *buf*.length > *q* **and** last trial + q ≤ *ti* **then**
10: last trial ← *ti*
11: novel ← DetectNovelClass(*M*,*buf*) // (Algorithm 11.3, Section 11.2.2)
12: **if** novel = **true** **then** remove novel (*buf*)
13: **end if**
14: **end if**

11.3.2 Classification

In line 2 of Algorithm 11.2, we first check whether the test instance *xj* is an *F outlier*, which is to be defined shortly. If any test instance *xj* falls outside the decision boundary *RE*(*Mi*) of a classifier *Mi*, then *xj* is an outlier. If *xj* is a novel class instance, it must be an outlier, which would be justified shortly. However, *xj* may also appear an outlier because of other reasons: noise, concept drift, or insufficient training data for *Mi*. Therefore, we apply filtering so that most of the outliers, which appear for any reason other than being novel class instance, are filtered out. The outliers that pass the filtering are called *F outliers*.

Definition 11.4 (F Outlier)

A test instance is an *F* outlier (i.e., filtered outlier) if it is outside the decision boundary of all classifiers

$$M_i \in M.$$

Intuitively, all novel class instances should be *F outliers*. Because, if any test instance x_j is not an *F outlier*, then it must be inside the decision boundary of some classifier M_i. Therefore, it must be inside *Re*(h') of some pseudopoint h'. This implies that x_j is closer to the centroid of h' than at least one training instance in h' (the one at the farthest distance from the centroid of h'), which leads to the conclusion that x_j is most likely an existing class instance having the same class label as the instances in h'. So, if x_j is not an *F outlier*, we classify it immediately using the ensemble voting (line 3).

11.3.3 Novel Class Detection

The buffer *buf* temporarily holds potential novel class instances. These instances are analyzed periodically in order to detect novel class, which is explained in the next paragraph. *buf* needs to be cleared periodically (line 6, Algorithm 11.2) to remove instances that no longer contribute to novel class detection. Besides, instances in *buf* that has reached classification deadline *Tc* are classified immediately. An instance is removed from *buf* if it fulfills either of the three conditions:

1. Age > S: the front of *buf* contains the oldest element in *buf*. It is removed if its age is >*S*, the chunk size. Therefore, at any moment in time, there can be at most *S* instances in *buf*.
2. Ensemble update: the ensemble may be updated while an instance *xk* is waiting inside *buf*. As a result, *xk* may no longer be an *F4 outlier* for the new ensemble of models, and it must be removed if so. If *xk* is no longer an *F outlier*, and it is not removed, it could be falsely

identified as a novel class instance, and also it could interfere with other valid novel class instances, misleading the detection process.

3. Existing class: any instance is removed from *buf* if it has been labeled, and it belongs to one of the existing classes. If it is not removed, it will also mislead novel class detection.

When an instance is removed from *buf*, it is classified immediately using the current ensemble (if not classified already).

Lines 7–14 are executed only if *xj* is an *F outlier*. At first, *xj* is enqueued into *buf* (line 8). Then we check whether *buf*.length, that is, the size of *buf* is at least *q*, and the last check on *buf* for detecting novel class had been executed (i.e., *last trial*) at least *q* time units earlier (line 9). Since novel class detection is more expensive than simple classification, this operation is performed at most once in every *q* time units.

In line 11, Algorithm 11.3 (DetectNovelClass) is called, which returns true if a novel class is found. Finally, if a novel class is found, all instances that are identified as novel class are removed from *buf* (line 12).

Next, we examine Algorithm 11.3 to understand how *buf* is analyzed to detect presence of novel class. First, we define *q*-neighborhood silhouette coefficient, or *q*-NSC, as follows:

Definition 11.5 (*q*-NSC)

Let $\bar{D}_{c_{out},q}(x)$ be the mean distance from an *F* outlier x to $\lambda_{c_{out},q}(x)$ defined by Equation 11.1, where $\lambda_{c_{out},q}(x)$ is the set of *q*-nearest neighbors of x within the *F* outlier instances. Also, let $\bar{D}_{c_{\min},q}(x)$ be the minimum among all $\bar{D}_{c,q}(x)$, where c is an existing class. Then *q-NSC* of x is given by

$$q\text{-NSC}(x) = \frac{\bar{D}_{c_{\min},q}(x) - \bar{D}_{c_{out},q}(x)}{\max(\bar{D}_{c_{\min},q}(x), \bar{D}_{c_{out},q}(x))} \quad (11.3)$$

q-NSC, which is a unified measure of cohesion and separation, yields a value between –1 and + 1. A positive value indicates that *x* is closer to the *F outlier* instances (more cohesion) and farther away from existing class instances (more separation), and vice versa. Note that *q*-NSC(*x*) of an *F outlier x* must be computed separately for each classifier $Mi \in M$. We declare a *new class* if there are at least *q! (>q) F outliers* having positive *q*-NSC for all classifiers $Mi \in M$. The justification behind this decision is discussed in the next subsection.

Speeding up the computation of q-NSC: For each classifier $Mi \in M$, computing *q*-NSC for all *F outlier* instance takes quadratic time in the number of *F outliers*. Let $B = buf$.length. In order to compute *q*-NSC for one element *x* in *buf*, we need *O(B)* time to compute the distances from *x* to all other elements in *buf*, and *O(K)* time to compute the distances from *x* to all existing class pseudopoints $h \in Mi$. Therefore, the total time to compute *q*-NSC of all elements in *buf* is $O(B(B + K)) = O(B2)$, since $B \gg K$. In order to make the computation faster, we create $Ko\ (=(B/S) * K)$ pseudopoints from *F outliers* using *K*-means clustering and perform the computations on the pseudopoints (referred to as *F pseudopoints*), where *S* is the chunk size. The time required to apply *K*-means clustering on *B* instances is *O(KoB)*. The time complexity to compute *q*-NSC of all of the *F pseudopoints* is $O(Ko * (Ko + K))$, which is constant, since both *Ko* and *K* are independent of the input size. Therefore, the overall complexity for computing *q*-NSC including the overhead for clustering becomes $O(Ko * (Ko + K) + KoB) = O(Ko(B + Ko + K) = O(KoB)$, since $B \gg K \geq Ko$. So, the running time to compute *q*-NSC after speedup is linear in *B* compared to quadratic in *B* before speedup. *q*-NSC of a *F pseudopoint* computed in this way is actually an approximate average of the *q*-NSC of each *F outlier* in that *F pseudopoint*. By using this approximation, although we gain speed, we also lose some precision. However, this drop in precision is negligible, as shown in the analysis to be presented shortly. This approximate *q*-NSC of an *F pseudopoint h* is denoted by q-*NSC′* (h).

Algorithm 11.3 Detect NovelClass(*M,buf*)

Input: *M* : Current ensemble of best *L* classifiers
buf : buffer holding temporarily deferred instances
Output: true, if novel class is found; false, otherwise
1: Make *Ko*=(*K* **buf*.length/*S*) clusters with the instances in *buf* using *K*-means clustering, and create *Ko F pseudopoints*
2: Let *Ho* be the set of *F pseudopoints*
3: **for** each classifier $Mi \in M$ **do**
4: **for** each $h \in Ho$ **do** Compute *q-NSC*′ (*h*)
5: $Hp \leftarrow \{h \setminus\setminus h \in Ho$ and *q-NSC*′ $(h) > 0\}$ //*F pseudopoints* with positive *q-NSC*′ ()
6: $w(Hp) \leftarrow Sumh \in Hp\ (w(h))$. //*w*(*h*) is the weight of *h* that is, # of instances in the *F pseudopoint h*.
7: **if** $w(Hp) > q$ **then** NewClassVote++
8: **end for**
9: **if** NewClassVote = *L* **then** return true **else** return false

In line 1 of Algorithm 11.3, we create *F pseudopoints* using the *F outliers* as explained earlier. For each classifier $Mi \in M$, we compute *q*-NSC′ (*h*) of every *F pseudopoint h* (line 4). If the total weight of the *F pseudopoints* having positive *q*-NSC′ () is $>q$, then *Mi* votes for novel class (line 7). If all classifiers vote for novel class, then we decide that a novel class has really appeared (line 9). Once novel class is declared, we need to find the instances of the novel class. This is done as follows: suppose *h* is an *F pseudopoint* having positive *q*-NSC′ (*h*) with respect to all classifiers $Mi \in M$ (note that *q*-NSC′ (*h*) is computed with respect to each classifier separately). Therefore, all *F outlier* instances belonging to *h* are identified as novel class instances.

This algorithm can detect one or more novel classes concurrently as long as each novel class follows property 1 and contains at least *q* instances. This is true even if the class distributions are skewed. However, if more than one such novel class appears concurrently, our algorithm will identify the instances belonging those classes as novel, without imposing any distinction between dissimilar novel class instances (i.e., it will treat them simply as "novel"). But the distinction will be learned by our model as soon as the true labels of those novel class instances arrive, and a classifier is trained with those instances.

It should be noted that the larger the value of *q*, the greater the confidence with which we can decide whether a novel class has arrived. However, if *q* is too large, then we may also fail to detect a new class if the total number of instances belonging to the novel class is $\leq q$. An optimal value of *q* is obtained empirically (Section 11.3).

Impact of evolving class labels on ensemble classification: As the reader might have realized already, the arrival of novel classes in the stream causes the classifiers in the ensemble to have different sets of class labels. There are two scenarios to consider. Scenario (a): suppose an older (earlier) classifier *Mi in* the ensemble has been trained with classes *c*0 and *c*1, and an younger (later) classifier *Mj* has been trained with classes *c*1, and *c*2, where *c*2 is a new class that appeared after *Mi* had been trained. This puts a negative effect on voting decision, since the *Mi* obviously misclassifies instances of *c*2. So, rather than counting the votes from each classifier, we selectively count their votes as follows. If a younger classifier *Mj* classifies a test instance *x* as class *c*, but an older classifier *Mi* had not been trained with training data of *c*, then the vote for *Mi* will be ignored if *x* is found to be an outlier for *Mi*. Scenario (b): the opposite situation may also arise where the oldest classifier is trained with some class *c!*, but none of the newer classifiers are trained with that class. This means class *c!* has been outdated, and in that case, we remove *Mi* from the ensemble.

Figure 11.6a illustrates scenario (a). The classifier in the ensemble are sorted according to their age, with *M*1 being the oldest, and *M*4 being the youngest. Each classifier *Mi* is marked with the classes

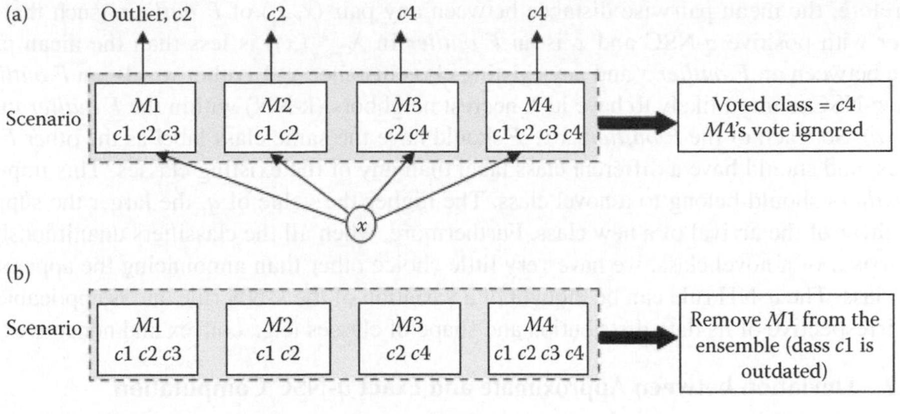

FIGURE 11.6 Impact of evolving class label on ensemble.

with which it has been trained. For example, $M1$ has been trained with classes $c1$, $c2$, and $c3$, and so on. Note that class $c4$ appears only in the two youngest classifiers. x appears as an outlier to $M1$. Therefore, $M1$'s vote is not counted since x is classified as $c4$ by an younger classifier $M3$, and $M1$ does not contain class $c4$. Figure 11.6b illustrates scenario (b). Here $M1$ contains class $c1$, which is not contained by any younger classifiers in the ensemble. Therefore, $c1$ has become outdated, and $M1$ is removed from the ensemble. In this way we ensure that older classifiers have less impact in the voting process. If class $c1$ later reappears in the stream, it will be automatically detected again as a novel class (see Definition 11.3).

11.3.4 Analysis and Discussion

In this subsection at first we justify the novel class detection algorithm, then analyze the extent of precision loss in computing q-NSC, and finally analyze the time complexity of ECSMiner.

11.3.4.1 Justification of the Novel Class Detection Algorithm

In Algorithm 11.3, we declare a novel class if there are at least $q'(>q)$ *F outliers* that have positive q-NSC for all the classifiers in the ensemble. First, we illustrate the significance of this condition, that is, "$>q$ *F outliers* have positive q-NSC." Equation 11.3 deals with the mean distance between an *F outlier* and its *nearest neighborhood*. Now we go one step further to examine the mean distances between any pair of *F outliers*.

Let $\mathcal{F}$ be the set of *F outliers* having positive q-NSC. Therefore, for any $x \in \mathcal{F}$:

$$\begin{aligned} &\bar{D}_{c_{\min},q}(x) - \bar{D}_{c_{out},q}(x) > 0 \\ &\Rightarrow \bar{D}_{c_{\min},q}(x) > \bar{D}_{c_{out},q}(x) \end{aligned} \tag{11.3}$$

Summing up for all *F outliers* $x \in$F:

$$\begin{aligned} &\sum_{x\in\mathcal{F}} \bar{D}_{c_{\min},q}(x) > \sum_{x\in\mathcal{F}} \bar{D}_{c_{out},q}(x) \\ &\Rightarrow \sum_{x\in\mathcal{F}} \frac{1}{q} \sum_{x_i \in \lambda_{c_{\min},q}(x)} D(x,x_i) > \sum_{x\in\mathcal{F}} \frac{1}{q} \sum_{x_j \in \lambda_{c_{out},q}(z)} D(x,x_j) \\ &\Rightarrow \frac{1}{m}\frac{1}{q} \sum_{x\in\mathcal{F}} \sum_{x_i \in \lambda_{c_{\min},q}(x)} D(x,x_i) > \frac{1}{m}\frac{1}{q} \sum_{x\in\mathcal{F}} \sum_{x_i \in \lambda_{c_{out},q}(x)} D(x,x_i) \text{ (letting m} = |\mathcal{F}|) \end{aligned} \tag{11.4}$$

Therefore, the mean pairwise distance between any pair (x, x_j) of *F outliers* (such that x is an *F outlier* with positive q-NSC and x_j is an *F outlier* in $\lambda_{C_{out,q}}(x)$) is less than the mean pairwise distance between an *F outlier* x and any existing class instance x_i. In other words, an *F outlier* with positive q-NSC is more likely to have its k-nearest neighbors (k-NN) within the *F outlier* instances (for $k \leq q$). So, each of the *F outliers* $x \in \mathcal{F}$ should have the same class label as the other *F outlier* instances, and should have a different class label than any of the existing classes. This implies that the *F outliers* should belong to a novel class. The higher the value of q, the larger the support we have in favor of the arrival of a new class. Furthermore, when all the classifiers unanimously agree on the arrival of a novel class, we have very little choice other than announcing the appearance of a novel class. The q-NH rule can be thought of a variation of the k-NN rule and is applicable to any dataset irrespective of its data distribution and shape of classes (e.g., convex and nonconvex).

11.3.4.2 Deviation between Approximate and Exact *q*-NSC Computation

As discussed earlier, we compute q-NSC for each *F pseudopoint*, rather than each *F outlier* individually in order to reduce time complexity. The resultant q-NSC is an approximation of the exact value. However, the following analysis shows that the deviation of the approximate value from exact value is negligible.

As shown in Figure 11.7 which illustrates the computation of deviation, ϕ_i is an *F pseudopoint*, that is, a cluster of *F outliers*, and ϕ_j is an existing class pseudopoint, that is, a cluster of existing class instances. In this particular example, all instances in ϕ_i belong to a novel class.

Without loss of generality, let ϕ_i be an *F pseudopoint* having weight q_1, and ϕ_j be an existing class pseudopoint having weight q_2, which is the closest existing class pseudopoint from ϕ_i. We compute q-$NSC'(\phi_i)$, the approximate q-NSC of ϕ_i using the following formula:

$$q\text{-NSC}'(\phi_i) = \frac{D(\mu_i, \mu_j) - \bar{D}_i}{\max(D(\mu_i, \mu_j), \bar{D}_i)} \tag{11.5}$$

where μ_i is the centroid of ϕ_i, μ_j is the centroid of ϕ_j, and $\bar{D}_i$ is the mean distance from centroid μ_i to the instances in ϕ_i. The exact value of q-NSC follows from Equation 11.3:

$$q\text{-NSC}(\phi_i) = \frac{1}{q_1} \sum_{x \in \phi_i} \frac{\frac{1}{q} \sum_{x_j \in \lambda_{c_{\min}, q}(x)} D(x, x_j) - \frac{1}{q} \sum_{x_i \in \lambda_{c_{out}, q}(x)} D(x, x_i)}{\max\left(\frac{1}{q} \sum_{x_j \in \lambda_{c_{\min}, q}(x)} D(x, x_j), \frac{1}{q} \sum_{x_i \in \lambda_{c_{out}, q}(x)} D(x, x_i)\right)} \tag{11.6}$$

where $\lambda_{c_{out},q}(x)$ is the set of q nearest neighbors of x within *F pseudopoint* ϕ_i, and $\lambda_{c_{min},q}(x)$ is the set of q nearest neighbors of x within pseudopoint ϕ_j, for some $x \in \phi_i$. Therefore, the deviation from the exact value, $\varepsilon_{qnsc} = q\text{-NSC}(\phi_i) - q\text{-NSC}'(\phi_i)$. Applying Equations 11.5 and 11.6,

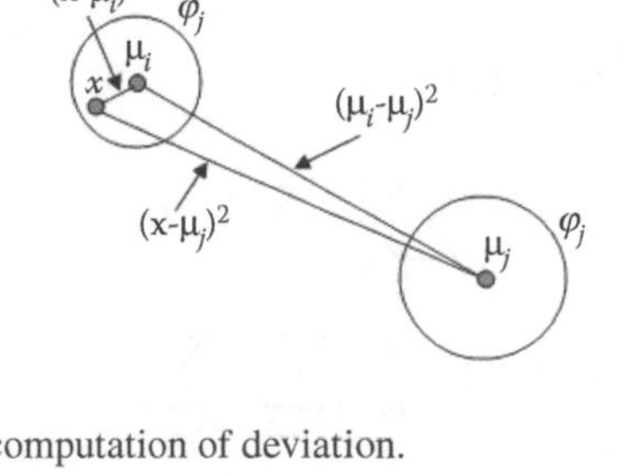

FIGURE 11.7 Illustration of the computation of deviation.

$$\mathcal{E}_{q\text{-NSC}} = \frac{1}{q_1}\sum_{x\in\phi_i} \frac{\frac{1}{q}\sum_{x_j\in\lambda_{c_{\min},q}(x)} D(x,x_j) - \frac{1}{q}\sum_{x_j\in\lambda_{c_{out},q}(x)} D(x,x_i)}{\max\left(\frac{1}{q}\sum_{x_j\in\lambda_{c_{\min},q}(x)} D(x,x_j), \frac{1}{q}\sum_{x_j\in\lambda_{c_{out},q}(x)} D(x,x_i)\right)} - \frac{D(\mu_i,\mu_j)-\bar{D}_i}{\max(D(\mu_i,\mu_j)-\bar{D}_i)} \tag{11.7}$$

In order to simplify the equations, we assume that $q_1 = q_2 = q$, and q-NSC is positive for any $x \in \phi_i$. Therefore, $\lambda_{c_{out},q}(x) = \phi_i$, $\lambda_{c_{min},q}(x) = \phi_j$. Also, we consider square of Eucledian distance as the distance metric, that is, $D(x, y) = (x - y)^2$. Since q-NSC is positive for any $x \in \phi_i$, we can deduce following relationships:

R_1: $\max(D(\mu_i,\mu_j),\bar{D}_i) = D(\mu_i,\mu_j)$—as the q-NSC for each $x \in \phi_i$ is positive, the overall q-NSC of ϕ_i (i.e., q-NSC$'(\phi_i)$) is also positive. Therefore, this relationship follows from Equation 11.5.

R_2: $\max\left(\frac{1}{q}\sum_{x_j\in\lambda_{c_{\min},q}(x)} D(x,x_j), \frac{1}{q}\sum_{x_j\in\lambda_{c_{out},q}(x)} D(x,x_i)\right) = \frac{1}{q}\sum_{x_j\in\lambda_{c_{\min},q}(x)} D(x,x_j)$, which follows, since the mean q-NSC of the instances in ϕ_i is positive.

Also, $\bar{D}_i = \frac{1}{q}\sum_{x\in\phi_i}(x-\mu_i)^2 = \sigma_i^2$, the mean distance of the instances in ϕ_i from the centroid. Therefore, q-NSC$'(\phi_i)$ can be rewritten as

$$\begin{aligned} q\text{-NSC}'(\phi_i) &= \frac{(\mu_i-\mu_j)^2-\sigma^2}{(\mu_i-\mu_j)^2} = \frac{1}{q}\sum_{x\in\phi_i}\frac{(\mu_i-\mu_j)^2-(x-\mu_i)^2}{(\mu_i-\mu_j)^2} \\ &= \frac{1}{q}\sum_{x\in\phi_i} q\text{-NSC}'(x) \end{aligned} \tag{11.8}$$

where q-NSC$'(x)$ is an approximate value of q-NSC(x). Now we can deduce the following inequalities:

I_1: $(x - \mu_i)^2 \le (\mu_i - \mu_j)^2$—since q-NSC$'(x)>0$ for all $x \in \phi_i$.
I_2: $\sigma_i^2 \le (\mu_i-\mu_j)^2$—from Equation 11.8, since q-NSC$'(\phi_i)>0$.
I_3: $(x - \mu_j)^2 \le (x - \mu_i)^2 + (\mu_i - \mu_j)^2$—by triangle inequality (see Figure 11.7)
I_4: $\sigma_j^2 \le (\mu_i-\mu_j)^2$—because ϕ_j represents an existing class, and similar inequality as I_2 is applicable to the instances of ϕ_j.

Continuing from Equation 11.7:

$$\begin{aligned} \mathcal{E}_{qnsc} &= \frac{1}{q}\sum_{x\in\phi_i}\frac{\frac{1}{q}\sum_{x_j\in\phi_j}(x-x_j)^2-\frac{1}{q}\sum_{x_j\in\phi_i}(x-x_i)^2}{\frac{1}{q}\sum_{x_j\in\phi_j}(x-x_j)^2} - \frac{(\mu_i-\mu_j)^2-\sigma_i^2}{(\mu_i-\mu_j)^2} \\ &= \frac{1}{q}\sum_{x\in\phi_i}\left(\frac{\frac{1}{q}\sum_{x_j\in\phi_j}(x-x_j)^2-\frac{1}{q}\sum_{x_j\in\phi_i}(x-x_i)^2}{\frac{1}{q}\sum_{x_j\in\phi_j}(x-x_j)^2} - \frac{(\mu_i-\mu_j)^2-(x-\mu_i)^2}{(\mu_i-\mu_j)^2}\right) \end{aligned}$$

It is easy to show that $\frac{1}{q}\sum_{x\in\phi_i}(x-x_i)^2-(x-u_i)^2=\sigma_i^2$ and $\frac{1}{q}\sum_{x\in\phi_j}(x-x_j)^2-(x-u_j)^2=\sigma_j^2$. Substituting these values, we obtain

$$\begin{aligned}
\mathcal{E}_{qnsc} &= \frac{1}{q}\sum_{x\in\phi_i}\left(\frac{\sigma_j^2+(x-\mu_j)^2-\sigma_i^2-(x-\mu_i)^2}{\sigma_j^2+(x-\mu_j)^2}-\frac{(\mu_i-\mu_j)^2-(x-\mu_i)^2}{(\mu_i-\mu_j)^2}\right)\\
&= \frac{1}{q}\sum_{x\in\phi_i}\left(1-\frac{\sigma_i^2+(x-\mu_i)^2}{\sigma_j^2+(x-\mu_j)^2}-1+\frac{(x-\mu_i)^2}{(\mu_i-\mu_j)^2}\right)\\
&= \frac{1}{q}\sum_{x\in\phi_i}\left(\frac{(x-\mu_i)^2}{(\mu_i-\mu_j)^2}-\frac{\sigma_i^2+(x-\mu_i)^2}{\sigma_j^2+(x-\mu_j)^2}\right)\\
&= \frac{\sigma_i^2}{(\mu_i-\mu_j)^2}-\frac{1}{q}\sum_{x\in\phi_i}\frac{\sigma_i^2}{\sigma_j^2+(x-\mu_j)^2}-\frac{1}{q}\frac{(x-\mu_i)^2}{\sigma_j^2+(x-\mu_j)^2}\\
&\le \frac{\sigma_i^2}{(\mu_i-\mu_j)^2}-\frac{\sigma_i^2}{\sigma_i^2+\sigma_j^2+(\mu_i-\mu_j)^2}-\frac{1}{q}\sum_{x\in\phi_i}\frac{(x-\mu_i)^2}{\sigma_j^2+(x-\mu_j)^2}
\end{aligned} \tag{11.9}$$

The last line follows since using the relationship between harmonic mean and arithmetic mean it can be shown that

$$\begin{aligned}
&\frac{1}{q}\sum_{x\in\phi_i}\frac{\sigma_i^2}{\sigma_j^2+(x-\mu_j)^2}\\
&\ge \frac{\sigma_i^2}{\frac{1}{q}\sum_{x\in\phi_i}(\sigma_j^2+(x-\mu_j)^2)}=\frac{\sigma_i^2}{\sigma_j^2+\frac{1}{q}\sum_{x\in\phi_i}(x-\mu_j)^2}=\frac{\sigma_i^2}{\sigma_j^2+\sigma_i^2+(\mu_i-\mu_j)^2}
\end{aligned}$$

Applying inequalities I_1–I_4, and after several algebraic manipulations, we obtain

$$\mathcal{E}_{qnsc}\le\frac{\sigma_i^2}{(\mu_i-\mu_j)^2}-\frac{\sigma_i^2}{3(\mu_i-\mu_j)^2}-\frac{\sigma_i^2}{3(\mu_i-\mu_j)^2}=\frac{\sigma_i^2}{3(\mu_i-\mu_j)^2} \tag{11.10}$$

Usually, if ϕ_i belongs to a novel class, it is empirically observed that q-NSC$'(\phi_i)\ge 0.9$. Putting this value in Equation 11.8 and solving, we obtain $\sigma_i^2\le(1-0.9)(\mu_i-\mu_j)^2$. Therefore, from Equation 11.10, we obtain $\varepsilon_{qnsc}\le 0.1/3\simeq 0.03$. Since the range of q-NSC is −1 to +1, a deviation of 0.03 (3%) from the exact value is really negligible, and does not affect the outcome of the algorithm. Similar reasoning can be carried out for the cases where q-NSC of the instances in ϕ_i is negative.

11.3.4.3 Time and Space Complexity

Line 1 of Algorithm 11.3 (clustering) takes $O(KS)$ time, and the for loop (lines 3–8) takes $O(K^2L)$ time. The overall time complexity of Algorithm 11.3 is $O(K^2L+KS)=O(KS)$, since $S\gg KL$. Lines 1–5 of Algorithm 11.2 takes $O(S(KL+Lf_c))$ per chunk, where f_c is the time to classify an instance using a classifier, and $O(KL)$ is the time to determine whether an instance is an *F outlier*. Line 6 takes $O(S)$ time. Line 11 (Algorithm 11.3) is executed at most once in every q time units. Therefore, the worst case complexity of lines 7–14 is $O((KS)*(S/q))$, where $O(KS)$ is the time required to execute line 11 (Algorithm 11.3). So, the overall complexity of Algorithm 11.1 is $O(S(KL+Lf_c+KSq^{-1}))$ per chunk. For most classifiers, $f_c=O(1)$. Also, let $S/q=m$. So, the overall complexity of algorithm becomes $O(KLS + LS + mS)$, since $m \gg KL$. Finally, the overall complexity of Algorithm 11.2 (ECSMiner) is $O(mS + f_t(S))$ per chunk, where $f_t(S)$ is the time to train a classifier with S training instances, and $m \ll S$.

ECSMiner keeps three buffers: *buf*, the training buffer $\mathcal{L}$, and the unlabeled data buffer U. Both *buf* and $\mathcal{L}$ hold at most S instances, whereas U holds at most T_l instances. Therefore, the space required to store all three buffers is $O(\max(S,T_l))$. The space required to store a classifier (along with the pseudopoints) is much $<S$. So, the overall space complexity remains $O(\max(S,T_l))$.

11.4 EXPERIMENTS

In this section, we describe the datasets, experimental environment, and discuss and analyze the results.

11.4.1 Datasets

11.4.1.1 Synthetic Data with only Concept Drift (SynC)

SynC simulates only concept drift, with no novel classes. This is done to show that concept drift does not erroneously trigger a new class detection in our approach. SynC data are generated with a moving hyperplane. The equation of a hyperplane is as follows: $\sum_{i=1}^{d} a_i x_i = a_0$. If $\sum_{i=1}^{d} a_i x_i \le a_0$, then an example is negative, otherwise it is positive. Each example is a randomly generated d-dimensional vector $\{x_1, \ldots, x_d\}$, where $x_i \in [0,1]$. Weights $\{a_1, \ldots, a_d\}$ are also randomly initialized with a real number in the range [0, 1]. The value of a_0 is adjusted so that roughly the same numbers of positive and negative examples are generated. This can be done by choosing $a_0 = \frac{1}{2}\sum_{i=1}^{d} a_i$. We also introduce noise randomly by switching the labels of p% of the examples, where $p = 5$ is set in our experiments.

There are several parameters that simulate concept drift. The parameter m specifies the percent of total dimensions whose weights are involved in changing, and it is set to 20%. The parameter t specifies the magnitude of the change in every N examples. In our experiments, t is set to 0.1, and N is set to 1000. s_i, $i \in \{1, \ldots, d\}$ specifies the direction of change for each weight. Weights change continuously, that is, a_i is adjusted by $s_i.t/N$ after each example is generated. There is a possibility of 10% that the change would reverse direction after every N examples are generated. We generate a total of 250,000 records.

11.4.1.2 Synthetic Data with Concept Drift and Novel Class (SynCN)

This synthetic data simulates both concept drift and novel class. Data points belonging to each class are generated using Gaussian distribution having different means (–5.0 to + 5.0) and variances (0.5–6) for different classes. Besides, in order to simulate the evolving nature of data streams, the probability distributions of different classes are varied with time. This caused some classes to appear and some other classes to disappear at different times. In order to introduce concept drift, the mean values of a certain percentage of attributes have been shifted at a constant rate. As done in the SynC dataset, this rate of change is also controlled by the parameters m, t, s, and N in a similar way. The dataset is normalized so that all attribute values fall within the range [0,1]. We generate the SynCN dataset with 20 classes and 40 real-valued attributes, having a total of 400K data points.

11.4.1.3 Real Data—KDDCup 99 Network Intrusion Detection (KDD)

We have used the 10% version of the dataset, which is more concentrated, hence more challenging than the full version. It contains around 490,000 instances. Here different classes appear and disappear frequently, making the new class detection challenging. This dataset contains TCP connection records extracted from LAN network traffic at MIT Lincoln Labs over a period of 2 weeks. Each record refers to either to a normal connection or an attack. There are 22 types of attacks, such as buffer-overflow, portsweep, guess-passwd, neptune, rootkit, smurf, spy, and so on. So, there are 23 different classes of data. Most of the data points belong to the normal class. Each record consists of 42 attributes, such as connection duration, the number bytes transmitted, number of root accesses, and so on. We use only the 34 continuous attributes and remove the categorical attributes. This dataset is also normalized to keep the attribute values within [0,1].

11.4.1.4 Real Data—Forest Covers Dataset from UCI Repository (Forest)

The dataset contains geospatial descriptions of different types of forests. It contains seven classes, 54 attributes and around 581,000 instances. We normalize the dataset and arrange the data so that in any chunk at most three and at least two classes co-occur, and new classes appear randomly.

11.4.2 Experimental Set-Up

We implemented our algorithm in Java. The code for decision tree has been adapted from the Weka machine learning open source repository (http://www.cs.waikato.ac.nz/ml/weka/). The experiments were run on an Intel P- IV machine with 2 GB memory and 3 GHz dual processor CPU. Our parameter settings are as follows, unless mentioned otherwise: (i) K (number of pseudopoints per classifier) = 50, (ii) q (minimum number of instances required to declare novel class) = 50, (iii) L (ensemble size) = 6, and (iv) S (chunk size) = 2000. These values of parameters are tuned to achieve an overall satisfactory performance.

11.4.3 Baseline Approach

To the best of our knowledge, there is no approach that can classify data streams and detect novel class. So, we compare ECSMiner with a combination of two baseline techniques: *OLI N DDA* [SPIN08] and weighted classifier ensemble (*WCE*) [WANG03], where the former works as novel class detector and the latter performs classification, respectively. This is done as follows. For each test instance, we delay its classification for *Tc* time units. That is, *OLI N DDA* is given *Tc* time units to determine whether the instance is novel. If by that time the test instance is identified as a novel class instance, then it is considered novel and not classified using *WCE*. Otherwise, the instance is assumed to be an existing class instance and its class is predicted using *WCE*. We use *OLI N DDA* as the novelty detector, since it is a recently proposed algorithm that is shown to have outperformed other novelty detection techniques in data streams [SPIN08].

However, *OLI N DDA* assumes that there is only one "normal" class, and all other classes are "novel." So, it is not directly applicable to the multiclass novelty detection problem, where any combination of classes can be considered as the "existing" classes. Therefore, we propose two alternative solutions. First, we build parallel *OLI N DDA* models, one for each class, which evolve simultaneously. Whenever the instances of a novel class appear, we create a new *OLI N DDA* model for that class. A test instance is declared as novel, if *all the existing class models* identify this instance as novel. We will refer to this baseline method as WCE-OLINDDA PARALLEL. Second, we initially build an *OLI N DDA* model using all the available classes with the first *init number* instances. Whenever a novel class is found, the class is absorbed into the existing *OLI N DDA* model. Thus, only one "normal" model is maintained throughout the stream. This will be referred to as WCE-OLINDDA SINGLE. In all experiments, the ensemble size and chunk size are kept the same for all three baseline techniques. Besides, the same base learner is used for *WCE* and ECSMiner. The parameter settings for *OLI N DDA* are (i) number of clusters built in the initial model, $K = 30$, (ii) least number of normal instances needed to update the existing model = 100, (iii) least number of instances needed to build the initial model = 100, and (iv) maximum size of the "unknown memory" = 200. These parameters are chosen either according to the default values used in [SPIN08] or by trial and error to get an overall satisfactory performance. *We will henceforth use the acronyms XM for ECSMiner, W-OP for WCE-OLINDDA PARALLEL and W-OS for WCE-OLINDDA SINGLE.*

11.4.4 Performance Study

11.4.4.1 Evaluation Approach

Let

- Fn = total novel class instances misclassified as existing class,
- Fp = total existing class instances misclassified as novel class,
- Fe = total existing class instances misclassified (other than Fp),
- Nc = total novel class instances in the stream, and
- N = total instances the stream.

We use the following performance metrics to evaluate our technique: M_{new} = % of novel class instances Misclassified as existing class, that is,

$$M_{new} = \frac{F_n \times 100}{N_c}$$

F_{new} = % of existing class instances Falsely identified as novel class, that is,

$$F_{new} = \frac{F_p \times 100}{N - N_c}$$

ERR = Total misclassification error (%)(including M_{new} and F_{new}), that is,

$$ERR = \frac{(F_p + F_n + F_e) * 100}{N}$$

From the definition of the error metrics, it is clear that ERR is not necessarily equal to the sum of M_{new} and F_{new}.

Evaluation is done as follows: we build the initial models in each method with the first *init number* instances. In our experiments, we set *init number* = 3S (first three chunks). From the fourth chunk onward, we evaluate the performances of each method on each data point using the time constraints. We update the models with a new chunk whenever all data points in that chunk are labeled.

11.4.4.2 Results

Figure 11.8a through c shows the total number of novel class instances missed (i.e., misclassified as existing class) and Figure 11.8d through f shows the overall error rates (ERR) of each of the techniques for decision tree classifier up to a certain point in the stream in different datasets. We omit SynC from the figures since it does not have any novel class. k-NN classifier also has similar results. For example, in Figure 11.8a at the *X*-axis = 100, the *Y* values show the total number of novel class instances missed by each approach in the first 100 K data points in the stream (Forest). At this point, XM misses only 15 novel class instances, whereas W-OP, and W-OS misses 1937, and 7053 instances, respectively. Total number of novel class instances appeared in the stream by this

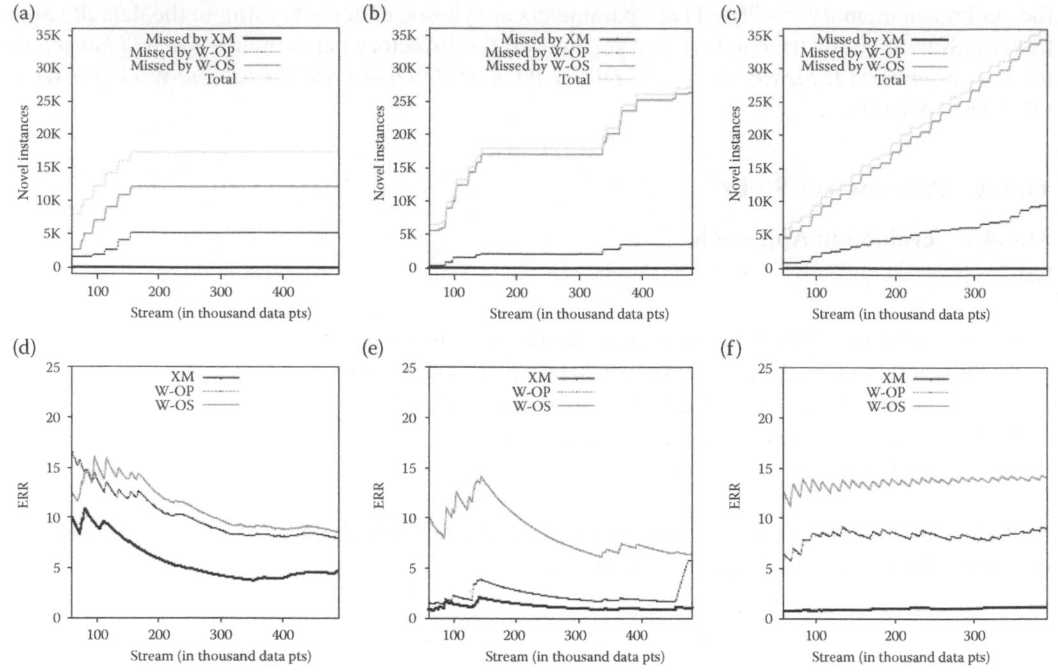

FIGURE 11.8 Novel class instances missed by each method (top row) and overall error of each method ($Tl = 1000$, $Tc = 400$) (bottom row).

point of time is shown by the corresponding Y value of the curve "Total," which is 12,226. Likewise, in Figure 11.8d, the ERR rates are shown throughout the stream history. In this figure, at the same position ($X = 100$), Y values show the ERR of each of the three techniques up to the first 100K data points in the stream. The ERR rates of XM, W-OP, and W-OS at this point are: 9.2%, 14.0%, and 15.5%, respectively.

Table 11.1 summarizes the error metrics for each of the techniques in each dataset for decision tree and KNN. The columns headed by ERR, M_{new}, and F_{new} report the value of the corresponding metric on an entire dataset. For example, while using decision tree in KDD dataset, XM, W-OP, and W-OS have 1.0%, 5.8%, and 6.7% ERR, respectively. Also, their corresponding M_{new} are 1.0%, 13.2%, and 96.9%, respectively. Note that there is no novel class in SynC, and so, there is no M_{new} for

TABLE 11.1
Performance Comparison in All Datasets

		ERR			M_{new}			F_{new}		
Classifier	**Dataset**	**XM**	**W-OP**	**W-OS**	**XM**	**W-OP**	**W-OS**	**XM**	**W-OP**	**W-OS**
Decision tree	SynC	**6.9**	14.1	12.8	–	–	–	**0.0**	2.4	1.1
	SynCN	**1.2**	8.9	13.9	**0.0**	26.5	96.2	**0.02**	1.6	0.1
	KDD	**1.0**	5.8	6.7	**1.0**	13.2	96.9	0.9	4.3	**0.03**
	Forest	**4.7**	7.9	8.5	**0.2**	30.7	70.1	3.0	1.1	**0.2**
k-NN	SynC	**0.0**	2.4	1.1	–	–	–	**0.0**	2.4	1.1
	SynCN	**0.01**	8.9	13.9	**0.0**	26.5	96.2	**0.0**	1.6	0.1
	KDD	**1.2**	4.9	5.2	**5.9**	12.9	96.5	0.9	4.4	**0.03**
	Forest	**3.6**	4.1	4.6	**8.4**	32.0	70.1	1.3	1.1	**0.2**

Note: Bold numbers in this table represent the best run times.

any approach. Both W-OP and W-OS have some F_{new} in SynC dataset, which appears since W-OP and W-OS are less sensitive to concept drift than XM. Therefore, some existing class instances are m is classified as novel class because of concept drift. In general, XM outperforms the baseline techniques in overall classification accuracy and novel class detection. The main reason behind the poorer performance of W-OP in detecting novel classes is the way OLINDDA detects novel class. OLINDDA makes two strong assumptions about a novel class and normal classes. First, it assumes a spherical boundary (or, convex shape) of the normal model. It updates the radius and centroid of the sphere periodically and declares anything outside the sphere as a novel class if there is evidence of sufficient cohesion among the instances outside the boundary. The assumption that a data class must have a convex/spherical shape is too strict to be maintained for a real-world problem. Second, it assumes that the data density of a novel class must be at least that of the normal class. If a novel class is sparser than the normal class, the instances of that class would never be recognized as a novel class. But in a real-world problem, two different classes may have different data densities. OLINDDA would fail in those cases where any of the assumptions are violated. On the other hand, XM does not require that an existing class must have convex shape, or that the data density of a novel class should match that of the existing classes. Therefore, XM can detect novel classes much more efficiently. Besides, OLINDDA is less sensitive to concept drift, which results in falsely declaring novel classes when drift occurs in the existing class data. On the other hand, XM correctly distinguishes between concept drift and concept evolution, avoiding false detection of novel classes in the event of concept drift. W-OS performs worse than W-OP since W-OS "assimilates" the novel classes into the normal model, making the normal model too generalized. Therefore, it considers most of the future novel classes as normal (nonnovel) data, yielding very high false negative rate.

Figure 11.9a and b shows how XM and W-OP respond to the constraints *Tl* and *Tc* in Forest dataset. Similar characteristics are observed for other datasets and W-OS. From Figure 11.9a, it is evident that increasing *Tl* increases error rates. This is because of the higher delay involved in labeling, which makes the newly trained models more outdated. Naturally, M_{new} rate decreases with increasing *Tc* as shown in Figure 11.9b because higher values of *Tc* means more time to detect novel classes. As a result, ERR rates also decreases.

Figure 11.10a through d illustrates how the error rates of XM change for different parameter settings on Forest dataset and decision tree classifier. These parameters have similar effects on other datasets, and k-NN classifier. Figure 11.10a shows the effect of chunk size on ERR, F_{new}, and M_{new} rates for default values of other parameters. We note that ERR and F_{new} rates decrease up to a certain point (2000) then increases. The initial decrement occurs because larger chunk size means more training data for the classifiers, which leads to lower error rates. However, if chunk size is increased

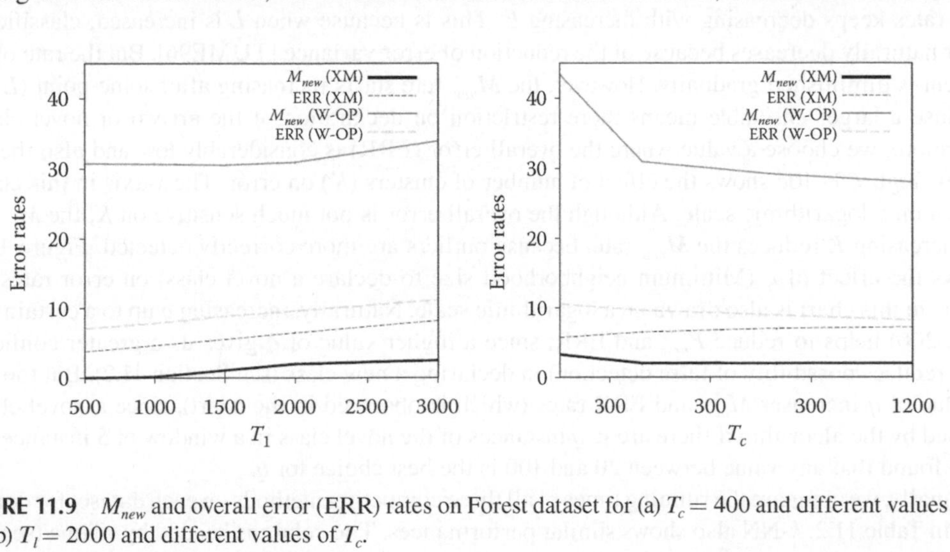

FIGURE 11.9 M_{new} and overall error (ERR) rates on Forest dataset for (a) $T_c = 400$ and different values of T_l and (b) $T_l = 2000$ and different values of T_c.

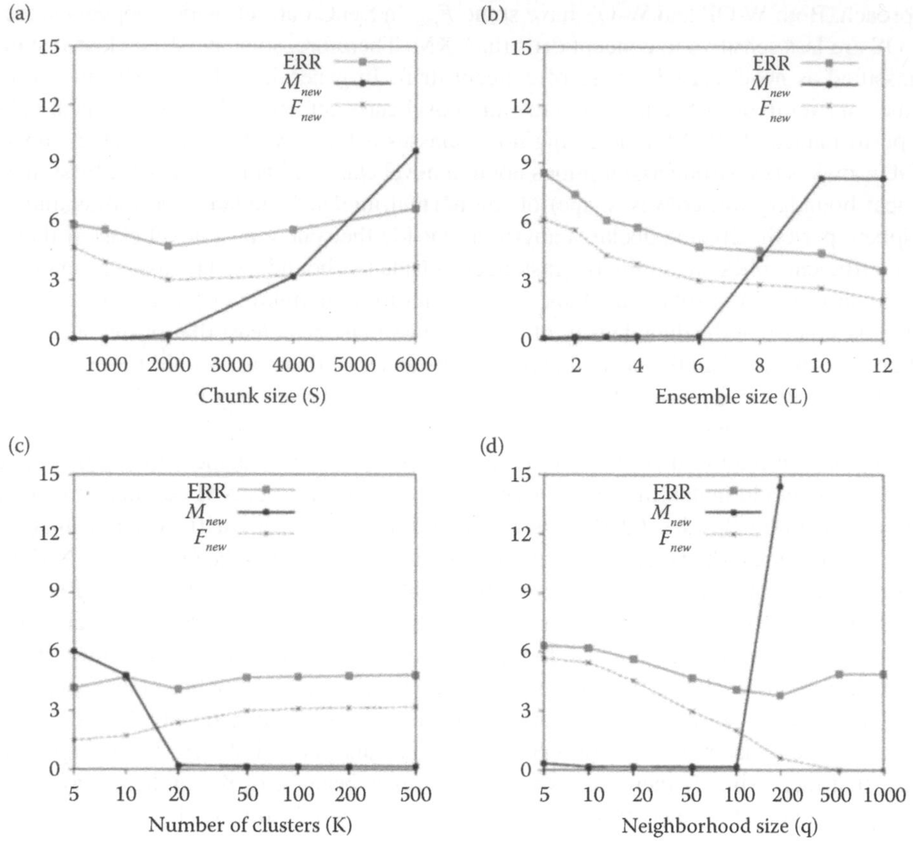

FIGURE 11.10 Parameter sensitivity.

too much, then we have to wait much longer to build the next classifier. As a result, the ensemble is updated less frequently than desired, meaning, the ensemble remains outdated for longer period of time. This causes increased error rates.

Figure 11.10b shows the effect of ensemble size (L) on error rates. We observe that the ERR and F_{new} rates keeps decreasing with increasing L. This is because when L is increased, classification error naturally decreases because of the reduction of error variance [TUME96]. But the rate of decrement is diminished gradually. However, the M_{new} rate starts increasing after some point ($L = 6$), because a larger ensemble means more restriction on declaration of the arrival of novel classes. Therefore, we choose a value where the overall error (ERR) is considerably low and also the M_{new} is low. Figure 11.10c shows the effect of number of clusters (K) on error. The x-axis in this chart is drawn on a logarithmic scale. Although the overall error is not much sensitive on K, the M_{new} rate is. Increasing K reduces the M_{new} rate, because outliers are more correctly detected. Figure 11.10d shows the effect of q (Minimum neighborhood size to declare a novel class) on error rates. The x-axis in this chart is also drawn on a logarithmic scale. Naturally, increasing q up to a certain point (e.g., 200) helps to reduce F_{new} and ERR, since a higher value of q gives us a greater confidence (i.e., reduces possibility of false detection) in declaring a new class (see Section 11.2). But too large a value of q increases M_{new} and ERR rates (which is observed in the chart), since a novel class is missed by the algorithm if there are $< q$ instances of the novel class in a window of S instances. We have found that any value between 20 and 100 is the best choice for q.

Finally, we compare the running times of all three competing methods on each dataset for decision tree in Table 11.2. k-NN also shows similar performances. The columns headed by "Time (sec)/1K"

TABLE 11.2
Running Time Comparison in All Datasets

	Time (second)/1K			Points/second			Speed Gain	
Dataset	**XM**	**W-OP**	**W-OS**	**XM**	**W-OP**	**W-OS**	**XM over W-OP**	**XM over W-OS**
SynC	0.33	0.41	**0.2**	2960	2,427	**5062**	**1.2**	0.6
SynCN	**1.7**	14.2	2.3	**605**	71	426	**8.5**	**1.4**
KDD	1.1	30.6	**0.5**	888	33	**1964**	**26.9**	0.45
Forest	0.93	8.3	**0.36**	1068	120	**2792**	**8.9**	0.4

Note: Bold numbers in this table represent the best run times.

show the average running times (train and test) in seconds per 1000 points, the columns headed by "Points/sec" show how many points have been processed (train and test) per second on average, and the columns headed by "speed gain" shows the ratio of the speed of XM to that of W-OP and W-OS, respectively.

For example, XM is 26.9 times faster than W-OP on KDD dataset. Also, XM is 1.2, 8.5, and 8.9 times faster than W-OP in SynC, SynCN, and Forest datasets, respectively.

In general, W-OP is roughly C times slower than XM in a dataset having C classes. This is because W-OP needs to maintain C parallel models, one for each class. Besides, *OLI N DDA* model creates cluster using the "unknown memory" every time a new instance is identified as unknown and tries to validate the clusters. As a result, the processing speed becomes diminished when novel classes occur frequently, as observed in KDD dataset. However, W-OS seems to run a bit faster than XM in three datasets, although W-OS shows much poorer performance in detecting novel classes and in overall error rates (see Table 11.1). For example, W-OS fails to detect 70% or more novel class instances in all datasets, but XM correctly detects 91% or more novel class instances in any dataset. Therefore, W-OS is virtually incomparable to XM for the novel class detection task. Thus, XM outperforms W-OP both in speed and accuracy and dominates W-OS in accuracy.

We also test the scalability of XM on higher dimensional data having larger number of classes. Figure 11.11 shows the results. The tests are done on synthetically generated data, having different dimensions (20–60) and number of classes (10–40). Each dataset has 250,000 instances. It is evident from the results that the time complexity of XM increases linearly with total number of dimensions in the data, as well as total number of classes in the data. Therefore, XM is scalable to high-dimensional data.

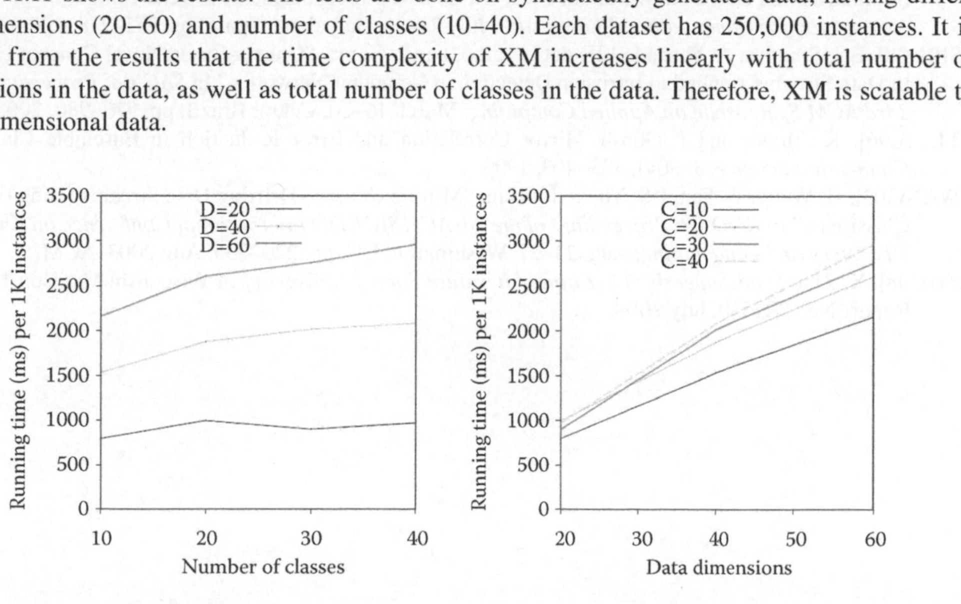

FIGURE 11.11 Scalability test.

11.5 SUMMARY AND DIRECTIONS

In this chapter, we have presented a novel technique to detect new classes in concept-drifting data streams. Most of the novelty detection techniques either assume that there is no concept drift or build a model for a single "normal" class and consider all other classes as novel. But our approach is capable of detecting novel classes in the presence of concept drift and even when the model consists of multiple "existing" classes. Besides, our novel class detection technique nonparametric, meaning, it does not assume any specific distribution of data. We also show empirically that our approach outperforms the state-of-the-art data stream based novelty detection techniques in both classification accuracy and processing speed. It might appear to readers that in order to detect novel classes we are in fact examining whether new clusters are being formed, and therefore, the detection process could go on without supervision. But supervision is necessary for classification. Without external supervision, two separate clusters could be regarded as two different classes, although they are not. Conversely, if more than one novel class appears in a chunk, all of them could be regarded as a single novel class if the labels of those instances are never revealed.

In the future, we would like to apply our technique in the domain of multiple-label instances. Some of our work toward this will be discussed in Chapter 12. Application to insider threat detection will be discussed in Section III.

REFERENCES

[COVE67]. T.M. Cover and P.E. Hart. Nearest Neighbor Pattern Classification. *IEEE Transactions on Information Theory*, 13 (1), 21–27, January 1967.

[MASU08]. M.M. Masud, J. Gao, L. Khan, J. Han, and B.M. Thuraisingham. "A Practical Approach to Classify Evolving Data Streams: Training with Limited Amount of Labeled Data," In *ICDM'08: Proceedings of the 2008 International Conference on Data Mining*, Dec. 15–19, Pisa, Italy, pp. 929–934, IEEE Computer Society, 2008.

[MASU09]. M.M. Masud, J. Gao, L. Khan, J. Han, and B.M. Thuraisingham. "Integrating Novel Class Detection with Classification for Concept-Drifting Datastreams," In *ECMLPKDD'09: Proceedings of the 2009 European Conference on Machine Learning and Principles and Practice in Knowledge Discovery in Databases*, II, September 7–11, Bled, Slovenia, pp. 79–94, Springer-Verlag, 2009.

[PANG04]. B. Pang and L. Lee. "A Sentimental Education: Sentiment Analysis using Subjectivity Summarization Based on Minimum Cuts," In *ACL'04:Proceedings of the 42nd Annual Meeting of the Association for Computational Linguistics*, July 21–26, Barcelona, Spain, pp. 271–278, 2004.

[SPIN08]. E.J. Spinosa, A. Poncede L.F. deCarvalho, and J. Gama. "Cluster-Based Novel Concept Detection in Data Streams Applied to Intrusion Detection in Computer Networks," In *SAC'08: Proceedings of the 23rd ACM Symposium on Applied Computing*, March 16–20, Ceara, Brazil, pp. 976–980, 2008.

[TUME96]. K. Tumer and J. Ghosh, "Error Correlation and Error Reduction in Ensemble Classifiers," *Connection Science*, 8 (304), 385–403, 1996.

[WANG03]. H. Wang, W. Fan, P.S. Yu, and J. Han, "Mining Concept-Drifting Data Streams Using Ensemble Classifiers," In *KDD'03: Proceedings of the 9th ACMSIGKDD International Conference on Knowledge Discovery and Data mining*, Aug. 24–27, Washington, DC, pp. 226–235, Aug 2003. ACM.

[ZHU08]. X. Zhu, *Semi-Supervised Learning Literature Survey*. University of Wisconsin Madison Technical Report No. TR1530, July 2008.

12 Data Stream Classification with Limited Labeled Training Data

12.1 INTRODUCTION

As stated in [MASU08], recent approaches in classifying evolving data streams are based on supervised learning algorithms, which can be trained with labeled data only. Manual labeling of data is both costly and time-consuming. Therefore, in a real-streaming environment, where huge volumes of data appear at a high speed, labeled data may be very scarce. Thus, only a limited amount of training data may be available for building the classification models, leading to poorly trained classifiers. We apply a novel technique to overcome this problem by building a classification model from a training set having both unlabeled and a small number of labeled instances. This model is built as microclusters using a semisupervised clustering technique and classification is performed with *k*-nearest neighbor algorithm. An ensemble of these models is used to classify the unlabeled data. Empirical evaluation on both synthetic data and real-botnet traffic reveals that our approach, using only a small amount of labeled data for training, outperforms state-of-the-art stream classification algorithms that use 20 times more labeled data than our approach. In this chapter, we describe our proposed solution for the limited labeled training data. It is based on our work discussed in [MASU08].

The organization of this chapter is as following. A description of our techniques is given in Section 12.2. Training with limited labeled data is discussed in Section 12.3. Ensemble classification is discussed in Section 12.4. Our experiments are discussed in Section 12.5. This chapter is summarized in Section 12.6.

12.2 DESCRIPTION OF REASC

ReaSC stands for Realistic Data Stream Classifier. Before describing ReaSC, we informally define the data stream classification problem. We assume that data arrive in chunks as follows:

$$D_1 = x_1, \ldots, x_S$$
$$D_2 = x_{S+1}, \ldots, x_{2S}$$
$$\vdots$$
$$D_n = x(n-1)S+1, \ldots, x_{nS}$$

where x_i is the *i*th instance in the stream, *S* is the chunk size, D_i is the *i*the data chunk, and D_n is the latest data chunk. Assuming that the class labels of all the instances in D_n are unknown, the problem is to predict their class labels. Let y_i and $\hat{y}_i$ be the actual and predicted class labels of x_i, respectively. If $\hat{y}_i = y_i$, then the prediction is correct, otherwise it is incorrect. The goal is to minimize the prediction error. Figure 12.1 shows the top level architecture of ReaSC.

We train a classification model from a data chunk D_i as soon as *P* % ($P \ll 100$) randomly chosen instances from the chunk have been correctly labeled by an independent labeling mechanism

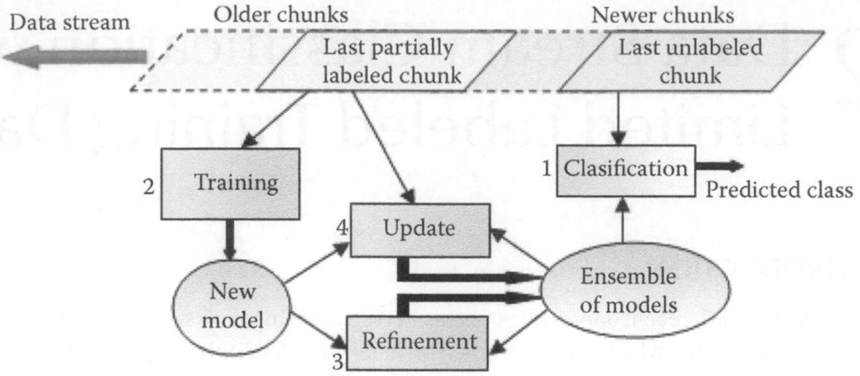

FIGURE 12.1 Overview of ReaSC.

(e.g., human experts). Note that this assumption is less strict than other stream classification techniques such as [WANG03] which assumes that all the instances of D_i must have been labeled before it can be used to train a model. We build the initial ensemble M of L models $= \{M_1, \ldots, M_L\}$ from the first L data chunks, where M_i is trained from chunk D_i. Then the following algorithm is applied for each of the following chunk.

Algorithm 12.1 ReaSC

Input: D_n: Latest datachunk
  M: current ensemble of L models$\{M_1, \ldots, M_L\}$
Output: Updated ensemble M
  1: **forall** $x_i \in D_n$ **do** $\hat{y}i \leftarrow$ **Classify** (M,x_i) (Section 12.3.1)
  /* Assuming that $P\%$ instances in D_n has now been labeled */
  2: $M' \leftarrow$ **Train** (D_n) (Section 12.2)/* Build a new model M' */
  3: $M \leftarrow$ **Refine-Ensemble** (M, M') (Section 12.3.2)
  4: $M \leftarrow$ **Update-Ensemble** (M, M', D_n) (Section 12.3.3)
  5: **return** M

The main steps of Algorithm 12.1 (ReaSC) are explained below.

1. *Classification*: The existing ensemble is used to predict the labels of each instance in Dn using nearest neighbor (NN) classification, and majority voting (Section 12.4.1). As soon as Dn has been partially labeled, the following steps are performed.
2. *Training*: Training is done by applying semisupervised clustering on the partially labeled training data to build K clusters (Section 12.3). The semisupervised clustering is based on the expectation-maximization (E-M) algorithm that locally minimizes an objective function. The objective function takes into account the dispersion between each point and its corresponding cluster centroid, as well as the impurity measure of each cluster. Then we extract a statistical summary from the data points of each cluster, save the summary as a microcluster, and remove the raw data points (Section 12.3.5). In this way, we get a new classification model M' that can be used to classify unlabeled data using the NN algorithm.
3. *Ensemble refinement*: In this step, M' is used to refine the existing ensemble of models if required (Section 12.4.2). Refinement is required if M' contains some data of a particular class c, but no model in the ensemble M contains any data of that class. This situation may occur because of concept evolution. In this case, the existing ensemble M does not have any

knowledge of class c, and so, it must be refined so that it learns to classify instances of this class. Refinement is done by injecting microclusters of M', which contain labeled instances of class c, into the existing models of the ensemble.

4. *Ensemble update*: In this step, we select the best L models from the $L + 1$ models: $\{M \cup M'\}$, based on their accuracies on the labeled instances of Dn (Section 12.3.3). These L best models construct the new ensemble M. The ensemble technique helps the system to cope with concept drift.

Table 12.1 illustrates a schematic example of ReaSC. In this example, we assume that $P\%$ data in data chunk D_i are labeled by the time chunk D_{i+1} arrives. The initial ensemble is built with the first L chunks. Then the ensemble is used to classify the latest chunk (D_{L+1}). From the next (L + 2nd) chunk onward, a sequence of operations is performed with the arrival of a new chunk. For example, the sequence of operations at the arrival of chunk D_{L+i} ($i > 1$) is as follows:

1. The previous chunk D_{L+i-1} has been partially labeled by now. Train a new model M' using D_{L+i-1}.
2. Refine the existing ensemble M using the new model M'.
3. Update the ensemble M by choosing the best L models from $M \cup M'$.
4. Classify each instance in D_{L+i} using ensemble M.

TABLE 12.1
An Example of ReaSC Actions with Stream Progression

Stream Progression	
Arrival of Chunk	**Action(s)**
D_1	—
D_2	$M_1 \leftarrow$ Train(D_1)
…	…
…	…
D_{L+1}	$D_L \leftarrow$ Train(D_L), Initial model $M = \{M_1, \ldots, M_L\}$ $\forall x_j \in DL + 1\hat{y}_j \leftarrow$ Classifiy (M, x_j)
D_{L+2}	$M' \leftarrow$ Train($D_L + 1$) $M \leftarrow$ Refine-Ensemble (M, M') $M \leftarrow$ Update-Ensemble (M, M', D_{L+1}) $\forall x_j \in D_L + 2\hat{y}_j \leftarrow$ Classifiy(M,x_j)
…	…
…	…
D_{L+i}	$M' \leftarrow$ Train(D_{L+i-1}) $M \leftarrow$ Refine-Ensemble (M, M') $M \leftarrow$ Update-Ensemble (M, M', D_{L+i-1}) $\forall x_j \in D_L + i \ldots \hat{y}_j \leftarrow$ Classifiy(M,x_j)
…	…

12.3 TRAINING WITH LIMITED LABELED DATA

12.3.1 Problem Description

As mentioned earlier, we train a classification model from each partially labeled data chunk. The classification model is a collection of *K* microclusters obtained using semisupervised clustering. Training consists of two basic steps: semisupervised clustering and storing the cluster summaries as microclusters.

In the semisupervised clustering problem, we are given a set of *m* data points

$$\mathcal{X} = \{x_1,\ldots,x_l,x_{l+1},\ldots,x_m\},$$

where the first *l* instances are labeled, that is, $y_i \in \{1, \ldots, C\}$, $i \leq l$, and the remaining instances are unlabeled; *C* being the total number of classes. We assign the class label $y_i = 0$ for all unlabeled instance x_i, $i > l$. We are to create *K* clusters maintaining the constraint that all points in the same cluster have the same class label. We restrict the value of parameter *K* to be greater than *C* since intuitively there should be at least one cluster for each class of data. We will first reexamine the unsupervised *K*-means clustering in Section 12.3.2 and then propose a new semisupervised clustering technique using cluster-impurity minimization in Section 12.3.3.

12.3.2 Unsupervised *K*-Means Clustering

The unsupervised *K*-means clustering creates *K*-partitions of the data points based on the only available information, the similarity/dispersion measure among the data points. The objective is to minimize the sum of dispersion between each data point and its corresponding cluster centroid (i.e., intracluster dispersion). Given *m* unlabeled data points $X = \{x_1, x_2, \ldots, x_m\}$, *K*-means creates *K*-partitions $\{X_1, \ldots, X_K\}$ of *X*, minimizing the objective function:

$$K_{\text{means}} = \sum_{i=1}^{K} \sum_{x \in \mathcal{X}_i} \| x - u_i \|^2 \tag{12.1}$$

where u_i is the centroid of cluster *i*, and $\|x - u_i\|$ is the Eucledian distance between *x* and u_i.

12.3.3 *K*-Means Clustering with Cluster-Impurity Minimization

Given a limited amount of labeled data, the goal for *K*-means with minimization of cluster impurity (MCI-K means) is to minimize the intracluster dispersion (same as unsupervised *K*-means) and at the same time minimize the impurity of each cluster. A cluster is completely pure if it contains only unlabeled instances, or labeled instances from only one class. Thus, the objective function should penalize each cluster for being impure. The general form of the objective function is as follows:

$$\text{MCI-}K_{\text{means}} = \sum_{i=1}^{K} \sum_{x \in \mathcal{X}_i} \| x - u_i \|^2 + \sum_{i=1}^{K} \mathcal{W}_i * Imp_i \tag{12.2}$$

where $\mathcal{W}_i$ is the weight associated with cluster *i* and Imp_i is the impurity of cluster.

In order to ensure that both the intracluster dispersion and cluster impurity are given the same importance, the weight associated with each cluster should be adjusted properly. Besides, we would want to penalize each data point that contributes to the impurity of the cluster. So, the weight associated with each cluster is chosen to be

$$\mathcal{W}_i = |\mathcal{L}_i| * \bar{D}_{\mathcal{L}_i} \tag{12.3}$$

where $\mathcal{W}_i$ is the set of data points in cluster i and DL_i is the average dispersion of each of these points from the cluster centroid. Thus, each instance has a contribution to the total penalty, which is equal to the cluster impurity multiplied by the average dispersion of the data points from the centroid. We observe that Equation 12.3 is equivalent to the sum of dispersions of all the instances from the cluster centroid. That is, we may rewrite Equation 12.3 as

$$\mathcal{W}_i = \sum_{x \in \mathcal{X}_i} \|x - u_i\|^2$$

Substituting this value of $\mathcal{W}_i$ in Equation 12.2 we obtain

$$\begin{aligned} \text{MCI-}K \text{ means} &= \sum_{i=1}^{K} \sum_{x \in \mathcal{X}_i} \| x - u_i \|^2 + \sum_{i=1}^{K} \sum_{x \in \mathcal{X}_i} \| x - u_i \|^2 * Imp_i \\ &= \sum_{i=1}^{K} \left(\sum_{x \in \mathcal{X}_i} \| x - u_i \|^2 + (1 + Imp_i) \right) \end{aligned} \tag{12.4}$$

Impurity measures: Equation 12.4 should be applicable to any impurity measure in general. Entropy and Gini index are most commonly used impurity measures. We use the following impurity measure: $Imp_i = ADC_i * Ent_i$, where ADC_i is the "aggregated dissimilarity count" of cluster i and Ent_i is the entropy of cluster i. The reason for using this impurity measure will be explained shortly. In order to understand ADC_i, we first need to define "Dissimilarity count."

Definition 12.1 (Dissimilarity Count)

Dissimilarity count $DC_i(x, y)$ of a data point x in cluster i having class label y is the total number of instances in that cluster having class label other than y.

In other words,

$$\mathcal{DC}_i(x, y) = |\mathcal{X}_i| - |\mathcal{X}_i(y)| \tag{12.5}$$

where $X_i(y)$ is the set of instances in cluster i having class label = y. Recall that unlabeled instances are assumed to have class label = 0. Note that $DC_i(x, y)$ can be computed in constant time, if we keep an integer vector to store the counts $|\chi_i(c)|$, $c \in \{0, 1, \ldots, C\}$. "Aggregated dissimilarity count" or ADC_i is the sum of the dissimilarity counts of all the points in cluster i:

$$\mathcal{ADC}_i = \sum_{x \in \mathcal{X}_i} DC_i(x, y). \tag{12.6}$$

The entropy of a cluster i is computed as

$$Ent_i = \sum_{c=0}^{C} \left(-p_c^i * \log\left(p_c^i\right)\right)$$

where p_c^i is the prior probability of class c, that is,

$$p_c^i = \frac{|\mathcal{X}_i(c)|}{|\mathcal{X}_i|}. \tag{12.7}$$

The use of Ent_i in the objective function ensures that clusters with higher entropy get higher penalties. However, if only Ent_i had been used as the impurity measure, then each point in the same cluster would have received the same penalty. But we would like to favor the points belonging to the majority class in a cluster, and disfavor the points belonging to the minority classes. Doing so would force more points of the majority class to be moved into the cluster, and more points of the minority classes to be moved out of the cluster, thus making the clusters purer. This is ensured by introducing ADC_i to the equation. We call the combination of ADC_i and Ent_i as "compound impurity measure" since it can be shown that ADC_i is proportional to the "gini index" of cluster i. Following from Equation 12.6, we obtain

$$\begin{aligned}
\mathcal{ADC}_i &= \sum_{x \in \mathcal{X}_i} DC_i(x,y) = \sum_{c=0}^{C} \sum_{x \in \mathcal{X}_i(x)} DC_i(x,y) \\
&= \sum_{c=0}^{C} \sum_{x \in \mathcal{X}_i(x)} (|\mathcal{X}_i| - |\mathcal{X}_i(x)|, \quad \text{(using Equation 12.5)} \\
&= \sum_{c=0}^{C} (|\mathcal{X}_i(c)|)(|\mathcal{X}_i| - |\mathcal{X}_i(c)|) = (|\mathcal{X}_i|)^2 \sum_{c=0}^{C} \left(\frac{\mathcal{X}_i(c)}{\mathcal{X}_i}\right)\left(1 - \frac{\mathcal{X}_i(c)}{\mathcal{X}_i}\right) \\
&= (|\mathcal{X}_i|)^2 \sum_{c=0}^{C} \left(p_c^i\right)\left(1 - p_c^i\right) \quad \text{(using Equation 12.7)} \\
&= (|\mathcal{X}_i|)^2 \left(1 - \sum_{c=0}^{C} \left(p_c^i\right)^2\right) = (|\mathcal{X}_i|)^2 * Gini_i
\end{aligned}$$

where $Gini_i$ is the gini index of cluster i.

12.3.4 Optimizing the Objective Function with Expectation Maximization (E-M)

The problem of minimizing Equation 12.4 is an *incomplete-data problem* because the cluster labels and the centroids are all unknown. The common solution to this problem is to apply E-M [DEMP77]. The E-M algorithm consists of three basic steps: initialization, E-step, and M-step. Each of them is discussed here.

Initialization with proportionate $k_c = K^*(|\mathcal{L}(c)|)/(|\mathcal{L}|)$, $c \in \{1, \ldots, C\}$ *cluster distribution*: For each class c appearing in the data, we initialize $k_c \leq K$ centroids by choosing k_c points from the labeled data of class c. The ratio of k_c to K is chosen to be equal to the ratio of the number of labeled points having class label c to the total number of labeled points in the dataset. That is,

$$k_c = K\frac{|\mathcal{L}(c)|}{|\mathcal{L}|}, c \in \{1,\ldots,C\},$$

where $\mathcal{L}$ is the set of all labeled points in X, and $\mathcal{L}(c)$ is the subset of points in $\mathcal{L}$ belonging to class c. We observed in our experiments that this initialization works better than initializing equal number of centroids of each class. This is because if we initialize the same number of centroids from each class, then larger classes (i.e., classes having more instances) tend to create larger and sparser clusters, which leads to poorer classification accuracy for the nearest neighbor classification.

Let there be η_c labeled points of class c in the dataset. If $\eta c > k_c$, then we choose k_c centroids from η_c points using the farthest-first traversal heuristic [HOCH85]. To apply this heuristic, we first initialize a "visited set" of points with a randomly chosen point having class label c. At each iteration, we find a point x_j of class c that maximizes the minimum distance from all points in the visited set, and add it to the visited set. This process continues until we have k_c points in the set. If $\eta_c < k_c$, then we choose remaining centroids randomly from the unlabeled points. After initialization, E-step and M-step are iterated until the convergence condition is fulfilled.

E-Step: In E-step, we assign each data point x to a cluster i such that its contribution to the global objective function, $k_{MCI\,Keans}(x)$, is minimized:

$$\mathcal{O}_{MCIKeans}(x) = \| x - u_i \|^2 * (1 + Ent_i * \mathcal{DC}_i(x, y)) \tag{12.8}$$

Note that the value of the global objective function $\mathcal{O}_{MCI\,Keans}$ depends on the order in which the labeled points are assigned to clusters. It is computationally intractable to try all possible orderings and choose the best one. However, there are some heuristic approaches that approximate the optimal solution. We follow the *iterative conditional mode* or ICM algorithm [BESA86]. This is implemented as follows: at each iteration of ICM, we first randomly order the points. Then we assign the points (in that order) to the cluster i that minimizes $\mathcal{O}_{MCI\,Keans}(x)$. This is continued until no point changes its cluster in successive iterations, which indicates convergence. According to [BESA86], ICM is guaranteed to converge. The E-step completes after termination of ICM, and the program moves to the M-step.

M-Step: In the M-Step, we recompute each cluster centroid by averaging all the points in that cluster:

$$u_i = \frac{\sum_{x \in \mathcal{X}_i} x}{|\mathcal{X}_i|} \tag{12.9}$$

After performing this step, the convergence condition is checked. If fulfilled, the procedure terminates, otherwise another iteration of E-step and M-step is performed.

12.3.5 Storing the Classification Model

After building the K clusters, we create a summary of the statistics of the data points belonging to each cluster. The summary contains the following statistics: (i) N: the total number of points; (ii) L_t: the total number of labeled points; (iii) $\{Lp[c]\}_{c=1}^{C}$: a vector containing the total number of labeled points belonging to each class; (iv) u: the centroid of the cluster; and (v) $\{Sum[r]\}_{r=1}^{d}$: the majority class, that is, the class having the highest frequency in the microcluster.

This summary will be referred to henceforth as a "microcluster." Note that with these statistics, the additive property of microclusters [AGGA06] remains valid. This property is essential for merging two microclusters. After creating the microclusters, we discard the raw data points. Besides, we also discard all microclusters that do not contain any labeled point (i.e., have $L_t = 0$) because these microclusters do not play any role in classification. The remaining set of microclusters serves as a classification model. Note that the number of microclusters in the model will become less than K if any such deletions take place.

12.4 ENSEMBLE CLASSIFICATION

12.4.1 Classification Overview

The ensemble consists of L models, where each model is trained with a partially labeled data chunk according to Section 12.3. The initial ensemble consists of the first L models trained with the first L chunks in the stream. The ensemble is used to classify future unlabeled instances. Besides, the ensemble undergoes several modifications in each successive chunk to keep it up-to-date with the most recent concept.

Classification is done using nearest neighbor technique. In order to classify an unlabeled data point $\boldsymbol{x}$ with a model M_i, we perform the following steps: (i) find the nearest microcluster from $\boldsymbol{x}$ in M_i, by computing the distance between the point and the centroids of the microclusters. (ii) Select the class with the highest frequency of labeled instances as the predicted class of x. Recall that the frequencies of labeled instances for each class are stored in the microcluster data structure. In order to classify x with the *ensemble M*, we perform the following steps: (i) find the nearest microcluster from $\boldsymbol{x}$ in each model $M_i \in M$. Let the nearest microcluster from $\boldsymbol{x}$ in M_i be m_i. (ii) Select the class with the highest "cumulative frequency" in these L microclusters $\{m_1, \ldots, m_L\}$ as the predicted class of $\boldsymbol{x}$. The classification by the ensemble can be thought of a kind of majority voting among all the voters (i.e., labeled points) in the L nearest microclusters $\{m_1, \ldots, m_L\}$.

As an example, suppose there are three models (M_1, M_2, M_3) in the ensemble (i.e., $L = 3$), and $C = 2$. The nearest microclusters from the test point $\boldsymbol{x}$ in M_1, M_2 and M_3 have the following class frequencies, respectively: [1,5], [3,1], and [0,3], where the first number in each pair represents the frequency of class $c = 1$, and the second number represents the frequency of class $c = 2$. Since the class-wise cumulative frequencies of the three microclusters are $[1 + 3 + 0{,}5 + 1 + 3] = [4{,}9]$, the predicted label of $\boldsymbol{x}$ by the ensemble M will be $\hat{y} = 2$.

12.4.2 Ensemble Refinement

After a new model M' has been trained with a partially labeled data chunk, the existing ensemble M is refined with this model (line 3, Algorithm 12.1). Refinement is done if the latest partially labeled data chunk D_n contains a class c, which is absent in all models of the ensemble M. This is possible if either a completely new class appears in the stream or an old class reappears that has been absent in the stream for a long time. Both of these happen because of concept evolution, and the class c is denoted as an *evolved class*. Note that there may be more than one evolved classes in the stream. If there is any evolved class, M must be refined so that it can correctly classify future instances of that class. Algorithm 12.2 describes how the existing model is refined.

Algorithm 12.2 Refine-Ensemble

Input: M: current ensemble of L models $\{M_1, \ldots, M_L\}$
M': the new model built from the new data chunk D_n
Output: Refine densemble M
1: **if Need-to-refine**(M) = false **then return** M
2: **for** each microcluster $m \in M'$ **do**
3: **if** the majority class of M' is an evolved class **then**
4: **for** each Model $M_i \in M$ **do**
5: $Q \leftarrow$ The closest pair of microclusters in M_i having the same majority class

6: **if** $Q \neq null$ **and** $||M_i|| = K$ **then** Merge the pair of microclusters in Q
7: $M_i \leftarrow M_i \cup m$/*Injection*/
8: **end for**
9: **end if**
10: **end for**
11: **return** M

Description of Refine-Ensemble (Algorithm 12.2): The algorithm starts (line 1) by checking whether ensemble refinement is needed. This can be done in constant time by keeping a Boolean vector V of size C per model, and setting $V[c] = true$ during training if there is any labeled training instance from class c. The function Need-to-refine (M) checks whether there is any class c such that $V[c]$ is false for all models $M_i \in M$, but true for M'. If there is such a class c, then c is an evolved class. Refinement is needed only if there is an evolved class. Then the algorithm looks into each microcluster m of the new model M' (line 2). If the majority class of m is an evolved class (line 3), then we do the following: for each model $M_i \in M$, we inject the microcluster m in M_i (line 7). Before injecting a microcluster, we try to merge the closest pair of microclusters in M_i having the same majority class (line 6). This is done to keep the number of microclusters constant ($=K$). However, merging is done only if such a closet pair is found, and $|M_i|$, the total number of microclusters in M_i equals K. Note that the first condition may occur (i.e., no such closest pair found) if $|M_i| < C$. In this case, $|M_i|$ is incremented after the injection. This ensures that if C, the number of classes, increases due to concept evolution, the number of microclusters in each model also increases. In the extreme case (not shown in the algorithm) when C exceeds K due to evolution, K is also incremented to ensure that the relation $K > C$ remains valid. The reasoning behind the refinement is as follows. Since no model in ensemble M has knowledge of an evolved class c, the models will certainly misclassify any data belonging to the class. By injecting microclusters of the class c, we introduce some data from this class into the models, which reduces their misclassification rate. Figure 12.2 illustrates the ensemble

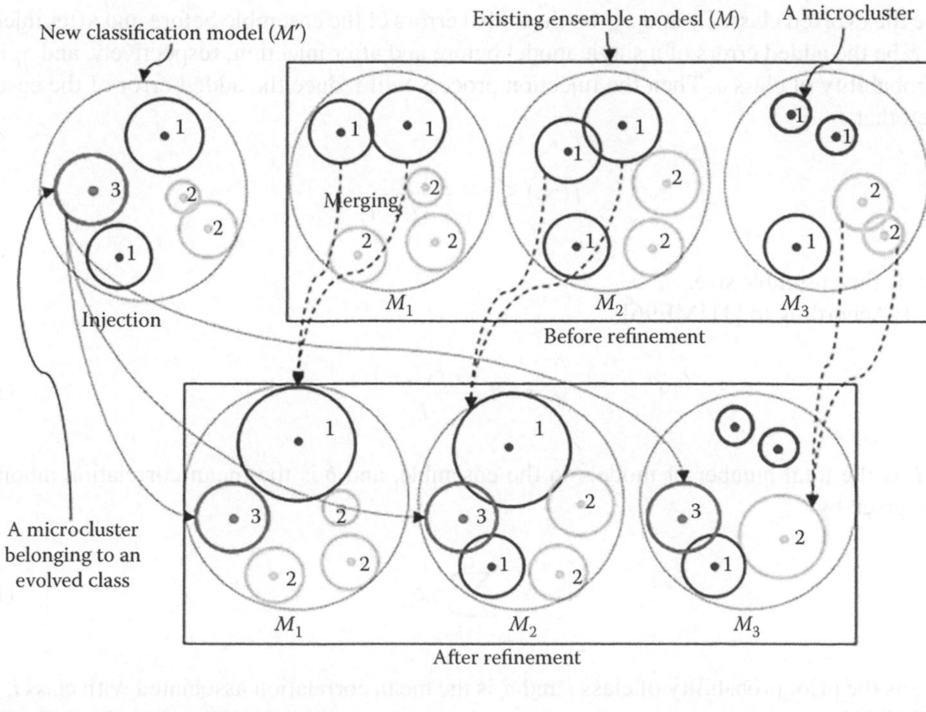

FIGURE 12.2 The ensemble refinement operation.

refinement process. The existing ensemble M consists of three models = $\{M_1, M_2, M_3\}$. The circles inside each model represent the microclusters. The numbers inside each microcluster represent the class label of its majority class. None of the existing models contains any microcluster of class 3, but the new model M' has such a microcluster. Therefore, class 3 is an evolved class. All microclusters belonging to class 3 are injected into the existing models. In order to keep the total number of clusters constant, two nearest (same class) microclusters in each model are merged before the injection.

It is obvious that when more training instances are provided to a model, its classification error is more likely to reduce. However, if the same set of microclusters are injected in all the models, the correlation among the models may increase, resulting in reduced prediction accuracy of the *ensemble*. According to [TUME96], if the errors of the models in an L-model ensemble are independent, then the added error (i.e., the error in addition to Bayes error) of the ensemble is $1/L$ times the added error of a single model. However, the ensemble error may be higher if there is correlation among the errors of the models. But even if correlation is introduced by injecting the microclusters, according to Lemma 12.1, under certain conditions the overall added error of the ensemble is reduced after injection. The lemma is based on the assumption that after injection, single model error monotonically decreases with increasing prior probability of class c. In other words, we assume that there is a continuous monotonic decreasing function $f(x)$, $f(x) \in [0, 1]$ and $x \in [0, 1]$, such that

$$\mathcal{E} = f(\gamma c) * \mathcal{E}^0 \tag{12.11}$$

where $\mathcal{E}^0$ and $\mathcal{E}$ are the single model errors before and after injection, respectively, and γc is the prior probability of class c. This function has the following special property: $f(0) = 1$, since $\gamma c = 0$ means class c has not appeared at all, and no injection has been made. Lemma 12.1 quantifies an upper bound of the function, that is, necessary for ensemble error reduction.

***Lemma 12.1*:**

Let c be the evolved class, $\mathcal{E}_M^0$ and $\mathcal{E}_M$ be the added errors of the ensemble before and after injection; $\mathcal{E}^0$ and $\mathcal{E}$ be the added errors of a single model before and after injection, respectively, and γ_c be the prior probability of class c. Then the injection process will reduce the added error of the ensemble provided that

$$f(\gamma_c) \le \frac{1}{1+\gamma_c^2(L-1)}$$

where L is the ensemble size.

Proof: According to [TUME96],

$$\mathcal{E}_M = \mathcal{E} * \frac{1+\delta(L-1)}{L} \tag{12.12}$$

where L is the total number of models in the ensemble, and δ is the mean correlation among the models, given by

$$\delta = \sum_{i=1}^{C} \gamma_i \delta_i \tag{12.13}$$

where γ_i is the prior probability of class i and δ_i is the mean correlation associated with class i, given by [TUME96]

$$\delta_i = \frac{1}{L(L-1)} \sum_{m=1}^{L} \sum_{l \neq m} \mathrm{Corr}\left(\eta_i^m, \eta_i^l\right) \tag{12.14}$$

where $\mathrm{Corr}\left(\eta_i^m, \eta_i^l\right)$ is the correlation between η_i^m, the error of model m, and η_i^l, the error of model l. For simplicity, we assume that the correlation between two models is proportional to the number of instances that are common to both these models. That is, the correlation is 1 if they have all instances in common, and 0 if they have no instances in common. So, before injection, the correlation between any pair of models is zero (since the models are trained using disjoint training data). As a result

$$\mathcal{E}_M^0 = \frac{\mathcal{E}^0}{L} \tag{12.15}$$

After injection, some instances of class c may be common among a pair of models, leading to $\delta_c \geq 0$, where c is the evolved class.

Consider a pair of models m and l whose prior probabilities of class c are γ_c^m and γ_c^l, respectively, after injection. So, the correlation between m and l reduces to

$$\mathrm{Corr}\left(\eta_c^m, \eta_c^l\right) = \frac{1}{2}\left(\gamma_c^m + \gamma_c^l\right),$$

Substituting this value in Equation 12.14, we obtain

$$\begin{aligned}\delta_c &= \frac{1}{L(L-1)} \frac{1}{2} \sum_{m=1}^{L} \sum_{l \neq m} \left(\gamma_c^m + \gamma_c^l\right) \\ &= \frac{1}{L(L-1)} \frac{1}{2} 2(L-1) \sum_{m=1}^{L} (\gamma_c^m) = \frac{1}{L} \sum_{m=1}^{L} (\gamma_c^m) = \bar{\gamma}_c\end{aligned} \tag{12.16}$$

where $\bar{\gamma}_c$ is the mean prior probability of class c in each model. Note that the mean prior probability $\bar{\gamma}_c$ represents the actual prior probability γc, so they can be used interchangeably. Substituting this value of δ_i in Equation 12.13,

$$\delta = \sum_{i=1}^{C} \gamma_i \delta_i = \gamma_c \delta_c + \sum_{i=1, i \neq c}^{C} \gamma_i \delta_i = (\gamma_c)^2 + 0 = (\gamma_c)^2$$

since $\delta_i = 0$ for all nonevolved class as no instance of those classes is common between any pair of models. Now, substituting this value of δ in Equation 12.12, we obtain

$$\begin{aligned}\mathcal{E}_M &= \mathcal{E} * \frac{1 + \gamma_c^2 (L-1)}{L} \\ &= f(\gamma_c) * \mathcal{E}^0 * \frac{1 + \gamma_c^2 (L-1)}{L} \quad \text{using Equation 12.11} \\ &= \frac{\mathcal{E}^0}{L} * \left(f(\gamma_c) * \left(1 + \gamma_c^2 (L-1)\right)\right) \\ &= \mathcal{E}_M^0 * \left(f(\gamma_c) * \left(1 + \gamma_c^2 (L-1)\right)\right) \quad \text{using Equation 12.15}\end{aligned} \tag{12.17}$$

Now, we will have an error reduction provided that $\mathcal{E}_M \leq \mathcal{E}_M^0$, which leads to

$$(f(\gamma_c)*\left(1+\gamma_c^2(L-1)\right)\leq 1$$

$$f(\gamma_c)\leq\frac{1}{1+\gamma_c^2(L-1)}$$

From Lemma 12.1, we can infer that the function $f(\cdot)$ becomes more restricted as the value of γ_c and/or L are increased. For example, for $\gamma_c = 0.5$, if $L = 10$, then $f(\gamma_c)$ must be ≤ 0.31, meaning, $\mathcal{E} \leq 0.31*\mathcal{E}_0$ is required for error reduction. For the same value of γ_c, if $L = 2$, then $\mathcal{E} \leq 0.8*\mathcal{E}_0$ is required for error reduction. However, in our experiments, we have always observed error reduction after injection, that is, inequality (12.17) has always been satisfied. Still, we recommend that the value of L be kept within 10 for minimizing the risk of violating inequality (12.17). ■

12.4.3 Ensemble Update

After the refinement, the ensemble is updated to adapt to the concept drift in the stream. This is done as follows. We have now $L + 1$ models: L models from the ensemble and the newly trained model M'. One of these $L + 1$ models is discarded, and the rest of them construct the new ensemble. The victim is chosen by evaluating the accuracy of each of these $L + 1$ models on the labeled instances in the training data D_n. The model having the worst accuracy is discarded.

12.4.4 Time Complexity

The ensemble training process consists of three main steps: (1) creating clusters using E–M; (2) refining the ensemble; and (3) updating the ensemble. Step (2) requires $O(K\ L)$ time, and step (3) requires $O(K\ LP\ S)$ time, where P is the proportion of labeled data ($P \leq 1$) in the chunk and S is the chunk size. Step (1) (E-M) requires $O(K\ SIicmIem)$ time, where $Iicm$ is the average number of ICM iterations per E-step and Iem is the total number of E-M iterations. Although it is not possible to find the exact values of $Iicm$ and Iem analytically, we obtain an approximation by observation. We observe from our experiments that Iem depends only on the chunk-size S, and $Iicm$ is constant ($\approx$2) for any dataset. On average, a data chunk having 1000 instances requires 10 E-M iterations to converge. This increases sublinearly with chunk size. For example, a 2000 instance chunk requires 14 E-M iterations and so on. There are several reasons for this fast convergence of E-M, such as: (1) proportionate initial seed selection from the labeled data using the farthest-fast traversal and (2) using the compound impurity measure in the objective function. Therefore, the overall time complexity of the ensemble training process of SmS Cluster is $O(K\ S * (LP + g(S)))$, where $g(.)$ is a sublinear function. This complexity is almost linear in S for a moderate chunk size. The time complexity of ensemble classification is $O(K\ LS)$, which is also linear in S for a fixed value of K and L.

12.5 EXPERIMENTS

In this section, we discuss the datasets used in the experiments, the system setup, and the results.

12.5.1 Dataset

We apply our technique on two synthetic and two real datasets. We generate two different kinds of synthetic datasets: concept drifting and concept drifting with concept evolving. The former dataset simulates only concept drift, whereas the latter simulates both concept drift and concept evolution. One of the two real datasets is the 10% version of the KDD cup 1999 intrusion detection dataset

[KDD99]. The other one is the Aviation Safety Reporting Systems (ASRS) dataset obtained from NASA [NASA]. All of these datasets are discussed in the following paragraphs.

Concept-drifting synthetic dataset (SynD): We use this dataset in order to show that our approach can handle concept drift. SynD data are generated using a moving hyperplane technique. The equation of a hyperplane is as follows:

$$\sum_{i=1}^{d} a_i x_i = a_0$$

where d is the total number of dimensions, a_i is the weight associated with dimension i, and x_i is the value of ith dimension of a datapoint x. If $\Sigma_{i=1}^{d} a_i x_i \leq a_0$ then an example is considered as negative; otherwise, it is considered positive. Each instance is a randomly generated d-dimensional vector $\{x_1, \ldots, x_d\}$, where $x_i \in [0, 1]$. Weights $\{a_1, \ldots, a_d\}$ are also randomly initialized with a real number in the range [0, 1]. The value of a_0 is adjusted so that roughly the same number of positive and negative examples is generated. This can be done by choosing$a_0 = (1/2)\Sigma_{i=1}^{d} a_i$. We also introduce noise randomly by switching the labels of $p\%$ of the examples, where $p = 5$ is set in our experiments.

There are several parameters that simulate concept drift. The parameter m specifies the percent of total dimensions whose weights are involved in changing, and it is set to 20%. The parameter t specifies the magnitude of the change in every N examples. In our experiments, t is varied from 0.1 to 1.0, and N is set to 1000. s_i, $i \in \{1, \ldots, d\}$ specifies the direction of change for each weight. Weights change continuously, that is, a_i is adjusted by $si.t/N$ after each example is generated. There is a possibility of $r\%$ that the change would reverse direction after every N example is generated. In our experiments, r is set to 10%. We generate a total of 250,000 instances and divide them into equal-sized chunks.

Concept drifting with concept-evolving synthetic dataset (SynDE): SynDE dataset simulates both concept drift and concept evolution. That is, new classes appear in the stream as well as old classes disappear, and at the same time, the concept for each class gradually changes over time. The dataset size is varied from 100 to 1000K points. The number of class labels is varied from 5 to 40, and data dimensions are varied from 20 to 80. Data points belonging to each class are generated by following a normal distribution having different mean (−5.0 to +5.0) and variance (0.5–6) for different classes. In order to simulate the evolving nature of data streams, the prior probabilities of different classes are varied with time. This has caused some classes to appear and some other classes to disappear at different times in the stream history. In order to simulate the drifting nature of the concepts, the class mean for each class is gradually changed in a way similar to the Syn-D dataset. Different synthetic datasets are identified by an abbreviation: <size> *C* < #of classes> *D* <#of dimensions>. For example, 300KC5D20 denotes a dataset having 300K points, 5 classes, and 20 dimensions.

Real dataset-KDDC up 99 network intrusion detection (KDD): This dataset contains TCP connection records extracted from LAN network traffic at MIT Lincoln Labs over a period of two weeks. We have used the 10% version of the dataset, which is more concentrated than the full version. Here different classes appear and disappear frequently. Each instance in the dataset refers to either to a normal connection or an attack. There are 22 types of attacks, such as buffer-overflow, port sweep, guess-passwd, neptune, rootkit, smurf, spy, etc. So, there are 23 different classes of data, most which are normal. Each record consists of 42 attributes, such as connection duration, the number bytes transmitted, number of root accesses, etc. We use only the 34 continuous attributes, and remove the categorical attributes.

Real dataset-Aviation Safety Reporting Systems (ASRS): This dataset contains around 150,000 text documents. Each document is actually a report corresponding to a flight anomaly. There are a total of 55 anomalies, such as "aircraft equipment problem: critical," "aircraft equipment problem: less severe," "inflight encounter: birds," "inflight encounter: skydivers," "maintenance problem: improper documentation," etc. Each of these anomalies is considered as a "class." These documents represent a data stream since it contains the reports in order of their creation time, and new reports are being added to the dataset on a regular basis.

We perform several preprocessing steps on this dataset. First, we discard the classes that contain very few (less than 100) documents. We choose 21 classes among the 55, which reduced the total number of selected documents to 125,799. Second, each text report is "normalized" by removing capitalization, expanding some abbreviations, and so on. Third, we extract word features from this corpus, and select the best 1000 features based on information gain. Then each document is transformed into a binary feature vector, where the value corresponding to a feature is "one" if the feature (i.e., word) is present or "zero" if it is not present in the document. The instances in the dataset are multilabel, meaning, an instance may have more than one class label. We transform the multilabel classification problem into 21 separate binary classification problems by generating 21 different datasets from the original dataset, one for each class. The dataset for *i*th class is generated by marking the instances belonging to class *i* as positive, and all other instances as negative. When reporting the accuracy, we report the average accuracy of the 21 datasets.

An example of a normalized text report is as follows:

> cleared direct private very high frequency omnidirectional radio range after takeoff bos. using right navigation flight management system and omega bos center advised we missed private very high frequency omnidirectional radio range by 20 miles. upon checking found both flight management system and omega in gross error. advised center of same and requested airways flight plan. received same. malfunction recorded in aircraft log for maintenance action.

This report is classified into three anomaly categories:

1. Aircraft equipment problem: less severe
2. Nonadherence: clearance
3. Other spatial deviation

12.5.2 Experimental Setup

Hardware and software: We implement the algorithms in Java. The experiments were run on a Windows-based Intel P-IV machine with 2 GB memory and 3 GHz dual processor CPU.

Parameter settings: The default parameter settings are as follows, unless mentioned otherwise:

1. K (number of microclusters) = 50 for all datasets.
2. S (chunk size) = 1600 records for real datasets, and 1000 records for synthetic datasets.
3. L (ensemble size) = 10 for all datasets.

Baseline method: We compare our algorithm with "On Demand Stream," proposed by Aggarwal et al. [AGGA06]. We will refer to this approach as "OnDS." We run our own implementation of the OnDS and report the results. For the OnDS, we use all the default values of its parameters, and set buffer size = 1600 and stream speed = 80 for real datasets, and buffer size = 1000 and stream speed = 200 for synthetic datasets, as proposed by the authors. However, in order to ensure a fair comparison, we make a small modification to the original OnDS algorithm. The original algorithm assumed that in each data chunk, 50% of the instances are labeled, and the rest of them are unlabeled. The labeled instances were used for training, and the unlabeled instances are used for testing and validation. As mentioned earlier, this assumption is even more impractical than assuming that a single stream contains both training and test instances. Therefore, in the modified algorithm, we assume that all the instances in a new data chunk are unlabeled, and test all of them using the existing model. After testing, the data chunk is assumed to be completely labeled, and all the instances are used for training.

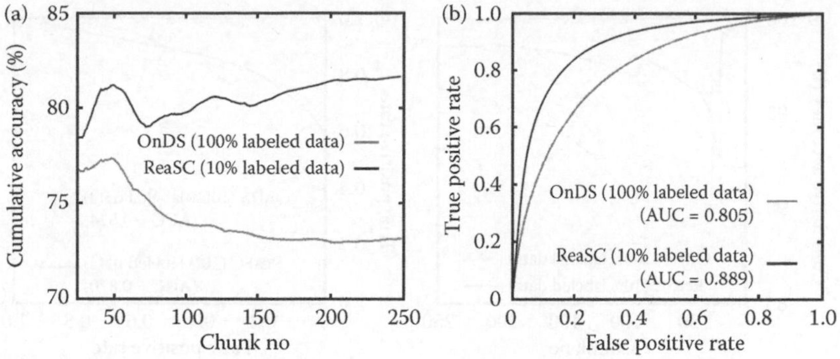

FIGURE 12.3 Cumulative accuracy (a) and ROC curve (b) for SynD dataset.

When training ReaSC, we consider that only 20% randomly chosen instances in a chunk have labels (i.e., $P = 20$), whereas for training OnDS, 100% instances in the chunk are assumed to have labels. So, if there are 100 data points in a chunk, then OnDS has 100 labeled training data points, but ReaSC has only 20 labeled and80 unlabeled training instances. Also, for a fair comparison, the chunk size of ReaSC is always kept equal to the buffer size of OnDS. Note that P is not a parameter of ReaSC, rather, it is a threshold assigned by the user based on the available system resources to label data points.

Evaluation: For each competing approach, we use the first three chunks to build the initial classification model, which can be thought of as a warm-up period. From the fourth chunk onward, we first evaluate the classification accuracy of the model on that chunk, then use the chunk as training data to update the model. Each method is run 20 times on each dataset, and the average result is reported.

12.5.3 Comparison with Baseline Methods

Figure 12.3a and b compares the accuracies and receiver operating characteristic (ROC) curves for each dataset. Each of these graphs is generated by averaging 20 runs for each method for the same parameter settings.

Figure 12.3a shows the cumulative accuracy of each competing method for each chunk on SynD dataset. In this figure, the X-axis represents chunk number and the Y-axis represents accuracy of a particular method from the beginning of the stream. For example, in Figure 12.3a at chunk 250 ($X = 250$), the Y values for ReaSC and OnDS represent the cumulative accuracies of ReaSC and OnDS from the beginning of the stream to chunk 250, which are 82.61% and 73%, respectively. This curve shows that as the stream progresses, accuracy of OnDS declines. This is because OnDS is not capable of handling concept-drift properly. Figure 12.3b shows the ROC curve for SynD dataset. The ROC curve is a good visual representation of the overall performance of a classifier in classifying all the classes correctly. Sometimes only the accuracy measure does not properly reflect the true classification performance if the class distribution is skewed. ROC curves reflect the true performance even if the class distributions are skewed. The area under the ROC curve (AUC) is higher for a better classifier. The AUCs for each ROC curve is reported in each graph. For the SynD dataset, AUC of ReaSC is almost 10% higher than that of OnDS.

Figure 12.4a shows the chunk number versus cumulative accuracy for SynDE dataset. In this dataset, ReaSC performs better (90%) than SynD because SynDE is generated using Gaussian distribution, which is easier to learn for ReaSC. On the other hand, accuracy of OnDS is much worse in this dataset. In fact, the average accuracy of OnDS is always less than 55%. Recall that SynDE simulates both concept drift and concept evolution. Since OnDS performance poorly in a dataset having only concept drift, it is natural that it performs even poorer in a dataset that has an additional hurdle: concept evolution. The ROC of ReaSC on this dataset shown in Figure 12.4b also has more than 20% higher AUC than OnDS.

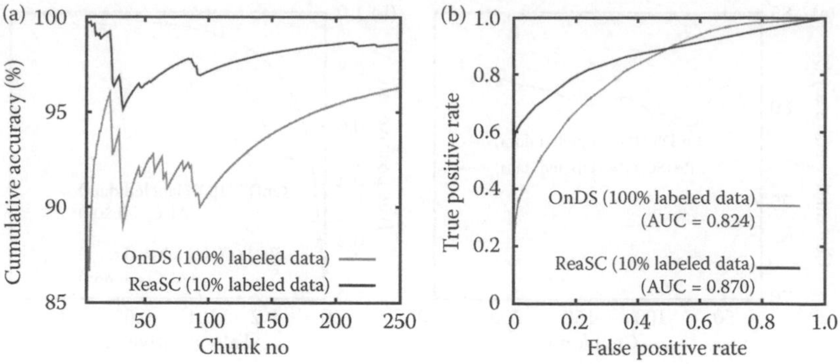

FIGURE 12.4 Cumulative accuracy (a) and ROC curve (b) for SynDE dataset.

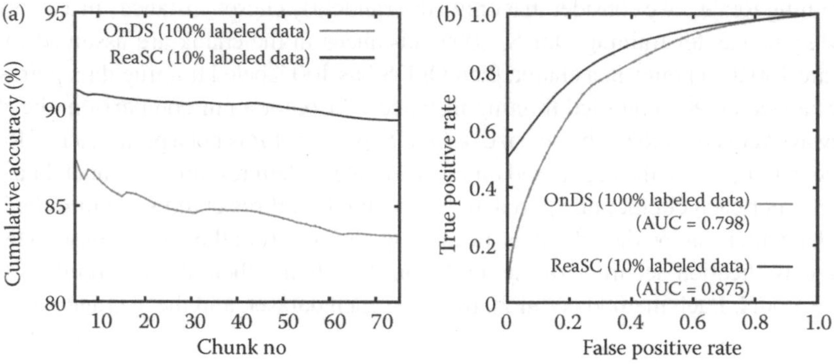

FIGURE 12.5 Cumulative accuracy (a) and ROC curve (b) for KDD dataset.

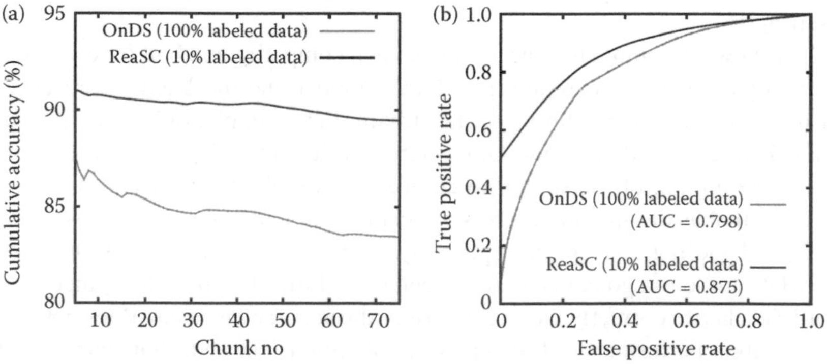

FIGURE 12.6 Cumulative accuracy (a) and ROC curve (b) for ASRS dataset.

Figure 12.5 shows the chunk number (No) vs. cumulative accuracy and ROC curves for KDD dataset. The KDD dataset has a lot of concept evolution, almost all of which occurs within the first 120 chunks. The accuracy of OnDS is 2%–12% lower than ReaSC in this region. So, ReaSC handles concept evolution better than OnDS in real data too. However, in the KDD dataset, most of the instances belong to the "normal" class. As a result, the class distribution is skewed, and simple accuracy does not reflect the true difference in performances. The ROC curves shown in Figure 12.5b reflect the performances of these two methods more precisely. The AUC of ReaSC is found to be 10% higher than OnDS, which is a great improvement. Finally, Figure 12.6 shows the accuracy and ROC curves for ASRS dataset. Recall that these graphs are generated by averaging the accuracies and ROC curves from 21 individual binary classification results.

Again, here ReaSC achieves 3% or higher accuracy than OnDS in all stream positions. Besides, the AUC of ReaSC in this dataset is 8% higher than OnDS. OnDS performs comparatively better in this dataset because this dataset does not have any concept drift.

Again recall that in all these experiments, OnDS uses five times more labeled data for training than ReaSC, still ReaSC outperforms OnDS in all datasets, both in accuracy and AUC.

12.5.4 Running Times, Scalability, and Memory Requirement

Table 12.2 compares the running times and classification speeds between ReaSC and OnDS. The columns headed by "Time (sec/1000 pts)" report the total running times (training plus testing) in *seconds per thousand points* of each of these methods. Note that these running times do not consider the data labeling time, which is an essential part of classifier training, and is a major bottleneck for OnDS, to be explained shortly. The columns headed by "classification speed (pts/sec)" report classification speed of each of these methods in *points* per *second*. The total running times of ReaSC in synthetic datasets are slightly higher than OnDS, but lower in real datasets. It is worth mentioning that the dimensions of the datasets are in increasing order: (SynD = 10, SynDE = 20, KDD = 34, ASRS = 1000), so are the running times. Both OnDS and ReaSC appear to have linear growth of running time with increasing dimensionality and class labels. But the running time of OnDS certainly grows at a higher rate than that of ReaSC with the increasing number of dimensions and class labels, as suggested by the data presented in Table 12.2. This is because, there is a classification overhead associated with OnDS, which increases with both stream length, data dimension and class labels, but there is no such overhead with ReaSC. The reason is that OnDS keeps snapshots of the microclusters for different time stamps in stream history. When classification is needed, OnDS needs to find the best time horizon by searching through the saved snapshots. This searching time is directly related with the data dimension, number of class labels, and stream length. As a result, OnDS takes relatively higher time on higher dimensions and larger datasets than ReaSC. As also shown in Table 12.2, classification speed of OnDS is much lower than ReaSC for the same reason.

If we include data labeling time, we get a more real picture of the total running time. Suppose the labeling time for each data point for KDD dataset is 1 s, and the same for ASRS dataset is 60 s. In fact, real annotation times would be much higher for any text dataset [HUYS07]. Table 12.3 shows the comparison. The labeling time for OnDS is five times higher than that of ReaSC, since per 1000 instances OnDS requires 1000 instances to have label, whereas ReaSC requires only 200 instances to have label. The net effect is ReaSC is five times faster than OnDS in both datasets.

TABLE 12.2
Comparison of Running Time (Excluding Labeling Time) and Classification Speed between OnDS (with 100% Labeled Data) and ReaSC (With 20% Labeled Data)

	Time (s/1000 pts)		Classification Speed (pts/s)	
Data Set	**OnDS (100% Labeled)**	**ReaSC (20% Labeled)**	**OnDS (100% Labeled)**	**ReaSC (20% Labeled)**
SynD	**0.88**	1.34	1222	**6248**
SynDE	**1.57**	1.72	710	**4033**
KDD	1.54	**1.32**	704	**3677**
ASRS	30.90	**10.66**	38	**369**

Note: Bold numbers in this table represent the best run times.

TABLE 12.3
Comparison of Running Time Including Labeling Time on Real Datasets

	Labeling Time (s/1000 pts)		Total Time (s/1000 pts)	
Data Set	**OnDS (100% Labeled)**	**ReaSC (20% Labeled)**	**OnDS (100% Labeled)**	**ReaSC (20% Labeled)**
KDD	1000	200	1001.54	**201.32**
ASRS	60,000	12,000	60,030.92	**12,010.66**

Note: Bold numbers in this table represent the best run times.

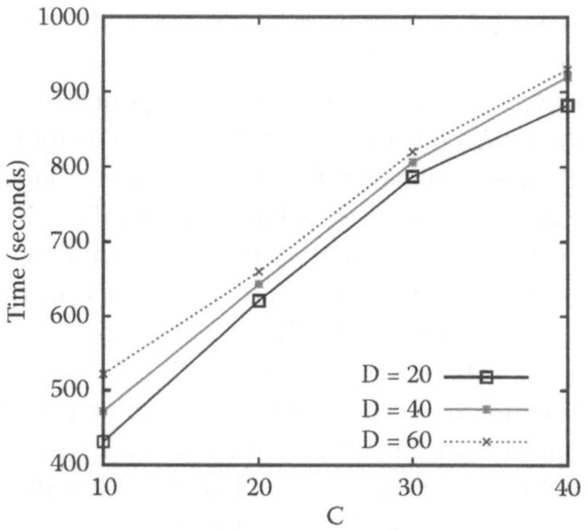

FIGURE 12.7 Running times on different datasets having higher dimensions (D) and number of classes (C).

In Figure 12.7, we report the scalability of ReaSC on high-dimensional and multiclass SynDE data. This graph reports the running times of ReaSC for different dimensions (20–60) of synthetic data with different number of classes (10–40). Each of these synthetic datasets has 250K points. For example, for $C = 10$, and $D = 20$, the running time is 431 s, and it increases linearly with the number of classes in the data. On the other hand, for a particular value of C (e.g., $D = 20$), the running time increases very slowly (linearly) with increasing the number of dimensions in the data. For example, for $C = 10$, running times for 20, 40, and 60 dimensions of datasets are 431, 472, and 522 s, respectively. Thus, we may conclude that ReaSC scales linearly to higher dimensionality and class labels.

The memory requirement for ReaSC is $O(D * K * L)$, whereas that of OnDS is $O(D * microcluster\ ratio * max\ capacity * C * \log(N))$, where N is the total length of the stream. Thus, the memory requirement of ReaSC is constant, whereas that of OnDS grows with stream length. For high-dimensional datasets, this requirement may not be practical. For example, for the ASRS dataset, ReaSC requires less than 10 MB memory, whereas OnDS requires approximately 700 MB memory.

12.5.5 Sensitivity to Parameters

All the following results are obtained using a SynDE dataset (B250K, C10, D20). Figure 12.8 shows how accuracy varies with chunk size (S) and the percentage of labeled instances in each chunk (P). It is obvious that higher values of P lead to better classification accuracy since each model is better trained. For any particular chunk size, the improvement gradually diminishes as P approaches to 100. For example, a stream with $P = 10$ has five times more labeled data than the one with $P = 2$. As a result, the accuracy improvement is also rapid from $P = 2$ to $P = 10$. But a stream with $P = 75$ has only 1.5

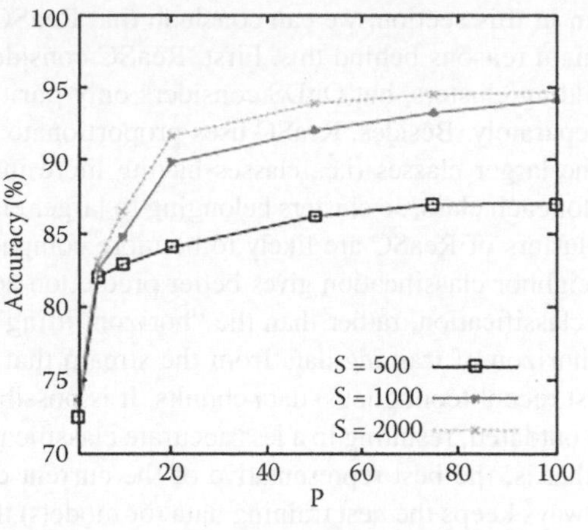

FIGURE 12.8 Sensitivity to chunk size (*S*) for different percentage of labeled data (*P*).

times more labeled data than a stream with $P = 50$, so the accuracy improvement in this case is much less than the former case. We also observe higher accuracy for larger chunk sizes. This is because, as chunk size is increased, each model gets trained with more data, which leads to a better classification accuracy. This improvement also diminishes gradually because of concept drift. According to [WANG03], if there is concept drift in the data, then a larger chunk contains more outdated points, canceling out any improvement expected to be gained by increasing the training set size.

Figure 12.9a shows how classification accuracy varies for ReaSC with the number of microclusters (K). We observe that higher values of K lead to better classification accuracies. This happens because when K is larger, smaller and more compact clusters are formed, leading to a finer-grained classification model for the nearest neighbor classifier. However, there is no significant improvement after $K = 50$ for this dataset, where $C = 10$. It should be noted that K should always be much larger than C. Experimental results suggest that K should be between $2C$ and $5C$ for best performance.

Figure 12.9b shows the effect of accuracy on ensemble size (L). Intuitively, increasing the ensemble size helps to reduce error. Significant improvement is achieved by increasing the ensemble size from 1 (i.e., single classifier) to 2. After that, the improvement diminishes gradually. Increasing the ensemble size also increases the classification time. Besides, correlation among the classifiers increases in the event of concept evolution, which diminishes the improvement intended by the ensemble. So, a reasonable value is chosen depending on the specific requirements of a system.

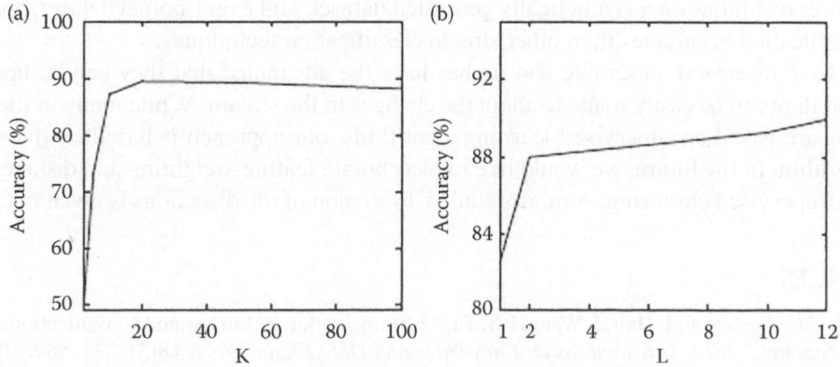

FIGURE 12.9 Sensitivity to number of clusters (*K*) (a) and ensemble size (*L*) (b).

From the results shown in this section, we can conclude that ReaSC outperforms OnDS in all datasets. There are two main reasons behind this. First, ReaSC considers both the dispersion and impurity measures in building clusters, but OnDS considers only purity, since it applies *K*-means algorithm to each class separately. Besides, ReaSC uses proportionate initialization, so that more clusters are formed for the larger classes (i.e., classes having more instances). But OnDS builds equal number of clusters for each class, so clusters belonging to larger classes tend to be bigger (and more sparse). Thus, the clusters of ReaSC are likely to be more compact than those of the OnDS. As a result, the nearest neighbor classification gives better prediction accuracy in ReaSC. Second, ReaSC applies ensemble classification, rather than the "horizon fitting" technique used in OnDS. Horizon fitting selects a horizon of training data from the stream that corresponds to a variable-length window of the most recent (contiguous) data chunks. It is possible that one or more chunks in that window have been outdated, resulting in a less accurate classification model. This is because the set of training data, that is, the best representative of the current concept are not necessarily contiguous. But ReaSC always keeps the best training data (or models) that are not necessarily contiguous. So, the ensemble approach is more flexible in retaining the most up-to-date set of training data, resulting in a more accurate classification model.

It would be interesting to compare ReaSC with some other baseline approaches. First, consider a *single* combined model that contains all the $K * L$ clusters in the ensemble *M*. We argue that this combined model is no better than the ensemble of models because our analysis shows that increasing the number of clusters beyond a certain threshold (e.g., 100) does not improve classification accuracy. Since *K* is chosen to be close to this threshold, it is most likely that we would not get a better model out of the $K* L$ clusters. Second, consider a single model having *K* clusters (not exceeding the threshold) built from *L* data chunks. Increasing the training set size would most likely improve classification accuracy. However, in the presence of concept drift, it can be shown that a single model built from *L* consecutive data chunks has a prediction error no less than an ensemble of *L* models, each built on a single data chunk [WANG03]. This also follows from our experimental results that a single model built on *L* chunks has 5%–10% worse accuracy than ReaSC, and is at least *L*-times slower than ReaSC.

12.6 SUMMARY AND DIRECTIONS

In this chapter, we have addressed a more realistic problem of stream mining and, that is, training with a limited amount of labeled data. Our technique is a more practical approach to the stream classification problem since it requires a fewer amount of labeled data, saving much time and cost that would be otherwise required to manually label the data. Previous approaches for stream classification did not address this vital problem. We designed and implemented a semisupervised clustering-based stream classification algorithm to solve this limited labeled data problem. We tested our technique on a synthetically generated dataset, and a real-botnet dataset, and received better classification accuracies than other stream classification techniques.

As we have discussed, ensemble approaches have the advantage that they can be updated efficiently, and they can be easily made to adopt the changes in the stream. While many of the ensemble approaches are based on supervised learning algorithms, our approach is based on the semisupervised algorithm. In the future, we would like to incorporate feature-weighting and distance-learning in the semisupervised clustering. A more detailed discussion of the directions is given in Chapter 13.

REFERENCES

[AGGA06]. C.C. Aggarwal, J. Han, J. Wang, P.S. Yu, "A Framework for On-Demand Classification of Evolving Data Streams," *IEEE Transactions on Knowledge and Data Engineering*, 18(5), 577–589, 2006.

[BESA86]. J. Besag, "On the Statistical Analysis of Dirty Pictures," *Journal of the Royal Statistical Society, Series B (Methodological)*, 48(3), 259–302, 1986.

[DEMP77]. A.P. Dempster, N.M. Laird, D.B. Rubin, "Maximum Likelihood from Incomplete Data via the Em Algorithm," *Journal of the Royal Statistical Society B*, 39, 1–38, 1977.

[HOCH85]. D. Hochbaum and D. Shmoys, "A Best Possible Heuristic for the K-Center Problem," *Mathematics of Operations Research*, 10(2), 180–184, 1985.

[HUYS07]. G.B. van Huyssteen, M.J. Puttkammer, S. Pilon, H.J. Groenewald, "Using Machine Learning to Annotate Data for NLP Tasks Semi-Automatically," In *CALP '07: Proceedings of the RANLP-07 Workshop: Computer-Aided Language Processing Computer-Aided Language Processing*, 27–29 Sep, Borovets, Bulgaria, 2007. http://rgcl.wlv.ac.uk/events/CALP07/papers/3.pdf.

[KDD99]. KDD Cup 1999 Intrusion Detection Dataset. http://kdd.ics.uci.edu/databases/kddcup99/kddcup99.html.

[MASU08]. M.M. Masud, J. Gao, L. Khan, J. Han, B.M. Thuraisingham, "A Practical Approach to Classify Evolving Data Streams: Training with Limited Amount of Labeled Data," In *ICDM '08: Proceedings of the 2008 International Conference on Data Mining*, Pisa, Italy, 15–19 Dec, pp. 929–934, 2008, IEEE Computer Society.

[NASA]. NASA Aviation Safety Reporting System. http://akama.arc.nasa.gov/ASRSDBOnline/QueryWizard_Begin.aspx.

[TUME96]. K. Tumer and J. Ghosh, "Error Correlation and Error Reduction in Ensemble Classifiers," *Connection Science*, 8(304), 385–403, 1996.

[WANG03]. H. Wang, W. Fan, P.S. Yu, J. Han, "Mining Concept-Drifting Data Streams Using Ensemble Classifiers," In *KDD '03: Proceedings of the Ninth ACM SIGKDD International Conference on Knowledge Discovery and Data Mining*, Washington, DC, USA, Aug 24–27, pp. 226–235, 2003, ACM.

13 Directions in Data Stream Classification

13.1 INTRODUCTION

We have discussed three major approaches for stream analytics in Chapters 10 through 12. In Chapter 10, we described our innovative technique for classifying concept-drifting data streams using a novel ensemble classifier originally discussed in [MASU09a]. It is a multiple partition, multiple chunk (MPC) ensemble classifier-based data mining technique to classify concept-drifting data streams. Existing ensemble techniques in classifying concept-drifting data streams follow a single-partition, single-chunk approach in which a single data chunk is used to train one classifier. In our approach, we train a collection of *v* classifiers from *r* consecutive data chunks using *v*-fold partitioning of the data, and build an ensemble of such classifiers. By introducing this MPC ensemble technique, we significantly reduce classification error compared to the single-partition, single-chunk ensemble approaches. We have theoretically justified the usefulness of our algorithm, and empirically proved its effectiveness over other state-of-the-art stream classification techniques on synthetic data and real botnet traffic.

In Chapter 11, we described a novel and efficient technique that can automatically detect the emergence of a novel class in the presence of concept drift by quantifying cohesion among unlabeled test instances and separation of the test instances from training instances. Our approach is nonparametric, meaning, it does not assume any underlying distributions of data. Comparison with the state-of-the-art stream classification techniques proves the superiority of our approach. In this chapter, we discuss our proposed framework for classifying data streams with automatic novel class detection mechanism. It is based on our previous work [MASU09a].

In Chapter 12, we discussed the building of a classification model from a training set having both unlabeled and a small number of labeled instances. This model is built as microclusters using a semisupervised clustering technique and classification is performed with *k*-nearest neighbor algorithm. An ensemble of these models is used to classify the unlabeled data. Empirical evaluation on both synthetic data and real botnet traffic reveals that our approach, using only a small amount of labeled data for training, outperforms state-of-the-art stream classification algorithms that use 20 times more labeled data than our approach. We describe our proposed solution for the limited labeled training data. It is based on our work discussed in [MASU08].

In this chapter, we will compare the three approaches we have developed. That is, we discuss the three data stream classification approaches described in previous chapters and give directions to possible extensions to those approaches. The organization of this chapter is as follows. A summary of the three approaches is provided in Section 13.2. Some extensions are discussed in Section 13.3. Summary and directions are provided in Section 13.4.

13.2 DISCUSSION OF THE APPROACHES

We summarize each of our proposed works under the respective headings.

13.2.1 MPC Ensemble Approach

We have introduced an MPC ensemble method for classifying concept-drifting data streams. MPC ensemble approach keeps the best *Lv* classifiers, where a batch of *v* classifiers are trained with *v* overlapping partitions of r consecutive data chunks. It is a generalization over previous ensemble approaches that train a single classifier from a single data chunk. By introducing this MPC ensemble, we have reduced error significantly over the single-partition, single-chunk approach. We have proved our claims theoretically, tested MPC ensemble approach on both synthetic data and real botnet data, and obtained better classification accuracies compared to other approaches.

13.2.2 Classification and Novel Class Detection in Data Streams (ECSMiner)

We have addressed several real-world problems related to data stream classification. We have proposed a solution to the concept-evolution problem, which has been ignored by most of the existing data stream classification techniques. Existing data stream classification techniques assume that the total number of classes in the stream is fixed. Therefore, when a novel class appears in the stream, instances belonging to that class are misclassified by the existing techniques. We show how to detect novel classes automatically even when the classification model is not trained with the novel class instances. Novel class detection becomes more challenging in the presence of concept drift.

Existing novel class detection techniques have limited applicability, since those are similar to one-class classifiers. That is, they assume that there is only one normal class, and all other classes are novel. However, ECSMiner is applicable to the more realistic scenario where there is more than one existing class in the stream. Besides, our novel class detection technique is nonparametric and it does not require any specific data distribution, nor does it require the classes to have convex shape. We have also shown how to effectively classify stream data under different time constraints. ECSMiner outperforms the state-of-the art data stream-based classification techniques in both classification accuracy and processing speed. We believe that our proposed technique will inspire more research toward solving real-world stream classification problems.

It might appear to readers that in order to detect novel classes, we are in fact examining whether new clusters are being formed, and therefore, the detection process could go on without supervision. But supervision is necessary for classification. Without external supervision, two separate clusters could be regarded as two different classes, although they are not. Conversely, if more than one novel class appears simultaneously, all of them could be regarded as a single novel class if the labels of those instances are never revealed.

13.2.3 Classification with Scarcely Labeled Data (ReaSC)

We address a more realistic problem of stream mining: training with a limited amount of labeled data. ReaSC is a more practical approach to the stream classification problem since it requires a lower amount of labeled data, saving much time and cost that would be otherwise required to manually label the data. Previous approaches for stream classification did not address this vital problem.

We propose and implement a semisupervised clustering-based stream classification algorithm to solve this limited labeled-data problem. We show that ReaSC, using much fewer labeled training instances than other stream classification techniques, works better than those techniques. We evaluate ReaSC on two synthetically generated datasets and two real datasets, and achieve better classification accuracies than state-of-the-art stream classification approaches in all datasets.

13.3 EXTENSIONS

Our proposed data stream classification techniques can be extended in various ways. The first and obvious extension would be developing a *unified framework that integrates all three proposed techniques*. We consider the novel class detection and limited labeled data problems separately. In the unified framework, the classification model should be able to detect the novel class even if there is only a few labeled data per chunk. It would be interesting to see how the scarcity of labeled data affects the proposed novel class detection technique. All of the following extensions are applicable to this unified framework.

Dynamic Feature Vector: We would like to address the data stream classification problem under dynamic feature vector. Currently, we assume that the feature vector is fixed. We would like to relax this assumption, and provide a more general framework for data stream classification where the feature vector may change over time. This would be useful for classifying text stream, and other similar data streams, where new features evolve over time. For example, suppose the data stream is a stream of text documents where the feature vector consists of a list of all words that appeared so far in the stream. Since the vocabulary is supposed to increase with the arrival of new documents, the feature vector also grows over time. As a result, each classifier in the ensemble would be built on a different feature vector. Also, a test instance would likely have a different feature vector from the training instances of a classifier. It would be a challenging task to classify the test instances and detect novel classes in these scenarios.

Multilabel Instances: In some classification problems, an instance may have multiple class labels, which are known as multilabel instances. The multilabel classification problem is more generalized than the traditional classification problem where each instance belongs to only one class. An example of this multilabel instance is the NASA Aviation Safety Reporting Systems dataset [NASA] which has been discussed in detail in Section 12.5. Although there are many existing solutions to the multilabel classification problem ([CHEN07], [CLAR01], [GAOS04], [LUO05] [MCDO05] [STRE08] [THAB04], [VELO07], [ZHAN07]), none of them are applicable to data streams. Besides, the problem becomes more complicated in the presence of concept drift and novel classes. It will be interesting to investigate the effects of multilabel instances on our proposed stream classification technique and extend it to cope with them.

Cloud Computing and Big Data: With so much streaming data being generated for various applications, we need to develop scalable stream data mining techniques that can handle massive amounts of data. Therefore, we need to extend our techniques to operate in a cloud computing framework. As data streams grow larger and faster, it would be difficult to mine them using a stand-alone computing machine and limited data storage. Therefore, in the future we would need to utilize the computing power and storage capacities from several computing machines. This would necessitate adapting our proposed technique on the cloud computing infrastructure. One such infrastructure is the Hadoop Distributed File System ([CHU07], [DEAN08], [HUSA09]). In order to facilitate classification, raw data will be distributed among different nodes in the system. Hadoop is a distributed file system and stream data will be stored in this system by partitioning each data chunk into a number of blocks and storing each block in a separate node as illustrated in Figure 13.1.

For example, without loss of generality, let us assume that a node can hold at least 128 MB data on hard disk and block size is 64 MB. If chunk size is 256 MB, the chunk will be partitioned into four data blocks. These four data blocks will be distributed across two nodes (without replication). On the other hand, if the chunk size is 64 MB, the whole chunk can be stored into a single node. Hence, a chunk will be processed in parallel by each node independently, which can speed up query processing and classification. Each node will train its own classification model from the raw data that is stored in that node. After training, raw data will be discarded. However, there should be a way to combine the classification output of each node to get a global output, such as majority voting.

In addition to using a cloud computing framework, we also need to explore the use of the big data management and analytics (BDMA) technologies discussed in Chapter 7. For example, the streaming data may need to be stored in systems such as HBase and CouchDB. Furthermore, the enhanced Weka techniques discussed in Chapter 7 to handle big data have to be examined for stream mining for big data.

Dynamic Chunk Size and Ensemble Size: In the proposed approach, we use fixed chunk size and ensemble size. In the future, we would like to make the system more adaptive to concept drift and concept evolution by adapting both the chunk size and ensemble size. It is shown in the past that if the chunk size is increased when concept drift is slow, and decreased when it is faster, it is

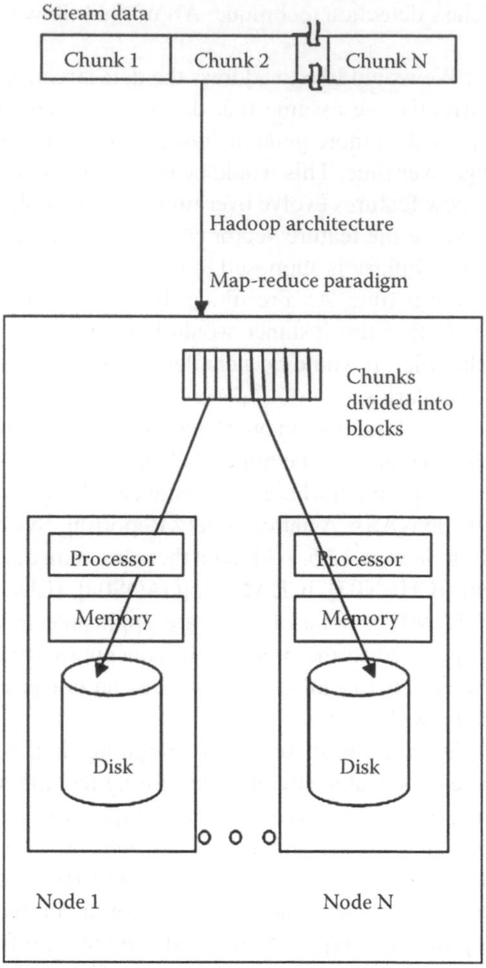

FIGURE 13.1 Architecture for stream data classification using Hadoop Distributed File System.

possible to improve classification performance ([KLIN00], [WIDM96]). Also, keeping older classifiers in the ensemble hurts performance when concept drift and concept evolution occur too fast, and improve performance when they are slow. Therefore, dynamically changing the ensemble size also adds to the overall improvement in classification accuracy. However, the main challenge is to determine whether concept drift and concept evolution are occurring and at what pace ([GARC06], [DRIE09], [GAMA04], [HIDO08]).

Parameter Reduction: We also have several other parameters that need to be tuned to optimum performance, for example, the number of clusters, K, and the minimum neighborhood size, q. In the future, we would like to make these parameters adapt to the dynamic nature of the data streams and change their values accordingly.

Real-Time Classification: We would like to extend our system to perform real-time stream classification. Real-time data stream classification is important in many applications such as the intrusion detection systems. We need to optimize both classification and training times for the system to be applicable to a real-time environment. In order to get a fast and accurate classification decision, we need to consider a number of issues. First, an instance must be classified using a fast classification model. Second, the classification model must be updated quickly, and also the update should not delay the classification of a test instance. Third, the system should be able to extract features from raw data quickly, and present the feature vector to the classification model.

Feature Weighting: We would like to incorporate feature weighting and distance learning in the semisupervised clustering, which should lead to a better classification model. Feature weighting and distance learning have been used in many semisupervised computing tasks in the past ([BASU04], [BASU06], [BILE04]). However, the learning process would be more challenging in a streaming environment in the presence of concept drift and novel classes.

13.4 SUMMARY AND DIRECTIONS

This chapter has examined the three approaches we have developed for data stream classification and discussed directions for further work. In particular, we need to enhance the algorithms by providing greater accuracy and fewer false positives and negatives. Furthermore, we need to enhance the performance of the algorithms to handle massive amounts of data. Towards this end, we believe that a cloud-based implementation is a viable approach for high-performance data analytics. In addition, the BDMA technologies that we discussed in Chapter 7 need to be examined for stream mining for big data.

In Section III of this book, we will discuss an application of stream data analytics and that is for insider threat detection. Some other systems that utilize stream mining with big data analytics including a discussion of malware detection systems in the cloud will be discussed in Section IV.

REFERENCES

[BASU04]. S. Basu, A. Banerjee, R.J. Mooney, "Active Semi-Supervision for Pairwise Constrained Clustering," *SDM '04: Proceedings of the 2004 SIAM International Conference on Data Mining*, April 22–24, Lake Buena Vista, FL, pp. 333–344, SIAM, 2004.

[BASU06]. S. Basu, M. Bilenko, A. Banerjee, R.J. Mooney, "Probabilistic Semi-Supervised Clustering with Constraints," *Semi-Supervised Learning*, O. Chapelle, B. Schoelkopf, A. Zien, editors, MIT Press, Cambridge, MA, 73–102, 2006.

[BILE04]. M. Bilenko, S. Basu, R.J. Mooney, "Integrating Constraints and Metric Learning in Semi-Supervised Clustering," *ICML '04: Proceedings of the Twenty-First International Conference on Machine Learning*, July 4–8, Banff, Canada, pp. 81–88, Morgan Kaufmann, 2004.

[CHEN07]. W. Chen, J. Yan, B. Zhang, Z. Chen, Q. Yang, "Document Transformation for Multi-Label Feature Selection in Text Categorization," *ICDM '07: Proceedings of the 2007 International Conference on Data Mining*, October 28–31, Omaha, NE, pp. 451–456, IEEE Computer Society, 2007.

[CHU07]. C.-T. Chu, S.K. Kim, Y.-A. Lin, Y.Y. Yu, G. Bradski, A.Y. Ng, "Map-Reduce for Machine Learning on Multicore," *NIPS '07: Proceedings of the 21st Annual Conference on Neural Information Processing Systems*, December 3–7, Vancouver, B.C., Canada, pp. 281–288, MIT Press, 2007.

[CLAR01]. A. Clare and R.D. King, "Knowledge Discovery in Multi-Label Phenotype Data," *PKDD '01: Proceedings of the 5th European Conference on Principles of Data Mining and Knowledge Discovery*, September 3–7, Freiburg, Germany, pp. 42–53, Springer-Verlag, 2001.

[DEAN08]. J. Dean and S. Ghemawat, "Mapreduce: Simplified Data Processing on Large Clusters," *Communications of the ACM*, 51(1):107–113, January 2008.

[DRIE09]. A. Dries and U. Rückert, "Adaptive Concept Drift Detection," *SDM 09: Proceedings of the 2009 Siam International Conference on Data Mining*, April 30 to May 2, Sparks, NV, pp. 233–244, SIAM, 2009.

[GAMA04]. J. Gama, P. Medas, G. Castillo, P.P. Rodrigues, "Learning with Drift Detection," *SBIA '04: Proceedings of the 17th Brazilian Symposium on Artificial Intelligence (SBIA)*, September 29 to October 1, Sao Luis, Maranhao, Brazil, pp. 286–295, Springer, 2004.

[GAOS04]. S.G. Gaosheng, W. Wu, C.H. Lee, "A MFoM Learning Approach to Robust Multiclass Multi-Label Text Categorization," *ICML '04: Proceedings of the 21st International Conference on Machine Learning*, July 4–8, Banff, Canada, pp. 329–336, Morgan Kaufmann, 2004.

[GARC06]. M. Baena-Garcia, J. del Campo-Avila, R. Fidalgo, A. Bifet, R. Gavalda, R. Morales-Bueno, "Early Drift Detection Method," *ECML PKDD 2006 Workshop on Knowledge Discovery from Data Streams*, September 18, Berlin, Germany, Springer-Verlag, 2006.

[HIDO08]. S. Hido, T. Ide, H. Kashima, H. Kubo, H. Matsuzawa, "Unsupervised Change Analysis Using Supervised Learning," *Advances in Knowledge Discovery and Data Mining*, 148–159, 2008.

[HUSA09]. M.F. Husain, P. Doshi, L. Khan, B. Thuraisingham, "*Storage and Retrieval of Large RDF Graph Using Hadoop and Mapreduce*," Technical Report No. UTDCS-40-09, Computer Science Department, University of Texas, Dallas, TX, 2009.

[KLIN00]. R. Klinkenberg and T. Joachims, "Detecting Concept Drift with Support Vector Machines," *ICML '00: Proceedings of the 17th International Conference on Machine Learning*, June 29 to July 2, Stanford University, CA, pp. 487–494, Morgan Kaufmann, 2000.

[LUO05]. X. Luo and A. Nur Zincir-Heywood, "Evaluation of Two Systems on Multi-Class Multi-Label Document Classification," *ISMIS '05: Proceedings of the 15th International Symposium on Methodologies for Intelligent Systems*, Saratoga Springs, New York, May 25–28, pp. 161–169, Springer, 2005.

[MCDO05]. R. Mcdonald, K. Crammer, F. Pereira, "Flexible Text Segmentation with Structured Multilabel Classification," *HLT-EMNLP '05: Proceedings of the 2005 Human Language Technology Conference and Conference on Empirical Methods in Natural Language Processing*, October 6–8, Vancouver, B.C., Canada, pp. 987–994, 2005.

[MASU08]. M.M. Masud, J. Gao, L. Khan, J. Han, B.M. Thuraisingham, "A Practical Approach to Classify Evolving Data Streams: Training with Limited Amount of Labeled Data," *ICDM '08: Proceedings of the 2008 International Conference on Data Mining*, December 15–19, Pisa, Italy, pp. 929–934, IEEE Computer Society, 2008.

[MASU09]. M.M. Masud, J. Gao, L. Khan, J. Han, B.M. Thuraisingham, "Integrating Novel Class Detection with Classification for Concept-Drifting Data Streams," *ECML PKDD '09: Proceedings of the 2009 European Conference on Machine Learning and Principles and Practice in Knowledge Discovery in Databases*, Vol. II, September 7–11, Bled, Slovenia, pp. 79–94, Springer-Verlag, 2009.

[NASA]. NASA Aviation Safety Reporting System, http://akama.arc.nasa.gov/ASRSDBOnline/QueryWizard_Begin.aspx.

[STRE08]. A.P. Streich and J.M. Buhmann, "Classification of Multi-Labeled Data: A Generative Approach," *ECML PKDD '08: Proceedings of the 2008 European Conference on Machine Learning and Principles and Practice in Knowledge Discovery in Databases*, Vol. II, September 15–19, Antwerp, Belgium, pp. 390–405, Springer, 2008.

[THAB04]. F.A. Thabtah, P. Cowling, Y. Peng," Mmac: A New Multi- Class, Multi-Label Associative Classification Approach," *ICDM '05: Proceedings of the 5th IEEE International Conference on Data Mining*, November 1–4, Brighton, UK, pp. 217–224, IEEE Computer Society, 2004.

[VELO07]. A. Veloso, W. Meira Jr, M. Goncalves, M. Zaki, "Multi-Label Lazy Associative Classification," *ECML PKDD '07: Proceedings of the 2007 European Conference on Machine Learning and Principles and Practice in Knowledge Discovery in Databases*, September 17–21, Warsaw, Poland, pp. 605–612, Springer-Verlag, 2007.

[WIDM96]. G. Widmer and M. Kubat, "Learning in the Presence of Concept Drift and Hidden Contexts," *Machine Learning*, 23(1):69–101, 1996.

[ZHAN07]. M.-L. Zhang and Z.-H. Zhou, "Multi-Label Learning by Instance Differentiation," *AAAI-07: Proceedings of the 22nd Conference on Artificial Intelligence*, July 22–26, Vancouver, British Columbia, Canada, pp. 669674, 2007.

Conclusion to Part II

Part II, consisting of six chapters, described our approach to stream data analytics, which we also called stream data mining. In particular, we discussed various techniques for detecting novel classes in data streams.

Chapter 8 stressed the need for mining data streams and discussed the challenges. The challenges include infinite length, concept drift, concept evolution, and limited labeled data. We also provided an overview of our approach to mining data streams. Specifically, our approach determines whether an item belongs to a pre-existing class or whether it is a novel class. Chapter 9 described prior approaches as well as our approach on stream analytics. For example, in the single model classification approach, incremental learning techniques are used. The ensemble-based techniques are more efficiently built than the single model approach. Our novel class detection approach integrated both data stream classification and novelty detection. Our data stream classification technique with limited labeled data uses a semi-supervised technique. Chapter 10 introduced a multiple partition, multiple chunk (MPC) ensemble method for classifying concept-drifting data streams. Our ensemble approach is a generalization over previous ensemble approaches that trains a single classifier from a single data chunk. By introducing this MPC ensemble, we have reduced error significantly over the single-partition, single-chunk approach. In Chapter 11, we presented a novel technique to detect new classes in concept-drifting data streams. Our approach is capable of detecting novel classes in the presence of concept drift, even when the model consists of multiple "existing" classes. Besides, our novel class detection technique is nonparametric, meaning, it does not assume any specific distribution of data. In Chapter 12, we addressed a more realistic problem of stream mining and that is training with a limited amount of labeled data. We designed and implemented a semisupervised, clustering-based stream classification algorithm to solve this limited labeled data problem. Finally, in Chapter 13, we examined the three approaches we developed for data stream classification and discussed in Chapters 10 through 12 and provided directions for further work. In particular, we discussed the need to use cloud computing and BDMA techniques to scale our stream mining techniques.

Now that we have discussed our techniques for stream data analytics, in Part III, we will show how we can apply our techniques for the insider threat detection problem.

Part III

Stream Data Analytics for Insider Threat Detection

Introduction to Part III

Part III, consisting of nine chapters, describes big data analytics techniques for insider threat detection. In particular, both supervised and unsupervised learning methods for insider threat detection are discussed.

Chapter 14 provides a discussion of the problem addressed and the solutions provided by big data analysis. In particular, stream data mining that addresses the big data issues for insider threat detection is discussed. Chapter 15 describes related work. Both insider threat detection and stream mining aspects are discussed. In addition, issues on handling big data techniques are also discussed. Chapter 16 describes ensemble-based classification and details both unsupervised and supervised learning techniques for insider threat detection. Chapter 17 describes supervised and unsupervised learning methods for nonsequence data. Chapter 18 describes our experiments and testing methodology and presents our results and findings on insider threat detection for nonsequence data. Chapter 19 describes both supervised and unsupervised learning algorithms for insider threat detection for sequence data. Chapter 20 presents our experiments and results on insider threat detection for sequence data. Chapter 21 describes scalability issues using the Hadoop/MapReduce framework and solutions for quantized dictionary construction. Finally, Chapter 22 concludes with an assessment of the viability of stream mining for real-world insider threat detection and the relevance to big data aspects.

14 Insider Threat Detection as a Stream Mining Problem

14.1 INTRODUCTION

There is a growing consensus within the intelligence community that malicious insiders are perhaps the most potent threats to information assurance in many or most organizations ([BRAC04], [HAMP99], [MATZ04], [SALE11]). One traditional approach to the insider threat detection problem is supervised learning, which builds data classification models from training data. Unfortunately, the training process for supervised learning methods tends to be time-consuming and expensive, and generally requires large amounts of well-balanced training data to be effective. In our experiments, we observe that <3% of the data in realistic datasets for this problem is associated with insider threats (the minority class) and over 97% of the data is associated with nonthreats (the majority class). Hence, traditional support vector machines (SVM) ([CHAN11], [MANE02]), trained from such imbalanced data are likely to perform poorly on test datasets.

One-class SVMs (OCSVM) [MANE02] address the rare-class issue by building a model that considers only normal data (i.e., nonthreat data). During the testing phase, test data is classified as normal or anomalous based on geometric deviations from the model. However, the approach is only applicable to bounded-length, static data streams. In contrast, insider threat-related data is typically continuous and threat patterns evolve over time. In other words, the data is a stream of unbounded length. Hence, effective classification models must be adaptive (i.e., able to cope with evolving concepts) and highly efficient in order to build the model from large amounts of evolving data. Data, that is, associated with insider threat detection and classification is often continuous. In these systems, the patterns of average users and insider threats can gradually evolve. A novice programmer can develop his skills to become an expert programmer over time. An insider threat can change his actions to more closely mimic legitimate user processes. In either case, the patterns at either end of these developments can look drastically different when compared directly to each other. These natural changes will not be treated as anomalies in our approach. Instead, we classify them as natural concept drift. The traditional static supervised and unsupervised methods raise unnecessary false alarms with these cases because they are unable to handle them when they arise in the system. These traditional methods encounter high false positive rates (FPR). Learning models must be adept in coping with evolving concepts and highly efficient at building models from large amounts of data to rapidly detecting real threats. For these reasons, the insider threat problem can be conceptualized as a stream mining problem that applies to continuous data streams. Whether using a supervised or unsupervised learning algorithm, the method chosen must be highly adaptive to correctly deal with concept drifts under these conditions. Incremental learning and ensemble-based learning ([MASU10a], [MASU10b] [MASU11a], [MASU11b], [MASU08], [MASU13], [MASU11c], [ALKH12a], [MASU11d], [ALKH12b]) are two adaptive approaches in order to overcome this hindrance. An ensemble of K models that collectively vote on the final classification can reduce the false negatives and false positives for a test set. As new models are created and old ones are updated to be more precise, the least accurate models are discarded to always maintain an ensemble of exactly K current models. An alternative approach to supervised learning is unsupervised learning, which can be effectively applied to purely unlabeled data—that is, data in which no points are explicitly identified as anomalous or nonanomalous. Graph-based anomaly detection (GBAD) is one important form of unsupervised learning ([COOK07], [EBER07], [COOK00]) but has traditionally been limited to static, finite-length datasets. This limits its application to streams related to insider threats which tend to have unbounded length and threat patterns that evolve over time. Applying GBAD to the insider threat problem therefore requires that the models used be adaptive and efficient. Adding these qualities allows effective models to be built from vast amounts of evolving data.

In this book, we cast insider threat detection as a stream mining problem and propose two methods (supervised and unsupervised learning) for efficiently detecting anomalies in stream data [PARV13]. To cope with concept evolution, our supervised approach maintains an evolving ensemble of multiple OCSVM models [PARV11a]. Our unsupervised approach combines multiple GBAD models in an ensemble of classifiers [PARV11b]. The ensemble updating process is designed in both cases to keep the ensemble current as the stream evolves. This evolutionary capability improves the classifier's survival of concept drift as the behavior of both legitimate and illegitimate agents varies over time. In experiments, we use test data that records system call data for a large, Unix-based, multiuser system.

This chapter deserves our approach to insider threat detection using stream data mining. In Section 14.2, we discuss sequence stream data. Big data issues are discussed in Section 14.3. Our contributions are discussed in Section 14.4. This chapter is summarized in Section 14.5.

14.2 SEQUENCE STREAM DATA

The above approach may not work well for sequence data ([PARV12a], [PARV12b]). For sequence data, our approach maintains an ensemble of multiple unsupervised stream-based sequence learning (USSL) [PARV12a]. During the learning process, we store the repetitive sequence patterns from a user's actions or commands in a model called a quantized dictionary. In particular, longer patterns with higher weights due to frequent appearances in the stream are considered in the dictionary. An ensemble in this case is a collection of K models of type quantized dictionary. When new data arrives or is gathered, we generate a new quantized dictionary model from this new dataset. We will take the majority voting of all models to find the anomalous pattern sequences within this new dataset. We will update the ensemble if the new dictionary outperforms others in the ensemble and will discard the least accurate model from the ensemble. Therefore, the ensemble always keeps the models current as the stream evolves, preserving high detection accuracy as both legitimate and illegitimate behaviors evolve over time. Our test data consists of real-time-recorded user command sequences for multiple users of varying experience levels and a concept-drift framework to further exhibit the practicality of this approach.

14.3 BIG DATA ISSUES

Quantized dictionary construction is time-consuming. Scalability is a bottleneck here. We exploit distributed computing to address this issue. There are two ways we can achieve this goal. The first one is parallel computing with shared memory architecture that exploits expensive hardware. The latter approach is distributing computing with shared nothing architecture that exploits commodity hardware. For our case, we exploit the latter choice. Here, we use a MapReduce-based framework to facilitate quantization using Hadoop Distributed File System (HDFS). We propose a number of algorithms to quantize dictionary. For each of them we discuss the pros and cons and report performance results on a large dataset.

It should be noted that there are several directions for further work on applying big data technologies. For example, in addition to the Hadoop/MapReduce framework, we also need to examine the use of Spark and Storm technologies. Also, the big data management and analytics systems discussed in Chapter 7 have to be examined for developing scalable stream data analytics techniques for insider threat detection.

14.4 CONTRIBUTIONS

The main contributions of this work can be summarized as follows (see Figure 14.1).

1. We show how stream mining can be effectively applied to detect insider threats.
2. With regard to nonsequence data:
   a. We propose a supervised learning solution that copes with evolving concepts using one-class SVMs.
   b. We increase the accuracy of the supervised approach by weighting the cost of false negatives.
   c. We propose an unsupervised learning algorithm that copes with changes based on GBAD.
   d. We effectively address the challenge of limited labeled training data (rare instance issues).
   e. We exploit the power of stream mining and graph-based mining by effectively combining the two in a unified manner. This is the first work to our knowledge to harness these two approaches for insider threat detection.
   f. We compare one and two class SVMs on how well they handle stream insider threat problems.
   g. We compare supervised and unsupervised stream learning approaches and show which has superior effectiveness using real-world data.
3. With regard to sequence data:
   a. For sequence data, we propose a framework that exploits an unsupervised learning (USSL) to find pattern sequences from successive user actions or commands using stream-based sequence learning.
   b. We effectively integrate multiple USSL models in an ensemble of classifiers to exploit the power of ensemble-based stream mining and sequence mining.

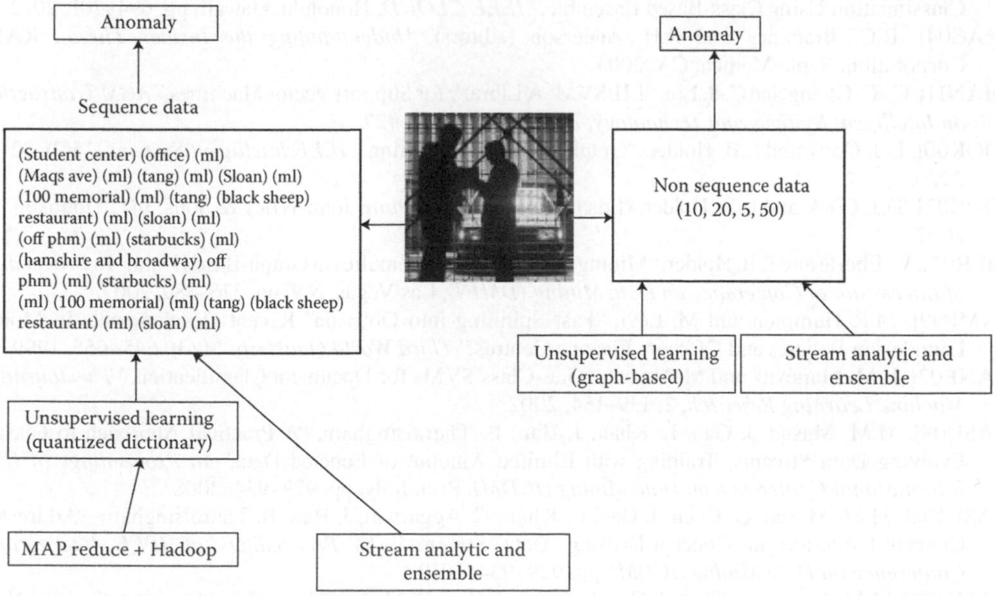

FIGURE 14.1 Contribution in visual form.

   c. We compare our approach with the supervised model for stream mining and show the effectiveness of our approach in terms of true positive rate (TPR) and FPR on a benchmark dataset.
4. With regard to big data:
   a. Scalability is an issue to construct benign pattern sequences for quantized dictionary. For this, we exploit the MapReduce-based framework and show effectiveness of our work.

14.5 SUMMARY AND DIRECTIONS

Our approach is to define the insider threat detection as a stream mining problem and propose two methods (supervised and unsupervised learning) for efficiently detecting anomalies in stream data. To cope with concept evolution, our supervised approach maintains an evolving ensemble of multiple OCSVM models. Our unsupervised approach combines multiple GBAD models in an ensemble of classifiers. The ensemble updating process is designed in both cases to keep the ensemble current as the stream evolves. This evolutionary capability improves the classifier's survival of concept drift as the behavior of both legitimate and illegitimate agents varies over time. In the experiments, we use test data that records system call data for a large, Unix-based, multiuser system.

This chapter has provided an overview of our approach to insider threat detection using stream analytics and discussed the big data issue with respect to the problem. That is, massive amounts of stream data are emanating from various devices and we need to analyze this data for insider threat detection. We essentially adapt the techniques discussed in Section II for insider threat detection. These techniques are discussed in the ensuing chapters of Section III.

REFERENCES

[ALKH12a]. T. Al-Khateeb, M.M. Masud, L. Khan, C.C. Aggarwal, J. Han, B.M. Thuraisingham, "Stream Classification with Recurring and Novel Class Detection Using Class-Based Ensemble," *ICDM*, Brussels, Belgium, pp. 31–40, 2012.

[ALKH12b]. T. Al-Khateeb, M.M. Masud, L. Khan, B.M. Thuraisingham, "Cloud Guided-Stream Classification Using Class-Based Ensemble," *IEEE CLOUD*, Honolulu, Hawaii, pp. 694–701, 2012.

[BRAC04]. R.C. Brackney and R.H. Anderson (editors). *Understanding the Insider Threat*. RAND Corporation, Santa Monica, CA, 2004.

[CHAN11]. C.-C. Chang and C.-J. Lin, "LIBSVM: A Library for Support Vector Machines," *ACM Transactions on Intelligent Systems and Technology*, 2(3), 2011, Article #27.

[COOK00]. D.J. Cook and L.B. Holder, "Graph-Based Data Mining," *IEEE Intelligent Systems*, 15(2), 32–41, 2000.

[COOK07]. D.J. Cook and L.B. Holder, (Eds.). *Mining Graph Data*. John Wiley & Sons, Inc., Hoboken, NJ, 2007.

[EBER07]. W. Eberle and L.B. Holder, "Mining for Structural Anomalies in Graph-Based Data," In *Proceedings of International Conference on Data Mining (DMIN)*, Las Vegas, NV, pp. 376–389, 2007.

[HAMP99]. M.P. Hampton and M. Levi, "Fast Spinning into Oblivion? Recent Developments in Money-Laundering Policies and Offshore Finance Centres," *Third World Quarterly*, 20(3), 645–656, 1999.

[MANE02]. L.M. Manevitz and M. Yousef, "One-Class SVMs for Document Classification," *The Journal of Machine Learning Research*, 2, 139–154, 2002.

[MASU08]. M.M. Masud, J. Gao, L. Khan, J. Han, B. Thuraisingham, "A Practical Approach to Classify Evolving Data Streams: Training with Limited Amount of Labeled Data," In *Proceedings of IEEE International Conference on Data Mining (ICDM)*, Pisa, Italy, pp. 929–934, 2008.

[MASU10a]. M.M. Masud, Q. Chen, J. Gao, L. Khan, C. Aggarwal, J. Han, B. Thuraisingham, "Addressing Concept-Evolution in Concept-Drifting Data Streams," In *Proceedings of IEEE International Conference on Data Mining (ICDM)*, pp. 929–934, 2010.

[MASU10b]. M.M. Masud, Q. Chen, J. Gao, L. Khan, J. Han, B. M. Thuraisingham, "Classification and Novel Class Detection of Data Streams in A Dynamic Feature Space," *CML/PKDD (2)*, pp. 337–352, 2010.

[MASU11a]. M.M. Masud, J. Gao, L. Khan, J. Han, B.M. Thuraisingham, "Classification and Novel Class Detection in Concept-Drifting Data Streams Under Time Constraints," *IEEE Transactions on Knowledge and Data Engineering*, 23(6), 859–874, 2011.

[MASU11b]. M.M. Masud, J. Gao, L. Khan, J. Han, B.M. Thuraisingham, "Classification and Novel Class Detection in Concept-Drifting Data Streams under Time Constraints," *IEEE Transactions on Knowledge and Data Engineering*, 23(6), 859–874, 2011.

[MASU11c]. M.M. Masud, C. Woolam, J. Gao, L. Khan, J. Han, K.W. Hamlen, N.C. Oza, "Facing The Reality of Data Stream Classification: Coping with Scarcity of Labeled Data," *Knowledge and Information Systems*, 33(1), 213–244, 2011.

[MASU11d]. M.M. Masud, T. Al-Khateeb, L. Khan, C.C. Aggarwal, J. Gao, J. Han, B.M. Thuraisingham, "Detecting Recurring and Novel Classes in Concept-Drifting Data Streams," *ICDM*, pp. 1176–1181, 2011.

[MASU13]. M.M. Masud, Q. Chen, L. Khan, C.C. Aggarwal, J. Gao, J. Han, A.N. Srivastava, N.C. Oza, "Classification and Adaptive Novel Class Detection of Feature-Evolving Data Streams," *IEEE Transactions on Knowledge and Data Engineering*, 25(7), 1484–1497, 2013.

[MATZ04]. S. Matzner and T. Hetherington, "Detecting Early Indications of A Malicious Insider," *IA Newsletter*, 7(2), 42–45, 2004.

[PARV11a]. P. Parveen, J. Evans, B. Thuraisingham, K.W. Hamlen, L. Khan, "Insider Threat Detection Using Stream Mining and Graph Mining," In *Proceedings of the 3rd IEEE Conference on Privacy, Security, Risk and Trust (PASSAT) MIT*, October, Boston, MA. (acceptance rate 8%) (Nominated for Best Paper Award), pp. 1102–1110, 2011.

[PARV11b]. P. Parveen, Z.R. Weger, B. Thuraisingham, K.W. Hamlen, L. Khan, "Supervised Learning for Insider Threat Detection Using Stream Mining," In *Proceedings of the 23rd IEEE International Conference on Tools with Artificial Intelligence*, November 7–9, Boca Raton, FL (acceptance rate 30%) (Best Paper Award), pp. 1032–1039, 2011.

[PARV12a]. P. Parveen, N. McDaniel, B. Thuraisingham, L. Khan, "Unsupervised Ensemble Based Learning for Insider Threat Detection," In *Proceedings of 4th IEEE International Conference on Information Privacy, Security, Risk and Trust (PASSAT)*, September, Amsterdam, the Netherlands, pp. 718–727, 2012.

[PARV12b]. P. Parveen and B. Thuraisingham, "Unsupervised Incremental Sequence Learning for Insider Threat Detection," In *Proceedings of IEEE International Conference on Intelligence and Security (ISI)*, June, Washington DC, pp. 141–143, 2012.

[PARV13]. P. Parveen, N. McDaniel, J. Evans, B. Thuraisingham, K.W. Hamlen, L. Khan, "Evolving Insider Threat Detection Stream Mining Perspective," *International Journal on Artificial Intelligence Tools (World Scientific Publishing)*, 22(5), 1360013-1–1360013-24, 2013.

[SALE11]. M.B. Salem and S.J. Stolfo, "Modeling User Search Behavior for Masquerade Detection," In *Proceedings of Recent Advances in Intrusion Detection (RAID)*, pp. 181–200, 2011.

15 Survey of Insider Threat and Stream Mining

15.1 INTRODUCTION

As we have discussed in Chapter 7, the effective detection of insider threats requires monitoring mechanisms that are far more fine-grained than for external threat detection. These monitors must be efficiently and reliably deployable in the software environments where actions endemic to malicious insider missions are caught in a timely manner. Such environments typically include user-level applications, such as word processors, email clients, and web browsers for which reliable monitoring of internal events by conventional means is difficult.

To be able to detect the insider threats, we need to capture as accurately as possible not only the attributes of such insiders but also their behavior and communication. In Chapter 14, we argued that the data about the insiders arrive continuously and therefore could be modeled as data streams. Therefore, insider threat detection amounts to a stream data mining problem.

In this chapter, first, we will present related work with regard to insider threat and stream mining. Next, we will present related work with regard to big data and analytics perspective. The organization of this chapter is as follows. Related work on insider threat detection will be discussed in Section 15.2. Related work in stream mining will be discussed in Section 15.3. Big data issues will be discussed in Section 15.4. This chapter is summarized in Section 15.5.

15.2 INSIDER THREAT DETECTION

Insider threat detection work has applied ideas from both intrusion detection and external threat detection ([SCHO01], [WANG03], [MAXI03], [SCHU02]). Supervised learning approaches collect system call trace logs, containing records of normal and anomalous behavior ([FORR96], [HOFM98], [NGUY03], [GAO04]), extract *n*-gram features from the collected data and use the extracted features to train classifiers. Text classification approaches treat each system call as a word in a bag-of-words model [LIAO02]. Various attributes of system calls, including arguments, object path, return value, and error status, have been exploited as features in various supervised learning methods ([KRUG03], [TAND03]).

Hybrid high-order Markov chain models detect anomalies by identifying a *signature behavior* for a particular user based on their command sequences [JU01]. The probabilistic anomaly detection (PAD) algorithm [STOL05] is a general-purpose algorithm for anomaly detection (in the windows environment) that assumes that anomalies or noise is a rare event in the training data. Masquerade detection is argued over by some individuals. A number of detection methods were applied to a dataset of "truncated" UNIX shell commands for 70 users [SCHO01]. Commands were collected using the UNIX acct auditing mechanism. For each user, a number of commands were gathered over a period of time. The detection methods were supervised by a multistep Markovian model and a combination of Bayes and Markov approaches. It was argued that the dataset was not appropriate for the masquerade detection task [MAXI03]. It was pointed out that the period of data gathering varied greatly from user to user (from several days to several months). Furthermore, commands were not logged in the order in which they were typed. Instead, they were coalesced when the application terminated the audit mechanism. This leads to the unfortunate consequence of possible faulty analysis of strict sequence data. Therefore, in this proposed work, we have not considered this dataset. These approaches differ from our supervised approach in that these learning approaches are static in nature and do not learn over evolving streams. In other words, stream characteristics of data are not explored further. Hence, static learning performance may degrade over time. On the other hand, our supervised approach will learn from evolving data streams. Our proposed work is based on supervised learning, and it can handle dynamic data or stream data well by learning from evolving streams. In anomaly detection, a one-class SVM (OCSVM) algorithm is used [STOL05]. OCSVM builds a model by training on normal data, and then it classifies test data as benign or anomalous based on geometric deviations from that normal training data. For masquerade detection, OCSVM training is as effective as two-class training [STOL05]. Investigations have been made into SVMs using binary features and frequency-based features. The OCSVM algorithm with binary features performed the best.

Recursive mining has been proposed to find frequent patterns [SZYM04]. OCSVM classifiers were used for masquerade detection after the patterns were encoded with unique symbols and all sequences rewritten with this new coding. To the best of our knowledge, there is no work that extends this OCSVM in a stream domain. Although our approach relies on OCSVM, it is extended to the stream domain so that it can cope with changes ([PARV11b], [PARV13]). Works have also explored unsupervised learning for insider threat detection, but only to static streams to our knowledge ([LIU05], [ESKI02]). Static graph-based anomaly detection (GBAD) approaches ([COOK07], [EBER07], [COOK00], [YAN02]) represent threat and nonthreat data as a graph and apply unsupervised learning to detect anomalies. The *minimum description length* (MDL) approach to GBAD has been applied to email, cell phone traffic, business processes, and cybercrime datasets ([STAN96], [KOWA08]). Our work builds upon GBAD and MDL to support dynamic, evolving streams ([PARV11a], [PARV13]).

Stream mining is a relatively new category of data mining research that applies to continuous data streams [FAN04]. In such settings, both supervised and unsupervised learning must be adaptive in order to cope with data whose characteristics change over time. There are two main approaches to adaptation: *incremental learning* ([DOMI01], [DAVI98]) and *ensemble-based learning* ([MASU10a], [MASU11a], [FAN04]). The past work has demonstrated that ensemble-based approaches are the more effective of the two, thus motivating our approach.

Ensembles have been used in the past to bolster the effectiveness of positive/negative classification ([MASU08], [MASU11a]). By maintaining an ensemble of K models that collectively vote on the final classification, the number of *false negatives* (FN) and *false positives* (FP) for a test set can be reduced. As better models are created, poorer models are discarded to maintain an ensemble of size exactly K. This helps the ensemble evolve with the changing characteristics of the stream and keeps the classification task tractable. A comparison of the above related works is summarized in Table 15.1. A more complete survey is available in [SALE08].

Insider threat detection work has utilized ideas from intrusion detection or external threat detection areas ([SCHO01], [WANG03]). For example, supervised learning has been applied to detect insider threats. System call traces from normal activity and anomaly data are gathered [HOFM98];

TABLE 15.1
Capabilities and Focuses of Various Approaches for Nonsequence Data

Approach	Learning	Concept Drift	Insider Threat	Sequence-Based
[JU01]	S	×	✓	✓
[MAXI03]	S	×	✓	×
[LIU05]	U	×	✓	✓
[WANG03]	S	×	✓	×
[MASU11a]	S	✓	×	×
(Parveen, Weger et al., 2011b)	U	✓	✓	×
(Parveen, McDaniel et al., 2012)	U	✓	✓	✓

features are extracted from this data using *n*-gram and, finally, trained with classifiers. Authors [LIAO02] exploit the text classification idea in the insider threat domain where each system call is treated as a word in a bag-of-words model. System call, and related attributes, arguments, object path, return value, and error status of each system call are served as features in various supervised methods ([KRUG03], [TAND03]). A supervised model based on a hybrid high-order Markov chain model was adopted by researchers [JU01]. A *signature behavior* for a particular user based on the command sequences that the user executed is identified and then anomaly is detected.

Schonlau et al. [SCHO01] applied a number of detection methods to a dataset of "truncated" UNIX shell commands for 70 users. Commands were collected using the UNIX acct auditing mechanism. For each user, a number of commands were gathered over a period of time. The detection methods are supervised based on the multistep Markovian model and the combination of the Bayes and Markov approaches. Maxion et al. [MAXI03] argued that the Schonlau dataset was not appropriate for the masquerade detection task and created a new dataset using the Calgary dataset and applying the static supervised model.

These approaches differ from our work in the following ways. These learning approaches are static in nature and do not learn over evolving stream. In other words, stream characteristics of data are not explored further. Hence, static learner performance may degrade over time. On the other hand, our approach will learn from evolving data stream. We show that our approach is unsupervised and is as effective as a supervised model (incremental). Researchers have explored *unsupervised learning* [LIU05] for insider threat detection. However, this learning algorithm is static in nature. Although our approach is unsupervised, it learns at the same time from evolving stream over time, and more data will be used for unsupervised learning. In anomaly detection, an OCSVM algorithm is used. OCSVM builds a model from training on normal data and then classifies a test data as benign- or anomaly-based on geometric deviations from normal training data. Wang et al. [WANG03] showed for masquerade detection that OCSVM training is as effective as two-class training. The authors have investigated SVMs using binary features and frequency-based features. The one-class SVM algorithm with binary features performed the best. To find frequent patterns, Szymanski et al. [SZYM04] proposed recursive mining, encoded the patterns with unique symbols, and rewrote the sequence using this new coding. They used an OCSVM classifier for masquerade detection. These learning approaches are static in nature and do not learn over evolving stream.

15.3 STREAM MINING

Stream mining is a new data mining area where data is continuous ([MASU11a], [MASU11b], [ALKH12a], [MASU11c], [MASU10b], [MASU13]). In addition, characteristics of data may change over time (concept drift). Here, supervised learning and unsupervised learning need to be adaptive to cope with changes. There are two ways through which adaptive learning can be developed: one is incremental learning and the other is ensemble-based learning. Incremental learning is used in user action prediction [DOMI01] but not for anomaly detection. Davidson et al. [DAVI98] introduced incremental probabilistic action modeling (IPAM), based on one-step command transition probabilities estimated from the training data. The probabilities were continuously updated with the arrival of a new command and modified with the usage of an exponential decay scheme. However, the algorithm is not designed for anomaly detection. Therefore, to the best of our knowledge, there is almost no work from other researchers that handles insider threat detection in the stream mining area. This is the first attempt to detect insider threat using stream mining ([PARV11a], [PARV11b], [PARV12b]).

Recently, unsupervised learning has been applied to detect insider threat in a data stream ([PARV13], [PARV11b]). This work does not consider sequence data for threat detection. Recall that sequence data is very common in an insider threat scenario. Instead, it considers data as a graph/vector and finds normative patterns and applies an ensemble-based technique to cope with changes. On the other hand, in our proposed approach, we consider user command sequences for anomaly detection and construct a quantized dictionary for normal patterns.

TABLE 15.2
Capabilities and Focuses of Various Approaches for Sequence Data

Approach	Learning	Concept Drift	Insider Threat	Sequence-Based
[JU01]	S	×	✓	✓
[MAXI03]	S	×	✓	×
[LIU05]	U	×	✓	✓
[WANG03]	S	×	✓	×
[MASU11a]	S	✓	×	×
(Parveen, Weger et al., 2011b)	U	✓	✓	×
(Parveen, McDaniel et al., 2012)	U	✓	✓	✓

Users' repetitive daily or weekly activities may constitute user profiles. For example, a user's frequent command sequences may represent a normative pattern of that user. Finding normative patterns over dynamic data streams of unbounded length is challenging due to the requirement of a one-pass algorithm. For this, an unsupervised learning approach is used by exploiting a compressed/quantized dictionary to model common behavior sequences. This unsupervised approach needs to identify a normal user's behavior in a single pass ([PARV12a], [PARV12b], [CHUA11]). One major challenge with these repetitive sequences is their variability in length. To combat this problem, we generate a dictionary that will contain any combination of possible normative patterns existing in the gathered data stream. In addition, we have incorporated the power of stream mining to cope with gradual changes. We have done experiments and shown that our USSL approach works well in the context of the concept drift and anomaly detection.

Our work ([PARV12a], [PARV12b]) differs from that of [CHUA11] in the following ways. First, the work in [CHUA11] focuses on dictionary construction to generate normal profiles. In other words, their work does not address the insider threat issue, which is our focus. Second, [CHUA11] does not consider ensemble-based techniques; our work exploits the ensemble-based technique with the combination of unsupervised learning (i.e., dictionary for benign sequences). Finally, when a number of users will grow, dictionary construction will become a bottleneck. The work of [CHUA11] does not consider the scalability issue; in our case, we address the scalability issue using a MapReduce framework.

In [PARV12a], an incremental approach is used. Ensemble-based techniques are not incorporated, but the literature used shows that ensemble-based techniques are more effective than those of the incremental variety for stream mining ([MASU10a], [MASU11a], [FAN04]). Therefore, our approach focuses on ensemble-based techniques [PARV12b].

Refer to Table 15.2 in which related approaches are unsupervised or supervised, and it has been explained whether they focus on concept-drift, detecting insider threat, and sequenced data from stream mining.

15.4 BIG DATA TECHNIQUES FOR SCALABILITY

Stream data are continuously coming with high velocity and large size [ALKH12b]. This conforms to the characteristics of big data. "Big data" is data whose scale, diversity, and complexity require new architecture, techniques, algorithms, and analytics to manage it and extract value and hidden knowledge from it. Therefore, big data researchers are looking for tools to manage, analyze, summarize, visualize, and discover knowledge from the collected data in a timely manner and in a scalable fashion. Here, we will list some and discuss what problems we are solving in big data.

With regard to big data management, there are a number of techniques available that allow massively scalable data processing over grids of inexpensive commodity hardware such as the following.

The Google File System ([CHAN06], [DEAN08]) is a scalable distributed file system that utilizes clusters of commodity hardware to facilitate data-intensive applications. The system is fault tolerant where the failure of the machine is normal due to the usage of commodity hardware. To cope with failure, data will replicate into multiple nodes. If one node is failing, the system will utilize the other node where replicated data exists.

MapReduce ([CHAN06], [DEAN08]) is a programming model that supports data-intensive applications in a parallel manner. The MapReduce paradigm supports map and reduce functions. Map generates a set of intermediate key and value pairs, and then the reduce function combines the results and deduces it. In fact, the map/reduce paradigm can solve many real-world problems as shown in ([CHAN06], [DEAN08]).

Hadoop ([BU10], [XU10], [ABOU09]) is an open-source apache project that supports the Google File System and the MapReduce paradigm. Hadoop is widely used to address the scalability issue along with MapReduce. For example, with the huge amount of semantic web datasets, Husain et al. ([HUSA09], [HUSA10], [HUSA11]) showed that Hadoop can be used to provide scalable queries. In addition, MapReduce technology has been exploited by the BioMANTA project [DING05] and SHARD (see also [BIOM] and [SHAR]).

Amazon developed Dynamo [DECA07], a distributed key-value store. Dynamo does not support master–slave architecture, which is supported by Hadoop. Nodes in Dynamo communicate via a gossip network. To achieve high availability and performance, Dynamo supports a model called eventual consistency by sacrificing rigorous consistency. In eventual consistency, updates will be propagated to nodes in the cluster asynchronously and a new version of the data will be produced for each update.

Google developed BigTable ([CHAN06], [CHAN08]), a column-oriented data storage system. BigTable utilizes the Google File System and Chubby [BURR06], a distributed lock service. BigTable is a distributed multidimensional sparse map based on row keys, column names, and time stamps.

Researchers [ABOU09] exploited the combined power of MapReduce and relational database technology. With regard to big data analytics, there are handfuls of works related to this topic. For example, on the one hand, some researchers focus on generic analytics tools to address the scalability issue. On the other hand, other researchers focus on specific analytics problems.

With regard to tools, Mahout is an open-source big data analytics tool to support classification, clustering, and a recommendation system for big data. In [CHU06], researchers customized well-known machine learning algorithms to take advantage of multicore machines and the MapReduce programming paradigm. MapReduce has been widely used for mining petabytes of data [MORE08].

With regard to specific problems, Al-Khateeb et al. [ALKH12b] and Haque et al. ([HAQU13a], [HAQU13b]) proposed scalable classification over evolving stream by exploiting the MapReduce and Hadoop frameworks. There are some research works on parallel boosting with MapReduce. Palit et al. [PALI12] proposed two parallel boosting algorithms, ADABOOST.PL and LOGITBOOST.PL.

15.5 SUMMARY AND DIRECTIONS

Many of the learning techniques that have been proposed in the literature do not handle data streams. As a result, these techniques do not address the evolving nature of streams. Our goal is to adapt SVM techniques for data streams so that such techniques can be used to handle the insider threat problem. This chapter has discussed aspects of stream mining as well as applying stream mining for massive data.

In the ensuing chapters of Part III we will discuss the techniques we have designed for insider threat detection. In particular, we argue that data relevant to insider threats is typically accumulated over many years of organization and system operations, and is therefore best characterized as an unbounded data stream. We then show how learning techniques including ensemble-based learning can be used for insider threat detection.

REFERENCES

[ABOU09]. A. Abouzeid, K. Bajda-Pawlikowski, D. J. Abadi, A. Rasin, A. Silberschatz, "HadoopDB: An Architectural Hybrid of MapReduce and DBMS Technologies for Analytical Workloads," In *Proceedings of the VLDB Endowment* 2 (1), 922–933, 2009.

[ALKH12a]. T. Al-Khateeb, M. M. Masud, L. Khan, C. C. Aggarwal, J. Han, B. M. Thuraisingham, "Stream Classification with Recurring and Novel Class Detection Using Class-Based Ensemble," In *ICDM'2012: Proceedings of the 12th IEEE Conference on Data Mining*, December 10–13, 2012, Brussels, Belgium, pp. 31–40, 2012.

[ALKH12b]. T. Al-Khateeb, M. M. Masud, L. Khan, B. M. Thuraisingham, "Cloud Guided Stream Classification Using Class-Based Ensemble." In *CLOUD'2012: Proceedings of the 5th IEEE Conference on Cloud Computing*, June 24–29, Honolulu, HI, USA, pp. 694–701, 2012.

[BIOM]. http://www.itee.uq.edu.au/eresearch/projects/biomanta.

[BU10]. Y. Bu, B. Howe, M. Balazinska, M. Ernst, "Haloop: Efficient Iterative Data Processing on Large Clusters," *Proceedings of the VLDB Endowment* 3 (1), 285–296, 2010.

[BURR06]. M. Burrows, "The Chubby Lock Service for Loosely-Coupled Distributed Systems," In *OSDI'06: Proceedings of the 7th Symposium on Operating Systems Design and Implementation*, November 6–8, Seattle, Washington, D.C., pp. 335–350, 2006.

[CHAN06]. F. Chang, J. Dean, S. Ghemawat, W. C. Hsieh, D. A. Wallach, M. Burrows, T. Chandra, A. Fikes, R. Gruber, "Bigtable: A Distributed Storage System for Structured Data (Awarded Best Paper)," In *OSDI'06: 7th USENIX Symposium on Operating Systems Design and Implementation*, November 6–8, Seattle, Washington, D.C., pp. 205–218, 2006.

[CHAN08]. F. Chang, J. Dean, S. Ghemawat, W. C. Hsieh, D. A. Wallach, M. Burrows, T. Chandra, A. Fikes, R. E. Gruber, "BigTable: A Distributed Storage System for Structured Data," *ACM Transactions on Computer Systems* 26 (2), Article #4, 2008.

[CHU06]. C. T. Chu, S. K. Kim, Y. A. Lin, Y. Yu, G. R. Bradski, A. Y. Ng, K. Olukotun, "Map-Reduce for Machine Learning on Multicore," B. Sch¨ opf, J. C. Platt, T. Hoffman (eds.), *Neural Information Processing Systems*, MIT Press, Cambridge, MA, pp. 281–288, 2006.

[CHUA11]. S.-L. Chua, S. Marsland, H. W. Guesgen, "Unsupervised Learning of Patterns in Data Streams Using Compression and Edit Distance," In *IJCAI'2011: Proceedings of the 22nd International Joint Conference on Artificial Intelligence*, July 16–22, Catalonia, Spain, pp. 1231–1236, 2011.

[COOK00]. D. J. Cook and L. B. Holder, "Graph-Based Data Mining," *IEEE Intelligent Systems* 15 (2), 32–41, 2000.

[COOK07]. D. J. Cook and L. B. Holder, editors. *Mining Graph Data*, John Wiley & Sons, Inc., Hoboken, NJ, 2007.

[DAVI98]. B. D. Davison and H. Hirsh, "Predicting Sequences of User Actions. In Working Notes of the Joint Workshop on Predicting the Future: AI Approaches to Time Series Analysis." *15th National Conference on Artificial Intelligence and Machine*, AAAI Press, Madison, WI, pp. 5–12, 1998.

[DEAN08]. J. Dean and S. Ghemawat, "MapReduce: Simplified Data Processing on Large Clusters," *Communications of the ACM*, 51(1), 107–113, 2008.

[DECA07]. G. DeCandia, D. Hastorun, M. Jampani, G. Kakulapati, A. Lakshman, A. Pilchin, S. Sivasubramanian, P. Vosshall, W. Vogels, "Dynamo: Amazon's Highly Available Key-Value Store," T. C. Bressoud, M. F. Kaashoek (eds.), In *SOSP'07: Proceedings of the 21st ACM Symposium on Operating Systems Principles*, Oct. 14–17, Stevenson, Washington, D.C., pp. 205–220, 2007.

[DING05]. L. Ding, T. Finin, Y. Peng, P. P. da Silva, D. L. Mcguinness, "Tracking RDF Graph Provenance Using RDF Molecules," Technical Report (TR-S-05-06), University of Maryland Baltimore County, 2005. http://ebiquity.umbc.edu/paper/html/id/240/.

[DOMI01]. P. Domingos and G. Hulten, "Catching Up with the Data: Research Issues in Mining Data Streams," In *DMKD'01: 2001 ACM SIGMOD Workshop on Research Issues in Data Mining and Knowledge Discovery*, May 20, Santa Barbara, CA, USA, 2001.

[EBER07]. W. Eberle and L. B. Holder, "Mining for Structural Anomalies in Graph-Based Data," In *DMIN'07: Proceedings of International Conference on Data Mining*, Las Vegas, NV, pp. 376–389, 2007.

[ESKI02]. E. Eskin, A. Arnold, M. Prerau, L. Portnoy, S. Stolfo, "A Geometric Framework for Unsupervised Anomaly Detection: Detecting Intrusions in Unlabeled data," D. Barbar´, S. Jajodia (eds.), *Applications of Data Mining in Computer Security*, Chapter 4. Springer, New York, NY, 2002.

[FAN04]. W. Fan, "Systematic Data Selection to Mine Concept-Drifting Data Streams," In *Proceedings of ACM SIGKDD*, Seattle, Washington, D.C., pp. 128–137, 2004.

[FORR96]. S. Forrest, S. A. Hofmeyr, A. Somayaji, T. A. Longstaf, "A Sense of Self for Unix Processes," In *Proceedings of the IEEE Symposium on Computer Security and Privacy (S&P)*, Oakland, CA, pp. 120–128, 1996.

[GAO04]. D. Gao, M. K. Reiter, D. Song, "On Gray-Box Program Tracking for Anomaly Detection," In *Proceedings of the USENIX Security Symposium*, pp. 103–118, 2004.

[HAQU13a]. A. Haque, B. Parker, L. Khan, "Intelligent MapReduce Based Frameworks for Labeling Instances in Evolving Data Stream" In *CloudCom'2013: Proceedings of the 5th International Conference on Cloud Computing Technology and Science*, December 2–5, Bristol, UK, pp. 299–304, 2013.

[HAQU13b]. A. Haque, B. Parker, L. Khan, "Labeling Instances in Evolving Data Streams with Mapreduce," *BigData*, Santa Clara, CA, pp. 387–394, 2013.

[HOFM98]. S. A. Hofmeyr, S. Forrest, A. Somayaji, "Intrusion Detection Using Sequences of System Calls," *Journal of Computer Security* 6 (3), 151–180, 1998.

[HUSA09]. M. Husain, P. Doshi, L. Khan, B. Thuraisingham, "Storage and Retrieval of Large RDF Graph Using Hadoop and MapReduce," In *CloudCom'09: Proceedings of the 1st International Conference on Cloud Computing*, pp. 680–686. Springer-Verlag, Berlin, 2009.

[HUSA10]. M. F. Husain, L. Khan, M. Kantarcioglu, B. Thuraisingham, "Data Intensive Query Processing for Large RDF Graphs Using Cloud Computing Tools," In *CLOUD'10: Proceedings of the 2010 IEEE 3rd International Conference on Cloud Computing*, Washington, DC, pp. 1–10, 2010.

[HUSA11]. M. F. Husain, J. P. McGlothlin, M. M. Masud, L. R. Khan, B. M. Thuraisingham, "Heuristics-Based Query Processing for Large RDF Graphs Using Cloud Computing," *IEEE Transactions on Knowledge and Data Engineering* 23 (9), 1312–1327, 2011.

[JU01]. W.-H. Ju and Y. Vardi, "A Hybrid High-Order Markov Chain Model for Computer Intrusion Detection," *Journal of Computational and Graphical Statistics* 10 (2), 277–295, 2001.

[KOWA08]. E., Kowalski, T. Conway, S. Keverline, M. Williams, D. Cappelli, B. Willke, A. Moore, "*Insider Threat Study: Illicit Cyber Activity in the Government Sector*," Technical Report, U.S. Department of Homeland Security, U.S. Secret Service, CERT, and the Software Engineering Institute (Carnegie Mellon University), 2008. http://resources.sei.cmu.edu/library/asset-view.cfm?assetID=52227.

[KRUG03]. C. Krugel, D. Mutz, F. Valeur, G. Vigna, "On the Detection of Anomalous System Call Arguments," In *ESORICS'03: Proceedings of the 8th European Symposium on Research in Computer Security*, Gjovik, Norway, pp. 326–343, 2003.

[LIAO02]. Y. Liao and V. R. Vemuri, "Using Text Categorization Techniques for Intrusion Detection," In *Proceedings of the 11th USENIX Security Symposium*, Berkeley, CA, pp. 51–59, 2002.

[LIU05]. A. Liu, C. Martin, T. Hetherington, S. Matzner, "A Comparison of System Call Feature Representations for Insider Threat Detection," In *IAW'05: Proceedings of the IEEE Information Assurance Workshop*, West Point, NY, pp. 340–347, 2005.

[MASU08]. Masud, M. M., J. Gao, L. Khan, J. Han, B. Thuraisingham, "A Practical Approach to Classify Evolving Data Streams: Training with Limited Amount of Labeled Data," In *ICDM'08: Proceedings of the IEEE International Conference on Data Mining*, West Point, NY, pp. 929–934, 2008.

[MASU10a]. M. M. Masud, Q. Chen, J. Gao, L. Khan, C. Aggarwal, J. Han, B. Thuraisingham, "Addressing Concept-Evolution in Concept-Drifting Data Streams," In *ICDM'10: Proceedings of the IEEE International Conference on Data Mining*, Sydney, New South Wales, pp. 929–934, 2010.

[MASU10b]. M. M. Masud, J. Gao, L. Khan, J. Han, B. M. Thuraisingham, "Classification and Novel Class Detection in Data Streams with Active Mining," In *PKDD'10: Advances in Knowledge Discovery and Data Mining (Lecture Notes in Computer Science Series, vol. 6119, part 2)*, Springer, New York, NY, pp. 311–324, 2010.

[MASU11a]. M. M. Masud, J. Gao, L. Khan, J. Han, B. M. Thuraisingham, "Classification and Novel Class Detection in Concept-drifting Data Streams under Time Constraints," *IEEE Transactions on Knowledge and Data Engineering* 23 (6), 859–874, 2011.

[MASU11b]. M. M., Masud, C. Woolam, J. Gao, L. Khan, J. Han, K. W. Hamlen, N. C. Oza, "Facing the Reality of Data Stream Classification: Coping with Scarcity of Labeled Data," *Knowledge and Information Systems* 33 (1), 213–244, 2011.

[MASU11c]. M. M. Masud, T. Al-Khateeb, L. Khan, C. C. Aggarwal, J. Gao, J. Han, B. M. Thuraisingham, "Detecting Recurring and Novel Classes in Concept-Drifting Data Streams," In *ICDM'2011: Proceedings of the 11th IEEE Conference on Data Mining*, December 11–14, Vancouver, BC, Canada, pp. 1176–1181, 2011.

[MASU13]. M. M., Masud, Q. Chen, L. Khan, C. C. Aggarwal, J. Gao, J. Han, A. N. Srivastava, N. C. Oza, "Classification and Adaptive Novel Class Detection of Feature-evolving Data Streams," *IEEE Transactions on Knowledge and Data Engineering* 25 (7), 1484–1497, 2013.

[MAXI03]. R. A. Maxion, "Masquerade Detection Using Enriched Command Lines," In *DSN'03: Proceedings of the IEEE International Conference on Dependable Systems and Networks*, San Francisco, CA, pp. 5–14, 2003.

[MORE08]. C. Moretti, K. Steinhaeuser, D. Thain, N. V. Chawla, "Scaling Up Classifiers to Cloud Computers," In *Proceedings of the 2008 8th IEEE International Conference on Data Mining*, Washington, D.C., pp. 472–481, 2008.

[NGUY03]. N. Nguyen, P. Reiher, and G. H. Kuenning, "Detecting Insider Threats by Monitoring System Call Activity," In *IAW'03: Proceedings of the IEEE Information Assurance Workshop*, West Point, NY, pp. 45–52, 2003.

[PALI12]. I. Palit and C. K. Reddy, "Scalable and Parallel Boosting with Mapreduce," *IEEE Transactions on Knowledge and Data Engineering* 24 (10), 1904–1916, 2012.

[PARV11a]. P. Parveen, J. Evans, B. Thuraisingham, K. W. Hamlen, L. Khan, "Insider Threat Detection Using Stream Mining and Graph Mining," In *PASSAT'2011: Proceedings of the 3rd IEEE Conference on Privacy, Security, Risk and Trust, MIT*, Boston, MA, USA, pp. 1102–1110, 2011.

[PARV11b]. P. Parveen, Z. R. Weger, B. Thuraisingham, K. W. Hamlen, L. Khan, "Supervised Learning for Insider Threat Detection Using Stream Mining," In *Proceedings of the 23rd IEEE International Conference on Tools with Artificial Intelligence*, November 7–9, Boca Raton, FL, pp. 1032–1039, 2011.

[PARV12a]. P. Parveen and B. Thuraisingham, "Unsupervised Incremental Sequence Learning for Insider Threat Detection," In *ISI'2012: Proceedings of the. IEEE International Conference on Intelligence and Security*, June, Washington, DC, pp. 141–143, 2012.

[PARV12b]. P. Parveen, N. McDaniel, B. Thuraisingham, L. Khan, "Unsupervised Ensemble Based Learning for Insider Threat Detection," In *PASSAT'2012: Proceedings of the 4th IEEE International Conference on Information Privacy, Security, Risk and Trus*, September, Amsterdam, The Netherlands, pp. 718–727, 2012.

[PARV13]. P. Parveen, N. McDaniel, J. Evans, B. Thuraisingham, K. W. Hamlen, L. Khan, "Evolving Insider Threat Detection Stream Mining Perspective," *International Journal on Artificial Intelligence Tools* 22 (5), 1360013, 2013.

[SALE08]. M. B., Salem, S. Herkshkop, S. J. Stolfo, "A Survey of Insider Attack Detection Research," *Insider Attack and Cyber Security* 39, 69–90, 2008.

[SCHO01]. M. Schonlau, W. DuMouchel, W.-H. Ju, A. F. Karr, M. Theus, Y. Vardi, "Computer Intrusion: Detecting Masquerades," *Statistical Science* 16 (1), 1–17, 2001.

[SCHU02]. E. E. Schultz, "A Framework for Understanding and Predicting Insider Attacks," *Computers and Security* 21 (6), 526–531, 2002.

[SHAR]. http://www.cloudera.com/blog/2010/03/how-raytheon-esearchers-are-using-hadoop-to-build-a-scalable-distributed-triple-store.

[STAN96]. S. Staniford-Chen, S. Cheung, R. Crawford, M. Dilger, J. Frank, J. Hoagland, K. Levitt, C. Wee, R. Yip, D. Zerkle, "GrIDS—A Graph Based Intrusion Detection System for Large Networks," In *Proceedings of the 19th National Information Systems Security Conference*, Baltimore, MD, pp. 361–370, 1996.

[STOL05]. S. J. Stolfo, F. Apap, E. Eskin, K. Heller, S. Hershkop, A. Honig, K. Svore, "A Comparative Evaluation of Two Algorithms for Windows Registry Anomaly Detection," *Journal of Computer Security* 13 (4), 659–693, 2005.

[SZYM04]. B. K. Szymanski and Y. Zhang, "Recursive Data Mining for Masquerade Detection and Author Identification," *13th Annual IEEE Information Assurance Workshop*, Washington, DC, pp. 424–431, 2004.

[TAND03]. G. Tandon and P. Chan, "Learning Rules from System Call Arguments and Sequences for Anomaly Detection," In *DMSEC'03: Proceedings of the ICDM Workshop on Data Mining for Computer Security*, Melbourne, FL, pp. 20–29, 2003.

[WANG 03]. H. Wang, W. Fan, P. S. Yu, J. Han, "Mining Concept-Drifting Data Streams Using Ensemble Classifiers," In *Proceedings of SIGKDD*, Washington, DC, pp. 226–235, 2003.

[XU10]. Y. Xu, P. Kostamaa, L. Gao, "Integrating Hadoop and Parallel DBMS," In *SIGMOD'2010: Proceedings of the 2010 International Conference on Management of Data*, New York, NY, pp. 969–974, 2010.

[YAN02]. X. Yan and J. Han, "gSpan: Graph-Based Substructure Pattern Mining," In *ICDM'02: Proceedings of the International Conference on Data Mining*, Maebashi City, Japan, pp. 721–724, 2002.

16 Ensemble-Based Insider Threat Detection

16.1 INTRODUCTION

Data relevant to insider threats is typically accumulated over many years of organization and system operations, and is therefore best characterized as an unbounded data stream. Such a stream can be partitioned into a sequence of discrete *chunks*; for example, each chunk might comprise a week's worth of data. Figure 16.1 illustrates how a classifier's decision boundary changes when such a stream observes the concept drift. Each circle in the picture denotes a data point with unfilled circles representing *true negatives* (TNs) (i.e., nonanomalies) and solid circles representing *true positives* (TPs) (i.e., anomalies). The solid line in each chunk represents the decision boundary for that chunk, whereas the dashed line represents the decision boundary for the previous chunk. Shaded circles are those that embody a new concept that have drifted relative to the previous chunk. In order to classify these properly, the decision boundary must be adjusted to account for the new concept. There are two possible varieties of *misapprehension* (false detection):

1. The decision boundary of chunk 2 moves upward relative to chunk 1. As a result, some nonanomalous data is incorrectly classified as anomalous, causing the false positive (FP) rate to rise.
2. The decision boundary of chunk 3 moves downward relative to chunk 2. As a result, some anomalous data is incorrectly classified as nonanomalous, causing the false negative (FN) rate to rise.

In general, the old and new decision boundaries can intersect, causing both of the above cases to occur simultaneously for the same chunk. Therefore, both FP and FN counts may increase. These observations suggest that a model built from a single chunk or any finite prefix of chunks is inadequate to properly classify all data in the stream. This motivates the adoption of our ensemble approach, which classifies data using an evolving set of *K* models.

The organization of this chapter is as follows. Ensemble learning will be discussed in Section 16.2. Ensemble for unsupervised learning will be discussed in Section 16.3. Ensemble learning for supervising learning will be discussed in Section 16.4. This chapter is summarized in Section 16.5.

16.2 ENSEMBLE LEARNING

The ensemble classification procedure is illustrated in Figure 16.2. We first build a model using one-class SVM (OCSVM) (supervised approach) or graph-based anomaly detection (GBAD) (unsupervised approach) from an individual chunk ([PARV11a], [PARV13], [PARV11b]). In the case of GBAD, *normative substructures* are identified in the chunk, each represented as a subgraph. To identify an anomaly, a test substructure is compared against each model of the ensemble. A model will classify the test substructure as an anomaly based on how much the test differs from the model's normative substructure. Once all models cast their votes, weighted majority voting is applied to make a final classification decision. Ensemble evolution is arranged so as to maintain a set of exactly *K* models at all times. As each new chunk arrives, a $(K + 1)$st model is created from the new chunk and one victim model of these $(K + 1)$st models is discarded. The discarded victim can be selected in a number of ways. One approach is to calculate the prediction error of each of the $K + 1$

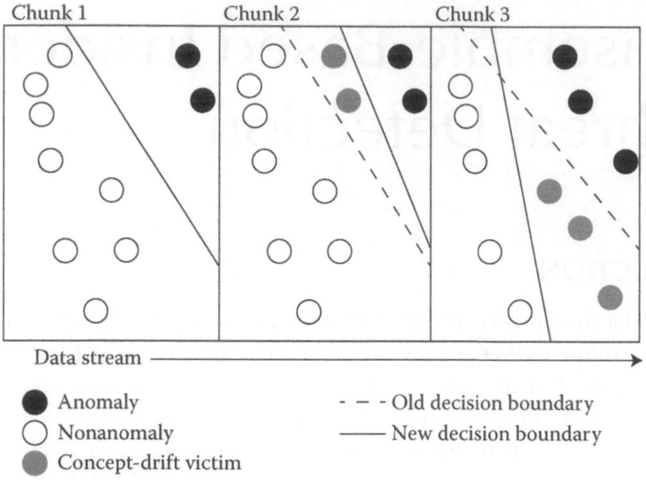

FIGURE 16.1 Concept drift in stream data.

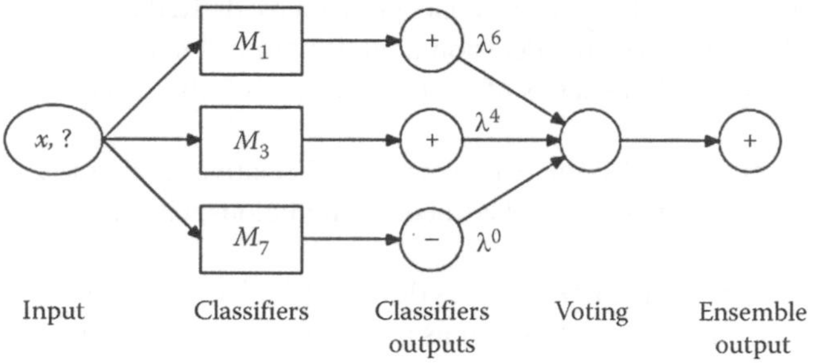

FIGURE 16.2 Ensemble classification.

models on the most recent chunk and discard the poorest predictor. This requires the *ground truth* to be immediately available for the most recent chunk so that the prediction error can be accurately measured. If the ground truth is not available, we instead rely on majority voting; the model with least agreement with the majority decision is discarded. This results in an ensemble of the K models that best match the current concept.

Algorithm 16.1 Unsupervised Ensemble Classification and Updating

```
Input: E (ensemble), t (test graph), and S (chunk)
Output: A (anomalies), and E (updated ensemble)
M ← NewModel(S)
E ← E∪{M}
for each model M in ensemble E do
   cM ← 0
   for each q in model M do
         A1 ← GBADP (t, q)
         A2 ← GBADMDL(t, q)
         A3 ← GBADMPS (t, q)
         AM ← ParseResults(A1, A2, A3)
   end for
end for
```

```
14: for each candidate a in M ∈ E AM do
15:   if round(WeightedAverage(E',a)) = 1 then then
16:     A ← A∪{a}
17:     for each model M in ensemble E do
18:       if a ∈ AM then then
19:           cM ← cM + 1
20:       end if
21:   end for
22: else
23:       for each model M in ensemble E do
24:           if a ∈ AM then then
25:           cM ← cM + 1
26:       end if
27:    end for
28:  end if
29: end for
30: E ← E–{choose(arg minM (cM))}
```

16.3 ENSEMBLE FOR UNSUPERVISED LEARNING

Algorithm 16.1 summarizes the unsupervised classification and ensemble-based updating algorithm. Lines 3–4 build a new model from the most recent chunk and temporarily add it to the ensemble. Next, Lines 5–13 apply each model in the ensemble to test graph *t* for possible anomalies. We use three varieties of GBAD for each model (P, MDL, and MPS); each discussed in Section 17.3. Finally, Lines 14–30 update the ensemble by discarding the model with the most disagreements from the weighted majority opinion. If multiple models have the most disagreements, an arbitrary poorest performing one is discarded. Note that no ground truth is used. However, majority voting of models serve the so-called ground truth. Weighted majority opinions are computed in Line 15 using the formula

$$WA(E,a) = \frac{\sum \{i \mid M_i \in E, a \in A_{M_i}\}^{\lambda^{\ell-i}}}{\sum \{i \mid M_i \in E\}^{\lambda^{\ell-i}}} \tag{16.1}$$

where $M_i \in E$ is a model in ensemble E that was trained from chunk i, A_{M_i} is the set of anomalies reported by model M_i, $\lambda \in [0, 1]$ is a constant *fading factor* [CHEN09] and is the index of the most recent chunk. Model M_i's vote therefore receives weight $\lambda - i$, with the most recently constructed model receiving weight $\lambda 0 = 1$, the model trained from the previous chunk receiving weight $\lambda 1$ (if it still exists in the ensemble), etc. This has the effect of weighting the votes of more recent models above those of potentially outdated ones when $\lambda < 1$. Weighted average *WA(E, a)* is then rounded to the nearest integer (0 or 1) in Line 15 to obtain the weighted majority vote. For example, in Figure 16.2, models M_1, M_3, and M_7 vote positive, positive, and negative, respectively, for the input sample *x*. If = 7 is the most recent chunk, these votes are weighted $\lambda 6$, $\lambda 4$, and 1, respectively. The weighted average is therefore $WA(E, x) = (\lambda 6 + \lambda 4)/(\lambda 6 + \lambda 4 + 1)$. If $\lambda \leq 0.86$, the negative majority opinion wins in this case; however, if $\lambda \geq 0.87$, the newer model's vote outweighs the two older dissenting opinions, and the result is a positive classification. The parameter λ can thus be tuned to balance the importance of large amounts of older information against smaller amounts of newer information. Our approach uses the results from the previous iterations of GBAD to identify anomalies in subsequent data chunks. That is, normative substructures found in the previous GBAD iterations may persist in each model. This allows each model to consider all data since the model's introduction to the ensemble, not just that of the current chunk. When streams observe the concept drift, this can be a significant advantage because the ensemble can identify patterns that are normative over the entire data stream or a significant number of chunks but not in the current chunk. Thus, insiders whose malicious behavior is infrequent can still be detected.

Algorithm 16.2 Supervised Ensemble Classification Updating

1: Input: *Du* (most recently labeled chunk), and *A* (ensemble)
2: Output: *A* (updated ensemble)
3: **for** each model *M* in ensemble *A* **do**
4: test(M, Du)
5: end for
6: $Mn \leftarrow OCSVM(Du)$
7: *test(Mn, Du)*
8: $A \leftarrow \{K : Mn \cup A\}$

Algorithm 16.3 Supervised Testing Algorithm

1: Input: *Du* (most recent unlabeled chunk), and *A* (ensemble)
2: Output: *Du* (labeled/predicted *Du*)
3: $F_u \leftarrow ExtractandSelectFeatures(Du)$
4: **for** each feature $xj \in F_u$ **do**
5: R ← NULL
6: **for** each model M in ensemble A **do**
7: R ← R∪ predict(xj, M)
8: **end for**
9: anomalies ← MajorityVote(R)
10: end for

16.4 ENSEMBLE FOR SUPERVISED LEARNING

Algorithm 16.2 shows the basic building blocks of our supervised algorithm. Here, we first present how we update the model. Input for Algorithm 16.2 will be as follows: D_u is the most recently labeled data chunk (most recent training chunk) and *A* is the ensemble. Lines 3–4 calculate the prediction error of each model on D_u. Line 6 builds a new model using OCSVM on D_u. Line 7 produces $K + 1$ models. Line 8 discards the model with the maximum prediction error, keeping the *K* best models. Algorithm 16.3 focuses on ensemble testing. Ensemble *A* and the latest unlabeled chunk of instance D_u will be the input. Line 3 performs feature extraction and selection using the latest chunk of unlabeled data. Lines 4–9 will take each extracted feature from D_u and do an anomaly prediction. Lines 6–7 use each model to predict the anomaly status for a particular feature. Finally, Line 9 predicts anomalies based on majority voting of the results.

Our ensemble method uses the results from previous iterations of OCSVM executions to identify anomalies in subsequent data chunks. This allows the consideration of more than just the current data being analyzed. Models found in previous OCSVM iterations are also analyzed, not just the models of the current dataset chunk. The ensemble handles the execution in this manner because patterns identified in previous chunks may be normative over the entire data stream or a significant number of chunks but not in the current execution chunk. Thus, insiders whose malicious behavior is infrequent will be detected. It is important to note that we always keep our ensemble size fixed. Hence, an outdated model, which is performing the worst on the most recent chunks, will be replaced by the new one.

It is important to note that the size of the ensemble remains fixed over time. Outdated models that are performing poorly are replaced by better performing, newer models that are more suited to the current concept. This keeps each round of classification tractable, even though the total amount of data in the stream is potentially unbounded.

16.5 SUMMARY AND DIRECTIONS

This chapter has discussed ensemble-based learning for insider threat detection. In particular, we have described techniques for both supervised and unsupervised learning and discussed the issues involved. We believe that ensemble-based approaches are suited for data streams as they are unbounded. In the ensuing chapters, we will discuss additional techniques for nonsequence and sequence data, and provide experimental results.

It should be noted that our goal is to provide a variety of stream mining methods for insider threat detection. These methods can be enhanced with respect to accuracy, false positives, and false negatives as more is known about the insider threat problem.

REFERENCES

[CHEN09]. L. Chen, S. Zhang, L. Tu, "An Algorithm for Mining Frequent Items on Data Stream Using Fading Factor," In *COMPSAC'09: Proceedings of the IEEE International Computer Software and Applications Conference*, Seattle, WA, pp. 172–177, 2009.

[PARV11a]. P. Parveen, Z. R. Weger, B. Thuraisingham, K. W. Hamlen, L. Khan, "Supervised Learning for Insider Threat Detection Using Stream Mining," In *Proceedings of the 23rd IEEE International Conference on Tools with Artificial Intelligence*, November 7–9, Boca Raton, FL, 2011.

[PARV11b]. P. Parveen, J. Evans, B. Thuraisingham, K. W. Hamlen, L. Khan, "Insider Threat Detection Using Stream Mining and Graph Mining," In *PASSAT'2011: Proceedings of the 3rd IEEE Conference on Privacy, Security, Risk and Trust, MIT*, October Boston, MA, pp. 1102–1110, 2011.

[PARV13]. P. Parveen, N. McDaniel, J. Evans, B. Thuraisingham, K. W. Hamlen, L. Khan, "Evolving Insider Threat Detection Stream Mining Perspective," *International Journal on Artificial Intelligence Tools* 22 (5), 1360013.

17 Details of Learning Classes

17.1 INTRODUCTION

Insider threats are veritable needles within the haystack. Their occurrence is rare and when they do occur are usually masked well within normal operation. The detection of these threats requires identifying these rare anomalous needles in a contextualized setting where behaviors are constantly evolving over time. To this refined search, we have designed approaches based on both supervised and unsupervised, ensemble-based learning algorithms that maintain a compressed dictionary of repetitive sequences found throughout dynamic data streams of unbounded length to identify anomalies. For example, in unsupervised learning, compression-based techniques are used to model common behavior sequences. This results in a classifier, exhibiting a substantial increase in classification accuracy for data streams containing insider threat anomalies. This ensemble of classifiers allows the unsupervised approach to outperform traditional static learning approaches and boosts the effectiveness over supervised learning approaches.

This chapter will describe the different classes of learning techniques for nonsequence data ([PARV11a], [PARV13], [PARV11b]). It serves the purpose of providing more detail as to exactly how each method arrives at detecting insider threats and how ensemble models are built, modified, and discarded. The first subsection focusses on supervised learning in detail, and the second subsection focuses on unsupervised learning. Both contain the formulas necessary to understand the inner workings of each class of learning.

The organization of this chapter is as follows. Supervised learning will be discussed in Section 17.2, while unsupervised learning will be discussed in Section 17.3. Section 17.4 will provide a summary of this chapter.

17.2 SUPERVISED LEARNING

In a chunk, a model is built using the OCSVM [MANE02]. The OCSVM approach first maps training data into a high-dimensional feature space (via a kernel). Next, the algorithm iteratively finds the maximal margin hyper-plane that best separates the training data from the origin. The OCSVM may be considered as a regular two-class SVM. Here, the first class entails all the training data and the second class is the origin. Thus, the hyper-plane (or linear decision boundary) corresponds to the classification rule:

$$f(x) = w, x + b \tag{17.1}$$

where w is the normal vector and b is a bias term. The OCSVM solves an optimization problem to find the rule with the maximal geometric margin. This classification rule will be used to assign a label to a test example x. If $f(x) < 0$, we label x as an anomaly; otherwise, it is labeled normal. In reality, there is a trade-off between maximizing the distance of the hyper-plane from the origin and the number of training data points contained in the region separated from the origin by the hyper-plane.

17.3 UNSUPERVISED LEARNING

Algorithm 17.1 uses three varieties of GBAD ([COOK07] [EBER07], [COOK00], [YAN02]) to infer potential anomalies using each model. GBAD is a graph-based approach to find anomalies in data

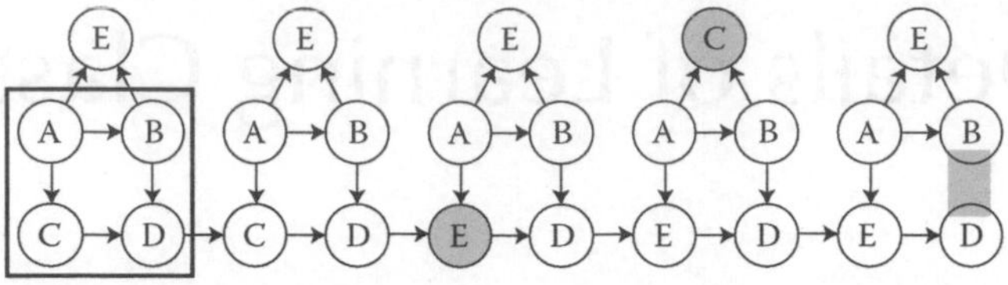

FIGURE 17.1 A graph with a normative substructure (boxed) and anomalies (shaded).

by searching for three factors: modifications, insertions, and deletions of vertices and edges. Each unique factor runs its own algorithm that finds a normative substructure and attempts to find the substructures that are similar but not completely identical to the discovered normative substructure. A normative substructure is a recurring subgraph of vertices and edges that, when coalesced into a single vertex, most compresses the overall graph. The rectangle in Figure 17.1 identifies an example of normative substructure for the depicted graph.

Our implementation uses SUBDUE [KETK05] to find normative substructures. The best normative substructure can be characterized as the one with minimal description length (MDL):

$$L(S,G) = DL(G \mid S) + DL(S) \tag{17.2}$$

where G is the entire graph, S is the substructure being analyzed, $DL(G \mid S)$ is the description length of G after being compressed by S, and $DL(S)$ is the description length of the substructure being analyzed. Description length $DL(G)$ is the minimum number of bits necessary to describe graph G [EBER11].

Insider threats appear as small percentage differences from the normative substructures. This is because insider threats attempt to closely mimic legitimate system operations except for small variations embodied by illegitimate behavior. We apply three different approaches for identifying such anomalies, discussed as follows.

17.3.1 GBAD-MDL

Upon finding the best compressing normative substructure, GBAD-MDL searches for deviations from that normative substructure in subsequent substructures. By analyzing substructures of the same size as the normative one, differences in the edges and vertices' labels and in the direction or endpoints of edges are identified. The most anomalous of these are those substructures for which the fewest modifications is required to produce a substructure isomorphic to the normative one. In Figure 17.1, the shaded vertex labeled E is an anomaly discovered by GBAD-MDL.

17.3.2 GBAD-P

In contrast, GBAD-P searches for insertions that, if deleted, yield the normative substructure. Insertions made to a graph are viewed as extensions of the normative substructure. GBAD-P calculates the probability of each extension based on edge and vertex labels, and therefore exploits label information to discover anomalies. The probability is given by

$$P(A = v) = P(A = v \mid A)P(A) \tag{17.3}$$

where A represents an edge or vertex attribute and v represents its value. The probability $P(A = v \mid A)$ can be generated by a Gaussian distribution:

$$\rho(x) = \frac{1}{\sigma\sqrt{2\pi}} \exp\left(-\frac{(x-\mu)^2}{2\sigma^2}\right) \tag{17.4}$$

where μ is the mean and σ is the standard deviation. Higher values of $\rho(x)$ correspond to more anomalous substructures.

Using GBAD-P therefore ensures that malicious insider behavior that is reflected by the actual data in the graph (rather than merely its structure) can be reliably identified as anomalous by our algorithm. In Figure 17.1, the shaded vertex labeled *C* is an anomaly discovered by GBAD-P.

17.3.3 GBAD-MPS

Finally, GBAD-MPS considers deletions that, if re-inserted, yield the normative substructure. To discover these, GBAD-MPS examines the parent structure. Changes in size and orientation in the parent signify deletions amongst the subgraphs. The most anomalous substructures are those with the smallest transformation cost required to make the parent substructures identical. In Figure 17.1, the last substructure of *A–B–C–D* vertices is identified as anomalous by GBAD-MPS because of the missing edge between *B* and *D* marked by the shaded rectangle.

17.4 SUMMARY AND DIRECTIONS

This chapter has described the different classes of learning techniques for nonsequence data. It describes exactly how each method arrives at detecting insider threats and how ensemble models are built, modified, and discarded. First, we discussed supervised learning in detail and then unsupervised learning. Both contain the formulas necessary to understand the inner workings of each class of learning. Experimental results of our algorithms will be provided in Chapter 18.

Throughout this book, we have stressed the need for big data analytics. This is because the amount of data being collected by organizations is massive. We need scalable techniques for mining very large data streams. In Part IV, we will discuss cloud-based data analytics techniques that can be adapted for mining data streams.

REFERENCES

[COOK00]. D. J. Cook and L. B. Holder, "Graph-Based Data Mining," *IEEE Intelligent Systems*, 15 (2), 32–41, 2000.

[COOK07]. D. J. Cook and L. B. Holder, editors. *Mining Graph Data*. John Wiley & Sons, Inc., Hoboken, NJ, 2007.

[EBER07]. W. Eberle and L. B. Holder, "Mining for Structural Anomalies in Graph-Based Data," In *DMIN'07: Proceedings of the International Conference on Data Mining*, pp. 376–389, 2007.

[EBER11]. W. Eberle, J. Graves, and L. Holder, "Insider Threat Detection Using a Graph-Based Approach," *Journal of Applied Security Research*, 6 (1), 32–81, 2011.

[KETK05]. N. S. Ketkar, L. B. Holder, and D. J. Cook, "Subdue: Compression-Based Frequent Pattern Discovery in Graph Data," In *Proceedings of the ACM KDD Workshop on Open-Source Data Mining*, Chicago, IL, pp. 71–76, 2005.

[MANE02]. L. M. Manevitz and M. Yousef, "One-class SVMs for Document Classification," *The Journal of Machine Learning Research*, 2, 139–154, 2002.

[MASU09]. M. Masud, J. Gao, L. Khan, J. Han, and B. Thuraisingham, *A Multi-Partition Multi-Chunk Ensemble Technique to Classify Concept-Drifting Data Streams, Advances in Knowledge Discovery and Data Mining*, Springer, Berlin, pp. 363–375, 2009.

[PARV11a]. P. Parveen, J. Evans, B. Thuraisingham, K. W. Hamlen, and L. Khan, "Insider Threat Detection Using Stream Mining and Graph Mining," In *PASSAT'2011: Proceedings of the 3rd IEEE Conference on Privacy, Security, Risk and Trust,* MIT Press, Boston, MA, pp. 1102–1110, 2011.

[PARV11b]. P. Parveen, Z. R. Weger, B. Thuraisingham, K. W. Hamlen, and L. Khan, "Supervised Learning for Insider Threat Detection Using Stream Mining," In *Proceedings of the 23rd IEEE International Conference on Tools with Artificial Intelligence*, November 7–9, Boca Raton, FL, pp. 1032–1039, 2011.

[PARV13]. P. Parveen, N. McDaniel, J. Evans, B. Thuraisingham, K. W. Hamlen, and L. Khan, "Evolving Insider Threat Detection Stream Mining Perspective," *International Journal on Artificial Intelligence Tools*, 22 (5), 1360013.

[YAN02]. X. Yan and J. Han, "gSpan: Graph-Based Substructure Pattern Mining," In *ICDM'02: Proceedings of the International Conference on Data Mining*, pp. 721–724, 2002.

18 Experiments and Results for Nonsequence Data

18.1 INTRODUCTION

Chapters 16 and 17 described our stream mining techniques for insider threat detection. In particular, ensemble-based techniques for nonsequence data were discussed. We also discussed both supervised and unsupervised earning methods. We also discussed stream mining for nonsequence data. We have argued that we need scalable stream mining techniques as massive amounts of data streams have to be analyzed for insider threat detection.

In this chapter, we will discuss our testing methodology and experimental results. The organization of this chapter is as follows. The dataset we used is discussed in Section 18.2. Experimental setup is discussed in Section 18.3. Results are presented in Section 18.4. This chapter is summarized in Section 18.5.

18.2 DATASET

We tested both of our algorithms on the 1998 Lincoln Laboratory Intrusion Detection dataset [KEND98]. This dataset consists of daily system logs, containing all system calls performed by all processes over a 7-week period. It was created using the Basic Security Mode (BSM) auditing program. Each log consists of tokens that represent system calls using the syntax exemplified in Figure 18.1.

The token arguments begin with a header line and end with a trailer line. The header line reports the size of the token in bytes, a version number, the system call, and the date and time of execution in milliseconds. The second line reports the full path name of the executing process. The optional attribute line identifies the user and group of the owner, the file system and node, and the device. The next line reports the number of arguments to the system call, followed by the arguments themselves on the following line. The subject line reports the audit ID, effective user and group IDs, real user and group IDs, process ID, session ID, and terminal port, and address, respectively. Finally, the return line reports the outcome and return value of the system call.

Since many system calls are the result of automatic processes not initiated by any particular user, they are therefore not pertinent to the detection of insider threat. We limit our attention to user-affiliated system calls. These include calls for exec, execve, utime, login, logout, su, setegid, seteuid, setuid, rsh, rexecd, passwd, rexd, and ftp. All of these correspond to logging in/out or file operations initiated by users, and are, therefore, relevant to insider threat detection. Restricting our attention to such operations helps to reduce extraneous noise in the dataset. Further, some tokens contain calls made by users from the outside, via web servers, and are not pertinent to the detection of *insider* threats. There are six such users in this dataset that have been pulled out. Table 18.1 reports statistics for the dataset after all irrelevant tokens have been filtered out and the attribute data in Figure 18.2 has been extracted. Preprocessing extracted 62K tokens spanning 500K vertices. This reflected the activity of all users over nine weeks.

Figure 18.3 shows the features extracted from the output data in Figure 18.1 for our supervised approach and Figure 18.2 depicts the subgraph structure yielded for our unsupervised approach. The first number in Figure 18.3 is the classification of the token as either anomalous (–1) or normal (1). The classification is used by a two-class support vector machine (SVM) for training the model, but is unused (although required) for the one-class SVM (OCSVM). The rest of the line is a list

```
header,129,2,execve(2),,Tue Jun 16 08:14:29 1998, +
    518925003 msec
path/op/local/bin/tcsh
attribute,100755,root,other,8388613,79914,0
exec_args,1,
-tcsh
subject,2142,2142,rjm,2142,rjm,401,400,24
    1 135.13.216.191
return,success,0
trailer,129
```

FIGURE 18.1 A sample system call record from the MIT Lincoln dataset.

TABLE 18.1
Dataset Statistics after Filtering and Attribute Extraction

Statistic	Value
No. of vertices	500,000
No. of tokens	62,000
No. of normative substructures	5
No. of users	All
Duration	9 weeks

of index–value pairs that are separated by a colon (:). The index represents the dimension for use by SVM, and the value is the value of the token along that dimension. The value must be numeric, and the list must be ascending by the index. Indices that are missing are assumed to have a value of 0. Attributes that are categorical in nature (and can take the value of any one of *N* categories) are represented by *N* dimensions. In Figure 18.2, 1:29669 means that the time of day (in seconds) is 29669. 6:1 means that the user's ID (which is categorical) is 2142, 8:1 means that the machine IP address (also categorical) is 135.13.216.191, 21:1 means that the command (categorical) is execve, 32:1 means that the path begins with /opt, and 36:0 means that the return value is 0. The mappings between the data values and the indices were set internally by a configuration file.

All of these features are important for different reasons. The time of day could indicate that the user is making system calls during normal business hours, or, alternatively, is logging in late at night, which could be anomalous. The path could indicate the security level of the system call being made for instance, a path beginning with */sbin* could indicate the use of important system files, while a path like */bin/mail* could indicate something more benign, like sending mails. The user ID is important to distinguish events; what is anomalous for one user may not be anomalous

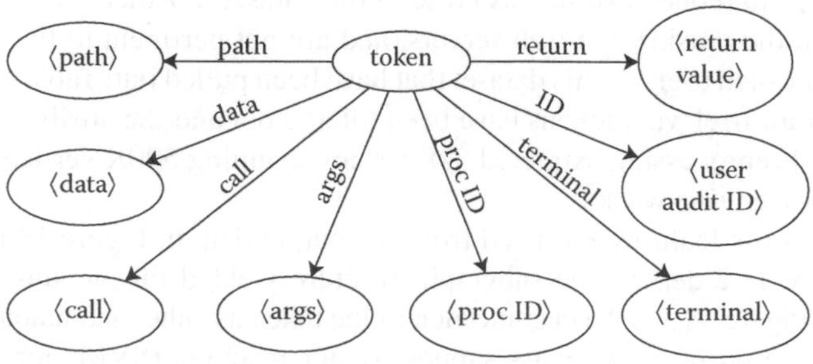

FIGURE 18.2 A token subgraph.

```
Time, userID, machineIP, command, arg, path, return
1 1:29669 6:1 8:1 21:1 32:1 36:0
```

FIGURE 18.3 Feature set extracted from Figure 18.1.

for another. A programmer that normally works from 9 a.m. to 5 p.m. would not be expected to login at midnight, but a maintenance technician (who performs maintenance on server equipment during off hours, at night) would. Frequent changes in machine IP addresses or changes that are not frequent enough could indicate something anomalous. Finally, the system call itself could indicate an anomaly most users would be expected to login and logout, but only administrators would be expected to invoke super-user privileges with a command such as *su*.

18.3 EXPERIMENTAL SETUP

18.3.1 Supervised Learning

We used LIBSVM [CHAN11] to build our models and to generate predictions for our test cases in our supervised approach. First, we will give an overview of our use of SVM software, which is a standard procedure and is well documented in LIBSVM's help files. We chose to use the radial-based function (RBF) kernel for the SVM. It was chosen because it gives good results for our dataset. Parameters for the kernel (in the case of two-class SVM, C and γ, and in the case of OCSVM, ν and γ) were chosen so that the $F1$ measure was maximized. We chose to use the $F1$ measure in this case (over other measures of accuracy) because, for the classifier to do well according to this metric, it must minimize FPs while also minimizing FNs. Before training a model with our feature set, we used LIBSVM to scale the input data to the range [0, 1]. This was done to ensure that dimensions that take on high values (like time) do not outweigh dimensions that take on low values (such as dimensions that represent categorical variables). The parameters that were used to scale the training data for the model are the same parameters that were used to scale that model's test data. Therefore, the model's test data will be in the vicinity of the range [0, 1].

We conducted two experiments with the SVM. The first, as shown in Table 18.2, was designed to compare an OCSVM with a two-class SVM for the purposes of insider threat detection, and the second, as shown in Table 18.3, was designed to compare a stream classification approach with a more traditional approach to classification. We will begin by describing our comparison of an OCSVM and a two-class SVM. For this experiment, we took 7 weeks of data, and randomly divided it into halves. We deemed the first half training data and the other half testing data. We constructed a simple one-class and two-class model from the training data and recorded the accuracy of the model in predicting the test data.

For the insider threat detection approach, we use an ensemble-based approach that is scored in real time. The ensemble maintains K models that use the OCSVM, each constructed from a single

TABLE 18.2
Exp. A: One Class vs. Two Class SVM

	One Class SVM	Two Class SVM
False positives	3706	0
True negatives	25,701	29,407
False negatives	1	5
True positives	1	0
Accuracy	0.87	0.99
False positive rate	0.13	0.0
False negative rate	0.2	1.0

TABLE 18.3
Exp. B: Updating vs. Nonupdating Stream Approach

	Updating Stream	Nonupdating Stream
False positives	13,774	24,426
True negatives	44,362	33,710
False negatives	1	1
True positives	9	9
Accuracy	0.76	0.58
False positive rate	0.24	0.42
False negative rate	0.1	0.1

TABLE 18.4
Summary of Data Subset *A* (Selected/Partial)

Statistic	Dataset *A*
User	Donaldh
No. of vertices	269
No. of edges	556
Week	2–8
Weekday	Friday

day and weighted according to the accuracy of the model's previous decisions. For each test token, the ensemble reports the majority vote of its models.

The aforementioned stream approach is more practical for detecting insider threats because insider threats are stream in nature and occur in real time. A situation like that in the first experiment above is not one that will occur in the real world. In the real world, insider threats must be detected as they occur, not after months of data has piled in. Therefore, it is reasonable to compare our updating stream ensemble with a simple OCSVM model constructed once and tested (but not updated) as a stream of new data becomes available (see Table 18.3).

18.3.2 Unsupervised Learning

For our unsupervised approach (based on graph-based anomaly detection), we needed to accurately depict the effects of two variables. Those variables are K, the number of ensembles maintained, and q, the number of normative substructures maintained for each model in the ensemble. We used a subset of data during this wide variety of experiments, as depicted in Table 18.4, in order to complete them in a manageable time. The decision to use the small subset of data was arrived at due to the exponential growth in cost for checking subgraph isomorphism.

Each ensemble iteration was run with q values between 1 and 8. Iterations were made with ensemble sizes of K values between 1 and 6.

18.4 Results

18.4.1 Supervised Learning

Performance and accuracy were measured in terms of total FPs and FNs throughout 7 weeks of test data as discussed in Table 18.4 (weeks 2–8). The Lincoln Laboratory dataset was chosen because of both its large size and its well-known set of anomalies, facilitating an accurate performance assessment via misapprehension counts. Table 18.2 shows the results for the first experiment using our supervised method. The OCSVM outperforms the two-class SVM in the first experiment. Simply, the two-class SVM is unable to detect any of the positive cases correctly. Although the two-class SVM does achieve a higher accuracy, it is at the cost of having a 100% FN rate. By varying the parameters for the two-class SVM, we found it possible to increase the FP rate (the SVM made an attempt to discriminate between anomaly and normal data), but in no case could the two-class SVM predict even one of the truly anomalous cases correctly. The OCSVM, on the other hand, achieves a moderately low FN rate (20%), while maintaining a high accuracy (87.40%). This demonstrates the superiority of the OCSVM over the two-class SVM for insider threat detection. The superiority of the OCSVM over two-class SVM for insider threat detection further justifies our decision to use OCSVM for our test of stream data. Table 18.3 gives a summary of our results for the second experiment using our supervised method. The updating stream achieves much higher accuracy than the nonupdating stream, while maintaining an equivalent and minimal FN rate (10%). The accuracy of the updating stream is 76%, while that of the nonupdating stream is 58%.

The superiority of updating stream over nonupdating stream for insider threat detection further justifies our decision to use updating stream for our test of stream data. By using labeled data, we establish a ground truth for our supervised learning algorithm. This ground truth allows us to place higher weights on FNs or FPs. By weighing one more than the other, we punish a model more for producing that which we have increased the weight for. When detecting insider threats, it is more important that we do not miss a threat (FN) than identify a false threat (FP). Therefore, we weigh FN more heavily, that is, we add an *FN cost*. Figures 18.4 and 18.5 show the results of weighting the

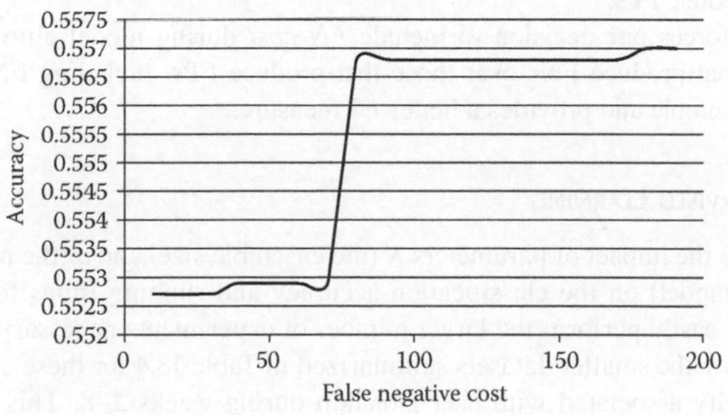

FIGURE 18.4 Accuracy by FN cost.

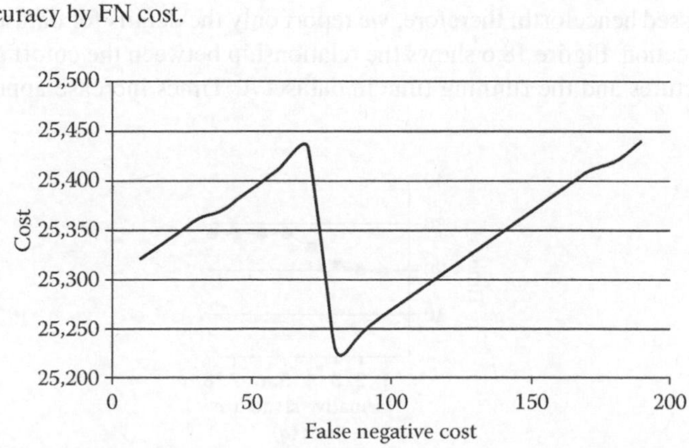

FIGURE 18.5 Total cost by FN cost.

TABLE 18.5
Impact of FN Cost

	Accuracy	F_2 Measure
w/ FN cost	0.55682	0.00159
w/o FN cost	0.45195	0.00141

FNs more heavily than FPs with this established ground truth. This is to say that at an FN cost of 50, an FN that is produced will count against a model 50 times more than an FP will. Increasing the FN cost also increases the accuracy of our OCSVM, updating the stream approach. We can see that that increasing the FN cost up to 30 only increases the total cost without affecting the accuracy, but after this, the accuracy climbs and the total cost comes down. Total cost, as calculated by Equation 18.1, represents the total number of FPs and FNs after they have been modified by the increased FN cost. We see this trend peak at an FN cost of 80 where accuracy reaches nearly 56% and the total cost is at a low of 25,229.

$$\text{Total Cost} = \text{Total False Positives} + (\text{Total False Negatives} * \text{FN Cost}) \qquad (18.1)$$

The FNs are weighted by cost more heavily than FPs because it is more important to catch all insider threats. FPs are acceptable in some cases, but an insider threat detection system is useless if it does not catch all positive instances of insider threat activity. This is why models that fail to catch positive cases and produce these FNs are punished, in our best-case result, 80 times more heavily than those who produce FPs.

Table 18.5 reinforces our decision to include *FN cost* during model elimination that heavily punishes models that produce FNs over those that produce FPs. Including FN cost increases the accuracy of the ensemble and provides a better *F*2 measure.

18.4.2 Unsupervised Learning

We next investigate the impact of parameters *K* (the ensemble size) and *q* (the number of normative substructures per model) on the classification accuracy and running times for our unsupervised approach. To more easily perform the larger number of experiments necessary to chart these relationships, we employ the smaller datasets summarized in Table 18.4 for these experiments. Dataset *A* consists of activity associated with user Donaldh during weeks 2–8. This user displays malicious insider activity during the respective time period. This dataset evidences similar trends for all relationships discussed henceforth; therefore, we report only the details for dataset *A* throughout the remainder of this section. Figure 18.6 shows the relationship between the cutoff *q* for the number of normative substructures and the running time in dataset *A*. Times increase approximately linearly

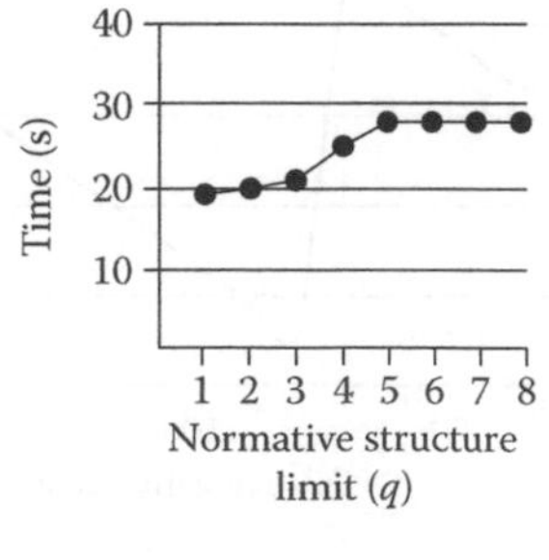

FIGURE 18.6 The effect of *q* on runtimes for fixed $K = 6$ on dataset *A*.

until $q = 5$ because there are only four normative structures in dataset *A*. The search for a fifth structure therefore fails (but contributes running time), and higher values of q have no further effect.

Figure 18.7 shows the impact of ensemble size K and runtimes for dataset *A*. As expected, runtimes increase approximately linearly with the number of models (2 s per model on average in this dataset). Increasing q and K also tends to aid in the discovery of TPs. Figures 18.8 and 18.9 illustrate the positive relationships of q and K, respectively, with TP. Once $q = 4$, normative substructures are considered per model and $K = 4$ models are consulted per ensemble, the classifier reliably detects all seven TPs in dataset *A*. These values of q and K therefore strike the best balance between the coverage of all insider threats and the efficient runtimes necessary for high responsiveness.

Increasing q to 4 does come at the price of raising more false alarms, however. Figure 18.10 shows that the FP rate increases along with the TP rate until $q = 4$. Dataset *A* has only four normative structures, so increasing q beyond this point has no effect. This is supported with $q = 4, 5, 6$ showing no increase in TP.

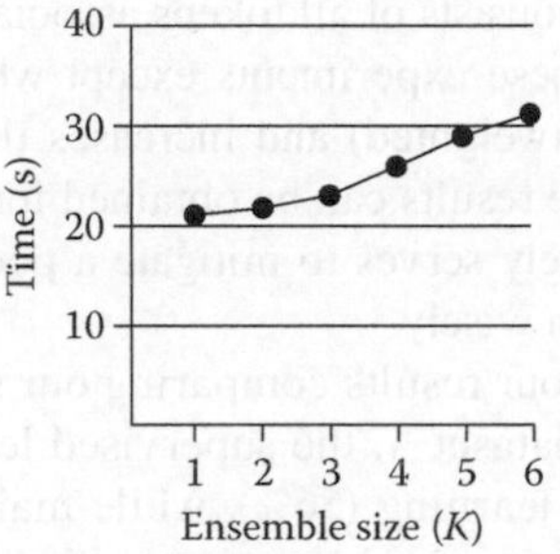

FIGURE 18.7 The effect of K on runtimes for fixed $q = 4$ on dataset *A*.

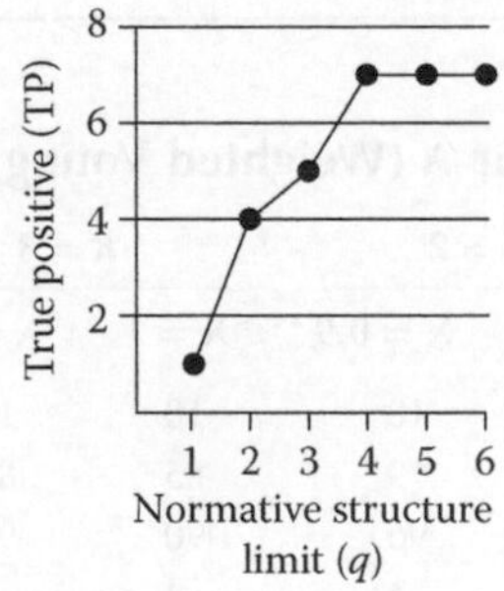

FIGURE 18.8 The effect of q on TP rates for fixed $K = 6$ on dataset *A*.

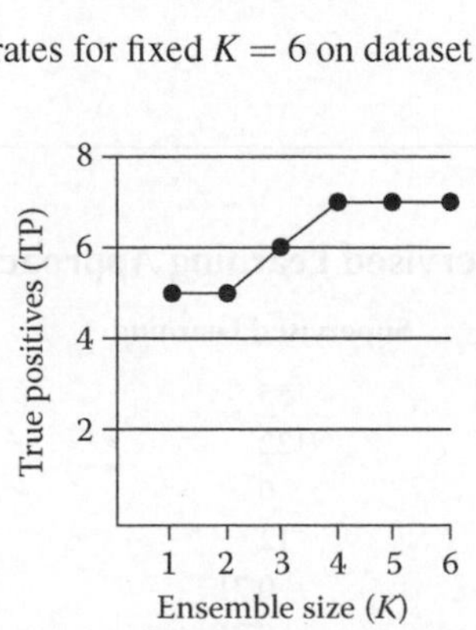

FIGURE 18.9 The effect of K on TP rates for fixed $q = 4$ on dataset *A*.

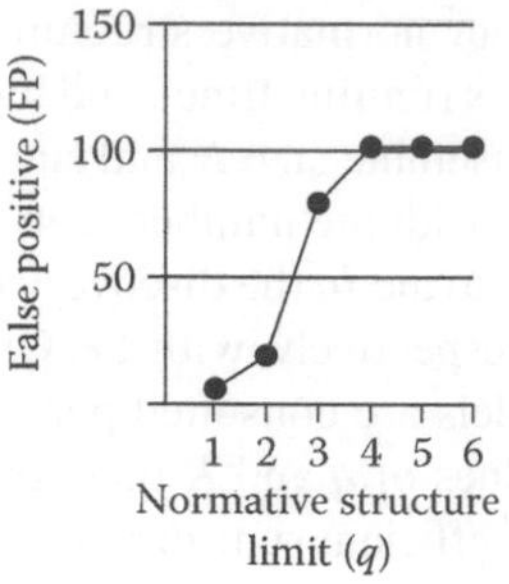

FIGURE 18.10 The effect of q on FP rates for fixed $K = 6$ on dataset A.

Table 18.6 considers the impact of weighted versus unweighted majority voting on the classification accuracy. The unweighted columns are those for $\lambda = 1$ and the weighted columns use the fading factor $\lambda = 0.9$. The dataset consists of all tokens associated with the user ID 2143. Weighted majority voting has no effect in these experiments except when $K = 4$, where it reduces the FP rate from 124 (unweighted) to 85 (weighted) and increases the TN rate from 51 (unweighted) to 90 (weighted). However, since these results can be obtained for $K = 3$ without weighted voting, we conclude that weighted voting merely serves to mitigate a poor choice of K; weighted voting has little or no impact when K is chosen wisely.

Table 18.7 gives a summary of our results comparing our supervised and unsupervised learning approaches. For example, on dataset A, the supervised learning achieves much higher accuracy (71%) than the unsupervised learning (56%), while maintaining a lower FP (31%) and FN rate (0%). On the other hand, unsupervised learning achieves 56% accuracy, 54% FP rate, and 42% FN rate.

TABLE 18.6
Impact of Fading Factor λ (Weighted Voting)

	$K = 2$		$K = 3$		$K = 4$	
	$\lambda = 1$	$\lambda = 0.9$	$\lambda = 1$	$\lambda = 0.9$	$\lambda = 1$	$\lambda = 0.9$
TP	10	10	10	10	14	14
FP	79	79	85	85	124	85
TN	96	96	90	90	51	90
FN	4	4	4	4	0	0

TABLE 18.7
Supervised vs. Unsupervised Learning Approach on Dataset A

	Supervised Learning	Unsupervised Learning
False positives	55	95
True negatives	122	82
False negatives	0	5
True positives	12	7
Accuracy	0.71	0.56
False positive rate	0.31	0.54
False negative rate	0	0.42

18.5 SUMMARY AND DIRECTIONS

In this chapter, we discussed our testing methodology and experimental results for mining data streams consisting of nonsequence data. In particular, the datasets used, our experimental setup, and results were discussed. We examined various aspects such as false positives, false negatives, and accuracy. Our results indicate that supervising learning yields better results for certain datasets. However, we need to carry out more extensive experiments for a variety of datasets. Nevertheless, our work has given guidance to experimentation for insider threat detection.

Our focus in Chapters 17 and 18 has been on handling nonsequence data. In Chapters 19 and 20, we will discuss how sequence data may be mined for insider threat detection.

REFERENCES

[CHAN11]. C.-C. Chang and C.-J. Lin, "LIBSVM: A Library for Support Vector Machines," *ACM Transactions on Intelligent Systems and Technology* 2 (3), 2:27:1–227:27, 2011. Software available at http://www.csie.ntu.edu.tw/cjlin/libsvm.

[KEND98]. K. Kendall, "A Database of Computer Attacks for the Evaluation of Intrusion Detection Systems," *Masters thesis*, Massachusetts Institute of Technology, 1998.

19 Insider Threat Detection for Sequence Data

19.1 INTRODUCTION

In this chapter, we will discuss inside threat detection for sequence data. A sequence is an ordered list of objects (or events). Sequence contains members (also called elements or terms). In a set, element order does not matter. On the other hand, in a sequence, order matters, and, hence, exactly the same elements can appear multiple times at different positions in the sequence [QUMR13]. For example, (U, T, D) is a sequence of letters with the letter "U" first and "D" last. This sequence differs from (D, T, U).

The sequence (U, T, D, A, L, L, A, S) that contains the alphabet "A" at two different positions is a valid sequence. Figure 19.1 illustrates some sequence of the movement pattern of a user. The first row represents a particular user's one movement pattern sequence: student center, office, and media lab (ml). In this sequence, the user was first at student center and ml (media lab) last [EAGL06].

The organization of this chapter is as follows. Classifying sequence data will be discussed in Section 19.2. Unsupervised stream-based sequence learning will be discussed in Section 19.3. Anomaly detection aspects will be discussed in Section 19.4. Complexity analysis will be provided in Section 19.4. This chapter is summarized in Section 19.5.

19.2 CLASSIFYING SEQUENCE DATA

As the length of the sequence is defined as the number of ordered elements, sequence data can be finite or infinite in length. Infinite sequences are known as stream sequence data. Insider threat detection-related sequence data is stream-based in nature. Sequence data may be gathered over time, maybe even years. In this case, we assume a data stream will be converted into a number of chunks. For example, each chunk may represent a week and contain the sequence data that arrived during that time period.

Figure 19.2 demonstrates how the classifier decision boundary changes over time (from one chunk to the next chunk). Data points are associated with two classes (normal and anomalous). In particular, a user command or a subsequence of commands may form a pattern/phrase that will be called here as a data point. A nonrepetitive pattern/phrase for a user may form an anomaly. There are three contiguous data chunks as shown in Figure 19.2. The dark straight line represents the decision boundary of its own chunk, whereas the dotted straight line represents the decision boundary of the previous chunk. If there were no concept drift in the data stream, the decision boundary would be the same for both the current chunk and its previous chunk (the dotted and straight lines). White dots represent the normal data (True Negative), blue dots represent anomaly data (True Positive), and striped dots represent the instances victim of the concept drift.

We show that the two different cases in Figure 19.2 are as follows:

Case 1: The decision boundary of the second chunk moves upward compared to that of the first chunk. As a result, more normal data will be classified as anomalous by the decision boundary of the first chunk; thus, FP will go up. Recall that a test point having a true benign (normal) category classified as an anomalous by a classifier is known as an FP.

Case 2: The decision boundary of the third chunk moves downward compared to that of the first chunk. So, more anomalous data will be classified as normal data by the decision boundary of the first chunk; thus, the FN will go up. Recall that a test point having a true malicious category classified as benign by a classifier is known as an FN.

Movement Pattern

(student center)(office)(ml)
(maqs ave)(ml)(tang)(ml)(sloan)(ml)
(100 memorial)(ml)(tang)(black sheep restaurant)(ml)(sloan)(ml)
(off phm)(ml)(starbucks)(ml)
(hamshire&broadway)(off phm)(ml)(starbucks)(ml)
(ml)(100 memorial)(ml)(tang)(black sheep restaurant)(ml)(sloan)(ml)

FIGURE 19.1 Example of sequence data related to movement pattern.

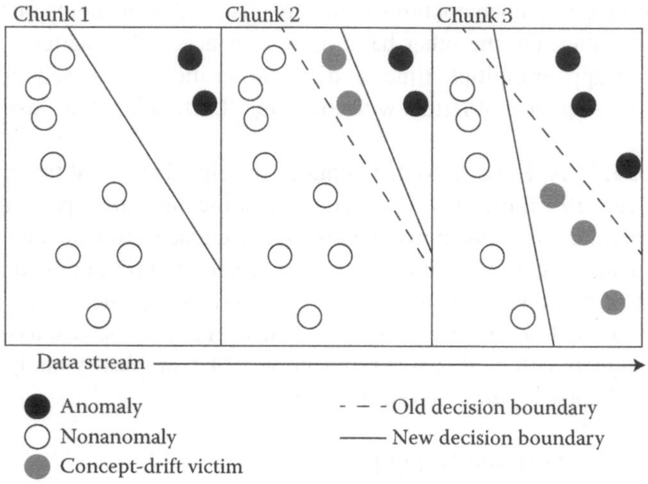

FIGURE 19.2 Concept drift in stream data.

In the more general case, the decision boundary of the current chunk can vary, which causes the decision boundary of the previous chunk to misclassify both normal and anomalous data. Therefore, both FP and FN may go up at the same time.

This suggests that a model built from a single chunk will not suffice. This motivates the adoption of adaptive learning. In particular, we will exploit two approaches as follows:

Incremental Learning: A single dictionary is maintained [PARV12a]. When a normative sequence pattern is learned from a chunk, it will be simply added to the dictionary. To find the normative pattern, we will exploit unsupervised stream-based sequence learning (USSL). The incremental learning classification procedure is illustrated in Figure 19.3. Here, first from a new chunk, patterns will be extracted and next these patterns will be merged with the old quantized dictionary (QD) from previous chunks. Finally, a new merged dictionary will be quantized in Figure 19.4.

Ensemble Learning: A number of dictionaries are maintained [PARV12b]. In the ensemble, we maintain K models. For each model, we maintain a single dictionary. Our ensemble approach classifies data using an evolving set of K models. The ensemble classification procedure is illustrated in Figure 19.5. Recall that we use USSL to train models from an individual chunk. USSL identifies the normative patterns in the chunk and stores it in a QD. In the literature ([MASU10], [MASU11], [MASU08]), it shows that ensemble-based learning is more effective than incremental learning. Here, we will focus on ensemble-based learning. To identify an anomaly, a test point will be compared against each model of the ensemble.

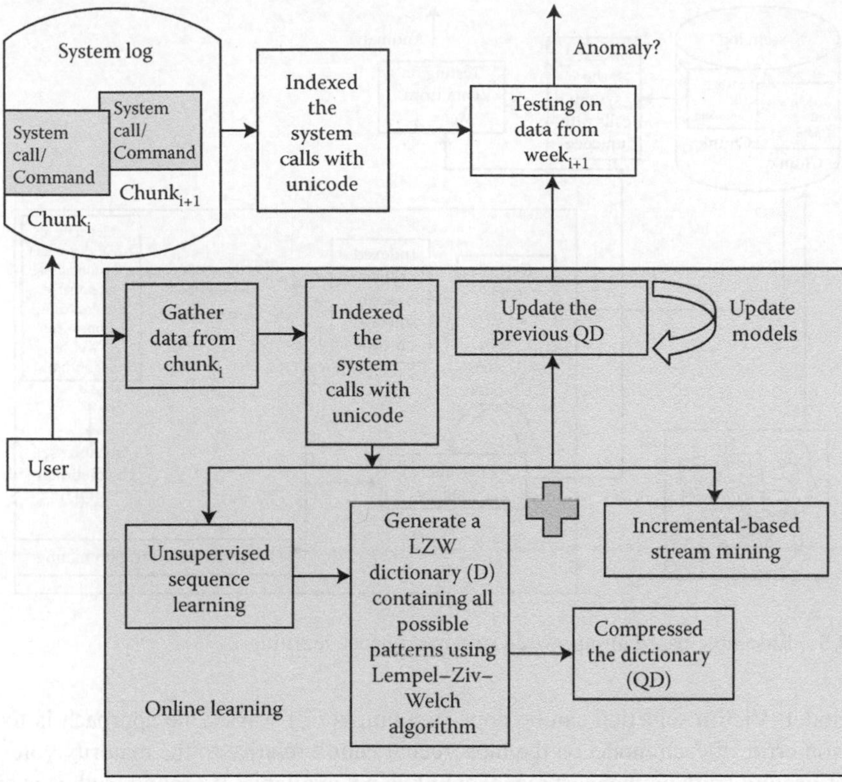

FIGURE 19.3 Unsupervised stream sequence learning using incremental learning.

Recall that a model will declare the test data as anomalous based on how much the test differs from the model's normative patterns. Once all models cast their vote, we will apply majority voting to make the final decision as to whether the test point is anomalous or not (as shown in Figure 16.2).

Model Update: We always keep an ensemble of fixed size models (K in that case). Hence, when a new chunk is processed, we already have K models in the ensemble, and the (K + 1)st model will be created from the current chunk. We need to update the ensemble by replacing a victim model with

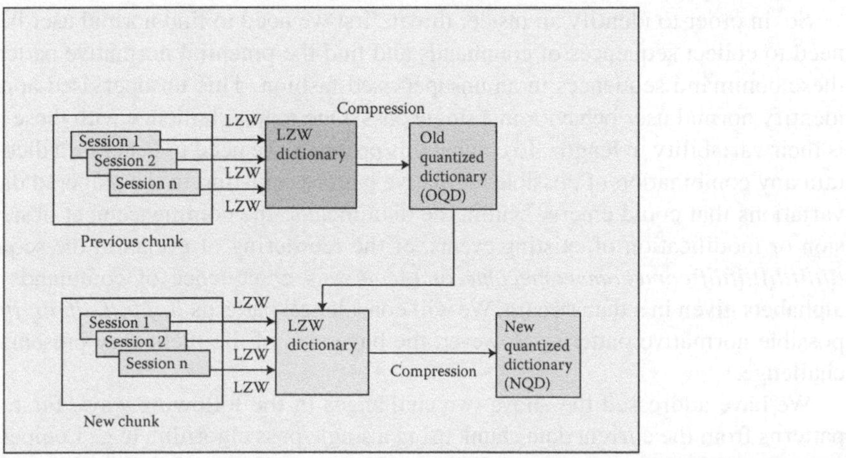

FIGURE 19.4 Block diagram of incremental learning.

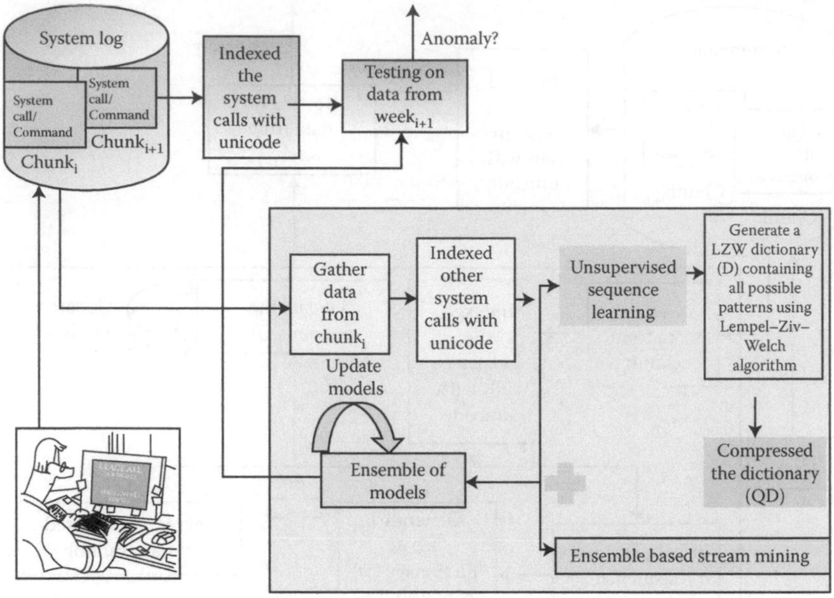

FIGURE 19.5 Ensemble-based unsupervised stream sequence learning.

this new model. Victim selection can be done in a number of ways. One approach is to calculate the prediction error of each model on the most recent chunk relative to the majority vote. Here, we assume that *ground truth* on the most recent chunk is not available. If ground truth is available, we can exploit this knowledge for training. The new model will replace the existing model from the ensemble that gives the maximum prediction error.

19.3 UNSUPERVISED STREAM-BASED SEQUENCE LEARNING (USSL)

Normal user profiles are considered to be repetitive daily or weekly activities that are frequent sequences of commands, system calls, etc. These repetitive command sequences are called normative patterns. These patterns reveal the regular, or normal, behavior of a user. When a user suddenly demonstrates unusual activities that indicate a significant excursion from normal behavior, an alarm is raised for potential insider threat.

So, in order to identify an insider threat, first we need to find normal user behavior. For that, we need to collect sequences of commands and find the potential normative patterns observed within these command sequences in an unsupervised fashion. This unsupervised approach also needs to identify normal user behavior in a single pass. One major challenge with these repetitive sequences is their variability in length. To combat this problem, we need to generate a dictionary that will contain any combination of possible normative patterns existing in the gathered data stream. Potential variations that could emerge within the data include the commencement of new events, the omission or modification of existing events, or the reordering of events in the sequence. For example, *liftliftliftliftliftcomecomecomecomecome-come,* is a sequence of commands represented by the alphabets given in a data stream. We will consider all patterns *li,if,ft,tl, lif, ift, ftl, lift, iftl* etc., as our possible normative patterns. However, the huge size of the dictionary presents another significant challenge.

We have addressed the above two challenges in the following ways. First, we extract possible patterns from the current data chunk using a single pass algorithm (e.g., Lempel–Ziv–Welch, LZW, algorithm [ZIV77]) to prepare a dictionary that we called the LZW dictionary. This dictionary has a set of patterns and their corresponding weights according to

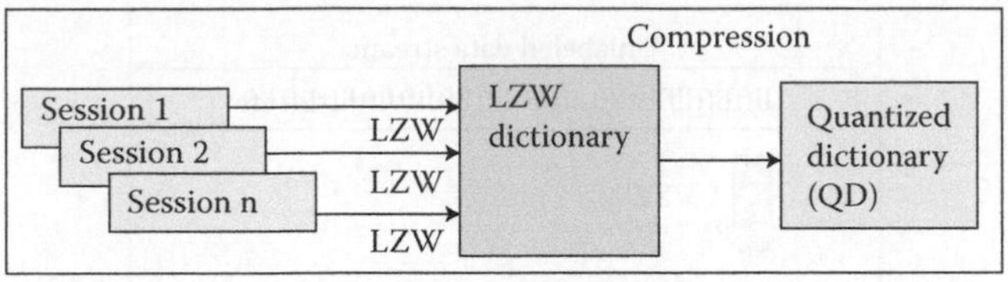

FIGURE 19.6 Unsupervised stream-based sequence learning (USSL) from a chunk in ensemble-based case.

$$w_i = \frac{f_i}{\sum_{i=1}^{n} f_i} \tag{19.1}$$

where w_i is the weight of a particular pattern p_i in the current chunk, f_i is the number of times the pattern p_i appears in the current chunk, and n is the total number of distinct patterns found in that chunk.

Next, we compress the dictionary by keeping only the longest, frequent unique patterns according to their associated weight and length, while discarding other subsumed patterns. This technique is called the compression method (CM), and the new dictionary is a QD. The QD has a set of patterns and their corresponding weights. Here, we use the edit distance to find the longest pattern. The edit distance is a measure of similarity between pairs of strings ([BORG11], [VLAD66]). It is the minimum number of actions required to transfer one string to another, where an action can be substitution, addition, or deletion of a character into the string. As in the case of the earlier example, the best normative pattern in the QD would be lift, come, etc.

This process is a lossy compression, but is sufficient enough to extract the meaningful normative patterns. The reason behind this is that the patterns that we extract are the superset of the subsumed patterns. Moreover, as frequency is another control parameter in our experiment, the patterns which do not appear often cannot be regular user patterns.

Data relevant to insider threat is typically accumulated over many years of organization and system operations, and is therefore best characterized as an unbounded data stream. As our data is a continuous stream of data, we use ensemble-based learning to continuously update our compressed dictionary. This continuous data stream is partitioned into a sequence of discrete chunks. For example, each chunk might be comprised of a day or weeks' worth of data and may contain several user sessions. We generate our QD and their associated weight from each chunk. Weight is measured as the normalized frequency of a pattern within that chunk.

When a new chunk arrives, we generate a new QD model and update the ensemble as mentioned earlier. Figure 19.6 shows the flow diagram of our *dynamic*, ensemble-based, unsupervised stream sequence learning method. Algorithm 19.1 shows the basic building block for updating the ensemble. It takes the most recent data chunk *S*, ensemble *E*, and test chunk *T*. Lines 3–4 generate a new QD model from the most recent chunk *S* and temporarily add it to the ensemble *E*. Lines 5–9 test chunk *T* for anomalies for each model in the ensemble. Lines 13–24 find and label the anomalous patterns in test chunk *T* according to the majority voting of the models in the ensemble. Finally, line 29 updates the ensemble by discarding the model with the lowest accuracy. An arbitrary model is discarded in the case of multiple models having the same low performance.

19.3.1 Construct the LZW Dictionary by Selecting the Patterns in the Data Stream

At the beginning, we consider that our data is not annotated (i.e., unsupervised). In other words, we do not know the possible sequence of future operations by the user. So, we use the LZW algorithm [ZIV77] to extract the possible sequences that we can add to our dictionary. These can also be commands like *liftliftliftliftliftcomecomecomecomecomecome* where each unique letter represents

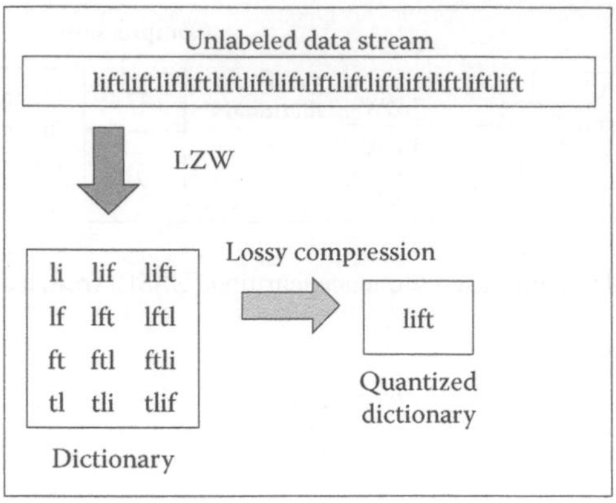

FIGURE 19.7 Quantization of dictionary.

a unique system call or command. We have used a unicode to index each command. For example, ls, cp, and find are indexed as *l*, *c*, and *f*, respectively. The possible patterns or sequences are added to our dictionary would be *li, if,ft,tl, lif,ift, ftl, lift, iftl, ftli, tc, co, om, mc, com, come*, and so on. When the sequence *li* is seen in the data stream for the second time, in order to avoid repetition, it will not be included in the LZW dictionary. Instead, we increase the frequency by 1 and extend the pattern by concatenating it with the next character in the data stream, thus turning up a new pattern *lif*. We will continue the process until we reach the end of the current chunk. Figure 19.7 demonstrates how we generate an LZW dictionary from the data stream.

19.3.2 Constructing the Quantized Dictionary

Once we have our LZW dictionary, we keep the longest and most frequent patterns and discard all their subsumed patterns. Algorithm 19.2 shows step by step how a QD is generated from the LZW dictionary. Inputs of this algorithm are as follows: the LZW dictionary *D* that contains a set of patterns *P* and their associated weight *W*. Line 5 picks a pattern (e.g., li). Lines 7–9 find all the closest patterns that are 1 edit distance away. Lines 13–16 keep the pattern that has the highest weight multiplied by its length and discard the other patterns. We repeat the steps (line 5–16) until we find the longest, frequent pattern (*lift*). After that, we start with a totally different pattern (*co*) and repeat the steps until we have explored all the patterns in the dictionary. Finally, we end up with a more compact dictionary that will contain many meaningful and useful sequences. We call this dictionary our QD. Figure 19.7 demonstrates how we generate a QD from the LZW dictionary. Once, we identify different patterns *lift*, *come*, etc., any pattern with *X*% ($\geq$ %30 in our implementation) deviation from all these patterns would be considered as anomaly. Here, we will use edit distance to identify the deviation.

Algorithm 19.1 Update the Ensemble

Input: *E* (ensemble), *T* (test chunk), *S* (chunk)
Output: *E* (updated ensemble)
$M \leftarrow$ NewModel(*S*)
$E \leftarrow E \cup \{M\}$
for each model *M* in ensemble *E* **do**
    $AM \leftarrow T$
    for each pattern *p* in *M* **do**
        if *EditDistance*(*x, p*) $\leq \alpha = \underline{1}$ of length **then** 3

```
            AM = AM − x
        end if
    end for
end for
for each candidate a in M∈E AM do
    if round(WeightedAverage(E, a)) = 1 then
        A ← A ∪ {a}
        for each model M in ensemble E do
            if a ∈ AM then
                cM ← cM + 1
            end if
        end for
    else
        for each model M in ensemble E do
            if a ∈ AM then
                cM ← cM + 1
            end if
        end for
    end if
end for
E ← E − {choose(arg minM (cM))}
```

Algorithm 19.2 Quantized Dictionary

```
Input: D = {Pattern, Weight} (LZW Dictionary)
Output: QD (Quantized Dictionary)
Visited ← 0
while D = 0 do
    X ← D_j | j ∈ Visited, D_j ∈ D
    Visited ← Visited ∪ j
    for each pattern i in D do
        if EditDistance(X, D_i) = 1 then
            P ← P ∪ i
        end if
    end for
    D ← D − X
    if P = 0 then
        X ← choose(arg max_i(w_i · l_i)) | l_i = Length(P_i), w_i = Weight(P_i), P_i ∈
        QD ← QD ∪ X
        D ← D − P
    end if
    X ← D_j | j ∈ Visited, D_j ∈ D
    Visited ← Visited ∪ j
end while
```

19.4 ANOMALY DETECTION

Given a QD, we need to find out the sequences in the data stream, which may raise a potential threat. To formulate the problem, given the data stream S and ensemble E, where $E = QD1, QD2, QD3, \ldots$, and $QDi = qdi1, qdi2, \ldots$, any pattern in the data stream is considered as an anomaly if it deviates from all the patterns *qdij* in *E* by more than *X*% (say $> 30\%$). In order to find the anomalies, we need to first find the matching patterns and delete those from the stream *S*. In particular, we find the pattern from the data stream *S* that is an exact match or α edit distance away from any pattern, *qdij*, in *E*. This pattern will be considered as the matching pattern. α can be half, one-third, or one-fourth of the length of that particular pattern in *qdij*. Next, remaining patterns in the stream will be considered as anomalies.

In order to identify the nonmatching patterns in the data stream *S*, we compute a distance matrix *L* that contains the edit distance between each pattern, *qdij* in *E*, and the data stream *S*. If we have a perfect match, that is, the edit distance 0 between a pattern *qdij* and *S*, we can move backward exactly the length of *qdij* in order to find the starting point of that pattern in *S*, and then delete it from the data stream. On the other hand, if there is an error in the match that is greater than 0 but less than α, in order to find the starting point of that pattern in the data stream, we need to traverse either left, or diagonal, or up within the matrix according to which one among the mentioned value ($L[i,j-1]$, $L[i-1,j-1]$, $L[i-1, j]$) gives the minimum, respectively. Finally, once we find the starting point, we can delete that pattern from the data stream. The remaining patterns in the data stream will be considered as anomalous.

19.5 COMPLEXITY ANALYSIS

Here, we will report time complexity of QD construction. In order to calculate edit distance between two patterns of length *K* (in worst case maximum length would be *K*), our worst case time complexity would be *O*(*K*2).

Suppose we have *n* patterns in our LZW dictionary. We have to construct a QD from this LZW dictionary. In order to do this, we need to find patterns in the LZW dictionary, which have 1 edit distance from a particular pattern (say *p*). We have to calculate edit distance between all the patterns and the pattern *p*. Recall that time complexity to find the edit distance between two patterns is *O*(*K*2). Since there are total *n* number of distinct patterns, the total time complexity between *p* and the rest of patterns is *O*(*n K*2). Note that *p* is one of the members of *n* patterns. Therefore, the total time complexity between the pair of patterns is *O*(*n*2*K*2). This is valid for a single user. If there is *u* of distinct users, the total time complexity across *u* user is *O*(*u n*2*K*2) (see Table 19.1).

19.6 SUMMARY AND DIRECTIONS

Insider threat detection-related sequence data is stream-based in nature. Sequence data may be gathered over time, maybe even years. In this case, we assume a continuous data stream will be converted into a number of chunks. For example, each chunk may represent a week and contain the sequence data that arrived during that time period. We described both supervised and unsupervised learning techniques for mining data streams for sequence data. Experimental results for our techniques are provided in Chapter 20.

TABLE 19.1
Time Complexity of Quantization Dictionary Construction

Description	Time Complexity
Pair of patterns	$O(n^2 \times K^2)$
u number of user	$O(u \times n^2 \times K^2)$

Future work should examine how our techniques can be enhanced to provide better accuracy and fewer false positives and negatives. Scalability of the techniques to handle massive data streams also needs to be investigated.

REFERENCES

[BORG11]. E. N., Borges, M. G. de Carvalho, R. Galante, M. A. Gones, A. H. F. Laender, "An Unsupervised Heuristic-Based Approach for Bibliographic Metadata Deduplication," *Information Processing and Management* 47 (5), 706–718, 2011.

[EAGL06]. N. Eagle and A. (Sandy) Pentland, "Reality Mining: Sensing Complex Social Systems," *Personal and Ubiquitous Computing* 10 (4), 255–268, 2006.

[MASU08]. M. M. Masud, J. Gao, L. Khan, J. Han, B. Thuraisingham, "A Practical Approach to Classify Evolving Data Streams: Training with Limited Amount of Labeled Data," In *ICDM'08: Proceedings of the IEEE International Conference on Data Mining*, Pisa, Italy, pp. 929–934, 2008.

[MASU09]. M. Masud, J. Gao, L. Khan, J. Han, B. Thuraisingham, *A Multi-Partition Multi-Chunk Ensemble Technique to Classify Concept-Drifting Data Streams, Advances in Knowledge Discovery and Data Mining*, Springer, Berlin, pp. 363–375, 2009.

[MASU10]. M. M. Masud, Q. Chen, J. Gao, L. Khan, C. Aggarwal, J. Han, B. Thuraisingham, "Addressing Concept-Evolution in Concept-Drifting Data Streams," In *ICDM'10: Proceedings of the IEEE International Conference on Data Mining*, Sydney, Australia, pp. 929–934, 2010.

[MASU11]. M. M., Masud, J. Gao, L. Khan, J. Han, B. M. Thuraisingham, "Classification and Novel Class Detection in Concept-Drifting Data Streams Under Time Constraints," *IEEE Transactions on Knowledge and Data Engineering* 23 (6), 859–874, 2011.

[PARV12a]. P. Parveen and B. Thuraisingham, "Unsupervised Incremental Sequence Learning for Insider Threat Detection," In *IS'2012: Proceedings of the IEEE International Conference on Intelligence and Security*, June, Washington, D.C., 2012.

[PARV12b]. P. Parveen, N. McDaniel, B. Thuraisingham, L. Khan, "Unsupervised Ensemble Based Learning for Insider Threat Detection. In *PASSAT'2012: Proceedings of the 4th IEEE International Conference on Information Privacy, Security, Risk and Trust*, September, Amsterdam, The Netherlands, 2012.

[QUMR13]. S. M. Qumruzzaman, L. Khan, B. M. Thuraisingham, "Behavioral Sequence Prediction for Evolving Data Stream," In *IRI'2013: Proceedings of the 14th IEEE Conference on Information Reuse and Integration*, August 14–16, San Francisco, CA, pp. 482–488, 2013.

[VLAD66]. L. Vladimir, "Binary Codes Capable of Correcting Deletions, Insertions and Reversals," *Soviet Physics—Doklady* 10 (8), 707–710, 1966.

[ZIV77]. J. Ziv and A. Lempel, "A Universal Algorithm for Sequential Data Compression," *IEEE Transactions on Information Theory* 23 (3), 337–343, 1977.

20 Experiments and Results for Sequence Data

20.1 INTRODUCTION

Chapter 19 described in detail our approach to insider threat detection for sequence data. In particular, both supervised and unsupervised learning techniques for streaming data were discussed. In this chapter, we will provide an overview of the testing methodology and the experimental results. We will present sequence dataset that we used for our experiments. Second, we present how we inject concept drift in the dataset. Finally, we present results showing the anomaly detection rate in the presence of concept drift[1].

The organization of this chapter is as follows. The dataset used is discussed in Section 20.2. Concept-drift aspects are discussed in Section 20.3. Results are presented in Section 20.4. This chapter is summarized in Section 20.5.

20.2 DATASET

The datasets used for training and testing have been created from Trace Files received from the University of Calgary project [GREE88]. As a part of that, 168 trace files were collected from 168 different users of Unix csh. There were four groups of people, namely novice programmers, experienced programmers, computer scientists, and nonprogrammers. The model that we have tried to construct is that of a novice programmer who has been gaining experience over the weeks and is gradually using more and more command sequences similar to that of an experienced user. These gradual normal behavior changes will be known here as concept drift. Anomaly detection in the presence of concept drift is difficult to achieve. Hence, our scenario is more realistic. This is a slow process that takes place over several weeks.

The Calgary dataset [GREE88] as described above was modified by Maxion [MAXI03] for masquerade detection. Here, we followed the same guidelines to inject masquerade commands. From the given list of users, those users who have executed >2400 commands (that did not result in an error) were filtered out to form the valid user pool. This list had 37 users. The remaining users were part of the invalid user pool. Out of the list of invalid users, 25 of them were chosen at random and a block of 100 commands from the commands that they had executed were extracted and put together to form a list of 2500 (25×100) commands. The 2500 commands were brought together as 250 blocks of 10 commands each. Out of these 250 blocks, 30 blocks were chosen at random as the list of masquerade commands (300 commands). For each user in the valid users list, the total number of commands was truncated to 2400. These 2400 commands were split into eight chunks of 300 commands each. The first chunk was kept aside as the training chunk (this contains no masquerade data). The other seven chunks are the testing chunks. In the testing chunks, a number of masquerade data blocks (each block comprising of 10 commands) were inserted at random positions. As a result, for each user, we have one training chunk with 300 commands (no masquerade data) and seven testing chunks which together have 2100 nonanomalous commands and 300 masquerade commands (see Table 20.1 and Figure 20.1).

TABLE 20.1
Description of the Dataset

Description	Number
No. of valid users	37
No. of invalid users	131
No. of valid commands per user	2400
No. of anomalous commands in testing chunks	300

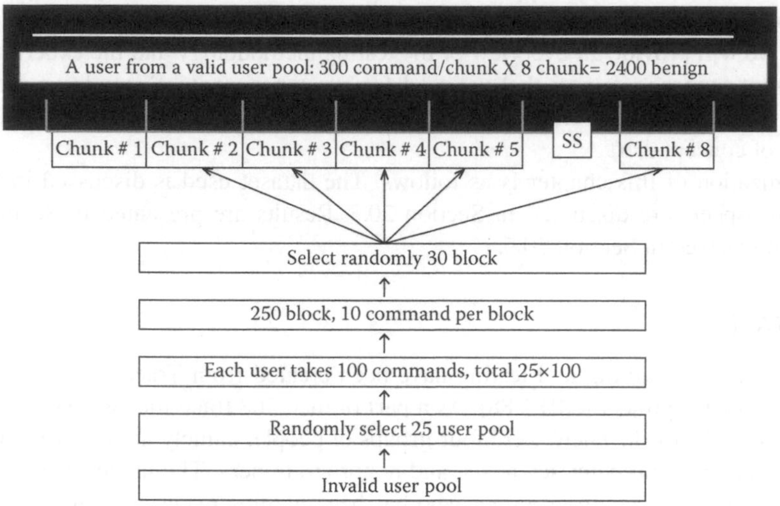

FIGURE 20.1 Pictorial representation for anomalous data generation process.

20.3 CONCEPT DRIFT IN THE TRAINING SET

Here, we present a framework for concept drift with the goal of introducing artificial drift into data generators. First, we generate a number of chunks having normal and anomalous sequences as described above. Note that the above process does not take into account concept drift. Next, we take sequences of each chunk as input and generate a new sequence with a particular drift for that chunk. New sequences will have concept-drift property. The framework processes each training example of user commands once and only once to produce variation predictions at any time. The framework is passed the next available sequence of commands (say thousand commands for a chunk) from the user data. The framework then processes these commands, updating the data structures with distribution and bounded concept-drift variance. The framework is then ready to process the next set of commands, and upon request can produce predicted variants based on the concept drift.

The data being passed into the framework is a set number of commands from different users in sequential order of execution by the user. Although commands are passed into the framework in large groups, each command is treated as an individual observation of that person's behavior. To calculate predicted variations, the following drift formula is used [KRAN12]:

$$\text{drift} = \sqrt{\frac{\log \frac{1}{\delta}}{2 \times d \times n}} \tag{20.1}$$

where δ is the variation constant, d is the current distribution of the command over the current number of individual observations, and n is the number of current observations made. A good value for the variation constant is 1×10^{-5}. The variation constant shares an inverse relation to the overall drift values. The expected range in distribution among produced variations is calculated by adding and subtracting the calculated drift from the current distribution.

Upon the processing of a sample of user commands, predicted variations can be produced by the framework upon request. The request can be made of any designated size and the concept drift will provide new distributions that fall within the range of the calculated drift for a set of commands of this size. The produced set of commands or new ones can be used to update the concept drift and provide for a constantly evolving command distribution that represents an individual. Sudden changes that do not fit within a calculated concept drift can be flagged as suspicious and therefore possibly representative of an insider threat.

Algorithm 20.1 shows how the distribution is calculated for a set of commands and how the predicted variation is produced. As an example we take 10 commands, instead of 1000 per chunk, such that we have [C_1, C_2, C_1, C_2, C_3, C_1, C_4, C_5, C_1, C_1]. The distributions will be [$C_1 = 0.5$, $C_2 = 0.2$, $C_3 = 0.1$, $C_4 = 0.1$, $C_5 = 0.1$]. With a value of $\delta = 1\times10^{-5}$ the *predicted variance* for each command comes out

$$C_1 = \sqrt{\frac{\log\frac{1}{1\times1^{-5}}}{2\times.5\times10}} \approx 0.7071\,\#\text{of occurrence} \tag{20.2}$$

We divide by the number of observation occurrences, in this case 10, because we want the concept drift per occurrence, not just for a sample of 10. Our predicted variation (PV) values are [$C_1 \approx 0.07071$, $C_2 \approx 0.11180$, $C_3 \approx 0.15811$, $C_4 \approx 0.15811$, $C_5 \approx 0.15811$]. The adjusted min/max drift comes out to be [$C_1 = 0.42929/0.57071$, $C_2 = 0.08820/0.31180$, $C_3 = 0/0.25811$, $C_4 = 0/0.25811$, $C_5 = 0/0.25811$]. From these drift values, we can produce a requested predicted variation for another 10, or any number of, user command values. We look at the original sequence and assemble at least the minimum drift value worth of commands in the variation. In this example, the first value is C_1 with a minimum of 0.42929 distribution. So we add it, bringing its current distribution to 1/10 or 0.1. This is the case for the first three values resulting in [C_1, C_2, C_1]. The fourth value is C_2 who has met its minimum distribution drift. Adding it will not go over the maximum distribution so it is either randomly added or not. The new predicted variation could look like [C_1, C_2, C_1, C_2, C_1, C_1, C_1, C_2, C_3, C_4] or [C_1, C_2, C_1, C_3, C_1, C_4, C_1, C_5, C_3, C_1] of which both have command distributions similar to the original that fall within the new variance bounds.

Algorithm 20.1 Concept Drift in Sequence Stream

Input: F (file), (size of PV)
Output: PV, (prediction variation)
for each command $C \in F$ **do**
    $D_C \leftarrow distribution(C)$
    $V_C \leftarrow variation(D_C)$
    $MaxDrift_C \leftarrow D_C + V_C$
    $MinDrift_C \leftarrow D_C - V_C$
end for
$PV \leftarrow newPredictedVariation()$
for each command $C \in F$ **do**
if $D_C < MinDrift_C$ **then**

```
        PV ← PV ∪ C
else
        if D_C + 1 < MaxDrift_C then
                flipCoin(PV ← PV ∪ C)
        else
                discard(C)
        end if
    end if
end if
```

We compare our approach, unsupervised stream-based sequence learning (USSL), with a supervised method modified from the baseline approach suggested by Maxion [MAXI03] which uses naive Bayes' (NB) classifier. The modified version compared in this book is more incremental in its model training, and thus will be referred to as *NB-INC*. All instances of both algorithms were tested using eight chunks of data. At every test chunk the NB-INC method uses all previously seen chunks to build the model and train for the current test chunk. For test chunk 3, NB builds the classification model and trains on chunks 1 and 2. For test chunk 5 NB builds a model and collectively trains on chunks 1 through 4. These USSL statistics are gathered in a "Grow as you Go" (GG) fashion. This is to say that, as the ensemble size being used grows larger, the amount of test chunks to go through decreases. For an ensemble size of 1, models are built from chunk 1 and chunks 2 through 8 are considered testing chunks. For an ensemble size of 3, chunks 4 through 8 are considered to be testing chunks. Every new chunk, starting at 4 in this case, is used to update the models in each ensemble after a majority vote is reached and the test data is classified as an anomaly or not. To clarify, in the example of ensemble size of three after the new model is built, all models vote on the possible anomaly and contribute to deciding which model is considered the least accurate and thus discarded. However, only models that have survived an elimination round (i.e., deemed not to be least accurate at least once) are used to measure the false positive (FP), true positive (TP), false negative (FN), and true negative (TN) for an ensemble. In particular, at chunk 4, the ensemble has three models from chunks 1 through 3. From chunk 4, a new model is built. During the elimination round, chunk 3 is eliminated based on accuracy. In other words, at chunk 4, the ensemble will have models created from chunks 1, 2, and 4 but not 3. The model updating process makes use of compression and model replacement. After models are updated, the least accurate one is discarded to maintain the highest accuracy and maintain the status quo since a new model is created before every update and anomaly classification step. There are other ways of updating models and selecting chunks for testing during the classification process not explored here. For this purpose, the limited USSL method used for the shown results will be referred to as USSL-GG.

20.4 RESULTS

We have compared the *NB* and *USSL-GG* algorithms on the basis of true positive rate (TPR), false positive rate (FPR), execution time, accuracy, F_1 measure, and F_2 measure. TPR and FPR as measured by

$$\text{TPR} = \frac{\text{true positives}}{\text{true positives} + \text{false negatives}} \tag{20.3}$$

$$\text{FPR} = \frac{\text{false positives}}{\text{false positives} + \text{true negatives}} \tag{20.4}$$

are the rates at which actual insider threats are correctly and incorrectly identified by the algorithm. For these calculations a TP is an identified anomaly, that is, actually an anomaly, a TN is an identified piece of normal data, that is, not an anomaly, a FP is an identified anomaly, that is, actually just normal data, and a FN is an identified piece of normal data, that is, actually an anomaly.

Accuracy better measures the algorithm's ability to pick out correct and incorrect insider threat instances on a whole. F_1 and F_2 measure are weighted variables calculated from the generic Equation 20.6 that penalize for incorrectly identified insider threats (FP) and positive threats that were not identified (FN). The F_1 measure penalizes FP and FN equally while the F_2 measure penalizes FN much more. These values are calculated by

$$\text{Accuracy} = \frac{(\text{TP} + \text{TN})}{(\text{TP} + \text{TN} + \text{FP} + \text{FN})} \tag{20.5}$$

$$F_n = \frac{(1 = n^2) + \text{TP}}{(1 + n^2)\text{TP} + (n^2) + \text{FN} + \text{FP}} \tag{20.6}$$

Tables 20.2 through 20.4 show the details of the value comparisons between NB-INC and USSL-GG for various drift values. USSL-GG has lower FPR and runtime values and higher everything else than NB-INC across the board. USSL-GG runs faster with less false threat identifications while maintaining higher success rates at catching real threats than NB-INC.

The USSL-GG data in Tables 20.2 through 20.4 are for its optimum results at ensemble size 3, which will be shown why this is optimal later.

With our optimization results for USSL-GG, we make our final comparison with NB. Figures 20.2 and 20.3 show the TPR and FPR, respectively. USSL-GG maintains higher TPR and lower FPR than NB-INC.

TABLE 20.2
NB-INC versus USSL-GG for Various Drift Values on TPR and FPR

Drift	TPR for NB-INC	TPR for USSL-GG	FPR for NB-INC	FPR USSL-GG
0.000001	0.34	**0.49**	0.12	**0.10**
0.00001	0.36	**0.58**	0.12	**0.09**
0.0001	0.37	**0.51**	0.11	**0.10**
0.001	0.38	**0.50**	0.11	**0.10**

Note: Bold numbers in this table represent the best run times.

TABLE 20.3
NB-INC versus USSL-GG for Various Drift Values on Accuracy and Runtime

Drift	ACC for NB-INC	ACC for USSL-GG	Time for NB-INC	Time USSL-GG
0.000001	0.80	**0.85**	52.0	**3.60**
0.00001	0.79	**0.87**	50.8	**3.54**
0.0001	0.82	**0.86**	51.0	**3.55**
0.001	0.81	**0.85**	53.4	**3.60**

Note: Bold numbers in this table represent the best run times.

TABLE 20.4
NB-INC versus USSL-GG for Various Drift Values on F_1 and F_2 Measure

Drift	F_1 Msr for NB-INC	F_1 Msr for USSL-GG	F_2 Msr for NB-INC	F_2 Msr USSL-GG
0.000001	0.34	**0.44**	0.34	**0.47**
0.00001	0.36	**0.50**	0.36	**0.54**
0.0001	0.37	**0.45**	0.37	**0.49**
0.001	0.38	**0.44**	0.38	**0.47**

Note: Bold numbers in this table represent the best run times.

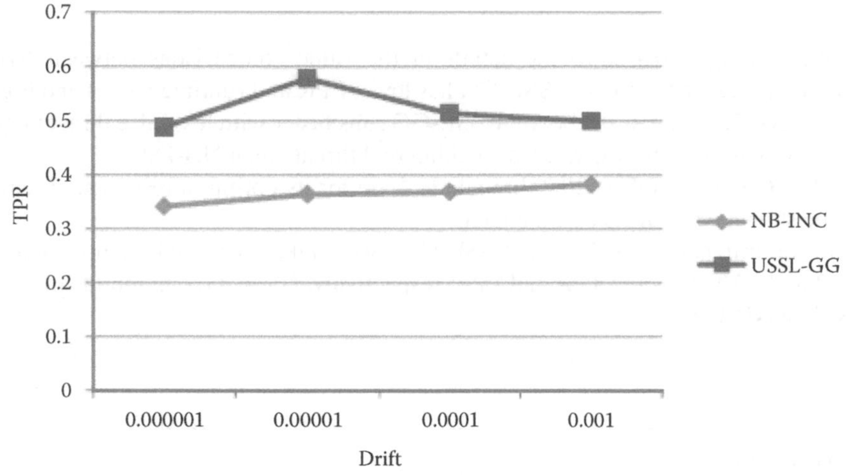

FIGURE 20.2 Comparison between NB-INC vs. our optimized model, USSL-GG in terms of TPR.

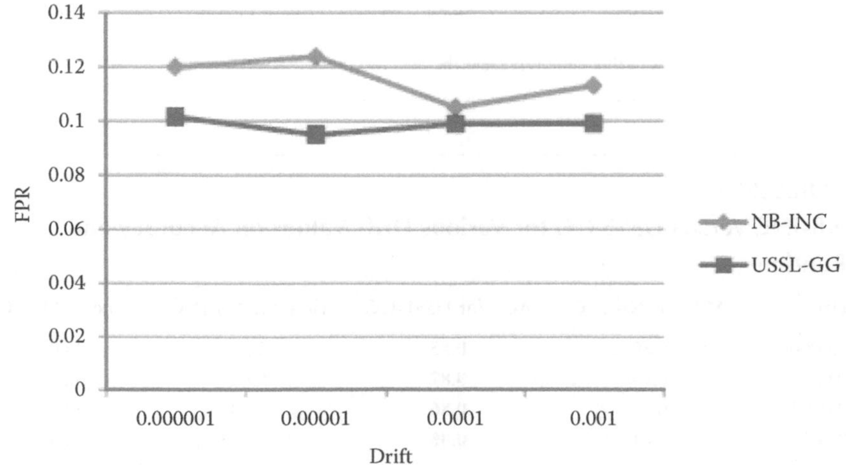

FIGURE 20.3 Comparison between NB-INC vs. our optimized model, USSL-GG in terms of FPR.

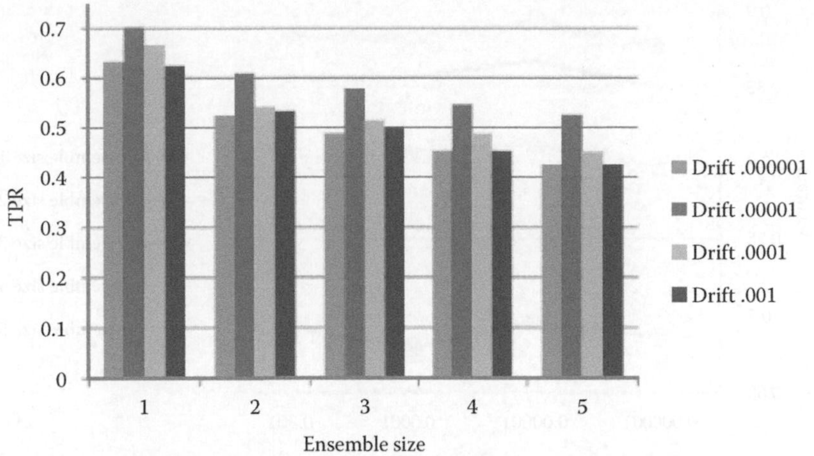

FIGURE 20.4 Comparison of USSL-GG across multiple drifts and ensemble sizes in terms of TPR.

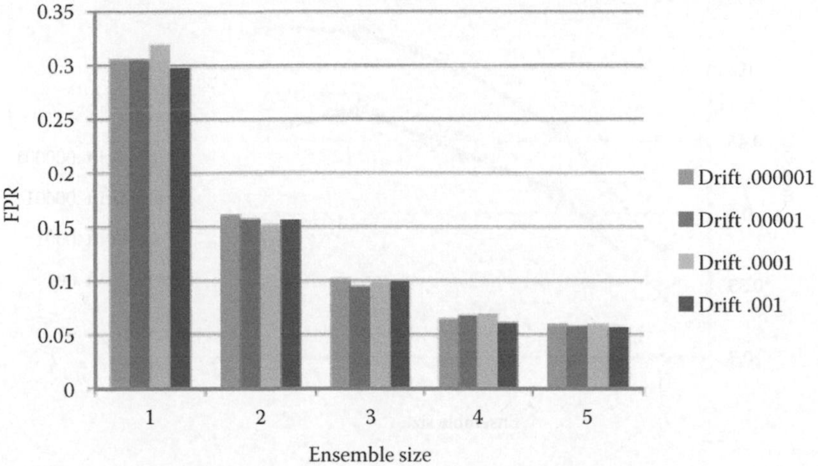

FIGURE 20.5 Comparison of USSL-GG across multiple drifts and ensemble sizes in terms of FPR.

20.4.1 Choice of Ensemble Size

In Figure 20.4, we show the various concept drifts and ensemble sizes of USSL-GG compared in terms of TPR. As ensemble size increases, TPR decreases. This is not desired. In Figure 20.5, we show the same set of concept drifts and ensemble sizes compared in terms of FPR. We can see a steady decrease in TPR across all drifts as ensemble size increases. However, we see a much larger decrease in FPR from ensemble size 1 to 2 and from 2 to 3 than from 3 to 4 and 4 to 5 across all drift values. As ensemble size increases we achieve a desired lower FPR at the expense of also lowering TPR.

In Figure 20.6, we show that when considering the rate at which positive and negative instances are correctly identified without punishing the algorithms for wrong classifications with the accuracy metric, USSL-GG performs better as the ensemble size increases.

Figure 20.7 shows $F1$ measure and Figure 20.8 shows $F2$ measure. With these two figures, we can see that USSL-GG performs better as the ensemble size increases until size 4 or 5. This is due

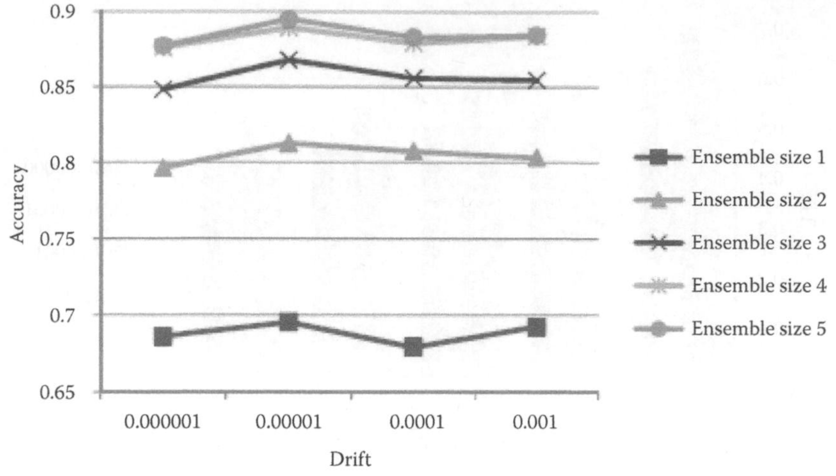

FIGURE 20.6 Comparison of USSL-GG across multiple drifts and ensemble sizes in terms of accuracy.

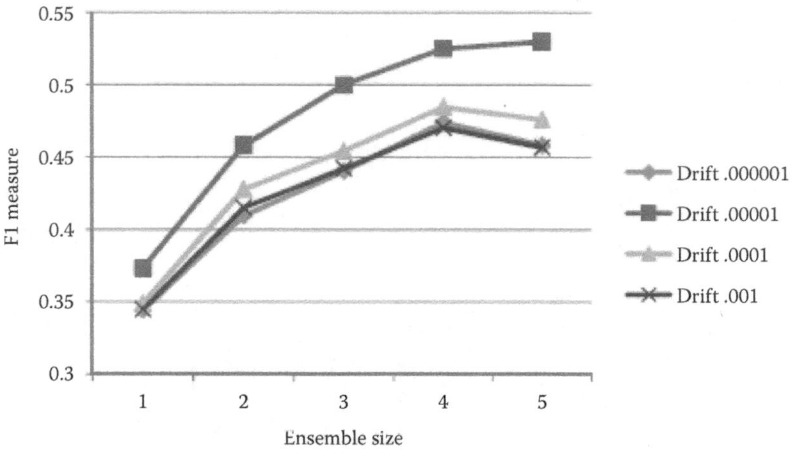

FIGURE 20.7 Comparison of USSL-GG across multiple drifts and ensemble sizes in terms of F_1 measure.

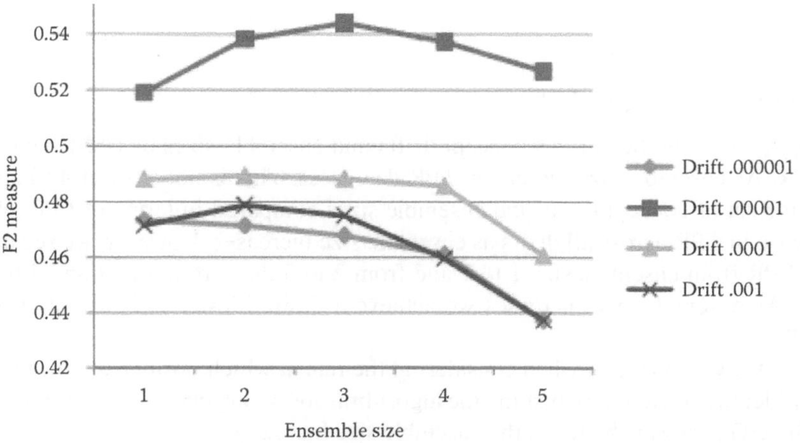

FIGURE 20.8 Comparison of USSL-GG across multiple drifts and ensemble sizes in terms of F_2 measure.

to F measure values penalizing missed insider threats and wrongly classifying harmless instances as threats. It does not give any direct bonuses for how many threats are correctly identified. This is important in insider threat detection because missing even one insider threat can be very detrimental to the system being protected. Wrongly classifying harmless instances are not as important, but they increase the problem of having to double-check-detected instances. In Figure 20.8, we show a decrease in $F2$ measure after ensemble size 3. This makes USSL-GG most effective at ensemble size 3 because $F2$ measure penalizes FN more than the FPs and low FN is the most important part of insider threat detection as stated previously. This makes our final optimization of USSL-GG to include ensemble size 3. With an ensemble size of 3, it is also worthy to note that runtimes are slower than that of ensemble sizes 1 or 2. For ensemble sizes >3, the runtimes grow exponentially. These greatly increased times are not desired and therefore ensemble sizes such as 4 or 5 are not optimal.

20.5 SUMMARY AND DIRECTIONS

In this chapter, we discussed our testing methodology and experimental results for mining data streams consisting of sequence data. In particular, the datasets used, our experimental set-up, and results were discussed. We examined various aspects such as FP, FN, and accuracy. We have also explained the results obtained.

While our focus in Chapters 17 and 18 has been on handling nonsequence data, in Chapters 19 and 20, we discussed how sequence data may be mined for insider threat detection. Future work should carry out experimentation with additional datasets and also examine the scalability of the algorithms to handle massive datasets. Some of the aspects of the big data issues will be discussed in Chapter 21.

REFERENCES

[GREE88]. S. Greenberg, "Using Unix: Collected Traces of 168 Users," Research Report 88/333/45, Department of Computer Science, University of Calgary, Calgary, Canada, 1988. http://grouplab.cpsc.ucalgary.ca/papers/.

[KRAN12]. P. Kranen, H. Kremer, T. Jansen, T. Seidl, A. Bifet, G. Holmes, B. Pfahringer, J. Read, "Stream Data Mining Using The Moa Framework," *DASFAA*, 2, 309–313, 2012.

[MAXI03]. R.A. Maxion, "Masquerade Detection Using Enriched Command Lines," In *Proceedings of IEEE International Conference on Dependable Systems & Networks (DSN)*, San Francisco, CA, pp. 5–14, 2003.

21 Scalability Using Big Data Technologies

21.1 INTRODUCTION

Several of the techniques we have discussed in Part III are computationally intensive. For example, the construction of the Lempel–Ziv–Welch (LZW) dictionary and quantized dictionary (QD) is time-consuming. Therefore, we need to address scalability issues of these algorithms. One possible solution is to adopt parallel/distributed computing. Here, we would like to exploit cloud computing based on commodity hardware. Cloud computing is a distributed parallel solution. For our approach, we utilize a Hadoop- and MapReduce-based framework to facilitate parallel computing.

This chapter will be organized in the following ways. First, we will discuss Hadoop/MapReduce in Section 21.2. Second, we will describe scalable LZW and QD construction algorithm using MapReduce (MR) in Section 21.3. Finally, we will present details of the results of various MR algorithms for the construction of QD in Section 21.4. This chapter is summarized in Section 21.5.

21.2 HADOOP MAPREDUCE PLATFORM

As discussed in Chapter 7, Hadoop MapReduce is a software framework that stores large volumes of data using large clusters and retrieves relevant data in parallel from large clusters. Those large clusters are built on commodity hardware in a reliable fault-tolerant manner. A MapReduce job usually splits input data into a number of independent chunks. These independent chunks will be run by map tasks in a parallel manner across clusters. Map tasks emit intermediate key–value pairs. The framework sorts output of the maps based on intermediate keys and passes these sorted intermediate key–value pairs to the reducer. The reducer accepts the intermediate key and a list of values. Intermediate (key, value) pairs having the same key will be directed to the same reducer. In other words, intermediate (key, value) pairs having the same key cannot go to different reducers. However, intermediate (key, value) pairs having a different key may end up at the same reducer. In general, both the input and the output of the job are stored in a Hadoop distributed file system (HDFS). The compute node is a node where map and reduce tasks are run. The storage node is a node where HDFS is running to store chunk data. In Hadoop, the compute node and storage node are the same to exploit locality. In other words, a MapReduce job strives to work on the local HDFS data to save network bandwidth across clusters.

Here is a simple example for a word count from a set of documents as illustrated in Figure 21.1. Split input files consist of a set of documents. Each line represents a document. Each line/document is passed to an individual mapper instance. The mapper emits each word as an intermediate key and the value will be counted as 1. Intermediate output values are not usually reduced together. All values with the same key (word) are presented to a single reducer together. In particular, each distinct word (subset of a different keyspace) is assigned to each reducer. These subsets are known as *partitioner*. After shuffling and sorting, reducer will get the intermediate key (word) and a list of values (counts). In Figure 21.1, the topmost reducer will get Apple key and a list of values will be "{1, 1, 1, 1}."

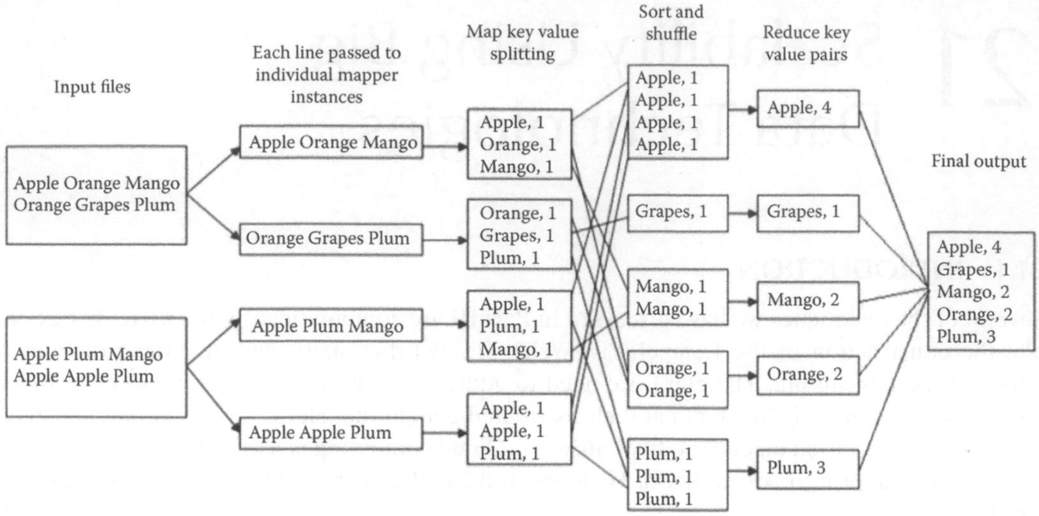

FIGURE 21.1 Word count example using MapReduce.

Algorithm 21.1 Concept Drift in Sequence Stream

1: Input: *filename*, *file−contents*
2: Output: *word*, *sum*
3: mapper (filename, file-contents)
4: **for** each word in file-contents **do**
5: *emit*(*word*, 1)
6: **end for**
7: reducer (word, values):
8: sum = 0
9: **for** each value in values **do**
10: *sum* = *sum* + *value*
11: **end for**
12: *emit*(*word*, *sum*)

Here, we have a simple word count program using the MapReduce framework (see Algorithm 21.1). Mapper tasks input document ID as key and the value is the content of the document. Mapper emits (term, 1) as intermediate key–value pair where each term appeared in a document is a key (see line 5 in Algorithm 21.1). The outputs are sorted by key and then partitioned per reducer. The reducer emits each distinct word as key and frequency count in the document as value (see line 12 in Algorithm 21.1).

21.3 SCALABLE LZW AND QD CONSTRUCTION USING MAPREDUCE JOB

We address the scalability issue using the following two approaches. Approaches are illustrated in Figure 21.2. Our proposed approach exploits in one case two MapReduce jobs (2MRJ) and the other case exploits a single map reduce job (1MRJ) [PARV13].

21.3.1 2MRJ Approach

This is a simple approach and requires 2MRJ. It is illustrated in Figures 21.3 and 21.4. The first MR job is dedicated for LZW dictionary construction in (Figure 21.3) and the second MR job is

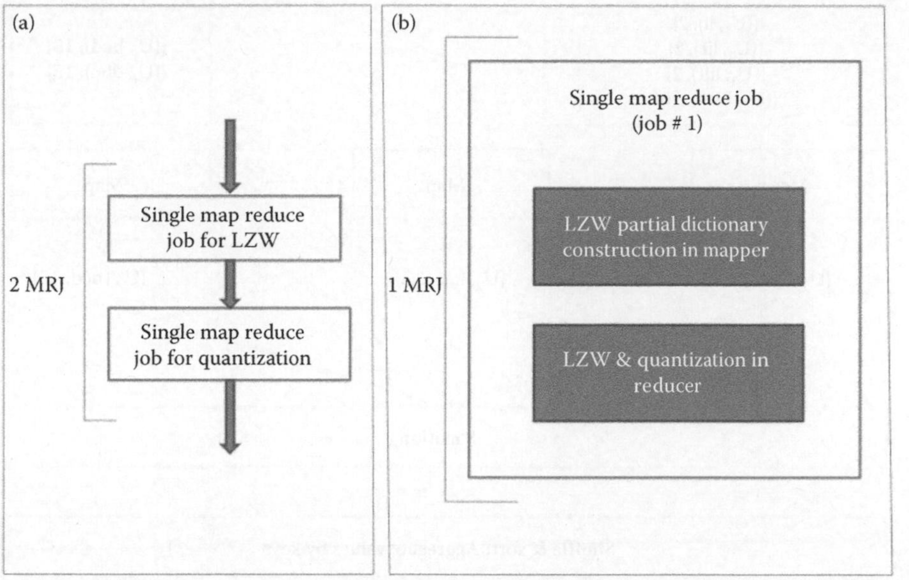

FIGURE 21.2 Approaches for scalable LZW and quantized dictionary construction using MapReduce job.

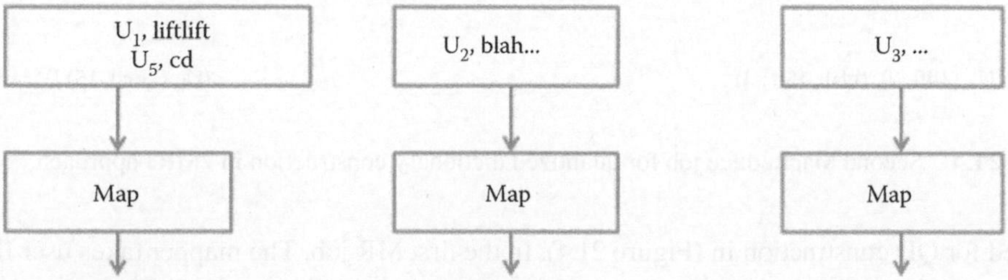

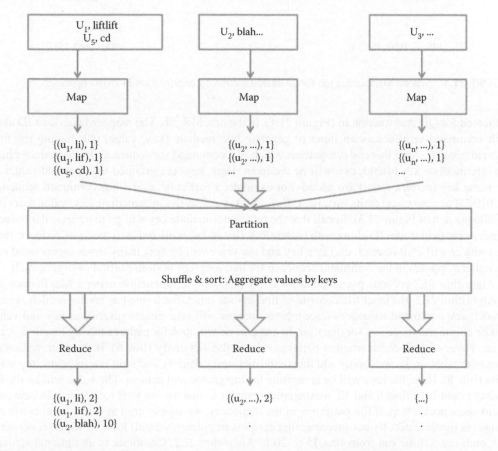

FIGURE 21.3 First MapReduce job for scalable LZW construction in 2MRJ approach.

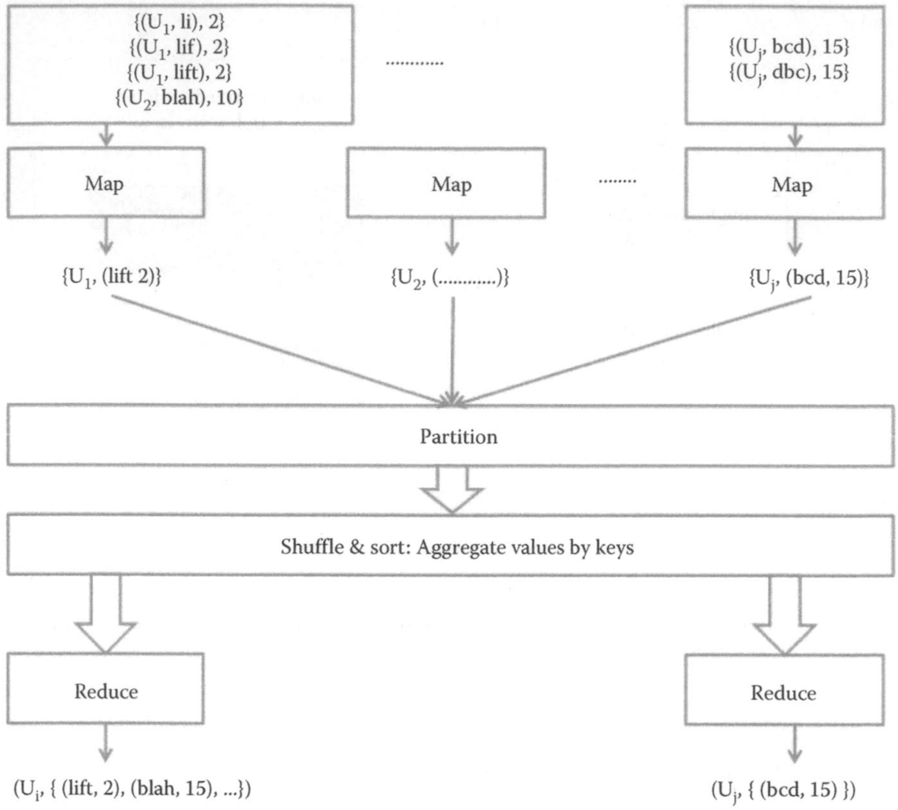

FIGURE 21.4 Second MapReduce job for quantized dictionary construction in 2MRJ approach.

dedicated for QD construction in (Figure 21.4). In the first MR job, The mapper takes user ID along with command sequence as an input to generate intermediate (key, value) pair having the form ((userid, css), 1). Note that css is a pattern which is a command subsequence. In the reduce phase, the intermediate key (userid, css) will be the input. Here, keys are grouped together and values for the same key (pattern count) are added. For example, a particular user 1 has command sequences "liftlift." The map phase emits ((u1, li), 1) ((u1, lif), 1) value as the intermediate key–value pairs (see middle portion of Figure 21.3). Recall that the same intermediate key will go to a particular reducer. Hence, a particular user ID along with pattern/css, that is, key, will arrive to the same reducer. Here, the reducer will emit (user id, css) as a key and the value will be how many times (aggregated one) the pattern appears in the command sequence for that user (see bottom portion of Figure 21.3).

Algorithm 21.2 presents pseudocode for LZW dictionary construction using a MapReduce job. In Algorithm 21.2, the input file consists of line-by-line input. Each line has entries namely, gname (userid) and command sequences (cseq). Next, mapper will take gname (userid) as key and values will be command sequences for that user. In mapper, we will look for patterns having length 2, 3, and so on. Here, we will check whether patterns exist in the dictionary (line 6). If the pattern does not exist in the dictionary, we simply add that in the dictionary (line 7), and emit intermediate key–value pairs (line 8). Here, the keys will be composite having gname and pattern. The value will be the frequency count 1. At lines 9 and 10, we increment pointer so that we can look for patterns in new command sequences (cseq). If the pattern is in the dictionary, we simply emit at line 12 and cseq's end pointer is incremented. By not incrementing cseq's start pointer, we will look for superset patterns.

Combiner will be run from line 15 to 20 in Algorithm 21.2. Combiner is an optional step and acts as "min reducer." For the same user, the same pattern may be emitted multiple times with the frequency count 1. In combiner, we aggregate them at line 18. Finally, in line 20, we emit the composite key (gname and pattern) and aggregate the frequency count. Combiner helps us to overcome unnecessary communication costs and therefore, improves processing time. Recall that combiner is optional; it may run 0 times or 1 or many times. Hence, the signature of the combiner method (input/output parameters) needs to match the output signature of mappers and the input signature of reducers. At reducer from line 21 to 26, aggregation is carried as shown in "Combiner."

In the second MR job, quantization of the dictionary will be carried out (see Figure 21.4). Mapper will carry simple transformation by generating a key based on user ID and value based on pattern frequency. In Algorithm 21.3, mapper will take each line as an input from the input file produced by the first MapReduce job. Here, mapper will take input (userid, pattern) as key and frequency as value. Mapper emits the intermediate key–value pair where the key will be user ID and the value will be concatenation of pattern and frequency (see middle portion of Figure 21.4 and see from line 4 to 7 in Algorithm 21.3). All patterns of a particular user and corresponding frequency will arrive at the same reducer. The reducer will conduct all pairwise edit distance calculation among all patterns for a particular user. Finally, user ID as key and longest frequent patterns as the value will be emitted by the reducer (see bottom portion of Figure 21.4).

At the reducer, each user (gname) will be input and list of values will be patterns and their frequency count. Here, compression of patterns will be carried out for that user. Recall that some patterns will be pruned using Edit distance. For a user, each pattern will be stored into Hashmap, H. Each new entry in the H will be pattern as key and value as frequency count 1. For existing pattern in the dictionary, we will simply update frequency count (line 11). At line 13, the dictionary will be quantized and H will be updated accordingly. Now, from the QD, patterns along frequency count will be emitted as values and key will be gname (at line 14).

21.3.2 1MRJ Approach

Here, we will utilize 1MRJ. It is illustrated in Figure 21.5. We are expecting that by reducing the number of jobs, we can reduce total processing costs. Running a job in Hadoop takes a significant overhead. Hence, by minimizing the number of jobs, we can construct the dictionary quickly. The overhead for a Hadoop job is associated with disk I/O and network transfers. When a job is submitted to Hadoop cluster, the following actions will take place:

1. The Executable file is moved from client machine to Hadoop JobTracker [JOB].
2. The JobTracker determines TaskTrackers [TASK] that will execute the job.
3. The Executable file is distributed to the TaskTrackers over the network.
4. Map processes initiates reading data from HDFS.
5. Map outputs are written to local discs.
6. Map outputs are read from discs, shuffled (transferred over the network to TaskTrackers.
7. Reduce processes initiate reading the input from local discs.
8. Reduce outputs are written to discs.

Therefore, if we can reduce the number of jobs, we can avoid expensive disk operations and network transfers. That is, the reason we prefer 1MRJ over 2MRJ.

Algorithm 21.2 LZW Dictionary Construction Using MapReduce (2MRJ)

1: Input: *gname*: *groupname*, *cseq* : *commandsequences*
2: Output: *Key*: (*gname*, *commandpattern*(*css*)), *count*
3: *map*(*stringgname*, *stringcseq*)
4: *start* ← 1, *end* ← 2
5: *css* = (*csstart* • • • *csend*)

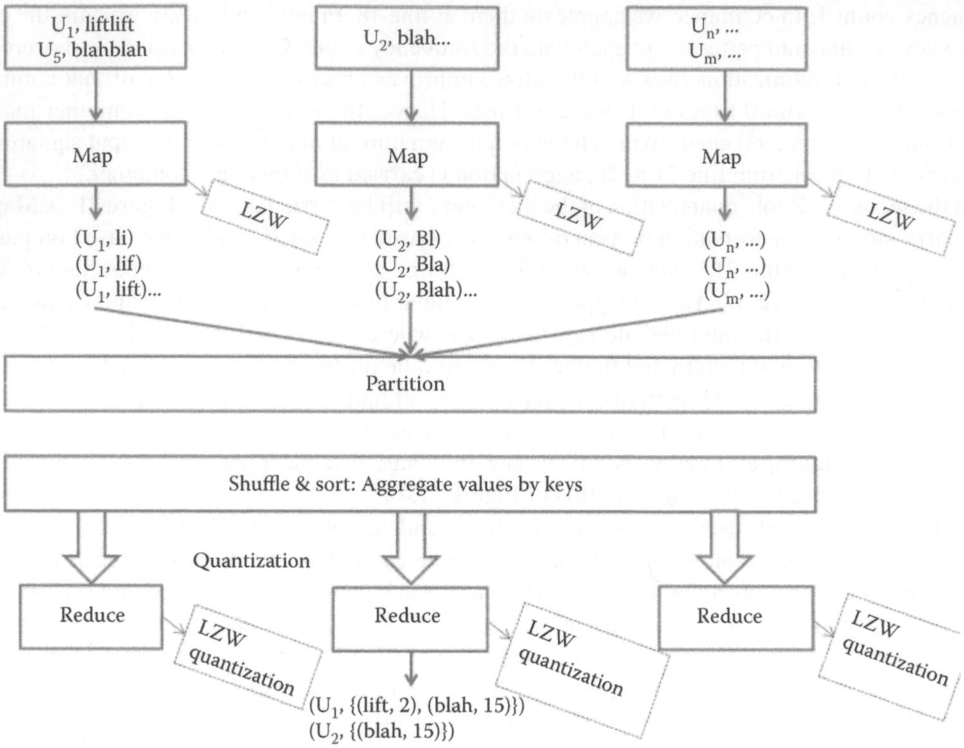

FIGURE 21.5 1MRJ: 1 MR job approach for scalable LZW and quantized dictionary construction.

```
if css ∈ dictionary then
    Add css to thedictionary
    emit(pairs(gname, css), integer1)
    start ← start + 1
    end ← end + 1
else
    emit(pairs(gname, css), integer1)
    end ← end + 1
end if
combine(pair(gname, css), (cnt1, cnt2, • • •))
Sum ← 0
for all cnt ∈ (cnt1, cnt2, • • •) do
    sum ← sum + cnt
end for
emit(pair(gname, css), integersum)
reduce(pair(gname, css), (cnt1, cnt2, • • •))
Sum ← 0
for all cnt ∈ (cnt1, cnt2, • • •) do
    sum ← sum + cnt
end for
emit(pair(gname, css), integersum)
```

Algorithm 21.3 Compression/Quantization Using MapReduce (2MRJ)

```
Input: line : gname, commandsequence(css), f requencycount(cnt)
Output: Key : (gname, commandpattern(css))
map(stringline, string)
gname ← Spilt(line)
css ← Spilt(line)
cnt ← Spilt(line)
emit(gname, pair(css, cnt))
reduce(gname, (pair(css1, cnt1), pair(css2, cnt2), • • •))
Sum ← 0
for all pair(cssi, cnti) ∈ ((pair(css1, cnt1), pair(css2, cnt2) • • •) do
    H ← H + pair(cssi, cnti)
end for
QD = QuantizedDictionary(H)
emit(gname, pair(css, integer sum))
for all cssi ∈ QD do
    emit(gname, pair(cssi, count(cssi)))
end for
```

Algorithm 21.4 Dictionary Construction and Compression Using Single MapReduce (1MRJ)

```
Input: gname: groupname, cseq : commandsequences
Output: Key: gname, commandpattern(css)
map(stringgname, stringcseq)
start ← 1, end ← 2
css = (csstart • • • csend)
if css ∈ dictionary then
    Add css to thedictionary
    emit(gname, css)
    start ← end
    end ← end + 1
else
    emit(gname, css)
    end ← end + 1
end if
reduce(gname, (css1, css2, • • •)
H←0
for all cssi ∈ ((css1, css2, • • •) do
    if css ∈ H then
    H ← H + (cssi, 1)
    else
        count ← getf requency(H(cssi))
    count ← count + 1
    H ← H + (cssi, count)
    end if
end for
QD = QuantizedDictionary(H)
```

```
27: for all cssi ∈ QD do
28:     emit(gname, pair(cssi, count(cssi)))
29: end for
```

Mapper will emit user ID as key and value will be pattern (see Algorithm 21.1). Recall that in mapper, partial LZW operation will be completed. The same user ID will arrive at the same reducer since user is the intermediate key. For that user ID, a reducer will have a list of patterns. In the reducer, incomplete LZW will be completed here. In addition, full quantization operation will be implemented as described in Chapter 19.3. Parallelization will be achieved at the user level (*interuser parallelization*) instead of within users (*intrauser parallelization*). In mapper, parallelization will be carried out by dividing large files into a number of chunks and processing a certain number of files in parallel.

Algorithm 21.1 illustrates the idea. The input file consists of line-by-line input. Each line has entries namely, gname (userid), and command sequences (cseq). Next, mapper will take gname (userid) as the key, and values will be command sequences for that user. In mapper, we will look for patterns having length 2, 3, and so on. Here, we will check whether patterns exist in the dictionary (line 6). If the pattern does not exist in the dictionary, we simply add that in the dictionary (line 7) and emit intermediate key–value pairs (line 8) having keys as gname and values as patterns with length 2, 3, and so on. At lines 9 and 10, we increment pointer so that we can look for patterns in new command sequences (cseq). If the pattern is in the dictionary, we simply emit at line 12 and cseq's end pointer is incremented so that we can look for superset command sequence.

At the reducer, each user (gname) will be input and the list of values will be patterns. Here, compression of patterns will be carried for that user. Recall that some patterns will be pruned using edit distance. For a user, each pattern will be stored into Hashmap, *H*. Each new entry in the *H* will be pattern as key and value as frequency count. For an existing pattern in the dictionary, we will simply update the frequency count (line 18). At line 20, the dictionary will be quantized, and *H* will be updated accordingly. Now, from the QD all distinct patterns from *H* will emitted as values along with key gname.

21.4 EXPERIMENTAL SETUP AND RESULTS

21.4.1 Hadoop Cluster

Our Hadoop cluster (cshadoop0-cshadoop9) is comprised of virtual machines (VM) that run in the Computer Science vmware esx cloud,—so there are 10 VM. Each VM is configured as a quad core with 4 GB of RAM and a 256 GB virtual hard drive. The virtual hard drives are stored on the CS SAN (3PAR).

There are three ESX hosts which are Dell PowerEdge R720 s with 12 cores @2.99 GHZ, 128 GB of RAM, and fiber to the 3PAR SAN. The VMs are spread across the three ESX hosts in order to balance the load. "cshadoop0" is configured as the "name node." A "cshadoopl" through "cshadoop9" are configured as the slave "data nodes."

We have implemented our approach using Java JDK version 1.6.0.39. For the MapReduce implementation we have used Hadoop version 1.0.4.

21.4.2 Big Dataset for Insider Threat Detection

The datasets used are created from the trace files from the University of Calgary project. A total of 168 files have been collected from different levels of users of UNIX as described in [GREE88] and [MAXI03]. The different levels of users are

- Novice programmers (56 users)
- Experienced programmers (36 users)

- Computer scientists (52 users)
- Nonprogrammers (25 users)

Each file contains the commands used by each of the users over several weeks. Now, in order to get the big data, first we replicated the user files randomly so that we have

- Novice programmers—(1320 users), that is, file starting from "novice-0001" to "novice-1320"
- Experienced programmers—(576 users)
- Computer scientists—(832 users)
- Nonprogrammers—(1600 Users)

Total Number of Users = 4328; size is 430 MB; and one command file is for one user. Next, we gave these files as input to our program (written in Python) which gave unique unicode for each distinct command provided by all users. The output file for all users is 15.5 MB. We dubbed it as *original data* (*OD*).

Finally, we replicated this data 12 times for each user. And we ended up 187 MB of input file which was given as an input to Map Reduce job of LZW and Compression. We dubbed this as *duplicate big data* (*DBD*).

21.4.3 Results for Big Data Set Related to Insider Threat Detection

First, we experiment on OD, and next, we concentrate on DBD.

21.4.3.1 On OD Dataset

We have compared our approaches, namely 2MRJ and 1MRJ, on OD dataset. Here, we have a varied number of reducers and a fixed number of mappers (e.g., HDFS block size equals 64 MB). In case of 2MRJ, we have a varied number of reducers in second job's reducer and not in first map reducer job. 1MRJ outperforms 2MRJ in terms of processing time on a fixed number of reducers except in the first case (number of reducers equals to 1). With the latter case, parallelization is limited at the reducer phase. Table 21.1 illustrates this. For example, for number of reducers equals 9, total time taken is 3.47 and 2.54 s for 2MRJ and 1MRJ approaches, respectively.

TABLE 21.1
Time Performance of 2MRJ vs. 1MRJ for Varying Number of Reducers

# of Reducer	Time for 2MRJ (M:S)	Time for lMRJ (M:S)
1	13.5	16.5
2	9.25	9.00
3	6.3	5.37
4	5.45	5.25
5	5.21	4.47
6	4.5	4.20
7	4.09	3.37
8	3.52	3.04
9	3.47	2.54
10	3.38	2.47
11	3.24	2.48
12	3.15	2.46

TABLE 21.2
Details of LZW Dictionary Construction and Quantization Using MapReduce in 2MRJ on OD Dataset

Description	Size/Entries in Second Job	Size/Entries in First Job
Map Input	95.75 MB (size)	15.498 MB (size)
Map Output	45,75,120 (entries)	65,37,040 (entries)
Reduce Input	17,53,590 (entries)	45,75,120 (entries)
Reduce Output	37.48 MB	95.75 MB (size)

With regard to 2MRJ case, Table 21.2 presents input/output statistics of both MapReduce jobs. For example, for first map reduce job mapper emits 6,537,040 intermediate key–value pairs and reducer emits 95.75-MB output. This 95.75 MB will be the input for mapper for the second MapReduce job.

Here, we will show how the HDFS block size will have an impact on the LZW dictionary construction in the 2MRJ case. First, we vary the HDFS block size that will control the number of mappers. With a 64-MB HDFS block size and a 15.5-MB input size, the number of mappers equals to 1. For a 4-MB HDFS block size, the number of mappers equals 4. Here, we assume that the input file split size equals the HDFS block size. The smaller HDFS block size (smaller file split size) increases performance (reduces time). More mappers will be run in various nodes in parallel.

Table 21.3 presents total time taken by mapper (part of first MapReduce job) in 2MRJ case on the OD dataset. Here, we have varied partition size for LZW dictionary construction. For a 15.498-MB input file size with an 8-MB partition block size, MapReduce execution framework used two mappers.

21.4.3.2 On DBD Dataset

Table 21.4 shows the details of the value comparisons of 1MRJ across a varying number of reducers and HDFS block size values. Here, we have used the DBD dataset.

In particular, in Figure 21.6, we show the total time taken for a varying number of reducers with a fixed HDFS block size. Here, *X* axis represents the number of reducer and *Y* axis represents the total time taken for 1MRJ with a fixed HDFS block size. We demonstrate that with an increasing number of reducers, total time taken will drop gradually. For example, with regard to reducer 1, 5, and 8, the total time taken in 1MRJ approach is 39.24, 13.04, 10.08 min, respectively. This number

TABLE 21.3
Time Performance of Mapper for LZW Dictionary Construction with Varying Partition Size in 2MRJ

Partition Block Size (MB)	Map (s)	No of Mappers
1	31.3	15
2	35.09	8
3	38.06	5
4	36.06	4
5	41.01	3
6	41.03	3
7	41.01	3
8	55.0	2
64	53.5	1

TABLE 21.4
Time Performance of 1MRJ for Varying Reducer and HDFS Block Size on DBD

No of Reducer	64 MB	40 MB	20 MB	10 MB
1	39:24	27:20	23:40	24:58
2	17:36	16:11	13:09	14:53
3	15:54	11:25	9:54	9:12
4	13:12	11:27	8:17	7:41
5	13:06	10:29	7:53	6:53
6	12:05	9:15	6:47	6:05
7	11:18	8:00	6:05	6:04
8	10:29	7:58	5:58	5:04
9	10:08	7:41	5:29	4:38
10	11:15	7:43	5:30	4:42
11	10:40	7:30	4:58	4:41
12	11:04	8:21	4:55	3:46

validates our claim. With more reducers running in parallel, we can run quantization/compression algorithms for various users in parallel. Recall that in 1MRJ reducer will get each distinct user as key and values will be LZW dictionary pattern. Let us assume that we have 10 distinct users and their corresponding patterns. For compression with one reducer, compression for 10 user patterns will be carried out in a single reducer. On the other hand for five reducers, it is expected that each reducer will get two users' patterns. Consequently, 5 reducers will run in parallel and each reducer will execute the compression algorithm for 2 users serially instead of 10. Therefore, with an increasing number of reducers, performance (decreases time) improves.

Now, we will show how the number of mappers will affect the total time taken in 1MRJ case. The number of mappers is usually controlled by the number of HDFS blocks (dfs.block.size) in the input files. The number of HDFS blocks in the input file is determined by HDFS block size. Therefore, people adjust their HDFS block size to adjust the number of maps.

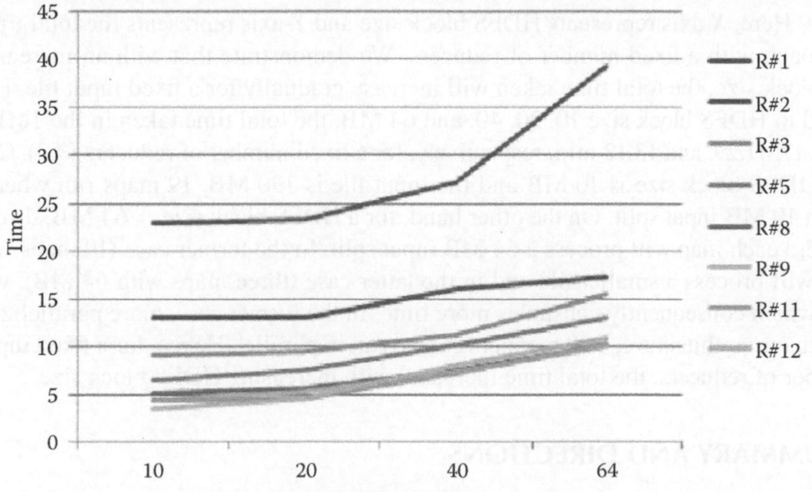

FIGURE 21.6 Time taken for varying number of HDFS block size in 1MRJ.

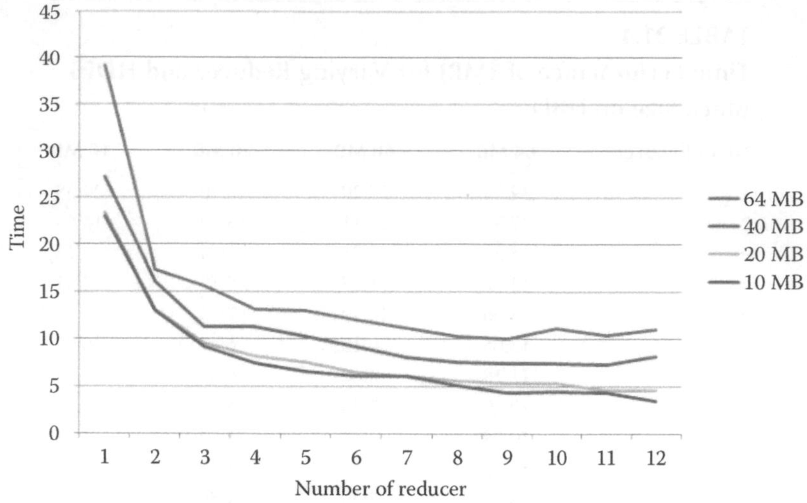

FIGURE 21.7 Time taken for varying number of reducer in 1MRJ 86.

Setting the number of map tasks is not as simple as setting up the number of reduce tasks. Here, first we determine whether the input file is isSplitable. Next, three variables, mapred.min.split.size, mapred.max.split.size, and dfs.block.size, determine the actual split size. By default, min split size is 0 and max split size is Long.MAX and block size 64 MB. For actual split size, minSplitSize and blockSize set the lower bound and blockSize and maxSplitSize together set the upper bound. Here is the function to calculate:

$$max(minsplitsize, min(maxsplitsize, blocksize))$$

For our case we use min split size is 0; max split size is Long.MAX and blockSize vary from 10 to 64 MB. Hence, the actual split size will be controlled by the HDFS block size. For example, the 190 MB input file with DFS block size 64 MB file will be split into three with each split having two 64 MB and the rest with 62 MB. Finally, we will end up with three maps.

In Figure 21.7, we show the impact of HDFS block size on the total time taken for a fixed number of reducers. Here, X axis represents HDFS block size and Y-axis represents the total time taken for 1MR approach with a fixed number of reducers. We demonstrate that with an increasing number of HDFS block size, the total time taken will increase gradually for a fixed input file. For example, with regard to HDFS block size 10, 20, 40, and 64 MB, the total time taken in the 1MRJ approach was 7.41, 8.17, 11.27, and 13.12 min, respectively, for a fixed number of reducers (=4). On one hand, when the HDFS block size is 10 MB and the input file is 190 MB, 19 maps run where each map processes a 10 MB input split. On the other hand, for a HDFS block size = 64 MB, three maps will be run where each map will process a 64 MB input split. In the former case (19 maps with 10 MB), each map will process a smaller file and in the latter case (three maps with 64 MB), we process a larger file which consequently consumes more time. In the former case, more parallelization can be achieved. In our architecture, >10 mappers can be run in parallel. Hence, for a fixed input file and a fixed number of reducers, the total time increases with increasing HDFS block size.

21.5 SUMMARY AND DIRECTIONS

Chapters 14 through 20 discussed stream mining techniques for insider threat detection. In addition, experiential results were also provided both for sequence data and nonsequence data. We argued that the data streams are massive and therefore we need scalable techniques. In this chapter, we discuss the scalability of our techniques and the issues in designing big data analytic techniques for insider threat detection.

The work discussed in this chapter is the first step towards big data analytics for handling massive data streams for insider threat detection. We need to examine the various techniques for stream mining for insider threat detection that we have discussed and examine the scalability of the solutions that have been proposed.

REFERENCES

[GREE88]. S. Greenberg, "*Using Unix: Collected Traces of 168 Users*," Research Report 88/333/45, Department of Computer Science, University of Calgary, Calgary, Canada, 1988. http://grouplab.cpsc.ucalgary.ca/papers/.

[JOB]. http://wiki.apache.org/hadoop/JobTracker.

[MAXI03]. R.A. Maxion, "Masquerade Detection Using Enriched Command Lines," In *Proc. IEEE International Conference on Dependable Systems & Networks (DSN)*, pp. 5–14, 2003.

[PARV13]. P. Parveen, B. Thuraisingham, L. Khan, "Map Reduce Guided Scalable Compressed Dictionary Construction for Repetitive Sequences," In *9th IEEE International Conference on Collaborative Computing: Networking, Applications and Worksharing*, 2013b, October.

[TASK]. http://wiki.apache.org/hadoop/TaskTracker.

22 Stream Mining and Big Data for Insider Threat Detection

22.1 INTRODUCTION

Insider threat detection is a very important problem requiring critical attention. This chapter presents a number of approaches to detect insider threats through augmented unsupervised and supervised learning techniques on evolving stream. We have considered both *sequence* and *nonsequence* stream data.

The supervised learning approach to insider threat detection outperformed the unsupervised learning approach. The supervised method succeeded in identifying all 12 anomalies in the 1998 Lincoln Laboratory Intrusion Detection dataset with zero false negatives (FN) and a lower false positive (FP) rate than the unsupervised approach.

For unsupervised learning, graph-based anomaly detection (GBAD) ([COOK00], [COOK07], [EBER07]) is used. However, applying GBAD to the insider threat problem requires an approach, that is, sufficiently adaptive and efficient so effective models can be built from vast amounts of evolving data.

In Section 22.2, we will provide a discussion of our approaches. Future work will be discussed in Section 22.3. This chapter is summarized in Section 22.4.

22.2 DISCUSSION

Our technique combines the power of GBAD and one-class support vector machines (SVMs) with the adaptiveness of stream mining to achieve effective practical insider threat detection for unbounded evolving data streams. Increasing the weighted cost of FN increased accuracy and ultimately allowed our approach to perform well. Though FP could be further reduced through more parameter tuning, our approach accomplished the goal of detecting all insider threats.

We examined the problem of insider threat detection in the context of command sequences and propose an unsupervised ensemble-based learning approach that can take into account concept drift. The approach adopts advantages of both compression and incremental learning. A classifier is typically built and trained using large amount of legitimate data. However, training a classifier is very expensive, and furthermore, it has problems when the baseline changes as is the case in real-life networks. We acknowledge this continuously changing feature of legitimate actions and introduce the notion of concept drift to address the changes. The proposed unsupervised learning system adapts directly to the changes in command sequence data. In addition, to improve accuracy we use an ensemble of K classifiers, instead of a single one. Voting is used, and a subset of classifiers is used because classifiers with more recent data gradually replace those that are outdated. We address an important problem and propose a novel approach.

For sequence data, our stream-guided sequence learning performed well with limited number of FP as compared to static approaches. This is because the approach adopts advantages from both compression and ensemble-based learning. In particular, compression offered unsupervised learning in a manageable manner; on the other hand, ensemble-based learning offered adaptive learning. The approach was tested on a real command line dataset and shows effectiveness over static approaches in terms of true positive and FP.

Compressed/quantized dictionary construction is computationally expensive. It does not scale well with a number of users. Hence, we look for distributed solution with parallel computing with commodity hardware. For this, all users' quantized dictionaries are constructed using a MapReduce framework on Hadoop. A number of approaches are suggested, experimented with on the benchmark dataset, and discussed. We have shown with one 1 MapReduce job that a quantized dictionary can be constructed and demonstrates effectiveness over other approaches.

22.3 FUTURE WORK

We plan to extend the work in the following directions.

22.3.1 Incorporate User Feedback

For unsupervised learning, we assume that no ground truth is available. In fact, over time some ground truth may be available in terms of feedback. Once a model is created in an unsupervised manner, we would like to update the model based on user feedback. Right now, once the model is created, it remains unchanged. When ground truth is available over time, we will refine all our models based on this feedback immediately (see also [MASU10a, MASU10b, MASU10c]).

22.3.2 Collusion Attack

During unsupervised learning (see Chapter 17), when we update models, collusion attack ([ZHAO05], [WANG09]) may take place. In that case, a set of models among K models will not be replaced for a while. Each time, when a victim will be selected, these colluded models will survive. Recall that "collusion" is an agreement between two or more models so that they will always agree on the prediction. In particular, if we have $K = 3$ models, two models may maintain secretive agreement and their prediction will be the same and used as ground truth. Therefore, two colluded/secretive models will always survive and never be victim in model update case. Recall that the learning is unsupervised and majority voting will be taken as ground truth. Hence, we will not be able to catch an insider attack. Our goal is to identify a colluded attack. For this, during victim selection of models, we will take into account agreement of models over time. If agreement of models persists for a long time and survives, we will choose the victim from there.

22.3.3 Additional Experiments

We will perform additional experiments on more sophisticated scenarios including chunk size. Currently, we assume that chunk size is fixed or uniform. Fixed chunk is easy to implement. But it fails to capture concept drift or anomaly in the stream. Assume that concept drift happens at the end of a chunk (fixed size). We may not be able to detect anomaly until we process the next chunk. For this, the better approach will be creation of dynamic chunk size. Here, chunk size will vary. Variable chunk size will be estimated by using change point detection ([CANG06], [BARO06]). Once we observe a new distribution, the current chunk ends and new chunk will emerge.

Instead of a one class SVM, we may use other classifiers [PARV06]. When we apply insider threat detection across multiple data sources/domains, we need to address heterogeneity issues of schema/sources. For this, we will utilize schema matching/ontology alignment ([PART11], [ALIP10a], [ALIP11], [ALIP10b], [KHAN02], [KHAN04]).

22.3.4 Anomaly Detection in Social Network and Author Attribution

Anomaly detection will be carried out in social networks using our proposed supervised and unsupervised approaches.

Twitter, an online social network, allows friends to communicate and stay connected via exchanging short messages (up to 140 characters). Spammer presence is prevalent in Twitter now.

Spammers post malicious links, send unsolicited messages to legitimate users, and hijack trending topics. At least 3% of messages can be categorized as spam. We can extend our framework to detect spam by exploiting anomaly detection.

New authors may appear in a blog. Our goal is to identify these new authors in the stream. For this, our anomaly detection can be applied. Feature extraction needs to be changed (i.e., stylometric feature [JAMA12]. We would like to carry out our techniques for author attribution ([AKIV12], [KOPP09], [SEKE13]).

22.3.5 Stream Mining as a Big Data Mining Problem

Stream data can be treated as big data. This is due to well-known properties of stream data such as infinite length, high-speed data arrival, online/timely data processing, changing characteristics of data, need for one-pass techniques (i.e., forgotten raw data), and so on. In particular, data streams are infinite, therefore efficient storage and incremental learning are required. The underlying concept changes over time are known as concept drift. The learner should adapt to this change and be ready for veracity and variety. New classes evolving in the stream are known as concept evolution which makes classification difficult. New features may also evolve in the stream such as text streams.

All of these properties conform to characteristics of big data. For example, infinite length of stream data constitutes a large "volume" of big data. High-speed data arrival and online processing holds the characteristics of a large "velocity" of big data. Stream data can be sequence or nonsequence data (vector). This conforms to "verity" characteristics of big data.

Characteristics of stream data can be changed over time. New patterns may emerge in evolving streams. Old patterns may be outdated. These properties may support the notion of "veracity" of big data. Therefore, stream data possesses characteristics of big data. In spite of the success and extensive studies of stream mining techniques, there is no single work dedicated to a unified study of the new challenges introduced by big data and evolving stream data.

The big data community adopts big data infrastructures that are used to process unbounded continuous streams of data (e.g., S4, Storm). However, their data mining support is rudimentary. A number of open source tools for big data mining have been released to support traditional data mining. Only a few tools support very basic stream mining. Research challenges such as change detection, novelty detection, and feature evolution over evolving streams have been recently studied in traditional stream mining ([DOMI01], [DAVI98], [MASU10a], [MASU11], [FAN04]), but not in big data.

Here, we need a unified picture of how these challenges and proposed solutions can be augmented in these open source tools. In addition to presenting the solutions to overcome stream mining challenges, experience with real applications of these techniques to data mining and security will be shared across the world.

- Big Data Stream Infrastructure: Apache S4 [NEUM10], Storm, Cassandra [LAKS10], and so on, including batch processing Hadoop.
- Big Data Mining Tool: Apache Mahout [OWEN11], MOA [ZLIO11], PEGASUS [KANG11], GraphLab, SAMOA, and their support for Stream Mining.

22.4 SUMMARY AND DIRECTIONS

In this chapter, we provided a discussion of our approaches for insider threat detection and described future work. The chapters in Part III have essentially discussed how the stream mining techniques in Part II can be applied for insider threat detection. We discussed various techniques as well as provided experimental results. We also discussed how our techniques can be scaled for handling very large datasets.

While there has been a lot of work on stream mining as well as on insider threat detection, the approaches discussed in this part are some of the early efforts to apply stream mining for insider threat detection. We also discussed the need to develop scalable techniques to handle massive datasets and provided some directions.

In Part IV of this book, we will discuss our experimental systems on applying big data management and analytics for various security applications. These systems will provide a better understanding on how the techniques discussed in Parts II and III could be scaled for large datasets.

REFERENCES

[AKIV12]. N. Akiva and M. Koppel, "Identifying Distinct Components of a Multi-Author Document," In *Proceedings of EISIC*, Odense, Denmark, pp. 205–209, 2012.

[ALIP10a]. N. Alipanah, P. Parveen, S. Menezes, L. Khan, S. Seida, B.M. Thuraisingham. "Ontology-Driven Query Expansion Methods to Facilitate Federated Queries," *SOCA*, Perth, Australia, pp. 1–8, 2010.

[ALIP10b]. N. Alipanah, P. Srivastava, P. Parveen, B.M. Thuraisingham, "Ranking Ontologies using Verified Entities to Facilitate Federated Queries," In *Proceedings of Web Intelligence Conference*, pp. 332–337, 2010.

[ALIP11]. N. Alipanah, P. Parveen, L. Khan, and B.M. Thuraisingham. "Ontology-Driven Query Expansion Using Map/Reduce Framework to Facilitate Federated Queries." In *ICWS*, Washington, DC, pp. 712–713, 2011.

[BARO06]. M. Baron and A. Tartakovsky. "Asymptotic Optimality of Change-Point Detection Schemes in General Continuous-Time Models," *Sequential Analysis*, 25(3), 257–296, 2006.

[CANG06]. J.W. Cangussu and M. Baron, "Automatic Identification of Change Points for the System Testing Process," *COMPSAC (1)*, 377–384, 2006.

[COOK00]. D.J. Cook and L.B. Holder "Graph-Based Data Mining," *IEEE Intelligent Systems*, 15(2), 32–41, 2000.

[COOK07]. D.J. Cook and L.B. Holder (Eds.) *Mining Graph Data*. John Wiley & Sons, Inc., Hoboken, NJ, 2007.

[DAVI98]. B.D. Davison and H. Hirsh. "Predicting Sequences of User Actions. Working Notes of The Joint Workshop on Predicting the Future: AI Approaches to Time Series Analysis," *15th National Conference on Artificial Intelligence and Machine*, Madison, WI, pp. 5–12, AAAI Press, 1998.

[DOMI01]. P. Domingos and G. Hulten, "Catching up with the Data: Research Issues in Mining Data Streams," *ACM SIGMOD Workshop on Research Issues on Data Mining and Knowledge Discovery (DMKD)*, Santa Barbara, CA, May 20, 2001. http://www.cs.cornell.edu/johannes/papers/dmkd2001-papers/p9_kollios.pdf.

[EBER07]. W. Eberle and L.B. Holder, "Mining for Structural Anomalies in Graph-Based Data," In *Proceedings of International Conference on Data Mining (DMIN)*, San Jose, CA, pp. 376–389, 2007.

[FAN04]. W. Fan, "Systematic Data Selection to Mine Concept-Drifting Data Streams," In *Proceedings of ACM SIGKDD*, Seattle, WA, pp. 128–137, 2004.

[JAMA12]. A. Jamak, S. Alen, M. Can, "Principal Component Analysis for Authorship Attribution," *Business Systems Research*, 3(2), 49–56, 2012.

[KANG11]. U. Kang, C.E. Tsourakakis, C. Faloutsos, "Pegasus: Mining Peta-Scale Graphs," *Knowledge and Information Systems*, 27(2), 303–325, 2011.

[KHAN02]. L. Khan and F. Luo, "Ontology Construction for Information Selection," In *Proceedings of ICTAI*, Washington, DC, pp. 122–127, 2002.

[KHAN04]. L. Khan, D. McLeod, E.H. Hovy, "Retrieval Effectiveness of an Ontology-Based Model for Information Selection," *VLDB Journal*, 13(1), 71–85, 2004.

[KOPP09]. M. Koppel, J. Schler, S. Argamon, "Computational Methods in Authorship Attribution," *JASIST*, 60(1), 9–26, 2009.

[LAKS10]. A. Lakshman and P. Malik. Cassandra: A decentralized structured storage system. *SIGOPS Operating Systems Review* 44(2), 35–40, 2010.

[MASU10a]. M.M. Masud, Q. Chen, J. Gao, L. Khan, C. Aggarwal, J. Han, B. Thuraisingham, "Addressing Concept-Evolution in Concept-Drifting Data Streams," In *Proceedings of IEEE International Conference on Data Mining (ICDM)*, Sydney, Australia, pp. 929–934, 2010a.

[MASU10b]. M.M. Masud, Q. Chen, J. Gao, L. Khan, J. Han, B.M. Thuraisingham, "Classification and Novel Class Detection of Data Streams in a Dynamic Feature Space," In *Proceedings of ECML/PKDD (2)*, Barcelona, Spain, pp. 337–352, 2010b.

[MASU10c]. M.M. Masud, J. Gao, L. Khan, J. Han, B.M. Thuraisingham, "Classification and Novel Class Detection in Data Streams with Active Mining," In *Proceedings of PAKDD (2)*, Barcelona, Spain, pp. 311–324, 2010.

[MASU11]. M.M. Masud, J. Gao, L. Khan, J. Han, B.M. Thuraisingham, "Classification and Novel Class Detection in Concept-Drifting Data Streams Under Time Constraints," *IEEE Transactions on Knowled ge and Data Engineering (TKDE)*, 23(6), 859–874, 2011a.

[NEUM10]. L. Neumeyer, B. Robbins, A. Nair, and A. Kesari. "S4: Distributed Stream Computing Platform." In *ICDM Workshops*, Sydney, Australia, pp. 170–177, 2010.

[OWEN11]. S. Owen, R. Anil, T. Dunning, E. Friedman, Mahout in Action, Manning Publications, Shelter Island, NY, 2011.

[PART11]. J. Partyka, P. Parveen, L. Khan, B.M. Thuraisingham, S. Shekhar, "Enhanced Geographically Typed Semantic Schema Matching," *Journal of Web Semantics*, 9(1), 52–70, 2011.

[PARV06]. P. Parveen and B.M. Thuraisingham, "Face Recognition Using Multiple Classifiers," In *Proceedings of ICTAI*, Arlington, VA, pp. 179–186, 2006.

[SEKE13]. S.E. Seker, K. Al-Naami, L. Khan, "Author Attribution on Streaming Data," *Information Reuse and Integration (IRI) 2013 IEEE 14th International Conference on*, San Francisco, CA, pp. 497–503, 2013.

[WANG09]. X. Wang, L. Qian, H. Jiang, "Tolerant Majority-Colluding Attacks For Secure Localization in Wireless Sensor Networks," In *WiCom '09: Proceedings of 5th International Conference on Wireless Communications, Networking and Mobile Computing, 2009*, Beijing, China, pp. 1–5, 2009.

[ZHAO05]. H. Zhao, M. Wu, J. Wang, K. Liu, "Forensic Analysis of Nonlinear Collusion Attacks for Multimedia Fingerprinting," *Image Processing, IEEE Transactions on*, 14(5), 646–661, 2005.

[ZLIO11]. I. Zliobaite, A. Bifet, G. Holmes, B. Pfahringer, "MOA Concept Drift Active Learning Strategies for Streaming Data," *Journal of Machine Learning Research—Proceedings Track*, 17, 48–55, 2011.

Conclusion to Part III

Part III, consisting of nine chapters, described stream data analytics techniques with emphasis on big data for insider threat detection. In particular, both supervised and unsupervised learning methods for insider threat detection were discussed.

Chapter 14 provided a discussion of our approach to insider threat detection using stream data analytics and discussed the big data issue with respect to the problem. That is, massive amounts of stream data are emanating from various devices and we need to analyze this data for insider threat detection. Chapter 15 described related work in both insider threat detection and stream data mining. In addition, aspects of the big data issue were also discussed. Chapter 16 described ensemble-based learning for insider threat detection. In particular, we have described techniques for both supervised and unsupervised learning and discussed the issues involved. We believe that ensemble-based approaches are suited for data streams as they are unbounded. Chapter 17 described the different classes of learning techniques for nonsequence data. It described exactly how each method arrives at detecting insider threats and how ensemble models are built, modified, and discarded. First, we discussed supervised learning in detail and then discussed unsupervised learning. In Chapter 18, we discussed our testing methodology and experimental results for mining data streams consisting of nonsequence data. We examined various aspects such as false positives, false negatives, and accuracy. Our results indicate that supervising learning yields better results for certain datasets. In Chapter 19, we described both supervised and unsupervised learning techniques for mining data streams for sequence data. Experimental results of the techniques discussed in Chapter 19 were presented in Chapter 20. In particular, we discussed our datasets and testing methodology as well as our experimental results. Chapter 21 discussed how big data technologies can be used for stream mining to handle insider threats. In particular, we examine one of the techniques we have designed and showed how it can be redesigned using big data technologies. We also discussed our experimental results. Finally, Chapter 22 concluded with an assessment of the viability of stream mining for real-world insider threat detection and the relevance to big data aspects.

Now that we have discussed the various aspects of stream data analytics, handling massive data streams, as well as applying the techniques for insider threat detection, in Part IV we will describe the various experimental systems we have designed and developed for BDMA and BDSP.

Part IV

Experimental BDMA and BDSP Systems

Introduction to Part IV

Parts II and III focused on stream data analytics with applications in insider threat detection. There was also a special emphasis on handling massive amounts of data streams and the use of cloud computing. We described various stream data analytics algorithms and provided our experimental results. While Parts II and III focused on big data management and analytics (BDMA) and big data security and privacy (BDSP) with respect to stream data analytics and insider threat detection, in Part IV we describe several experimental systems we have designed and developed that are related to BDMA and BDSP. While these systems have also been discussed in our previous book, in Part IV, we will emphasize extending our systems to handle big data.

Part IV, consisting of six chapters, describes the various experimental systems we have designed and developed. In Chapter 23, we discuss a query processing system that functions in the cloud and manages a large number of RDF triples. These RDF triples can be used to represent big data applications such as social networks. Chapter 24 describes a cloud-based system called InXite that is designed to detect evolving patterns and trends in streaming data for security applications. Chapter 25 describes our cloud-centric assured information sharing system that addresses the information sharing requirements of various organizations including social media users in a secure manner. In Chapter 26, we describe the design and implementation of a secure information integration framework that uses the Intelligence Community's data integration framework Blackbook as well as the Amazon cloud. Chapter 27 describes one of our data mining techniques that is dedicated to the automated generation of signatures to defend against malware attacks. Due to the need for near real-time performance of the malware detection tools, we have implemented our data mining tool in the cloud. This implementation technique shows how BDMA techniques can be applied for cyber security problems. Finally, in Chapter 28, we have described the design and implementation of an inference controller for provenance data. We have also argued that there is a need for the inference controller to manage massive amounts of data as the knowledge base could grow rapidly as it has to store the data, the metadata, the release data as well as real-world knowledge.

While we have designed and developed several additional systems for BDMA and BDSP, we believe that the systems we have described in Part IV provide a representative sample of the systems we have developed.

23 Cloud Query Processing System for Big Data Management

23.1 INTRODUCTION

As stated in some of the earlier chapters, cloud computing is an emerging paradigm in the information technology and data processing communities. Enterprises utilize cloud computing services to outsource data maintenance that can result in significant financial benefits. Businesses store and access data at remote locations in the "cloud." As the popularity of cloud computing grows, the service providers face ever increasing challenges. They have to maintain huge quantities of heterogeneous data while providing efficient information retrieval. Thus, the key emphasis for cloud computing solutions is scalability and query efficiency. In other words, cloud computing is a critical technology for big data management and analytics.

Semantic web technologies are being developed to present data in a standardized way such that such data can be retrieved and understood by both humans and machines. Historically, webpages are published in plain HTML (Hypertext Markup Language) files that are not suitable for reasoning. Instead, the machine treats these HTML files as a bag of keywords. Researchers are developing semantic web technologies that have been standardized to address such inadequacies. The most prominent standards are Resource Description Framework (RDF) [W3b], SPARQL Protocol and RDF Query Language [W3C] (SPARQL). RDF is the standard for storing and representing data and SPARQL is a query language to retrieve data from an RDF store. RDF is being used extensively to represent social networks. Cloud computing systems can utilize the power of these semantic web technologies to represent and manage the social networks so that the users of these networks have the capability to efficiently store and retrieve data for data-intensive applications.

Semantic web technologies could be especially useful for maintaining data in the cloud. Semantic web-based social networks provide the ability to specify and query heterogeneous data in a standardized manner. Moreover, using the Web Ontology Language (OWL), ontologies, different schemas, classes, data types, and relationships can be specified without sacrificing the standard RDF/SPARQL interface. Conversely, cloud computing solutions could be of great benefit to the semantic web-based big data community, such as the social network community. Semantic web datasets are growing exponentially. In the web domain, scalability is paramount. Yet, high speed response time is also vital in the web community. We believe that the cloud computing paradigm offers a solution that can achieve both of these goals.

Existing commercial tools and technologies do not scale well in cloud computing settings. Researchers have started to focus on these problems recently. They are proposing systems built from scratch. In [WANG10], researchers propose an indexing scheme for a new distributed database [COMP] that can be used as a cloud system. When it comes to semantic web data such as RDF, we are faced with similar challenges. With storage becoming cheaper and the need to store and retrieve large amounts of data, developing systems to handle billions of RDF triples requiring terabytes of disk space is no longer a distant prospect. Researchers are already working on billions of triples ([NEWM08], [ROHL07]). Competitions are being organized to encourage researchers to build efficient repositories [CHAL]. At present, there are just a few frameworks (e.g., RDF-3X [NEUM08], Jena [CARR04], Sesame [OPEN], BigOWLIM [KIRY05]) for semantic web technologies, and these

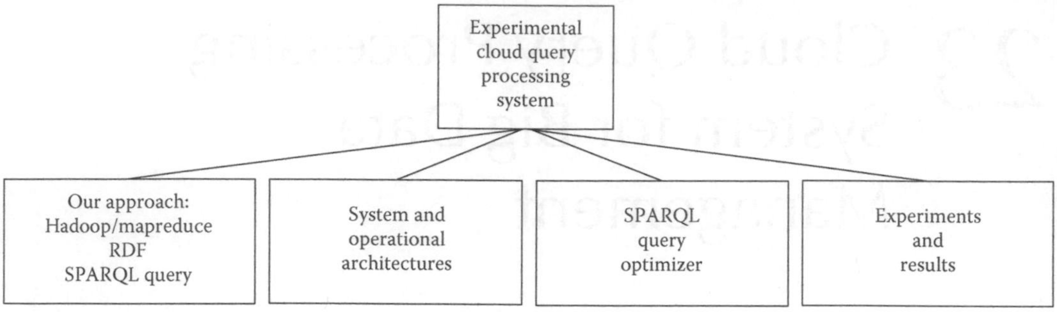

FIGURE 23.1 Experimental cloud query-processing system.

frameworks have limitations for large RDF graphs. Therefore, storing a large number of RDF triples and efficiently querying them is a challenging and important problem.

In this chapter, we discuss a query-processing system that functions in the cloud and manages a large number of RDF triples. These RDF triples can be used to represent big data applications such as social networks as discussed in our previous book [THUR15]. The organization of this chapter is as follows. Our approach is discussed in Section 23.2. In Section 23.3, we discuss related work. In Section 23.4, we discuss our system architecture. In Section 23.5, we discuss how we answer an SPARQL query. In Section 23.6, we present the results of our experiments. In section 23.7, we discuss our work on security policy enforcement that was built on top of our prototype system. Finally, in Section 23.8, we draw some conclusions and discuss areas we have identified for improvement in the future. Key concepts discussed in this chapter are illustrated in Figure 23.1. A more detailed discussion of the concepts, architectures and experiments are provided in [HUSA11a] and [HUSA11b]. Since semantic web technologies can be used to model big data systems such as social network systems, our query-processing system can be utilized to query social networks and related big data systems.

23.2 OUR APPROACH

A distributed system can be built to overcome the scalability and performance problems of current semantic web frameworks. Databases are being distributed in order to provide such scalable solutions. However, to date, there is no distributed repository for storing and managing RDF data. Researchers have only recently begun to explore the problems and technical solutions that must be addressed in order to build such a distributed system. One promising line of investigation involves making use of readily available distributed database systems or relational databases. Such database systems can use relational schema for the storage of RDF data. SPARQL queries can be answered by converting them to SQL first ([CHEB07], [CHON05], [CYGA05]). Optimal relational schemas are being probed for this purpose [ABAD07]. The main disadvantage with such systems is that they are optimized for relational data. They may not perform well for RDF data, especially because RDF data are sets of triples [W3a] (an ordered tuple of three components called subject, predicate, and object, respectively) that form large directed graphs. In an SPARQL query, any number of triple patterns (TPs) [W3e] can join on a single variable [W3d] which makes a relational database query plan complex. Performance and scalability will remain a challenging issue due to the fact that these systems are optimized for relational data schemata and transactional database usage.

Yet another approach is to build a distributed system for RDF from scratch. Here, there will be an opportunity to design and optimize a system with specific application to RDF data. In this approach, the researchers would be reinventing the wheel. Instead of starting with a blank slate, we built a solution with a generic distributed storage system that utilizes a cloud computing platform. We then tailored the system and schema specifically to meet the needs of semantic web data. Finally, we built a semantic web repository using such a storage facility.

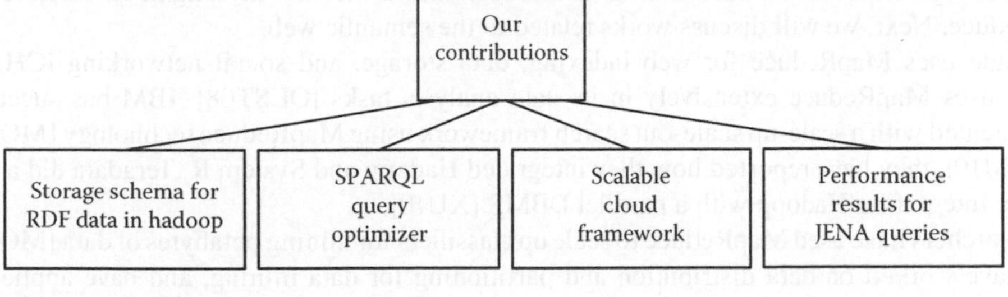

FIGURE 23.2 Our contributions.

Hadoop [HADOa] is a distributed file system where files can be saved with replication. It is an ideal candidate for building a storage system. Hadoop features high fault tolerance and great reliability. In addition, it also contains an implementation of the MapReduce [DEAN04] programming model, a functional programming model that is suitable for the parallel processing of large amounts of data. Through partitioning data into a number of independent chunks, MapReduce processes run against these chunks, making parallelization simpler. Moreover, the MapReduce programming model facilitates and simplifies the task of joining multiple triple patterns.

In this chapter, we will describe a schema to store RDF data in Hadoop, and we will detail a solution to process queries against these data. In the preprocessing stage, we process RDF data and populate files in the distributed file system. This process includes partitioning and organizing the data files, and executing dictionary encoding. We will then detail a query engine for information retrieval. We will specify exactly how SPARQL queries will be satisfied using MapReduce programming. Specifically, we must determine the Hadoop "jobs" that will be executed to solve the query. We will present a greedy algorithm that produces a query plan with the minimal number of Hadoop jobs. This is an approximation algorithm using heuristics, but we will prove that the worst case has a reasonable upper bound. Finally, we will utilize two standard benchmark datasets to run experiments. We will present results for the dataset ranging from 0.1 to over 6.6 billion triples. We will show that our solution is exceptionally scalable. We will show that our solution outperforms leading state-of-the-art semantic web repositories using standard benchmark queries on very large datasets. Our contributions are listed in the following, and illustrated in Figure 23.2. More details are given in [HUSA11a].

1. We designed a storage scheme to store RDF data in Hadoop distributed file system (HDFS) [HADOb].
2. We developed an algorithm that is guaranteed to provide a query plan whose cost is bounded by the log of the total number of variables in the given SPARQL query. It uses summary statistics for estimating join selectivity to break ties.
3. We built a framework that is highly scalable and fault-tolerant and supports data-intensive query processing.
4. We demonstrated that our approach performs better than Jena for all queries and BigOWLIM and RDF-3X for complex queries having large result sets.

23.3 RELATED WORK

MapReduce, though a programming paradigm, is rapidly being adopted by researchers. This technology is becoming increasingly popular in the community that handles large amounts of data. It is the most promising technology to solve the performance issues researchers are facing in cloud computing. In [ABAD09a], the author discusses how MapReduce can satisfy most of the requirements to build an ideal Cloud DBMS. Researchers and enterprises are using MapReduce technology for web indexing, searches, and data mining. In this section, we will first investigate research related to MapReduce. Next, we will discuss works related to the semantic web.

Google uses MapReduce for web indexing, data storage, and social networking [CHAN06]. Yahoo! uses MapReduce extensively in its data analysis tasks [OLST08]. IBM has successfully experimented with a scale-up scale-out search framework using MapReduce technology [MORE07]. In [SISM10], they have reported how they integrated Hadoop and System R. Teradata did a similar work by integrating Hadoop with a parallel DBMS [XU10].

Researchers have used MapReduce to scale up classifiers for mining petabytes of data [MORE08]. They have worked on data distribution and partitioning for data mining, and have applied three data mining algorithms to test the performance. Data mining algorithms are being rewritten in different forms to take advantage of MapReduce technology. In [CHU06], researchers rewrite well-known machine learning algorithms to take advantage of multicore machines by leveraging the MapReduce programming paradigm. Another area where this technology is successfully being used is simulation [MCNA07]. In [ABOU09], researchers reported an interesting idea of combining MapReduce with existing relational database techniques. These works differ from our research in that we use MapReduce for semantic web technologies. Our focus is on developing a scalable solution for storing RDF data and retrieving them by SPARQL queries.

In the semantic web arena, there has not been much work done with MapReduce technology. We have found two related projects: BioMANTA [ITEE] project and Scalable, High-Performance, Robust and Distributed (SHARD) [CLOU]. BioMANTA proposes extensions to RDF molecules [DING05] and implements a MapReduce-based molecule store [NEWM08]. They use MapReduce to answer the queries. They have queried a maximum of four million triples. Our work differs in the following ways: first, we have queried one billion triples. Second, we have devised a storage schema that is tailored to improve query execution performance for RDF data. We store RDF triples in files based on the predicate of the triple and the type of the object. Finally, we also have an algorithm to determine a query-processing plan whose cost is bounded by the log of the total number of variables in the given SPARQL query. By using this, we can determine the input files of a job and the order in which they should be run. To the best of our knowledge, we are the first ones to come up with a storage schema for RDF data using flat files in HDFS and a MapReduce job determination algorithm to answer an SPARQL query.

SHARD is an RDF triple store using the Hadoop Cloudera distribution. This project shows initial results demonstrating Hadoop's ability to improve scalability for RDF datasets. However, SHARD stores its data only in a triple store schema. It currently does no query planning or reordering, and its query processor will not minimize the number of Hadoop jobs. There has been significant research into semantic web repositories with particular emphasis on query efficiency and scalability. In fact, there are too many such repositories to fairly evaluate and discuss each. Therefore, we will pay attention to semantic web repositories that are open source or available for download and which have received favorable recognition in the semantic web and database communities.

In [ABAD09b] and [ABAD07], researchers reported a vertically partitioned DBMS for storage and retrieval of RDF data. Their solution is a schema with a two-column table for each predicate. Their schema is then implemented on top of a column-store relational database such as CStore [STON05] or MonetDB [BONC06]. They observed performance improvement with their scheme over traditional relational database schemes. We have leveraged this technology in our predicate-based partitioning within the MapReduce framework. However, in the vertical partitioning research, only small databases (<100 million) were used. Several papers [SIDI08], [MCGL09], and [WEIS08] have shown that vertical partitioning's performance is drastically reduced as the dataset size is increased.

Jena [CARR04] is a semantic web framework for Jena. True to its framework design, it allows integration of multiple solutions for persistence. It also supports inference through the development of reasoners. However, Jena is limited to a triple store schema. In other words, all data are stored in a single three column table. Jena has very poor query performance for large datasets. Furthermore, any change to the dataset requires complete recalculation of the inferred triples.

BigOWLIM [KIRY05] is among the fastest and most scalable semantic web frameworks available. However, it is not as scalable as our framework and requires very high end and costly machines. It requires expensive hardware (a lot of main memory) to load large datasets and it has a long loading time. As our experiments show, it does not perform well when there is no bound object in a query. However, the performance of our framework is not affected in such a case.

RDF-3X [NEUM08] is considered the fastest existing semantic web repository. In other words, it has the fastest query times. RDF-3X uses histograms, summary statistics, and query optimization to enable high performance semantic web queries. As a result, RDF-3X is generally able to outperform any other solution for queries with bound objects and aggregate queries. However, RDF-3X's performance degrades exponentially for unbound queries, and queries with even simple joins if the selectivity factor is low. This becomes increasingly relevant for inference queries that generally require unions of subqueries with unbound objects. Our experiments show that RDF-3X is not only slower for such queries, but also it often aborts and cannot complete the query. For example, consider the simple query "Select all students." This query in LUBM requires us to select all graduate students, select all undergraduate students, and union the results together. However, there are a very large number of results in this union. While both subqueries complete easily, the union will abort in RDF-3X for LUBM (30,000) with 3.3 billion triples.

RDF Knowledge Base (RDFKB) [MCGL10] is a semantic web repository using a relational database schema built upon bit vectors. RDFKB achieves better query performance than RDF-3X or vertical partitioning. However, RDFKB aims to provide knowledge base functions such as inference forward chaining, uncertainty reasoning, and ontology alignment. RDFKB prioritizes these goals ahead of scalability. RDFKB is not able to load LUBM (30,000) with three billion triples, so it cannot compete with our solution for scalability.

Hexastore [WEIS08] and BitMat [ATRE08] are main memory data structures optimized for RDF indexing. These solutions may achieve exceptional performance on hot runs, but they are not optimized for cold runs from persistent storage. Furthermore, their scalability is directly associated with the quantity of main memory RAM available. These products are not available for testing and evaluation.

In our previous work [HUSA09], [HUSA10], we proposed a greedy and an exhaustive search algorithm to generate a query-processing plan. However, the exhaustive search algorithm was expensive and the greedy one was not bounded and its theoretical complexity was not defined. In this chapter, we present a new greedy algorithm with an upper bound. Also, we did observe scenarios in which our old greedy algorithm failed to generate the optimal plan. The new algorithm is able to obtain the optimal plan in each of these cases. The Join Executer component runs the jobs using MapReduce framework. It then relays the query answer from Hadoop to the user.

23.4 ARCHITECTURE

Our system architecture is illustrated in Figure 23.3. It essentially consists of an SPARQL query optimizer and a RDF data manager implemented in the cloud. The operational architecture is illustrated in Figure 23.4. It consists of two components. The upper part of Figure 23.4 depicts the data preprocessing component and the lower part shows the query answering one. We have three subcomponents for data generation and preprocessing. We convert RDF/XML [W3f] to N-triples [W3a] serialization format using our N-triples converter component. The predicate split (PS) component takes the N-triples data and splits it into predicate files. The predicate files are then fed into the Predicate Object Split (POS) component that splits the predicate files into smaller files based on the type of objects. These steps are described below.

Data Generation and Storage: For our experiments, we use the LUBM [GUO05] dataset. It is a benchmark dataset designed to enable researchers to evaluate a semantic web repository's performance [GUO04]. The LUBM data generator generates data in RDF/XML serialization format. This format is not suitable for our purpose because we store data in HDFS as flat files and so to

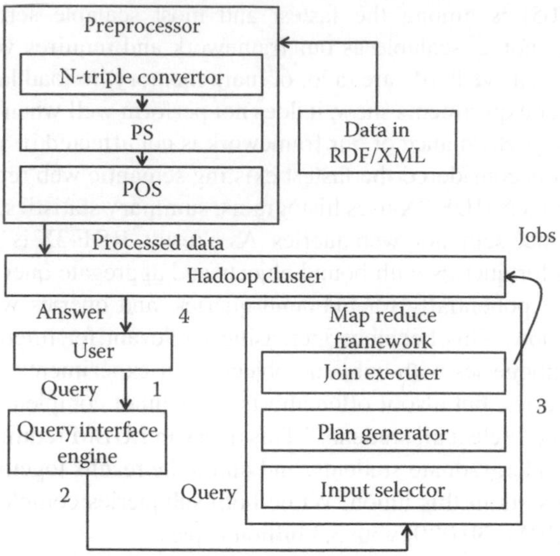

FIGURE 23.3 System architecture.

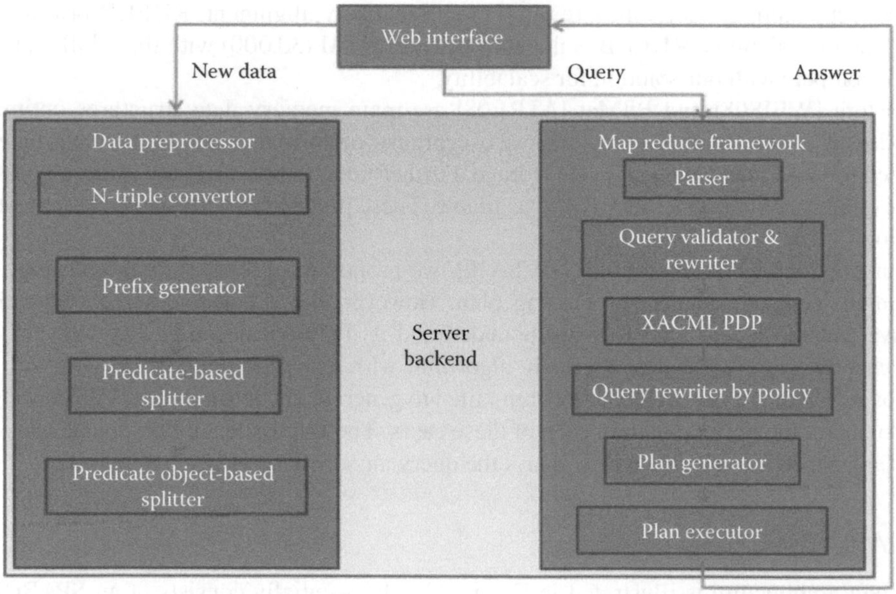

FIGURE 23.4 Operational architecture.

retrieve even a single triple, we would need to parse the entire file. Therefore, we convert the data to N-triples to store the data, because with that format, we have a complete RDF triple (Subject, Predicate, and Object) in one line of a file that is very convenient to use with MapReduce jobs. The processing steps to go through to get the data into our intended format are described in following sections.

File Organization: We do not store the data in a single file because, in a Hadoop and MapReduce framework, a file is the smallest unit of input to a MapReduce job and in the absence of caching, a file is always read from the disk. If we have all the data in one file, the whole file will be input to jobs for each query. Instead, we divide the data into multiple smaller files. The splitting is done in two steps, which we discuss in the following sections.

Predicate Split: In the first step, we divide the data according to the predicates. This division immediately enables us to cut down the search space for any SPARQL query that does not have a variable predicate. For such a query, we can just pick a file for each predicate and run the query on those files only. For simplicity, we name the files with predicates, for example, all the triples containing a predicate p1:pred go into a file named p1-pred. However, in case we have a variable predicate in a triple pattern [W3e] and if we cannot determine the type of the object, we have to consider all files. If we can determine the type of the object, then we consider all files having that type of object. We discuss more on this in Section 23.5. In real-world RDF datasets, the number of distinct predicates is in general not a large number [STOC08]. However, there are datasets having many predicates. Our system performance does not vary in such a case because we just select files related to the predicates specified in an SPARQL query.

Split Using Explicit Type Information of Object: In the next step, we work with the explicit type information in the rdf_type file. The predicate rdf:type is used in RDF to denote that a resource is an instance of a class. The rdf_type file is first divided into as many files as the number of distinct objects the rdf:type predicate has. For example, if in the ontology, the leaves of the class hierarchy are $c_1, c_2, \ldots, c_n$, then we will create files for each of these leaves and the file names will be like type_c_1, type_c_2; ..., type_c_n. Please note that the object values $c_1, c_2, \ldots, c_n$ are no longer needed to be stored within the file as they can be easily retrieved from the file name. This further reduces the amount of space needed to store the data. We generate such a file for each distinct object value of the predicate rdf:type.

Split Using Implicit Type Information of Object: We divide the remaining predicate files according to the type of the objects. Not all the objects are URIs (Uniform Resource Identifier); some are literals. The literals remain in the file named by the predicate; no further processing is required for them. The type information of a URI object is not mentioned in these files but they can be retrieved from the type_*files. The URI objects move into their respective file named as predicate type. For example, if a triple has the predicate p and the type of the URI object is c_i, then the subject and object appear in one line in the file p_c_i. To do this split, we need to join a predicate file with the type_*files to retrieve the type information.

Our MapReduce framework, described in Section 23.5, has three subcomponents in it. It takes the SPARQL query from the user and passes it to the Input and Plan Generator. This component selects the input files by using our algorithm described in Section 23.5, decides how many MapReduce jobs are needed, and passes the information to the Join Executer component that runs the jobs using the MapReduce framework. It then relays the query answer from Hadoop to the user.

23.5 MAPREDUCE FRAMEWORK

23.5.1 Overview

The MapReduce framework is at the heart of our cloud computing efforts. We will discuss MapReduce in various chapters of this book as it relates to the contents of that chapter. In this section, we discuss how we answer SPARQL queries in our MapReduce framework component.

Section 23.5.2 discusses our algorithm to select input files for answering the query. Section 23.5.3 describes the cost estimation needed to generate a plan to answer an SPARQL query. It introduces a few terms that we use in the following discussions. We also describe the ideal model we should follow to estimate the cost of a plan, and introduce the heuristics-based model we use in practice. Section 23.5.4 presents our heuristics-based greedy algorithm to generate a query plan that uses the cost model introduced in Section 23.5.3. We face tie situations in order to generate a plan in some cases. In Section 23.5.5, we discuss how we handle these special cases. Section 23.5.6 shows how we implement a join in a Hadoop MapReduce job by working through an example query.

23.5.2 Input Files Selection

Before determining the jobs, we select the files that need to be input to the jobs. We have some query rewriting capability which we apply at this step of query processing. We take the query submitted by the user and iterate over the triple patterns. We may encounter the following cases:

1. In a triple pattern, if the predicate is variable, we select all the files as input to the jobs and terminate the iteration.
2. If the predicate is rdf:type and the object is concrete, we select the type file having that particular type. For example, for LUBM query 9 (Listing 1), we could select file type_Student as part of the input set. However, this brings up an interesting scenario. In our dataset, there is actually no file named type_Student because Student class is not a leaf in the ontology tree. In this case, we consult the LUBM ontology [LEHI] to determine the correct set of input files. We add the files type_GraduateStudent, type_UndergraduateStudent, and type_ResearchAssistant as GraduateStudent; UndergraduateStudent, and ResearchAssistant are the leaves of the subtree rooted at node Student.
3. If the predicate is rdf:type and the object is variable, then if the type of the variable is defined by another triple pattern, we select the type file having that particular type. Otherwise, we select all type files.
4. If the predicate is not rdf:type and the object is variable, then we need to determine if the type of the object is specified by another triple pattern in the query. In this case, we can rewrite the query and eliminate some joins. For example, in LUBM Query 9 (Listing 1), the type of Y is specified as Faculty and Z as Course and these variables are used as objects in the last three triple patterns. If we choose files advisor_Lecturer, advisor_PostDoc, advisor_FullProfessor, advisor_AssociateProfessor, advisor_AssistantProfessor, and advisor_ VisitingProfessor as part of the input set, then the triple pattern in line 2 becomes unnecessary. Similarly, triple pattern in line 3 becomes unnecessary if files takesCourse_Course and takesCourse_GraduateCourse are chosen. Hence, we get the rewritten query shown in Listing 2. However, if the type of the object is not specified, then we select all files for that predicate.
5. If the predicate is not rdf:type and the object is concrete, then we select all files for that predicate.

Listing 1. LUBM Query 9

```
SELECT ?X ?Y ?Z WHERE {
?X rdf:type ub:Student.
?Y rdf:type ub:Faculty.
?Z rdf:type ub:Course.
?X ub:advisor ?Y.
?Y ub:teacherOf ?Z.
?X ub:takesCourse ?Z}
```

Listing 2. Rewritten LUBM Query 9

```
SELECT ?X ?Y ?Z WHERE {
?X rdf:type ub:Student.
?X ub:advisor ?Y.
?Y ub:teacherOf ?Z.
?X ub:takesCourse ?Z}
```

23.5.3 Cost Estimation for Query Processing

We run Hadoop jobs to answer an SPARQL query. In this section, we discuss how we estimate the cost of a job. However, before doing that, we introduce some definitions that we will use later:

Definition 23.1

Triple Pattern, TP: A triple pattern is an ordered set of subject, predicate, and object that appears in an SPARQL query WHERE clause. The subject, predicate, and object can be either a variable (unbounded) or a concrete value (bounded).

Definition 23.2

Triple Pattern Join, TPJ: A triple pattern join is a join between two TPs on a variable.

Definition 23.3

MapReduceJoin, MRJ: A MapReduceJoin is a join between two or more triple patterns on a variable.

Definition 23.4

Job, JB: A job JB is a Hadoop job where one or more MRJs are done. JB has a set of input files and a set of output files.

Definition 23.5

Conflicting MapReduceJoins, CMRJ: Conflicting MapReduceJoins is a pair of MRJs on different variables sharing a triple pattern.

Definition 23.6

Nonconflicting MapReduceJoins, NCMRJ: Nonconflicting MapReduceJoins is a pair of MRJs either not sharing any triple pattern or sharing a triple pattern and the MRJs are on same variable.

An example will illustrate these terms better. In Listing 3, we show LUBM Query 12. Lines 2, 3, 4, and 5 each have a triple pattern. The join between TPs in lines 2 and 4 on variable ?X is an MRJ. If we do two MRJs, one between TPs in lines 2 and 4 on variable ?X and the other between TPs in lines 4 and 5 on variable ?Y, there will be a CMRJ as TP in line 4 (?X ub:worksFor ?Y) takes part in two MRJs on two different variables ?X and ?Y. This type of join is called CMRJ because in a Hadoop job, more than one variable of a TP cannot be a key at the same time and MRJs are performed on keys. An NCMRJ, one MRJ would be shown between triple patterns in lines 2 and 4 on variable ?X and another MRJ between triple patterns in lines 3 and 5 on variable ?Y . These two MRJs can make up a JB.

Listing 3. LUBM Query 12

```
SELECT ?X WHERE {
?X rdf:type ub:Chair.
?Y rdf:type ub:Department.
?X ub:worksFor ?Y.
?Y ub:subOrganizationOf www.utdallas.edu}
```

Ideal Model

To answer an SPARQL query, we may need more than one job. Therefore, in an ideal scenario, the cost estimation for processing a query requires the individual cost estimation of each job that is needed to answer that query. A job contains three main tasks that are reading, sorting, and writing. We estimate the cost of a job based on these three tasks. For each task, a unit cost is assigned to each triple pattern it deals with. In the current model, we assume that costs for reading and writing are the same:

$$\text{Cost} = \left(\sum_{i=1}^{n-1} \text{MI}_i + \text{MO}_i + \text{RI}_i + \text{RO}_i \right) + \text{MI}_n + \text{MO}_n + \text{RI}_n \tag{23.1}$$

$$= \left(\sum_{i=1}^{n-1} \text{Job}_i \right) + \text{MI}_n + \text{MO}_n + \text{RI}_n \tag{23.2}$$

$$\text{Job}_i = +\text{MI}_i + \text{MO}_i + \text{RO}_i + \text{RI}_i (\text{if } i < n) \tag{23.3}$$

where,

$$\text{MI}_i = \text{Map input phase for job } i$$

$$\text{MO}_i = \text{Map output phase for job } i$$

$$\text{RI}_i = \text{Reduce input phase for job } i$$

$$\text{RO}_i = \text{Reduce output phase for job } i$$

Equation 23.1 is the total cost of processing a query. It is the summation of the individual costs of each job and only the map phase of the final job. We do not consider the cost of the reduce output of the final job because it would be the same for any query plan as this output is the final result that is fixed for a query and a given dataset. A job essentially performs a MapReduce task on the file data. Equation 23.2 shows the division of the MapReduce task into subtasks. Hence, to estimate the cost of each job, we will combine the estimated cost of each subtask.

Map input (MI) phase: This phase reads the triple patterns from the selected input files stored in the HDFS. Therefore, we can estimate the cost for the MI phase to be equal to the total number of triples in each of the selected files.

Map output (MO) phase: The estimation of the MO phase depends on the type of query being processed. If the query has no bound variable (e.g., [?X ub:worksFor ?Y]), then the output of the Map phase is equal to the input. All of the triple patterns are transformed into key–value pairs and given as output. Therefore, for such a query, the MO cost will be the same as the MI cost. However, if the query involves a bound variable, (e.g., [?Y ub:subOrganizationOf <http://www.U0.edu>]), then before making the key–value pairs, a bound component selectivity estimation can be applied. The resulting estimate for the triple patterns will account for the cost of the Map output phase. The selected triples are written to a local disk.

Reduce input (RI) phase: In this phase, the triples from the Map output phase are read via HTTP and then sorted based on their key values. After sorting, the triples with identical keys are grouped together. Therefore, the cost estimation for the RI phase is equal to the MO phase. The number of key–value pairs that are sorted in RI is equal to the number of key–value pairs generated in the MO phase.

Reduce output (RO) phase: The RO phase deals with performing the joins. Therefore, it is in this phase we can use the join triple pattern selectivity summary statistics to estimate the size of its output. In the following, we talk in detail about the join triple pattern selectivity summary statistics needed for our framework.

However, in practice, the earlier discussion is applicable for the first job only. For the subsequent jobs, we lack both the precise knowledge and estimate of the number of triple patterns selected after applying the join in the first job. Therefore, for these jobs, we can take the size of the RO phase of the first job as an upper bound on the different phases of the subsequent jobs.

Equation 23.3 shows a very important postulation. It illustrates the total cost of an intermediate job, when $i < n$ includes the cost of the RO phase in calculating the total cost of the job.

Heuristic Model

In this section, we show that the ideal model is not practical or cost-effective. There are several issues that make the ideal model less attractive in practice. First, the ideal model considers simple abstract costs, namely, the number of triples read and written by the different phases, ignoring the actual cost of copying, sorting, etc., these triples, and the overhead for running jobs in Hadoop. But accurately incorporating those costs in the model is a difficult task. Even making a reasonably good estimation may be nontrivial. Second, to estimate intermediate join outputs, we need to maintain comprehensive summary statistics. In a MapReduce job in Hadoop, all the joins on a variable are joined together. For example, in the rewritten LUBM Query 9 (Listing 2), there are three joins on variable X. When a job is run to do the join on X, all the joins on X between triple patterns 1, 2, and 4 are done. If there were more than three joins on X, all will still be handled in one job. This shows that in order to gather summary statistics to estimate join selectivity, we face an exponential number of join cases. For example, between triple patterns having p_1, p_2, and p_3, there may be multiple types of joins because in each triple pattern, a variable can occur either as a subject or an object. In the case of the rewritten Query 9, it is a subject–subject–subject join between 1, 2, and 4. There can be more types of join between these three, for example, subject–object–subject and object–subject–object. This means that between P predicates, there can be 2^P types of joins on a single variable (ignoring the possibility that a variable may appear both as a subject and as an object in a triple pattern). If there are P predicates in the dataset, a total number of cases for which we need to collect summary statistics can be calculated by the formula:

$$2^2 \times C_2^P + 2^3 \times C_3^P + \cdots + 2^P \times C_P^P$$

In the LUBM dataset, there are 17 predicates. So, in total, there are 129,140,128 cases, which is a large number. Gathering summary statistics for such a large number of cases would be very time- and space-consuming. Hence, we took an alternate approach.

We observe that there is significant overhead for running a job in Hadoop. Therefore, if we minimize the number of jobs to answer a query, we get the fastest plan. The overhead is incurred by several disk I/O and network transfers that are an integral part of any Hadoop job. When a job is submitted to a Hadoop cluster, at least the following set of actions takes place:

1. The Executable file is transferred from the client machine to the Hadoop JobTracker [WIKIa].
2. The JobTracker decides which TaskTrackers [WIKIb] will execute the job.
3. The Executable file is distributed to the TaskTrackers over the network.
4. Map processes start by reading data from HDFS.
5. Map outputs are written to disks.
6. Map outputs are read from disks, shuffled (transferred over the network to TaskTrackers, which would run Reduce processes), sorted, and written to disks.
7. Reduce processes start by reading the input from the disks.
8. Reduce outputs are written to disks.

These disk operations and network transfers are expensive operations even for a small amount of data. For example, in our experiments, we observed that the overhead incurred by one job is almost equivalent to reading a billion triples. The reason is that in every job, the output of the map process is always sorted before feeding the reduce processes. This sorting is unavoidable even if it is not needed by the user. Therefore, it would be less costly to process several hundred million more triples in n jobs, rather than processing several hundred million less triples in $n + 1$ jobs.

To further investigate, we did an experiment where we used the query shown in Listing 4. Here, the join selectivity between TPs 2 and 3 on ?Z is the highest. Hence, a query plan generation algorithm that uses selectivity factors to pick joins would select this join for the first job. As the other TPs 1 and 4 share variables with either TP 2 or 3, they cannot take part in any other join; moreover, they do not share any variables so the only possible join that can be executed in this job is the join between TPs 2 and 3 on ?X. Once this join is done, the two joins left are between TP 1 and the join output of the first job on variable ?X and between TP 4 and the join output of first job on variable ?Y. We found that the selectivity of the first join is greater than the latter one. Hence, the second job will do this join and TP 4 will again not participate. In the third and last job, the join output of the second job will be joined with TP 4 on ?Y. This is the plan generated using join selectivity estimation. But the minimum job plan is a two job plan where the first job joins TPs 1 and 2 on ?X and TPs 3 and 4 on ?Y. The second and final job joins the two join outputs of the first job on ?Z. The query runtimes we found are given in [HUSA11a].

Listing 4. Experiment Query

```
?S1 ub:advisor ?X.
?X ub:headOf ?Z.
?Z ub:subOrganizationOf ?Y.
?S2 ub:mastersDegreeFrom ?Y
```

For each dataset, we found that the two job plan is faster than the three job plan, even though the three job plan produced less intermediate data because of the join selectivity order. We can explain this by an observation we made in another small experiment. We generated files of sizes 5 and 10 MB containing random integers. We put the files in HDFS. For each file, we first read the file by a program and recorded the time needed to do it. While reading, our program reads from one of the three available replicas of the file. Then, we ran a MapReduce job that rewrites the file with the numbers sorted. We utilized MapReduce sorting to have the sorted output. Please also note that when it writes the file, it writes three replications of it. We found that the MapReduce job, which does reading, sorting, and writing, takes 24.47 times longer to finish for 5 MB. For 10 MB, it is 42.79 times. This clearly shows how the write and data transfer operations of a MapReduce job are more expensive than a simple read from only one replica. Because of the number of jobs, the three job plan is doing much more disk read and write operations as well as network data transfers, and, as a result, is slower than the two job plan, even if it is reading less input data.

Because of these reasons, we do not pursue the ideal model. We follow the practical model, which is to generate a query plan having minimum possible jobs. However, while generating a minimum job plan, whenever we need to choose a join to be considered in a job among more than one joins, instead of choosing randomly, we use the summary join statistics. This is described in Section 23.5.6. More details of our experimental results with the charts are provided in [HUSA11a].

23.5.4 Query Plan Generation

In this section, first we define the query plan generation problem and show that generating the best (i.e., least cost) query plan for the ideal model as well as for the practical model is computationally expensive. Then, we will present a heuristic and a greedy approach to generate an approximate solution to generate the best plan.

Running example. We will use the following query as a running example in this section:

Listing 5. Running Example

```
SELECT ?V,?X,?Y,?Z WHERE{
?X rdf:type ub:GraduateStudent
```

?Y rdf:type ub:University
?Z ?V ub:Department
?X ub:memberOf ?Z
?X ub:undergraduateDegreeFrom ?Y}

In order to simplify the notations, we will only refer to the TPs by the variable in that pattern. For example, the first TP (?X rdf:type ub:GraduateStudent) will be represented as simply *X*. Also, in the simplified version, the whole query would be represented as follows: {*X,Y,Z,XZ,XY*}.

We will use the notation *join(XY,X)* to denote a join operation between the two TPs XY and X on the common variable *X*.

Definition 23.7

The Minimum Cost Plan Generation Problem (Bestplan Problem): For a given query, the Bestplan problem is to generate a job plan so that the total cost of the jobs is minimized. Note that Bestplan considers the more general case where each job has some cost associated with it (i.e., the ideal model).

Example: Given the query in our running example, two possible job plans are as follows:
Plan1. $job_1 = \{X,XY,XZ\}$,
resultant TPs = $\{YZ,YZ\}$. $job_2 = \{Y,YZ\}$,
resultant TPs = $\{Z,Z\}$,. $job_3 = \{Z,Z\}$. Total cost = $cost(job_1) + cost(job_2)$.
Plan 2. $job_1 = \{XZ,Z\}$ and $join(XY,Y)$
resultant TPs = $\{X,X,X\}$.$job_2 = join(X,X,X)$.
Total cost = $cost(job_1) + cost(job_2)$.
The Bestplan problem is to find the least cost job plan among all possible job plans.

Definition 23.8

Joining Variable: A variable that is common in two or more triple patterns. For example, in the running example query, *X*, *Y*, *Z* are joining variables, but V is not.

Definition 23.9

Complete Elimination: A join operation that eliminates a joining variable. For example, in the example query, *Y* can be completely eliminated if we join (*XY,Y*).

Definition 23.10

Partial Elimination: A join operation that partially eliminates a joining variable. For example, in the example query, if we perform join (*XY,Y*) and join (*X,ZX*) in the same job, the resultant triple patterns would be {*X,Z,X*}. Therefore, *Y* will be completely eliminated, but *X* will be partially eliminated. So, the join(*X,ZX*) performs a partial elimination.

Definition 23.11

E-Count(v): E-count(v) is the number of joining variables in the resultant triple pattern after a complete elimination of variable v. In the running example, *join(X,XY,XZ)* completely eliminates *X* and the resultant triple pattern (*YZ*) has two joining variables *Y* and *Z*. So, E-count(*X*) = 2. Similarly, E-count(*Y*) = 1 and E-count(*Z*) = 1.

Computational Complexity of Bestplan: It can be shown that generating the least cost query plan is computationally expensive, since the search space is exponentially large. At first, we formulate the problem, and then show its complexity.

Problem Formulation: We formulate Bestplan as a search problem. Let $G = (V, E)$ be a weighted directed graph, where each vertex $v_i \in V$ represents a state of the triple patterns, and each edge $e_i \in (v_{i_1}, v_{i_2}) \in E$ represents a job that makes a transition from state v_{i_1} to state v_{i_2}. v_0 is the initial state, where no joins have been performed, that is, the given query. Also, v_{goal} is the goal state, which represents a state of the triple pattern where all joins have been performed. The problem is to find the shortest weighted path from v_0 to v_{goal}.

For example, in our running example query, the initial state $v_0 = \{X,Y,Z,XY,XZ\}$, and the goal state, $v_{goal} = \varnothing$, that is, no more triple patterns left. Suppose the first job (jobl) performs join(X,XY,XZ). Then, the resultant triple patterns (new state) would be $v_1 = \{Y,Z,YZ\}$, and jobl would be represented by the edge (v_0, v_1). The weight of edge (v_0, v_1) is the cost of $job_1 = cost(job_1)$, where cost is the given cost function. Figure 23.4 shows the partial graph for the example query.

Search Space Size: Given a graph $G = (V, E)$, Dijkstra's shortest path algorithm can find the shortest path from a source to all other nodes in $O(|V|\log|V|+|E|)$ time. However, for Bestplan, it can be shown that in the worst case, $|V| \geq 2^K$, where K is the total number of joining variables in the given query. Therefore, the number of vertices in the graph is exponential, leading to an exponential search problem. In [HUSA11a], we have shown that the worst-case complexity of the Bestplan problem is exponential in K, the number of joining variables in the given query.

Relaxed Bestplan Problem and Approximate Solution: In the Relaxed Bestplan problem, we assume uniform cost for all jobs. Although this relaxation does not reduce the search space, the problem is reduced to finding a job plan having the minimum number of jobs. Note that this is the problem for the practical version of the model.

Definition 23.12

Relaxed Bestplan Problem: The Relaxed Bestplan problem is to find the job plan that has the minimum number of jobs.

Next, we show that if joins are reasonably chosen, and no eligible join operation is left undone in a job, then we may set an upper bound on the maximum number of jobs required for any given query. However, it is still computationally expensive to generate all possible job plans. Therefore, we resort to a greedy algorithm (Algorithm 23.1) that finds an approximate solution to the Relaxed Bestplan problem, but is guaranteed to find a job plan within the upper bound.

Algorithm 23.1 Relaxed-Bestplan (Query Q)

1: $Q \leftarrow$ Remove non–joining variables(Q)
2: **while** $Q \neq$ Empty **do**
3: $J \leftarrow$ 1//Total number of jobs
4: $U = \{u_1,\ldots,u_K\} \leftarrow$ All variables sorted in non-decreasing order of their E-counts
5: $Job_J \leftarrow$ Empty // List of join operations in the // current job
6: $tmp \leftarrow$ Empty // Temporarily stores resultant // triple patterns
7: **for** $i = 1$ to K **do**
8: **if** *Can–Eliminate* $(Q,u_i) = true$ **then**
//complete or partial elimination possible
9: $tmp \leftarrow tmp \cup$ *Join–result*$(TP(Q,u_i))$
10: $Q \leftarrow Q - TP(Q,u_i)$
11: $Job_J \leftarrow Job_J \cup$ *join*$(TP(Q,u_i))$

12: **end if**
13: **end for**
14: $Q \leftarrow Q \cup tmp$
15: $J \leftarrow J + 1$
16: **end while**
17: *return* $\{Job_1, \ldots, Job_{J-1}\}$

Definition 23.13

Early Elimination Heuristic: The early elimination heuristic makes as many complete eliminations as possible in each job.

This heuristic leaves the fewest number of variables for join in the next job. In order to apply the heuristic, we must first choose the variable in each job with the least E-count. This heuristic is applied in Algorithm 23.1.

Description of Algorithm 23.1

The algorithm starts by removing all the nonjoining variables from the query Q. In our running example, $Q = \{X,Y,VZ,XY,XZ\}$, and removing the nonjoining variable V makes $Q = \{X,Y,Z,XY,XZ\}$. In the while loop, the job plan is generated, starting from Job_1. In line 4, we sort the variables according to their E-count. The sorted variables are: $U = \{Y,Z,X\}$, since Y and Z have E-count $= 1$, and X has E-count $= 2$. For each job, the list of join operations is stored in the variable Job_J, where J is the ID of the current job. Also, a temporary variable *tmp* is used to store the resultant triples of the joins to be performed in the current job (line 6). In the for loop, each variable is checked to see if the variable can be completely or partially eliminated (line 8). If yes, we store the join result in the temporary variable (line 9), update Q (line 10), and add this join to the current job (line 11). In our running example, this results in the following operations: Iteration 1 of the for loop: $u_1 = (Y)$ can be completely eliminated. Here, $TP(Q,Y)$ the triple patterns in Q containing Iteration 3 of the for loop: $u_3 = (X)$ cannot be completely or partially eliminated, since there is no other TP left to join with it. Therefore, when the for loop terminates, we have $job_1 = \{join(Y,XY), join(Z,XZ)\}$, and $Q = \{X,X,X\}$. In the second iteration of the while loop, we will have $\{job_2 = \{X,X,X\}$. Since after this join, Q becomes Empty, the while loop is exited. Finally, $\{job_1, job_2\}$ are returned from the algorithm.

In [HUSA11a], we have proved that for any given query Q, containing K joining variables and N triple patterns, Algorithm Relaxed-Bestplan (Q) generates a job plan containing at most J jobs, where

$$J = \begin{cases} 0 & N = 0 \\ 1 & N = 1 \text{ or } K = 1 \\ \min(1.71 \log_2 N, K) & N, K > 1 \end{cases} \tag{23.4}$$

23.5.5 Breaking Ties by Summary Statistics

We frequently face situations where we need to choose a join for multiple join options. These choices can occur when both query plans (i.e., join orderings) require the minimum number of jobs. For example, the query shown in Listing 6 poses such a situation.

Listing 6. Query Having Tie Situation

?X rdf:type ub:FullProfessor.
?X ub:advisorOf ?Y.
?Y rdf:type ub:ResearchAssistant.

The second triple pattern in the query makes it impossible to answer and solve the query with only one job. There are only two possible plans: we can join the first two triple patterns on *X* first and then join its output with the last triple pattern on *Y* or we can join the last two patterns first on *Y* and then join its output with the first pattern on *X*. In such a situation, instead of randomly choosing a join variable for the first job, we use join summary statistics for a pair of predicates. We select the join for the first job which is more selective to break the tie. The join summary statistics we use are described in [STOC08].

23.5.6 MapReduce Join Execution

In this section, we discuss how we implement the joins needed to answer SPARQL queries using the MapReduce framework of Hadoop. Algorithm 23.1 determines the number of jobs required to answer a query. It returns an ordered set of jobs. Each job has associated input information. The Job Handler component of our MapReduce framework runs the jobs in the sequence they appear in the ordered set. The output file of one job is the input of the next. The output file of the last job has the answer to the query.

Listing 7. LUBM Query 2

```
SELECT ?X, ?Y, ?Z WHERE {
?X rdf:type ub:GraduateStudent.
?Y rdf:type ub:University.
?Z rdf:type ub:Department.
?X ub:memberOf ?Z.
?Z ub:subOrganizationOf ?Y.
?X ub:undergraduateDegreeFrom ?Y }
```

Listing 7 shows LUBM Query 2, which we will use to illustrate the way we do a join using map and reduce methods. The query has six triple patterns and nine joins between them on the variable *X*, *Y*, and *Z*.

Our input selection algorithm selects files *type_GraduateStudent*, type_ University, *type_ Department*, all files having the prefix *memberOf*, all files having the prefix *subOrganizationOf*, and all files having the prefix *underGraduateDegreeFrom* as the input to the jobs needed to answer the query.

The query plan has two jobs. In job 1, triple patterns of lines 2, 5, and 7 are joined on *X* and triple patterns of lines 3 and 6 are joined on *Y*. In job 2, triple pattern of line 4 is joined with the outputs of previous two joins on *Z* and also the join outputs of job 1 are joined on *Y*.

The input files of job 1 are type_GraduateStudent, type_University, all files having the prefix memberOf, all files having the prefix subOrganizationOf, and all files having the prefix underGraduateDegreeFrom. In the map phase, we first tokenize the input value which is actually a line of the input file. Then, we check the input file name and, if input is from type_GraduateStudent, we output a key–value pair having the subject URI prefixed with X# the key and a flag string GS# as the value. The value serves as a flag to indicate that the key is of type GraduateStudent. The subject URI is the first token returned by the tokenizer. Similarly, for input from file type_University output a key–value pair having the subject URI prefixed with Y# the key and a flag string U# as the value. If the input from any file has the prefix memberOf, we retrieve the subject and object from the input line by the tokenizer and output a key–value pair having the subject URI prefixed with X# the key and the object value prefixed with MO# as the value. For input from files having the prefix subOrganizationOf, we output key–value pairs making the object prefixed with Y# the key and the subject prefixed with SO# the value. For input from files having the prefix underGraduateDegreeFrom, we output key–value pairs making the subject URI prefixed with X# the key and the object value prefixed with UDF# the value. Hence, we make either the subject or the object a map output key based on which we are joining. This is the reason why the object is made the key for the triples from files having the prefix subOrganizationOf because the joining variable *Y* is an object in the triple pattern in line 6. For all other inputs, the subject is made the key because the joining variables *X* and *Y* are subjects in the triple patterns in lines 2, 3, 5, and 7.

In the reduce phase, Hadoop groups all the values for a single key and for each key provides the key and an iterator to the values collection. Looking at the prefix, we can immediately tell if it is a value for *X* or *Y* because of the prefixes we used. In either case, we output a key–value pair using the same key and concatenating all the values to make a string value. So after this reduce phase, join on *X* is complete and on *Y* is partially complete.

The input files of job 2 are type_Department file and the output file of job 1, jobl.out. Like the map phase of job 1, in the map phase of job 2, we also tokenize the input value which is actually a line of the input file. Then, we check the input file name and if input is from type_Department, we output a key–value pair having the subject URI prefixed with Z# the key and a flag string D# as the value. If the input is from jobl.out, we find the value having the prefix Z#. We make this value the output key and concatenate the rest of the values to make a string and make it the output value. Basically, we make the *Z#* values the keys to join on *Z*.

In the reduce phase, we know that the key is the value for *Z*. The values collection has two types of strings. One has *X* values, which are URIs for graduate students and also *Y* values from which they got their undergraduate degree. The *Z* value, that is, the key, may or may not be a subOrganizationOf the *Y* value. The other types of strings have only *Y* values which are universities and of which the *Z* value is a suborganization. We iterate over the values collection and then join the two types of tuples on *Y* values. From the join output, we find the result tuples which have values for *X*, *Y*, and *Z*.

23.6 RESULTS

23.6.1 Experimental Setup

In this section, we first present the benchmark datasets with which we experimented. Next, we present the alternative repositories we evaluated for comparison. Then, we detail our experimental setup. Finally, we present our evaluation results.

Datasets: In our experiments with SPARQL query processing, we use two synthetic datasets: LUBM [GUO05] and SP2B [SCHM09]. The LUBM dataset generates data about universities by using an ontology [LEHI]. It has 14 standard queries. Some of the queries require inference to answer. The LUBM dataset is very good for both inference and scalability testing. For all LUBM datasets, we used the default seed. The SP2B dataset is good for scalability testing with complex queries and data access patterns. It has 16 queries most of which have complex structures.

Baseline Frameworks: We compared our framework with RDF-3X [NEUM08], Jena [JENA], and BigOWLIM [ONTO]. RDF-3X is considered the fastest semantic web framework with persistent storage. Jena is an open source framework for semantic web data. It has several models which can be used to store and retrieve RDF data. We chose Jena's in-memory and SDB models to compare our framework with. As the name suggests, the in-memory model stores the data in main memory and does not persist data. The SDB model is a persistent model and can use many off-the-shelf database management systems. We used MySQL database as SDB's back-end in our experiments. BigOWLIM is a proprietary framework which is the state-of-the-art significantly fast framework for semantic web data. It can act both as a persistent and nonpersistent storage. All of these frameworks run in a single machine setup.

Hardware: We have a 10-node Hadoop cluster which we use for our framework. Each of the nodes has the following configuration: Pentium IV 2.80 GHz processor, 4 GB main memory, and 640 GB disk space. We ran Jena, RDF-3X, and BigOWLIM frameworks on a powerful single machine having 2.80 GHz quad core processor, 8 GB main memory, and 1 TB disk space.

Software: We used hadoop-0.20.1 for our framework. We compared our framework with Jena-2.5.7 which used MySQL 14.12 for its SDB model. We used BigOWLIM version 3.2.6. For RDF-3X, we utilized version 0.3.5 of the source code.

23.6.2 Evaluation

We present performance comparison between our framework, RDF-3X, Jena In-Memory and SDB models, and BigOWLIM. More details are found in [HUSA11a]. We used three LUBM datasets: 10,000, 20,000, and 30,000 which have more than 1.1, 2.2, and 3.3 billion triples, respectively. Initial population time for RDF-3X took 655, 1756, and 3353 min to load the datasets, respectively. This shows that the RDF-3X load time is increasing exponentially. LUBM (30,000) has three times as many triples as LUBM (10,000) yet it requires more than five times as long to load.

For evaluation purposes, we chose LUBM Queries 1, 2, 4, 9, 12, and 13 to be reported in this work. These queries provide a good mixture and include simple and complex structures, inference, and multiple types of joins. They are representatives of other queries of the benchmark and so reporting only these covers all types of variations found in the queries we left out and also saves space. Query 1 is a simple selective query. RDF-3X is much faster than HadoopRDF for this query. RDF-3X utilizes six indexes [NEUM08] and those six indexes actually make up the dataset. The indexes provide RDF-3X a very fast way to look up triples, similar to a hash table. Hence, a highly selective query is efficiently answered by RDF-3X. Query 2 is a query with complex structures, low selectivity, and no bound objects. The result set is quite large. For this query, HadoopRDF outperforms RDF-3X for all three dataset sizes. RDF-3X fails to answer the query at all when the dataset size is 3.3 billion triples. RDF-3X returns memory segmentation fault error messages and does not produce any query results. Query 4 is also a highly selective query, that is, the result set size is small because of a bound object in the second triple pattern but it needs inferencing to answer it. The first triple pattern uses the class Person which is a superclass of many classes. No resource in LUBM dataset is of type Person, rather there are many resources which are its subtypes. RDF-3X does not support inferencing so we had to convert the query to an equivalent query having some union operations. RDF-3X outperforms HadoopRDF for this query. Query 9 is similar in structure to Query 2 but it requires significant inferencing. The first three triple patterns of this query use classes which are not explicitly instantiated in the dataset. However, the dataset includes many instances of the corresponding subclasses. This is also the query that requires the largest dataset join and returns the largest result set out of the queries we evaluated. RDF-3X is faster than HadoopRDF for 1.1 billion triples dataset but it fails to answer the query at all for the other two datasets. Query 12 is similar to Query 4 because it is both selective and has inferencing in one triple pattern. RDF-3X beats HadoopRDF for this query. Query 13 has only two triple patterns. Both of them involve inferencing. There is a bound subject in the second triple pattern. It returns the second largest result set. HadoopRDF beats RDF-3X for this query for all datasets. RDF-3X's performance is slow because the first triple pattern has very low selectivity and requires low selectivity joins to perform inference via backward chaining.

These results lead us to some simple conclusions. RDF-3X achieves the best performance for queries with high selectivity and bound objects. However, HadoopRDF outperforms RDF-3X for queries with unbound objects, low selectivity, or large dataset joins. RDF-3X cannot execute the two queries with unbound objects (Queries 2 and 9) for a 3.3 billion triples dataset. This demonstrates that HadoopRDF is more scalable and handles low selectivity queries more efficiently than RDF-3X.

We also compared our implementation with the Jena In-Memory, the SDB and BigOWLIM models. Due to space and time limitations, we performed these tests only for LUBM Queries 2 and 9 from the LUBM dataset. We chose these queries because they have complex structures and require inference. It is to be noted that BigOWLIM needed 7 GB of Java heap space to successfully load the billion triples dataset. We ran BigOWLIM only for the largest three datasets as we are interested in its performance with large datasets. For each set we obtained the results for the Jena In-Memory model, Jena SDB model, our Hadoop implementation and BigOWLIM, respectively. At times the query could not complete or it ran out of memory. In most of the cases, our approach was the fastest. For Query 2, Jena In-Memory and Jena SDB models were faster than our approach, giving results in 3.9 and 0.4 s, respectively. However, as the size of the dataset grew, the Jena In-Memory model ran out of memory space. Our implementation was much faster than the Jena SDB model for large datasets. For example, for 110 million triples, our approach took 143.5 s as compared to about 5000 s for Jena SDB model. We found that the Jena SDB model could not finish answering Query 9. Jena In-Memory model worked well for small datasets but became slower than our implementation as the dataset size grew and eventually ran out of memory.

For Query 2, BigOWLIM was slower than ours for the 110 and 550 million datasets. For the 550 million dataset, it took 22693.4 s, which is abruptly high compared to its other timings. For the billion triple dataset, BigOWLIM was faster. It should be noted that our framework does not have any indexing or triple cache whereas BigOWLIM exploits indexing which it loads into main memory when it starts. It may also prefetch triples into main memory. For Query 9, our implementation is faster than BigOWLIM in all experiments.

It should also be noted that our RDF-3X and HadoopRDF queries were tested using cold runs. What we mean by this is that main memory and file system cache were cleared prior to execution. However, for BigOWLIM, we were forced to execute hot runs. This is because it takes a significant amount of time to load a database into BigOWLIM. Therefore, we will always easily outperform BigOWLIM for cold runs. So, we actually tested BigOWLIM for hot runs against HadoopRDF for cold runs. This gives a tremendous advantage to BigOWLIM, yet for large datasets, HadoopRDF still produced much better results. This shows that HadoopRDF is much more scalable than BigOWLIM, and provides more efficient queries for large datasets.

The final tests we have performed are an in-depth scalability test. For this, we repeated the same queries for eight different dataset sizes, all the way up to 6.6 billion.

In our experiments we found that Query 1 is simple and requires only one join, thus it took the least amount of time among all the queries. Query 2 is one of the two queries having the greatest number of triple patterns. Even though it has three times more triple patterns, it does not take thrice the time of Query 1 answering time because of our storage schema. Query 4 has one less triple pattern than Query 2, but it requires inferencing. As we determine inferred relations on the fly, queries requiring inference take longer times in our framework. Queries 9 and 12 also require inferencing. Details are given in [HUSA11a].

As the size of the dataset grows, the increase in time to answer a query does not grow proportionately. The increase in time is always less. For example, there are 10 times as many triples in the dataset of 10,000 universities than 1000 universities, but for Query 1, the time only increases by 3.76 times and for query 9 by 7.49 times. The latter is the highest increase in time, yet it is still less than the increase in the size of the datasets. Due to space limitations, we do not report query runtimes with PS schema here. We found that PS schema is much slower than POS schema.

23.7 SECURITY EXTENSIONS

We have implemented a security models based on XACML on top of the SPARQL Query Optimizer. This section described our security model. More details of the system can be found in [KHAL10]. It should be noted that we have also designed and developed a second secure query-processing system using XACML for relational data. This system uses the HIVE relational database system and also operates in the cloud. The details design and implementation of the HIVE-based systems is discussed in [THUR10].

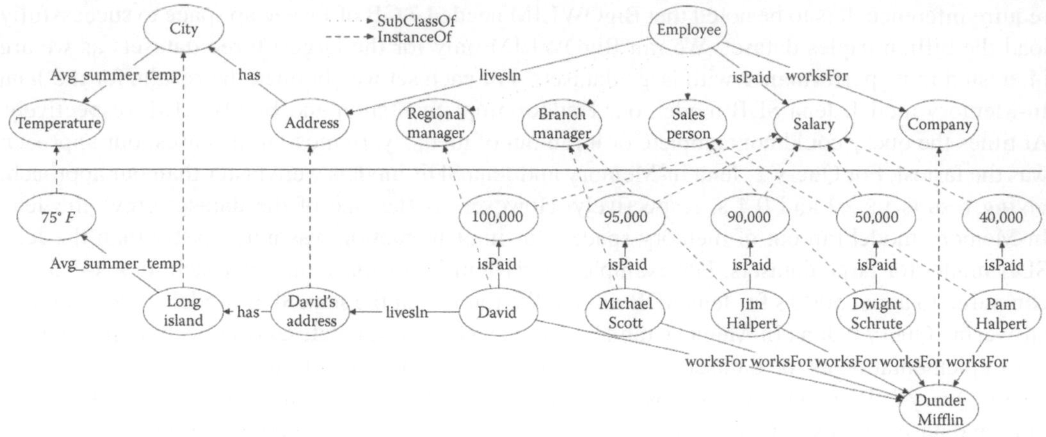

FIGURE 23.5 Knowledge base.

23.7.1 Access Control Model

Definition 23.14

Access Tokens (*AT*) permit access to security-relevant data. An agent in possession of an AT may view the data permitted by that AT. We denote ATs by positive integers.

Definition 23.15

Access Token Tuples (ATT) have the form *AccessToken, Element, ElementType, ElementName*, where *Element* can be *Subject, Object*, or Predicate, and *ElementType* can be described as *URI*, DataType, *Literal, Model*, or *BlankNode.* Model is used to access subject models, and will be explained later in this section.

For example, in the ontology/knowledge base in Figure 23.5, *David* is a subject and 1, *Subject, URI, David* is an ATT. Any agent having AT 1 may retrieve *David*'s information over all files (subject to any other security restrictions governing access to URIs, literals, etc., associated with *David*'s objects). While describing ATT's for, we leave the *ElementName* blank (_).

Based on the record organization, we support six access levels along with a few subtypes described below. Agents may be assigned one or more of the following access levels. Access levels with a common AT combine conjunctively, while those with different ATs combine disjunctively.

1. *Predicate data access*: If an object type is defined for one particular predicate in an access level, then an agent having that access level may read the whole predicate file (subject to any other policy restrictions). For example, 1,*Predicate, is Paid,*_ is an ATT that permits its possessor to read the entire predicate file *is Paid.*
2. *Predicate and subject data access*: Agents possessing a subject ATT may access data associated with a particular subject, where the subject can be either a *URI* or a *DataType.* Combining one of these subject ATTs with a predicate data access ATT having the same AT, grants the agent access to a specific subject of a specific predicate. For example:
   a. Predicate and subject as URIs: Combining ATT's 1, *Predicate, is Paid*, and 1, *Subject,URI, MichaelScott* (drawn from the ontology in Figure 23.5) permits an agent with AT 1 to access a subject with URI *MichaelScott* of predicate *is Paid.*

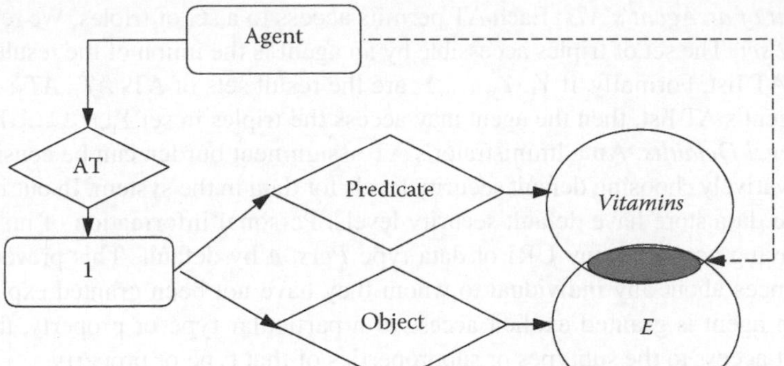

FIGURE 23.6 Conjunctive combination of ATTs with a common AT.

b. Predicate and subject as DataTypes: Similarly, Predicate and DataType ATT's can be combined to permit access to subjects of a specific data type over a specific predicate file.

For brevity, we omit descriptions of the different subject and object variations of each of the remaining access levels.

3. *Predicate and object*: This access level permits a principal to extract the names of subjects satisfying a particular predicate and object. For example, with ATT's 1, *Predicate,hasVitamins,_*, and 1, *Object,URI,E,* an agent possessing AT 1 may view the names of subjects (e.g., foods) that have vitamin *E*. More generally, if X_1 and X_2 are the set of triples generated by Predicate and Object triples (respectively) describing an AT, then agents possessing the AT may view set $X1 \cap X2$ of triples. An illustration of this example is displayed in Figure 23.6.
4. *Subject access*: With this access level, an agent may read the subject's information over all the files. This is one of the less restrictive access levels. The subject can be a *DataType* or *BlankNode.*
5. *Object access*: With this access level, an agent may read the object's subjects over all the files. Like the previous level, this is one of the less restrictive access levels. The object can be a *URI*, *DataType*, *Literal*, or *BlankNode*.
6. *Subject model level access*: Model level access permits an agent to read all necessary predicate files to obtain all objects of a given subject. Of these objects, the ones that are URIs are next treated as subjects to extract their respective predicates and objects. This process continues iteratively until all objects finally become literals or blank nodes. In this manner, agents possessing model level access may generate models on a given subject.

The following example drawn from Figure 23.5 illustrates *David* lives in *LongIsland*. *LongIsland* is a subject with an *Avg_SummerTemp* predicate having object 75° F. An agent with model level access of *David* read the average summer temperature of.

23.7.2 Access Token Assignment

Definition 23.16

An *Access Token List* (AT-list) is an array of one or more ATs granted to a given agent, along with a time stamp identifying the time at which each was granted. A separate AT list is maintained for each agent.

When a system administrator decides to add an AT to an agent's AT list, the AT and time stamp are first stored in a temporary variable. Before committing the change, the system must first detect potential conflicts in the new AT list.

Final output of an Agent's ATs: Each AT permits access to a set of triples. We refer to this set as the AT's *result set*. The set of triples accessible by an agent is the union of the result sets of the ATs in the agent's AT list. Formally, if $Y_1, Y_2, \ldots, Y_n$ are the result sets of ATs $AT_1, AT_2, \ldots, AT_n$ (respectively) in an agent's AT list, then the agent may access the triples in set $Y_1 \cup Y_2 \cup \ldots \cup Y_n$.

Security Level Defaults: An administrator's AT assignment burden can be considerably simplified by conservatively choosing default security levels for data in the system. In our implementation, all items in the data store have default security levels. Personal information of individuals is kept private by denying access to any URI of data type *Person* by default. This prevents agents from making inferences about any individual to whom they have not been granted explicit permission. However, if an agent is granted explicit access to a particular type or property, the agent is also granted default access to the subtypes or subproperties of that type or property.

As an example, consider a predicate file *Likes* that lists elements that an individual likes. Assume further that *Jim* is a person who likes *Flying*, *SemanticWeb*, and *Jenny*, which are URIs of type *Hobby*, *ResearchInterest*, and *Person*, respectively, and 1 is an AT with ATTs 1,*Subject,URI,Jim* and 1,*Likes,Predicate,_*. By default, agent *Ben*, having only AT 1, cannot learn that *Jenny* is in *Jim's Likes* list since *Jenny*'s data type is *Person*. However, if *Ben* also has AT 2 described by ATT 2,*Object,URI,Jenny*, then *Ben* will be able to see *Jenny* in *Jim*'s *Likes* list.

23.7.3 Conflicts

A conflict arises when the following three conditions occur: (1) An agent possesses two ATs 1 and 2, (2) the result set of AT 2 is a proper subset of AT 1, and (3) the time stamp of AT 1 is earlier than the time stamp of AT 2. In this case the latter, more specific AT supersedes the former, so AT 1 is discarded from the AT list to resolve the conflict. Such conflicts arise in two varieties, which we term *subset conflicts* and *subtype conflicts*.

A subset conflict occurs when AT 2 is a conjunction of ATTs that refines those of AT 1. For example, suppose AT 1 is defined by ATT 1,*Subject,URI,Sam* and AT 2 is defined by ATTs 2,*Subject,URI,Sam* and 2,*Predicate,HasAccounts,_*. In this case the result set of AT 2 is a subset of the result set of AT 1. A conflict will therefore occur if an agent possessing AT 1 is later assigned AT 2. When this occurs, AT 1 is discarded from the agent's AT list to resolve the conflict.

Subtype conflicts occur when the ATTs in AT 2 involve data types that are subtypes of those in AT 1. The data types can be those of subjects, objects or both.

Conflict resolution is summarized by Algorithm 23.2. Here, Subset(AT_1, AT_2) is a function that returns true if the result set of AT_1 is a proper subset of the result set of AT_2, and SubjectSubType(AT_1, AT_2) returns true if the subject of AT_1 is a subtype of the subject of AT_2. Similarly, ObjectSubType (AT_1, AT_2), decides subtyping relations for objects instead of subjects.

Algorithm 23.2 Conflict Detection and Resolution

Input: AT *newAT* with time stamp TS_{newAT}
Result: Detect conflict and, if none exists, add
(*newAT*, TS_{newAT}) to the agent's AT-list
1 *currentAT*[]← the ATs and their time stamps;
2 if (!Subset(newAT, tempATTS) AND
!Subset(tempATTS, newAT) AND
!SubjectSubType(newAT, tempATTS)) AND
!SubjectSubType(tempATTS, newAT) AND
!ObjectSubType(newAT, tempATTS)) AND
!ObjectSubType(tempATTS, newAT)) then

```
    currentAT[length_currentAT].AT←newAT;
    currentAT[length_currentAT].TS←TS newAT;
else
    count←0;
    while count<length_currentAT do
        ATtempATTS←currentAT[count].AT;
        tempTS←currentAT[count].TS;
        /* the timestamp during the AT assignment */
        if (Subset(newAT, tempATTS) AND (TS_newAT≥tempTS)) then
            /* a conflict occurs */
            currentAT[count].AT←newAT;
            currentAT[count].TS←TSnewAT;
        else if (Subset(tempATTS, newAT) AND (tempTS<TS_newAT)) then
            currentAT[count].AT←newAT;
            currentAT[count].TS←TSnewAT ;
        else if ((SubjectSubType(newAT,tempATTS)OR)
            ObjectSubType (newAT,tempATTS)) AND TS_newAT≥tempTS) then
            /* a conflict occurs */
            currentAT[count].AT←newAT;
            currentAT[count].TS←TSnewAT;
    else if ((SubjectSubType(tempATTS,newAT)ORObjectSubType(tempATTS,newAT))
AND (tempATTS<TS_newAT) then
            currentAT[count].AT←newAT;
            currentAT[count].TS←TSnewAT ;
        end
        count←count+1;
    end
end
```

23.8 SUMMARY AND DIRECTIONS

We have presented a framework capable of handling enormous amounts of RDF data that can be used to represent big data systems such as social networks. Since our framework is based on Hadoop, which is a distributed and highly fault tolerant system, it inherits these two properties automatically. The framework is highly scalable. To increase capacity of our system, all that needs to be done is to add new nodes to the Hadoop cluster. We have proposed a schema to store RDF data, an algorithm to determine a query-processing plan, whose worst case is bounded, to answer an SPARQL query and a simplified cost model to be used by the algorithm. Our experiments demonstrate that our system is highly scalable. If we increase the data volume, the delay introduced to answer a query does not increase proportionally. The results indicate that for very large datasets (over one billion triples), Hadoop RDF is preferable and more efficient if the query includes low selectivity joins or significant inference. Other solutions may be more efficient if the query includes bound objects which produce high selectivity. We also provided an overview of our security model that we built on top of the query-processing system.

In the future, we would like to extend the work in multiple directions. First, we will investigate a more sophisticated query model. We will cache statistics for the most frequent queries and use dynamic programming to exploit the statistics. Second, we will evaluate the impact of the number of reducers, the only parameter of a Hadoop job specifiable by user, on the query runtimes. Third, we will investigate indexing opportunities and further usage of binary formats. Fourth, we will handle more complex SPARQL patterns, for example, queries having OPTIONAL blocks. Fifth, we will demonstrate our system with realistic big data applications such as social networking systems. Finally, we will incorporate security at all levels of the system. That is, security should not be just an add-on to the query-processing prototype. It has to be built into the SPARQL query optimizer.

REFERENCES

[ABAD07]. D. J. Abadi, A. Marcus, S. R. Madden, K. Hollenbach, "Scalable Semantic Web Data Management Using Vertical Partitioning," In *Proceedings of 33rd International Conference of Very Large Data Bases*, Vienna, Austria, 2007.

[ABAD09a]. D. J. Abadi, "Data Management in the Cloud: Limitations and Opportunities," *IEEE Data Engineering Bulletin*, 32 (1), 3–12, 2009.

[ABAD09b]. D. J. Abadi, A. Marcus, S. R. Madden, K. Hollenbach, "SW-Store: A Vertically Partitioned DBMS for Semantic Web Data Management," *VLDB Journal*, 18 (2), 385–406, 2009.

[ABOU09]. A. Abouzeid, K. Bajda-Pawlikowski, D. J. Abadi, A. Silberschatz, A. Rasin, "HadoopDB: An Architectural Hybrid of MapReduce and DBMS Technologies for Analytical Workloads," *Proceedings of the VLDB Endowment*, 2 (1), 922–933, 2009.

[ATRE08]. M. Atre, J. Srinivasan, J. A. Hendler, "BitMat: A Main-Memory Bit Matrix of RDF Triples for Conjunctive Triple Pattern Queries," In *Proceedings of the 5th International Workshop on Semantic Web Conference*, Karlsruhe, Germany, 2008.

[BONC06]. P. Boncz, T. Grust, M. van Keulen, S. Manegold, J. Rittinger, J. Teubner, "MonetDB/XQuery: A Fast XQuery Processor Powered by a Relational Engine," In *Proceedings of ACM SIGMOD International Conference on Management of Data*, Chicago, IL, pp. 479–490, 2006.

[CARR04]. J. J. Carroll, I. Dickinson, C. Dollin, D. Reynolds, A. Seaborne, K. Wilkinson, "Jena: Implementing the Semantic Web Recommendations," In *Proceedings of 13th International World Wide Web Conference on Alternate Track Papers and Posters*, New York, NY, pp. 74–83, 2004.

[CHAL]. Semantic Web Challenge, http://challenge.semanticweb.org.

[CHAN06]. F. Chang, J. Dean, S. Ghemawat, W. C. Hsieh, D. A. Wallach, M. Burrows, T. Chandra, A. Fikes, R. E. Gruber, "Bigtable: A Distributed Storage System for Structured Data," In *Proceedings of the 7th USENIX Symposium on Operating System Design and Implementation*, Seattle, WA, pp. 205–218, Nov. 2006.

[CHEB07]. A. Chebotko, S. Lu, F. Fotouhi, "Semantics Preserving SPARQL-to-SQL Translation," *Technical Report*, TR-DB-112007-CLF, 2007.

[CHON05]. E. I. Chong, S. Das, G. Eadon, J. Srinivasan, "An Efficient SQL- Based RDF Querying Scheme," In *VLDB '05: Proceedings of 31st International Conference on Very Large Data Bases*, Trondheim, Norway, pp. 1216–1227, 2005.

[CHU06]. C. T. Chu, S. K. Kim, Y. A. Lin, Y. Yu, G. Bradski, A. Y. Ng, K. Olukotun, "Map-Reduce for Machine Learning on Multicore," In *Proceedings of the 19th International Conference on Neural Information Processing Systems (NIPS)*, Vancouver, BC, Canada, pp. 281 – 288, 2006.

[CLOU]. Cloudera University, http://www.cloudera.com/blog/2010/03/how-raytheon-researchers-are-using-hadoop-to-build-a-scalable-distributed-triple-store.

[COMP]. National University of Singapore School of Computing, http://www.comp.nus.edu.sg/~epic/.

[CYGA05]. R. Cyganiak, "A Relational Algebra for SPARQL," *Technical Report*, HPL-2005-170, 2005.

[DEAN04]. J. Dean and S. Ghemawat, "MapReduce: Simplified Data Processing on Large Clusters," In *Proceedings of the 6th Conference Symposium on Operating Systems Design and Implementation*, San Francisco, CA, pp. 137–150, 2004.

[DING05]. L. Ding, T. Finin, Y. Peng, P. P. da Silva, D. L. Mcguinness, "Tracking RDF Graph Provenance Using RDF Molecules," In *Proceedings of the 4th International Semantic Web Conference*, Galway, Ireland, 2005.

[GUO04]. Y. Guo, Z. Pan, J. Heflin, "An Evaluation of Knowledge Base Systems for Large OWL Datasets," In *Proceedings of the International Semantic Web Conference*, Hiroshima, Japan, 2004.

[GUO05]. Y. Guo, Z. Pan, J. Heflin, "LUBM: A Benchmark for OWL Knowledge Base Systems," *Web Semantics: Science, Services and Agents on the World Wide Web*, 3 (2–3), 158–182, 2005.

[HADOa]. Apache Software Foundation, http://hadoop.apache.org.

[HADOb]. Apache Software Foundation, http://hadoop.apache.org/core/docs/r0.18.3/hdfs_design.html.

[HUSA09]. M. F. Husain, P. Doshi, L. Khan, B. Thuraisingham, "Storage and Retrieval of Large RDF Graph Using Hadoop and MapReduce," In *Proceedings of the 1st International Conference on Cloud Computing*, Bejing, China, 2009, http://www.utdal- las.edu/mfh062000/techreport1.pdf.

[HUSA10]. M. F. Husain, L. Khan, M. Kantarcioglu, B. Thuraisingham, "Data Intensive Query Processing for Large RDF Graphs Using Cloud Computing Tools," In *Proceedings of the IEEE International Conference on Cloud Computing*, Miami, FL, pp. 1–10, July 2010.

[HUSA11a]. M. F. Husain, J. P. McGlothlin, M. M. Masud, L. R. Khan, B. M. Thuraisingham, "Heuristics-Based Query Processing for Large RDF Graphs Using Cloud Computing," *IEEE Transactions on Knowledge and Data Engineering*, 23 (9), 1312–1327, 2011.

[HUSA11b]. M. F. Husain, "Data Intensive Query Processing for Semantic Web Data Using Hadoop and MapReduce," PhD thesis, The University of Texas at Dallas, May 2011.

[ITEE]. The University of Queensland Australia, School of Information Technology and Electrical Engineering, http://www.itee.uq.edu.au/eresearch/projects/biomanta.

[JENA]. Apache Software Foundation, http://jena.sourceforge.net.

[KHAL10]. A. Khaled, M. F. Husain, L. Khan, K. W. Hamlen, B. M. Thuraisingham, "A Token-Based Access Control System for RDF Data in the Clouds," In *CloudCom: 2010 IEEE 2nd International Conference on Cloud Computing Technology and Science*, Indianapolis, IN, USA, 2010.

[KIRY05]. A. Kiryakov, D. Ognyanov, D. Manov, "OWLIM: A Pragmatic Semantic Repository for OWL," In *SSWS'05: Proceedings of the 2005 International Workshop on Scalable Semantic Web Knowledge Base Systems*, New York, NY, 2005.

[LEHI]. Lehigh University, http://www.lehigh.edu/~zhp2/2004/0401/univ-bench.owl.

[MCGL09]. J. P. McGlothlin and L. R. Khan, "RDFKB: Efficient Support for RDF Inference Queries and Knowledge Management," In *IDEAS'09: Proceedings of the International Database Engineering and Applications Symposium*, Cetraro, Italy, 2009.

[MCGL10]. J. Ps. McGlothlin and L. Khan, "Materializing and Persisting Inferred and Uncertain Knowledge in RDF Datasets," In *Proceedings of AAAI Conference on Artificial Intelligence*, Atlanta, GA, 2010.

[MCNA07]. A. W. Mcnabb, C. K. Monson, K. D. Seppi, "MRPSO: MapReduce Particle Swarm Optimization," In *GECCO: Proceedings of the Annual Conference on Genetic and Evolutionary Computation*, London, England, UK, 2007.

[MORE07]. J. E. Moreira, M. M. Michael, D. Da Silva, D. Shiloach, P. Dube, L. Zhang, "Scalability of the Nutch Search Engine," In *ICS'07: Proceedings of the 21st Annual International Conference on Supercomputing*, Rotterdam, The Netherlands, pp. 3–12, June 2007.

[MORE08]. C. Moretti, K. Steinhaeuser, D. Thain, N. Chawla, "Scaling Up Classifiers to Cloud Computers," In *ICDM'08: Proceedings of the IEEE International Conference on Data Mining*, Pisa, Italy, 2008.

[NEUM08]. T. Neumann and G. Weikum, "RDF-3X: A RISC-Style Engine for RDF," *Proceedings of VLDB Endowment*, 1 (1), 647–659, 2008.

[NEWM08]. A. Newman, J. Hunter, Y. F. Li, C. Bouton, M. Davis, "A Scale-Out RDF Molecule Store for Distributed Processing of Biomedical Data," In *Proceedings of the Semantic Web for Health Care and Life Sciences Workshop*, Karlsruhe, Germany, 2008.

[OLST08]. C. Olston, B. Reed, U. Srivastava, R. Kumar, A. Tomkins, "Pig Latin: A Not-So-Foreign Language for Data Processing," In *Proceedings of ACM SIGMOD International Conference on the Management of Data*, Vancouver, BC, Canada, 2008.

[ONTO]. Ontotext AD, http://www.ontotext.com/owlim/big/index.html.

[OPEN]. Eclipse RDF4J, http://docs.rdf4j.org/migration/.

[ROHL07]. K. Rohloff, M. Dean, I. Emmons, D. Ryder, J. Sumner, "An Evaluation of Triple-Store Technologies for Large Data Stores," In *Proceedings of the OTM Confederated International Conference on the Move to Meaningful Internet Systems*, Vilamoura, Portugal, 2007.

[SCHM09]. M. Schmidt, T. Hornung, G. Lausen, C. Pinkel, "SP2Bench: A SPARQL Performance Benchmark," In *ICDE '09: Proceedings of the 25th International Conference on Data Engineering*, Shanghai, China, 2009.

[SIDI08]. L. Sidirourgos, R. Goncalves, M. Kersten, N. Nes, S. Manegold, "Column-Store Support for RDF Data Management: Not All Swans Are White," *Proceedings of VLDB Endowment*, 1 (2), 1553–1563, 2008.

[SISM10]. Y. Sismanis, S. Das, R. Gemulla, P. Haas, K. Beyer, J. McPherson, "Ricardo: Integrating R and Hadoop," In *SIGMOD'10: Proceedings of the ACM SIGMOD International Conference Management of Data*, Indianapolis, IN, USA, 2010.

[STOC08]. M. Stocker, A. Seaborne, A. Bernstein, C. Kiefer, D. Reynolds, "SPARQL Basic Graph Pattern Optimization Using Selectivity Estimation," In *WWW '08: Proceedings of the 17th International Conference on World Wide Web*, Beijing China, 2008.

[STON05]. M. Stonebraker et al. "C-Store: A Column-Oriented DBMS," In *VLDB '05: Proceedings of the 31st International Conference on Very Large Data Bases*, Trondheim, Norway, pp. 553–564, 2005.

[THUR10]. B. M. Thuraisingham, V. Khadilkar, A. Gupta, M. Kantarcioglu, L. Khan, "Secure Data Storage and Retrieval in the Cloud," In *CollaborateCom'10: Proceedings of the 6th International Conference on Collaborative Computing: Networking, Applications and Worksharing*, Chicago, IL, USA, 2010.

[THUR15]. B. Thuraisingham, S. Abrol, R. Heatherly, M. Kantarcioglu, V. Khadilkar, L. Khan, *Analyzing and Securing Social Networks*. CRC Press, Boca Raton, FL, 2016.

[W3a]. World Wide Web Consortium, http://www.w3.org/2001/sw/RDFCore/ntriples.

[W3b]. World Wide Web Consortium, http://www.w3.org/TR/rdf-concepts/#dfn-rdf-triple.

[W3c]. World Wide Web Consortium, http://www.w3.org/TR/rdf-primer.

[W3d]. World Wide Web Consortium, http://www.w3.org/TR/rdf-sparql-query/#defn_QueryVariable.

[W3e]. World Wide Web Consortium, http://www.w3.org/TR/rdf-sparql-query/#defn_TriplePattern.

[W3f]. World Wide Web Consortium, http://www.w3.org/TR/rdf-syntax-grammar.

[WANG10]. J. Wang, S. Wu, H. Gao, J. Li, B. C. Ooi, "Indexing Multi-Dimensional Data in a Cloud System," In *SIGMOD'10: Proceedings of ACM SIGMOD International Conference on the Management of Data*, Indianapolis, IN, USA, 2010.

[WEIS08]. C. Weiss, P. Karras, A. Bernstein, "Hexastore: Sextuple Indexing for Semantic Web Data Management," *Proceedings of VLDB Endowment*, 1 (1), 1008–1019, 2008.

[WIKIa]. http://wiki.apache.org/hadoop/JobTracker.

[WIKIb]. http://wiki.apache.org/hadoop/TaskTracker.

[XU10]. Y. Xu, P. Kostamaa, L. Gao, "Integrating Hadoop and Parallel DBMs," In *SIGMOD'10: Proceedings of the ACM SIGMOD International Conference on the Management of Data*, Indianapolis, IN, USA, 2010.

24 Big Data Analytics for Multipurpose Social Media Applications

24.1 INTRODUCTION

This chapter describes a cloud-based system called InXite, also called InXite-Security (Stream-based Data Analytics for Threat Detection and Prediction), that is designed to detect evolving patterns and trends in streaming data. InXite comprises four major modules: InXite Information Engine, InXite Profile Generator, InXite Psychosocial Analyzer, and InXite Threat Evaluator and Predictor, each of which is outlined in this chapter. We also describe the novel methods we have developed for stream data analytics that are at the heart of InXite.

InXite integrates information from a variety of online social media sites such as Twitter, Foursquare, Google+, and LinkedIn builds people profiles through correlation, aggregation, and analyses in order to identify persons of interest who pose a threat. Other applications include garnering user feedback on a company's products, providing inexpensive-targeted advertising, and monitoring the spread of an epidemic, among others.

InXite is designed to detect evolving patterns and trends in streaming data including emails, blogs, sensor data, and social media data such as tweets. InXite is designed on top of two powerful and patented data mining systems, namely Tweethood (location extraction for Tweets), with the explicit aim of detecting and predicting suspicious events and people, and stream-based novel class detection (SNOD). We also designed a separate system, SNOD++, an extension of SNOD, for detecting multiple novel classes of threats for InXite. Our goal is to decipher and monitor topics in data streams as well as to detect emerging trends. This includes general changes in topics such as sports or politics and also includes new, quickly emerging trends such as hurricanes and bombings. The problem of correctly associating data streams (e.g., Tweet messages) with trends and topics is a challenging one. The challenge is best addressed with a streaming model due to the continuous and large volume of incoming messages.

It should be noted that InXite is a general purpose system that can be adapted for a variety of applications including security, marketing, law enforcement, healthcare, emergency response, and finance. Also, the design of InXite is cloud based and can handle massive amounts of data. In other words, InXite is essentially a big data analytics system. This chapter mainly focuses on the adaptation of InXite for security applications which we call InXite-Security. Other adaptations of InXite are called InXite-Marketing, InXite-Law, InXite-Healthcare, InXite-Emergency, and InXite-Finance among others. That is, while InXite-Security is developed mainly for counter-terrorism and intelligence applications, all of the features can be tailored for marketing and law enforcement applications with some effort. We have completed the design and implementation of InXite-Security and InXite-Marketing. We have also completed an initial design and implementation of InXite-Law. Other applications such as healthcare and finance will be part of our future work. For convenience, we will use the term InXite to mean InXite-Security in this chapter.

The organization of this chapter is as follows. Our premise for InXite is discussed in Section 24.2. We will describe in detail the design of all the modules of InXite and the implementation in Section 24.3. A note on InXite-Marketing is discussed in Section 24.4. Related work is discussed in Section 24.5. This chapter is concluded in Section 24.6. Figure 24.1 describes the concepts

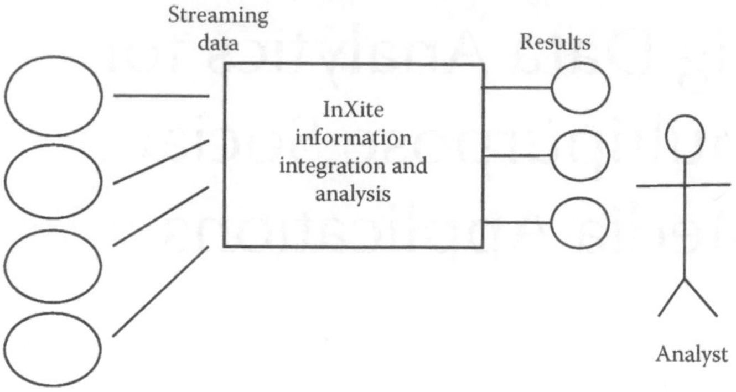

FIGURE 24.1 Big data analytics for social media applications.

discussed in this chapter. It should be noted that while we have focused on social media systems, the techniques we have designed and developed can be applied to various big data systems.

24.2 OUR PREMISE

Like a blunt instrument which destroys more than is intended, National Security Agency (NSA)'s PRISM program dredges the communications landscape and gathers more information than should be necessary to ferret out terrorists and terrorist cells communicating inside the USA and around the world. The NSA PRISM program is deemed necessary in order to prevent future terrorist acts against the USA. This top-down approach not only breaches the privacy of U.S. citizens and upset and angered them but it has also drawn the ire of foreign governments who have been spied upon.

By contrast, InXite utilizes a bottom-up approach that uses specific keywords designed to reveal people around the world tweeting about a topic of particular interest. For instance, the keyword pair "Egypt" and "Muslim-brotherhood" would display a list of people in Egypt tweeting to others around the world using the keyword "Muslim-brotherhood." In other words, InXite uses a targeted approach without needing to gather massive amounts of data.

Data streams are emanating from numerous data sources including blogs and social media data. Such data could be structured, unstructured, semistructured, and real-time/nonreal-time, static or dynamic data. It also includes relational and object data as well as semantic web data such as resource description framework (RDF) graphs and multimedia data such as video, audio, and images. With modern technology, it is possible to exchange numerous messages in a very short space of time. Furthermore, communication messages (e.g., blogs and tweets) are often abbreviated and difficult to follow. To understand the motives, sentiments, and behavior of individuals and groups, where some of them could be malicious, tools are needed to make sense out of the massive amounts of streaming data often represented as graphs. To address this need, we have designed a framework called InXite for analyzing stream-based data.

We have utilized Tweethood and SNOD to develop a sophisticated data analytics system called InXite. InXite is a multipurpose system that can be applied to security, law enforcement, marketing, healthcare, and financial applications among others. We have designed and developed two InXite applications. One is InXite-Security and the other one is InXite-Marketing. InXite-Security (which we will refer to as InXite for convenience since much of the InXite system initially focused on security applications) will detect and predict threats including potential terrorists, harmful events, and the time and place of such events. The data sources for InXite include blogs, sensor, and social media data among others. InXite is a cloud-based application due to the numerous advantages of clouds such as on-demand scalability, reliability, and performance improvements. InXite-Marketing utilizes the various modules of InXite and gives recommendations to businesses for selling products. The design of InXite uses Tweethood to obtain demographics information about individuals and SNOD and SNOD++ for detecting novel classes of threats and sentiments.

24.3 MODULES OF INXITE

24.3.1 Overview

Figure 24.2 illustrates the various modules of InXite, each of which is described in the ensuing subsections. InXite gets the data from various social media sites including streaming data from Twitter. The information is integrated by the information engine which carries out various functions such as entity resolution and ontology alignment. Then the information analytics engine will analyze the integrated data using data mining techniques.

The results are then given to the analyst. The major modules of InXite are common to our applications such as security, marketing, and law enforcement. Each application also has a small number of tailored components. InXite also follows a plug-and-play approach. That is, the analyst can plug his components if he or she has a preference for various tasks. In the ensuing sections we will describe each of the modules in more detail.

24.3.2 Information Engine

The first step is to extract concepts and relationships from the vast amount of data streams and categorize the messages. Then we provide *semantic* representation of the knowledge buried in the streams. This would enable an analyst to interact more directly with the hidden knowledge. The second step is to represent the concepts as ontologies, and subsequently integrate and align the ontologies. Once the multiple graphs extracted from the streams are integrated, then our analytics tools will analyze the graphs and subsequently predict threats.

The information engine module, illustrated in Figure 24.3, integrates the attributes of a user from multiple data streams including social networks (e.g., Twitter, LinkedIn, Foursquare, etc.) and performs entity resolution, ontology alignment, conflict resolution, data provenance, and reasoning under uncertain and incomplete information. At the heart of the Information Engine is Tweethood, a novel, patent-pending method/algorithm to determine user attributes including, but not limited to, location, age, age group, race, ethnicity, threat, languages spoken, religion, economic status,

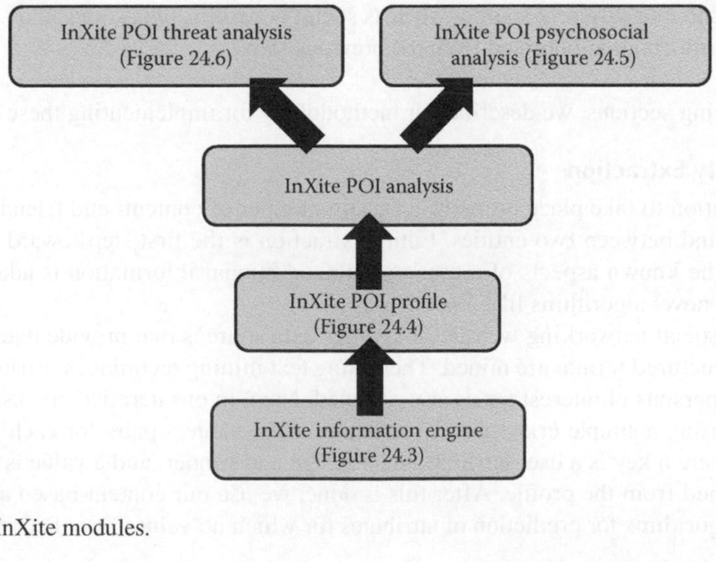

FIGURE 24.2 InXite modules.

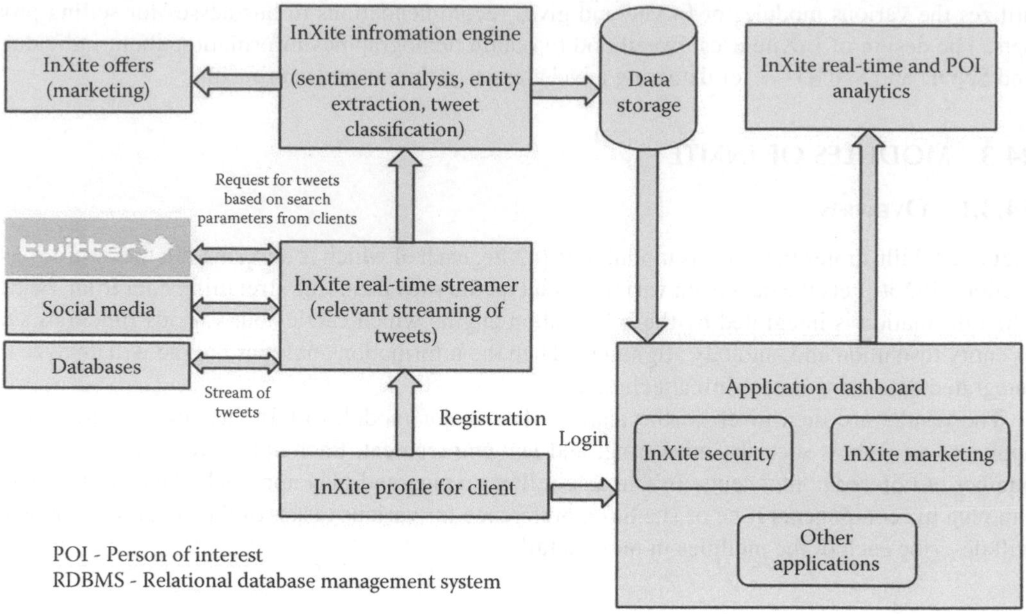

FIGURE 24.3 InXite information engine module.

education level, gender, hobbies, or interests based on the attribute values for the friends of the user [MOTO09].

While entity resolution algorithms have been around since the mid-1990s, InXite uses a combination of content-based similarity matching [TUNG06] and friends-based similarity matching [MOTO09] algorithms. The information engine module consists of two major components:

1. Entity extraction: The process of extracting (mining) and/or, in certain cases, predicting user specific attributes which include demographic information, such as, age, gender, and so on and information about his/her social networks, such as friends, followers, people he/she is following, and so on.
2. Information integration: The process of integrating or joining two or more user profiles from the same or different sources, such as social networks, blogs, and so on. This is done using the information obtained from the previous step.

In the following sections, we describe our methodology for implementing these two modules.

24.3.2.1 Entity Extraction

For data integration to take place properly, a certain number of content- and friend-based similarities must be found between two entities. Entity extraction is the first step toward that goal. Upon integrating all the known aspects of a user's profile, additional information is added through text mining and our novel algorithms like Tweethood.

All popular social networking websites and other data sources that provide data in either structured or semistructured format are mined. Then using text mining techniques, various entities associated with the persons of interest for us are extracted. Next, in our iterative process, the structured data is parsed using a simple crawler and we obtain <key, value> pairs for each profile from the information, where a key is a user attribute, such as age and gender, and a value is the corresponding value obtained from the profile. After this is done, we use our content-based and friend-based (Tweethood) algorithms for prediction of attributes for which no values have been found.

The pseudocode for entity extraction is as follows:

1. Using text mining techniques in the literature, extract relevant information about the user from the multiple sources of data (including social networks, databases, etc.).
2. Organize the information into (key, value) pairs.
3. Use Tweethood to predict values that are unknown for any keys.

24.3.2.2 Information Integration

In this step, we integrate or join two or more profiles from different data sources, which belong to the same individual based on matching of the attribute <key, value> pairs we obtained in the previous step. We pick one profile from data source A and try to find the closest match for it in data source B, by forming pairs and assigning them scores. This score is assigned based on the similarity of the two profiles, determined by the proximity of different user attributes in the two. If this score crosses a predetermined threshold and is also the highest for that chosen profile from data source A, then we link the two indicating that the two profiles point to the same user.

Finding a partial verification of entities and friends can be a difficult process. The amount of information similarities needed to make a conclusive match is constantly changing. These decisions therefore need to also be made from constantly changing ontologies. InXite constructs ontologies for partial entity resolution dynamically by observing patterns in complete resolutions. We define ontology for each data source, such as an online social network, blog, and so on. These ontologies are then linked so that the system understands that an attribute key A, such as gender, from one data source points to the same thing as attribute B, such as sex, from another data source. This linkage of ontology structures constructed from different data sources is essential for the integration/disambiguation of two or more profiles.

The pseudocode for information integration is as follows:

1. Construct ontologies for the entities extracted using various ontology construction techniques in the literature.
2. Carry out entity resolutions by determining whether two entities are the assigning scores as to how similar the entities are.
3. Apply data mining techniques to observe patterns in the entity resolution process.
4. For those entities that cannot be completely resolve, use the patterns observed in step 3 and resolve the entities.
5. Link the various ontologies constructed using the results from the entity resolution process to form a linkage of ontologies which are essentially person of interest (i.e., user) profiles.

24.3.3 Person of Interest Analysis

Once the information engine integrates the multiple data sources, extracts entities, constructs ontologies, resolves conflicts, determines similarities, and links the ontologies, the next step is to analyze a person of interest (POI) based on various attributes and algorithms. In this section, we will discuss our techniques for such an analysis. Note that in Section 24.3.4, we will discuss our data mining techniques for threat prediction.

24.3.3.1 InXite Person of Interest Profile Generation and Analysis

The InXite POI profile generation and analysis modules are illustrated in Figure 24.4. A generated profile represents one or more aggregated entities from the extraction step. If two profiles are determined to belong to the same person at any point before or after profile generation, then the attributes and data of the two are merged into a single profile. This may happen because of ontology shifts during analysis or manual discovery by an analyst. Even though attribute prediction happens during the entity extraction and alignment steps, SNOD is continuously used in several modules to detect

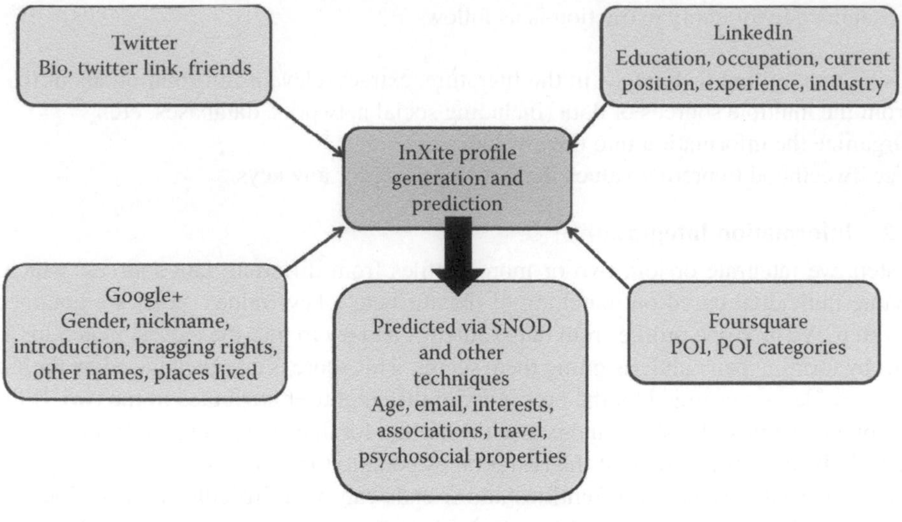

FIGURE 24.4 InXite person of interest profile generation and analysis.

novel information nodes as long as information is added or discovered in the searching process. This means that profiles are constantly edited, updated, and merged after profile generation.

24.3.3.2 InXite POI Threat Analysis

The InXite POI threat analysis (module 3 in Figure 24.2) is a core InXite feature which combines several individual scores, some based on existing studies and some novel, to come up with a final score for evaluating the seriousness of as a potential threat. Each of the individual scores and the final score has a range from 0 to 100 with 0 meaning a low threat and 100 meaning a high threat. Below listed are the seven major components of the Threat Evaluation Module that contribute to the final threat evaluation score:

1. *Demographics-based score computation*: InXite predicts and aggregates user-related attributes such as age, location, religion, and so on. Using existing studies done on terrorists such as the one by Marc Sageman [SAGE04], InXite determines if the POI fits the profile of a terrorist or not.

   Example: If (age between 22 and 35) AND (education = college) AND (ethnicity = Arab) → High Score
2. *Psychological score computation*: For calculating the psychological scores, we design algorithms that analyze the language used by the POI; in particular, we look at the adjectives and the nouns, to come up with five personality traits: sociability, evaluation, negativity, self-acceptance, fitting-in, psychological stability, and maturity. Based on these scores, we derive a final psychological score [SHAV92].

   Example: Sociability AND Negativity AND Psychological Instability AND Fitting In → High Score
3. *Content-based score computation*: An important source of information about a user is the messages/posts that he/she puts on his/her page. In order to calculate the content-based threat score for a user, we define a rule-based system that looks for suspicious nouns and verbs, analyzes their relationship, and assigns a score based on that.

   Example: I want to bomb the Pentagon → I/PRP want/VBP to/TO bomb/ VB the/DT Pentagon/NN → High Score.

   This metric is particularly useful for identifying mal-intent users who are expressive about their intents.

4. *Background check score computation*: For individuals located in the USA, we run background checks using existing software/websites. The integration and prediction of user attributes helps in successful user disambiguation and allows us to do an advanced search of the database.

   Based on the previous crimes committed by the individual, we assign a score which reflects the likelihood of him/her being a threat in the near future.

   Example: If criminal and Type_of_Crime = Violent or Federal → High Score
5. *Online reputation-based score computation*: InXite analyzes various online data sources such as newspapers, blogs, and social networking sites to analyze the sentiment about the user and determines his/her involvement in political events like rallies, riots, scams, frauds, robberies, among others. As in the case for other modules, the integration and prediction of other attributes allows for successful user disambiguation.

   Example: If user received award from president it could lead to a low score. On the other hand, an individual who is an active participant in rallies (news article in NY Times) → high score.
6. *Social graph-based score computation*: The final module is based on our patent pending algorithm, Tweethood. We predict the threat level for all friends of the POI (based on above listed = factors) and aggregate to obtain score for the central POI.

   Example: If Threat (friend1) = 0.9 AND Threat (friend2) = 0.1 AND Threat (friend3) = 0.8 AND Threat (friend4) = 0.7 AND Threat (friend5) = 0.5, then Threat (POI) = 0.6

Threat Assessment: Once the profiles of a user have been constructed, we then examine the various attributes to determine whether the given user is a potential terrorist. For example, a user's attributes (e.g., age, location, etc.) as well as their behavioral, social and psychological properties are extracted using our analytics algorithms. We then also apply existing algorithms (e.g., Mark Sageman's algorithms ([SAGE04], [SAGE08])) to enhance a user's psychological profile. These profiles will be used to determine whether the current user will carry out terrorist attacks, homicides, and so on. For threat assessment, here are some results that we have obtained using existing algorithms as well as our data analytics algorithms.

- *Demographics*: Up to 0.2 points are assigned to fitting into rages for the following categories: age, education, religion, politics, and hobbies. These are then added up for the final demographics score. The ranges for these categories are based on the research of Marc Sageman [SAGE08].
- *Psychology*: Verb usage is categorized into traits. Four of these traits are found to be indicative of low psychological stability. These four traits are measured by percentage of total verb usage and added together to form the psychology score. The psychology submodule is based on techniques given in [MARK03] and [SHAV92].
- *NLP* (Natural Language Processing): Weighted average of sentiment used between verbs and high-profile nouns (i.e., White House or Pentagon). Negative or threatening verb analyses have a weight of 1 while positive or benign verb analyses have a weight of 0.1. This allows strong statements such as a correlation of "bomb" and "Pentagon" to produce an overwhelmingly high score.
- *Social structure*: Standard means average of friends' threat scores. A friend's threat score is the average of their other scores (demographics, psychology, NLP, social structure, background, and online reputation).
- *Background checks*: Represents a DoD standard background check on the individual.
- *Online reputation*: If no previous association is found with this person or all associations are positive, the score will be 0. Any score higher than this directly represents the percentage of previous associations from mainstream media that are analyzed to have a negative sentiment.

Our design utilizes Tweethood and SNOD as well as existing algorithms to develop a comprehensive system for threat assessment/evaluation.

24.3.3.3 InXite Psychosocial Analysis

This module is illustrated in Figure 24.5. It consists of a variety of techniques including visualizing ontologies and generating word clouds. This module also uses two novel data analytics techniques that we have developed, namely microlevel location mining and sentiment mining. We begin the discussion with these two novel techniques, after which we discuss the remaining techniques.

Microlevel location mining refers to a method for determining specific or fine-grained locations that may be mentioned in communications between individuals or groups of individuals. In addition to locations, the technique can also be used to carry out fine-grained detection of other attributes such as hobbies, places traveled, and events. Our technique for microlevel location mining is unique and uses a crowd-sourced database, namely Foursquare. Furthermore, the technique uses the following tools/algorithms:

- WordNet is used for disambiguation of locations mentioned in communications between individuals/groups such as messages or tweets.
- Tweethood is used for identifying a city-level location which in turn is used to narrow the search for micro-level locations within the identified city.

The work in [KINS11] aims to identify zip codes/locations based on the particular language used in tweets and is thus a different approach toward location identification. We have considerably enhanced current efforts and have developed a novel technique for microlevel location mining.

The pseudocode for microlevel location mining is as follows:

1. Disambiguate locations mentioned in tweets using Wordnet.
2. Use Foursquare to find the general locations.
3. When locations are missing in the tweets, use Tweethood to find the locations as well as the city-level locations.
4. Use variations of Tweethood to mine further to pinpoint the exact location.

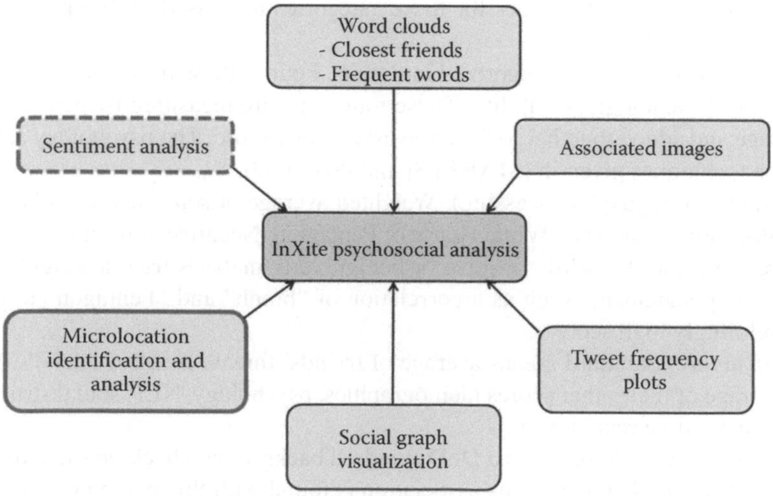

FIGURE 24.5 InXite psychosocial analysis and prediction.

24.3.3.4 Other Features

We have designed a number of features that would enhance psychosocial analysis including the following:

24.3.3.4.1 Sentiment mining

We have also designed sentiment mining techniques about a certain keyword/topic. For example, what does "John Smith" feel about "Tax Breaks" or what does "John Smith" feel about 'Osama bin Laden." Our methods use existing as well as our own algorithms (Tweethood, SNOD) for classifying user messages as positive, negative, or neutral or whether it belongs to a novel class. We use emotion mining and also social behavioral mining to determine sentiments. In particular, we use the following two techniques:

- User demographics-based: For example, if we know that 95% of all African Americans are pro-Obama, then our system will give a positive bias to a tweet from an African American about President Obama.
- Social factor-based (based on Tweethood): If we know that 9 out of 10 friends of a user are pro-Obama, then we will give a positive bias to tweets from that user.

Our training dataset is a labeled dataset—each tweet with its sentiment type positive or negative or neutral. We obtained the labeled training dataset from set of tweets which has emo-icons in it. Based on the emo-icon, we determined the label of the tweet and made the training dataset. For each of the training data/tweet, we first remove the stopwords in it. Then we remove all the words starting with "@" or "http." Then we convert each token of the tweet to standard form means: we convert a token like "hungryyyyyy" to "hungryy." Then from each tweet we make the list of unigrams and bigrams for that tweet with its sentiment type. We saved the list of unigrams and bigrams in a HashSet and also convert the tweet as unigram and bigrams.

Now, for each token in the HashSet and for each tweet, we check whether the tweet contains the token or not. Then we make the occurrence matrix based on their presence/absence. So, at this point we have a dataset of large numbers of dimensions. So to reduce the dimensionality we leverage the entropy concept. We choose best N attribute based on the higher information gain. Now, we have considerably good data and then we use WEKA for classifying purpose and we use naïve Bayesian classifier and decision tree (J48) classifier.

The pseudocode for the sentiment mining algorithm is as follows:

```
Input: Set of training tweets T, Bag of stopword S, Set of testing tweets R, number of attribute N
Output: Labels of each of the tweet of R.
For every tweet in T
   Remove all the stopwords in S.
   Remove the words starting with '@' or 'http' and make each token as standard form.
   Make the set G, of unigrams and bigrams, and convert each tweet as a set of those and make the
   set W. [W contains the unigrams and bigrams of each tweet.]
For each token g in G
   For each token in w in W
      If g matches w then encode it as 1 and fill up the occurrence matrix M.
      Else encode it as 0 and fill up the occurrence matrix M.
Choose the best N attribute from M based on the information gain and make new dataset D.
Use D as the training dataset and build the classifier NB or J48.
Use the trained classifier to classify the instances of test set R.
```

WORD CLOUDS: Shows frequently used words. More frequent words are shown with a larger font.

ENTITY CLOUDS: Shows frequently used entities. Entities of interest among the profile and their friends are shown in size by correlation to frequency of discussion.

TWEET FREQUENCY: Line graphs of tweets over time show useful timing information. Lack of tweets are as important as writing tweets. Sleeper agents are known to cut contact and go silent before acting.

SOCIAL GRAPH VISUALIZATION: Visually shows the threat level of the most popular friends that are associated with a given user online.

ASSOCIATED IMAGES: Brought to life in a slide show, all the images gathered from online sources for the given user profile.

24.3.4 InXite Threat Detection and Prediction

InXite threat detection and prediction is module 5 depicted in Figure 24.2. While the threat evaluation and assessment techniques described in the previous section will determine whether a person is a threat or not based on some predetermined attributes, we have also designed data mining techniques to determine whether a person will commit future terrorist attacks. That is, threat prediction in InXite is carried out through a series of stages either meant to find suggested threatening behavior in a user or to eliminate individuals who are unlikely to be a current or become a future threat. By leveraging both manually configured word analysis and automated data mining classifications, InXite is able to separate likely threats from a vast number of individuals.

A very broad list of users is created by first picking out those who use a list of specific nouns and verbs. This list is manually maintained and may include code words that are added after the discovery that they are being used. Persons who use enough of these words in a single statement are flagged and classified in the next stage. The number of statements or tweets that pass this stage contain a high number of false positives.

In the next stage, the flagged statements are tagged by part of speech similar to the content-based score in the threat evaluation section. Classifiers are trained on labeled and tagged data from statements manually confirmed by analysts or engineers to indicate imminent threats. Because many nonthreatening statements can contain threatening words like "kill," the classifiers are useful in removing false positives from the statements passed in from the first phase.

Phrases like "killing time" or "people would kill for this opportunity" are eliminated in this way. This method of classification also serves to solidify seemingly innocent sentences that may be using code words. Even if the words of the sentence are replaced, the sentences' structure and placement remain the same and compare similarly to sentences that explicitly state the obvious threatening language.

This automated method is so effective because every word in a statement contributes an equal probability to the statement's classification as a threat or not. Given enough samples of threats and nonthreats, as each word is compared to its individual threat level and placement within the whole statement, the algorithm can determine where it belongs. When the algorithm decides that a statement is threatening, it is grouped with similar statements based on identified threatening words and grammatical structure. Using feedback from the analyst or user, these groups can be solidified or changed to reflect similar threatening statements.

Predicting threats based on data content first requires that the threatening or useful data be separated from the extremely large amount of benign or useless data. This can be accomplished with high accuracy through the union of linear discriminate analysis and bag of words filtering. This process has the benefit of breaking possibly threatening content into feature groups and dynamically detecting new threatening content categories. However, it also produces a large amount of false positives. We have multiple methods. One is based on a naïve Bayes classifier to help eliminate false positives. The classifier trains threats and benign content based on individual words and their

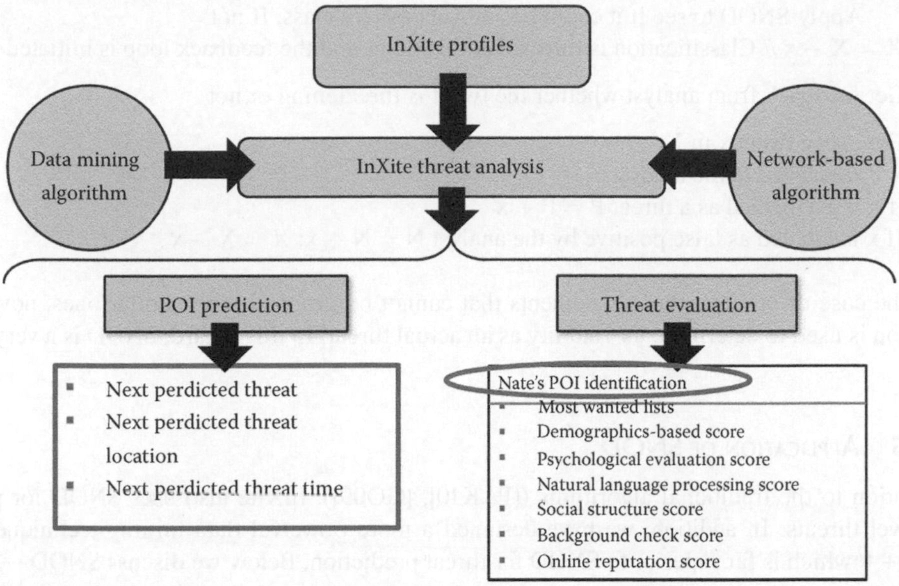

FIGURE 24.6 InXite threat analysis and prediction module.

part of speech obtained from a tagger developed by CMU specifically for twitter language usage instead of published text documents. The other is based on our patent-pending technology SNOD. Our integrated algorithms provide much higher accuracy than the current approaches. Figure 24.6 illustrates details of the threat prediction module (module 5 of Figure 24.2)

The pseudocode for the threat detection algorithm is as follows:

```
    1. Identifying Threatening Tweets
Input: Set of tweets T, Bag of words A, B, C
Output: Set of threatening tweets X
  For every tweet t in T,
    If t contains a word from set B then let n = location of this word
      If at least two words from (n−3, n−1) exist in set A, then
      If at least two words from (n+1, n+3) exist in set C
            Set X = X + t
// X now contains all preliminary identified threatening content and moves onto the classifier
    2. Naïve Bayes Classification (NB)
Input: Set of threatening tweets X; Set of training tweets P, N
// P is positively identified threats; N is originally empty until feedback loop initiated, are false positive nonthreats
Ouput: Revised threatening tweets X
  For every tweet p in P NB trained on positive threat
  For every tweet n in N NB trained on negative threat
  For every tweet x in X
    For every word w in x Part of speech is tagged
      For every set of three words from (w1,w3) to (wn-2,wn)
      Classify probability of threat based of part of speech using NB
      NB classifies x as real threat or false positive
      If false positive
```

Apply SNOD to see if it could be a novel positive class, If not
X = X − x // Classification is finished at this point and the feedback loop is initiated

3. Get feedback from analyst whether the tweet is threatening or not

For every tweet x in X
x is displayed to the analyst
if x is confirmed as a threat P = P + x
If x is labeled as false positive by the analyst N = N + x; X = X − x

In the case of outliers, those statements that cannot be grouped with similar ones, novel class detection is used to determine its viability as an actual threat. In this regard, SNOD is a very useful tool.

24.3.5 Application of SNOD

In addition to the traditional algorithms ([PAK10], [GO09]), InXite also uses SNOD for predicting novel threats. In addition, we have designed a more powerful data mining technique called SNOD++ which is far superior to SNOD for threat prediction. Below we discuss SNOD++.

24.3.5.1 SNOD++

InXite is based on SNOD which occurs because of the dynamic nature of the stream. Second, if more than one novel class appears in the stream, SNOD cannot detect them. Third, SNOD does not address the problem of high-dimensional feature spaces, which may lead to higher training and classification error. Finally, SNOD does not apply any optimizations for feature extraction and classification. Therefore, we have designed a practical and robust blogs and tweets detection tool using powerful systems called SNOD++. That is, we have enhanced SNOD into SNOD++ that is more practical and robust than SNOD. In addition to addressing the infinite-length, concept-drift, and concept-evolution problems, SNOD++ addresses feature evolution and multiple novel classes, as well as applies subspace clustering and other optimizations, all of which improve the robustness, power, and accuracy of the algorithm.

24.3.5.2 Benefits of SNOD++

Systems based on SNOD++ can handle massive volumes of training data and will also be able to cope with concept drift in the data. These attributes make it more practical and robust than blogs and tweets detectors that are trained with static data. Furthermore, it can be used in detecting one or more novel classes of blogs and tweets. Also, recall that existing blogs and tweets detection techniques may fail to detect completely new patterns, but InXite++ should be able to detect such novel classes and raise an alarm. The blogs would be later analyzed and characterized by human experts. In particular, InXite++ will be more robust and useful than InXite because InXite++ will be capable of detecting multiple novel blogs and tweets in the stream and will also exhibit much higher classification accuracy and a faster training time because of its robustness to higher feature dimensions and application of distributed feature extraction and selection.

24.3.6 Expert Systems Support

InXite provides basic support for expert systems to provide explanations for decisions and the ability to add additional modules as needed. Essentially, InXite integrates an expert system for analyzing and interpreting the results of the scores explained in previous paragraphs (e.g., reputation-based score, social grap-based score). This is meant to help the analyst to better interpret the information he/she is provided with. With the ability to customize and add additional modules, the inclusion of expert systems into In-Xite allows for near endless assistance and extensibility.

The pseudocode for the expert system is given below.

```
Input: Expert System E; Starting node n
Output: Result Graph R Explanation Graph Q Final Node N
While N = null
  Evaluate decision of n
    Q = Q + decision R = R + n
    If decision leads to end point N = destination node
    Else n = destination node
// N displays the final result of the expert system, while R displays the nodes that were evaluated in the process, and Q displays all of the logical steps used to reach N.
```

24.3.7 Cloud-Design of InXite to Hanndle Big Data

For InXite to function in real time and to handle massive numbers of tweets and data, we need a cloud to host all of the modules of InXite. In this section, we describe our cloud-based design for various InXite modules. The design uses two separate tools, namely Storm and HBase, for the development of the various InXite modules. A separate Storm topology is constructed for each of the InXite modules. Furthermore, HBase is used by all topologies for storage and retrieval of user profiles. We now present the design of the various topologies in the form of pseudocode-based algorithms.

InXite Information Engine in the Cloud

1. Identify a user of interest using a spout.
2. Perform the steps included in the entity extraction and information integration module for the user selected in step 1 in a custom bolt (this also includes the implementation of Tweethood in the Cloud).
3. Store the identified attribute <key, value> pairs in HBase.
4. Perform the steps for information integration for the user selected in step 1 using the attribute <key, value> pairs obtained in step 2 in a separate custom bolt.
5. Update the results stored in HBase with the results of step 4.

InXite Profile Generation and Prediction

1. Identify a user of interest using a spout.
2. Use the attribute <key, value> pairs created by the information engine to build a user profile in a bolt, which is stored in an HBase schema.
3. Update the user profile by predicting values for other attributes using the attribute <key, value> pairs in a separate custom bolt.
4. Conduct a threat assessment of the identified user with the help of the various scores described earlier (demographics-based, psychological, etc.) using a custom bolt.
5. Update the user profile with the results of threat assessment.

InXite Psychosocial Analysis and Prediction

1. Identify a user of interest using a spout.
2. Identify micro-level locations for the user and store them as a part of their profile using a custom bolt (this includes the implementation of Tweethood in the Cloud).
3. Perform a sentiment analysis of the user's messages/posts/tweets using a custom bolt and store the results as a part of their profile.

4. Use a separate custom bolt to construct word/entity clouds, graphs for tweet frequency, determine the threat score for the top friends of this user and download images associated with this user.
5. Store all information obtained in step 4a as a part of the user's profile.

InXite Threat Detection and Prediction

1. Identify a user of interest using a spout.
2. Perform threat prediction for the identified user in a custom bolt using the classification algorithms described earlier.
3. Store the results of threat prediction as a part of the user's profile.

In addition to Storm and Hbase, we are also exploring the use of other big data technologies such as Spark to implement InXite. In addition, NoSQL database systems such as CouchDB are also being explored to store the massive amounts of data collected from social media systems.

24.3.8 Implementation

All of the modules of InXite illustrated in Figure 24.2 have been implemented. These include entity extraction and information integration, profile generation and threat analysis, psychosocial analysis, as well as threat prediction. With respect to the cloud implementation, we have completed the implementation of Tweethood in the cloud as well as SNOD in the cloud. The remaining modules of InXite are yet to be implemented in the cloud.

Multiple demonstrations of InXite are available. These include canned demonstrations, real-time demonstrations (that requires access to numerous tweets) as well as Tweethood in the cloud. We have taken a plug-and-play (i.e., a component-based approach) to the development of InXite. This means that if a customer has a certain module of his/her own (e.g., sentiment mining) that he/she wishes to use, then he can replace our sentiment mining module with that of his/her choice. This feature is a great strength of InXite. Many of the products require an all or nothing approach. With InXite you can select the modules you want to meet your needs. It should also be noted that while the design of InXite does not limit the data to tweets, the implementation handles only tweets. That is, the design of InXite can handle any data whether it is structured data in databases or unstructured data in the form of social graphs or tweets.

24.4 OTHER APPLICATIONS

As we have stated in Section 24.1, InXite is a multipurpose system. In addition to InXite-Security described in Section 24.2, we have also designed and developed other applications for InXite including InXite-Marketing and InXite-Law. In this section, we discuss InXite-Marketing which will provide advice to businesses as to who to target for a particular product based on the user's social graphs and tweets.

InXite-Marketing carries out entity extraction and information integration and builds profiles of persons of interest. In this case, the person of interest is the user who is interested in a product such as iPhone or a particular kind if pizza. We can develop word clouds as well as associated images for this user. We can also carry out sentiment mining and obtain results such as John prefers iPhone to Android. InXite-Marketing also finds locations from Tweethood and novel classes using SNOD.

However, there are some differences between the features between InXite-Security and InXite-Marketing. It does not make sense to determine whether a person is a threat or whether he will commit a crime for InXite-Marketing. Furthermore, it does not make sense to determine the psychosocial profile of a user. What is useful for InXite-Marketing is integrating with a *recommender* system. For example, we can analyze the user preferences and make recommendations.

As we already discussed in the sentiment analysis section, we can predict the sentiment of tweet for a person, though it needs some further improvement like incorporating NLP techniques. Our system is easily workable for a particular person's tweet and a particular subject. For example, if we want to determine John Smith's sentiment about iPhone-5, we can go through all his tweets about the iPhone-5 and based on the sentiment of each of the tweet, we can determine the overall sentiment of John Smith about iPhone-5. So now, once we know the sentiment of John Smith about iPhone-5, say it is positive, we can recommend him some more i-products or products related to the iPhone-5, for example, headphone, charger, and so on. Here is another factor to consider that we call *peer effect*. The positive statements made by an individual's friends can be mined for individual products. Because the friends or associates of this individual talk positively about a product, especially one that the individual does not mention themselves, we can extrapolate these products for the recommender system. For example, if John Smith has ten friends and all of them have a positive sentiment about Android phones, then it is a good idea to recommend some Android products to John Smith. So, we can consider it as a weighted vector of "personal sentiment" and "peer sentiment." Based on the weighted factor, we can decide what product and in what extent we should recommend him. These weights will be mostly influenced by the individual's personal sentiment and the sentiment of his peers will help fill in the gaps and more greatly expand the recommendation options for this person.

The pseudocode for the recommender system is as follows:

Query: Find the John's sentiment about product X
Analyze John's Tweets about X applying data mining techniques
  If Positive, then give additional recommendation related to product X
Analyze the Tweets of John's friends using weighted vectors.
  If they are positive about X, then give recommendations to John about X

We have a demonstration system for InXite-Marketing (as well as InXite-Law) that has implemented all of the features that we have described above including the recommender system. There are also additional features we have implemented. For example, based on the interests of a user, we could predict the product he would be interested in the future and this way a business can market this product first to this user and gain a competitive advantage.

24.5 RELATED WORK

In addition to Tweethood, SNOD, and the information integration techniques, other works that have influenced our approach include those of Goyal et al., Katakis et al., Lin et al., Markou and Singh, Smith and Crane, Spinosa et al., Frigui and Nasraoui, Backstrom et al., and Wenerstrom and Giraud-Carrier, among others ([GOYA09], [KATA06], [LIN11], [MARK03], [SMIT01], [SPIN08], [BACK08], [FRIG04], [WENE06], [DONG05], [HUBE09]). In addition, much of our work has also been applied for the InXite system. These include the work discussed in [ABRO09], [AHME09], [AHME10], [CHAN11], [KHAN02], [MASU10], and [MASU11].

Many tools exist for entity extraction and location identification from web pages and other structured text. Although the details of some of these detection strategies are proprietary, it is well known that all of them use standard NLP or machine learning techniques that assume that the text is structured and consists of complete sentences with correct grammar. Our work on the other hand focuses on unstructured text consisting of slang and incomplete sentences which is usually associated with the social media. With regard to cloud-based stream mining and novel class detection framework, to the best of our knowledge, there is no significant commercial competition for a cloud-centric trend detection tool. The current work on trend detection (TwitterMonitor and Streaming Trend Detection in Twitter by James Benhardusis) is primitive and makes use of a keyword-based approach instead of choosing feature vectors. Additionally, since we have taken a modular approach to the creation of our tools, we can iteratively refine each component (novel class detection for trend analysis, entity extraction, scalability on cloud, and ontology construction) separately. All the frameworks and tools that we have used (or are using) for the development of InXite are open source and have been extensively used in our previous research and hence our tools will be able to accommodate any changes to the platform.

24.6 SUMMARY AND DIRECTIONS

In this chapter, we have described the design of the big data analytics system called InXite. InXite will be a great asset to the analysts who have to deal with massive amounts of data streams in the form of billions of blogs and messages among others. For example, by analyzing the behavioral history of a particular group of individuals as well as details of concepts such as events, analysts will be able to predict behavioral changes in the near future and take necessary measures. We have also discussed our use of cloud computing and various big data tools in the implementation of InXite.

New streams of data swarm the cyberspace every day. Analyzing such streams and updating the existing classification models is a daunting task. Most existing behavior-profiling techniques are manual, which require days to analyze a single blog sample and extract its behavioral profile. Even existing automated techniques have been tested only on a small sample of training data. By integrating our approach with a cloud computing framework, we have overcome this barrier and provided a highly scalable behavior modeling tool, thereby achieving higher accuracy in detecting new patterns. Furthermore, no existing profiling (manual or automated) technique addresses the evolving characteristics of data streams such as blogs and messages. Therefore, our product will have a tremendous advantage over other behavior-based products by quickly responding to the dynamic environment.

While InXite is a considerable improvement over currently available analysis tools, the underlying SNOD technology has some limitations. For example, SNOD lacks the ability to detect multiple novel classes emerging simultaneously. Since data streams such as blogs and messages could have multiple concurrent evolutions, we need a system that can detect multiple novel classes. Therefore, we have extended SNOD to achieve a more powerful detection strategy (SNOD++) that addresses these limitations. SNOD++ is utilized by InXite. We believe that InXite will be a novel product for streaming data analysis due to the fact that it can handle dynamic data, changing patterns, and dynamic emergence of novel classes. We have utilized our cloud computing framework to develop InXite for scalable solutions for mining streaming data.

REFERENCES

[ABRO09]. S. Abrol, L. Khan, T.M. Al-Khateeb, "MapIt: Smarter Searches using Location Driven Knowledge Discovery and Mining," *1st SIGSPATIAL ACM GIS 2009 International Workshop on Querying and Mining Uncertain Spatio-Temporal Data (QUeST)*, November 2009, Seattle, WA.

[AHME09]. M.S. Ahmed and L. Khan, "SISC: A Text Classification Approach Using Semi Supervised Subspace Clustering," *ICDM Workshops*, Miami, FL, pp. 1–6, 2009.

[AHME10]. M.S. Ahmed, L. Khan, M. Rajeswari, "Using Correlation Based Subspace Clustering for Multi-label Text Data Classification," *ICTAI*, 2, 296–303, 2010.

[BACK08]. L. Backstrom, J. Kleinberg, R. Kumar, J. Novak. "Spatial Variation in Search Engine Queries." In *Proceedings of the 17th International Conference on WWW*, New York, NY, 2008.

[CHAN11]. S. Chandra and L. Khan, "Estimating Twitter User Location Using Social Interactions A Content Based Approach," *The 3rd IEEE International Conference on Social Computing*, Oct. 9–11, MIT Press, Boston, MA, 2011.

[DONG05]. X. Dong, A.Y. Halevy, J. Madhavan, "Reference Reconciliation in Complex Information Spaces," In *SIGMOD Conference*, Baltimore, MD, pp. 85–96, 2005.

[FRIG04]. H. Frigui and O. Nasraoui, "Unsupervised Learning of Prototypes and Attribute Weights," *Pattern Recognition*, 37 (3), 567–581, 2004.

[GO09]. G. Alec, R. Bhayani, L. Huang, "*Twitter Sentiment Classification Using Distant Supervision*," CS224N Project Report, Stanford, 2009, 1–12.

[GOYA09]. M.A. Goyal, H. Daum, S. Venkatasubramanian, "Streaming for Large Scale NLP: Language Modeling," *Human Language Technologies: The 2009 Annual Conference of the North American Chapter of the Association for Computational Linguistics*, Boulder, CO, 2009.

[HUBE09]. B. Huberman and D. R. F. Wu, "Social Networks That Matter: Twitter Under the Microscope," *First Monday*, 14, 2009.

[KATA06]. I. Katakis, G. Tsoumakas, I. Vlahavas, "Dynamic Feature Space and Incremental Feature Selection for the Classification of Textual Data Streams," *ECML PKDD: 2006 International Workshop on Knowledge Discovery from Data Streams*, pp. 102–116, 2006.

[KHAN02]. L. Khan and F. Luo, "Ontology Construction for Information Selection," In *Proceedings of ICTAI*, Washington, DC, 2002.

[KINS11]. K. Sheila, V. Murdock, N. O'Hare. "I'm Eating a Sandwich in Glasgow: Modeling Locations with Tweets," In *Proceedings of the 3rd International Workshop on Search and Mining user-Generated Contents*, Glasgow, UK, pp. 61–68, 2011, ACM.

[LIN11]. J. Lin, R. Snow, W. Morgan, "Smoothing Techniques for Adaptive Online Language Models: Topic Tracking in Tweet Streams," In *Proceedings of ACM SIGKDD Conference on Knowledge Discovery and Data Mining*, August, San Diego, CA, 2011.

[MARK03]. M. Markou and S. Singh, "Novelty Detection: A Review. Part 1: Statistical Approaches, Part 2: Neural Network Based Approaches," *Signal Processing*, 83, 2481–2497, 2499–2521, 2003.

[MASU10]. M.M. Masud, Q. Chen, L. Khan, C.C. Aggarwal, J. Gao, J. Han, B.M. Thuraisingham, "Addressing Concept-Evolution in Concept-Drifting Data Streams," In *Proceedings of ICDM*, Sydney, Australia, 2010.

[MASU11]. M.M. Masud, J. Gao, L. Khan, J. Han, B.M. Thuraisingham, "Classification and Novel Class Detection in Concept-Drifting Data Streams Under Time Constraints," *IEEE TKDE*, 23 (1), 859–874, 2011.

[MOTO09]. M. Motoyama and G. Varghese, "I Seek You: Searching and Matching Individuals in Social Networks," In *ACM WIDM*, Hong Kong, 2009.

[PAK10]. P. Alexander and P. Paroubek, "Twitter as a Corpus for Sentiment Analysis and Opinion Mining," In *Proceedings of LREC*, Valletta, Malta, pp. 1320–1326, 2010.

[SAGE04]. S. Marc. *Understanding Terror Networks*. University of Pennsylvania Press, Philadelphia, PA, 2004.

[SAGE08]. M. Sageman and L. Jihad, *Terror Networks in the Twenty-First Century*, University of Pennsylvania Press, Philadelphia, PA, 2008.

[SHAV92]. S.R. Phillip and K.A. Brennan, "Attachment Styles and the "Big Five" Personality Traits: Their Connections with Each Other and with Romantic Relationship Outcomes," *Personality and Social Psychology Bulletin*, 18 (5), 536–545, 1992.

[SMIT01]. D.A. Smith and G. Crane, "Disambiguating Geographic Names in a Historical Digital Library," *5th European Conference on Research and Advanced Technology for Digital Libraries (ECDL01)*, Lecture Notes in Computer Science, Darmstadt, September 2001.

[SPIN08]. E.J. Spinosa, A.P. de Leon, F. de Carvalho, J. Gama, "Cluster-Based Novel Concept Detection in Data Streams Applied to Intrusion Detection in Computer Networks," In *Proceedings of ACM SAC*, Fortaleza, Ceara, Brazil, pp. 976–980, 2008.

[TUNG06]. A. Tung, R. Zhang, N. Koudas, B. Doi, "Similarity Search: A Matching Based Approach," In *Proceedings of VLDB*, Seoul, Korea, 2006.

[WENE06]. B. Wenerstrom and C. Giraud-Carrier. "Temporal Data Mining in Dynamic Feature Spaces," In *Proceedings of ICDM*, Hong Kong, pp. 1141–1145, 2006.

25 Big Data Management and Cloud for Assured Information Sharing

25.1 INTRODUCTION

The advent of cloud computing and the continuing movement toward software as a service (SaaS) paradigms have posed an increasing need for assured information sharing (AIS) as a service in the cloud. The urgency of this need was voiced in April 2011 by the National Security Agency (NSA) Chief Information Officer (CIO) Lonny Anderson in describing the agency's focus on a "cloud-centric" approach to information sharing with other agencies [NSA11]. Likewise, the Department of Defense (DoD) has been embracing cloud computing paradigms to more efficiently, economically, flexibly, and scalably meet its vision of "delivering the power of information to ensure mission success through an agile enterprise with the freedom of maneuverability across the information environment" ([DoD, DoD07]). Both agencies therefore have a tremendous need for effective AIS technologies and tools for cloud environments. Furthermore, there is also an urgent need for those in different social circles within agencies to share the information in the cloud securely and in a timely manner. Therefore, extending the AIS tools to function in a cloud-centric social media environment is becoming a need for many organizations.

Although a number of AIS tools have been developed in recent years for policy-based information sharing ([AWAD10, Fini09, RAO08, THUR08]), to our knowledge none of these tools operate in the cloud and hence do not provide the scalability needed to support large numbers of users such as social media users, involving massive amounts of data such as social media data including text, images, and video. The early prototype systems we developed for supporting cloud-based AIS have applied cloud-centric query engines (QEs) (e.g., the SPARQL query optimizer discussed in Chapter 23) that query large amounts of data in relational and semantic web databases by utilizing noncloud-based policy engines that enforce policies expressed in the eXtensible Access Control Markup Language (XACML) ([THUR10, THUR11]). While this is a significant improvement over prior efforts (and has given us insights into implementing cloud-based solutions), it nevertheless has at least three significant limitations. First, XACML-based policy specifications are not expressive enough to support many of the complex policies needed for AIS missions like those of the NSA and DoD, as well as applications such as social networks. Second, to meet the scalability and efficiency requirements of mission-critical tasks, the policy engine needs to operate in the cloud rather than externally. Third, secured query processing based on relational technology has limitations in representing and processing unstructured data needed for command and control applications.

To share the large amounts of data securely and efficiently, there clearly needs to be a seamless integration of the policy and data managers for social media in the cloud. Therefore, in order to satisfy the cloud-centric AIS needs of the DoD and NSA, we need (i) a cloud-resident policy manager that enforces information-sharing policies expressed in a semantically rich language and (ii) a cloud-resident data manager that securely stores and retrieves data and seamlessly integrates with the policy manager. To our knowledge, no such system currently exists. Therefore, our project has designed and developed such cloud-based AIS systems for social media users. Our policy engine as well as data are represented using semantic web technologies and therefore can represent and reason about social media data. That is, we have developed a cloud-centric policy manager that enforces

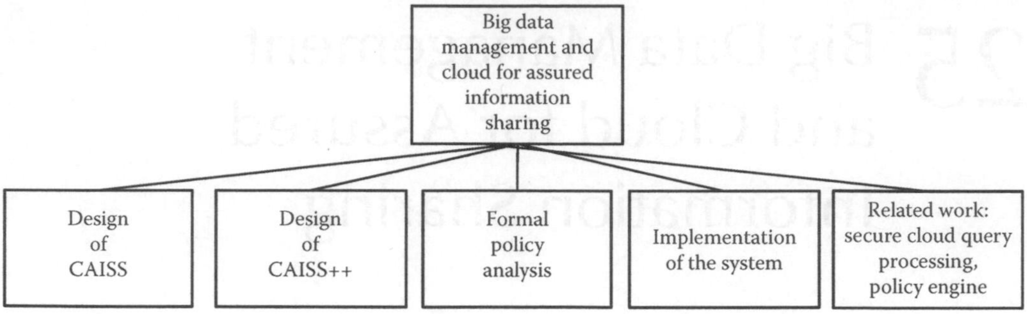

FIGURE 25.1 Big data management and cloud for assured information sharing.

policies specified in the resource description framework (RDF) and a cloud-centric data manager that will store and manage data, such as social graphs and associated data, also specified in RDF. This RDF data manager is essentially a QE for SPARQL, a language widely used by the semantic web community to query RDF data. Furthermore, our policy manager and data manager will have seamless integration since they both manage RDF data.

To address the AIS requirements of various organizations, including social media users, we have designed and developed a series of cloud-based AIS systems that handle massive amounts of data. That is, we have essentially used big data management techniques for AIS. This chapter provides an overview of our design. The organization of this chapter is as follows. Our design philosophy is discussed in Section 25.2. Our system design will be discussed in Section 25.3. In particular, we will discuss the design and implementation of CAISS in Section 25.3.1 and the design of CAISS++ in Section 25.3.2. Formal policy analysis and the implementation approach for CAISS++ will be provided in Sections 25.3.3 and 25.3.4, respectively. Related efforts are discussed in Section 25.4. Extending our approach to social media applications is discussed in Section 25.5. This chapter is concluded in Section 25.6. Figure 25.1 illustrates the contents of this chapter. Details of our work can also be found in [THUR12].

25.2 DESIGN PHILOSOPHY

Our design has proceeded in two phases. During phase 1, we have designed and implemented a proof of concept prototype of a cloud-centric assured information sharing system (CAISS) that utilizes the technology components we have designed in-house as well as open source tools. CAISS consists of two components: a cloud-centric policy manager that enforces policies specified in the RDF and a cloud-centric data manager that will store and manage data also specified in the RDF. This RDF data manager is essentially a QE for SPARQL (SPARQL protocol and RDF query language), a language widely used by the semantic web community to query RDF data. RDF is a semantic web language that is considerably more expressive than XACML for specifying and reasoning about policies. Furthermore, our policy manager and data manager will have seamless integration since they both manage RDF data. We have chosen this RDF-based approach for cloud-centric AIS during phase 1 because it satisfies the two necessary conditions stated in the previous paragraph, and we have already developed an RDF-based noncloud-centric policy manager [CADE11a] and an RDF-based cloud-centric data manager for Air Force Office of Scientific Research (AFOSR) [HUSA11]. Having parts of the two critical components needed to build a useful cloud-centric AIS system puts us in an excellent position to build a useful proof of concept demonstration system CAISS. Specifically, we are enhancing our RDF-based policy engine to operate on a cloud, extend our cloud-centric RDF data manager to integrate with the policy manager, and build an integrated framework for CAISS. Our goal is to extend CAISS for a social media environment.

While our initial CAISS design and implementation will be the first system supporting cloud-centric AIS, it will operate only on a single trusted cloud and will therefore not support information sharing across multiple clouds. Furthermore, while CAISS's RDF-based, formal semantics approach to policy specification will be significantly more expressive than XACML-based approaches, it will not support an enhanced machine interpretability of content since RDF does not provide a sufficiently rich vocabulary (e.g., support for classes and properties). Phase 2 will therefore develop a fully functional and robust AIS system called CAISS++ that addresses these deficiencies. The preliminary design for CAISS++ is completed and will be discussed later in this chapter. CAISS is an important stepping-stone toward CAISS++ because CAISS can be used as a baseline framework against which CAISS++ can be compared along several performance dimensions, such as storage model efficiency and ontology language (OWL)-based policy expressiveness. Furthermore, since CAISS and CAISS++ share the same core components (policy engine and query processor), the lessons learned from the implementation and integration of these components in CAISS will be invaluable during the development of CAISS++. Finally, the evaluation and testing of CAISS will provide us with important insights into the shortcomings of CAISS, which can then be systematically addressed in the implementation of CAISS++.

We will also conduct a formal analysis of policy specifications and the software-level protection mechanisms that enforce them to provide exceptionally high-assurance security guarantees for the resulting system. We envisage CAISS++ to be used in highly mission-critical applications. Therefore, it becomes imperative to provide guarantees that the policies are enforced in a provably correct manner. We have extensive expertise in formal policy analysis ([JONE10], [JONE11]) and their enforcement via machine-certified, in-line reference monitors ([HAML06a], [HAML06b], [SRID10]). Such analyses will be leveraged to model and certify security properties enforced by core software components in the trusted computing base of CAISS++.

CAISS++ will be a breakthrough technology for information sharing due to the fact that it uses a novel combination of cloud-centric policy specification and enforcement along with a cloud-centric data storage and efficient query evaluation. CAISS++ will make use of ontologies, a sublanguage of the web ontology language (OWL), to build policies. A mixture of such ontologies with a semantic web-based rule language (e.g., SWRL) facilitates distributed reasoning on the policies to enforce security. Additionally, CAISS++ will include an RDF-processing engine that provides cost-based optimization for evaluating SPARQL queries based on information sharing policies.

25.3 SYSTEM DESIGN

25.3.1 Design of CAISS

We are enhancing our tools developed for AFOSR on (i) secure cloud query processing with semantic web data and (ii) semantic web-based policy engine to develop CAISS. Details of our tools are given in Section 25.4 (under related work). In this section, we will discuss the enhancements to be made to our tools to develop CAISS.

First, our RDF-based policy engine enforces access control, redaction, and inference control policies on data represented as RDF graphs. Second, our cloud SPARQL QE for RDF data uses the Hadoop/MapReduce framework. Note that Hadoop is the Apache-distributed file system and MapReduce sits on top of Hadoop and carries out job scheduling. As in the case of our cloud-based relational query processor prototype [THUR10], our SPARQL QE also handles policies specified in XACML, and the policy engine implements the XACML protocol. The use of XACML as a policy language requires extensive knowledge about the general concepts used in the design of XACML. Thus, policy authoring in XACML requires a steep learning curve, and is therefore a task that is left to an experienced administrator. A second disadvantage of using XACML is related to performance. Current implementations of XACML require an access request to be evaluated against every policy in the system until a policy applies to the incoming request. This strategy is sufficient for systems with relatively few users and policies. However, for systems with a large number of users and a substantial number of access requests, the aforementioned strategy becomes a performance bottleneck. Finally, XACML is not sufficiently expressive to capture the semantics of information sharing policies. Prior research has shown that semantic web-based policies are far more expressive. This is because semantic web technologies are based on a description logic (DL) and have the power to represent knowledge as well as reason about knowledge. Therefore, our first step is to replace the XACML-based policy engine with a semantic web-based policy engine. Since we already have our RDF-based policy engine for the phase 1 prototype, we will enhance this engine and integrate it with our SPARQL query processor. Since our policy engine is based on RDF and our query processor also manages large RDF graphs, there will be no impedance mismatch between the data and the policies.

Enhanced Policy Engine: Our current policy engine has a limitation in that it does not operate in a cloud. Therefore, we will port our RDF policy engine to the cloud environment and integrate it with the SPARQL QE for federated query processing in the cloud. Our policy engine will benefit from the scalability and the distributed platform offered by Hadoop's MapReduce framework to answer SPARQL queries over large distributed RDF triple stores (billions of RDF triples). The reasons for using RDF as our data model are as follows: (1) RDF allows us to achieve data interoperability between the seemingly disparate sources of information that are catalogued by each agency/organization separately; (2) the use of RDF allows participating agencies to create data-centric applications that make use of the integrated data that is now available to them; and (3) since the RDF does not require the use of an explicit schema for data generation, it can be easily adapted to ever-changing user requirements. The policy engine's flexibility is based on its accepting high-level policies and executing them as query rules over a directed RDF graph representation of the data. While our prior work focusses on provenance data and access control policies, our CAISS prototype will be flexible enough to handle data represented in RDF and will include information-sharing policies. The strength of our policy engine is that it can handle any type of policy that could be represented using RDF and horn logic rules.

The second limitation of our policy engine is that it currently addresses certain types of policies such as confidentiality, privacy, and redaction policies. We need to incorporate information-sharing policies into our policy engine. We have however conducted simulation studies for incentive-based AIS as well as AIS prototypes in the cloud. We have defined a number of information-sharing policies such as "US gives information to UK provided UK does not share it with India." We specify such policies in RDF and incorporate them to be processed by our enhanced policy engine.

Enhanced SPARQL Query Processor: While we have a tool that will execute SPARQL queries over large RDF graphs on Hadoop, there is still the need for supporting path queries (i.e., SPARQL queries that provide answers to a request for paths in an RDF graph). An RDF triple can be viewed as an arc from the subject to object with the predicate used to label the arc. The answers to the SPARQL query are based on reachability (i.e., the paths between a source node and a target node). The concatenation of the labels on the arcs along a path can be thought of as a word belonging to the answer set of the path query. Each term of a word is contributed by some predicate label of a triple in the RDF graph. We have designed an algorithm to determine the candidate triples as an answer set in a distributed RDF graph. First, the RDF document is converted to an *N*-triple file that is split based on predicate labels. A term in a word could correspond to some predicate file. Second, we form the word by tracing an appropriate path in the distributed RDF graph. We use MapReduce jobs to build the word and to get the candidate RDF triples as an order set. Finally, we return all of the set of ordered RDF triples as the answers to the corresponding SPARQL query.

Integration Framework: Figure 25.2 provides an overview of the CAISS architecture. The integration of the cloud-centric RDF policy engine with the enhanced SPARQL query processor must address the following. First, we need to make sure that RDF-based policies can be stored in the existing storage schema used by the query processor. Second, we need to ensure that the enhanced query processor is able to efficiently evaluate policies (i.e., path queries) over

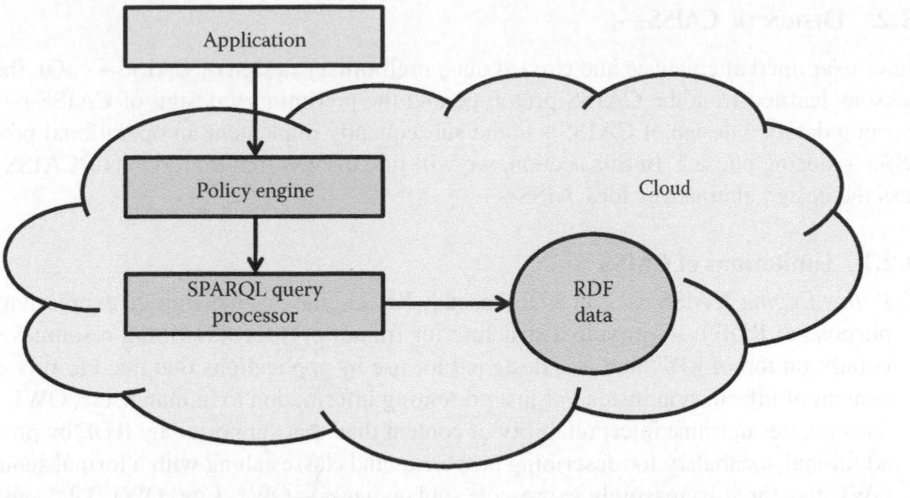

FIGURE 25.2 CAISS prototype overview.

the underlying RDF storage. Finally, we need to conduct a performance evaluation of CAISS to verify that it meets the performance requirements of various participating agencies. Figure 25.3 illustrates the concept of operation of CAISS. Here, multiple agencies will share data in a single cloud. The enhanced policy engine and the cloud-centric SPARQL query processor will enforce the information-sharing policies. This proof of concept system will drive the detailed design and implementation of CAISS++.

There are several benefits in developing a proof of concept prototype such as CAISS before we embark on CAISS++. First, CAISS itself is useful to share data within a single cloud. Second, we will have a baseline system that we can compare against with respect to efficiency and ease of use when we implement CAISS++. Third, this will give us valuable lessons with respect to the integration of the different pieces required for AIS in the cloud. Finally, by running different scenarios on CAISS, we can identify potential performance bottlenecks that need to be addressed in CAISS++.

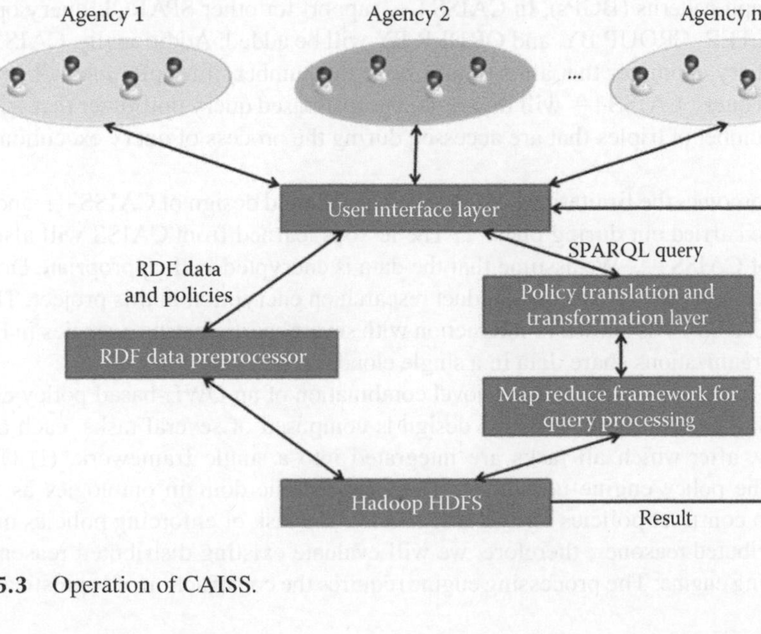

FIGURE 25.3 Operation of CAISS.

25.3.2 Design of CAISS++

We have examined alternatives and carried out a preliminary design of CAISS++. On the basis of the lessons learned from the CAISS prototype and the preliminary design of CAISS++, we will carry out a detailed design of CAISS++ and subsequently implement an operational prototype of CAISS++ during phase 2. In this section, we will first discuss the limitations of CAISS and then discuss the design alternatives for CAISS++.

25.3.2.1 Limitations of CAISS

1. *Policy Engine*: CAISS uses an RDF-based policy engine that has limited expressivity. The purpose of RDF is to provide a structure (or framework) for describing resources. OWL is built on top of RDF, and it is designed for use by applications that need to process the content of information instead of just presenting information to human users. OWL facilitates greater machine interpretability of content than that supported by RDF by providing additional vocabulary for describing properties and classes along with a formal semantics. OWL has three increasingly expressive sublanguages—OWL Lite, OWL DL, and OWL Full—and one has the freedom to choose a suitable sublanguage based on application requirements. In CAISS++, we plan to make use of OWL, which is much more expressive than RDF, to model security policies through organization-specific domain ontologies, as well as a system-wide upper ontology. (Note that CAISS++ will reuse an organization's existing domain ontology or facilitate the creation of a new domain ontology if it does not exist. Additionally, we have to engineer the upper ontology that will be used by the centralized component of CAISS++.) Additionally, CAISS++ will make use of a distributed reasoning algorithm that will leverage ontologies to enforce security policies.
2. *Hadoop Storage Architecture*: CAISS uses a static storage model wherein a user provides the system with RDF data only once during the initialization step. Thereafter, a user is not allowed to update the existing data. On the other hand, CAISS++ attempts to provide a flexible storage model to users. In CAISS++, a user is allowed to append new data to the existing RDF data stored in Hadoop Distributed File System (HDFS). Note that only allowing a user to append new data rather than deleting/modifying existing data comes from the append-only restriction for files that is enforced by HDFS.
3. *SPARQL Query Processor*: CAISS only supports simple SPARQL queries that make use of basic graph patterns (BGPs). In CAISS++, support for other SPARQL query operators such as FILTER, GROUP BY, and ORDER BY will be added. Additionally, CAISS uses a heuristic query optimizer that aims to minimize the number of MapReduce jobs required to answer a query. CAISS++ will incorporate a cost-based query optimizer that will minimize the number of triples that are accessed during the process of query execution.

CAISS++ overcomes the limitations of CAISS. The detailed design of CAISS++ and its implementation will be carried out during phase 2. The lessons learned from CAISS will also drive the detailed design of CAISS++. We assume that the data is encrypted with appropriate DoD encryption technologies and therefore will not conduct research on encryption in this project. The concept of operation for CAISS++ is shown in interaction with several participating agencies in Figure 25.4 where multiple organizations share data in a single cloud.

The design of CAISS++ is based on a novel combination of an OWL-based policy engine with an RDF-processing engine. Therefore, this design is composed of several tasks, each of which is solved separately, after which all tasks are integrated into a single framework. (1) OWL-based policy engine: The policy engine uses a set of agency-specific domain ontologies as well as an upper ontology to construct policies for the task of AIS. The task of enforcing policies may require the use of a distributed reasoner; therefore, we will evaluate existing distributed reasoners (DRs). (2) RDF-processing engine: The processing engine requires the construction of sophisticated storage

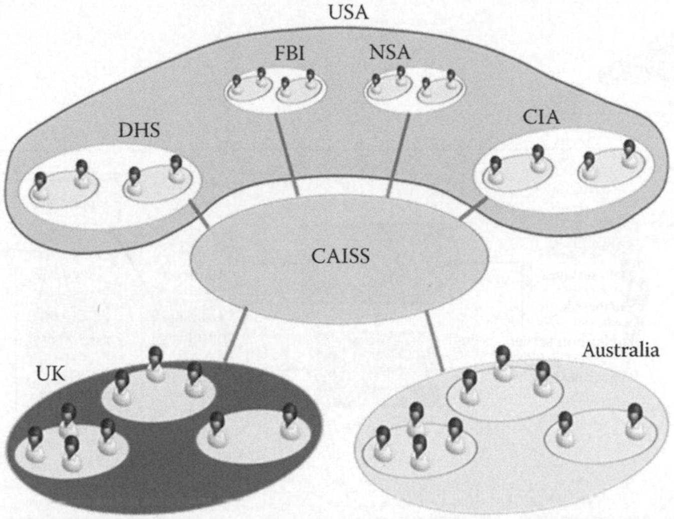

FIGURE 25.4 CAISS++ scenario.

architectures as well as an efficient query processor. (3) Integration Framework: The final task is to combine the policy engine with the processing engine into an integrated framework. The initial design of CAISS++ will be based on a trade-off between simplicity of design vs. its scalability and efficiency. The first design alternative is known as centralized CAISS++ and it chooses simplicity as the trade-off whereas the second design alternative (known as decentralized CAISS++) chooses scalability and efficiency as the trade-off. Finally, we also provide a hybrid CAISS++ architecture that tries to combine the benefits of both, centralized and decentralized CAISS++. Since CAISS++ follows a requirements-driven design, the division of tasks that we outlined above to achieve AIS are present in each of the approaches that we present next.

Centralized CAISS++: Figure 25.5 illustrates two agencies interacting through Centralized CAISS++. Centralized CAISS++ consists of shared cloud storage to store the shared data. All the participating agencies store their respective knowledge bases consisting of domain ontology with corresponding instance data. Centralized CAISS++ also consists of an upper ontology, a QE, and a DR. The upper ontology is used to capture the domain knowledge that is common across the domains of participating agencies, whereas domain ontology captures the knowledge specific to a given agency or a domain. Note that the domain ontology for a given agency will be protected from the domain ontologies of other participating agencies. Policies can either be captured in the upper ontology or in any of the domain ontologies depending on their scope of applicability. Note that the domain ontology for a given agency will be protected from domain ontologies of other participating agencies.

The design of an upper ontology as well as domain ontologies that capture the requirements of the participating agencies is a significant research area and is the focus of the ontology engineering problem. Ontologies will be created using suitable dialects of OWL that are based on DLs that are usually decidable fragments of the first-order logic and will be the basis for providing sound formal semantics. Having represented knowledge in terms of ontologies, reasoning will be done using existing optimized reasoning algorithms. Query answering will leverage reasoning algorithms to formulate and answer intelligent queries. The encoding of policies in OWL will ensure that they are enforced in a provably correct manner. Later, we present an ongoing research project at The University of Texas at Dallas that focusses on providing a general framework for enforcing policies in a provably correct manner using the same underlying technologies. This work can be leveraged toward modeling and enforcement of security policies in CAISS++. The instance data can choose between several available data storage formats. The QE receives queries from the participating agencies, parses the query,

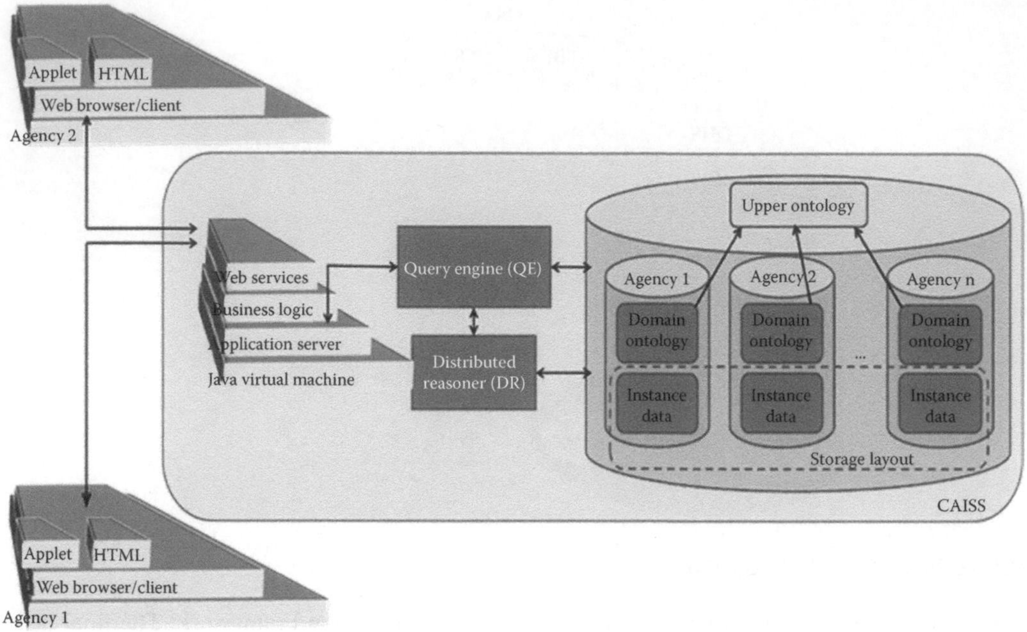

FIGURE 25.5 Centralized CAISS++.

and determines whether the computation requires the use of a DR. If the query is simple and does not require the use of a reasoner, the QE executes the query directly over the shared knowledge base. Once the query result has been computed, the result is returned to the querying agency. If, however, the query is complex and requires inferences over the given data, the QE uses the DR to compute the inferences and then returns the result to the querying agency. A distributed DL reasoner differs from a traditional DL reasoner in its ability to perform reasoning over cloud data storage using the MapReduce framework. During the preliminary design of CAISS++ in Phase 1, we will conduct a thorough investigation of the available DRs using existing benchmarks such as the Lehigh University Benchmark (LUBM) [GUO05]. The goal of this investigation is to determine whether we can use one of the existing reasoners or we need to build our own DR. In Figure 25.5, an agency is illustrated as a stack consisting of a web browser, an applet, and HTML. An agency uses the web browser to send the queries to CAISS++, which are handled by the query processor.

The main differences between centralized CAISS++ and CAISS are as follows: (1) CAISS will use RDF to encode security policies, whereas centralized CAISS++ will use a suitable sublanguage of OWL that is more expressive than RDF and can therefore capture the security policies better. (2) The SPARQL query processor in CAISS will support a limited subset of SPARQL expressivity, that is, it will provide support only for BGPs, whereas the SPARQL query processor in centralized CAISS++ will be designed to support the maximum expressivity of SPARQL. (3) The Hadoop storage architecture used in CAISS only supports data insertion during an initialization step. However, when data needs to be updated, the entire RDF graph is deleted and a new dataset is inserted in its place. On the other hand, centralized CAISS++, in addition to supporting the previous feature, also opens up HDFS's append-only feature to users. This feature allows users to append new information to the data that they have previously uploaded to the system.

Decentralized CAISS++: Figure 25.6 illustrates two agencies in interaction with decentralized CAISS++. It consists of two parts, namely, global CAISS++ and local CAISS++. The global CAISS++ consists of a shared cloud storage that is used by the participating agencies to store only their respective domain ontologies and not the instance data unlike the centralized CAISS++. Note that domain ontologies for various organizations will be sensitive; therefore, CAISS++ will make

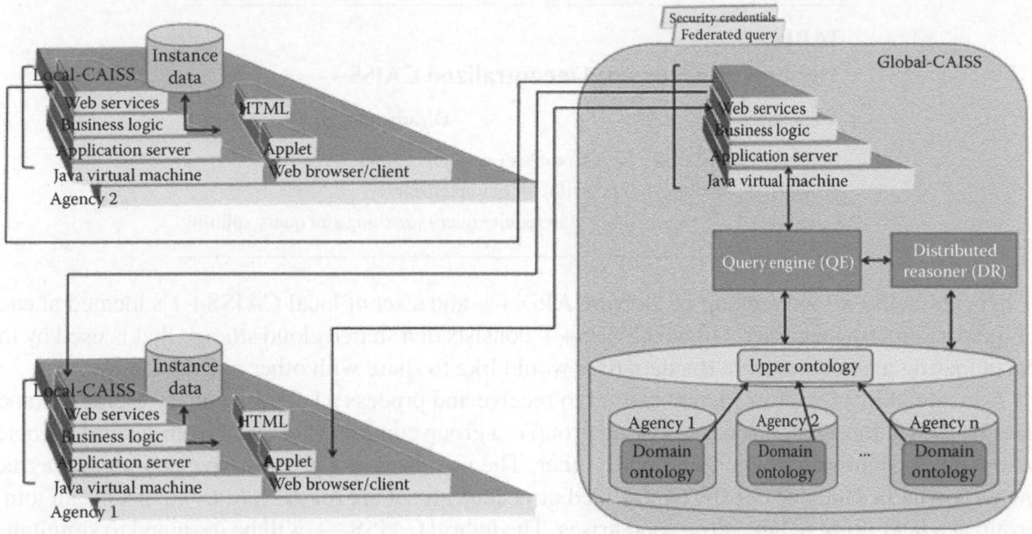

FIGURE 25.6 Decentralized CAISS++.

use of its own domain ontology to protect a participating agency from accessing other domain ontologies. When a user from an agency queries the CAISS++ data store, global CAISS++ processes the query in two steps. In the first step, it performs a check to verify whether the user is authorized to perform the action specified in the query. If the result of step 1 verifies the user as an authorized user, then it proceeds to step 2 of query processing. In the second step, global CAISS++ federates the actual query to the participating agencies. The query is then processed by the local CAISS++ of a participating agency. The result of computation is then returned to the global CAISS++ that aggregates the final result, and returns it to the user. Step 2 of query processing may involve query splitting if the data required to answer a query spans multiple domains. In this case, the results of subqueries from several agencies (their local CAISS++) will need to be combined for further query processing. Once the results are merged and the final result is computed, the result is returned to the user of the querying agency. The figure illustrates the agencies with a set of two stacks, one of which corresponds to the local CAISS++ and the other consisting of a web browser, an applet, and HTML, which is used by an agency to query global CAISS++. Table 25.1 shows the pros and cons of the centralized CAISS++ approach, while Table 25.2 shows the pros and cons of the decentralized CAISS++ approach.

Hybrid CAISS++: Figure 25.7 illustrates an overview of hybrid CAISS++ that leverages the benefits of centralized CAISS++ as well as decentralized CAISS++. A hybrid CAISS++ architecture is illustrated in Figure 25.8. It is a flexible design alternative as the users of the participating agencies have the freedom to choose between centralized CAISS++ and decentralized CAISS++.

TABLE 25.1
The Pros and Cons of Centralized CAISS++

Pros	Cons
Simple approach	Difficult to update data. Expensive approach as data needs to be migrated to central storage on each update or a set of updates
Ease of implementation	Leads to data duplication
Easier to query	If data is available in different formats it needs to be homogenized by translating it to RDF

TABLE 25.2
The Pros and Cons of Decentralized CAISS++

Advantages	Disadvantages
No duplication of data	Complex query processing
Scalable and flexible	Difficult to implement
Efficient	May require query rewriting and query splitting

A hybrid CAISS++ is made up of global CAISS++ and a set of local CAISS++'s located at each of the participating agencies. Global CAISS++ consists of a shared cloud storage that is used by the participating agencies to store the data they would like to share with other agencies.

A local CAISS++ of an agency is used to receive and process a federated query on the instance data located at the agency. A participating group is a group comprised of users from several agencies who want to share information with each other. The members of a group arrive at a mutual agreement on whether they opt for the centralized or decentralized approach. Additional users can join a group at a later point in time if the need arises. The hybrid CAISS++ will be designed to simultaneously support a set of participating groups. Additionally, a user can belong to several participating groups at the same time. We describe a few use-case scenarios that illustrate the operation.

1. The first case corresponds to the scenario where a set of users who want to securely share information with each other opt for a centralized approach. Suppose users from Agency 1 want to share information with users of Agency 2 and vice versa; then both the agencies store their knowledge bases comprising of domain ontology and instance data on the shared cloud storage located at global CAISS++. The centralized CAISS++ approach works by having the participating agencies arrive at mutual trust on using the central cloud storage. Subsequently, information sharing proceeds as in centralized CAISS++.
2. The second case corresponds to the scenario where a set of users opts for a decentralized approach. For example, Agencies 3, 4, and 5 wish to share information with each other and

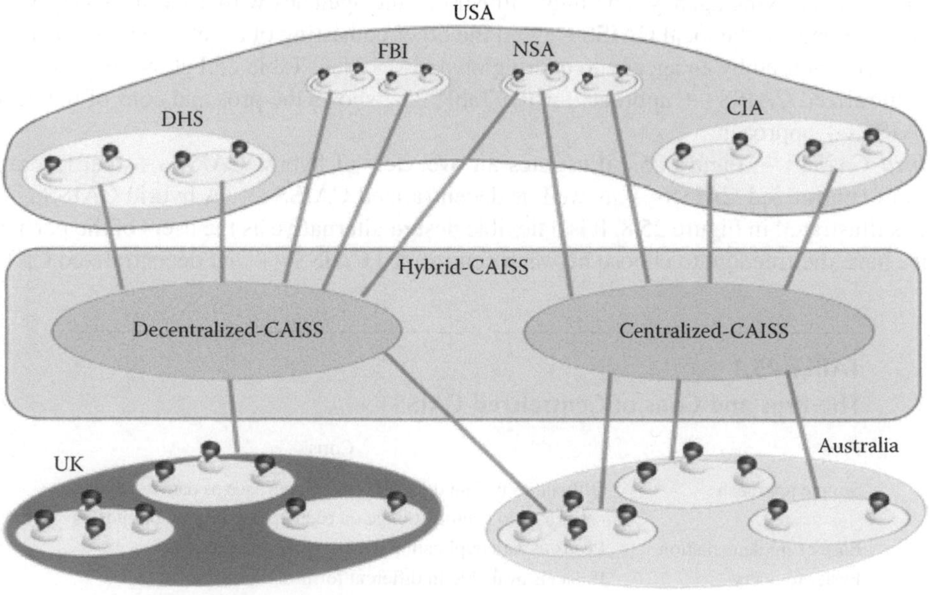

FIGURE 25.7 Hybrid CAISS++ overview.

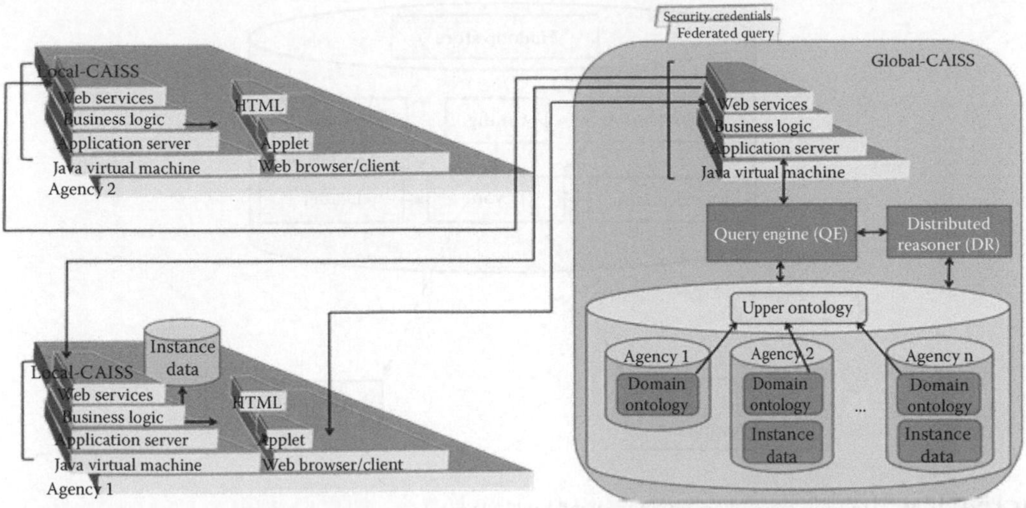

FIGURE 25.8 Hybrid CAISS++ architecture.

mutually opt for the decentralized approach. All the three agencies store their respective domain ontologies at the central cloud storage, and this information is only accessible to the members of this group. The subsequent information-sharing process proceeds in the manner described earlier for the decentralized CAISS++ approach.

3. The third case corresponds to the scenario where a user of an agency belongs to multiple participating groups, some of which opt for the centralized approach and others for the decentralized approach. Since the user is a part of a group using the centralized approach to sharing, he/she needs to make his/her data available to the group by shipping his/her data to the central cloud storage. Additionally, since the user is also a part of a group using the decentralized approach for sharing, he/she needs to respond to the federated query with the help of the local CAISS++ located at his/her agency.

Table 25.3 shows the trade-offs between the different approaches, and this will enable users to choose a suitable approach of AIS based on their application requirements. Next we describe details of the cloud storage mechanism that makes use of Hadoop to store the knowledge bases from various agencies and then discuss the details of distributed SPARQL query processing over the cloud storage.

In Figure 25.9, we present an architectural overview of our Hadoop-based RDF storage and retrieval framework. We use the concept of a "Store" to provide data loading and querying capabilities on RDF

TABLE 25.3
A Comparison of the Three Approaches Based on Functionality Hadoop Storage Architecture

Functionality	Centralized CAISS++	Decentralized CAISS++	Hybrid CAISS++
No data duplication	X	√	May be
Flexibility	X	X	√
Scalablility	X	√	√
Efficiency	√	√	√
Simplicity—No query rewriting	√	X	X
Trusted centralized cloud data storage	√	X	X

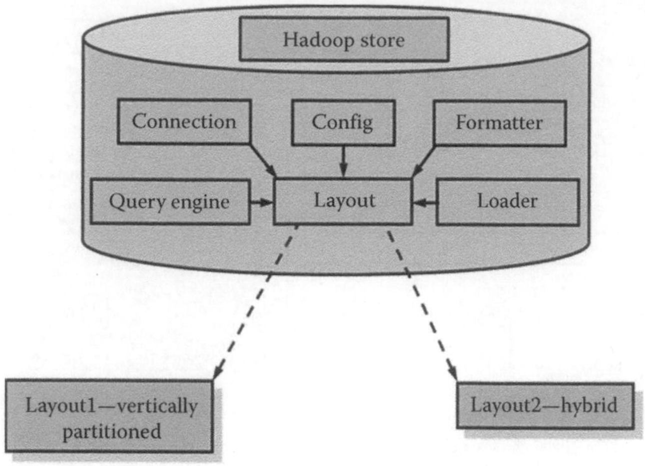

FIGURE 25.9 Hadoop storage architecture used by CAISS++.

graphs that are stored in the underlying HDFS. A store represents a single RDF dataset and can therefore contain several RDF graphs, each with its own separate layout. All operations on an RDF graph are then implicitly converted into operations on the underlying layout including the following:

- *Layout Formatter*: This block performs the function of formatting a layout, which is the process of deleting all triples in an RDF graph while preserving the directory structure used to store that graph.
- *Loader*: This block performs loading of triples into a layout.
- *Query Engine*: This block allows a user to query a layout using an SPARQL query. Since our framework operates on the underlying HDFS, the querying mechanism on a layout involves translating an SPARQL query into a possible pipeline of MapReduce jobs and then executing this pipeline on a layout.
- *Connection*: This block maintains the necessary connections and configurations with the underlying HDFS.
- *Config*: This block maintains configuration information such as graph names for each of the RDF graphs that make up a store.

Since RDF data will be stored under different HDFS folders in separate files as a part of our storage schema, we need to adopt certain naming conventions for such folders and files.

Naming Conventions: A Hadoop store can be composed of several distinct RDF graphs in our framework. Therefore, a separate folder will be created in HDFS for each such Hadoop Store. The name of this folder will correspond to the name that has been selected for the given store. Furthermore, an RDF graph is divided into several files in our framework depending on the storage layout that is selected. Therefore, a separate folder will be created in HDFS for each distinct RDF graph. The name of this folder is defined to be "default" for the default RDF graph, while for a named RDF graph, the uniform resource identifier (URI) of the graph is used as the folder name. We use the abstraction of a store in our framework for the reason that this will simplify the management of data belonging to various agencies. Two of the layouts to be supported by our framework are given below. These layouts use a varying number of HDFS files to store RDF data.

Vertically Partitioned Layout: Figure 25.10 presents the storage schema for the vertically partitioned layout. For every unique predicate contained in an RDF graph, this layout creates a separate file using the name of the predicate as the file name, in the underlying HDFS. Note that only the local name part of a predicate Universal Resource Identifier (URI) is used in a file name and a

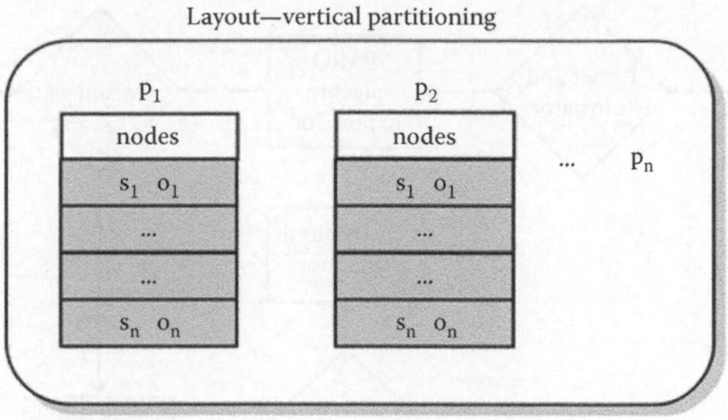

FIGURE 25.10 Vertically partitioned layout.

separate mapping exists between a file name and the predicate URI. A file for a given predicate contains a separate line for every triple that contains that predicate. This line stores the subject and object values that make up the triple. This schema will lead to significant storage space savings since moving the predicate name to the name of a file completely eliminates the storage of this predicate value. However, multiple occurrences of the same resource URI or literal value will be stored multiple times across all files as well as within a file. Additionally, an SPARQL query may need to look up multiple files to ensure that a complete result is returned to a user, for example, a query to find all triples that belong to a specific subject or an object.

Hybrid Layout: Figure 25.11 presents the storage schema for the hybrid layout. This layout is an extension of the vertically partitioned layout, since in addition to the separate files that are created for every unique predicate in an RDF graph, it also creates a separate triples file containing all the triples in the SPO (subject, predicate, object) format. The advantage of having such a file is that it directly gives us all triples belonging to a certain subject or an object. Recall that such a search operation required scanning through multiple files in the vertically partitioned layout. The storage space efficiency of this layout is not as good as the vertically partitioned layout due to the addition of the triples file. However, an SPARQL query to find all triples belonging to a certain subject or object could be performed more efficiently using this layout.

Distributed processing of SPARQL: Query processing in CAISS++ comprises of several steps (Figure 25.12). The first step is query parsing and translation where a given SPARQL query is first parsed to verify syntactic correctness, and then a parse tree corresponding to the input query is built. The parse tree is then translated into an SPARQL algebra expression. Since a given SPARQL query can have multiple equivalent SPARQL algebra expressions, we annotate each such expression with

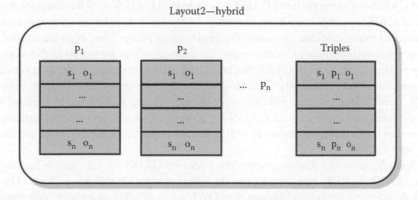

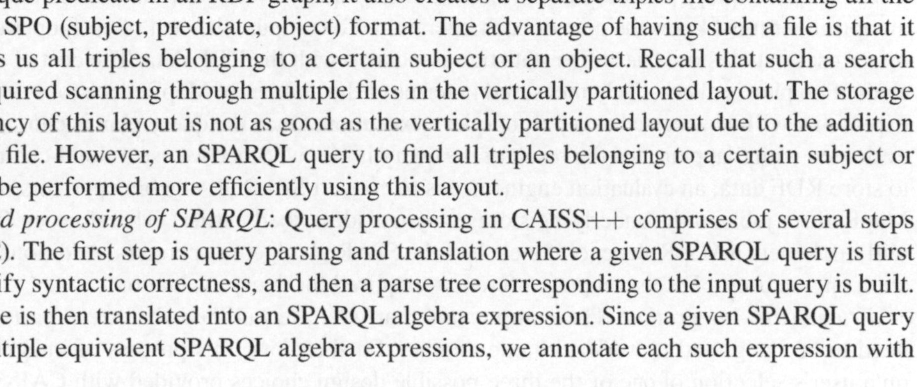

FIGURE 25.11 Hybrid layout.

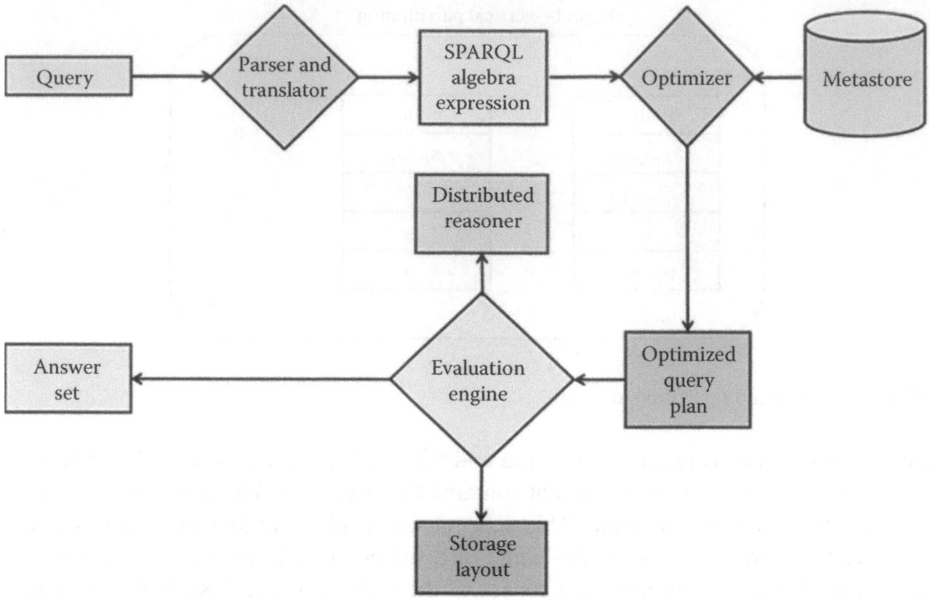

FIGURE 25.12 Distributed processing of SPARQL in CAISS++.

instructions on how to evaluate each operation in this expression. Such annotated SPARQL algebra expressions correspond to query-evaluation plans that serve as the input to the optimizer. The optimizer selects a query plan that minimizes the cost of query evaluation. In order to optimize a query, an optimizer must know the cost of each operation. To compute the cost of each operation, the optimizer uses a metastore that stores statistics associated with the RDF data. The cost of a given query-evaluation plan is alternatively measured in terms of the number of MapReduce jobs or the number of triples that will be accessed as a part of query execution. Once the query plan is chosen, the query is evaluated with that plan, and the result of the query is output. Since we use a cloud-centric framework to store RDF data, an evaluation engine needs to convert SPARQL algebra operators into equivalent MapReduce jobs on the underlying storage layouts (described earlier). Therefore, in CAISS++, we will implement a MapReduce job for each of the SPARQL algebra operators. Additionally, the evaluation engine uses a DR to compute inferences required for query evaluation.

Framework Integration: The components that we have outlined that are a part of CAISS++ need to be integrated to work with one another. Furthermore, this process of integration depends on a user's selection of one of the three possible design choices provided with CAISS++, namely, centralized CAISS++, decentralized CAISS++, or hybrid CAISS++. The integration of the various pieces of CAISS++ that have been presented so far needs to take into account several issues. First, we need to make sure that our ontology engineering process has been successful in capturing an agency's requirements and, additionally, the ontologies can be stored in the storage schema used by the Hadoop storage architecture. Secondly, we need to ensure that the distributed SPARQL query processor is able to efficiently evaluate queries (i.e., user-generated SPARQL queries as well as SPARQL queries that evaluate policies) over the underlying RDF storage. Finally, we need to conduct a performance evaluation of CAISS++ to verify that it meets the performance requirements of various participating agencies as well as leads to significant performance advantages when compared with CAISS.

Policy Specification and Enforcement: The users of CAISS++ can use a language of their choice (e.g., XACML, RDF, Rei, etc.) to specify their information sharing policies. These policies will be translated into a suitable sublanguage of OWL using existing or custom-built translators. We will extend our policy engine for CAISS to handle policies specified in OWL. In addition to RDF policies, our current policy engine can handle policies in OWL for implementing role-based access control, inference control, and social network analysis.

25.3.3 Formal Policy Analysis

Our framework is applicable to a variety of mission-critical, high-assurance applications that span multiple possibly mutually distrusting organizations. In order to provide maximal security assurance in such settings, it is important to establish strong formal guarantees regarding the correctness of the system and the policies it enforces. To that end, we examined the development of an infrastructure for constructing formal, machine-checkable proofs of important system properties and policy analyses for our system. While machine-checkable proofs can be very difficult and time-consuming to construct for many large software systems, our choice of SPARQL, RDF, and OWL as query, ontology, and policy languages opens unique opportunities to elegantly formulate such proofs in a logic programming environment. We will encode policies, policy-rewriting algorithms, and security properties as a rule-based, logical derivation system in Prolog, and will apply model-checking and theorem-proving systems such as ACL2 to produce machine-checkable proofs that these properties are obeyed by the system. Properties that we intend to consider in our model include soundness, transparency, consistency, and completeness. The results of our formal policy analysis will drive our detailed design and implementation of CAISS++. To our knowledge, none of the prior work has focused on such formal policy analysis for SPARQL, RDF, and OWL. Our extensive research on formal policy analysis with in-line reference monitors is discussed under related work.

25.3.4 Implementation Approach

The implementation of CAISS was carried out in Java, and is based on a flexible design where we can plug and play multiple components. A service provider and/or user will have the flexibility to use the SPARQL query processor as well as the RDF-based policy engine as separate components or combine them. The open source component used for CAISS will include the Pellet reasoner as well as our in-house tools such as the SPARQL query processor on the Hadoop/MapReduce framework and the cloud-centric RDF policy engine. CAISS will allow us to demonstrate basic AIS scenarios on our cloud-based framework.

We have also completed a preliminary implementation of CAISS+. In the implementation of CAISS++, we have used Java as the programming language. We have used Protégé as our ontology editor during the process of ontology engineering which includes designing domain ontologies as well as the upper ontology. In the future, we will evaluate several existing distributed reasoning algorithms such as WebPIE and QueryPIE to determine the best algorithm that matches an agency's requirements. The selected algorithm will then be used to perform reasoning over OWL-based security policies. Additionally, the design of the Hadoop storage architecture is based on Jena's SPARQL database (SDB) architecture and features some of the functionalities that are available with Jena SDB. The SPARQL QE also features the code written in Java. This code consists of several modules including query parsing and translation, query optimization, and query execution. The query execution module will consist of MapReduce jobs for the various operators of the SPARQL language. Finally, our web-based user interface makes use of several components such as JBoss, EJB, JSF, among others. We are also exploring the use of other big data technologies such as Storm and Spark for our cloud platform. In addition, NoSQL database systems such as Hbase and CouchDB are also being explored for integration into our AIS platform.

25.4 RELATED WORK

We will first provide an overview of our research directly relevant to our project and then discuss overall related work. We will also discuss product/technology competition.

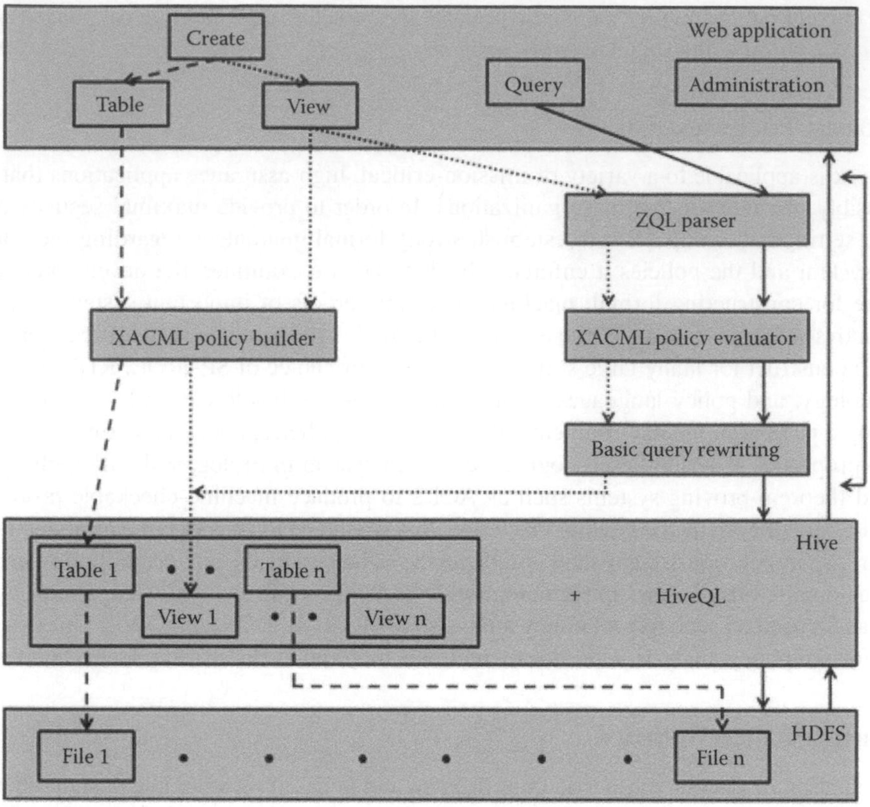

FIGURE 25.13 Hive-based assured cloud query processing.

25.4.1 Our Related Research

Secure Data Storage and Retrieval in the Cloud: We have built a web-based application that combines existing cloud computing technologies such as Hadoop, an open source distributed file system, and Hive data warehouse infrastructure built on top of Hadoop with an XACML policy-based security mechanism to allow collaborating organizations to securely store and retrieve large amounts of data ([HUSA11], [THUR10], [UTD1]). Figure 25.13 presents the architecture of our system. We use the services provided by the Hive layer and Hadoop including the Hadoop Distributed File System (HDFS) layer that makes up the storage layer of Hadoop and allows the storage of data blocks across a cluster of nodes. The layers we have implemented include the web application layer, the ZQL parser layer, the XACML policy layer, and the query rewriting layer. The web application layer is the only interface provided by our system to the user to access the cloud infrastructure. The ZQL parser [ZQL] layer takes as input any query submitted by a user and either proceeds to the XACML policy evaluator if the query is successfully parsed or returns an error message to the user. The XACML policy layer is used to build (XACML policy builder) and evaluate (XACML policy evaluation) XACML policies. The basic query rewriting layer rewrites SQL queries entered by the user. The Hive layer is used to manage relational data that is stored in the underlying HDFS [THUS09]. In addition, we have also designed and implemented secure storage and query processing in a hybrid cloud [KHAD11].

Secure SPARQL Query Processing on the Cloud: We have developed a framework to query RDF data stored over Hadoop as shown in Figure 25.14 (also discussed in Chapter 23). We used the Pellet reasoner to reason at various stages. We carried out real-time query reasoning using the pellet libraries coupled with Hadoop's MapReduce functionalities. Our RDF query

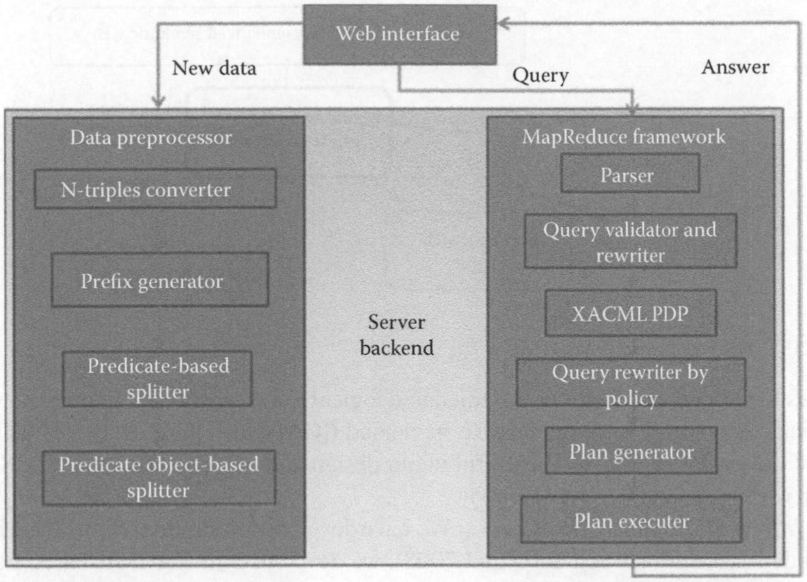

FIGURE 25.14. SPARQL-based assured cloud query processing.

processing is composed of two main steps: (1) the preprocessing and (2) the query optimization and execution.

Preprocessing: In order to execute an SPARQL query on RDF data, we carried out data preprocessing steps and stored the preprocessed data in HDFS. A separate MapReduce task was written to perform the conversion of RDF/XML data into *N*-triples as well as for prefix generation. Our storage strategy is based on predicate splits [HUSA11].

Query Execution and Optimization: We have developed an SPARQL query execution and optimization module for Hadoop. As our storage strategy is based on predicate splits, first, we examine the predicates present in the query. Second, we examine a subset of the input files that are matched with predicates. Third, SPARQL queries generally have many joins in them and all of these joins may not be possible to perform in a single MapReduce job. Therefore, we have developed an algorithm that decides the number of jobs required for each kind of query. As part of optimization, we applied a greedy strategy and cost-based optimization to reduce query-processing time. We have also developed an XACML-based centralized policy engine that will carry out federated RDF query processing on the cloud. Details of the enforcement strategy are given in [HAML10a], [HUSA11], and [KHAL10].

RDF Policy Engine: In our prior work [CADE11a], we have developed a policy engine to process RDF-based access control policies for RDF data. The policy engine is designed with the following features in mind: scalability, efficiency, and interoperability. This framework (Figure 25.15) can be used to execute various policies, including access control policies and redaction policies. It can also be used as a testbed for evaluating different policy sets over RDF data and to view the outcomes graphically. Our framework presents an interface that accepts a high-level policy, which is then translated into the required format. It takes a user's input query and returns a response that has been pruned using a set of user-defined policy constraints. The architecture is built using a modular approach; therefore, it is very flexible in that most of the modules can be extended or replaced by another application module. For example, a policy module implementing a discretionary access control (DAC) could be replaced entirely by an RBAC module or we may decide to enforce all our constraints based on a generalized redaction model. It should be noted that our policy engine also handles role-based access control policies specified in OWL and SWRL [CADE10]. In addition, it handles certain policies specified in OWL for inference control such as association-based policies

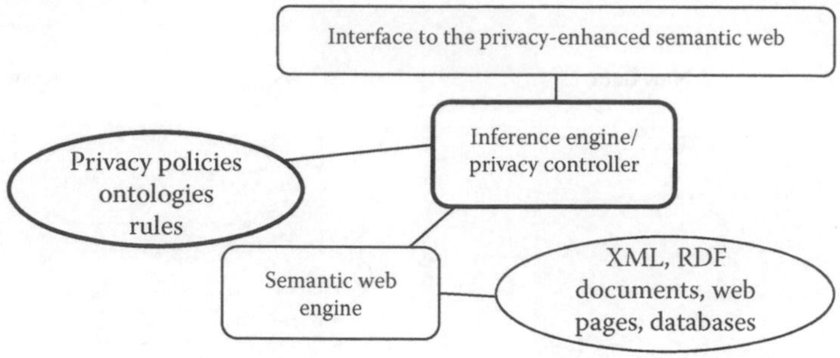

FIGURE 25.15 RDF policy engine.

where access to collections of entities is denied and logical policies where A implies B, and if access to B is denied, then access to A should also be denied ([CADE10], [CADE11b], [CARM09]). This capability of our policy engine will be useful in our design and implementation of CAISS++ where information is shared across multiple clouds.

Assured Information Sharing Prototypes: We have developed multiple systems for AIS. Under an AFOSR-funded project (between 2005 and 2008), we developed an XACML-based policy engine to function on top of relational databases and demonstrated the sharing of (simulated) medical data [THUR08]. In this implementation, we specified the policies in XACML and stored the data in multiple Oracle databases. When one organization requests data from another organization, the policies are examined and authorized data is released. In addition, we also conducted simulation studies on the amount of data that would be lost by enforcing the policies while information sharing. Under our Multidisciplinary University Research Initiative (MURI) project, also funded by AFOSR, we conducted simulation studies for incentive-based information sharing [KANT10]. We have also examined risk-based access control in an information-sharing scenario [CELI07]. In addition to access control policies, we have specified different types of policies including need-to-share policies and trust policies (e.g., A shared data with B provided B does not share the data with C). Note that the 9/11 Commission Report calls for the migration from the more restrictive need-to-know to the less restrictive need-to-share policies. These policies are key to support the specification of the directive concerning AIS obligations.

Formal Policy Analysis: By reducing high-level security policy specifications and system models to the level of the denotational and operational semantics of their binary-level implementations, our past work has developed formally machine-certifiable security enforcement mechanisms of a variety of complex software systems, including those implemented in .NET [HAML06b], ActionScript [SRID10], Java [JONE10], and native code [HAML10b]. Working at the binary level provides extremely high formal guarantees because it permits the tool chain that produces mission-critical software components to remain untrusted; the binary code produced by the chain can be certified directly. This strategy is an excellent match for CAISS++ because data-security-specification languages such as XACML and OWL can be elegantly reflected down to the binary level of bytecode languages with XML-aware system application program interfaces (APIs), such as Java bytecode. Our past work has applied binary instrumentation (e.g., in-lined reference monitoring) and a combination of binary type checking [HAML06b], model checking [SRID10], and automated theorem proving (e.g., via ACL2) to achieve fully automated machine certification of binary software in such domains.

25.4.2 Overall Related Research

While there are some related efforts, none of the efforts have provided a solution to AIS in the cloud, nor have they conducted such a formal policy analysis.

Secure Data Storage and Retrieval in the Cloud: Security for cloud has received recent attention [TALB09]. Some efforts on implementing at the infrastructure level have been reported [OMAL109].

Such development efforts are an important step toward securing cloud infrastructures but are only in their inception stages. The goal of our system is to add another layer of security above the security offered by Hadoop [UTD1]. Once the security offered by Hadoop becomes robust, it will only strengthen the effectiveness of our system. Similar efforts have been undertaken by Amazon and Microsoft for their cloud computing offerings ([AMAZ16], [MARS10]). However, this work falls in the public domain, whereas our system is designed for a private cloud infrastructure. This distinguishing factor makes our infrastructure "trusted" over public infrastructures where the data must be stored in an encrypted format.

SPARQL Query Processor: Only a handful of efforts have been reported on SPARQL query processing. These include BioMANTA [BIOM] and SHARD [SHAR11]. BioMANTA proposes extensions to RDF Molecules [DING05] and implements a MapReduce-based molecule store [NEWM08]. They use MapReduce to answer the queries. They have queried a maximum of 4 million triples. Our work differs in the following ways: first, we have queried 1 billion triples. Second, we have devised a storage schema which is tailored to improve query execution performance for RDF data. To our knowledge, we are the first to come up with a storage schema for RDF data using flat files in HDFS, and a MapReduce job determination algorithm to answer an SPARQL query. Scalable, high-performance, robust, and distributed (SHARD) is an RDF triple store using the Hadoop Cloudera distribution. This project shows initial results, demonstrating Hadoop's ability to improve scalability for RDF datasets. However, SHARD stores its data only in a triple store schema. It does no query planning or reordering, and its query processor will not minimize the number of Hadoop jobs. None of the efforts have incorporated security policies.

RDF-Based Policy Engine: There exists prior research devoted to the study of enforcing policies over RDF stores. These include the work in [CARM04] which uses RDF for policy specification and enforcement. In addition, the policies are generally written in RDF. In [JAIN06], the authors propose an access control model for RDF. Their model is based on RDF data semantics and incorporates RDF and RDF schema (RDFS) entailments. Here, protection is provided at the resource level, which adds granularity to their framework. Other frameworks enforcing policies over RDF\OWL include [KAGA02] and [USZO04]. [USZO04] describes KAoS, a policy and domain services framework that uses OWL, to represent both policies and domains. [KAGA02] introduces Rei, a policy framework that is flexible and allows different kinds of policies to be stated. Extensions to Rei have been proposed recently [KHAN10]. The policy-specification language allows users to develop declarative policies over domain-specific ontologies in RDF, DAML+OIL, and OWL. The authors in [REDD05] also introduced a prototype, RAP, for the implementation of an RDF store with integrated maintenance capabilities and access control. These frameworks, however, do not address cases where the RDF store can become very large or the case where the policies do not scale with the data. Under an IARPA-funded project, we have developed techniques for very large RDF graph processing [UTD2].

Hadoop Storage Architecture: There has been significant interest in large-scale distributed storage and retrieval techniques for RDF data. The theoretical designs of a parallel processing framework for RDF data are presented in the work done by Castagna et al. [CAST09]. This work advocates the use of a data-distribution model with varying levels of granularity such as the triple level, graph level, and dataset level. A query over such a distributed model is then divided into a set of subqueries over machines containing the distributed data. The results of all subqueries will then be merged to return a complete result to a user application. Several implementations of this theoretical concept exist in the research community. These efforts include the work done by Choi et al. [CHOI09] and Abraham et al. [ABRA10]. A separate technique that has been used to store and retrieve RDF data makes use of peer-to-peer systems ([ABER04], [CAI04], [HART07], [VALL06]). However, there are some drawbacks with such systems as peer-to-peer systems need to have super peers that store information about the distribution of RDF data among the peers. Another disadvantage is a need to federate an SPARQL query to every peer in the network.

Distributed Reasoning: The InteGrail system uses distributed reasoning, whose vision is to shape the European railway organization of the future [INTE09]. In [URBA09], authors have shown a scalable implementation of RDFS reasoning based on MapReduce, which can infer 30 billion triples from a real-world dataset in less than 2 hours, yielding an input and output throughput of 123.000 triples/s and 3.27 million triples/s, respectively. They have presented some nontrivial optimizations for encoding the RDFS ruleset in MapReduce and have evaluated the scalability of their implementation on a cluster of 64 compute nodes using several real-world datasets.

Access Control and Policy Ontology Modeling: There have been some attempts to model access control and policy models using semantic web technologies. In [CIRI07], authors have shown how OWL and DL can be used to build an access control system. They have developed a high-level OWL−DL ontology that expresses the elements of a role-based access control system and have built a domain-specific ontology that captures the features of a sample scenario. Finally, they have joined these two artifacts to take into account attributes in the dentition of the policies and in the access control decision. In [REUL10], authors first presented a security policy ontology based on the DOGMA, which is a formal ontology engineering framework. This ontology covers the core elements of security policies (i.e., condition, action, resource) and can easily be extended to represent specific security policies, such as access control policies. In [ANDE09], authors present an ontologically motivated approach to multilevel access control and provenance for information systems.

25.4.3 Commercial Developments

RDF Processing Engines: Research and commercial RDF processing engines include Jena by HP Labs, BigOWLIM, and RDF-3X. Although the storage schemas and query-processing mechanisms for some of these tools are proprietary, they are all based on some type of indexing strategy for RDF data. However, only a few tools exist that use a cloud-centric architecture for processing RDF data, and, moreover, these tools are not scalable to a very large number of triples. In contrast, our query processor in CAISS++ will be built as a planet-scale RDF processing engine that supports all SPARQL operators and will provide optimized execution strategies for SPARQL queries and can scale to billions of triples.

Semantic Web-Based Security Policy Engines: As stated in Section 25.2, the current work on semantic web-based policy specification and enforcement does not address the issues of policy generation and enforcement for massive amounts of data and support a large number of users.

Cloud: To the best of our knowledge, there is no significant commercial competition for cloud-centric AIS. Since we have taken a modular approach to the creation of our tools, we can iteratively refine each component (policy engine, storage architecture, and query processor) separately. Due to the component-based approach we have taken, we will be able to adapt to changes in the platforms we use (e.g., Hadoop, RDF, OWL, and SPARQL) without having to depend on the particular features of a given platform.

25.5 EXTENSIONS FOR BIG DATA-BASED SOCIAL MEDIA APPLICATIONS

There are several variations of the designs discussed in this chapter, which we can adapt for social media applications, utilizing big data management and analytics. First, members of a network may want to share data. Therefore, they could implement the information sharing policies, with each member having his/her own data store. In the second design, the members could use a shared space or a cloud to store the data and the policies and share the data securely.

The member could also belong to multiple social networks. That is, one person could belong to more than one network or a person could belong to just one network. In this case, a member could share more data with the members of his/her network while sharing limited data with members of another network. Also, different networks may use heterogeneous technologies for representation. Therefore, the heterogeneous representations have to be resolved. One could also develop a logical representation of the multiple networks and have mappings to the individual networks.

Over time the number of users in the multiple social networks could grow rapidly and the amount of data they store and share in the networks could be massive. Therefore, several of the BDMA technologies we have discussed in Chapter 7 as well as in other chapters in Sections I through III have to be explored for use in AIS between multiple social networks.

25.6 SUMMARY AND DIRECTIONS

This chapter has described our design and implementation of a cloud-based information-sharing system called CAISS that utilizes several technologies we have developed as well as open source tools. We also described the design of an ideal cloud-based assured information-sharing system called CAISS++.

We have developed a proof of concept prototype of both CAISS and a preliminary implementation of CAISS++. In the implementation of CAISS, we utilized our SPARQL query processor in the cloud with the policies specified in both XACML and RDF. Our policies include both access-control and information-sharing policies. In the implementation of CAISS+, we specified policies in OWL, developed the policy engine in the cloud, and integrated it with the SPARQL data engine. These systems are discussed in [CADE12a] and [CADE12b]. In the future, we will continue to enhance our prototypes by implementing more complex policies as well as implement the distributed version CAISS++. We will also carry out a formal analysis of the execution of the policies. Finally, we will examine AIS between users of multiple social networks and explore the use of technologies such as Spark, Storm and CouchDB in the implementation.

REFERENCES

[ABER04]. K. Aberer, P. Cudŕe-Mauroux, M. Hauswirth, T. Van Pelt, "GridVine: Building Internet-Scale Semantic Overlay Networks," In *Proceedings of International Semantic Web Conference*, Hiroshima, Japan, pp. 107–121, 2004.

[ABRA10]. J. Abraham, P. Brazier, A. Chebotko, J. Navarro, A. Piazza, "Distributed Storage and Querying Techniques for a Semantic Web of Scientific Workflow Provenance," In *Proceedings IEEE International Conference on Services Computing (SCC)*, Miami, FL, pp. 178–185, 2010.

[AMAZ16]. Overview of Security Processes. Available at: https://aws.amazon.com/whitepapers/overview-of-security-processes/, 2016.

[ANDE09]. B. Andersen and F. Neuhaus, "An Ontological Approach to Information Access Control and Provenance," In *Proceedings of Ontology for the Intelligence Community*, Fairfax, VA, USA, pp. 1–6, October 2009.

[AWAD10]. M. Awad, L. Khan, B. M. Thuraisingham. "Policy Enforcement System for Inter-Organizational Data Sharing," *Journal of Information Security and Privacy* 4 (3), 22–39, 2010.

[BIOM]. Biomanta http://www.itee.uq.edu.au/eresearch/projects/biomanta.

[CADE10]. T. Cadenhead, M. Kantarcioglu, B. Thuraisingham, "Scalable and Efficient Reasoning for Enforcing Role-Based Access Control," In *Proceedings of Data and Applications Security and Privacy XXIV, 24th Annual IFIP Working Group 11.3 Working Conference*, Rome, Italy, pp. 209–224, 2010.

[CADE11a]. T. Cadenhead, V. Khadilkar, M. Kantarcioglu, B. Thuraisingham, "Transforming Provenance Using Redaction," In *SACMAT'2011: Proceedings of ACM Symposium on Access Control Models and Technologies*, Innsbruck, Austria, pp. 93–102, 2011.

[CADE11b]. T. Cadenhead, V. Khadilkar, M. Kantarcioglu, B. Thuraisingham, "A Language for Provenance Access Control," In *CODASPY'2011: Proceedings of ACM Conference on Data Application Security and Privacy*, San Antonio, TX, USA, pp. 125–144, 2011.

[CADE12a]. T. Cadenhead, V. Khadilkar, M. Kantarcioglu, B. M. Thuraisingham, "A Cloud-Based RDF Policy Engine for Assured Information Sharing," In *SACMAT'2012: Proceedings of ACM Symposium on Access Control Models and Technologies*, Newark, NJ, USA, pp. 113–116, 2012.

[CADE12b]. T. Cadenhead, M. Kantarcioglu, V. Khadilkar, B. M. Thuraisingham, "Design and Implementation of a Cloud-based Assured Information Sharing System," *Proceedings of International Conference on Mathematical Methods, Models and Architectures for Computer Network Security*, St. Petersburg, Russia, pp. 36–50, 2012.

[CAI04]. M. Cai and M. Frank, "RDFPeers: A Scalable Distributed RDF Repository Based on a Structured Peer-to-Peer Network," In *Proceedings ACM World Wide Web Conference*, New York, NY, USA, pp. 650–657, 2004.

[CARM04]. B. Carminati, E. Ferrari, B.M. Thuraisingham,"Using RDF for Policy Specification and Enforcement," In *Proceedings of International Workshop on Database and Expert Systems Applications*, Zaragoza, Spain, pp. 163–167, 2004.

[CARM09]. B. Carminati, E. Ferrari, R. Heatherly, M. Kantarcioglu, B. M. Thuraisingham, "Design and Implementation of a Cloud-Based Assured Information Sharing System," In *Proceedings of ACM Symposium on Access Control Models and Technologies*, Stresa, Italy, pp. 177–186, 2009.

[CAST09]. P. Castagna, A. Seaborne, C. Dollin, "*Parallel Processing Framework for RDF Design and Issues,*" Technical Report, HP Laboratories, HPL-2009-346, 2009.

[CELI07]. E. Celikel, M. Kantarcioglu, B. Thuraisingham, E. Bertino, "Managing Risks in RBAC Employed Distributed Environments," *On the Move to More Meaningful Internet Systems 2007: CoopIS, DOA, ODBASE, GADA, and IS.* Volume 4804 of Lecture Notes in Computer Science, Springer, New York, pp. 1548–1566, 2007.

[CHOI09]. H. Choi, J. Son, Y. Cho, M. Sung, Y. Chung, "SPIDER: A System for Scalable, Parallel/Distributed Evaluation of Large-Scale RDF Data," In *CIKM'09: Proceedings of ACM Conference on Information and Knowledge Management*, Hong Kong, China, pp. 2087–2088, 2009.

[CIRI07]. L. Cirio, I. Cruz, R. Tamassia, "A Role and Attribute Based Access Control System Using Semantic Web Technologies," *IFIP Workshop on Semantic Web and Web Semantics*, Vilamoura, Algarve, Portugal, pp. 1256–1266, 2007.

[DING05]. L. Ding, T. Finin, Y. Peng, P. da Silva, D. McGuinness, "Tracking RDF Graph Provenance using RDF Molecules," In *Proceedings International Semantic Web Conference*, Galway, Ireland, 2005, https://github.com/lidingpku/iswc-archive/raw/master/paper/iswc-2005-poster-demo/PID-87.pdf.

[DoD]. DoD Information Enterprise Strategic Plan, 2010–2012, http://dodcio.defense.gov/Portals/0/Documents/DodIESP-r16.pdf.

[DoD07]. Department of Defense Information Sharing Strategy, 2007, http://www.defense.gov/releases/release.aspx?releaseid=10831.

[Fini09]. T. Finin et al., "Assured Information Sharing Life Cycle," In *Proceedings of Intelligence and Security Informatics*, Dallas, TX, USA, pp. 307–309, 2009.

[GUO05]. Y. Guo, Z. Pan, J. Heflin, "LUBM: A Benchmark for OWL Knowledge Base Systems," *Web Semantics* 3 (2, 5), 158–182, 2005.

[Haml06a]. K. Hamlen, G. Morrisett, F. Schneider, "Computability Classes for Enforcement Mechanisms," *ACM Transactions on Programming Languages and Systems* 28 (1), 175–205, 2006.

[Haml06b]. K. Hamlen, G. Morrisett, F. Schneider, "Certified In-Lined Reference Monitoring on .NET," In *Proceedings of the ACM Workshop on Programming Language and Analysis for Security*, Ottawa, Canada, pp. 7–16, 2006.

[Haml10a]. K. Hamlen, M. Kantarcioglu, L. Khan, B. Thuraisingham, "Security Issues for Cloud Computing," *Journal of Information Security and Privacy* 4 (2), 2010.

[Haml10b]. K. Hamlen, V. Mohan, R. Wartell, "*Reining in Windows API Abuses with In-lined Reference Monitors*," Technical Report UTDCS-18-10, Computer Science Department, The University of Texas at Dallas, 2010.

[HART07]. A. Harth, J. Umbrich, A Hogan, S. Decker, "YARS2: A Federated Repository for Searching nd Querying Graph Structured Data," In *Proceedings of International Semantic Web Conference*, Busan, Korea, pp. 211–224, 2007.

[HUSA11]. M. Husain, J. McGlothlin, M. Masud, L. Khan, B. Thuraisingham, "Heuristics-Based Query Processing for Large RDF Graphs Using Cloud Computing," *IEEE Transansactions on Knowledge and Data Engineering* 23, pp. 1312–1327, 2011.

[INTE09]. Distributed reasoning: Seamless integration and processing of distributed knowledge, http://www.integrail.eu/documents/fs04.pdf.

[JAIN06]. A. Jain and C. Farkas, "Secure Resource Description Framework: An Access Control Model," In *Proceedings of ACM Symposium on Access Control Models and Technologies*, Lake Tahoe, CA, pp. 121–129, 2006.

[JONE10]. M. Jones and K. Hamlen, "Disambiguating Aspect-Oriented Security Policies" In *Proceedings of 9th International Conference on Aspect-Oriented Software Development*, Rennes and St. Malo, France, pp. 193–204, 2010.

[JONE11]. M. Jones and K. Hamlen, "A Service-Oriented Approach to Mobile Code Security," In *MobiWIS'2011: Proceedings of the 8th International Conference on Mobile Web Information Systems*, Niagara Falls, ON, Canada, pp. 531–538, 2011.

[KAGA02]. L. Kagal, "Rei: A policy language for the me-centric project," HPL-2002-270, accessible online http://www.hpl.hp.com/techreports/2002/HPL-2002-270.html, 2002.

[KANT10]. M. Kantarcioglu, "Incentive-Based Assured Information Sharing," AFOSR MURI Review, October 2010.

[KHAD11]. V. Khadilkar, M. Kantarcioglu, B. Thuraisingham, S. Mehrotra, "Secure Data Processing in a Hybrid Cloud," In *CoRR'2011*: *Proceedings of Computering Research Repository*, abs/1105.1982, 2011.

[KHAL10]. A. Khaled, M. Husain, L. Khan, K. Hamlen, B. Thuraisingham, "A Token-Based Access Control System for RDF Data in the Clouds," In *Proceedings of CloudCom*, Indianapolis, IN, USA, pp. 104–111, 2010.

[KHAN10]. A. Khandelwal, J. Bao, L. Kagal, I. Jacobi, L. Ding, J. Hendler, "Analyzing the AIR Language: A Semantic Web (Production) Rule Language," In *Proceedings of International Web Reasoning and Rule Systems*, Bressanone, Brixen, Italy, pp. 58–72, 2010.

[MARS10]. A. Marshall, M. Howard, G. Bugher, B. Harden, *Security Best Practices in Developing Windows Azure Applications*, Microsoft Corp., Redmond, WA, USA, 2010.

[NEWM08]. A. Newman, J. Hunter, Y. Li, C. Bouton, M. Davis, "A Scale-Out RDF Molecule Store for Distributed Processing of Biomedical Data," *Semantic Web for Health Care and Life Sciences Workshop, World Wide Web Conference*, Beijing, China, 2008.

[NSA11]. http://www.informationweek.com/news/government/cloud-saas/229401646, 2011.

[OMAL109]. D. O'Malley, K. Zhang, S. Radia, R. Marti, C. Harrell, Hadoop Security Design. https://issues.apache.org/jira/secure/attachment/12428537/security-design.pdf.

[RAO08].P. Rao, D. Lin, E. Bertino, N. Li, J. Lobo, "EXAM: An Environment for Access Control Policy Analysis and Management," In *POLICY'08: Proceedings of IEEE Workshop on Policies for Distributed Systems and Networks*, Palisades, NY, USA, pp. 238–240, 2008.

[REDD05]. P. Reddivari, T. Finin, J. Joshi, A. "Policy-Based Access Control for an RDF Store. Policy Management for the Web," In *IJCAI'05*: *Proceedings of the International Joint Conference on Artificial Intelligence Workshop*, Edinburgh, Scotland, UK, 2005.

[REUL10]. Q. Reul, G. Zhao, R. Meersman, "Ontology-Based Access Control Policy Interoperability," In *MISC'2010*: *Proceedings of the 1st Conference on Mobility, Individualisation, Socialisation and Connectivity*, London, UK, 2010.

[SHAR11]. SHARD: http://blog.cloudera.com/blog/2010/03/how-raytheon-researchers-are-using-hadoop-to-build-a-scalable-distributed-triple-store/.

[SRID10]. M. Sridhar and K. Hamlen, "Model-Checking In-Lined Reference Monitors," *Proceedings of the 11th International Conference on Verification, Model Checking, and Abstract Interpretation*, Madrid, Spain, pp. 312–327, 2010.

[TALB09]. D. Talbot, "How Secure is Cloud Computing?" http://www.technologyreview.com/computing/23951/.

[THUR08]. B. Thuraisingham, H. Kumar, L. Khan, "Design and Implementation of a Framework for Assured Information Sharing Across Organizational Boundaries," *Journal of Information Security and Privacy* 2 (4), 67–90, 2008.

[THUR10]. B. Thuraisingham, V. Khadilkar, A. Gupta, M. Kantarcioglu, L. Khan, *Secure Data Storage and Retrieval in the Cloud*. CollaborateCom, Chicago, IL, USA, 2010.

[THUR11]. B. Thuraisingham and V. Khadilkar, "Toward the Design and Implementation of a Cloud-centric Assured Information System," TR# UTDCS, September 2011.

[THUR12]. B. M. Thuraisingham, V. Khadilkar, J. Rachapalli, T. Cadenhead, M. Kantarcioglu, K. W. Hamlen, L. Khan, M. F. Husain, "Cloud-Centric Assured Information Sharing," In *PAISI'2012: Proceedings of the Pacific Asia Workshop on Intelligence and Security Informatics*, Kuala Lumpur, Malaysia, pp. 1–26, 2012.

[THUS09]. A. Thusoo, J. Sharma, N. Jain, Z. Shao, P. Chakka, S. Anthony, H. Liu, P. Wyckoff, R. Murthy, "Hive - A Warehousing Solution Over a Map-Reduce Framework," In *Proceedings of VLDB Endowment*, Lyon, France, 2(2), 1626–1629, 2009.

[URBA09]. Urbani, J., S. Kotoulas, E. Oren, F. van Harmelen, "Scalable Distributed Reasoning using MapReduce," *Proceedings of the International Semantic Web Conference 2009*, Lecture Notes in Computer Science, Bernstein, A., Karger, D.R., Heath, T. et al., Vol. 5823, Springer, Berlin, Heidelberg, pp. 634–649, 2009

[USZO04]. A. Uszok, J. Bradshaw, M. Johnson, R. Jeffers, A. Tate, J. Dalton, S. Aitken, "KAoS Policy Management for Semantic Web Services," *IEEE Intelligent Systems* 19 (4), 32–41, 2004.

[UTD1]. UTD Secure Cloud Repository, http://cs.utdallas.edu/secure-cloud-repository/.

[UTD2]. UTD Semantic Web Repository, http://cs.utdallas.edu/semanticweb/.

[VALL06]. E. Valle, A. Turati, A. Ghioni. "AGE: A Distributed Infrastructure for Fostering RDF-Based Interoperability," In *DAIS'06: Proceedings of Distributed Applications and Inter-Operable Systems*, Bologna, Italy, 2006.

[ZQL]. Zql: a Java SQL parser. http://zql.sourceforge.net/.

26 Big Data Management for Secure Information Integration

26.1 INTRODUCTION

Cloud computing and big data services like Amazon S3 [AMAZ] are gaining a lot of popularity because of factors such as cost efficiency and ease of maintenance. We have evaluated the feasibility of using S3 storage services for storing semantic web data using the Intelligence Community's Blackbook system. Blackbook was an initiative by Intelligence Advanced Research Project Activity (IARPA) toward building a semantic web-based data integration framework [BLAC]. The main purpose of the Blackbook system is to provide intelligence analysts an easy-to-use tool to access data from disparate data sources, make logical inferences across the data sources, and share this knowledge with other analysts using the system. Besides providing a web application interface, it also exposes its services by means of web services. Blackbook integrates data from different data sources, thereby making it prudent to store the data sources in a shared environment like the one provided by cloud computing services. Blackbook essentially uses several semantic data sources to produce search results. But storing shared data in cloud environments in a secure manner is a big challenge. Our approach to solving this problem is discussed in this chapter.

In our approach, we stored one of the Blackbook data sources on Amazon S3 in a secure manner, thus leveraging cloud computing services within a semantic web-based framework. We encrypted the data source using Advanced Encryption Standard [AES] before storing it on Amazon S3. Also, we do not store the original key anywhere in our system. Instead, the key is generated by two separate components; each called a "Key Server." Then, the generated key is used to encrypt data.

To prevent replay attacks, we used the Lamport one time password (OTP) [LAMP81] scheme to generate the passwords that are used by the client for authentication with the "Key Servers." We used the role-based access control (RBAC) model [SAND96] to restrict system access to authorized users and implemented the RBAC policies using Sun's implementation of XACML [OASI].

In this chapter, we describe the design and implementation of a secure information integration framework that uses Blackbook. Details of Blackbook can be found in [BLAC]. In Section 26.2, we present a detailed description of our implementation. Section 26.3 presents our experimental results. This chapter summary and future directions are presented in Section 26.4. Additional details of our work can be found in [PARI09] and [PARI12]. Figure 26.1 illustrates the contents of this chapter.

26.2 INTEGRATING BLACKBOOK WITH AMAZON S3

As stated earlier, Blackbook, a semantic web-based data integration framework, allows data integration from various data sources. We have found that RDF resources are perfect candidates for publication via RESTful web services. Since RESTful web services and semantic web, both deal with resources, it makes sense to expose RDF resources via the RESTful interface. Technologies like semantic web can only work with web services that identify resources with Uniform Resource Identifiers (URIs), and, hence, REST is an ideal platform for implementing web services for semantic web-based systems [PARI09].

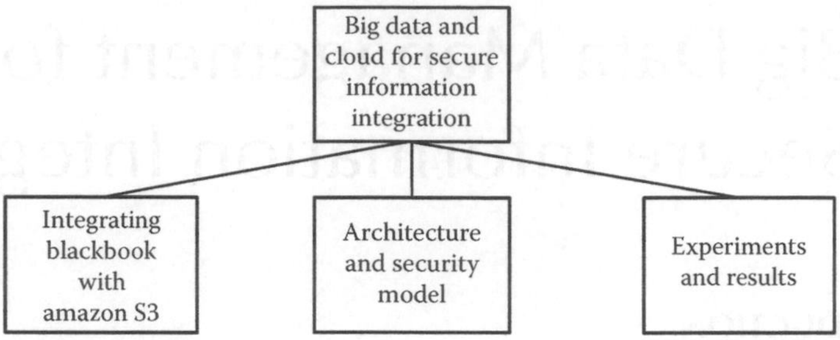

FIGURE 26.1 Big data and cloud for secure information integration.

Cloud computing is a paradigm of computing in which dynamically scalable and often virtualized resources are provided as a service over the Internet [CLOU]. The concept incorporates the following combinations:

Infrastructure as a Service (IaaS)
Platform as a Service (PaaS)
Software as a Service (SaaS)

Economic advantage is one of the main motivations behind the cloud computing paradigm, since it promises the reduction of capital expenditure (CapEx) and operational expenditure (OpEx) [JENS09]. Various organizations can share data and computational power using the cloud computing infrastructure. For instance, salesforce.com is an industry leader in customer relationship management (CRM) products and one of the pioneers to leverage the cloud computing infrastructure on a massive scale. Since Blackbook is a data-integration framework, it can search and integrate data from various data sources that may be located on local machines or remote servers. We utilized the data storage services provided by Amazon S3 to store data sources used by Blackbook.

The reasons we chose Amazon S3 are as follows:

- Cost Effective—Storage price as low as $0.125 per GB per month.
- Ease of use—Can be invoked via both REST and SOAP web services.
- Reliability—Amazon is a big player in cloud computing and is known for providing reliable cloud computing services.

One of the major challenges for current cloud computing systems is privacy risk. That is, privacy is an important concern for cloud computing services in terms of legal compliance and user trust. In [PEAR09], the author provides some interesting insights about how privacy issues should be taken into consideration when designing cloud computing services. The main privacy risks identified in [PEAR09] include the following:

- For the cloud service user—being forced to be tracked or give personal information against his/her will.
- For the organization using cloud service—noncompliance of enterprise policies, loss of reputation, and credibility.
- For implementers of cloud platforms—exposure of sensitive information stored on the platforms, loss of reputation, and credibility.
- For providers of applications on top of cloud platforms—legal noncompliance, loss of reputation.
- For the data subject—exposure of personal information.

We have used Amazon S3 in our implementation. "Amazon S3 is storage for the Internet. It is designed to make web-scale computing easier for developers. Amazon S3 provides a simple web services interface that can be used to store and retrieve any amount of data, at any time, from anywhere on the web. It gives any developer access to the same highly scalable, reliable, fast, inexpensive data storage infrastructure that Amazon uses to run its own global network of web sites. The service aims to maximize benefits of scale and to pass those benefits on to developers." [AMAZ].

Many organizations use services like Amazon S3 for data storage. Some important questions that need to be addressed include: Is the data we store on S3, secure? Is it accessible by any user outside our organization? How do we restrict access to files for users within the organization? To keep our data secure, we propose to encrypt the data using Advanced Encryption Standard (AES) before uploading the data files on Amazon S3. To restrict access to files to users within the organization, we propose to implement RBAC policies using XACML. In RBAC, permissions are associated with roles and users are made members of appropriate roles. This simplifies management of permissions [SAND96]. Our system architecture is illustrated in Figure 26.2.

The data sources are stored on an Amazon S3 server in an encrypted form. The two keys used to encrypt the data source are stored on two servers—key server 1 and key server 2. The policies associated with the data sources for different users are also stored on these servers.

The system uses the OTP for authentication. This password is only valid for a single session or transaction. OTPs avoid the shortcomings associated with static passwords [ONE]. Unlike static passwords, they are not vulnerable to replay attacks. So if an intruder manages to get hold of an OTP that was used previously to log into a service or carry a transaction, the system's security would not be compromised since that password will no longer be valid. The only drawback of OTP is that humans cannot memorize them and hence require additional technology in order to work.

OTP generation algorithms make use of randomness to prevent the prediction of future OTPs based on the previously observed OTPs. Some of the approaches to generate OTPs are as follows:

- Use of a mathematical algorithm to generate a new password based on the previous passwords.
- Based on time synchronization between the authentication server and the client providing the password.
- Use of a mathematical algorithm where the new password is based on a challenge (e.g., a random number chosen by the authentication server or transaction details) and/or a counter.

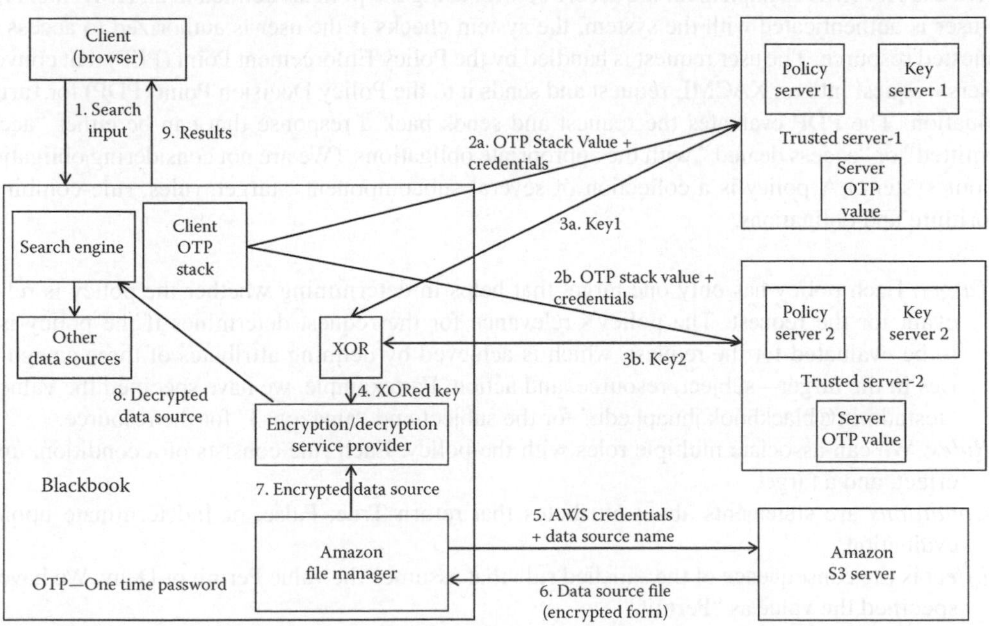

FIGURE 26.2 System architecture.

We use Lamport's OTP scheme for authentication. The Lamport OTP approach is based on a mathematical algorithm for generating a sequence of "passkey" values, and each successor value is based on the value of predecessor. The core of Lamport's OTP scheme requires that cooperating client/service components agree to use a common sequencing algorithm to generate a set of expiring OTPs (client side) and validate client-provided passkeys included in each client-initiated request (service side). In our case, the client is the Blackbook system and the service components are the "Key Servers." The client generates a finite sequence of values starting with a "seed" value and each successor value is generated by applying some transformation algorithm (or F(S) function) to the previous sequence value:

$$S1 = Seed,\ S2 = F(S1),\ S3 = F(S2),\ S4 = F(S3) \ldots\ S[n] = F(S[n-1])$$

We use the "password" of the user, which is salted with some randomly generated bytes (using SHA1PRNG) as a key to generate the seed value using SHA-256 [SECU02]. The next values in the sequence are generated using the obtained seed value using SHA-256. All these generated values are stored in a stack on the client machine. The topmost value on the stack is stored on both the "Key Servers" (1 and 2). If the client sends a request for the first time, the topmost value of the client stack is compared with that on the "Key Servers" (1 and 2). If the values match, the client is authenticated and the topmost value on the client stack is removed. For subsequent requests, the topmost value on the client stack is used to compute the successor value using the hash function (used to build the stack). If the generated value and the value on the "Key Servers" match, the user is authenticated; the topmost value on the client stack is stored on the "Key Servers" and subsequently removed from the client stack. If the client stack is exhausted, a new stack is generated and the topmost value on the stack is stored on the "Key Servers." Once the user is authenticated using the OTP scheme, the user request is evaluated against the policies applicable for the resource (data source in our case) requested by the user for access. The predefined policies are stored in the "Policy Server" component of the "Key Servers." If the policies for the resource are applicable for the user request, the "Key Server" sends the keys used to encrypt the resource requested by the user.

We use XACML to implement the access control using the policies defined in an XML file. After the user is authenticated with the system, the system checks if the user is authorized to access the requested resource. The user request is handled by the Policy Enforcement Point (PEP) that converts a users' request into an XACML request and sends it to the Policy Decision Point (PDP) for further evaluation. The PDP evaluates the request and sends back a response that can be either "access permitted" or "access denied," with the appropriate obligations. (We are not considering obligations for our system.) A policy is a collection of several subcomponents: target, rules, rule-combining algorithm, and obligations.

Target: Each policy has only one target that helps in determining whether the policy is relevant for the request. The policy's relevance for the request determines if the policy is to be evaluated for the request, which is achieved by defining attributes of three categories in the target—subject, resource, and action. For example, we have specified the value "testadmin@blackbook.jhuapl.edu" for the subject and "amazons3" for the resource.

Rules: We can associate multiple roles with the policy. Each rule consists of a condition, an effect, and a target.

Conditions are statements about attributes that return True, False, or Indeterminate upon evaluation.

Effect is the consequence of the satisfied rule that assumes the value Permit or Deny. We have specified the value as "Permit."

Target helps in determining if the rule is relevant for the request.

Rule-combining Algorithms: As a policy can have various rules, it is possible for different rules to generate conflicting results. Rule-combining algorithms resolve such conflicts to arrive at one outcome per policy per request. Only one rule-combining algorithm is applicable to one policy.

Obligations allow the mechanism to provide a finer level of access control than mere permit and deny decisions. They are the actions that must be performed by the PEP in conjunction with the enforcement of an authorization decision.

After successful authentication and authorization, the Amazon File Manager downloads the requested resource from the Amazon S3 server. More specifically, Key Server – 1 sends key1 and the Key Server – 2 sends key2 to the Amazon File Manager. These keys are XORED to get keyorg, that is,

$$keyorg = key1\ XOR\ key2$$

Then, keyorg is used to decrypt the resource by the Encryption/Decryption Service Provider.

The main motive behind using two key servers is to avoid a single point of failure. If any of the key servers is hacked, the data is not compromised as two keys; one from each of the key servers is needed to decrypt the data sources. In case one of the key servers is hacked and the keys stored on that server are compromised, we run into the risk of rendering the data source stored on Amazon useless as we need two keys, one from each key server, to retrieve the original key used to encrypt the data source. To avoid this, we propose to take periodic backups of the keys on each of the key server.

Scenario: We now describe a sample scenario, depicting an interaction with the Amazon S3 storage service, with respect to the Blackbook system.

1. The user U fires a search query to Blackbook (step 1 in Figure 26.2). Blackbook federates the query across various data sources, including the data source F that is securely stored on Amazon S3.
2. We follow the OTP scheme to authenticate the client (Blackbook in this case) for using the AWS S3 service. The client machine sends the topmost value on the OTP stack along with the user credentials and the request to key servers 1 & 2 (steps 2a and 2b in Figure 26.2).
3. If the value passed by the client matches that on the OTP stack of the key servers and the policies applicable for the user are valid for the request, the key servers send the "key" used to decrypt the data source (steps 3a and 3b in Figure 26.2).
4. The keys, key1 and key2, obtained from the key servers 1 & 2 are /XOR-ed to obtain the original key used to decrypt the data source F (step 4 in Figure 26.2).
5. The Amazon File Manager passes the Amazon account credentials and the data source name to retrieve the data source (steps 5 and 6 in Figure 26.2).
6. The Encryption/Decryption Service Manager retrieves the encrypted data source, and then, using the XOR-ed key, decrypts the data source (steps 7 and 8 in Figure 26.2).
7. Blackbook performs a search on the data source retrieved from Amazon along with other data sources and returns the results to the user (step 9 in Figure 26.2).

A sample XACML request: The subject, testadmin@blackbook.jhuapl.edu, which belongs to the users group (attribute of the subject), is trying to perform a read action on the resource amazons3. To create such a request, we need two subject attributes: one resource attribute and one action attribute. The two subject attributes are rfc822Name (e-mail ID) and the group to which the subject belongs. The one resource attribute is the URI of the resource, and the one action attribute is the read action on the resource. The complete listing, which demonstrates the creation of the PEP with all of these attributes, can be found in [PARI09].

26.3 EXPERIMENTS

In our approach, we have used the Advanced Encryption Standard to encrypt data before storing it on the Amazon S3 server. Uploading the data on the Amazon server is a one-time process. The data source needs to be uploaded again only when the stored data needs to be modified. But the data source stored on Amazon S3 needs to be downloaded every time the user issues a search query to the Blackbook system. Since the data source needs to be decrypted every time a query is issued, it may affect performance since encryption and decryption are costly operations.

We ran the experiments on a Dell desktop computer running on Ubuntu Gutsy 7.10 with the following hardware configuration: Intel® Pentium® 4 CPU 3.00 GHZ, 1 GB RAM. The network bandwidth while running the experiments varied between 250 and 300 Mbps. We generated the data files using the triple generation program provided by SP2B, the SPARQL Performance Benchmark [SPAR]. We experimented with 30 files of different sizes, ranging from 1 to 30 MB. Details of the experiments are given in [PARI09].

26.4 SUMMARY AND DIRECTIONS

Cloud computing paradigm is becoming increasingly important in today's world. Therefore, issues like data security and privacy in the context of cloud computing have gained a lot of attention. In this chapter, we described techniques to protect our data by encrypting it before storing on cloud computing servers like Amazon S3. Our approach is novel as we propose to use two key servers to generate and store the keys. Also, we assure more security than some of the other known approaches as we do not store the actual key used to encrypt the data. This assures the protection of our data even if one or both key servers are compromised. Our implementation utilizes Blackbook, a semantic web-based data integration framework, and allows data integration from various data sources.

In our current approach, we download the data source for every request from the user. In the future, we can make the provision to cache the data source requested by the user on our local server and provide the results to the user from the cached data source by treating it as a local data source. This approach will help to enhance performance. Also, we can divide the data source in chunks and then upload it. Since the search process takes place in an asynchronous manner, we can download the chunks, search for results, and display them to the user, one at a time. Meanwhile, the application can keep downloading other chunks. We can also keep track of search history for a user. When the user logs in to the system, we can download chunks that a user is most likely to query.

It should be noted that while we have used Amazon S3, which is considered to be a big data technology, our future work will include exploring the use of cloud systems based on Hadoop/MapReduce, Storm, and Spark. In addition, we will also explore the use of big data systems such as Hbase, CouchDB, and Cassandra that can replace Blackbook so that the data is stored in a more open environment. Nevertheless, the system we have discussed shows how a data integration framework such as Blackbook can be securely integrated with an open cloud system such as Amazon S3.

REFERENCES

[AES] Advanced Encryption Standard, http://en.wikipedia.org/wiki/Advanced_Encryption_Standard.

[AMAZ] Amazon S3, http://aws.amazon.com/s3/.

[BLAC] http://info.publicintelligence.net/IARPA_overview_UMD.pdf.

[CLOU] Cloud Computing, http://en.wikipedia.org/wiki/Cloud_computing.

[JENS09] M. Jensen, J. Schwenk, N. Gruschka, and L. L. Iacono, "On Technical Security issues in Cloud Computing," *In Proceedings of IEEE International Conference on Cloud Computing*, pp. 109–116, 2009.

[LAMP81] L. Lamport, "Password Authentication with Insecure Communication," *Communications of the ACM* 24 (11), 770–772, 1981.

[OASI] OASIS, https://www.oasis-open.org/committees/tc_home.php?wg_abbrev=xacml.

[ONE] One-time Password, http://en.wikipedia.org/wiki/One-time_password.

[PARI09] P. Parikh, "Secured Information Integration with a Semantic Web-Based Framework," *Master's thesis*, The University of Texas at Dallas, 2009.

[PARI12] P. Parikh, M. Kantarcioglu, V. Khadilkar, B. M. Thuraisingham, and L Khan, "Secure Information Integration with a Semantic Web-Based Framework," In *Proceedings of the IRI*, Las Vegas, NV, USA, pp. 659–663, 2012.

[PEAR09] S. Pearson, HP Labs, "Taking Account of Privacy when Designing Cloud Computing Services," In *Proceedings of IEEE ICSE Cloud09*, Workshop on Software Engineering Challenges in Cloud Computing, Vancouver, IEEE, pp. 44–52, 2009.

[SAND96] R. Sandhu, E. J. Coyne, H. L. Feinstein, and C. Youman, – "Role Based Access Control Models," *IEEE Computer* 29 (2), 38–47, 1996.

[SECU02] Secure Hash Standard, http://csrc.nist.gov/publications/fips/fips180-2/fips180-2.pdf, 2002.

[SPAR] SPARQL Performance Benchmark http://www.openlinksw.com/dataspace/vdb/weblog/vdb%27s%20BLOG%20%5B136%5D/1423.

27 Big Data Analytics for Malware Detection

27.1 INTRODUCTION

In the previous chapters in Part IV, we discussed sample big data management and analytics (BDMA) and big data security and privacy (BDSP) systems. These include systems such as the SPARQL query processor, InXite, CAISS, and the Secure Data Integration framework. In this chapter, we will discuss an experimental system that uses big data analytics and cloud for malware detection. In other words, we will show how big analytics techniques can be used for malware detection. In fact, some of our work discussed in Part III on stream data analytics for insider threat detection has been influenced by the system discussed in this chapter.

Malware is a potent vehicle for many successful cyber attacks every year, including data and identity theft, system and data corruption, and denial of service; it therefore constitutes a significant security threat to many individuals and organizations. The average direct malware cost damages worldwide per year from 1999 to 2006 have been estimated at $14 billion USD [COMP07]. This includes labor costs for analyzing, repairing and disinfecting systems, productivity losses, revenue losses due to system loss or degraded performance, and other costs directly incurred as a result of the attack. However, the direct cost does not include the prevention cost, such as antivirus software, hardware, and IT (information technology) security staff salary. Aside from these monetary losses, individuals and organizations also suffer identity theft, data theft, and other intangible losses due to successful attacks.

Malware includes viruses, worms, Trojan horses, time and logic bombs, botnets, and spyware. A number of techniques have been devised by researchers to counter these attacks; however, the more successful the researchers become in detecting and preventing the attacks, the more sophisticated malicious code appears in the wild. Thus, the arms race between malware authors and malware defenders continues to escalate. One popular technique applied by the antivirus community to detect malicious code is *signature detection*. This technique matches untrusted executables against a unique telltale string or byte pattern known as a *signature*, which is used as an identifier for a particular malicious code. Although signature detection techniques are widely used, they are not effective against zero-day attacks (new malicious code), polymorphic attacks (different encryptions of the same binary), or metamorphic attacks (different code for the same functionality) [CRAN05]. There has therefore been a growing need for fast, automated, and efficient detection techniques that are robust to these attacks.

This chapter describes a data mining technique that is dedicated to the automated generation of signatures to defend against these kinds of attacks. Due to the need for the near real-time performance of the malware detection tools, we have developed our data mining tool in the cloud. We describe the detailed design and implementation of this cloud-based tool in the remaining sections of this chapter.

This chapter is organized as follows. Section 27.2 discusses malware detection. Section 27.3 discusses related work. Section 27.4 discusses the classification algorithm and proves its effectiveness analytically. Section 27.5 then describes the feature-extraction and feature-selection technique using cloud computing for malware detection, and Section 27.6 discusses data collection, experimental setup, evaluation techniques, and results. Section 27.7 discusses several issues related to our approach, and finally, Section 27.8 summarizes our conclusions. Figure 27.1 illustrates the concepts of this chapter.

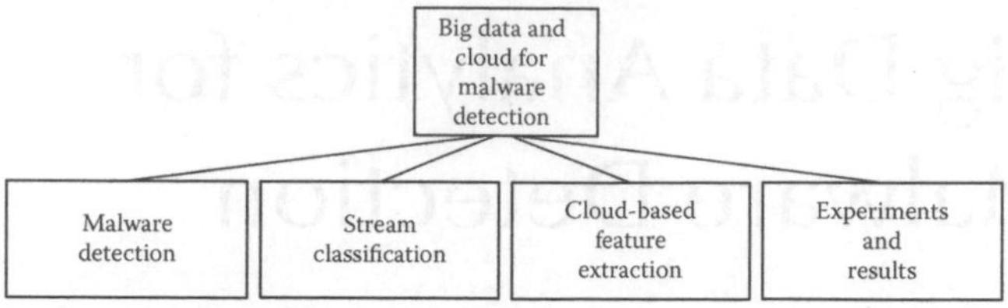

FIGURE 27.1 Big data and cloud for malware detection.

27.2 MALWARE DETECTION

27.2.1 Malware Detection as a Data Stream Classification Problem

The problem of detecting malware using data mining ([SCHU01], [KOLT04], [MASU08a]) involves classifying each executable as either *benign* or *malicious*. Most past work has approached the problem as a static data-classification problem, where the classification model is trained with fixed training data. However, the escalating rate of malware evolution and innovation is not well suited to static training. The detection of continuously evolving malware is better treated as a *data stream* classification problem. In this paradigm, the data stream is a sequence of executables in which each data point is one executable. The stream is of *infinite length*. It also observes *concept drift* as attackers relentlessly develop new techniques to avoid detection, changing the characteristics of the malicious code. Similarly, the characteristics of benign executables change with the evolution of compilers and operating systems.

Data stream classification is a major area of active research in the data mining community, and requires surmounting at least three challenges. First, the storage and maintenance of potentially unbounded historical data in an infinite-length, concept-drifting stream for training purposes is infeasible. Second, the classification model must be adapted continuously to cope with concept drift. Third, if there is no predefined feature space for the data points in the stream, new features with high discriminating power must be selected and extracted as the stream evolves, which we call *feature evolution*.

Solutions to the first two problems are related. The concept drift necessitates the refinement of the hypothesis to accommodate the new concept; most of the old data must be discarded from the training set. Therefore, one of the main issues in mining concept-drifting data streams is the selection of training instances adequate to learn the evolving concept. Solving the third problem requires a feature-selection process that is ongoing, since new and more powerful features are likely to emerge and old features are likely to become less dominant as the concept evolves. If the feature space is large, then the running time and memory requirements for feature-extraction and feature-selection become a bottleneck for the data stream classification system.

One approach to address the concept drift is to select and store the training data that are most consistent with the current concept [FAN04]. Other approaches such as Very Fast Decision Trees (VFDTs) [DOMI00] update the existing classification model when new data appear. However, past work has shown that ensemble techniques are often more robust for handling unexpected changes and concept drifts ([WANG03], [SCHO05], [KOLT05]). These maintain an ensemble of classifiers and update the ensemble when new data appear.

We design and develop a multipartition, multichunk ensemble classification algorithm that generalizes existing ensemble methods. The generalization leads to significantly improved classification accuracy relative to existing single-partition, single-chunk (SPC) ensemble approaches when tested on real-world data streams. The ensemble in our approach consists of Kv classifiers, where K is a constant and v is the number of partitions, to be explained shortly.

Our approach divides the data stream into equal-sized chunks. The chunk size is chosen so that all data in each chunk fits into the main memory. Each chunk, when labeled, is used to train classifiers. Whenever a new data chunk is labeled, the ensemble is updated as follows. We take the

r most recent labeled consecutive data chunks, divide these r chunks into v partitions, and train a classifier with each partition. Therefore, v classifiers are trained using the r consecutive chunks. We then update the ensemble by choosing the best Kv classifiers (based on accuracy) among the newly trained v classifiers and the existing Kv classifiers. Thus, the total number of classifiers in the ensemble remains constant. Our approach is therefore parameterized by the number of partitions v, the number of chunks r, and the ensemble size K.

Our approach does not assume that new data points appearing in the stream are immediately labeled. Instead, it defers the ensemble updating process until labels for the data points in the latest data chunk become available. In the meantime, new unlabeled data continue to be classified using the current ensemble. Thus, the approach is well suited to applications in which misclassifications solicit corrected labels from an expert user or other source. For example, consider the online credit card fraud detection problem. When a new credit card transaction takes place, its class (*fraud* or *authentic*) is predicted using the current ensemble. Suppose a fraudulent transaction is misclassified as *authentic*. When a customer receives the bank statement, he or she identifies this error and reports it to the authority. In this way, the actual labels of the data points are obtained and the ensemble is updated accordingly.

27.2.2 Cloud Computing for Malware Detection

If the feature space of the data points is not fixed, a subproblem of the classification problem is the extraction and selection of features that describe each data point. As in previous work (e.g., [KOLT04]), we use binary n-grams as features for malware detection. However, since the total number of possible n-grams is prohibitively large, we judiciously select n-grams that have the greatest discriminatory power. This selection process is ongoing; as the stream progresses, newer n-grams appear that dominate the older n-grams. These newer n-grams replace the old in our model in order to identify the best features for a particular period.

Naïve implementation of the feature-extraction and feature-selection process can be both time- and storage-intensive for large datasets. For example, our previous work [MASU08a] extracted roughly a quarter billion n-grams from a corpus of only 3500 executables. This feature extraction process required extensive virtual memory (with associated performance overhead), since not all of these features could be stored in main memory. Extraction and selection required about 2 hours of computation and many gigabytes of disk space for a machine with a quad-core processor and 12 GB of memory. This is despite the use of a purely static dataset; when the dataset is a dynamic stream, extraction and selection must recur, resulting in a major bottleneck. In this chapter, we consider a much larger dataset of 105,000 executables for which our previous approach is insufficient.

We therefore design and develop a scalable feature-selection and feature-extraction solution that leverages a cloud computing framework [DEAN08]. We show that depending on the availability of cluster nodes, the running time for feature-extraction and feature-selection can be reduced by a factor of m, where m is the number of nodes in the cloud cluster. The nodes are machines with inexpensive commodity hardware. Therefore, the solution is also cost-effective as high-end computing machines are not required.

27.2.3 Our Contributions

Our contributions can therefore be summarized as follows. We design and develop a generalized multipartition, multichunk ensemble technique that significantly reduces the expected classification error over existing SPC ensemble methods. A theoretical analysis justifies the effectiveness of the approach. We then formulate the malware detection problem as a data stream classification problem and identify drawbacks of traditional malicious code detection techniques relative to our data mining approach.

We design and develop a scalable and cost-effective solution to this problem using a cloud computing framework. Finally, we apply our technique to synthetically generated data as well as real botnet traffic and real malicious executables, achieving better detection accuracy than other stream data-classification techniques. The results show that our ensemble technique constitutes a powerful tool for intrusion detection based on data stream classification.

27.3 RELATED WORK

Our work is related to both malware detection and stream mining. Both are discussed in this section. Traditional *signature-based* malware detectors identify malware by scanning untrusted binaries for distinguishing byte sequences or *features*. Features unique to malware are maintained in a *signature database* that must be continually updated as new malware is discovered and analyzed. Traditionally, signature databases have been manually derived, updated, and disseminated by human experts as new malware appears and is analyzed. However, the escalating rate of new malware appearances and the advent of self-mutating, polymorphic malware over the past decade have made manual signature updating less practical. This has led to the development of automated data mining techniques for malware detection (e.g., [KOLT04], [SCHU01], [MASU08a], and [HAML09b]) that are capable of automatically inferring signatures for previously unseen malware.

Data-mining-based approaches analyze the content of an executable and classify it as malware if a certain combination of features are found (or not found) in the executable. These malware detectors are first trained so that they can generalize the distinction between malicious and benign executables, and thus detect future instances of malware. The training process involves feature extraction and model building using these features. Data mining-based malware detectors differ mainly on how the features are extracted and which machine learning technique is used to build the model. The performance of these techniques largely depends on the quality of the features that are extracted.

In the work reported in [SCHU01], the authors extract DLL (Dynamic-Link Library) call information (using *GNU binutils*) and character strings (using *GNU strings*) from the headers of Windows PE executables, as well as 2-byte sequences from the executable content. The DLL calls, strings and bytes are used as features to train models. Models are trained using two different machine learning techniques, RIPPER [COHE96] and Naïve Bayes (NB) [MICH94], to compare their relative performances. In [KOLT04], the authors extract binary *n*-gram features from executables and apply them to different classification methods, such as *k*-nearest neighbor (KNN) [AHA91], NB, support vector machines (SVM) [BOSE92], decision trees [QUIN03], and boosting [FREU96]. Boosting is applied in combination with various other learning algorithms to obtain improved models (e.g., boosted decision trees). Our previous work on data-mining-based malware detection [MASU08a] extracts binary *n*-grams from the executable, assembly instruction sequences from the disassembled executables, and DLL call information from the program headers. The classification models used in this work are SVM, decision tree, NB, boosted decision tree, and boosted NB.

Hamsa and Polygraph ([LI06], [NEWS05]) apply a simple form of data mining to generate worm signatures automatically using binary *n*-grams as features. Both identify a collection of *n*-grams as a worm signature if they appear only in malicious binaries (i.e., positive samples) and never in benign binaries. This differs from the traditional data mining approaches already discussed (including ours) in two significant respects: First, Polygraph and Hamsa limit their attention to *n*-grams that appear only in the malicious pool, whereas traditional data mining techniques also consider *n*-grams that appear in the benign pool to improve the classification accuracy. Second, Polygraph and Hamsa define signature matches as simply the presence of a set of *n*-grams, whereas traditional data mining approaches build classification models that match samples based on both the presence and absence of features. Traditional data mining approaches therefore generalize the approaches of Polygraph and Hamsa, with corresponding increases in power.

Almost all past work has approached the malware detection problem as a static data-classification problem in which the classification model is trained with fixed training data. However, the rapid emergence of new types of malware and new obfuscation strategies adopted by malware authors introduces a dynamic component to the problem that violates the static paradigm. We therefore argue that effective malware detection must be increasingly treated as a data stream classification problem in order to keep pace with attacks.

Many existing data stream classification techniques target infinite-length data streams that exhibit concept drift ([AGGA06], [WANG03], [YANG05], [KOLT05], [HULT01], [FAN04], [GAO07], [HASH09], [ZHAN9]). All of these techniques adopt a one-pass incremental update approach, but with differing approaches to the incremental updating mechanism. Most can be grouped into two main classes: single-model incremental approaches and hybrid batch incremental approaches.

Single-model incremental updating involves dynamically updating a single model with each new training instance. For example, decision tree models can be incrementally updated with incoming data [HULT01]. In contrast, hybrid batch incremental approaches build each model from a batch of training data using a traditional batch learning technique. Older models are then periodically replaced by newer models as the concept drifts ([WANG03], [BIFE09], ([YANG05], [FAN04], [GAO07]). Some of these hybrid approaches use a single model to classify the unlabeled data (e.g., [YANG05], [CHEN08]), while others use an ensemble of models (e.g., [WANG03], [SCHO05]). Hybrid approaches have the advantage that model updates are typically far simpler than in single-model approaches; for example, classifiers in the ensemble can simply be removed or replaced. However, other techniques that combine the two approaches by incrementally updating the classifiers within the ensemble can be more complex [KOLT05].

Accuracy-weighted classifier ensembles (AWEs) ([WANG03], [SCHO05]) are an important category of hybrid incremental updating ensemble classifiers that use weighted majority voting for classification. These divide the stream into equal-sized chunks, and each chunk is used to train a classification model. An ensemble of K such models classifies the unlabeled data. Each time a new data chunk is labeled, a new classifier is trained from that chunk. This classifier replaces one of the existing classifiers in the ensemble. The replacement victim is chosen by evaluating the accuracy of each classifier on the latest training chunk. These ensemble approaches have the advantage that they can be built more efficiently than a continually updated single model and they observe higher accuracy than their single-model counterparts [TUME96].

Our ensemble approach is most closely related to AWE, but with a number of significant differences. First, we apply multipartitioning of the training data to build v classifiers from that training data. Second, the training data consists of r consecutive data chunks (i.e., a multichunk approach) rather than from a single chunk. We prove both analytically and empirically that both of these enhancements, that is, multipartitioning and multichunk, significantly reduce the ensemble classification error. Third, when we update the ensemble, v classifiers in the ensemble are replaced by v newly trained classifiers. The v classifiers that are replaced may come from different chunks; thus, although some classifiers from a chunk may have been removed, other classifiers from that chunk may still remain in the ensemble. This differs from AWE in which removal of a classifier means total removal of the knowledge obtained from one whole chunk. Our replacement strategy also contributes to error reduction. Finally, we use simple majority voting rather than weighted voting, which is more suitable for data streams, as shown in [GAO07]. Thus, our multipartition, multichunk ensemble approach is a more generalized and efficient form of that implemented by AWE.

Our work extends our previously published work [MASU09]. Most existing data stream classification techniques, including our previous work, assume that the feature space of the data points in the stream is fixed. However, in some cases, such as text data, this assumption is not valid. For example, when features are words, the feature space cannot be fully determined at the start of the stream since new words appear frequently. In addition, it is likely that much of this large lexicon of words has low discriminatory power, and is therefore best omitted from the feature space. It is therefore more effective and efficient to select a subset of the candidate features for each data point. This feature selection must occur incrementally as newer, more discriminating candidate features arise and older features become outdated. Therefore, feature-extraction and feature-selection should be an integral part of data stream classification. In this chapter, we describe the design and

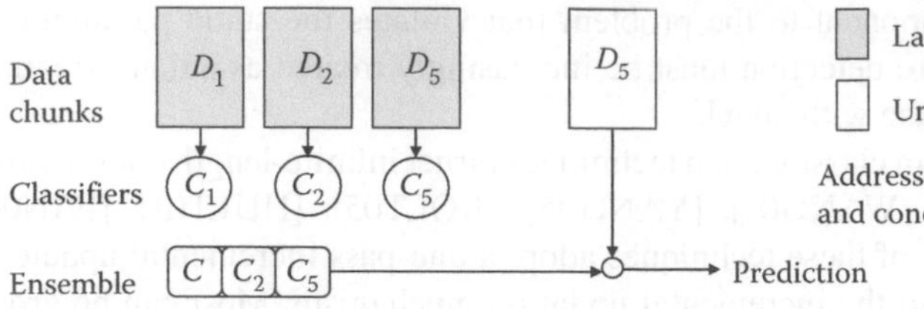

FIGURE 27.2. Ensemble construction.

implementation of an efficient and scalable feature-extraction and feature-selection technique using a cloud computing framework ([ZHAO09], [DEAN08]). This approach supersedes our previous work in that it considers the real challenges in data stream classification that occur when the feature space cannot be predetermined. This facilitates the application of our technique to the detection of real malicious executables from a large, evolving dataset, showing that it can detect newer varieties of malware as malware instances evolve over time.

27.4 DESIGN AND IMPLEMENTATION OF THE SYSTEM

27.4.1 Ensemble Construction and Updating

Our *extended, multipartition, multichunk (EMPC)* ensemble learning approach maintains an ensemble $A = \{A1, A2, \ldots, AKv\}$ of the most recent, best Kv classifiers. Each time a new data chunk Dn arrives, it tests the data chunk with the ensemble A. The ensemble is updated once chunk Dn is labeled. The classification process uses simple majority voting.

The ensemble construction updating process is illustrated in Figure 27.2 and summarized in Algorithm 27.1. Lines 1–3 of the algorithm compute the error of each classifier $Ai \in A$ on chunk Dn where Dn is the most recent data chunk that has been labeled. Let D be the data of the most recently labeled r data chunks, including Dn. Line 5 randomly partitions D into v equal parts $\{d1, \ldots, dv\}$ such that all the parts have roughly the same class distributions. Lines 6–9 train a new batch of v classifiers, where each classifier An is trained with dataset $D - dj$. The error of each classifier $An \in An$ is computed by testing it on its corresponding test data. Finally, line 10 selects the best Kv classifiers from the $Kv + v$ classifiers in $An \cup A$ based on the errors of each classifier computed in lines 2 and 8. Note that any subset of the nth batch of v classifiers may be selected for inclusion in the new ensemble.

27.4.2 Error Reduction Analysis

As explained in Algorithm 27.1, we build ensemble A of Kv classifiers. A test instance x is classified using a majority vote of the classifiers in the ensemble. We use simple majority voting rather than weighted majority voting (refer to [WANG03]), since simple majority voting has been theoretically proven the optimal choice for data streams [GAO07]. Weighted voting can be problematic in these contexts because it assumes that the distribution of training and test data is the same. However, in data streams, this assumption is violated because of concept-drift. Simple majority voting is therefore a better alternative. Our experiments confirm this in practice, obtaining better results with simple rather than weighted majority voting.

We have shown in [MASU11] that EMPC can further reduce the expected error in classifying concept-drifting data streams compared to *single-partition, single-chunk* (*SPC*) approaches that use only one data chunk for training a single classifier (i.e., $r = v = 1$). Intuitively, there are two main reasons for the error reduction. First, the training data per classifier is increased by introducing the multichunk concept. Larger training data naturally lead to a better trained model, reducing the error. Second, rather than training only one model from the training data, we partition the data into v partitions, and train one model from each partition. This further reduces error because the mean expected error of an ensemble of v classifiers is theoretically v times lower than that of a single classifier [TUME96]. Therefore, both the multichunk and multipartition strategies contribute to error reduction.

Algorithm 27.1 Updating the Classifier Ensemble

Input: $\{D_{n-r+1}, \ldots, D_n\}$: the r most recently labeled data chunks
A: the current ensemble of best Kv classifiers
Output: an updated ensemble A
for each classifier $A_i \in A$ **do**
  $e(A_i) \leftarrow$ *error of* A_i on D_n // test and compute error
end for
$D \leftarrow \cup_{j=n-r+1}^{n} D_j$
Partition D into equal parts $\{d_1, d_2, \ldots, d_v\}$
for $j = 1$ to v **do**
  $A_j^n \leftarrow n$ newly trained classifier from data $D - d_j$
  $e(A_j) \leftarrow$ error of A_j on d_j // test and compute error
end for
  $A \leftarrow$ best Kv from $A^n \cup A$ based on computed error $e(\cdot)$

27.4.3 Empirical Error Reduction and Time Complexity

For a given partition size v, increasing the window size r only yields reduced error up to a certain point. After that, increasing r actually hurts the performance of our algorithm, because inequality (18) is violated. The upper bound of r depends on the magnitude of drift ρd. We have shown in [MASU11] the relative error ER for $v = 2$, and different values of ρd, for increasing r. It is clear from the graph that for lower values of ρd, increasing r reduces the relative error by a greater margin. However, in all cases after r exceeds a certain threshold, ER becomes greater than 1. Although it may not be possible to know the actual value of ρd from the data, we may determine the optimal value of r experimentally. In our experiments, we found that for smaller chunk sizes, higher values of r work better, and vice versa. However, the best performance-cost trade-off is found for $r = 2$ or $r = 3$. We have used $r = 2$ in our experiments. Similarly, the upper bound of v can be derived from inequality (18) for a fixed value of r. It should be noted that if v is increased, running time also increases. From our experiments, we obtained the best performance-cost trade-off for $v = 5$.

The time complexity of the algorithm is $O(vn(Ks + f(rs)))$, where n is the total number of data chunks, s is the size of each chunk, and $f(z)$ is the time required to build a classifier on a training data of size z. Since v is constant, the complexity becomes $O(n(Ks + f(rs)))$. This is at most a constant factor rv slower than the closest related work [WANG03] but with the advantage of the significantly reduced error.

27.4.4 Hadoop/MapReduce Framework

We used the open-source Hadoop [APAC10] MapReduce framework to implement our experiments. Here, we provide some of the algorithmic details of the Hadoop MapReduce feature-extraction and feature-selection algorithm. The *Map* function in a MapReduce framework takes a key-value pair as input and yields a list of intermediate key-value pairs for each.

$$Map: (MKey \times MVal) \rightarrow (RKey \cdot RVal)^*$$

All the *Map* tasks are processed in parallel by each node in the cluster without sharing data with other nodes. Hadoop collates the output of the *Map* tasks by grouping each set of intermediate values $V \subseteq RVal$ that share a common intermediate key $k \in RKey$. The resulting collated pairs (k, V) are then streamed to *Reduce* nodes. Each reducer in a Hadoop MapReduce framework therefore receives a list of multiple (k, V) pairs, issued by Hadoop one at a time in an iterative fashion. *Reduce* can therefore be understood as a function having signature

$$Reduce\colon (RKey \times RVal^*)^* \rightarrow Val.$$

Co-domain *Val* is the type of the final results of the MapReduce cycle.

In our framework, *Map* keys (*MKey*) are binary file identifiers (e.g., filenames), and *Map* values (*MVal*) are the file contents in bytes. *Reduce* keys (*RKey*) are *n*-gram features, and their corresponding values (*RVal*) are the class labels of the file instances whence they were found. Algorithm 27.2 shows the feature extraction procedure that *Map* nodes use to map the former to the latter. Lines 5–10 of Algorithm 27.3 tally the class labels reported by *Map* to obtain positive and negative instance counts for each *n*-gram. These form a basis for computing the information gain of each *n*-gram in line 11. Lines 12–16 use a min-heap data structure *h* to filter all but the best *S* features as evaluated by the information gain. The final best *S* features encountered are returned by lines 18–20.

The *q* reducers in the Hadoop system therefore yield a total of *qS* candidate features and their information gains. These are streamed to a second reducer that simply implements the last half of Algorithm 27.3 to select the best *S* features.

Algorithm 27.2 Map(file_id, bytes)

Input: file file id with content bytes
Output: list of pairs (g, l), where g is an n-gram and l is file id's label

$T \leftarrow \varnothing$.
for all n-grams g in bytes **do**
$T \leftarrow T \cup \{g, labelof(file\ id)\}$ $\{(g, labelof(fil\_id))\}$
end for
for all $(g, l) \in T$ **do**
print (g, l)
end for

Algorithm 27.3 $\mathbf{Reduce}_{p,t}(F)$

Input: list F of (g, L) pairs, where g is an n-gram and L is a list of class labels; total size t of original instance set; total number p of positive instances
Output: S pairs (g, i), where i is the information gain of n-gram g

1: **heap** h/* empty min-heap*/
2: **for all** (g, L) in **F do**
3: $t' \leftarrow 0$
4: $p' \leftarrow 0$
5: **for all** l in L **do**
6: $t' \leftarrow t' + 1$
7: **if** $l = +$ **then**
8: $p \leftarrow p + 1$
9: **end if**
10: **end for**
11: $i \leftarrow \hat{G}(p', t', p, t)$/* see Equation 21*/

```
if h.size < S then
h.insert(i_(g))
else if (h.root < i) then
h.replace(h.root, i_(g))
end if
end for
for all i_(g) in h do
print (g, i)
end for
```

27.5 MALICIOUS CODE DETECTION

27.5.1 Overview

Malware is a major source of cyber attacks. Some malware varieties are purely static; each instance is an exact copy of the instance that propagated it. These are relatively easy to detect and filter once a single instance has been identified. However, a much more significant body of current day malware is polymorphic. Polymorphic malware self-modifies during propagation so that each instance has a unique syntax but carries a semantically identical malicious payload. The antivirus community invests significant effort and manpower toward devising, automating, and deploying algorithms that detect particular malware instances and polymorphic malware families that have been identified and analyzed by human experts. This has led to an escalating arms race between malware authors and antiviral defenders, in which each camp seeks to develop offenses and defenses that counter the recent advances of the other. With the increasing ease of malware development and the exponential growth of malware variants, many believe that this race will ultimately prove to be a losing battle for the defenders.

The malicious code detection problem can be modeled as a data mining problem for a stream having both infinite length and concept drift. Concept drift occurs as polymorphic malware mutates and as attackers and defenders introduce new technologies to the arms race. This conceptualization invites the application of our stream classification technique to automate the detection of new malicious executables.

Feature extraction using *n*-gram analysis involves extracting all possible *n*-grams from the given dataset (training set), and selecting the best *n*-grams among them. Each such *n*-gram is a feature. That is, an *n*-gram is a sequence of *n* bytes. Before extracting *n*-grams, we preprocess the binary executables by converting them to hexdump files. Here, the granularity level is 1 byte. We apply the UNIX hexdump utility to convert the binary executable files into text files (*hexdump files*) containing the hexadecimal numbers corresponding to each byte of the binary. This process is performed to ensure the safe and easy portability of the binary executables. In a nondistributed framework, the feature-extraction process consists of two phases: feature extraction and feature selection, described shortly. Our cloud computing variant of this traditional technique is presented in this chapter.

27.5.2 Nondistributed Feature Extraction and Selection

In a nondistributed setting, feature extraction proceeds as follows. Each hexdump file is scanned by sliding an *n*-byte window over its content. Each *n*-byte sequence that appears in the window is an *n*-gram. For each *n*-gram g, we tally the total number tg of file instances in which g appears, as well as the total number $pg \leq tg$ of these that are positive (i.e., malicious executables).

This involves maintaining a hash table T of all *n*-grams encountered so far. If g is not found in T, then g is added to T with counts $tg = 1$ and $pg \in \{0, 1\}$ depending on whether the current file has a negative or positive class label. If g is already in T, then tg is incremented and pg is conditionally incremented depending on the file's label. When all hexdump files have been scanned, T contains all the unique *n*-grams in the dataset along with their frequencies in the positive instances and in total.

It is not always practical to use all n-gram features extracted from all the files corresponding to the current chunk. The exponential number of such n-grams may introduce unacceptable memory overhead, slow the training process, or confuse the classifier with large numbers of noisy, redundant, or irrelevant features. To avoid these pitfalls, candidate n-gram features must be sorted according to a selection criterion so that only the best ones are selected.

We choose the *information gain* as the selection criterion, because it is one of the most effective criteria used in the literature for selecting the best features. The information gain can be defined as a measure of the effectiveness of an attribute (i.e., feature) for classifying the training data. If we split the training data based on the values of this attribute, then the information gain measures the expected reduction in entropy after the split. The more an attribute reduces entropy in the training data, the better that attribute is for classifying the data.

We have shown in [MASU11] as new features are considered, their information gains are compared against the heap's root. If the gain of the new feature is greater than that of the root, the root is discarded and the new feature inserted into the heap. Otherwise, the new feature is discarded and feature selection continues.

27.5.3 Distributed Feature Extraction and Selection

There are several drawbacks related to the nondistributed feature extraction and the selection approach just described.

- The total number of extracted n-gram features might be very large. For example, the total number of 4-grams in one chunk is around 200 million. It might not be possible to store all of them in main memory. One obvious solution is to store the n-grams in a disk file, but this introduces unacceptable overhead due to the cost of disk read/write operations.
- If colliding features in the hash table T are not sorted, then a linear search is required for each scanned n-gram during feature extraction to test whether it is already in T. If they are sorted, then the linear search is required during insertion. In either case, the time to extract all n-grams is worst case quadratic in the total number N of n-grams in each chunk, an impractical amount of time when $N \approx 108$. Similarly, the nondistributed feature-selection process requires a sort of the n-grams in each chunk. In general, this requires $O(N \log N)$ time, which is impractical when N is large.

In order to efficiently and effectively tackle the drawbacks of the nondistributed feature-extraction and feature-selection approach, we leverage the power of cloud computing. This allows feature extraction, n-gram sorting, and feature selection to be performed in parallel, utilizing the Hadoop *MapReduce* framework.

MapReduce [DEAN08] is an increasingly popular distributed programming paradigm used in cloud computing environments. The model processes large datasets in parallel, distributing the workload across many nodes (machines) in a share-nothing fashion. The main focus is to simplify the processing of large datasets using inexpensive cluster computers. Another objective is ease of usability with both load balancing and fault tolerance.

MapReduce is named for its two primary functions. The *Map* function breaks jobs down into subtasks to be distributed to available nodes, whereas its dual, *Reduce*, aggregates the results of completed subtasks. We will henceforth refer to nodes performing these functions as *mappers* and *reducers*, respectively. The details of the MapReduce process for n-gram feature extraction and selection are explained in the appendix. In this section, we give a high-level overview of the approach.

Each training chunk containing N training files is used to extract the n-grams. These training files are first distributed among m nodes (machines) by the HDFS (Figure 27.3, step 1). Quantity m is selected by HDFS depending on system availability. Each node then independently extracts n-grams from the subset of training files supplied to the node using the technique discussed in

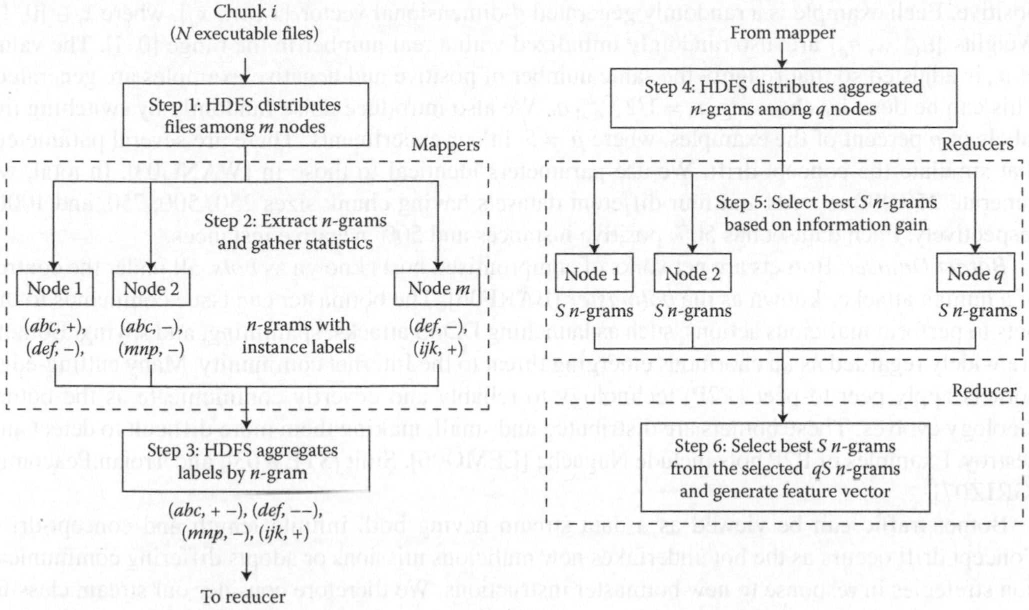

FIGURE 27.3 Distributed feature extraction and selection.

Section 4.1 (Figure 27.3, step 2). When all nodes finish their jobs, the *n*-grams extracted from each node are collated (Figure 27.3, step 3).

For example, suppose Node 1 observes *n*-gram *abc* in one positive instance (i.e., a malicious training file), while Node 2 observes it in a negative (i.e., benign) instance. This is denoted by pairs *abc*, + and *abc*, − under Nodes 1 and 2 (respectively) in Figure 27.3. When the *n*-grams are combined, the labels of instances containing identical *n*-grams are aggregated. Therefore, the aggregated pair for *abc* is *abc*, + −. The combined *n*-grams are distributed to *q* reducers (with *q* chosen by HDFS based on system availability). Each reducer first tallies the aggregated labels to obtain a positive count and a total count. In the case of *n*-gram *abc*, we obtain tallies of $pabc = 1$ and $tabc = 2$. The reducer uses these tallies to choose the best *S n*-grams (based on Equation 21) from the subset of *n*-grams supplied to the node (Figure 27.3, step 5). This can be done efficiently using a min-heap of size *S*; the process requires $O(W \log S)$ time, where *W* is the total number of *n*-grams supplied to each reducer. In contrast, the nondistributed version requires $O(W \log W)$ time. Thus, from the *q* reducer nodes, we obtain *qS n*-grams. From these, we again select the best *S* by running another round of the MapReduce cycle in which the Map phase does nothing, but the Reduce phase performs feature selection using only one node (Figure 27.3, step 6). Each feature in a feature set is binary; its value is 1 if it is present in a given instance (i.e., executable) and 0 otherwise. For each training or testing instance, we compute the feature vector whose bits consist of the feature values of the corresponding feature set. These feature vectors are used by the classifiers for training and testing.

27.6 EXPERIMENTS

We evaluated our approach on synthetic data, botnet traffic generated in a controlled environment, and a malware dataset. The results of the experiments are compared with several baseline methods.

27.6.1 Datasets

Synthetic Dataset. To generate synthetic data with a drifting concept, we use a moving hyperplane, given by $\sum_{i=1}^{d} a_i x_i = a_0$ [WANG03]. If $\sum_{i=1}^{d} a_i x_i \leq a_0$, then an example is negative; otherwise, it is positive. Each example is a randomly generated d-dimensional vector $\{x_1, \ldots, x_d\}$, where $x_i \in [0, 1]$. Weights $\{a_1, \ldots, a_d\}$ are also randomly initialized with a real number in the range [0, 1]. The value of a_0 is adjusted so that roughly the same number of positive and negative examples are generated. This can be done by choosing $a_0 = 1/2 \sum_{i=1}^{d} a_i$. We also introduce noise randomly by switching the labels of p percent of the examples, where $p = 5$ in our experiments. There are several parameters that simulate the concept-drift. We use parameters identical to those in [WANG03]. In total, we generate 250,000 records and four different datasets having chunk sizes 250, 500, 750, and 1000, respectively. Each dataset has 50% positive instances and 50% negative instances.

Botnet Dataset: Botnets are networks of compromised hosts known as *bots*, all under the control of a human attacker known as the *botmaster* [BARF06]. The botmaster can issue commands to the bots to perform malicious actions, such as launching DDoS attacks, spamming, and spying. Botnets are widely regarded as an enormous emerging threat to the Internet community. Many cutting-edge botnets apply peer-to-peer (P2P) technology to reliably and covertly communicate as the botnet topology evolves. These botnets are distributed and small, making them more difficult to detect and destroy. Examples of P2P bots include Nugache [LEMO06], Sinit [STEW03], and Trojan.Peacomm [GRIZ07].

Botnet traffic can be viewed as a data stream having both infinite length and concept-drift. Concept drift occurs as the bot undertakes new malicious missions or adopts differing communication strategies in response to new botmaster instructions. We therefore consider our stream classification technique to be well suited to detect the P2P botnet traffic.

We generate the real P2P botnet traffic in a controlled environment using the Nugache P2P bot [LEMO06]. The details of the feature extraction process are discussed in Masud et al. [MASU08b]. There are 81 continuous attributes in total. The whole dataset consists of 30,000 records, representing 1 week's worth of network traffic. We generate four different datasets having chunk sizes of 30 min, 60 min, 90 min, and 120 min, respectively. Each dataset has 25% positive (botnet traffic) instances and 75% negative (benign traffic).

Malware Dataset: We extract a total of 38,694 benign executables from different Windows machines, and a total of 66,694 malicious executables collected from an online malware repository VX Heavens [VX10] that contains a large collection of malicious executables (viruses, worms, trojans, and back-doors). The benign executables include various applications found at the Windows installation folder, as well as other executables in the default program installation directory.

We select only the Win32 Portable Executables (PEs) in both cases. Experiments with the ELF executables are a potential direction of future work. The collected 105,388 files (benign and malicious) form a data stream of 130 chunks, each consisting of 2000 instances (executable files). The stream order was chosen by sorting the malware by version and discovery date, simulating the evolving nature of Internet malware. Each chunk has 1500 benign executables (75% negative) and 500 malicious executables (25% positive). The feature-extraction and feature-selection process for this dataset is described in earlier sections.

Note that all these datasets are dynamic in nature. Their unbounded (potentially infinite-length) size puts them beyond the scope of purely static classification frameworks. The synthetic data also exhibits concept-drift. Although it is not possible to accurately determine whether the real datasets have concept-drift, theoretically the stream of executables should exhibit concept drift when observed over a long period of time. The malware data exhibits feature evolution as evidenced by the differing set of distinguishing features identified for each chunk.

27.6.2 Baseline Methods

For classification, we use the Weka machine learning open-source package [HALL09]. We apply two different classifiers: J48 decision tree and Ripper. We then compare each of the following baseline techniques to our EMPC algorithm.

BestK: This is an SPC ensemble approach, where an ensemble of the best K classifiers is used. The ensemble is created by storing all the classifiers seen so far and selecting the best K based on the expected error on the most recent training chunk. An instance is tested using simple majority voting.

Last: In this case, we only keep the classifier trained on the most recent training chunk. This can be considered an SPC approach with $K = 1$.

AWE: This is the SPC method implemented using accuracy-weighted classifier ensembles [WANG03]. It builds an ensemble of K models where each model is trained from one data chunk. The ensemble is updated as follows. Let Cn be the classifier built on the most recent training chunk. From the existing K models and the newest model Cn, the K best models are selected based on their error on the most recent training chunk. Selection is based on weighted voting where the weight of each model is inversely proportional to the error of the model on the most recent training chunk.

All: This SPC uses an ensemble of all the classifiers seen so far. The new data chunk is tested with this ensemble by simple voting among the classifiers. Since this is an SPC approach, each classifier is trained from only one data chunk.

We obtain the optimal values of r and v to be between 2 and 3, and 3 and 5, respectively, for most datasets. Unless mentioned otherwise, we use $r = 2$ and $v = 5$ in our experiments. To obtain a fair comparison, we use the same value for K (ensemble size) in EMPC and all baseline techniques.

Hadoop Distributed System Setup: The distributed system on which we performed our experiments consists of a cluster of 10 nodes. Each node has the same hardware configuration: an Intel Pentium IV 2.8 GHz processor, 4 GB main memory, and 640 GB hard disk space. The software environment consists of a Ubuntu 9.10 operating system, the Hadoop-0.20.1 distributed computing platform, the JDK 1.6 Java development platform, and a 100 MB LAN network link.

27.7 DISCUSSION

Our work considers a feature space consisting of purely syntactic features: binary n-grams drawn from executable code segments, static data segments, headers, and all other content of untrusted files. Higher level structural features such as call- and control-flow graphs, and dynamic features such as runtime traces, are beyond our current scope. Nevertheless, n-gram features have been observed to have very high discriminatory power for malware detection, as demonstrated by a large body of prior work as well as our experiments. This is in part because n-gram sets that span the entire binary file content, including headers and data tables, capture important low-level structural details that are often abstracted away by higher level representations. For example, malware often contains the handwritten assembly code that has been assembled and linked using nonstandard tools. This allows attackers to implement binary obfuscations and low-level exploits not available from higher level source languages and standard compilers. As a result, malware often contains unusual instruction encodings, header structures, and link tables whose abnormalities can only be seen at the raw binary level, not in assembly code listings, control flow graphs, or system API call traces. Expanding the feature space to include these additional higher level features requires an efficient and reliable method of harvesting them and assessing their relative discriminatory power during feature selection, and is reserved as a subject of future work.

The empirical results reported in [MASU11] confirm our analysis that shows that multipartition, multichunk approaches should perform better than single-chunk, single-partition approaches. Intuitively, a classifier trained on multiple chunks should have better prediction accuracy than a classifier trained on a single chunk because of the larger training data. Furthermore, if more than one classifier is trained by multipartitioning the training data, the prediction accuracy of the resulting ensemble of classifiers should be higher than a single classifier trained from the same training data because of the error reduction power of an ensemble over single classifier. In addition, the accuracy advantages of EMPC can be traced to two important differences between our work and that of AWE. First, when a classifier is removed during ensemble updating in AWE, all information obtained from the corresponding chunk is forgotten; but in EMPC, one or more classifiers from an earlier chunk may survive. Thus, EMPC ensemble updating tends to retain more information than that of AWE, leading to a better ensemble. Second, AWE requires at least Kv data chunks, whereas EMPC requires at least $K + r - 1$ data chunks to obtain Kv classifiers. Thus, AWE tends to keep much older classifiers in the ensemble than EMPC, leading to some outdated classifiers that can have a negative effect on the classification accuracy.

However, the higher accuracy comes with an increased cost in running time. Theoretically, EMPC is at most rv times slower than AWE, its closest competitor in accuracy. This is also evident in the empirical evaluation, which shows that the running time of EMPC is within 5 times that of AWE (for $r = 2$ and $v = 5$). However, some optimizations can be adopted to reduce the runtime cost. First, the parallelization of training for each partition can be easily implemented, reducing the training time by a factor of v. Second, classification by each model in the ensemble can also be done in parallel, thereby reducing the classification time by a factor of Kv. Therefore, the parallelization of training and classification should reduce the running time at least by a factor of v, making the runtime close to that of AWE. Alternatively, if parallelization is not available, parameters v and r can be lowered to sacrifice prediction accuracy for lower runtime cost. In this case, the desired balance between runtime and prediction accuracy can be obtained by evaluating the first few chunks of the stream with different values of v and r, and choosing the most suitable values.

27.8 SUMMARY AND DIRECTIONS

Many intrusion detection problems can be formulated as classification problems for infinite-length, concept-drifting data streams. Concept drift occurs in these streams as attackers react and adapt to defenses. We formulated both malicious code detection and botnet traffic detection as such problems, and introduced EMPC, a novel ensemble learning technique for the automated classification of infinite-length, concept-drifting streams. Applying EMPC to real-data streams obtained from polymorphic malware and botnet traffic samples yielded better detection accuracies than other data stream classification techniques. This shows that the approach is useful and effective for both intrusion detection and more general data stream classification.

EMPC uses generalized, multipartition, multichunk ensemble learning. Both theoretical and empirical evaluations of the technique show that it significantly reduces the expected classification error over existing SPC ensemble methods. Moreover, we show that EMPC can be elegantly implemented in a cloud computing framework based on MapReduce [DEAN08]. The result is a low-cost scalable stream classification framework with high classification accuracy and low runtime overhead.

At least two extensions to our technique offer promising directions of future work. First, our current feature-selection procedure limits its attention to the best S features based on information gain as the selection criterion. The classification accuracy could potentially be improved by leveraging recent work on supervised dimensionality reduction techniques [RISH08]; [SAJA05] for improved feature selection. Second, the runtime performance of our approach could be improved by exploiting additional parallelism available in the cloud computing architecture. For example, the classifiers of an ensemble could be run in parallel as mappers in a MapReduce framework with reducers that aggregate the results for voting. Similarly, the candidate classifiers for the next ensemble could be trained and evaluated in parallel. Reformulating the ensemble components of the system in this way could lead to significantly shortened processing times, and hence opportunities to devote more processing time to classification for improved accuracy. Other big data platforms such as Storm and Spark also need to be explored to host our algorithms. Finally, the amount of malware data collected for analysis could be massive; we need to explore the use of NoSQL database systems such as CouchDB to store, manage and query the data.

REFERENCES

[AGGA06]. C. C. Aggarwal, J. Han, J. Wang, P. S. Yu, "A Framework for On-Demand Classification of Evolving Data Streams," *IEEE Transactions on Knowledge and Data Engineering* 18 (5), 577–589, 2006.

[AHA91]. D. W. Aha, D. Kibler, M. K. Albert, "Instance-Based Learning Algorithms," *Machine Learning* 6 (1), 37–66, 1991.

[APAC10]. Hadoop. hadoop.apache.org, 2010.

[BARF06]. P. Barford and V. Yegneswaran, "An Inside Look at Botnets," *Malware Detection, Advances in Information Security*, M. Christodorescu, S. Jha, D. Maughan, D. Song, and C. Wang, editors, Springer, New York, NY, USA, pp. 171–192, 2006.

[BIFE09]. A. Bifet, G. Holmes, B. Pfahringer, R. Kirkby, R. Gavalda, "New Ensemble Methods for Evolving Data Streams," In *KDD'09: Proceedings of the 15th ACM International Conference on Knowledge Discovery and Data Mining*, Paris, France, pp. 139–148, 2009.

[BOSE92]. B. E. Boser, I. M. Guyon, V. N. Vapnik, "A Training Algorithm for Optimal Margin Classifiers," In *Proceedings of the 5th ACM Workshop on Computational Learning Theory*, Pittsburgh, PA, pp. 144–152, 1992.

[CHEN08]. S. Chen, H. Wang, S. Zhou, P. S. Yu, "Stop Chasing Trends: Discovering High Order Models in Evolving Data," In *ICDE'08: Proceedings of the 24th IEEE International Conference on Data Engineering*, Cancun, Mexico, pp. 923–932, 2008.

[COHE96]. W. W. Cohen, "Learning Rules that Classify E-mail," In *Proceedings of the AAAI Spring Symposium on Machine Learning in Information Access*, Portland, OR, pp. 18–27, 1996.

[COMP07]. Computer Economics, INC., *Malware Report: The Economic Impact of Viruses, Spyware, Adware, Botnets, and Other Malicious Code*, http://www.computereconomics.com/article.cfm?id=1227, 2007.

[CRAN05]. J. R. Crandall, Z. Su, S. F. Wu, F. T. Chong, "On Deriving Unknown Vulnerabilities from Zero-Day Polymorphic and Metamorphic Worm Exploits," In *CCS'05: Proceedings of the 12th ACM Conference on Computer and Communications Security*, Alexandria, VA, pp. 235–248, 2005.

[DEAN08]. J. Dean, S. Ghemawat, "MapReduce: Simplified Data Processing on Large Clusters," *Communicatioins of the ACM* 51 (1), 107–113, 2008.

[DOMI00]. P. Domingos, G. Hulten, "Mining High-Speed Data Streams," In *KDD'2000: Proceedings of the 6th ACM International Conference on Knowledge Discovery and Data Mining*, Boston, MA, pp. 71–80, 2000.

[FAN04]. W. Fan, "Systematic Data Selection to Mine Concept-Drifting Data Streams," In *KDD'04: Proceedings of the 10th ACM International Conference on Knowledge Discovery and Data Mining*, Seattle, WA, pp. 128–137, 2004.

[FREU96]. Y. Freund, R. E. Schapire, "Experiments with a New Boosting Algorithm," In *Proceedings of the 13th International Conference on Machine Learning*, Bari, Italy, pp. 148–156, 1996.

[GAO07]. J. Gao, W. Fan, J. Han, "On Appropriate Assumptions to Mine Data Streams: Analysis and Practice," In *ICDM'07: Proceedings of the 7th IEEE International Conference on Data Mining*, Omaha, NE, pp. 143–152, 2007.

[GRIZ07]. J. B. Grizzard, V. Sharma, C. Nunnery, B. B. Kang, D. Dagon, "Peer-to-Peer Botnets: Overview and Case Study," In *HotBots'07: Proceedings of the 1st Workshop on Hot Topics in Understanding Botnets*, pp. 1–8, 2007.

[HALL09a]. M. Hall, E. Frank, G. Holmes, B. Pfahringer, P. Reutemann, I. H. Witten, "The WEKA Data Mining Software: An Update," *ACM SIGKDD Explorations Newsletter* 11 (1), 10–18, 2009.

[HAML09b]. K. W. Hamlen, V. Mohan, M. M. Masud, L. Khan, B. M. Thuraisingham, "Exploiting An Antivirus Interface," *Computer Standards and Interfaces* 31 (6), 1182–1189, 2009.

[HASH09]. S. Hashemi, Y. Yang, Z. Mirzamomen, M. R. Kangavari, "Adapted One-versus-All Decision Trees for Data Stream Classification," *IEEE Transactions on Knowledge and Data Engineering* 21 (5), 624–637, 2009.

[HULT01]. G. Hulten, L. Spencer, P. Domingos, "Mining Time-Changing Data Streams," In *KDD'01: Proceedings of the 7th ACM International Conference on Knowledge Discovery and Data Mining*, San Francisco, CA, pp. 97–106, 2001.

[KOLT04]. J. Kolter, M. A. Maloof, "Learning to Detect Malicious Executables in the Wild," In *KDD'04: Proceedings of the 10th ACM International Conference on Knowledge Discovery and Data Mining*, Seattle, WA, pp. 470–478, 2004.

[KOLT05]. J. Z. Kolter and M. A. Maloof, "Using Additive Expert Ensembles to Cope with Concept Drift," In *ICML'05: Proceedings of the 22nd International Conference on Machine Learning*, Bonn, Germany, pp. 449–456, 2005.

[LEMO06]. R. Lemos, "Bot Software Looks to Improve Peerage," *SecurityFocus*, www.securityfocus.com/news/11390, 2006.

[LI06]. Z. Li, M. Sanghi, Y. Chen, M.-Y. Kao, B. Chavez, "Hamsa: Fast Signature Generation for Zero-Day Polymorphic Worms with Provable Attack Resilience," In *Proceedings of the IEEE Symposium on Security and Privacy*, Oakland, CA, pp. 32–47, 2006.

[MASU08a]. M. M. Masud, J. Gao, L. Khan, J. Han, B. Thuraisingham, "Mining Concept-Drifting Data Stream to Detect Peer to Peer Botnet Traffic, *Technical Reports*, UTDCS-05-08, The University of Texas at Dallas, Richardson, TX, www.utdallas.edu/mmm058000/reports/UTDCS-05-08.pdf, 2008.

[MASU08b]. M. M. Masud, L. Khan, B. Thuraisingham, "A Scalable Multi-Level Feature Extraction Technique to Detect Malicious Executables," *Information System Frontiers* 10 (1), 33–45, 2008.

[MASU09]. M. M. Masud, J. Gao, L. Khan, J. Han, , B. M. Thuraisingham, "A Multi-Partition Multi-Chunk Ensemble Technique to Classify Concept-Drifting Data Streams," In *Proceedings of the 13th Pacific-Asia Conference on Advances in Knowledge Discovery and Data Mining*, Bangkok, Thailand, 2009.

[MASU11]. M. M. Masud, T. Al-Khateeb, K. W. Hamlen, J. Gao, L. Khan, J. Han, B. M. Thuraisingham, "Cloud-Based Malware Detection for Evolving Data Streams," *ACM Transactions on Management Information Systems* 2 (3), 16, 2011.

[MICH94]. D. Michie, D. J. Spiegelhalter, C. C. Taylor, editors. *Machine Learning, Neural and Statistical Classification*, Ellis Horwood Series in Artificial Intelligence, Morgan Kaufmann, San Mateo, CA, pp. 50–83, 1994.

[NEWS05]. J. Newsome, B. Karp, D. Song, "Polygraph: Automatically Generating Signatures for Polymorphic Worms," In *S&P: Proceedings of the IEEE Symposium on Security and Privacy*, Oakland, CA, pp. 226–241, 2005.

[QUIN03]. J. R. Quinlan, *C4.5: Programs for Machine Learning* 5th Ed. Morgan Kaufmann, San Francisco, CA, USA, 2003.

[RISH08]. I. Rish, G. Grabarnik, G. Cecchi, F. Pereira, and G.J. Gordon. "Closed-Form Supervised Dimensionality Reduction with Generalized Linear Models." In *Proceedings of the 25th International Conference on Machine Learning (ICML '08)*. ACM, New York, NY, USA, pp. 832–839, 2008.

[SAJA05]. Sajama A. Orlitsky, "Supervised Dimensionality Reduction Using Mixture Models," In *ICML'05: Proceedings of the 22nd ACM International Conference on Machine Learning*, Bonn, Germany, pp. 768–775, 2005.

[SCHO05]. M. Scholz and R. Klinkenberg, "An Ensemble Classifier for Drifting Concepts," In *IWKDDS'05: Proceedings of the 2nd International Workshop on Knowledge Discovery in Data Streams*, Chicago, IL, pp. 53–64, 2005.

[SCHU01]. M. G. Schultz, E. Eskin, E. Zadok, S. J. Stolfo, "Data Mining Methods for Detection of New Malicious Executables," In *S&P: Proceedings of the IEEE Symposium on Security and Privacy*, Oakland, CA, pp. 38–49, 2001.

[STEW03]. J. Stewart, Sinit P2P Trojan Analysis, www.secureworks.com/research/threats/sinit, 2003.

[TUME96]. K. Tumer and J. Ghosh, "Error Correlation and Error Reduction in Ensemble Classifiers," *Connection Science* 8 (3), 385–404, 1996.

[VX10]. VX Heavens, VX Heavens. vx.netlux.org, 2010.

[WANG03]. H. Wang, W. Fan, P. S. Yu, J. Han, 2003. "Mining Concept-Drifting Data Streams Using Ensemble Classifiers," In *KDD'03: Proceedings of the 9th ACM International Conference on Knowledge Discovery and Data Mining*, Washington, DC, pp. 226–235, 2003.

[YANG05]. Y. Yang, X. Wu, X. Zhu, "Combining Proactive and Reactive Predictions for Data Streams," In *KDD'05: Proceedings of the 11th ACM International Conference on Knowledge Discovery and Data Mining*, Chicago, IL, pp. 710–715, 2005.

[ZHAN09]. P. Zhang, X. Zhu, L. Guo, "Mining Data Streams with Labeled and Unlabeled Training Examples," In *ICDM'09: Proceedings of the 9th IEEE International Conference on Data Mining*, Miami, FL, pp. 627–636, 2009.

[ZHAO09]. W. Zhao, H. Ma, Q. He, "Parallel K-Means Clustering Based on MapReduce," In *CloudCom'09: Proceedings of the 1st International Conference on Cloud Computing*, Beijing, China, pp. 674–679, 2009.

28 A Semantic Web-Based Inference Controller for Provenance Big Data

28.1 INTRODUCTION

Inference is the process of forming conclusions from premises. The inferred knowledge is harmful when the user is not authorized to acquire such information from legitimate responses that he/she receives. Providing a solution to the inference problem where users issue multiple requests and consequently infer unauthorized knowledge is an open problem. An inference controller is a device that is used to detect or prevent the occurrence of the inference problem. However, an inference controller will never know in full the inferences possible from the answers to a query request since there is always some prior knowledge available to the querying user. This prior knowledge could be any subset of all possible knowledge available from other external sources. The inference problem is complex and, therefore, an integrated and/or incremental domain-specific approach is necessary for its management. For a particular domain, one could take several approaches, such as (1) building inference controllers that act during query processing, (2) building inference controllers that enforce constraints during the knowledge base design, and (3) building inference controllers that provide explanations to a system security officer. Over time, the provenance data as well as the data deduced from the provenance data combined could become massive and therefore we need big data management techniques for handling the inference problem.

This chapter discusses the implementation of these incremental approaches for a prototype inference controller for provenance in a medical domain. The inference controller that we have designed and developed protects the sensitive information stored in a provenance database from unauthorized users. The provenance is represented as a directed acyclic graph. This graph-based structure of provenance can be represented and stored as an RDF graph [KLYN04], thereby allowing us to further exploit various semantic web technologies. In our work, we have built a prototype to evaluate the effectiveness of the proposed inference controller. We store the provenance information as an Web Ontology Language (OWL) knowledge base and use OWL-compliant reasoners to draw inferences from the explicit information in the provenance knowledge base. We enforce policy constraints at the design phase, as well as at runtime.

Provenance is metadata that captures the origin of a data source; the history or ownership of a valued object or a work of art or literature. It allows us to verify the quality of information in a data store to repeat manipulation steps and to discover dependences among data items in a data store. In addition, provenance can be used to determine the usefulness and trustworthiness of shared information. The utility of shared information relies on: (i) the quality of the source of information and (ii) the reliability and accuracy of the mechanisms (i.e., procedures and algorithms) used at each step of the modification (or transformation) of the underlying data items. Furthermore, provenance is a key component for the verification and correctness of a data item which is usually stored and then shared with information users.

Organizations and individual users rely on information sharing as a way of conducting their day-to-day activities. However, ease of information sharing comes with a risk of information misuse. An electronic patient record (EPR) is a log of all activities, including patient visits to a hospital, diagnoses and treatments for diseases, and processes performed by healthcare professionals on a patient. This EPR is often shared among several stakeholders (e.g., researchers, and insurance and pharmaceutical companies). Before this information can be made available to any third party, the sensitive information in an EPR must be circumvented or hidden before releasing any part of the EPR. This can be addressed by applying policies that completely or partially hide sensitive attributes within the information being shared. The protection of sensitive information is often required by regulations that are mandated by a company or by laws, such as Health Insurance Portability and Accountability Act (HIPAA) [ANNA03].

While the technologies that we have used are mainly semantic web technologies, we believe that the amount of data that has to be handled by the inference controller could be massive. This is because the data not only includes the data in the database, but also previously released data as well as real-world information. Therefore, traditional database management techniques will be inadequate for implementing the inference controllers. As an example, we designed and implemented inference controllers in the 1990s, and it took us almost two years for the implementation discussed in [THUR93] and [THUR95]. Furthermore, we could not store all of the released data as well as the real-world data. That is, we purged the data that was least recently used from the knowledge base. We re-implemented the inference controllers with semantic web technologies in the late 2000s and early 2010s, and it took us just a few months for these implementations. Furthermore, our knowledge base was quite large and stored much of the released data and the real-world data. However, for the inference controller to be truly effective, it needs to process massive amounts of data, and we believe that we need a cloud-based implementation with big data management technologies. Our initial implementation of a policy engine in the cloud, which is a form of the inference controller, was discussed in Chapter 25. We need to implement he complete inference controller in the cloud using big data technologies.

The organization of this chapter is as follows. Our system architecture will be discussed in Section 28.2. Some background on data provenance as well as semantic web technologies will be discussed in Section 28.3. Our system design with examples is presented in Section 28.4. Details regarding the implementation of the inference controller are provided in Section 28.5. Implementing the inference controller using big data management techniques is discussed in Section 28.6. Finally, this chapter is concluded in Section 28.7. Details of our inference controller are given in our prior book [THUR15].

28.2 ARCHITECTURE FOR THE INFERENCE CONTROLLER

In this section, we present the design of an inference controller that employs inference strategies and techniques built around semantic web technologies. Our architecture takes a user's input query and returns a response that has been pruned using a set of user-defined policies (i.e., constraints on the underlying data items and provenance). We assume that a user could interact with our system to obtain both traditional data and its associated provenance. However, since the emphasis of this chapter is on protecting the provenance of data items, we will mainly focus on the design of the inference controller with respect to provenance data and less on the protection of traditional data items. Note that our inference controller can complement policies used to protect traditional data items by adding an extra layer of protection for provenance data.

The architecture is built using a modular approach; therefore, it is very flexible in that most of the modules can be extended or replaced by another application module. A modular design also allows a policy designer to focus on designing policies and abstracts them from the management of user interaction tasks.

Provenance data has a logical graph structure; therefore, it can also be represented and stored in a graph data model, without being limited to any particular data format. Although our focus in this chapter is on building an inference controller over the graph representation of provenance, our inference controller could also be used to protect data within a traditional database. Also, the use of an RDF data model is not restrictive since other data formats are well served by an RDF data model.

Furthermore, tools such as D2RQ [BIZE03] could be used to convert traditional relational data into RDF data, thus allowing users to view both types of data as RDF graphs.

In our design, we will assume that the available information is divided into two parts: the actual data and provenance. Both the data and provenance can be represented as RDF graphs. The reader should note that we do not make any assumptions about how the actual information is stored. A user may have stored data and provenance in two different triple stores or in the same store. In addition, a user's application can submit a query for access to the data and its associated provenance or vice versa. Figure 28.1 presents the design of our proposed inference controller over provenance. We next present a description of the major modules in Figure 28.1.

User-Interface Manager: A user-interface manager is responsible for processing a user's requests, authenticating a user and providing suitable responses back to a user. The interface manager also provides an abstraction layer that allows a user to interact with the system. A user can therefore poses either a data query or a provenance query to this layer. The user-interface manager also determines whether the query should be evaluated against the data or its provenance.

The user interacts with the provenance inference controller via an interface layer. This layer accepts a user's credentials and authenticates the user. The interface manager hides the actual internal representation of an inference controller from a user by providing a simple question–answer mechanism. This mechanism allows a user to pose standard provenance queries such as why a data item was created, where in the provenance graph it was generated, and how the data item was generated and when and where it was created. This layer also returns results after they are examined against a set of policies. Figure 28.2 shows a more detailed view of the interface manager that allows a user to interact with the underlying provenance store(s) via the inference controller. The interface manager's role is to authenticate users, process input queries, and check for errors that may occur during query processing. In addition, it carries out other functions; for example, it performs some preprocessing operations before submitting a query to the inference controller layer.

Policy Manager: A policy manager is responsible for ensuring that the querying user is authorized to use the system. It evaluates policies against a user's query and associated query results to ensure that no confidential information is released to unauthorized users. The policy manager may enforce policies against data or its associated provenance. Each data type may have its own policy manager, for example, data may be stored in a different format from provenance data. Hence, we may require separate implementations of the policy manager for data and provenance. Figure 28.3 shows the

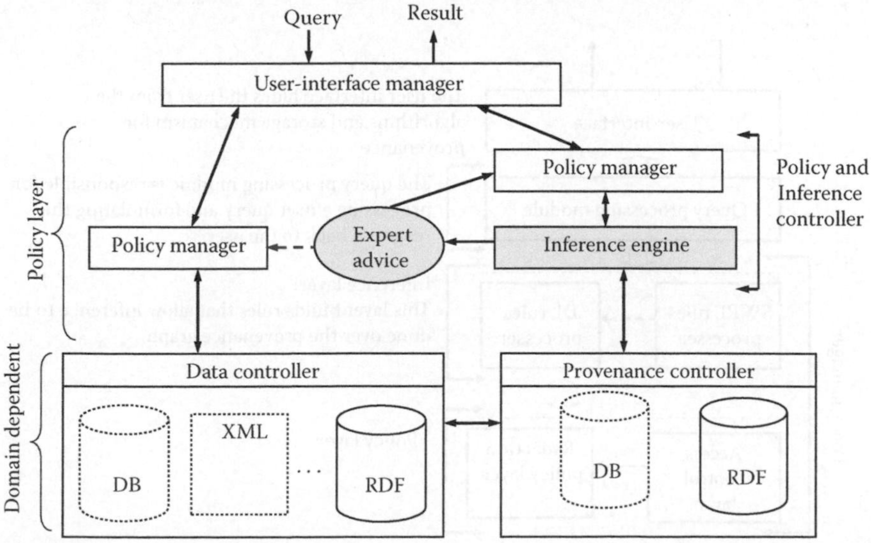

FIGURE 28.1 Architecture overview.

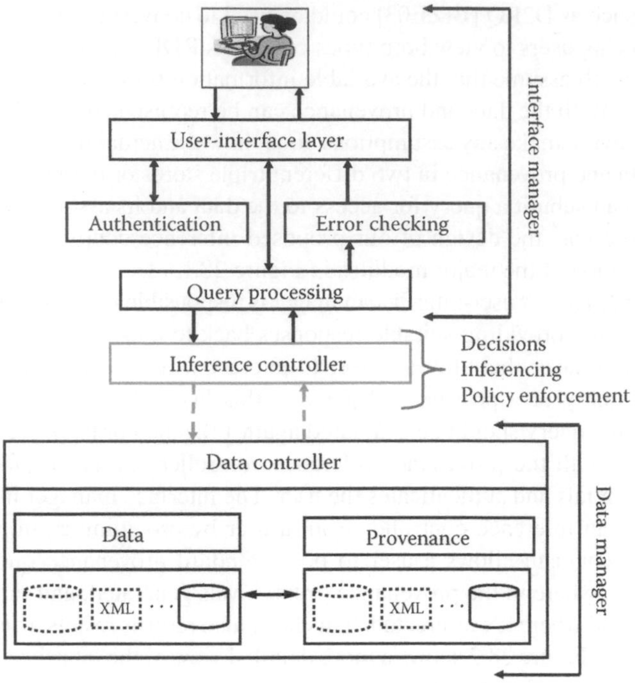

FIGURE 28.2 Interface manager.

details of the policy manager. The policy manager interacts with the user via the query-processing module. Each query passed to the policy manager from the query-processing module is evaluated against a set of policies. As previously mentioned, these policies can be encoded as access control rules via any access control mechanism or other suitable policy languages ([CADE11a], [CADE11b]). They can be expressed as rules that operate directly over a directed graph or they can be encoded as description logic (DL) [LEVY98] constraints or using web rule languages, such as the Semantic Web Rule Language (SWRL) [HORR04]. The policy layer is responsible for enforcing any high-level policy defined by an application user or administrator. The policies are not restricted to any particular

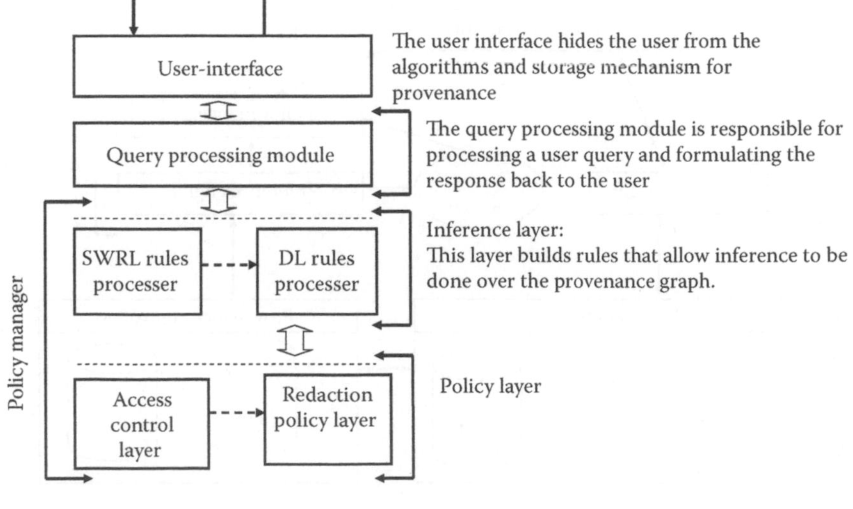

FIGURE 28.3 Policy manager.

security policy definition, model, or mechanism. In fact, we can support different policies, for example, role-based access control (RBAC), access control based on context, such as time (TRBAC) and location (LBAC). The policy manager also handles RBAC policies specified in OWL and SWRL [CADE10a]. In addition, it handles certain policies specified in OWL for inference control such as association-based policies. Besides the traditional and well-established security models built on top of access control mechanisms, the inference controller also supports redaction policies. Redaction policies are based on sharing data for ongoing mutual relationships among businesses and stakeholders. Redaction policies are useful when the results of a query are further sanitized. For example, the literal value of an assertion by an RDF triple in a result graph may contain the nine-digit social security number of employees, as *999-99-9999*, but for regulatory purposes, the four-digit format *9999* is the correct format for disclosure. The redaction policies can also be used to redact (block out or hide) any node in an RDF triple (i.e., block out a literal value, hide a resource, etc.).

Finally, the policy layer interacts with various reasoners in the inference layer, which offer further protection against inference attacks. The inference layer enforces policies that are in the form of DL constraints [ZHAN09], OWL restrictions [MCGU04a], or SWRL rules. Note that some of the access control policies can be expressed as inference rules (for more expressive power) or as queries via query rewriting ([OULM10a, OULM10b]), or in the form of view definitions [RIZV04]. The policy manager therefore has many layers equipped with security features, thus ensuring that we offer the maximal protection over the underlying provenance store.

The Query-Processing Module: It is responsible for accepting a user's query from the user interface, parsing it, and submitting it to the policy manager. In addition, the module also evaluates results against the user-defined set of policies and rules, after which the results are returned to the user via the user-interface layer. The query-processing module can accept any standard provenance query, as well as any query written using SPARQL [PRUD06]. The query-processing module also provides feedback to the user via the user interface. This feedback includes errors due to query syntax in addition to the responses constructed by the underlining processes of the policy and inference controller layers.

Inference Engine: The inference engine is the heart of the inference controller. The engine is equipped to use a variety of inference strategies, each requiring a reasoner. Since there are many implementations of reasoners available, our inference controller offers an added feature of flexibility, whereby we can select a reasoner from amongst a variety of OWL-compliant reasoning tools based on different reasoning tasks or domains. For example, decisions in a medical domain may require all the facts in a triple store or only the facts related to a particular EPR in the triple store. Therefore, one can limit a task involving inferences to the local information (available in the EPR and the related provenance).

A modular approach [CADE10b] can improve the efficiency of the inference controller. The approach given in [CADE10b] allows each inference process to be executed on a separate processor; therefore, we can take advantage of designs based on partitioning and parallelism. For example, the code implementing a strategy based on heuristic reasoning [THUR90] could be executed in parallel with the code that implements a strategy based on inference by semantic association [THUR93]. Furthermore, an inference engine typically uses software programs that have the capability of reasoning over a relevant subset of facts that are in some data representation of a domain, for example, a relational data model or an RDF graph representation.

Data Controller: The data controller is a suite of software programs that stores and manages access to data. The data could be stored in any format such as in a relational database, in XML files or in an RDF store. The controller accepts requests for information from the policy layer if a policy allows the requesting user to access the data items in the data stores (e.g., the triple stores). This layer then executes the request over the stored data and returns the results back to the policy layer where they are re-evaluated before being returned to the user-interface layer.

Provenance Controller: The provenance controller is used to store and manage provenance information that is associated with data items that are present in the data controller. In the case when we represent provenance as an RDF graph, the provenance controller stores information in the form of a logical graph structure in any appropriate data representation format (e.g., RDF serialization format). The provenance controller also records the ongoing activities associated with the data items stored in the data controller. The provenance controller takes as input a graph query and evaluates it over the provenance data. The provenance controller then returns a resultant RDF graph back to the policy layer where it is re-examined using a set of policies before returning it to the querying user. A re-examination of the resulting RDF graph allows the policy designer to transform the result graph further by applying other graph transformation techniques (e.g., redaction, sanitization, etc.) that can alter triples in the resulting RDF graph. Note that the original provenance graphs are not altered during the transformation; instead, copies of the original graph (created by queries) undergo transformations. This protects the integrity of the provenance data; the effect of modifying the provenance changes the provenance.

Policy Managers: An application user may wish to write policies at a high level using domain-specific business rules. Thus, an application user can continue using his/her business policies independent of our software implementation of the provenance inference controller. A suitable policy parser module could handle the parsing of high-level policies and their transformation into low-level policy objects used by the system. Therefore, modifying or extending a policy manager module is facilitated since it is not hard-wired to any implementation of other modules in the architecture.

Inference Tools: Newly published data, when combined with existing public knowledge, allows for complex and sometimes unintended inferences. Therefore, we need semi-automated tools for detecting these inferences prior to releasing provenance information. These tools should give data owners a fuller understanding of the implications of releasing the provenance information, as well as helping them adjust the amount of information they release in order to avoid unwanted inferences.

The inference controller is a tool that implements some of the inference strategies that a user could use to infer confidential information that is encoded into a provenance graph. Our inference controller leverages existing software tools that perform inferencing, for example, Pellet [SIRI07], Fact++ [TSAR06], Racer [HAAR01], Hermit [SHEA08], CWM [BERN00], and third party plugins [CARR04]. A modular design also takes advantage of theories related to a modular knowledge base in order to facilitate collaborative ontology construction, use, and reuse ([BAO06], [FARK02], [BAO04]). In addition, there exists a trade-off between expressivity and decidability; therefore, a policy designer or an administrator should have flexibility when selecting an appropriate reasoner software for a particular application. In addition to the reasoner, the policy designer should take into consideration the expressiveness of the representational language for the concepts in an application domain. For example, one may prefer urgency in a medical or intelligence domain when making appropriate decisions and therefore decide on an optimized reasoner for a representational language (e.g., RDF, RDFS, OWL-DL).

28.3 SEMANTIC WEB TECHNOLOGIES AND PROVENANCE

28.3.1 Semantic Web-Based Models

Provenance data can be stored in the relational data model, the XML data model, or the RDF data model. Each of these in their current form has drawbacks with respect to provenance [HOLL08]. The directed nature of a provenance graph presents major challenges. A relational model suffers from the fact that it needs expensive joins on relations (tables) for storing edges or paths. In addition, current SQL languages that support transitive queries are complex and awkward to write. XML supports path queries, but the current query languages such as XQuery and XPath only support a tree structure. RDF naturally supports a graph structure, but the current W3C recommendation for SPARQL (the standard query language for RDF) lacks many features needed for path queries. There are recent works on extending SPARQL with path expressions and variables. These include SPARQL Query 1.1 [HARR10], which is now a W3C recommendation. Of these three data models, we represent provenance using an RDF data model. This data model meets the specification of the open provenance model (OPM) recommendation [MORE11]. In addition, RDF allows the integration of multiple databases describing the different pieces of the lineage of a resource (or data item) and naturally supports the directed structure of provenance. This data model has also been successfully applied for provenance capture and representation ([DING05, ZHAO08]). In addition to RDF, [KLYN04], RDF Schema (RDFS) can be used for the reasoning capabilities.

Other representation schemes are the OWL [MCGU04a,b] and the SWRL [HORR04]. OWL is an ontology language that has more expressive power and reasoning capabilities than RDF and RDFS. It has an additional vocabulary along with a formal semantics. The formal semantics in OWL are based on DLs, which are a decidable fragment of first-order logics. OWL consists of a Tbox that comprises the vocabulary that defines the concepts in a domain, and an Abox that is made up of assertions (facts about the domain). The Tbox and Abox make up an OWL knowledge base. The SWRL extends the set of OWL axioms to include Horn-like rules, and it extends these rules to be combined with an OWL knowledge base. Using these languages allows us to later perform inference over the provenance graph. Therefore, we could determine the implicit information in the provenance graph.

28.3.2 Graphical Models and Rewriting

Graphs are a very natural representation of data in many application domains, for example, precedence networks, path hierarchy, family tree, and concept hierarchy. In addition, directed graphs are a natural representation of provenance ([BRAU08, MORE11, MORE10, ZHAO10]). We begin by giving a general definition of a labeled graph, and then we introduce a specific labeled graph representation for provenance. This specific representation is referred to as RDF, which will serve to represent and store a provenance graph. Note that an RDF graph is a set of triples, which may have one or more machine-processable formats, such as RDF/XML, TURTLE, and NTRIPLE.

The OPM [MORE11] is an abstract vocabulary that describes provenance as a set of objects that is represented by a causality graph that is a directed acyclic graph. This graph is enriched with annotations that capture information about an execution. The objects are nodes and their relationships are arcs. The provenance model of causality is timeless since time precedence does not imply causality. We define the nodes in the provenance graph using the nomenclature in [MORE11].

A graph-rewriting system is well suited for performing transformations over a graph. Furthermore, provenance is well represented in a graphical format. Thus, a graph-rewriting system is well suited for specifying policy transformations over provenance. Graph rewriting is a transformation technique that takes as input an original graph and replaces a part of that graph with another graph. This technique, also called graph transformation, creates a new graph from the original graph by using a set of production rules. Popular graph-rewriting approaches include the single-pushout approach and the double-pushout approach ([ROZE97, CORR97]).

A graph-rewriting system should be capable of specifying under what conditions a graph-manipulation operation is valid. The embedding instructions normally contain a fair amount of information and are usually very flexible; however, allowing the policy designer to specify the embeddings may become error-prone. The OPM nomenclature places a restriction on the set of admissible RDF graphs, which we call valid OPM graphs. These restrictions serve to control a graph-transformation process (also a graph-rewriting process) by ruling out transformations that lead to nonadmissible graphs.

28.4 INFERENCE CONTROL THROUGH QUERY MODIFICATION

28.4.1 Our Approach

An inference controller offers a mechanism that (1) protects confidential information, (2) mimics a user's strategy for inferring confidential information, and (3) performs inference over the provenance graph data. Data provenance in general contains both sensitive and public information.

We need to disclose provenance information in order to ensure that the user gets high-quality information. Provenance data has a unique characteristic that makes it different from traditional data [BRAU08]. This characteristic is the directed acyclic graph (DAG) structure of provenance that captures single-data items and the causal relationships between them. Additionally, the DAG structure complicates any efforts to successfully build an inference controller over provenance data and surprisingly this area has been unexplored by the research community. Although the research community has applied inference over provenance data, in particular, the inference web that has used provenance to provide proofs as justifications for data items [MCGU04b], it has not considered inferencing from the point of view of provenance security.

28.4.2 Domains and Provenance

Provenance and RDF define different domain spaces from traditional database problems. Provenance is mainly used for justification and proofs, verification and detection, gauging the trustworthiness of data items, for auditing and maintaining the history of a workflow process, establishing high integrity and quality data, and the reliability of information sources. RDF is mainly used for the knowledge representation of a domain, to formulate a problem with a graph representation, to name things with URIs and assert relationships between them, to link data in an open environment for information discovery, to support interoperability among data sources, and to add semantics to data and support reasoning. Traditional databases, on the other hand, are best suited for problems with fixed schemas. RDF technologies have been used to build inference engines that support inferences [CARR05] and also to represent and store provenance information ([CARR05], [DING05], [ZHAO08]). In addition, OWL has been used to model different domains with private information [FINI08], and DLs have been applied to the privacy problem [STOU09]. Our goal is to combine some of these efforts in order to build an inference controller over provenance. Therefore, provenance will be represented as RDF graphs, and DLs will be used to support the inference tasks of our inference controller.

Traditionally, we protect data using various policies. These include access control policies that specify what can be accessed, sanitization and anonymization policies that specify how to share released information, and randomization and encryption techniques that can be used to scramble the data in transmission. These techniques alone do not prevent the inference problem. Therefore, our inference controller will serve as a key security tool on top of the existing ones, thereby complementing the existing techniques in order to protect provenance data.

Different approaches have been used to apply access control policies to provenance ([NI09], [CADE11a], [SYAL09], [ROSE09]). For example, an approach that annotates OPM entities with access control attributes is given in [ROSE09]. Another approach that defines policies for artifacts, processes, and path dependences is given in [CADE11c]. Our approach takes into consideration the structure of provenance and instead represents it as RDF data in order to leverage existing SWRLs that have been used to encode extremely complicated access control policies ([ZHAN09], [FINI08], [LI05], [SHIE06]). Furthermore, our approach encodes some of the simpler access control policies as SPARQL queries (by the use of a rewrite procedure); we use DL to compactly write the rules formally to avoid ambiguity, and we also use SWRL to write rules that are very expressive. Note that there is a trade-off between expressiveness and decidability (e.g., SWRL [HORR05] vs. OWL-DL [MCGU04a,b]).

Protecting provenance by applying access control policies alone, however, ignores the utility of the provenance given to the querying user. Therefore, an important feature of our inference controller is to build mechanisms for associating a high utility with the query responses while ensuring that policies are not compromised. We rely on a formal graph-transformation approach for visualizing the provenance after a policy is enforced (see Definition 6). At each transformation step, the policy that preserves the highest utility is applied. We continue to apply policies at different transformation steps until all policies are enforced. Throughout this chapter, we refer to the policies that utilize a graph-transformation approach as redaction policies (see [CADE11b] for further details). This graph transformation technique can also be used to modify the triple patterns in an SPARQL query; this is called query rewriting. As previously mentioned, the inference controller will therefore use a combination of policies. When appropriate, we will: protect data by using access control policies to limit access to the provenance data; use redaction policies to share the provenance information; and also use the graph-transformation technique for sanitizing the initial query results.

Inferences may be obtained during two stages:

1. *Data collection*: This includes data in the data stores that is accessible to users and real-world knowledge (which is not represented in the data stores) about an application domain.
2. *Reasoning with the collected data*: This is the act of deriving new information from the collected data.

The data collection and the reasoning stages are performed repeatedly by the adversary (i.e., by a human user or an autonomous agent) until the intended inference is achieved or the adversary gives up. Each query attempts to retrieve data from the internal data stores, but the adversary may also collect data from external data stores as part of the background-knowledge-acquisition process. The data that adversaries want to infer may include the existence of a certain entity in the data stores (i.e., the knowledge base of the facts about a domain) or the associations among data (i.e., the relationships among the facts).

In some cases, instead of inferring the exact data (facts) in a knowledge base (precise inference), users may be content with a set of possible data values (imprecise inference or approximate inference). For instance, assume that a user wants to infer *the disease of a patient* from the patient's record, which is a part of the provenance graph. Further, assume that the provenance captures the record's history that records that a heart surgeon performed an operation on the patient. Revealing the fact that a heart surgeon is part of the provenance could enable the user to infer that the patient has *some disease related to heart problems* but not necessarily the exact nature of the surgery or the exact disease of the patient.

28.4.3 Inference Controller with Two Users

An approach to tackling the inference problem is to explicitly represent all information available to a user, and mimic the reasoning strategies of that user. A query log has a context ([BAI07], [SHEN05]) and therefore could be used to identify the activities of the user. In addition, a designated database could be used to record all information released to the user so far. This could help in identifying some background profile of the user, as well as to know what the user already knows [CADE10a]. However, there are major challenges to this approach. An example challenge is related to the storage used to track the released information. Another challenge is the duplication of facts (the facts in the released database are copies of facts in the original knowledge base). Instead of materializing the query results and storing them, another approach is to re-evaluate the queries from the query logs at query execution time, but this could impact the performance of the data manager. The query logs contain pieces of information that can be revealing and can therefore reveal queries targeting private information in the provenance stores. Queries for phone numbers, addresses, and names of individuals are all useful in narrowing down the target space for individuals, and thus increase the chance of a successful attack. In addition, the query logs show the distribution of queries for a user as well as the query sequencing; the query logs also aid the reconstructing of results for previous queries. Finally, it is possible to cluster users based on query behaviors. More significantly, there also exist correlations among queries (e.g., those who query for X also query for Y).

The inference controller comprises a knowledge base for storing provenance. This is represented by a set of RDF triples. The provenance is encoded using a provenance vocabulary. The user submits queries; each query is first examined to determine if it is a valid query before submitting it to the inference layer. The query is then submitted and executed over the knowledge base. We model this as two machines (or automated tools): the user (e.g., an automated agent) and the controller.

We assume that the user builds a machine, M', that contains the history of all the answers given to the user, the modified background knowledge with relevant domain information and a prior set of rules about the system. Further, the user can infer a subset of the private information using M'. Likewise, we build a machine M'' that simulates the inferencing mechanism of the user, but with certain modifications to compensate for any differences. This machine, M'', combines the history of all previous answers, the current query and associated provenance and the rules that enforce the security policies. We use M'' to determine certain inferences occurring in M'. The major difference between M' and M'' is the user's background information. M' and M'' contain different sets of rules and M'' keeps a repository of a user's input queries. This repository (or query log) is a rich source of information about the context of the user. For example, if the logged queries could compromise the knowledge base, the user is flagged as an attacker.

The inferencing capabilities of M'' are best realized by a language with formal semantics. The Resource Description Framework (RDF), RDFS and the Web Ontology Language (OWL) are knowledge representation languages that fit this criterion; these languages all use the RDF data model. RDF data model is also a natural fit for a directed graph such as provenance. Also, to realize policy rules using SWRL and DLs, the provenance is stored in an OWL knowledge base.

The queries are written in the SPARQL language. These queries are extended with regular expressions in order to select graph patterns for both the user's query and the protected resources. In order to write the policy constraints (as rules), we use a mixture of queries, DL rules and SWRL. These constraints (rules) specify the concepts, triples and facts that are to be protected. The concepts are the definitions (or descriptions) of resources in a provenance graph; these are normally written formally to avoid ambiguity in policy specification languages such as DLs. Each DL concept can also be successfully defined by an SPARQL query or an SWRL rule. In some cases, the constraints may require more expressive languages for defining the concept and so we sometimes choose SWRL rules over DL rules.

28.4.4 SPARQL Query Modification

RDF is being increasingly used to store information as assertions about a domain. This includes both confidential and public information. SPARQL has been selected as a query language that extracts data from RDF graphs. Since confidential data is accessed during the querying process, we need to filter the results of SPARQL queries so that only authorized information is released with respect to some confidentiality policy. Our aim is to rewrite the SPARQL queries so that the results returned are compliant with the confidentiality policies.

Existing work has been done in the area of data management, data warehousing and query optimization that apply query modification techniques ([RIZV04], [LEVY95], [BEER97]). These traditional approaches use rewrite procedures to modify the original query for purposes of query optimization, query pruning or fulfilling policy requirements. Other works [ORAC], [OULM10a], [OULM10b], [LE11], [HOLL10], and [CORR10] describe query modification techniques based on SPARQL queries over RDF data. Our focus will be on applying similar query modification techniques to the input SPARQL queries.

We design security mechanisms that control the evaluation of SPARQL queries in order to prevent the disclosure of confidential provenance information. Our approach is to modify the graph patterns in the SPARQL query by adding filters and/or property functions that are evaluated over the provenance data. These approaches may return answers different from the user's initial query intent. It may be necessary to decide on appropriate actions in these cases. We identify two approaches that may be followed. The first approach checks the query validity against that of the initial query and notifies the user that the query validity is not guaranteed. The second approach takes into consideration that a feedback about the validity of a query result may lead the user to draw undesirable inferences.

In some cases, it may be possible to return only the answers that comply with the policy constraints. One approach is to replace a set of triples satisfying a query with another set of triples by applying transformation rules over the first set of triples. Another approach may be to lie about the contents in the knowledge base. Yet another approach is to use polyinstantiation similar to that in multilevel secure databases, where users at different clearance levels see different versions of reality [STAC90].

Approaches for modifying the graph patterns in an SPARQL query make use of different techniques, for example, SPARQL filters and property functions, graph transformations and match/apply pattern. In order to determine the type of triple with respect to a security classification, the inference engine would use a domain ontology to determine the concept each data item belongs to as well as a query modification based on an SPARQL BGP transformation.

There is a difference between a query engine that simply queries an RDF graph but does not handle rules and an inference engine that also handles rules. In the literature, this difference is not always clear. The complexity of an inference engine is a lot higher than a query engine. The reason is that rules permit us to make sequential deductions. In the execution of a query, these deductions are to be constructed. This is not necessary in the case of a query engine. Note that there are other examples of query engines that rely on a formal model for directed labeled graphs such as DQL [FIKE02] and RQL [KARV12].

Rules also support a logic base that is inherently more complex than the logic in the situation without rules. For an RDF query engine, only the simple principles of entailment on graphs are necessary. RuleML is an important effort to define rules that are usable for the World Wide Web. The inference web [MCGU04a,b] is a recent realization that defines a system for handling different inference engines on the semantic web.

28.5 IMPLEMENTING THE INFERENCE CONTROLLER

28.5.1 Our Approach

We now present the design of an inference controller for provenance. The inference controller is implemented using a modular approach; therefore, it is very flexible in that most of the modules can be extended by a domain user. For example, an application user may substitute the policy parser module that handles the parsing of high-level policies into low-level policy objects with a custom-built parser. Internally, the rules associated with a policy could be converted to SPARQL queries so that they are evaluated over an RDF graph. Therefore, the application user can continue using his/her high-level business policies independent of our software implementation.

We describe the phases through which the knowledge base is populated with domain data and provenance. The first phase is the selection of a domain. This is followed by data collection and data representation of the concepts and relationships among the concepts in the domain. Once the domain data is represented in a suitable machine readable format (i.e., RDF, OWL), the next phase is to generate provenance workflow data, which is also recorded using a provenance vocabulary. The policies are internally written as suitable semantic web rules (e.g., SWRL, DL, and/or SPARQL). Once the policies are in place, a user can interact with the system by posing SPARQL queries which are then evaluated over the knowledge base.

28.5.2 Implementation of a Medical Domain

We describe a medical domain with respect to online sources (for example, WebMD, which is available at http://www.webmd.com/). The medical domain is made up of patients, physicians, nurses, technicians, equipments, medical procedures, etc. Note that we use a fictitious hospital, which complies with real procedures described at online sources (e.g., http://www.nlm.nih.gov/ and http://www.mghp.com/services/procedure/). These procedures include heart surgery, the hip replacement procedure, etc. Since the procedures are described by actual documents on the Web, the generated workflow structures encode a set of guidelines that are also known to the users of the system. However, most real-world hospitals follow guidelines related to a patient's privacy, so our fictitious hospital generates provenance workflows whose contents correspond to the confidential data found in patients' records. Therefore, the record (i.e., an artifact), the agent who generated a version of a record, the time when the record was updated and the processes that contributed to the changes of the record are part of the provenance. Furthermore, the laws governing the release of provenance (i.e., the contents of the generated workflow) are enforced by constraints which are implemented as semantic web rules in our prototype system. The use of a fictitious hospital here reflects the fact that real data and provenance from real hospitals are difficult to obtain and are usually not released in their original form, since they are protected by domain and regulatory laws.

28.5.3 Generating and Populating the Knowledge Base

A set of seeds, each consisting of a first name, a last name, a state and city, were used to create queries which are issued against the *yellowpages* and the *whitepages* web sites. The pages matching an initial query are crawled, and the results are converted and stored in an appropriate format for later use. The crawl routines were executed off-line in a predefined sequence. The first crawl gathers a list of patients. With the zip codes of the patients, we formulate web queries to further search for hospitals, doctors and their specialties. The results of these queries are also stored in a predetermined format. A set of generators are responsible for extracting background information which is normally available online. A provenance workflow generator also produces the provenance. Note that this workflow generator produces synthetic provenance data that is not available online.

We use real information on current web pages so that we can demonstrate the effectiveness of the inference controller with respect to the prior knowledge of the querying agent. Parameters such as city, state and zip in the USA were initialized and sent to freely available web sites, such as the yellow pages (http://www.yellowpages.com/) and white pages (http://www.whitepages.com/). These websites were crawled and important attributes such as the name, address, telephone numbers, age, sex, relatives of various individuals were extracted. These attributes make up the patients in our knowledge base.

We selected a list of hospitals which were located in the zip codes of the patients. Each hospital has a name, address, and telephone number. Because many hospitals do not release the names of their staff, additional searches for doctors and their specialties were carried out; these searches were also limited to the zip codes of the hospitals. Note that it is normal to assume most specialists are affiliated with a particular hospital close to their location of practice. Some insurance companies do provide a list of the doctors and their affiliations on their websites, but many of these websites require a login id or a different verification code each time it is accessed (i.e., preventing automated crawls). Due to these obstacles, the knowledge base reflects a less accurate picture of the personnel of an actual hospital. The procedures that populate the domain knowledge are independent of the user-interface and policy/inference layers of the architecture. Furthermore, the data manager is not integrated with any procedure for loading the domain data into the data stores. Therefore, application users will have the freedom to populate the knowledge base with their own domain data using their own procedures.

The choice of real-web data *vs.* pure synthetic data makes the inference controller more realistic. A querying user can combine the responses from the system with actual accessible background information (from the publicly available websites given previously) to draw inferences about the information in a knowledge base.

28.5.4 Background Generator Module

Figure 28.4 is a diagram of the different background generators. Each generator is built to target specific websites (or web pages) which contain some information of interest. For example, http://

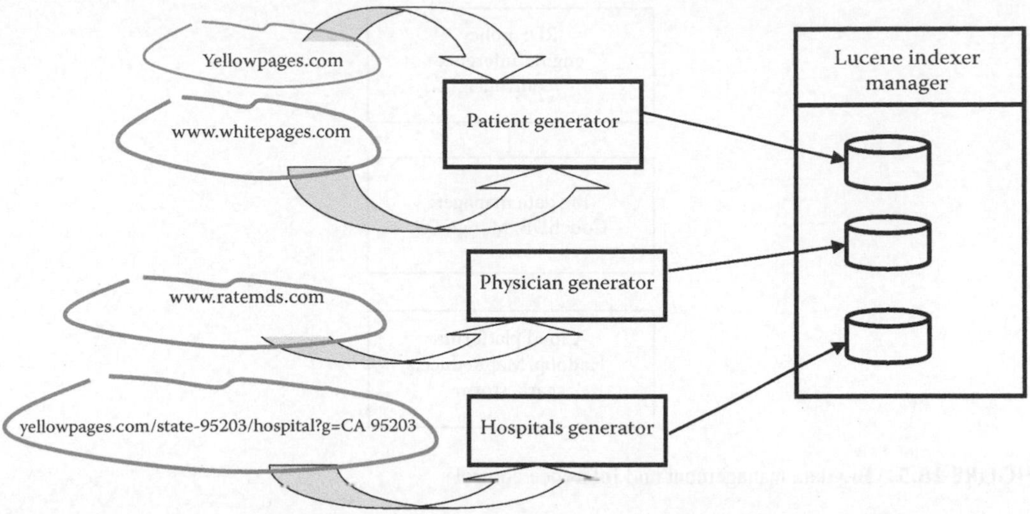

FIGURE 28.4 Background generator.

www.ratemd.com provides structured information about doctors at a specified zip code. The patient generator extracts the attributes of a person from a set of web pages. A provenance workflow generator updates the record for a patient. The recorded provenance is not publicly available and therefore can be treated as confidential data in the system. The intent here is to give the querying user an opportunity to guess the information in a patient's record and the associations between each electronic version of a patient's record. This information includes the patient's disease, medications, procedures or tests, physicians, etc. Provenance data is more challenging than the traditional data in a database (or the multilevel databases described in [THUR93], [STAC90], and [CHEN05] because the inference controller not only anticipates inferences involving the users prior knowledge, but also the inferences associated with the causal relationships among the provenance entities.

28.6 BIG DATA MANAGEMENT AND INFERENCE CONTROL

It should be noted that the RDF-based policy engine that we discussed in Chapter 25 has essentially adapted the inference controller discussed in this chapter to a cloud environment. That is, we have used the policy engine which is essentially our inference controller to determine whether access should be allowed to the data. Based on this access control decision, information is then shared between the organization that would also depend on the information sharing policies. That is, before the information is shared, the policy engine will determine whether the information sharing policy would permit the sharing of the information and then whether the receiver is authorized to access the data to be shared.

We note that by re-implementing the policy engine in the cloud we were able to achieve a significant improvement in performance. Massive amounts of provenance data are generated due to the inferencing capabilities, therefore our initial implementation the inference controller had to be implemented in the cloud to achieve scalability. In addition, some of the technologies such as the Lucene index manager also supported scalability.

However, as stated in Section 28.1, we believe that the knowledge base managed by the inference controller could become massive over time due to not just the raw data, but also the derived data, released data, and the real-world knowledge. Therefore, we believe that several of the big data technologies discussed in Chapter 7 including the Hadoop/MapReduce framework, the Apache Storm and Spark frameworks are needed to provide the infrastructure to handle the massive data generated by the inference controller. In addition, several of the big data management systems

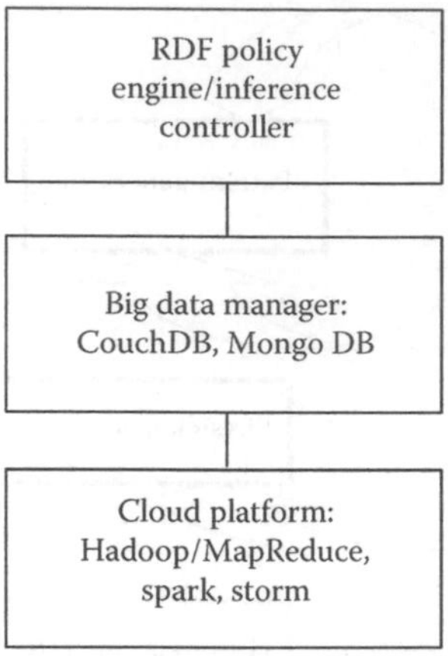

FIGURE 28.5 Big data management and inference control.

such as the NoSQL databases (e.g., HBase and CouchDB) need to be utilized to design a big data management system that can not only manage massive amounts of data but also be able to carry out inferencing and prevent unauthorized violations due to inference. Figure 28.5 illustrates our approach to Big Data Management and Inference Control.

28.7 SUMMARY AND DIRECTIONS

This chapter has described the first of a kind inference controller that will control certain unauthorized inferences in a data management system. Our approach is powerful due to the fact that we have applied semantic web technologies for both policy representation and reasoning. Furthermore, we have described inference control for provenance data represented as RDF graphs. Our approach can be applied for any kind of data represented in a graphical structure. We have also argued that inference control is an area that will need the use of BDMA systems for managing the data as well as reasoning about the data.

Our current work involves extending the inference controller to includc more sophisticated types of policies, such as information sharing policies, and implementing our policy engine on the cloud [CADE12]. We are also using big data management techniques to manage the massive amounts of data that has to be managed by the inference controller. Essentially, our cloud-based inference controller will process powerful policies applied to large quantities of data. This will enable multiple organizations to share data without violating confidentiality and privacy and at the same timc ensure that unauthorized inferences are controlled.

REFERENCES

[ANNA03]. G. J. Annas, "HIPAA Regulations—A New Era of Medical-Record Privacy?," *The New England Journal of Medicine*, 348 (15), 1486–1490, 2003.

[BAI07]. J. Bai, J. Y. Nie, G. Cao, H. Bouchard, "Using Query Contexts in Information Retrieval," In *SIGIR'07: Proceedings of the 30th Annual International ACM SIGIR Conference on Research and Development in Information Retrieval*, July 23–27, Amsterdam, The Netherlands, pp. 15–22, 2007.

[BAO04].J. Bao and V. G. Honavar, "*Ontology Language Extensions to Support Localized Semantics, Modular Reasoning, and Collaborative Ontology Design and Ontology Reuse.*" Technical Report, Computer Science, Iowa State University 2004.

[BAO06].J. Bao, D. Caragea, V. G. Honavar, "Modular Ontologies—A Formal Investigation of Semantics and Expressivity," In *ASWC 2006: Proceedings of the 1st Semantic Web Conference*, September 3–7, Beijing, China, pp. 616–631, 2006.

[BEER97]. C. Beeri, A. Y. Levy, M. C. Rousset, "Rewriting Queries Using Views in Description Logics," In *PODS'97: Proceedings of the 16th ACM SIGACT-SIGMOD-SIGART Symposium on Principles of Database Systems*, May 11–15, Tucson, AZ, USA, pp. 99–108, 1997.

[BERN00]. T. Berners-Lee and others. CWM: A General Purpose Data Processor for the Semantic Web, 2000, http://www.w3.org/2000/10/swap/doc/cwm.html.

[BIZE03]. C. Bizer, "D2R MAP—A Database to RDF Mapping Language," *WWW (Posters)*, May 20–24, 2003, Budapest, Hungary, 2003.

[BRAU08]. U. Braun, A. Shinnar, M. Seltzer, "Securing Provenance," In *Proceedings of the 3rd Conference on Hot Topics in Security*, USENIX Association, 2008.

[CADE10a]. T. Cadenhead, M. Kantarcioglu, B. Thuraisingham, "Scalable and Efficient Reasoning for Enforcing Role-Based Access Control," In *DBSec'10: Proceedings of the 24th Annual IFIP WG 11.3 Working Conference on Data and Applications Security and Privacy*, June 21–23, Rome, Italy, pp. 209–224, 2010.

[CADE10b]. T. Cadenhead, M. Kantarcioglu, B. Thuraisingham, "An Evaluation of Privacy, Risks and Utility with Provenance," In *SKM'10: Secure Knowledge Management Workshop*, New Brunswick, NJ, 2010.

[CADE11a]. T. Cadenhead, V. Khadilkar, M. Kantarcioglu, B. Thuraisingham, "A Language for Provenance Access Control" In *CODASPY'11: Proceedings of the 1st ACM Conference on Data and Application Security and Privacy*, February 21–23, San Antonio, TX, USA, pp. 133–144, 2011.

[CADE11b]. T. Cadenhead, V. Khadilkar, M. Kantarcioglu, B. Thuraisingham, "Transforming Provenance Using Redaction," In *SACMAT'11: Proceedings of the 16th ACM Symposium on Access Control Models and Technologies*, June 15–17, Innsbruck, Austria, pp. 93–102, 2011.

[CADE11c]. T. Cadenhead, M. Kantarcioglu, B. Thuraisingham, "A Framework for Policies over Provenance," In *TaPP'11: 3rd USENIX Workshop on the Theory and Practice of Provenance*, Heraklio, Crete, Greece, 2011.

[CADE12]. T. Cadenhead, V. Khadilkar, M. Kantarcioglu, B. Thuraisingham, "A Cloud-Based RDF Policy Engine for Assured Information Sharing," In *SACMAT'12: Proceedings of the 17th ACM Symposium on Access Control Models and Technologies*, June 20–22, Newark, NJ, USA, pp. 113–116, 2012.

[CARR04]. J. J. Carroll, I. Dickinson, C. Dollin, D. Reynolds, A. Seaborne, K. Wilkinson, "Jena: Implementing the Semantic Web Recommendations," In *ACM WWW 2004*, New York, NY, pp. 74–83, 2004.

[CARR05]. J. J. Carroll, C. Bizer, P. Hayes, P. Stickler, "Named Graphs, Provenance and Trust," In *ACM WWW*, Chiba, Japan, pp. 613–622, 2005.

[CHEN05]. X. Chen and R. Wei, "A Dynamic Method for Handling the Inference Problem in Multilevel Secure Databases," In *IEEE ITCC 2005*, Vol. II, Las Vegas, NV, pp. 751–756, 2005.

[CORR97]. A. Corradini, U. Montanari, F. Rossi, H. Ehrig, R. Heckel, M. Löwe, "Algebraic Approaches to Graph Transformation, Part I: Basic Concepts and Double Pushout Approach," *Handbook of Graph Grammars and Computing by Graph Transformation*, 1, 163–245, 1997.

[CORR10]. G. Correndo, M. Salvadores, I. Millard, H. Glaser, N. Shadbolt, "SPARQL Query Rewriting for Implementing Data Integration Over Linked Data," In *ACM EDBT*, Article #4, Lausanne, Switzerland, 2010.

[DING05]. L. Ding, T. Finin, Y. Peng, P. P. Da Silva, D. L. McGuinness, "Tracking RDF Graph Provenance Using RDF Molecules," *Technical Report*, 2005. http://ebiquity.umbc.edu/paper/html/id/263/Tracking-RDF-Graph-Provenance-using-RDF-Molecules.

[FARK02]. C. Farkas and S. Jajodia, "The Inference Problem: A Survey," *ACM SIGKDD Explorations Newsletter*, 4 (2), 6–11, 2002.

[FIKE02]. R. Fikes, P. Hayes, I. Horrocks, "DQL—A Query Language for the Semantic Web," *Knowledge Systems Laboratory*, 2002.

[FINI08]. T. Finin, A. Joshi, L. Kagal, J. Niu, R. Sandhu, W. Winsborough, B. Thuraisingham, "ROWLBAC: Representing Role Based Access Control in OWL," In *ACM SACMAT 2008*, Estes Park, CO, pp. 73–82, 2008.

[HAAR01]. V. Haarslev and R. Möller, "RACER System Description," *IJCAR 2001: Automated Reasoning*, Seattle, WA, pp. 701–705, 2001.

[HARR10]. S. Harris and A. Seaborne, "SPARQL 1.1 Query Language," *W3C Working Draft*, 14, 2010.

[HOLL08]. D. A. Holland, U. Braun, D. Maclean, K. K. Muniswamy-Reddy, M. Seltzer, "Choosing a Data Model and Query Language for Provenance," In *Provenance and Annotation of Data and Processes: Proceedings of the 2nd International Provenance and Annotation Workshop (IPAW '08)*, June 17–18, 2008, Salt Lake City, UT, ed. Juliana Freire, David Koop, and Luc Moreau. Berlin: Springer. Special Issue. Lecture Notes in Computer Science 5272.

[HOLL10]. V. Hollink, T. Tsikrika, A. Vries, "De.The Semantics of Query Modification," In *Le Centre De Hautes Etudes Internationales D'informatique Documentaire*, pp. 176–181, 2010.

[HORR04]. I. Horrocks, P. F. Patel-Schneider, H. Boley, S. Tabet, B. Grosof, M. Dean, "SWRL: A Semantic Web Rule Language Combining OWL and RuleML," *W3C Member Submission*, 21, 2004. https://www.w3.org/Submission/SWRL/.

[HORR05]. I. Horrocks, P. F. Patel-Schneider, S. Bechhofer, D. Tsarkov, "OWL Rules: A Proposal and Prototype Implementation," *Web Semantics: Science, Services and Agents on the World Wide Web*, 3 (1), 23–40, 2005.

[KARV12]. G. Karvounarakis, S. Alexaki, V. Christophides, D. Plexousakis, M. Scholl, RQL: A Declarative Query Language for RDF, In *ACM WWW 2002*, Honolulu, HI, pp. 592–603, 2002.

[KLYN04]. G. Klyne, J. J. Carroll, B. McBride, "Resource Description Framework (RDF): Concepts and Abstract Syntax," In *W3C Recommendation*, February 10, 2004. https://www.w3.org/TR/2004/REC-rdf-concepts-20040210/.

[LE11]. W. Le, S. Duan, A. Kementsietsidis, F. Li, M. Wang, "Rewriting Queries on SPARQL Views," In *ACM, WWW 2011*, Hyderabad, India, pp. 655–664, 2011.

[LEVY95]. A. Y. Levy, A. O. Mendelzon, Y. Sagiv, "Answering Queries Using Views," In *ACM PODS 1995*, San Jose, CA, pp. 95–104, 1995.

[LEVY98]. A. Y. Levy and M. C. Rousset, *Combining Horn Rules and Description Logics in CARIN*, Elsevier, New York, pp. 165–209, 1998.

[LI05]. H. Li, X. Zhang, H. Wu, Y. Qu, "Design and Application of Rule Based Access Control Policies," *Semantic Web and Policy Workshop*, Galway, Ireland, pp. 34–41, 2005.

[MCGU04a]. D. L. McGuinness, F. van Harmelen, and others. "OWL Web Ontology Language Overview," *W3C Recommendation*, 10, 2004–3, 2004.

[MCGU04b]. D. L. McGuinness P. Pinheiro da Silva, "Explaining Answers from the Semantic Web: The Inference Web Approach," *Web Semantics: Science, Services and Agents on the World Wide Web*, 397–413, 2004.

[MORE10]. L. Moreau, Open Provenance Model (OPM) OWL Specification. Latest version: http://openprovenance.org/model/opmo 2010.

[MORE11]. L. Moreau et al. "The Open Provenance Model Core Specification (v1. 1)," *Future Generation Computer Systems*, 27 (6), 743–756, 2011.

[NI09]. Q. Ni, S. Xu, E. Bertino, R. Sandhu, W. Han, "An Access Control Language for a General Provenance Model," *Secure Data Management, Proceedings of 6th VLDB Workshop, SDM 2009*, Lyon, France, pp. 68–88, August 28, 2009.

[ORAC]. Oracle® Database Semantic Technologies Developer's Guide 11 g Release 2 (11.2). Available at http://docs.oracle.com/cd/E14072_01/appdev.112/e11828/toc.htm.

[OULM10a]. S. Oulmakhzoune, N. Cuppens-Boulahia, F. Cuppens, S. Morucci, "fQuery: SPARQL Query Rewriting to Enforce Data Confidentiality," *Data and Applications Security and Privacy*, XXIV, 146–161, 2010.

[OULM10b]. S. Oulmakhzoune, N. Cuppens-Boulahia, F. Cuppens, S. Morucci, "Rewriting of SPARQL/Update Queries for Securing Data Access," *ICICS'10 Proceedings of the 12th International Conference on Information and Communications Security*, Barcelona, Spain, pp. 4–15, 2010.

[PRUD06]. E. Prud and A. Seaborne, Sparql query language for rdf, 2006.

[RIZV04]. S. Rizvi, A. Mendelzon, S. Sudarshan, P. Roy, "Extending Query Rewriting Techniques for Fine-Grained Access Control," In *ACM SIGMOD*, Paris, France, pp. 551–562, 2004.

[ROSE09]. A. Rosenthal, L. Seligman, A. Chapman, B. Blaustein, "Scalable Access Controls for Lineage," In *USENIX TAPP'09 First workshop on Theory and Practice of Provenance*, San Francisco, CA, Article No. 3, pp. 1–10, 2009.

[ROZE97]. G. Rozenberg and H. Ehrig, *Handbook of Graph Grammars and Computing by Graph Transformation*, World Scientific, River Edge, NJ, 1997.

[SHEA08]. R. Shearer, B. Motik, I. Horrocks, T. Hermi, "A Highly-Efficient OWL Reasoner," In *Proceedings of the 5th International Workshop on OWL: Experiences and Directions (OWLED 2008)*, pp. 26–27, 2008.

[SHEN05]. X. Shen, B. Tan, C. X. Zhai, "Context-Sensitive Information Retrieval Using Implicit Feedback," In *ACM SIGIR*, Salvador, Brazil, pp. 43–50, 2005.

[SHIE06]. B. Shields, O. Molloy, G. Lyons, J. Duggan, "Using Semantic Rules to Determine Access Control for Web Services" In *ACM WWW 2006*, Edinburgh, Scotland, pp. 913–914, 2006.

[SIRI07]. E. Sirin, B. Parsia, B. C. Grau, A. Kalyanpur, Y. Katz, "Pellet: A Practical Owl-dl Reasoner," *Web Semantics: Science, Services and Agents on the World Wide Web*, 5 (2), 51–53, 2007.

[STAC90]. P. D. Stachour and B. Thuraisingham, "Design of LDV: A Multilevel Secure Relational Database Management System," *Knowledge and Data Engineering, IEEE Transactions on*, 2 (2), 190–209, 1990.

[STOU09]. P. Stouppa and T. Studer, "Data Privacy for ALC Knowledge Bases," In *Intl Symposium of the LFCS 2009*, Deerfield Beach, FL, pp. 409–421, 2009.

[SYAL09]. A. Syalim, Y. Hori, K. Sakurai, "Grouping Provenance Information to Improve Efficiency of Access Control" *Advances in Information Security and Assurance, Third Intl Conference and Workshops, ISA*, Seoul, Korea, pp. 51–59, 2009.

[THUR90]. B. Thuraisingham, "Novel Approaches to Handle the Inference Problem" Proceedings of the 3rd RADC Database Security Workshop, New York, pp. 58–67, 1990.

[THUR93]. B. Thuraisingham, W. Ford, M. Collins, J. O'Keeffe, "Design and Implementation of a Database Inference Controller," *Data & Knowledge Engineering*, 11(3), 271–297, 1993.

[THUR95]. B. Thuraisingham, W. Ford. "Security Constraints in a Multilevel Secure Distributed Database Management System." *IEEE Transactions on Knowledge and Data Engineering*, 7 (2), 274–293, 1995.

[THUR15]. B. Thuraisingham, T. Cadenhead, M. Kantarcioglu, V. Khadilkar, *Secure Data Provenance and Inference Control with Semantic Web*. CRC Press, Boca Raton, FL, 2015.

[TSAR06]. D. Tsarkov and I. Horrocks, "FaCT++ Description Logic Reasoner: System Description," *International Joint Conference on Automated Reasoning*, Seattle, WA, pp. 292–297, 2006

[ZHAN09]. R. Zhang, A. Artale, F. Giunchiglia, B. Crispo, "Using Description Logics in Relation Based Access Control," In *CEUR Workshop Proceedings*, Grau, B. C., Horrocks, I., Motik, B., & Sattler, U. editors, 2009.

[ZHAO08]. J. Zhao, C. Goble, R. Stevens, D. Turi, "Mining Taverna's Semantic Web of Provenance," *Concurrency and Computation: Practice and Experience*, 20 (5), 463–472, 2008.

[ZHAO10]. J. Zhao, Open Provenance Model Vocabulary Specification. Latest version: http://open-biomed.sourceforge.net/opmv/ns.html 2010.

Conclusion to Part IV

Part IV, consisting of six chapters, described some of the experimental systems we have designed and developed that illustrate the key points of both big data management and analytics (BDMA) and big data security and privacy (BDSP) systems.

In Chapter 23, we presented a framework capable of handling enormous amounts of resource description framework (RDF) data that can be used to represent big data systems such as social networks. Our framework is based on the Hadoop/MapReduce technologies and implements a SPARQL query processor that can handle massive amounts of data. We also provided a brief overview of our security prototype that we built on top of the query processing system. In Chapter 24, we described the design of the big data analytics system called InXite. InXite will be a great asset to the analysts who have to deal with massive amounts of data streams in the form of billions of blogs and messages among others. For example, by analyzing the behavioral history of a particular group of individuals as well as details of concepts such as events, analysts will be able to predict behavioral changes in the near future and take necessary measures. We also discussed the use of cloud computing and various big data tools in the implementation of InXite. Chapter 25 described our design and implementation of a cloud-based information sharing system called CAISS. CAISS utilizes several of the technologies we have developed as well as open source tools. We also described the design of an ideal cloud-based assured information sharing system called CAISS++. In Chapter 26, we described techniques to protect our data by encrypting it before storing on cloud computing servers like Amazon S3. Our approach is novel as we propose to use two key servers to generate and store the keys. Also, we assure more security than some of the other known approaches as we do not store the actual key used to encrypt the data. This assures the protection of our data even if one or both key servers are compromised. Our implementation utilizes Blackbook, a semantic web-based data integration framework and allows data integration from various data sources. In Chapter 27, we formulated the intrusion detection problems as classification problems for infinite-length, concept-drifting data streams. Concept drift occurs in these streams as attackers react and adapt to defenses. We formulated both malicious code detection and botnet traffic detection as such problems, and introduced extended, multiple partition, multiple chunk, a novel ensemble learning technique for automated classification of infinite-length, concept-drifting streams. Finally, In Chapter 28, we described the first of a kind inference controller that will control certain unauthorized inferences for provenance data represented as RDF graphs. We also argued that inference control is an area that will need the use of BDMA systems for managing the data as well as reasoning about the data.

Now that we have described some of the experimental BDMA and BDSP systems we have developed in Part IV and focused on the details of stream data analytics in Parts II and III, we are now ready to describe several directions for BDMA and BDSP systems in Part V.

Part V

Next Steps for BDMA and BDSP

Introduction to Part V

Parts II and III focused on stream data analytics with applications in insider threat detection. There was also a special emphasis on handling massive amount of data streams and the use of cloud computing. We described various stream data analytics algorithms and provided our experimental results. Part IV discussed some of the experimental systems we have designed and developed on big data management and analytics (BDMA) and big data security and privacy (BDSP). While Parts II through IV focused on BDMA and BDSP with respect to the design and development of the systems with applications, in Part V, we describe some of our exploratory work we have carried out as well as plans for enhancing our work in BDMA and BDSP.

Part V, consisting of seven chapters, describes the various exploratory systems including Internet of Things (IoT) systems and experimental infrastructures. In Chapter 29, we discuss aspects of confidentiality, privacy, and trust for the semantic web and describe how they relate to big data systems such as social media systems. In Chapter 30, we integrate the various parts of a big data system into an automatic framework for carrying out analytics while at the same time ensuring security. In particular, we integrate the analytics techniques with the privacy and security techniques and at the same time preserve features such as scalability, efficiency, and interoperability in developing this framework. In Chapter 31, we discuss our approach to designing a cyber defense framework for IoT systems based on a layered architecture. We also discuss the use of BDMA systems for securing IoT applications. In Chapter 32, we focus on a particular IoT system and that is a connected smartphone system. These connected smartphone devices generate massive amounts of data and can be considered to be an IoT system. We discuss how big data analytics may be applied for detecting malware in smartphones. We also discuss an experimental and education infrastructure for securing smartphones. In Chapter 33, we illustrate the key points in big data analytics and security for a particular vertical domain and that is healthcare. In particular, we describe a planned case study where there is a need to manage and analyze massive amounts of data securely. In Chapter 34, we describe our planned experimental infrastructure and education programs for BDMA and BDSP. Finally, in Chapter 35, we summarize the discussion on BDSP and the applications of BDMA for cyber security at the NSF workshop we hosted on BDSP.

While we have explored additional systems and plans for BDMA and BDSP, we believe that the systems and plans we have described in Part V provide a representative sample of our exploratory work.

29 Confidentiality, Privacy, and Trust for Big Data Systems

29.1 INTRODUCTION

Security has many dimensions including confidentially, privacy, trust, availability, and dependability among others. Our work has examined confidentiality, privacy, and trust (CPT) aspects of security for big data systems such as social media systems and cloud data systems where the data is represented using semantic web technologies and how they relate to each other. Confidentiality is essentially secrecy. Privacy deals with not disclosing sensitive data about the individuals. Trust is about the assurance one can place on the data or on an individual. For example, even though John is authorized to get salary data, can we trust John not to divulge this data to others? Even though the website states that it will not give out social security numbers of individuals, can we trust the website? Our prior work has designed a framework called CPT based on semantic web technologies that provides an integrated approach to addressing CPT [THUR07]. In this chapter, we will revisit CPT and discuss how it relates to big data such as social media data.

The organization of this chapter is as follows. Our definitions of CPT as well as the current status on administering the semantic web will be discussed in Section 29.2. This will be followed by a discussion of our proposed framework for securing the social media data that we call CPT in Section 29.3. Next, we will take each of the features, CPT, and discuss various aspects as they relate to social media in Sections 29.4 through 29.6, respectively. We have used social media systems as an illustrative example for big data systems. An integrated architecture for CPT as well as inference and privacy control will be discussed in Section 29.7. Relationship to a big data system such as a social media system is discussed in Section 29.8. Finally, this chapter is summarized and future directions are given in Section 29.9.

Figure 29.1 illustrates the concepts of this chapter. It should be noted that while we have focused on social media data for illustration purposes, the techniques can be applied to any type of big data system. The reason is the fact that such systems have reasoning capabilities and can learn from experiences, and, therefore, can be prone to both privacy attacks and attacks due to security violations via inference.

29.2 TRUST, PRIVACY, AND CONFIDENTIALITY

In this section, we will discuss aspects of the security and privacy relationship to the inference problem with respect to social media data. In particular, confidentiality, privacy, trust, integrity, and availability will be briefly defined with an examination of how these issues specifically relate to the trust management and inference problem. Confidentiality is preventing the release of unauthorized information. One view of privacy is to consider it to be a subset of confidentiality in that it is the prevention of unauthorized information being released with regard to an individual. However, much of the recent research on privacy, especially relating to data mining, addresses the following aspect: How can we mine and extract useful nuggets about groups of people while keeping the values of the sensitive attributes of an individual private? That is, even though we can make inferences about groups, we want to maintain individual privacy. For example, we want to protect the fact that John has cancer. However, the fact that people who live in Dallas, Texas, are more prone to cancer is something we make public. More details on privacy and its relationship to data mining can be found in [AGRA00] and [KANT03].

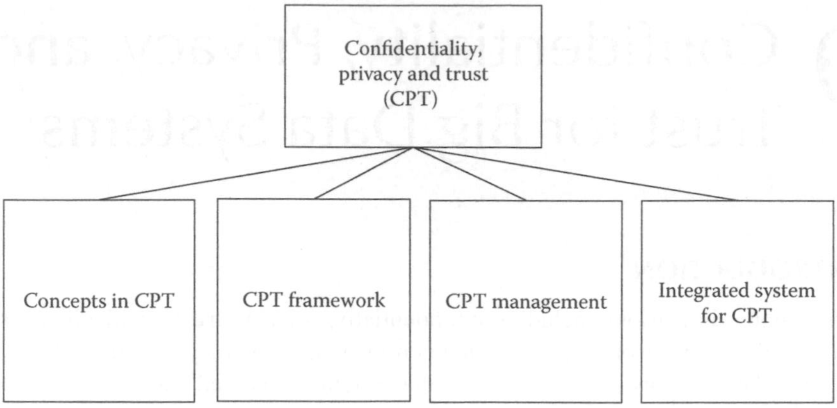

FIGURE 29.1 Confidentiality, privacy, and trust.

Integrity of data is the prevention of any modifications made by an unauthorized entity. Availability is the prevention of unauthorized omission of data. Trust is a measure of confidence in data correctness and legitimacy from a particular source. Integrity, availability, and trust are all very closely related in the sense that data quality is of particular importance and all require individuals or entities processing and sending information to not alter the data in an unauthorized manner. If confidentiality, privacy, trust, integrity, and availability are all guaranteed, a system can be considered secure. Thus, if the inference problem can be solved such that unauthorized information is not released, the rules of CPT will not be broken. A technique such as inference can be used to either aid or impair the cause of integrity, availability, and trust. If correctly used, inference can be used to infer trust management policies. Thus, inference can be used for good or bad purposes. The intention is to prevent inferred, unauthorized conclusions and to use inference to apply trust management.

29.2.1 Current Successes and Potential Failures

The World Wide Web Consortium [W3C] has proposed encryption techniques for securing XML documents. Furthermore, logic, proof, and trust belong to one of the layers of the semantic web. However, by trust, in that context, is meant whether the semantic web can trust the statements such as data and rules. In our definition, by trust we mean to what extent we can believe that the user and the website will enforce the confidentiality and privacy policies as specified. Privacy has been discussed by the semantic web community. The main contribution of this community is developing the Platform for Privacy Preferences (P3P).

P3P requires the web developer of the server to create a privacy policy, validate it, and then place it in a specific location on the server as well as write a privacy policy in English. When the user enters the website, the browser will discover the privacy policy and if the privacy policy matches the user's browser security specifications, then the user can simply enter the site. If the policy does not match the user's specifications, then the user will be informed of the site's intentions and the user can then choose to enter or leave.

While this is a great start, it is lacking in certain areas. One concern is the fact that the privacy policy must be placed in a specific location. If a website, for example, a student website on a school's server, is to implement P3P and cannot place it in a folder directly from the school's server, then the user's browser will not find the privacy policy.

Another problem with P3P is that it requires the data collector on the server side to follow exactly what is promised in the privacy policy. If the data collections services on the server side decide to abuse the policy and instead do other things not stated in the agreement, then no real consequences occur. The server's privacy policy can simply choose to state that it will correct the problem upon discovery, but if the user never knows it until the data is shared publicly, correcting it to show the data is private will not simply solve the problem. Accountability should be addressed, where it is not the server's decision, but rather the lawmaker's decisions. When someone breaks a law, or does not abide by contractual agreements, we do not turn to the accused and ask what punishment they deem necessary. Instead, we look to the law and apply each law when applicable.

Another point of contention is trust and inference. Before beginning any discussions of privacy, a user and a server must evaluate how much the other party can be trusted. If neither party trusts each other, how can either party expect the other to follow a privacy policy? Currently P3P only uses tags to define actions; it uses no web rules for inference or specific negotiations regarding confidentiality and privacy. With inference, a user can decide if certain information should not be given because it would allow the distrusted server to infer information that the user would prefer to remain private or sensitive.

29.2.2 Motivation for a Framework

While P3P is a great initiative to approaching the privacy problem for users of the semantic web, it becomes obvious from the above discussion that more work must be continued on this process. Furthermore, we need to integrate confidentiality and privacy within the context of trust management. A new approach to be discussed later must be used to address these issues such that the user can establish trust, preserve privacy and anonymity, and ensure confidentiality. Once the server and client have negotiated trust, the user can begin to decide what data can be submitted that will not violate his/her privacy. These security policies, one each for trust, privacy, and confidentiality, are described with web rules. Describing policies with web rules can allow an inference engine to determine what is in either the client or server's best interest and help advise each party accordingly. Also with web rules in place, a user and server can begin to negotiate confidentiality. Thus, if a user does not agree with a server's privacy policies but would still like to use some services, a user may begin negotiating confidentiality with the server to determine if the user can still use some services but not all (depending on the final conclusion of the agreement). The goal of this new approach is to simulate real-world negotiations, thus giving semantics to the current web and providing much needed security.

29.3 CPT FRAMEWORK

In this section, we will discuss a framework for enforcing CPT for the semantic web. We first discuss the basic framework where rules are enforced to ensure CPT. In the advanced framework, we include inference controllers that will reason about the application and determine whether CPT violations have occurred.

29.3.1 The Role of the Server

In the previous section, focus was placed on the client's needs; now we will discuss the server's needs in this process. The first obvious need is that the server must be able to evaluate the client in order to grant specific resources. Therefore, the primary goal is to establish trust regarding the client's identity and, based on this identity, grant various permissions to specific data. Not only must the server be able to evaluate the client but also be able to evaluate its own ability to grant permission with standards and metrics. The server also needs to be able to grant or deny a request appropriately without giving away classified information or instead of giving away classified information, the server may desire to give a cover story. Either scenario, a cover story or protecting classified resources, must be completed within the guidelines of a stated privacy policy in order to guarantee a client's confidentiality. One other key aspect is that all of these events must occur in a timely manner such that security is not compromised.

29.3.2 CPT Process

Now that the needs of the client and server have been discussed, focus will be placed on the actual process of our system CPT. First, a general overview of the process will be presented. After the reader has garnered a simple overview, this chapter will continue to discuss two systems—Advanced CPT and Basic CPT—based on the general process previously discussed. The general process of CPT is to first establish a relationship of trust and then negotiate privacy and confidentiality policies. Figure 29.2 shows the general process.

Notice that both parties partake in establishing trust. The client must determine the degree to which it can trust the server in order to decide how much trust to place in the resources supplied by the server and also to negotiate privacy policies. The server must determine the degree to which it can trust the client in order to determine what privileges and resources it can allow the client to access as well as how to present the data. The server and client will base their decisions of trust on credentials of each other. Once trust is established, the client and server must come to an agreement of privacy policies to be applied to the data that the client provides the server. Privacy must follow trust because the degree to which the client trusts the server will affect the privacy degree. The privacy degree affects what data the client chooses to send. Once the client is comfortable with the privacy policies negotiated, the client will then begin requesting data. Based on the initial trust agreement, the server will determine what and when the client views these resources. Based on its own confidentiality requirements and confidentiality degree, the client will make decisions regarding confidentiality and what data can be given to the user. It is also important to note that the server and client must make these decisions and then configure the system to act upon these decisions. The basic CPT system will not advise the client or server in any way regarding outcomes of any decisions. Figure 29.3 illustrates the communication between the different components.

29.3.3 Advanced CPT

The previous section discussed the basic CPT system, and the advanced CPT system is an extension of the basic system. The advanced CPT system is outlined in Figure 29.4, which incorporates three new entities not found in the basic system. These three new entities are the trust inference engine (TIE), the privacy inference engine (PIE), and the confidentiality inference engine (CIE). The first

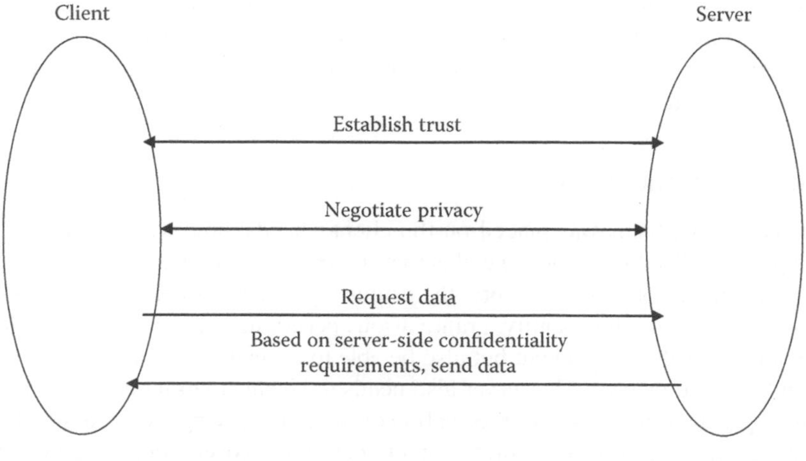

FIGURE 29.2 Basic framework for CPT.

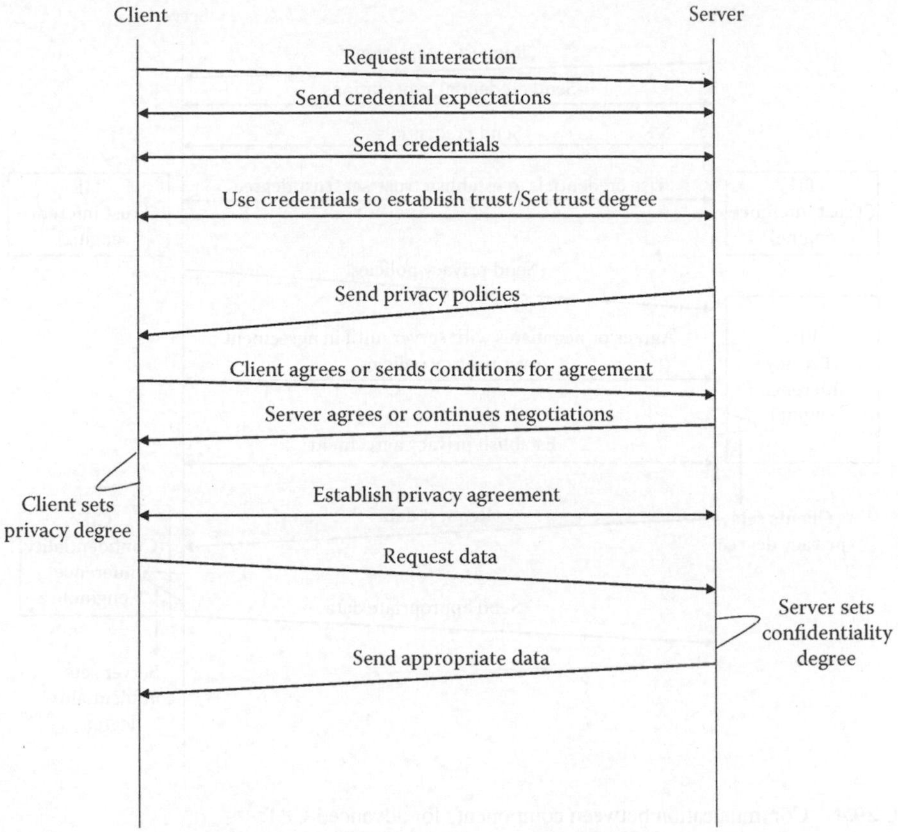

FIGURE 29.3 Communication between the components for basic CPT.

step of sending credentials and establishing trust is the same as the basic system except that both parties consult with their own TIE. Once each party makes a decision, the client receives the privacy policies from the server and then uses these policies in configuration with PIE to agree, disagree, or negotiate. Once the client and server have come to an agreement about the client's privacy, the client will send a request for various resources. Based on the degree of trust that the server has assigned to a particular client, the server will determine what resources it can give to the client. However, in this step the server will consult the CIE to determine what data is preferable to give to the client and what data, if given, could have disastrous consequences. Once the server has made a conclusion regarding data that the client can receive, it can then begin transmitting data over the network.

29.3.4 Trust, Privacy, and Confidentiality Inference Engines

With regard to trust, the server must realize that if it chooses to assign a certain percentage of trust, then this implies the client will have access to the specific privileged resources and can possibly infer other data from granted permissions. Thus, the primary responsibility of the TIE is to determine what information can be inferred and is this behavior acceptable. Likewise, the client must realize that the percentage of trust it assigns to the server will affect permissions of viewing the site as well as affecting how data given to the client will be processed. The inference engine in the client's scenario will guide the client regarding what can or will occur based on the trust assignment given to the server.

Once trust is established, the PIE will continue the inference process. It is important to note that the PIE only resides on the client side. The server will have its own privacy policies but these

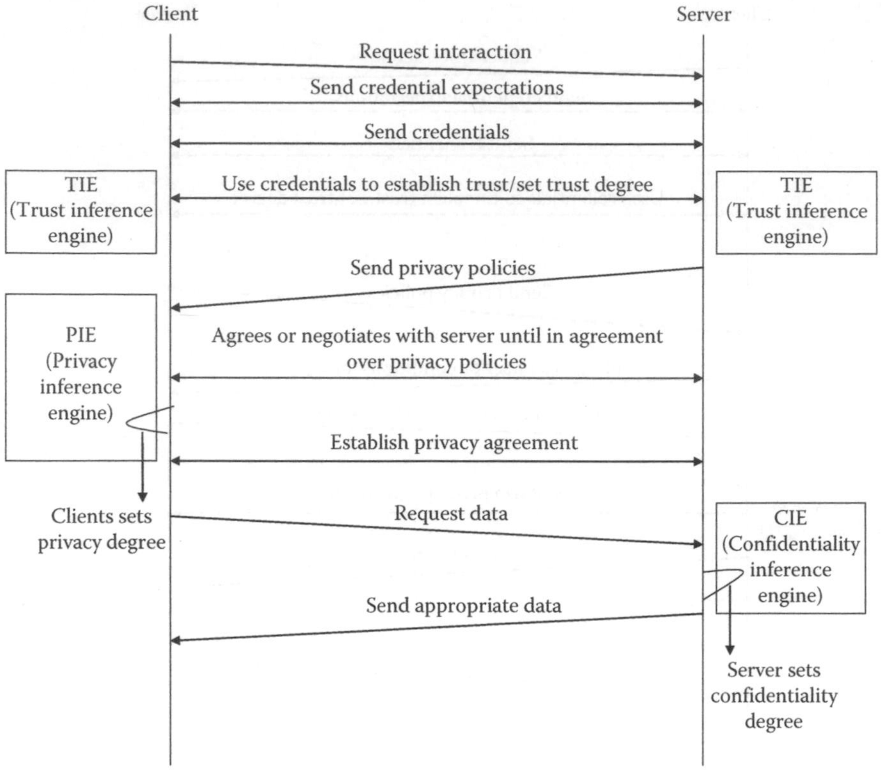

FIGURE 29.4 Communication between components for advanced CPT.

policies may not be acceptable to the client. It is impossible for the server to evaluate each client and determine how to implement an individual privacy policy without first consulting the client. Thus, the PIE is unnecessary on the server's side. The PIE must guide the client in negotiating privacy policies. In order to guide the client through negotiations, the inference engine must be able to determine how the server will use data the client gives it as well as who else will have access to the submitted data. Once this is determined, the inference engine must evaluate the data given by the client to the server. If the inference engine determines that this data can be used to infer other data that the client would prefer to remain private, the inference engine must warn the client and then allow the client to choose the next appropriate measure of either sending or not sending the data.

Once the client and server have agreed on the privacy policies to be implemented, the client will naturally begin requesting data and the server will have to determine what data to send, based on confidentiality requirements. It is important to note that the CIE is located only on the server side. The client has already negotiated its personal privacy issues and is ready to view the data thus leaving the server to decide what the next appropriate action is. The CIE must first determine what data will be currently available to the client, based on the current trust assignment. Once the inference engine has determined this, the inference engine must explore what policies or data can be potentially inferred if the data is given to the client. The primary objective of the CIE is to ponder how the client might be able to use the information given to it and then guide the server through the process of deciding a client's access to resources.

29.4 OUR APPROACH TO CONFIDENTIALITY MANAGEMENT

While much of our previous work focused on security control in relational databases, our work discussed in this book focuses on extending this approach to social media data. The social network

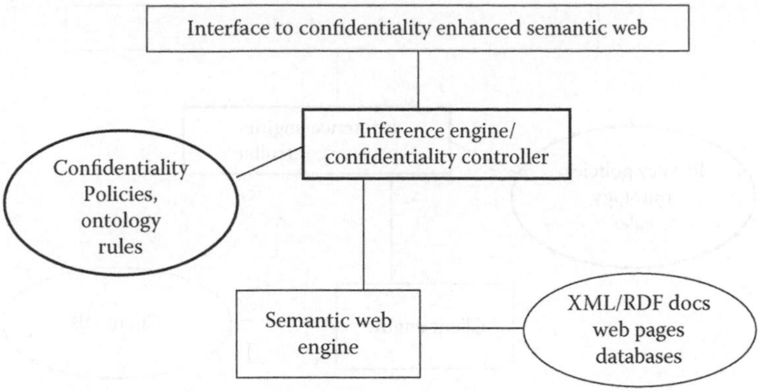

FIGURE 29.5 Confidentiality controller for the semantic web.

is augmented by an inference controller that examines the policies specified as ontologies and rules, and utilizes the inference engine embedded in the web rules language, reasons about the applications and deduces the security violations via inference. In particular, we focus on the design and implementation of an inference controller where the data is represented as RDF documents.

It should be noted that prior to the work discussed in this book, we designed and developed a preliminary confidentiality controller in 2005. Here, we utilized two popular semantic web technologies in our prototype called Intellidimension RDF Gateway and Jena (see [INTE] and [JENA]). RDF Gateway is a database and integrated web server, utilizing RDF and built from the ground up rather than on top of existing web servers or databases [RDF]. It functions as a data repository for RDF data and also as an interface to various data sources, external or internal, that can be queried. Jena is a Java application programming package to create, modify, store, query, and perform other processing tasks on RDF/XML documents from Java programs. RDF documents can be created from scratch or preformatted documents can be read into memory to explore various parts. The node-arc-node feature of RDF closely resembles how Jena accesses an RDF document. It also has a built-in query engine designed on top of RDFQL (RDF Query Language) that allows querying documents using standard RDFQL query statements. Our initial prototype utilized RDFQL while our current work has focused ion SPARQL queries.

Using these technologies, we specify the confidentiality policies. The confidentiality engine ensures that the policies are enforced correctly. If we assume the basic framework, then the confidentiality engine will enforce the policies and will not examine security violations via inference. In the advanced approach, the confidentiality engine will include what we call an inference controller. While our approach has been to store the data in RDF, as the amount of data to be managed could become very large over the years, we need to apply the big data management technologies discussed in Chapter 7. Figure 29.5 illustrates an inference/confidentiality controller for the semantic web that has been the basis of our book.

29.5 PRIVACY FOR SOCIAL MEDIA SYSTEMS

As discussed in Chapter 3, privacy is about protecting information about individuals. Furthermore, an individual can specify say to a web service provider the information that can be released about him or her. Social media systems are especially prone to privacy violations as the members post so much information about themselves. Therefore, such systems are prone to privacy attacks.

Privacy has been discussed to a great deal in the past, especially when it relates to protecting medical information about patients. Social scientists as well as technologists have been working on privacy issues. However, privacy has received enormous attention during the past year. This is mainly because of the advent of the web, the semantic web, counter-terrorism, and national security.

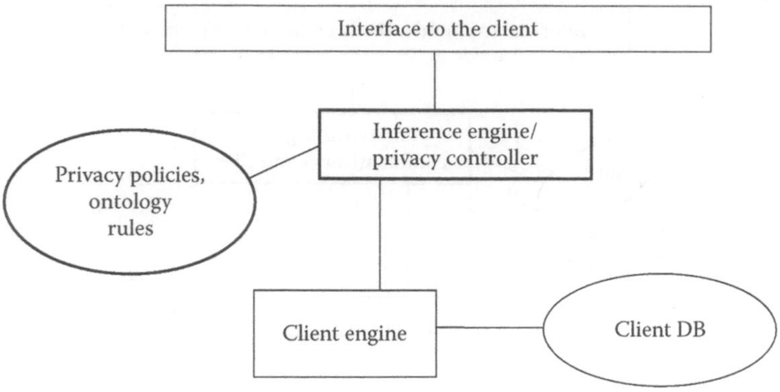

FIGURE 29.6 Privacy controller for the semantic web.

For example, in order to extract information about various individuals and perhaps prevent and/or detect potential terrorist attacks, data mining tools are being examined. We have heard much about national security versus privacy in the media. This is mainly due to the fact that people are now realizing that to handle terrorism, the government may need to collect data about individuals and mine the data to extract information. Data may be in relational databases or it may be text, video, and images. This is causing a major concern with the civil liberties union ([THUR02], [THUR05]).

From a technology policy of view, a privacy controller could be considered to be identical to the confidentiality controller we have designed and developed. The privacy controller is illustrated in Figure 29.6. However, it is implemented at the client side. Before the client gives out information to a website, it will check whether the website can divulge aggregated information to the third party and subsequently result in privacy violations. For example, the website may give out medical records without the identity so that the third party can study the patterns of flu or other infectious diseases. Furthermore, at some other time, the website may give out the names. However, if the website gives out the link between the names and diseases, then there could be privacy violations. The inference engine will make such deductions and determine whether the client should give out personal data to the website.

As we have stated earlier, privacy violations could also result due to data mining and analysis. In this case, the challenge is to protect the values of the sensitive attributes of an individual and make public the results of the mining or analysis. This aspect of privacy is illustrated in Figure 29.7. A CPT framework should handle both aspects of privacy. Our work on privacy aspects of social networks addresses privacy violations that could occur in social networks due to data analytics. It should be noted that the amount of data collected about the individuals might grow rapidly due to better data collection technologies. This data may be mined and that could result in privacy

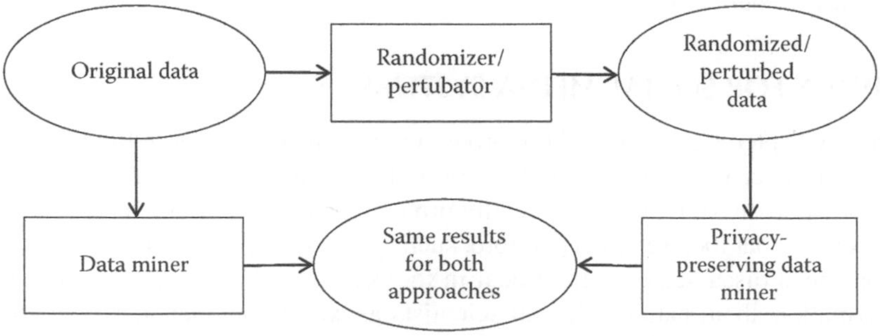

FIGURE 29.7 Privacy control for social network mining and analysis.

breaches. Therefore, we need privacy enhanced big data analytics techniques to be integrated with our reasoning system.

29.6 TRUST FOR SOCIAL NETWORKS

Researchers are working on protocols for trust management. Languages for specifying trust management constructs are also being developed. In addition, there is research on the foundations of trust management. For example, if A trusts B and B trusts C, then can A trust C? How do you share the data and information on the semantic web and still maintain autonomy? How do you propagate trust? For example, if A trusts B say 50% of the time and B trusts C 30% of the time, then what value do you assign for A trusting C? How do you incorporate trust into semantic interoperability? What are the quality of service primitives for trust and negotiation? That is, for certain situations, one may need 100% trust while, for certain other situations, 50% trust may suffice [YU03].

Another topic that is being investigated is trust propagation and propagating privileges. For example, if you grant privileges to A, what privileges can A transfer to B? How can you compose privileges? Is there an algebra and/or calculus for the composition of privileges? Much research still needs to be done here. One of the layers of the semantic web is logic, proof, and trust. Essentially, this layer deals with trust management and negotiation between different agents and examining the foundations and developing logics for trust management. Some interesting work has been carried out by Finin et al. ([DENK03], [FINI02], [KAGA03]). For example, if given data A and B can someone deduce classified data X (i.e., $A + B \rightarrow X$)? The inference engines will also use an inverse inference module to determine if classified information can be inferred if a user employs inverse resolution techniques. For example, if given data A and the user wants to guarantee that data X remains classified, the user can determine that B which combined with A implies X, must remain classified as well (i.e., $A + ? \rightarrow X$; the question mark results with B). Once the expert system has received the results from the inference engines, it can conclude a recommendation and then pass this recommendation to the client or server who will have the option to either accept or reject the suggestion.

29.7 INTEGRATED SYSTEM

In order to establish trust, privacy, and confidentiality, it is necessary to have an intelligent system that can evaluate the user's preferences. The system will be designed as an expert system to store trust, privacy, and confidentiality policies. These policies can be written using a web rules language with the foundations of the first-order logic. Traditional theorem provers can then be applied to the rules to check for inconsistencies and alert the user [ANTO08]. Once the user approves of all the policies, the system can take action and properly apply these policies during any transaction occurring on a site. Also, the user can place percentages next to the policies in order to apply probabilistic scenarios. Figure 29.8 gives an example of a probabilistic scenario occurring with a trust policy.

In Figure 29.8, the user sets the trust degree to 59%. Because the user trusts another person 59%, only policies 5–8 will be applied. Figure 29.9 shows some example policies. These example policies will be converted into a web rules language, such as the Semantics Web Rules Language [SWRL]

```
Trust degree = 59%
    90 Policy1
    75 Policy2
    70 Policy3
    60 Policy4
    50 Policy5
    35 Policy6
    10 Policy7
     0 Policy8
```

FIGURE 29.8 Trust probabilities.

```
Policy1: if A then B else C
Policy2: not A or B
Policy3: A or C
Policy4: A or C or D or not E
Policy5: not (A or C)
```

FIGURE 29.9 Example policies.

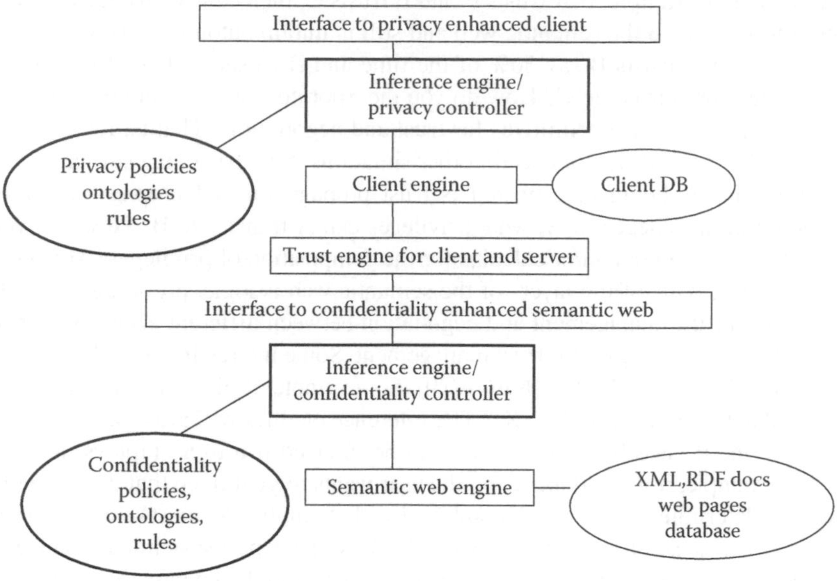

FIGURE 29.10 Integrated architecture for confidentiality, privacy, and trust.

and enforced by the trust engine. Figure 29.10 illustrates an integrated architecture for ensuring CPT for the semantic web. The web server as well as the client have trust management modules. The web server has a confidentiality engine, whereas client has a privacy engine. The inference controller is the first towards an integrated CPT system with XML, RDF, and web rules technologies. Some details of the modules are illustrated in Figure 29.11. Note that a version of an inference controller was discussed in Chapter 28.

In Figure 29.11, ontologies, CPT policies, and credentials are given to the expert system such that the expert system can advise the client or server who should receive access to what particular resource and how these resources should further be regulated. The expert system will send the policies to the WCOP (web rules, credentials, ontologies, and policies) parser to check for syntax errors and validate the inputs. The information contained within the dashed box is a part of the system that is only included in the Advanced TP&C system. The inference engines (e.g., TIE, PIE, and CIE) will use an inference module to determine if classified information can be inferred.

29.8 CPT WITHIN THE CONTEXT OF BIG DATA AND SOCIAL NETWORKS

CPT are crucial services that must be built into a big data system such as a social network. Confidentiality policies will enable the members of the network to determine what information is to be shared with their friends in the network. Privacy policies will determine what a network can release about a member, provided these policies are accepted by the member. Trust policies will provide a way for members of a network to assign trust values to the others. For example, a member may not share all the data with his/her friends in the network unless he trusts the friends. Similarly,

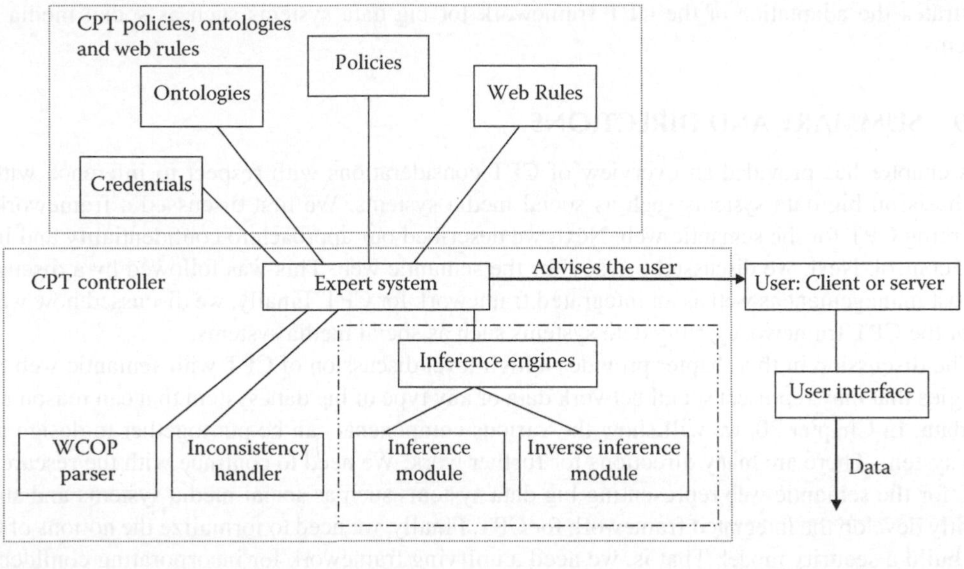

FIGURE 29.11 Modules of CPT controller.

a network may enforce certain privacy policies and if one does not approve of these policies or not trust the network, he/she may not join the network. Therefore, we see that many of the concepts discussed in the previous sections are directly applicable to social networks.

If the social networks are represented using semantic web technologies such as RDF graphs, then the reasoning techniques inherent in technologies such as RDF and OWL can be used to reason about the policies and determine whether any information should be shared with members. In addition to CPT policies, social networks also have to deal with information sharing policies, That is, member John of a network may share data with member Jane, provided Jane does not share with member Mary. We have carried out an extensive investigation of assured information sharing in the cloud and are extending this work to social media data and other big data systems. Figure 29.12

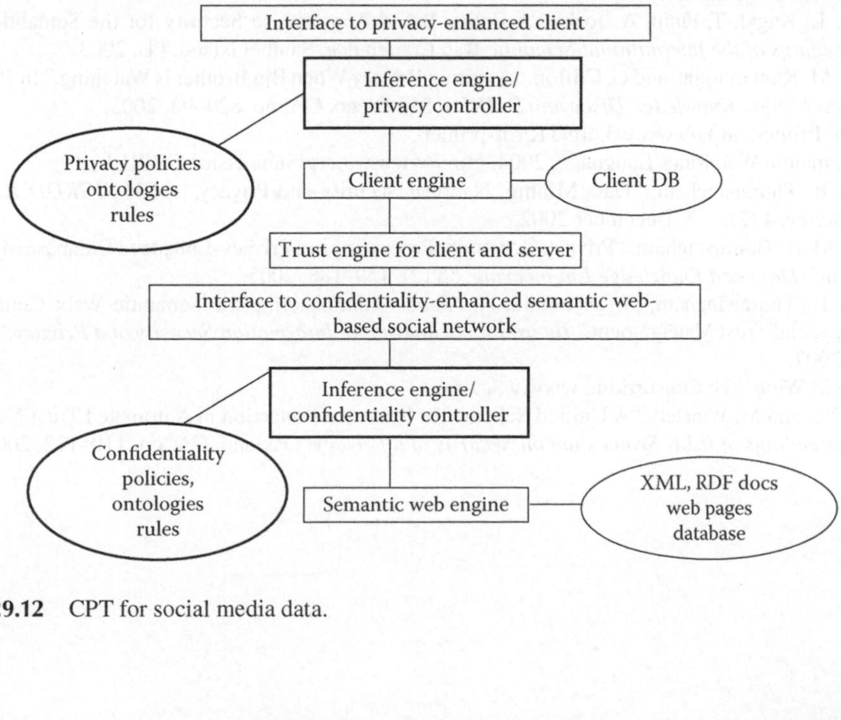

FIGURE 29.12 CPT for social media data.

illustrates the adaptation of the CPT framework for big data systems such as social media data systems.

29.9 SUMMARY AND DIRECTIONS

This chapter has provided an overview of CPT considerations with respect to inference with an emphasis on big data systems such as social media systems. We first discussed a framework for enforcing CPT for the semantic web. Next, we described our approach to confidentiality and inference control. Next, we discussed privacy for the semantic web. This was followed by a discussion of trust management as well as an integrated framework for CPT. Finally, we discussed how we can adapt the CPT framework for big data systems such as social media systems.

The discussion in this chapter provides a high-level discussion of CPT with semantic web technologies that may represent social network data or any type of big data system that can reason about the data. In Chapter 30, we will show the various components can be put together to design a big data system. There are many directions for further work. We need to continue with the research on CPT for the semantic web representing big data systems such as social media systems and subsequently develop the integrated framework for CPT. Finally, we need to formalize the notions of CPT and build a security model. That is, we need a unifying framework for incorporating confidentiality, privacy, trust, and information sharing policies for big data systems and some directions are provided in Chapter 30.

REFERENCES

[AGRA00]. A. Rakesh and R. Srikant, "Privacy-Preserving Data Mining," *SIGMOD Conference*, Dallas, TX, pp. 439–450, 2000.

[ANTO08]. G. Antoniou and F. V. Harmelen, *A Semantic Web Primer*, MIT Press, Cambridge, MA, 2008.

[DENK03]. G. Denker, L. Kagal, T. Finin, M. Paolucci, and K. Sycara, "Security for DAML Web Services: Annotation and Matchmaking," In *Proceedings of the International Semantic Web Conference*, Sanibel Island, FL, pp. 335–350, 2003.

[FINI02]. T. Finin and A. Joshi, "Agents, Trust, and Information Access on the Semantic Web," *ACM SIGMOD Record*, (4), 30–35, 2002.

[INTE]. Intellidimension, the RDF Gateway, http://www.intellidimension.com/.

[JENA]. Jena, http://jena.sourceforge.net/.

[KAGA03]. L. Kagal, T. Finin, A. Joshi, "A Policy Based Approach to Security for the Semantic Web," In *Proceedings of the International Semantic Web Conference*, Sanibel Island, FL, 2003.

[KANT03]. M. Kantarcioglu, and C. Clifton, "Assuring Privacy When Big Brother is Watching," In *Proceedings of Data Mining Knowledge Discover (DMKD)*, San Diego, CA, pp. 829–93, 2003.

[RDF]. RDF Primer, http://www.w3.org/TR/rdf-primer/.

[SWRL]. Semantic Web Rules Language, 2004. http://www.w3.org/Submission/SWRL/.

[THUR02]. B. Thuraisingham, "Data Mining, National Security and Privacy," *ACM SIGKDD Explorations Newsletter*, 4 (2), 1–5, December 2002.

[THUR05]. M. B. Thuraisingham, "Privacy Constraint Processing in a Privacy-Enhanced Database Management System," *Data and Knowledge Engineering*, 55 (2), 159–188, 2005.

[THUR07]. B. Thuraisingham, N. Tsybulnik, A. Alam, "Administering the Semantic Web: Confidentiality, Privacy, and Trust Management," *International Journal of Information Security and Privacy*, 1 (1), 129–134, 2007.

[W3C]. World Wide Web Consortium, www.w3c.org.

[YU03]. T. Yu, and M. Winslett, "A Unified Scheme for Resource Protection in Automated Trust Negotiation," In *Proceedings of IEEE Symposium on Security and Privacy*, Oakland, CA, pp. 110–122, 2003.

30 Unified Framework for Secure Big Data Management and Analytics

30.1 OVERVIEW

In this chapter, we integrate the various parts of a big data system into an automatic framework for carrying out analytics but at the same time ensuring security. In particular, we integrate the analytics techniques with the privacy and security techniques discussed in the previous parts. In developing this framework, we preserve features such as scalability, efficiency, and interoperability. This framework can be used to execute various policies, including access control policies, redaction policies, filtering policies, and information-sharing policies, as well as inference strategies. Our framework can also be used as a testbed for evaluating different policy sets over big data (e.g., social media) graphs. Our recent work discussed in [THUR15] proposes new mechanisms for developing a unifying framework of data provenance expressed as RDF graphs. Some of our design techniques was also discussed in Chapter 28. These methods were applied for social media systems represented using semantic web technologies, and the approach was discussed in [THUR16]. In this chapter, we adapt the discussions in our previous works (e.g., [THUR15] and [THUR16]) for big data systems.

The framework we present in this chapter is in the design stages. Specifically, we give guidelines for policy processing for big data systems, as well as metadata that includes data provenance both for access control and inference control, as well as information sharing. We can integrate features such as risk-based access control and inference into such a framework. In addition, we can also incorporate privacy-aware data analytics for big data systems such as social media systems. Our ultimate goal is to develop big data systems that not only carry out access control and inference control but also information sharing and risk-based policy processing, as well as privacy-aware analytics. Before we present our framework, we will describe various aspects of integrity and data provenance for big data systems. Our framework will incorporate several features such as security, privacy, trust, and integrity for big data systems. While confidentiality, privacy, and trust have been discussed in Chapter 29, in this chapter, we will focus on integrity and data provenance and discuss how the various components can be put together into a unified framework for secure big data systems.

The organization of this chapter is as follows. In Section 30.2, we discuss aspects of integrity and data provenance for big data systems. In Section 30.3, we discuss our framework. Aspects of what we call our global inference controller will be discussed in Section 30.4. Such an inference controller will handle unauthorized inference during access control as well as during data sharing. This chapter is summarized in Section 30.5. Figure 30.1 illustrates the contents of this chapter.

30.2 INTEGRITY MANAGEMENT AND DATA PROVENANCE FOR BIG DATA SYSTEMS

30.2.1 Need for Integrity

In this section, we will discuss integrity management for big data systems. Integrity includes several aspects. In the database world, integrity includes concurrency control and recovery, as well as enforcing integrity constraints. For example, when multiple transactions execute at the same time,

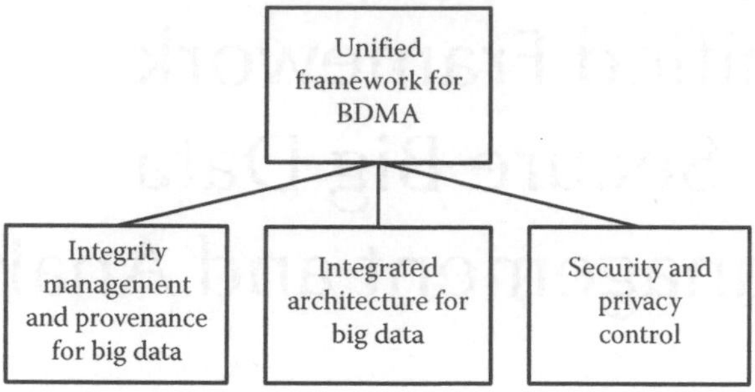

FIGURE 30.1 Unified framework for big data management and analytics.

the consistency of the data has to be ensured. When a transaction aborts, it has to be ensured that the database is recovered from the failure into a consistent state. Integrity constraints are rules that have to be satisfied by the data. Rules include "salary value has to be positive" and "age of an employee cannot decrease over time." More recently, integrity has included data quality, data provenance, data currency, real-time processing, and fault tolerance.

Integrity management is essential for big data systems such as social media systems in order to provide accurate and timely information to its users. For example, when users want to share information with their friends, they may want to share a certain version or the most recent version of the data. Furthermore, the member of the network may copy data from other sources and post it on their social media pages. In such situations, it would be useful to provide the sources of the information as well as from where the information was derived. In this section, we discuss aspects of integrity for big data as well as implementing integrity management as cloud services. For example, how do we ensure the integrity of the data and the processes? How do we ensure that data quality is maintained?

30.2.2 Aspects of Integrity

There are many aspects to integrity. For example, concurrency control, recovery, data accuracy, meeting real-time constraints, data accuracy, data quality, data provenance, fault tolerance, and integrity constraint enforcement are all aspects of integrity management. This is illustrated in Figure 30.2. In this section, we will examine each aspect of integrity.

Concurrency control: In data management, concurrent control is about transactions executing at the same time and ensuring consistency of the data. Therefore, transactions have to obtain locks or utilize time stamps to ensure that the data is left in a consistent state when multiple transactions attempt to access the data at the same time. Extensive research has been carried out on concurrency control techniques for transaction management both in centralized and distributed environments [BERN87].

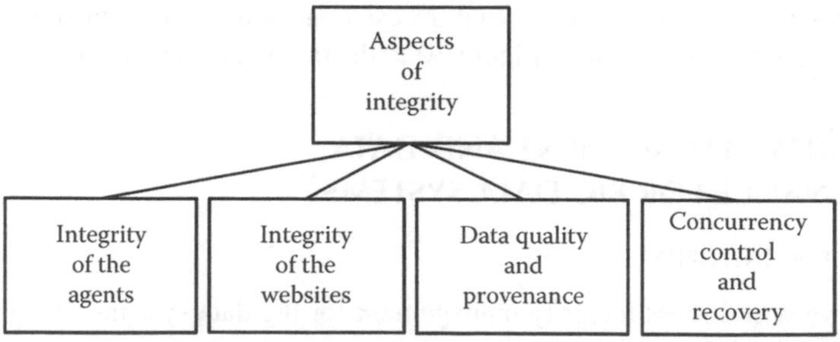

FIGURE 30.2 Aspects of integrity.

Data Recovery: When transactions abort before they complete execution, the database should be recovered to a consistent state such as it was before the transaction started execution. Several recovery techniques have been proposed to ensure the consistency of the data.

Data Authenticity: When the data is delivered to the user, its authenticity has to be ensured. That is, the user should get accurate data and the data should not be tampered with. We have conducted research on ensuring the authenticity of XML data during third party publishing [BERT04].

Data Completeness: Data that a user receives should not only be authentic but also be complete. That is, everything that the user is authorized to see has to be delivered to the user.

Data Currency: Data has to be current. That is, data that is outdated has to be deleted or archived and the data that the user sees has to be current data. Data currency is an aspect of real-time processing. If a user wants to retrieve the temperature, he has to be given the current temperature, not the temperature that is 24 hours old.

Data Accuracy: The question is how accurate is the data? This is also closely related to data quality and data currency. That is, accuracy depends on whether the data has been maliciously corrupted or whether it has come from an untrusted source.

Data Quality: Is the data of high quality? This includes data authenticity, data accuracy, and whether the data is complete or certain. If the data is uncertain, then can we reason with this uncertainty to ensure that the operations that use the data are not affected? Data quality also depends on the data source.

Data Provenance: This has to do with the history of the data, that is, from the time the data originated such as emanating from the sensors until the present time when it is given to the general. The question is who has accessed the data? Who has modified the data? How has the data traveled? This will determine whether the data has been misused.

Integrity Constraints: These are rules that the data has to satisfy, such as the age of a person cannot be a negative number. This type of integrity has been studied extensively by the database and the artificial intelligence communities.

Fault Tolerance: As in the case of data recovery, the processes that fail have to be recovered. Therefore, fault tolerance deals with data recovery as well as process recovery. Techniques for fault tolerance include check pointing and acceptance testing.

Real-time Processing: Data currency is one aspect of real-time processing where the data has to be current. Real-time processing also has to deal with transactions meeting timing constraints. For example, stock quotes have to be given within say 5 min. If not, it will be too late. Missing timing constraints could cause integrity violations.

30.2.3 Inferencing, Data Quality, and Data Provenance

Some researchers feel that data quality is an application of data provenance. Furthermore, they have developed theories for inferring data quality. In this section, we will examine some of the developments keeping in mind the relationship between data quality, data provenance, and the semantic cloud services.

Data quality is about accuracy, timeliness, and dependability (i.e., trustworthiness) of the data. It is however subjective, and it depends on the users and the domains. Some of the issues that have to be answered include the creation of the data, that is, where did it come from and why and how was the data obtained? Data quality information is stored as annotations to the data and should be part of data provenance. One could ask the question as to how we can obtain the trustworthiness of the data. This could depend on how the source is ranked and the reputation of the source.

As we have stated, researchers have developed theories for inferring data quality [PON]. The motivation is due to the fact that data could come from multiple sources; it is shared and prone to errors. Furthermore, data could be uncertain. Therefore, theories of uncertainty such as statistical reasoning, Bayesian theories, and Dempster Schafer theory of evidence are being used to infer the quality of the data. With respect to security, we need to ensure that the quality of the inferred data does not violate

Data Provenance

Who created the data?

Where has the data come from?

Who accessed the data?

What is the complete history of the data?

Has the data been misused?

FIGURE 30.3 Data provenance.

the policies. For example, at the unclassified level, we may say that the source is trustworthy, but at the secret level, we know that the source if not trustworthy. The inference controllers that we have developed could be integrated with the theories of interceding developed for data quality to ensure security.

Next, let us examine data provenance. For many of the domains including medical and healthcare, as well as defense, where the accuracy of the data is critical, we need to have a good understanding as to where the data came from and who may have tampered with the data. As stated in [SIMM05], data provenance, a kind of metadata, sometimes called "lineage" or "pedigree" is the description of the origin of a piece of data and the process by which it arrived in a database." Data provenance is information that helps determine the derivation history of a data product, starting from its original source.

Provenance information can be applied to data quality, auditing, and ownership, among others. By having records of who accessed the data, data misuse can be determined. Usually, annotations are used to describe the information related to the data (e.g., who accessed the data? where did the data come from?). The challenge is to determine whether one needs to maintain coarse-grained provenance data or fine-grained provenance data. For example, in a course-grained situation, the tables of a relation may be annotated, whereas in a fine-grained situation, every element may be annotated. There is, of course, the storage overhead to consider for managing provenance. XML, RDF, and OWL have been used to represent provenance data, and this way the tools developed for the semantic web technologies may be used to manage the provenance data.

There is much interest in using data provenance for misuse detection. For example, by maintaining the complete history of data such as who accessed the data, when and where was the data accessed, one can answer queries such as "who accessed the data between January and May 2010." Therefore, if the data is corrupted, one can determine who corrupted the data or when the data was corrupted. Figure 30.3 illustrates the aspects of data provenance. We have conducted extensive research on representing and reasoning about provenance data and policies represented using semantic web technologies ([CADE11a], [CADE11b], [THUR15]).

30.2.4 Integrity Management, Cloud Services and Big Data

Cloud Services for Integrity Management: There are two aspects here. One is that integrity management may be implemented with cloud services and the other is ensuring that the cloud services have high integrity. For implementing integrity management as cloud services, the idea is to invoke cloud services to ensure data quality as well as the integrity of the data and the system. Figure 30.4 illustrates implementing integrity management as a cloud service.

Like confidentiality, privacy, and trust, semantic web technologies such as XML may be used to specify integrity policies. Integrity policies may include policies for specifying integrity constraint as well as policies for specifying timing constraints, data currency, and data quality. Here are some examples of the policies:

FIGURE 30.4 Cloud services for integrity management.

Integrity Constraints: Age of an employee has to be positive. In a relational representation, one could specify this policy as

```
EMP.AGE>0.
In XML this could be represented as the following:
<Condition Object=”//Employe/Age”>
   <Apply FunctionId="greater-than">
      <AttributeValue DataType="http://www.w3.org/2001/
XMLSchema#integer">0
      </AttributeValue>
   </apply>
</Condition>
```

Data Quality Policy: The quality of the data in the employee table is LOW.
In the relational model, this could be represented as

```
EMP.Quality = LOW.
In XML, this policy could be represented as

<Condition Object=”//Employe/Quality”>
   <Apply FunctionId="equal">
      <AttributeValue DataType="http://www.w3.org/2001/
XMLSchema#string">LOW
      </AttributeValue>
   </Apply>
</Condition>
```

Data Currency: An example is: The salary value of EMP cannot be more than 365 days old. In a relational representation, this could be represented as

```
AGE (EMP.SAL) <=365 days.
In XML, this is represented as

<Condition Object=”//Employe/Salary”>
   <Apply FunctionId="AGE">
      <Apply FunctionId="less-than-or-equal">
         <AttributeValue DataType="http://www.w3.org/2001/
XMLSchema#integer">365
         </AttributeValue>
      </Apply>
   </Apply>
</Condition>
```

The above examples have shown how certain integrity policies may be specified. Note that there are many other applications of semantic web technologies to ensure integrity. For example, in order to ensure data provenance, the history of the data has to be documented. Semantic web technologies such as XML are being used to represent say the data annotations that are used to determine the quality of the data or whether the data has been misused. That is, the data captured is annotated with metadata information such as what the data is about, when it was captured, and who captured it. Then, as the data moves from place to place or from person to person, the annotations are updated so that, at a later time, the data may be analyzed for misuse. These annotations are typically represented in semantic web technologies, such as XML, RDF, and OWL.

Another application of semantic web technologies for integrity management is the use of ontologies to resolve semantic heterogeneity. That is, semantic heterogeneity causes integrity violations. This happens when the same entity is considered to be different at different sites and therefore compromises integrity and accuracy. Through the use of ontologies specified in say OWL, it can be expressed that a ship in one site and a submarine in another are one and the same.

Semantic web technologies also have applications in making inferences and reasoning under uncertainty or mining [THUR15]. For example, the reasoning engines based on RDF, OWL, or say rules may be used to determine whether the integrity policies are violated. We have discussed inference and privacy problems and building inference engines in earlier chapters. These techniques have to be investigated for the violation of integrity policies.

30.2.5 Integrity for Big Data

While integrity management can be provided as cloud services for big data systems such as social media and other systems, we ensure that the social media data has high integrity. The idea here is to not only ensure that the data shared by the social media members are accurate and current, it is also important to ensure that the big data system is not malicious and does not corrupt the data or other services. Figure 30.5 illustrates integrity management for big data systems.

Since many of the big data systems (e.g., social media) that we have developed utilize semantic web technologies for data resonation and reasoning, we need to ensure that integrity is maintained for semantic web technologies. Annotations that are used for data quality and provenance are typically represented in XML or RDF documents. These documents have to be accurate, complete, and current. Therefore, integrity has to be enforced for such documents. Another aspect of integrity is managing databases that consist of XML or RDF documents. These databases have all of the issues and challenges that are present for say relational databases. That is, the queries have to be optimized and transactions should execute concurrently. Therefore, concurrency control and recovery for XML and RDF documents become a challenge for managing XML and RDF databases. This is yet another aspect of integrity for semantic web documents.

The actions of the agents that make use of the semantic services to carry out operations such as searching, querying, and integrating heterogeneous databases, as well as information sharing in social media systems have to ensure that the integrity of the data is maintained. These agents cannot maliciously corrupt the data. They have to ensure that the data is accurate, complete, and consistent. Finally, when integrating heterogeneous databases, semantic web technologies such as OWL ontologies are being used to handle semantic heterogeneity. These ontologies have to be accurate and complete, and cannot be tampered with.

In summary, in order for the big data systems such as the social media systems to be useful to their members, they have to enforce data, system, and process integrity. Since many of the systems we have developed utilize semantic web technologies, we need to ensure that integrity is enforced on semantic web databases.

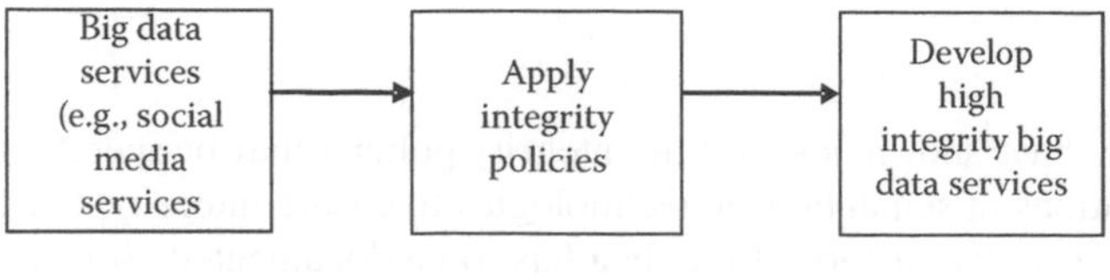

FIGURE 30.5 Integrity for big data systems.

30.3 DESIGN OF OUR FRAMEWORK

The architecture for our provenance manager discussed in Chapter 28 is extended to include an inference controller as well as a data-sharing manager and a risk manager. This enables us to add the risk-based mechanism into our framework. Our architecture takes a user's input query and returns a response that has been pruned using a set of user-defined policy constraints. We assume that a user could interact with our system to obtain both traditional data and provenance. In our design, we will assume that the available information is divided into two parts: the actual data and provenance. Both the data and provenance are represented as RDF graphs, but they are not limited to any data format since tools can map existing formats to RDF [BIZE03].

The architecture is built using a modular approach; therefore, it is very flexible in that most of the modules can be extended or replaced by another application module. For example, an application user may substitute a policy parser module that handles the parsing of high-level business policies to low-level policy objects, or replace or extend one policy layer without changing the inner workings of the other policy layer modules. This substitution or replacement of modules would allow the application user to continue using high-level business policies independent of our software implementation.

A user application can submit a query for access to the data and its associated provenance or vice versa. Figure 30.6 shows the design of our framework. All of the modules that comprise this framework make up our inference controller. We call this the global inference controller as it handles inference control for access control as well as for information sharing. We now present a description of these modules in Figure 30.6. Some aspects of our global inference controller will be discussed in Section 30.3. Next, we discuss the components of the framework.

Data Controller: The data controller is a suite of software programs that store and manage access to data such as social media data. The data could be stored in any format such as in a relational database, in XML files or in an RDF store. The controller accepts requests for information from the policy manager (and/or the inference engine layer) if a policy allows the requesting user access to

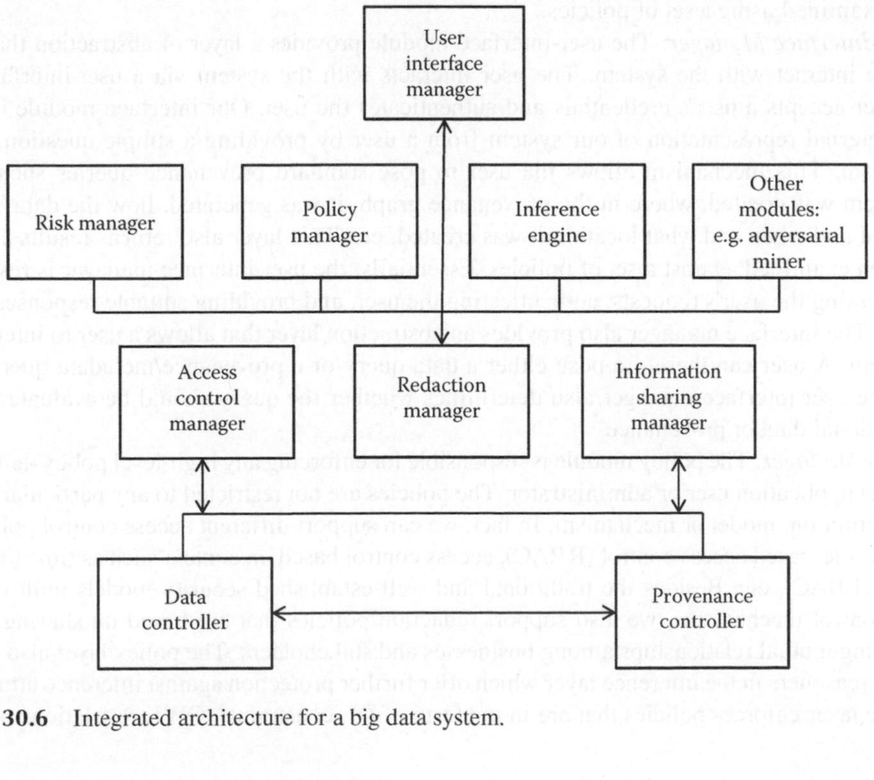

FIGURE 30.6 Integrated architecture for a big data system.

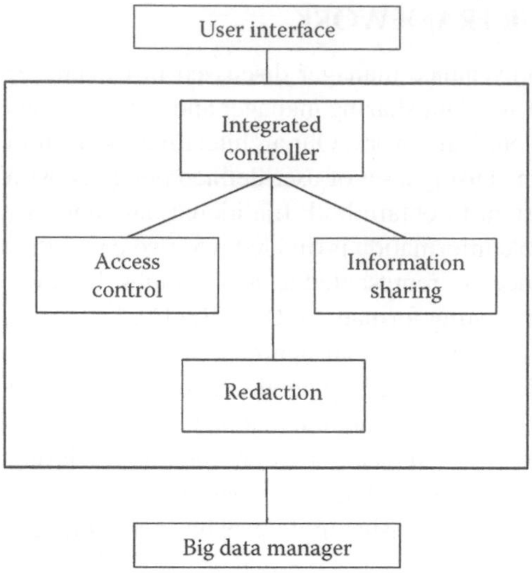

FIGURE 30.7 Global big data security and privacy controller.

the data item. This layer then executes the request over the stored data and returns results back to the policy layer (and/or the inference engine layer) where it is re-evaluated based on a set of policies.

Provenance/Metadata Controller: The provenance/metadata controller is used to store and manage provenance/metadata information, that is, associated with data items that are present in the data controller. In the case when we select a graph representation of provenance, the provenance controller stores information in the form of logical graph structures in any appropriate data representation format. This controller also records the ongoing activities associated with the data items stored in the data controller. This controller takes as input a graph query and evaluates it over the provenance information. This query evaluation returns a subgraph back to the inference controller layer where it is re-examined using a set of policies.

User-Interface Manager: The user-interface module provides a layer of abstraction that allows a user to interact with the system. The user interacts with the system via a user-interface layer. This layer accepts a user's credentials and authenticates the user. Our interface module hides the actual internal representation of our system from a user by providing a simple question–answer mechanism. This mechanism allows the user to pose standard provenance queries such as why a data item was created, where in the provenance graph, it was generated, how the data item was generated and when and what location it was created, etc. This layer also returns results after they have been examined against a set of policies. Essentially, the user-interface manager is responsible for processing the user's requests, authenticating the user, and providing suitable responses back to the user. The interface manager also provides an abstraction layer that allows a user to interact with the system. A user can therefore pose either a data query or a provenance/metadata query to this layer. The user-interface manager also determines whether the query should be evaluated against the traditional data or provenance.

Policy Manager: The policy module is responsible for enforcing any high-level policy defined by a high-level application user or administrator. The policies are not restricted to any particular security policy definition, model or mechanism. In fact, we can support different access control policies, for example, role-based access control (RBAC), access control based on context such as time (TRBAC), location (LBAC), etc. Besides the traditional and well-established security models built on top of access control mechanisms, we also support redaction policies that are based on sharing data for the ongoing mutual relationships among businesses and stakeholders. The policy layer also interacts with any reasoners in the inference layer which offer further protection against inference attacks. The inference layer enforces policies that are in the form of DL constraints, OWL restrictions or SWRL rules. We also observe that some of the access control policies can be expressed as inference rules or queries via query rewrite or views. Our policy module therefore has many layers equipped with security features, thus ensuring we are enforcing the maximal protection over the underlying provenance store. The policy module also handles the information-sharing policies.

Essentially, the policy manager is responsible for ensuring that the querying user is authorized to use the system. It evaluates the policies against a user's query and associated query results to ensure that no confidential information is released to unauthorized users. The policy manager may enforce the policies against the traditional data or against the provenance data. Each data type may have its own policy manager; for example, the traditional data may be stored in a different format from the provenance data. Hence, we may require different implementations for each policy manager.

Inference Engine: The inference engine is the heart of the inference controller. The engine is equipped to use a variety of inference strategies that are supported by a particular reasoner. Since there are many implementations of reasoners available, our inference controller offers an added feature of flexibility, whereby we can select from among any reasoning tool for each reasoning task. We can improve the efficiency of the inference controller since each inference strategy (or a combination of strategies) could be executed on a separate processor. An inference engine typically uses software programs that have the capability of reasoning over some data representation, for example, a relational data model or an RDF graph model representation.

The inference problem is an open problem and a lot of research has been pivoted around its implementations based on traditional databases ([MARK96], [HINK97]). However, since provenance has a logical graph structure, it can also be represented and stored in a graph data model, therefore it is not limited to any particular data format. Although our focus in this chapter is on building an inference controller over the directed graph representation of provenance, our inference controller could be used to protect the case when provenance is represented and stored in a traditional relational database model. Also, the use of an RDF data model does not overburden our implementation with restrictions, since other data formats are well served by an RDF data model. Furthermore, there are tools to convert say relational data into RDF and vice versa (see e.g., [D2RQ]).

Query Manager: The query processing module is responsible for accepting a user's query, parsing it and submitting it to the provenance knowledge base. After the query results are evaluated against a set of policies, it is returned to the user via the user-interface layer. The query processing module can accept any standard provenance query as well as any query written in the SPARQL format. The querying user is allowed to view the errors that are due to the syntax of a query, as well as the responses constructed by the underlying processes of the inference controller.

Information Sharing Manager: The information-sharing manager will implement the information-sharing policies. For example, if organization A wants to share data with organization B, then the information-sharing controller will examine the policies via the policy manager, determine whether there are any unauthorized inferences by communicating with the inference engine, and determine whether data is to be given to organization B.

Access Control Manager: This access control module is responsible for determining whether the user can access the data. The access control policies are obtained via the policy manager. The inference engine will determine whether any unauthorized information will be released by carrying out reasoning. The results are given to the user via the user-interface manager.

Redaction Manager: This module will determine which data has to be redacted before it is given to the user. It operates in conjunction with the access control manager. It also examines the information that has been released previously and determines whether the new information obtained as a result of executing the query should be given to the user.

Risk Analyzer: The risk analyzer will compute the risks for releasing the information and makes a determination whether the information should be released to the user. It interacts with other modules, such as the access control manager, the redaction manager, and the information-sharing manager, in making this determination. The results of the risk manager are then given to the access control manager, the redaction manager, and the information-sharing manager to execute the results.

Adversarial Data Miner: This module will implement the strategies to mine the adversary to see what his/her motives are. An adversary could be a human or some malicious code. In particular, such a data miner will determine how to thwart the adversary as well as apply game theoretic reasoning in determining what information is to be released to the user. It will work jointly with the inference engine.

30.4 THE GLOBAL BIG DATA SECURITY AND PRIVACY CONTROLLER

Our global controller should determine unauthorized inference during access control, redaction, and information sharing, as well as determine whether privacy violations have occurred through data mining. It has to compute the risks in disclosing the information as well as apply novel strategies such as adversarial monitoring to be ahead of the adversary. In this section, we will discuss some of the key points of such an inference controller illustrated in Figure 30.7.

Our prior work has developed models that can be used to determine the expected risk of releasing data and metadata. We need to extend such models in order to determine whether the addition of massive amounts of data such as social media data impacts security and privacy. The extended models would typically incorporate inference tools into the architecture.

Inference Tools: Newly published data, when combined with existing public knowledge, allows for complex and sometimes unintended inferences. Therefore, we need semi-automated tools for detecting these inferences prior to releasing provenance information. These tools should give data owners a fuller understanding of the implications of releasing the provenance information, as well as help them to adjust the amount of information they release in order to avoid unwanted inferences [STAD07]. The inference controller is a tool that implements some of the inference strategies that a user may utilize to infer confidential information, that is, encoded into a provenance graph. Our inference controller leverages from existing software tools that perform inferencing, for example, Pellet [SIRI07], Fact++ [TSAR06], Racer [HAAR01], Hermit [SHEA08], and CWM [CWM]. Therefore, we can add more expressive power by replacing the default base engine of our inference controller with a more powerful reasoner. Furthermore, since there is a trade-off of expressivity and decidability, an application user has more flexibility in selecting the most appropriate reasoner for his/her application domain.

For our default reasoner, we employ the services of Pellet [SIRI07]. Pellet has support for OWL-DL (SHOIN(D)) and is also extended to support OWL 2 specification (SROIQ(D)). The OWL 2 specification adds the following language constructs:

- Qualified cardinality restrictions
- Complex subproperty axioms (between a property chain and a property)
- Local reflexivity restrictions
- Reflexive, irreflexive, symmetric, and antisymmetric properties
- Disjoint properties
- Negative property assertions
- Vocabulary sharing (punning) between individuals, classes, and properties
- User-defined data ranges

In addition, Pellet provides all the standard inference services that are traditionally provided by DL reasoners. These are

- *Consistency checking*: This ensures that an ontology does not contain any contradictory facts. The OWL 2 Direct Semantics provide the formal definition of ontology consistency used by Pellet.
- *Concept satisfiability*: This determines whether it is possible for a class to have any instances. If a class is unsatisfiable, then defining an instance of that class will cause the whole ontology to be inconsistent.

- *Classification*: This computes the subclass relations between every named class to create the complete class hierarchy. The class hierarchy can be used to answer queries such as getting all or only the direct subclasses of a class [SIRI07].
- *Realization*: This finds the most specific classes that an individual belongs to; that is, realization computes the direct types for each of the individuals. Realization can only be performed after classification since direct types are defined with respect to a class hierarchy [SIRI07]. Using the classification hierarchy, it is also possible to get all the types for each individual.

The global inference controller has to reason with big data. Its operation has to be timely. Therefore, we propose a cloud-based implementation of such an inference controller. Our ultimate goal is to implement the entire inference controller in the cloud.

30.5 SUMMARY AND DIRECTIONS

This chapter has essentially integrated much of the design and implementation of the systems we have developed and described a unifying framework for big data systems. The framework includes components both for access control and inference control, as well as information-sharing control. Our framework can also include the modules for risk and game theoretic approaches for access and inference control. We discussed the modules of the framework as well as building the global inference controller.

We also provided an overview of data integrity that includes data quality and data provenance. We discussed the applications of semantic web technologies for data integrity, as well as discussed integrity for big data systems represented using semantic web technologies. Data provenance and data quality while important are only recently receiving attention. This is due to the fact that there are vast quantities of information stored in the cloud. Furthermore, massive amounts of data and information are managed and shared by members of a social media system. Therefore, it is important to know the extent to which such data and information are accurate. In addition, the members need to know that the data is copied and/or plagiarized. We also need to have answers to questions such as who owns the data. Has the data been misused? Therefore, data provenance is important to determine the security of the big data systems.

Our framework is in the design stages. Essentially, we have provided guidelines toward implementing such a framework. We can essentially plug and play various modules in order to develop such a framework. We believe that a cloud-based implementation of such a framework can provide scalability and efficiency. Our ultimate goal is to develop our global inference controller in the cloud with big data management technologies so that it can handle inferences for big data.

REFERENCES

[BERN87] P. Bernsteinet al., *Concurrency Control and Recovery in Database Systems*. Addison-Wesley, MA, 1987.

[BERT04] E. Bertinoet al., "Secure Third Party Publication of XML Documents," *IEEE Transactions on Knowledge and Data Engineering*, 16 (10), 1263–1278, 2004.

[BIZE03] C. Bizer, D2R MAP-A database to RDF mapping language. (WWW Posters) 2003.

[CADE11a] T. Cadenhead, V. Khadilkar, M. Kantarcioglu, and B.M. Thuraisingham, "A Language for Provenance Access Control," In *CODASPY' 2011: Proceedings of the 1st ACM Conference on Data and Application Security and Privacy*, pp. 133–144, San Antonio, TX, USA, 2011.

[CADE11b] T. Cadenhead, V. Khadilkar, M. Kantarcioglu, and B. M. Thuraisingham, "Transforming Provenance Using Redaction," In *SACMAT'2011: Proceedings of the 16th ACM Symposium on Access Control Models and Technologies*, pp. 93–102, Innsbruck, Austria, 2011.

[CWM] Closed World Machine, http://www.w3.org/2001/sw/wiki/CWM.

[D2RQ] D2RQ: Accessing Relational Databases as Virtual RDF Graphs, http://d2rq.org/.

[HAAR01] V. Haarslev and R. Möller, "RACER System Description," In *IJCAR'01: Proceedings of the 1st International Joint Conference on Automated Reasoning*, pp. 701–706, Springer-Verlag, London, 2001.

[HINK97] T. H. Hinke, H. S. Delugach, and R. P. Wolf, "Protecting Databases from Inference Attacks," *Computers & Security*, 16 (8), 687–708, 1997.

[MARK96] D. G. Marks, "Inference in MLS Database Systems," *IEEE Transacations on Knowledge Data Engineering*, 8 (1), 46–55, 1996.

[PON] R. K. Pon and A. F. Cárdenas, "Data Quality Inference," In *IQIS '05 Proceedings of the 2nd International Workshop on Information Quality in Information Systems*, Baltimore, MD, pp. 105–111, 2005.

[SHEA08] R. Shearer, B. Motik, and I. Horrocks, "HermiT: A Highly-Efficient OWL Reasoner," *OWLED'08: Proceedings of the 5th OWLED Workshop on OWL*, 432 (91), 378, 2008.

[SIMM05] Y.L. Simmhan, B. Plale, and D. Gannon, "*A Survey of Data Provenance in E-Science*," Indiana University Technical Report, *ACM SIGMOD Record*, 34 (3), 31–36, 2005.

[SIRI07] E. Sirin, B. Parsia, B.C. Grau, A. Kalyanpur, and Y. Katz, "Pellet: A practical Owl-Dl Reasoner," *Web Semantics: Science, Services and Agents on the World Wide Web*, 5 (2), 51–53, 2007.

[STAD07] J. Staddon, P. Golle, and B. Zimny, "Web-Based Inference Detection," In *Proceedings of 16th USENIX Security Symposium*, Article No. 6, Boston, MA, 2007.

[THUR15] B. Thuraisinghamet al., *Secure Data Provenance and Inference Control with Semantic Web Technologies*. CRC Press, Boca Raton, FL, 2015.

[THUR16] B. Thuraisinghamet al., *Analyzing and Securing Social Networks*. CRC Press, Boca Raton, FL, 2016.

[TSAR06] D. Tsarkov and I. Horrocks, "FaCT++ Description Logic Reasoner: System Description," In *IJCAR'06: Proceedings of the 3rd International Joint Conference on Automated Reasoning*, pp. 302–307, Seattle, Washington, D.C., 2006.

31 Big Data, Security, and the Internet of Things

31.1 INTRODUCTION

In this chapter, we will continue to discuss the next steps in BDMA and BDSP. In particular, we will provide an overview of the Internet of things (IoT) and various security issues for IoT as well as discuss the big data problem for IoT systems. IoT is one of the rapidly going technologies today with multiple devices from a few to millions connected through the cyberspace. These devices may include computers, controllers, smartphones, and embedded devices ranging from those used in smart grids to smart homes. Managing the connections of these devices as well as handling the large amounts of data generated by the devices has become a daunting challenge for corporations. For example, AT&T has stated that "as of Q1 2016 there are 27.8 million devices on the AT&T Network [ATT] and they expect the numbers of connected devices to grow from tens of millions to hundreds of millions to billions." Figure 31.1 shows a sample topology for IoT. Data is first collected from sensors and then aggregated. Finally, this data is analyzed.

The increasing complexity of cyberspace due to the IoT with heterogeneous components, such as different types of networks (e.g., fixed wired networks, mobile cellular networks, and mobile ad hoc networks), diverse computing systems (e.g., sensors, embedded systems, smartphones, and smart devices), and multiple layers of software (e.g., applications, middleware, operating systems [Oss], and hypervisors), results in massive security vulnerabilities as any of the devices or the networks or the data generated could be attacked. Adversaries will increasingly move into the cyberspace for IoT and will target all cyber-based infrastructures, including energy, transportation, and financial and health care infrastructures. Providing cyber security solutions for managing cyber conflicts and defending against cyber attacks for IoT in such a complex landscape is thus a major challenge.

We discuss our approach of a cyber-defense framework for IoT systems based on a layered architecture. In particular, we discuss a layered security framework for IoT applications. The goals are to (i) develop techniques for secure networks (both wired and wireless), hardware, software, and systems as well as data sources when faced with attacks and (ii) develop analytics solutions for detecting the attacks. It should be noted that there are several reported efforts on IoT security. But many of these projects focus on just one aspect (e.g., hardware, network, software, or data). We believe that we need an integrated framework to solve the challenging security problems.

While securing each layer of our framework is important for security, we believe that the IoT challenges are mainly data challenges. This is because the IoT devices generate data and combining all the devices together will make it a big data problem. This data has to be analyzing and secured. In addition, threat/attack data is also collected for IoT devices from all the layers. That is, the hardware, network, and systems layers generate threat/attack data that has to be integrated and analyzed to determine whether there are anomalies. Therefore, much of our focus in this chapter is on data-related security issues for IoT.

The organization of this chapter is as follows. Use cases covering various systems are given in Section 31.2. A layered security framework is discussed in Section 31.3. Data security challenges are discussed in Section 31.4. Scalable analytics for security applications are discussed in Section 31.5. This chapter is summarized in Section 31.6. It should be noted that there is no one architecture for an IoT. The architecture will depend on whether the IoT is for smart home or a smart grid or some other critical infrastructure. Therefore, the security solutions will depend on the particular architecture; for example, when the network is attacked, a device in a smart grid may be able to

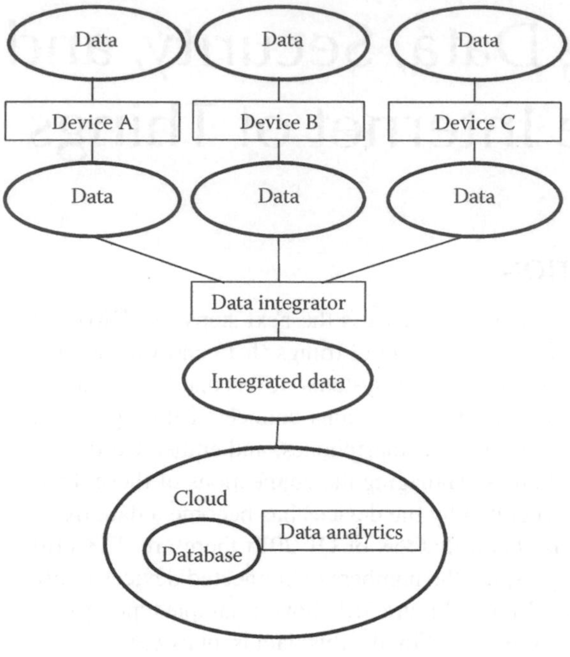

FIGURE 31.1 Internet of things: sample topology.

switch to another network or the system may divert the critical resources to another location. Such agility may not be possible say for a smart home IoT. Therefore, such considerations have to be taken into account when devising security solutions for IoT.

31.2 USE CASES

The IoT is expected to revolutionize the way we interact with devices at work, home, and public spaces. By providing network connectivity to embedded devices, everyday objects will be able to interact with each other, introducing new services and opportunities to end users. We now provide four domains where embedded smart devices are transforming the landscape, providing new functionalities but at the same time, if care is not taken to secure these systems, providing new vulnerabilities.

Intelligent transportation systems: Advances in computing and networking technologies have enabled a new generation of vehicular applications based on real-time measurements. Ubiquitous sensing and actuation capabilities, mobile and embedded computing with smartphones and wireless communication networks have been used for real-time traveler information systems (e.g., dynamic message signs), field actuation mechanisms (e.g., ramp and signal controllers), and improved evacuation responses to disasters.

The data collected in the four major domains of operations planning includes (1) traffic flow control which implements ramp metering at freeway on-ramps and signal timing plans at signalized intersections to reduce congestion; (2) demand management which focuses on reducing the excess demand during peak hours; (3) incident management which targets resources to alleviate incident hot spots; and (4) traveler information which is used to reduce traveler buffer time, that is, the extra time the travelers must account for when planning trips.

At the same time, collection of large-scale, potentially privacy sensitive sensor data has created significant security and privacy concerns. For example, modern transportation algorithms depend on the availability of real-time measurement data of traffic conditions. The sensing infrastructure used to collect this real-time traffic data includes point sensors like loop detectors, space sensors like surveillance cameras and satellite data, and mobile sensors like GPS-equipped vehicles and automatic vehicle location techniques. In order to meet the requirements of modern transportation algorithms, these sensors are collecting data at unprecedented levels of granularity, and because sensing is passive, users are generally unaware of the privacy risks.

Smart home: A typical *home area network* (HAN) can connect a set of devices such as fridges, smart meters, printers, thermostats, streaming clients, and set top boxes. The diversity of devices connected to these networks is expected to increase rapidly in the next couple of years. As new devices enter the market, the proliferation of heterogeneous technologies poses serious challenges for interactions among devices following different specifications and standards.

Smart homes will provide several new opportunities and functionalities for users, but at the same time, they present several security challenges that need to be addressed. These challenges include (1) secure interoperability among a wide range of manufacturers and service providers, (2) trust and authentication, (3) usability of security solutions, and (4) access control.

Consider, for example, a home network that controls appliances, heating and cooling, and lighting. In most networks available to consumers, there is typically a lack of fine-grained access control; access to the central controller implies total control of the system. However, adding such fine-grained access control runs the danger of making the system unusable.

There have been many examples of security problems, including smart refrigerators that give Google Calendar user passwords to untrusted devices, smartphone apps that control locks and temperature in homes that allow impersonators, home cameras sharing private images with anyone, insurance dongles in cars accepting software updates from untrusted services, and home alarm systems that allow attackers to intercept and modify messages.

Control systems: Control systems are computer-based systems that *monitor* and *control* physical processes. These systems represent a wide variety of networked information technology (IT) systems connected to the physical world. Depending on the application, these control systems are also called process control systems (PCS), supervisory control and data acquisition (SCADA) systems (in industrial control or in the control of the critical infrastructures), distributed control systems (DCS), or cyber-physical systems (CPS; to refer to embedded sensor and actuator networks).

Control systems are usually composed of a set of networked agents, consisting of sensors, actuators, control processing units such as programmable logic controllers (PLCs) and communication devices. For example, the oil and gas industry uses integrated control systems to manage refining operations at plant sites, remotely monitor the pressure and flow of gas pipelines, and control the flow and pathways of gas transmission. Water utilities can remotely monitor well levels and control the wells pumps; monitor flows, tank levels, or pressure in storage tanks; monitor pH, turbidity, and chlorine residual; and control the addition of chemicals to the water.

Several control applications can be labeled as *safety-critical*; their failure can cause irreparable harm to the physical system being controlled and to the people who depend on it. SCADA systems, in particular, perform vital functions in national critical infrastructures, such as electric power distribution, oil and natural gas distribution, water and wastewater treatment, and transportation systems. They are also at the core of health care devices, weapons systems, and transportation management. The disruption of these control systems could have a significant impact on public health and safety and lead to large economic losses.

Control systems are now at a higher risk to cyber attacks because their vulnerabilities are increasingly becoming exposed and available to an ever-growing set of motivated and highly skilled attackers.

Smart grid: Smart grid refers to multiple efforts around the globe to modernize aging power grid infrastructures with new technologies, enabling a more intelligently networked automated system. The goal of a smart grid is to deliver energy with greater efficiency, reliability, and security, and provide more transparency and choice to electricity consumers.

This modernization leverages recent advances in IT, wireless communications, and embedded systems (sensors and actuators with processing power, capable of communicating with each other).

These new technologies will provide real-time monitoring of the health of the power grid, collect and analyze data for better analytics and control, and accommodate the integration of new forms of energy supply (such as renewable sources) and delivery (energy storage and dynamic pricing).

While the smart grid promises many benefits, it raises many new security and privacy challenges. With the large-scale deployment of ubiquitous, remotely accessible networked devices to monitor and control the grid, it will be easier for attackers to find vulnerable points, including new smart devices, to access various parts of the grid and so the attack surface of the power grid will be vastly increased. Also, the new functionalities provided by the new devices such as the remote disconnect option provided by many smart meters may be exploited by the attackers resulting in major security risks to the system.

There are also many new privacy concerns related to smart grid deployments. The fine-grained energy usage data collected by new devices including smart meters, smart appliances, and electric cars will result in new privacy threats to consumers, especially because of the large-scale, more detailed, and more frequent collection of the usage data.

31.3 LAYERED FRAMEWORK FOR SECURE IOT

Protecting IoT devices requires a multifaceted layered approach to secure individual devices, securing how these devices communicate (network security) and securing applications that run on top of these systems. Figure 31.2 illustrates a layered framework for secure IoT. At the lowest layer is the device hardware. To prevent attackers from obtaining control of the device, we need to increase the resilience of individual devices under the constraints of embedded systems. Hardware-level security can be used to provide new and strong cryptographic keys with the help of hardware security modules (HSMs). Hardware-assisted security can be leveraged to provide security guarantees such as TrustZone security extensions for ARM devices or SGX extensions for Intel-based IoT processors. Hardware-assisted security can also help devices bootstrap with a secure root of trust, and can also help prevent vulnerable code to be abused by attackers and to prevent malware from taking full control of the device.

On top of the hardware, we have an embedded software platform/layer. As previously mentioned, one of the challenges for a variety of IoT devices is the patch cycle and the insecure-by-design vulnerabilities. One way to address these problems is through binary rewriting and binary analysis of the code. Next is the systems layer. This layer focuses on security issues such as virtual machine introspection as appropriate. That is, not all of the devices may have full-fledged systems. While the

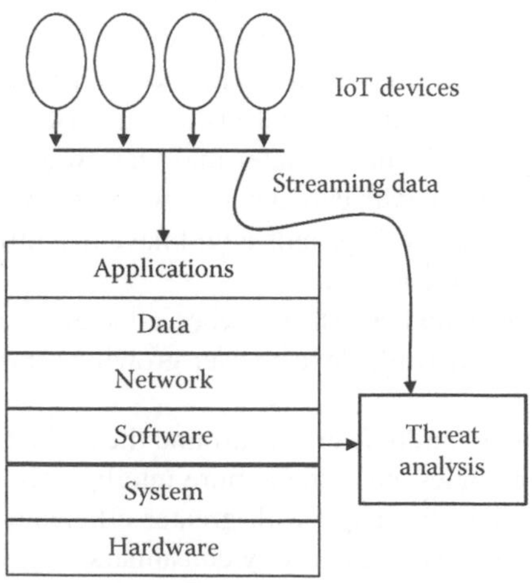

FIGURE 31.2 Layered architecture for IoT.

smart devices in a home network may be lightweight, those in a smart grid (e.g., for telecom, oil and gas, and power) may have more heavyweight systems.

Next, we have the network layer. IoT devices have a variety of network stacks and communication options, from embedded wireless communications in IEEE 802.15.4 to lightweight IPv6 packets for devices with small communication frames such as those provided by 6LoWPAN, new routing protocols such as the new IETF standard for ROLL and lightweight IP-based network stacks like LwIP. Networking additions to IoT devices are new and the security analysis of all these protocols is still ongoing. Network security, firewalls, and intrusion detection for IoT gateway hubs will be essential in future IoT deployments. Software-defined networking (SDN) solutions can be leveraged for orchestration and to launch desired defenses on demand. Due to the developments with SDN, we can monitor communications at a smart hub or IoT router and reconfigure the network in case we see threats or new vulnerabilities. Our work will continue this research by looking at current specifications and identifying threats and possible improvements to guarantee secure network operations. Specifically, we will focus on proactive security using multipath coding.

Next is the data layer. This layer ensures features such as access control to the resources and that the privacy of the individuals who access the IoT system are protected. For example, issues such as privacy-preserving data management and novel success control models need to be investigated for data management. Another aspect of data management is analyzing all the data collected. This aspect is represented in the threat management layer. That is, the devices are connected to the data centers via the wireless network and the data collected by the devices are sent to the data center for analysis. The applications (discussed in the use cases) drive the hardware, software, systems, and networks.

Our security investigation will focus on each of the layers under varying assumptions for IoT. The challenges for each of the layers as well as for threat analysis will be discussed in Section 31.4.

31.4 PROTECTING THE DATA

We believe that to create more value from the IoT ecosystem, we need to support more secure and privacy-preserving data-processing capabilities. Data collected using the IoT devices can be used in different ways to the benefit of the individual, others and society in general. For example, individual electric usage data could be shared and mined to understand overall trends and predict electricity demand. However, even though IoT data can be collected and shared for societal value, privacy/security concerns may impede such sharing. We thus need techniques to protect the potentially sensitive data while providing privacy guarantees to the individuals using the IoT-based systems such as smart grid, etc.

In certain scenarios, even directly releasing IoT data may disclose sensitive information, so instead we may want to share results that are mined locally. For example, IoT data collected by a medical device (e.g., heart rate monitor) may be mined locally to find interesting association rules or important events (e.g., notifying 911 if heart attack is detected). Furthermore, IoT systems could be updated to send only aggregate data to further protect privacy and security (e.g., electricity usage aggregated over few hours).

Also, data coming from different IoT devices may need to be integrated to create system-level models. One way to facilitate such data integration securely and privately would be to send data using techniques such as onion routing (e.g., using Tor [TOR]) to avoid data being linked to the specific IoT device (e.g., not providing the ID of smart meter when fine-grained data is collected from smart meters, and only sending ID for aggregate billing data). Also, potentially encrypt all the data in transit. However, previous research on identifiability [SWE02] clearly indicates that even if data contains no identifiers and is sent using onion routing, it can still be used to identify individuals. Another option could be to add noise to the data so that the shared data becomes less accurate (e.g., randomized response type application [DU03]) and, therefore, less likely to cause negative outcomes for individuals.

For IoT users to allow data sharing, they must have trust that their data will be protected in the manner that they intend and will not be vulnerable to attacks. Also, users must be able to comprehend the policy management options so that they understand their choices and the possible consequences of their selections. Because these options involve the data that can be collected and the contexts in which they can be collected, as well as who will be allowed access to their data, policy specification by the user will necessarily be a complex process. Consequently, the interactions with the interface necessary for a user to define his/her policies and set the data management options need to be as straightforward as possible and allow for personalization. Not all users may desire to have detailed control over their personal information, so the interface needs to support decisions at different levels of granularity.

Our approach to securing IoT data will consist of multiple components. The first component consists of an access control system supporting the specification and enforcement of access control policies for IoT data as well as the evolution and merging of different policies ranging from event-based sharing (e.g., share only when heart attack is detected) to emergency data release for critical situations (e.g., access to precise locations of certain cars when a traffic accident is detected). The second component is a data analytics system able to work on sanitized data. An important issue is to assess the quality of data analytics models derived from sets of sanitized data. More importantly, it is crucial to determine whether and how a data-mining model built from a large volume of IoT data coming from many devices can then be refined by using a nonanonymized specific IoT device to provide value to users. For example, based on the aggregate electricity usage data collected from a given region and the user's specific data, the most cost-effective plan can be recommended to the user. The goal would be to create global data-mining models based on the sanitized data of multiple IoT devices and then specialize these models for each specific IoT device to find optimal configurations for a given task.

Initially, we will build a framework where IoT data streams coming from different sources will be analyzed locally. Using the computational power of the IoT devices (many devices will have some computation power and small storage), important statics will be computed locally for detecting various events. In addition, as needed, important data and statistics will be sent to a cloud-based service in encrypted format for storage. Later on, these data and statistics will be shared based on the policies and events registered by the user. We will also develop cloud-based secure data-mining techniques. Based on the data-sharing policies, the data that will be submitted to data-mining models will be automatically extracted. In certain scenarios, the data will also be aggregated using the information coming from the peers (i.e., information coming from nearby IoT devices). In some cases, the information will be sanitized by adding noise before sharing with the cloud-based services (e.g., by leveraging randomized response-based differential-privacy techniques [DU03]). This locally computed information will be shared using secret sharing-based techniques with multiple servers located on the public cloud using service such as Tor [TOR] so that linking back the data to a particular IoT device will be harder. Furthermore, hacking into any one server will not disclose any sensitive information. Once the data is sent to multiple servers using secret sharing mechanisms, secret sharing-based secure protocols will be executed among the servers to build the global data-mining models from IoT data. To scale to a large number of users, we need to combine effective sampling and randomized response techniques in conjunction with secret sharing-based secure multiparty ideas. For example, we may want to combine IoT data from a certain subpopulation (e.g., smart meters) to build a linear regression model to understand the relationship between power usage and income on Sundays in say North Dallas.

31.5 SCALABLE ANALYTICS FOR IOT SECURITY APPLICATIONS

As the use and advances of sensor network become ubiquitous and the IoT becomes a reality, we increasingly need to deal with large volumes of heterogeneous dynamic stream data. For example, on the one hand, smart meters and other sensors continuously create physical system stream data (e.g., video, audio, pressure, voltage, altitude, etc.); on the other hand, (cyber) data can include logs, NetFlow data, content metadata telemetry, etc. These new sensors are constantly collecting more data, and as a result we have the need to analyze heterogeneous correlated information. Examples include (1) video signal and audio signal to detect events, target tracking, etc., (2) sensor signal (e.g., power consumption) and cyber signals (e.g., network intrusion detection data) to identify faults or potential attacks, and (3) multiple video signals from different angles having different and partial views of a scene. Furthermore, cyber threat/attack detection in a dynamic, heterogeneous IoT environment is a challenging task. The traditional detection approach based on prior knowledge from domain experts (e.g., signature-based detection) may capture some types of existing malicious activities (including threats) but may not be effective against untypical or stealthy attacks. As a more advanced approach, a unified learning framework can learn from data and incidents on the fly which may better detect zero-day or untypical malicious activities.

As stated in Section 31.1, Figure 31.1 shows a generic IoT topology where data is first collected from sensors (data acquisition) and devices. Second, the collected data is through a gateway (data aggregation) which may also involve some basic and localized data analysis. Third, the processed data is sent to a cloud for more complex analytics. These analytics will involve data from multiple gateways. An example of real-life implementation may be using Raspberry Pi as a gateway to collect temperature data from TMP36 sensors and send it to cloud. In the cloud, a big streaming analytics framework like Spark running on a Google Compute Engine will be used for further processing and to retrieve meaningful insights about the data. End users will be able to view the analytics result in real (or near-real) time through apps. The tasks for analytics are briefly enumerated below:

- *Preprocessing*: Cleaning, detecting, and correcting errors, omissions, and inconsistencies in gleaned data or across datasets are the main objectives at this task. In addition, for alignment relating, different representations of the same object is the focus here. At this stage, data needs to be captured in real time. For this, in the first step, as we are collecting data from distributed sensors, we may want to encode or reduce the amount of data being transmitted in order to preserve battery life. By encoding sensor data at the physical layer, the dependencies and correlation of heterogeneous sources become more robust. The second step focuses on real-time processing of data; Apache Spark streaming platform or Spark will be utilized.
- *Prediction and forecasting*: We would like to make decisions about upcoming future values of a variable of interest or determine future (time-stamped) values of a variable within a given time interval. For example, UAV could potentially be modeled by an ARMA process, while network logs could be analyzed by a machine-learning tool used to identify irregularities or infer the number and types of traffic incidents in an upcoming time interval based on historical data. For this, first we will focus prediction and forecasting on local aggregated data at a gateway using machine learning and data mining (i.e., supervised, unsupervised, and semi-supervised learning). Next, we will focus on the information fusion or correlation among these different data-analysis tools/gateways. Traditional machine-learning tools have generally used ensemble methods that use voting as a deciding factor, ignoring uncertainty. Voting is a linear decision function, but based on the potential correlations that may amend the datasets, some of optimal aggregation rules might not be linear. We have previously shown in [BARR08] one of the benefits of combining statistical detection theory and machine learning: all voting rules and ensemble methods can be considered as examples of Neyman Pearson theory and using this theory we can identify flaws in previous arguments and propose better decision rules.

Our goal is to build a comprehensive streaming analytics framework with applications to anomaly detection for IoT threat detection. Characteristics of streaming data are as follows:

- *Heterogeneity*: A sensor network deployed over a geographical area may consist of diverse types of sensors nodes with different degrees of dissimilarity of sourced data. This may add complexity in data representation and evaluation.
- *Scalability*: Mining on large networks is computationally intensive and requires a significant amount of resources. This makes real-time data analytics challenging.
- *Concept drift and Concept evolution*: Concept drift occurs in data streams when the underlying data distribution changes over time [WANG03]. Concept-evolution occurs when new classes evolve in streams [MASU11]. Furthermore, the topology of a network may also change (e.g., due to mobility). Therefore, statistical models representing the data streams distribution should adapt continuously to reduce misclassification errors.
- *Infinite length*: As streaming data occurs continuously, the streams can be assumed to be of unbounded length, making main memory data storage difficult.
- *Energy-efficient communication*: Communicating data is among the most energy-expensive routines across different types of wireless sensor networks (WSN). For instance, receiving and transmitting data in WSN consisting of Mica2 nodes running TinyDB applications constitutes about 59% of the total energy consumption [SHNA04]. Reducing the amount of data transmitted and/or energy consumed per transmission could lead to longer network lifetimes and significantly impact network functions. Therefore, we need to design energy-efficient communication for battery-powered wireless networks to significantly affect network performance and lifetime.

Neither multistep methodologies and techniques nor multiscan algorithms suitable for typical knowledge discovery and data mining can be readily applied to data streams due to well-known limitations such as bounded memory, online data processing, and the need for one-pass techniques (i.e., forgotten raw data). In spite of the success and extensive studies of stream-mining techniques, there is no effort (to the best of our knowledge) that focuses on a unified study of new challenges introduced by evolving data streams such as change detection, novelty detection, feature evolution/heterogeneity, scalability, and energy-aware communication.

In Figure 31.3, a scenario of anomaly detection over IoT network traffic is depicted. The sensors and IoT devices will be communicated by the rest of the Internet through their respective gateways. At the gateway, we will apply machine-learning techniques on those traffic data to detect anomalous traffic locally. The learning process will be continuous; feedback from the prediction module along with the stream of data will be used to build and update the model to detect the anomaly. Captured data will be IP packets or MQTT (MQTT, http://mqtt.org/) messages. Recall that MQTT is a simple lightweight publish-subscribe messaging protocol used in IoT which runs on top of TCP/IP protocol. There will be multiple such gateways with each generating their own views of anomalous traffic detection. Those views can be combined in the cloud for refinement producing a generic threat model. There might be some gateways where local threat detection will not be conducted. They will share data with the cloud and in cloud, an aggregated threat model will be detected based on the data from several such gateways.

We will focus on particular communication scenarios in the context of wireless networks' energy efficiency. In many cases of WSN deployments, for instance, clusters of spatially proximate nodes sense and potentially transmit very highly correlated, almost identical values to the sink [VURA06]. The scenario underlying the operation of cooperative transmission networks and related distributed transmit-beamforming physical layer protocols are analogous: a group of nodes transmits the same message in a carefully coordinated fashion. In both these scenarios, a group of source nodes has access to the same or highly correlated pieces of data that need to be sent to a common sink. We will introduce a novel scheme, encoded sensing (ES) that substantially reduces the energy required

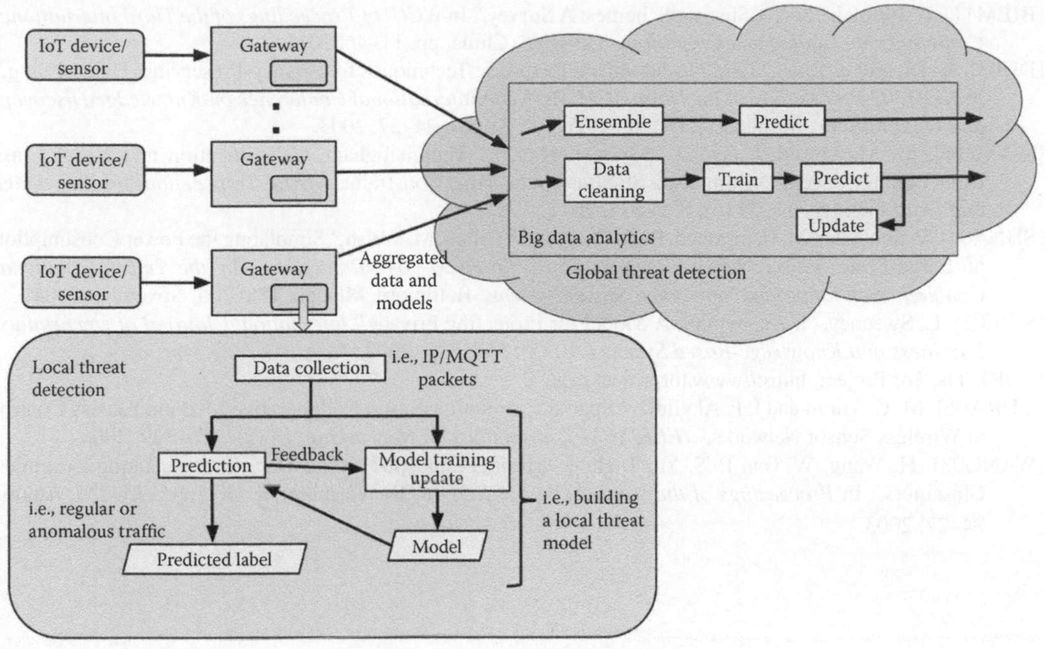

FIGURE 31.3 A scenario of anomaly detection over IoT network traffic.

for transmission of data in various types of wireless networks, where these settings hold. For analytics, a number of heterogeneous models will be maintained where models may be from relational learning, signal processing, or stochastic processes. Classification will be performed by efficiently aggregating the combined classifier resulting from heterogeneous models.

31.6 SUMMARY AND DIRECTIONS

In this chapter, we discussed the need for IoT security and provided some use cases. Next, we described a layered architecture for secure IoT. We argued that data security and analytics are at the heart of IoT security because data is being collected from the various IoT devices. This data has to be secured. In addition, the threat/attack data has to be analyzed to determine anomalies. While our focus has been mainly on the data aspects of security, the network, system, and applications also have to be secured for IoT systems. We should try and achieve end-to-end security. In addition, the risk analysis for IoT systems has to be carried out so that realistic solutions can be developed.

As stated earlier, it should be noted that there is no one architecture for an IoT. The architecture will depend on whether the IoT is for smart home or a smart grid or some other critical infrastructure. Therefore, the security solutions will depend on the particular architecture; for example, when the network is attacked, a device in a smart grid may be able to switch to another network or the system may divert the critical resources to another location. Such agility may not be possible say for a smart home IoT. Therefore, such considerations have to be taken into account when devising security solutions for IoT.

REFERENCES

[ATT]. "AT&T on Securing the Internet of Things: A Layered Approach Tackles Sophisticated New Threats," *CyberTrend*, 14 (6), Sandhills Publishing, June 2016.

[BARR08]. M. Barreno, A. Cardenas, J. D. Tygar, "Optimal ROC Curve for a Combination of Classifiers," In *Proceedings of NIPS 2008*, Vancouver, British Columbia, Canada, pp. 57–64, 2008.

[BIEM11]. A. Beimel, "Secret-Sharing Schemes: A Survey." In *WCC'11 Proceedings of the Third International Conference on Coding and Cryptology*, Qingdao, China, pp. 11–46, 2011.

[DU03]. K. Du and Z. Zhan, "Using Randomized Response Techniques for Privacy-Preserving, Data Mining," In *KDD '03 Proceedings of the Ninth ACM SIGKDD International Conference on Knowledge Discovery and Data Mining*, Washington, DC, pp. 505-510, August 24–27, 2003.

[MASU11]. M. M. Masud, J. Gao, L. Khan, J. Han, B. Thuraisingham, "Classification and Novel Class Detection in Concept-Drifting Data Streams Under Time Constraints," *IEEE Transactions on Knowledge and Data Engineering*, 23 (6), 859–874, 2011.

[SHNA04]. V. Shnayder, M. Hempstead, B. R. Chen, G. W. Allen, M. Welsh, "Simulating the Power Consumption of Large-Scale Sensor Network Applications," In *ACM '04: Proceedings of the 2nd International Conference on Embedded Networked Sensor Systems*, Baltimore, MD, pp. 188–200, November 2004.

[SWE02]. L. Sweeney, "k-Anonymity: A Model for Protecting Privacy," *International Journal of Uncertainty, Fuzziness and Knowledge-Based Systems*, 10 (5), 557–570, 2002.

[TOR]. The Tor Project, https://www.torproject.org/.

[VURA06]. M. C. Vuran and I. F. Akyildiz, "Spatial Correlation-Based Collaborative Medium Access Control in Wireless Sensor Networks," *IEEE/ACM Transactions on Networking*, 14 (2), 316–329, 2006.

[WANG03]. H. Wang, W. Fan, P. S. Yu, J. Han, "Mining Concept-Drifting Data Streams Using Ensemble Classifiers," In *Proceedings of the Ninth ACM SIGKDD KDD*, Washington, DC, pp. 226–235, August 24–27, 2003.

32 Big Data Analytics for Malware Detection in Smartphones

32.1 INTRODUCTION

As stated in Chapter 31, Internet of things (IoT) systems generate massive amounts of data that have to be managed, integrated, and analyzed to extract useful patterns and trends. However, the pervasive nature of these devices is also prone to attack. That is, it is not only the device that is attacked but also the data that is generated and integrated possibly in a cloud. In Chapter 31, we discussed some of the security challenges for IoT devices in general. In this chapter, we will focus on a particular IoT system, that is, a connected smartphone system. These connected smartphone devices generate massive amounts of data and can be considered to be an IoT system. We discuss how big data analytics may be applied for detecting malware in smartphones.

The smartphone has rapidly become an extremely prevalent computing platform, with just over 968 million devices sold in 2013 around the world [GART14b], a 36% increase in the fourth quarter of 2013. In particular, Android devices accounted for 78.4% of the market share, an increase of 12% year-on-year. This popularity has not gone unnoticed by malware authors. Despite the rapid growth of the Android platform, there are already well-documented cases of Android malware, such as DroidDream [BRAD11] which was discovered in over 50 applications on the official Android market in March 2011. Furthermore, a study by [ENCK11] found that Android's built-in security features are largely insufficient, and that even nonmalicious programs can (unintentionally) expose confidential information. A study of 204,040 Android applications conducted in 2011 found 211 malicious applications on the official Android market and alternative marketplaces [ZHOU12]. In addition, sophisticated Trojans have been reported recently [UNUC13], spreading via mobile botnets. Various researchers around the globe track reported security threats [SOPH14], wherein well over 300 Android malware families have been recorded.

On the other hand, smartphone apps on App Stores have been on a steady rise, with app download reaching 102 billion in 2013 [GART13] with a total revenue of $26 billion. This shows an ever increasing popularity in smartphone apps used in a multitude of applications including banking among others. In addition, private companies, military, and government organizations also develop apps to be used for processing and storing extremely strategic data including control jets, tanks, or machine guns. These applications make such apps targets for malicious attacks, where an attacker can gain information that negatively affects the peace and security of the users or the general population at large. This shows that it is prudent to empower app users with an ability to estimate the security thread of using an app in their smartphone. In addition, there is also a need to educate developers on various security threats and defense mechanisms and encourage them to incorporate these into the app design methods. A recent report [GART14c] suggested that by 2016, 25% of the top 50 banks would have an app. In addition, it is also reported in [GART14a] that 75% of mobile security breaches result from app misconfiguration.

To address the limitations of current secure mobile platforms, we have been conducting research as well as infrastructure development efforts in securing the connected smartphones for the past 6 years. In particular, we have designed and developed solutions for behavior-based intrusion detection/mitigation for mobile smartphones. In addition, we are also investigating privacy aspects for smartphones as well as integrating our secure mobile computing framework with the cloud. We are integrating the research in an experimental infrastructure for our students and developing a curriculum for them which will eventually be a part of an IoT education program.

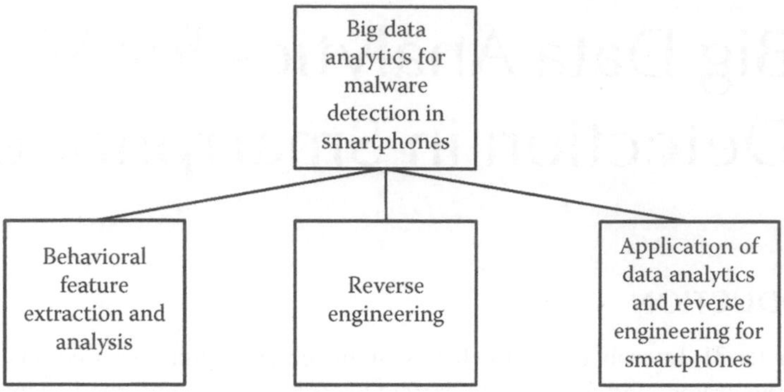

FIGURE 32.1 Big data analytics for malware detection in smartphones.

The organization is as follows. Our approach is discussed in Section 32.2. The experimental evaluation efforts will be discussed in Section 32.3. The infrastructure we are developing is discussed in Section 32.4. Finally, our education program for connected smartphones will be discussed. The concepts discussed in this chapter are illustrated in Figure 32.1.

32.2 OUR APPROACH

32.2.1 Challenges

Behavioral analysis offers a promising approach to malware detection since behavioral signatures are more obfuscation resilient than the binary ones. Indeed, changing behavior while preserving the desired (malicious) functions of a program is much harder than changing only the binary structure. More importantly, to achieve its goal, malware usually has to perform some system operations (e.g., registry manipulation). Since system operations can be easily observed and they are difficult to obfuscate or hide, malicious programs are more likely to expose themselves to behavioral detection. This approach requires a database of specific *behavioral* signatures, but its size and the rate of increase of such a database are incomparably lower than those in the case of *binary* signatures. However, the behavioral detector has to be able to distinguish malicious operations from benign ones (executed by benign programs) which is often difficult. Moreover, maliciousness of an executed functionality can often be determined only by its context or environment. Therefore, the challenge of behavioral detection is in devising a good model of behavior which is descriptive enough to allow for discrimination of benign versus malicious programs and which can be tuned to the target environment.

In principle, there are two kinds of behavior detection mechanisms: misuse detection and anomaly detection. Misuse detection looks for specific behavioral patterns known to be malicious, while the anomaly-based approach responds to unusual (unexpected) behavior. The advantage of anomaly-based detection is in its ability to protect against previously unseen threats; however, it usually suffers from a high false positive rate. Misuse detection is usually more reliable in terms of detection performance (fewer false positives and often no false negatives) but it has two major drawbacks. First, defining a set of malicious patterns (signatures) is a time-consuming and error-prone task that calls for periodic updating, similarly to how binary signatures are used today. Second, it cannot detect any malicious code that does not expose known malicious behavior patterns and thus its capabilities to detect a zero day attack are limited. Consequently, it seems logical to combine both detection mechanisms thus resulting in a highly dependable intrusion detection systems (IDS) technology.

The main challenge of the approach is the development of the appropriate behavior models suitable for the task of dependable and efficient intrusion detection. Behavior analysis can be performed on the basis of system call data. To facilitate kernel-level operations, a computer issues system calls that being monitored and properly processed provide ample information for understanding the process behavior. However, system calls represent the lowest level of behavior semantics and mere aggregation of system calls has inherent limitations in terms of behavior analysis. Instrumental behavior analysis must involve all levels of the semantic pyramid, from its foundation to application program interface (API) functions and to its highest level, that is, functionality defined as a sequence of operations achieving well-recognized results in the programs environment. In our approach functionalities constitute the basis of the behavioral model.

We need to achieve the expressiveness of behavioral signatures, that is, crucial for the success of IDS in detecting new realizations of the same malware. Since most malware incidents are derivatives of some original code, a successful signature must capture invariant generic features of the entire malware family, that is, the signature should be expressive enough to reflect the most possible malware realizations. We also need to address possible behavioral obfuscation, that is, attempts to hide the malicious behavior of software, including the multipartite attacks perpetrated by a coordinated operation of several individually benign codes. This is an emerging threat that, given the extensive development of behavior-based detection, is expected to become a common feature of future information attacks. Finally, we need to develop an efficient model building process utilizing system call data and incorporating unsupervised learning (where no training is required) along with supervised learning (where training is required), as well as mathematically rigorous and heuristic data mining procedures. Some of the work we have carried with respect to big data analytics for malware detection in smartphones will be discussed next.

32.2.2 Behavioral Feature Extraction and Analysis

The main goal of behavior mining is to construct behavioral models that have a low false positive rate and a high detection rate. The traditional approach to generating behavioral models requires human effort and expertise which is an expensive, time-consuming, and error-prone process that does not provide any guarantee regarding the quality of the resultant models. Therefore, developing an automatic technique for building such models is a major goal for the cyber security community. An automated technique will not only reduce the response time to new attacks, but also guarantee more accurate behavioral models.

32.2.2.1 Graph-Based Behavior Analysis

Malware behavior modeling is a more effective approach than purely syntax-directed modeling. This is because although polymorphic and metamorphic obfuscations can defeat content-based signature detection techniques, they cannot easily defeat the behavior-based detection techniques as the behavior of malware is more difficult to obfuscate automatically. Specifications of malware behavior have long been generated manually which are both time and cost intensive. Graph-based behavior analysis is an effort to build malware specifications automatically. The basic approach followed here is to build a malware behavior specification from a sample of malicious and benign applications. A graph is generated for each executable in the sample, where each node in the graph represents an event (such as a system call) and the edges represent a dependency (such as a dataflow from one system call's output to another's input) between two events. We build upon the graph-based behavior analysis for detecting malicious executables [MASU11a]. The approach we use is supervised learning.

We also explore unsupervised learning to detect malware. Eberle and Holder. treat data as a graph and apply unsupervised learning to detect anomalies [EBER07]. They find the normative substructures of the graph and identify anomalies as a small *X%* difference from the normative substructure. Finding the best normative substructure in this case means minimizing the description length *M*, which is represented as

$$M(S,G) = DL(G|S) + DL(S)$$

where G is the entire graph, S is the substructure being analyzed, $DL(G|S)$ is the description length of G after being compressed by S, and $DL(S)$ is the description length of the substructure being analyzed. The description length $DL(G)$ of a graph G is the minimum number of bits necessary to describe G. This framework is not easily extensible to dynamic/evolving streams (dynamic graphs) because the framework is static in nature. Our work relies on their normative substructure-finding methods but extends it to handle dynamic graphs or stream data by learning from evolving streams. Recently we have tested this graph-based algorithm with stream analysis on insider threat data and observed better results relative to traditional approaches ([PARV11a], [PARV11b]). Therefore, we intend to apply both unsupervised and supervised learning in the graph-based technique.

32.2.2.2 Sequence-Based Behavior Analysis

Gathered data stream can be repeated sequences of events (i.e., system calls) of variable length. These repeated sequences of events could reveal the regular/normal behavior of an android application.

It is very important to identify sequences of events in an unsupervised manner and find the potential normative patterns/sequences observed within these sequences that identify the normal pattern. In order to achieve this, we need to generate a dictionary which contains any combination of possible potential patterns existing in the gathered data. Potential variations that could emerge within the data are caused/occurred by commence of new events, missing or modification of existing events, or reordering of events in the sequence.

One way to extract patterns having variable length is to preprocess and manually segment the data which is not very suitable with this continuous incoming flow of data.

Therefore, in our automated method, we consider how we can continually generate the possible patterns for the dictionary using a single pass. Another challenge would be the size of the dictionary that could be extraordinarily large in bulk as it contains any possible observed patterns. Hence, we address the above two challenges in the following ways. First, we extract patterns using single-pass algorithm (e.g., Lempel–Ziv–Welch (LZW) algorithm [WELC84]) to prepare a dictionary. Next, our goal would be to compress the dictionary by keeping the longest frequent set of patterns and discarding other patterns [CHUA11]. We use edit distance to find the longest patterns. This process is a lossy compression, but would be sufficient enough to handle the gathered data.

For example, suppose the sequences of system call traces are liftliftliftlift, where each unique letter represents a particular system call. The possible patterns in our dictionary would be li, if,ft, lif,ift, ftl, lift, iftl, ftli, and so on. Then, we extract the longest and frequent pattern "lift" from this dictionary while discarding the others. There could be many possible patterns.

Once, we identify the pattern "lift," any X% (=%30 say) deviation from the original pattern would be considered as anomaly. Here, we use edit distance to identify the deviation.

32.2.2.3 Evolving Data Stream Classification

Model update (Figure 32.2) can be done in a number of ways. Since we have continuous flows of data, namely stream data, our techniques need to be adaptive in nature. In real-world data stream classification problems, such as malware applications, novel classes may appear at any time in the stream (e.g., a new intrusion). Traditional data stream classification techniques (supervised one) would be unable to detect the novel class until the classification models are trained with labeled instances of the novel class. Thus, all novel class instances go undetected (i.e., misclassified) until the novel class is manually detected by experts, and training data with the instances of that class is made available to the learning algorithm. For example, in case of malware detection, a new kind of android malware application might go undetected by a traditional classifier, but our approach should not only be able to detect the malware but also deduce that it is a new kind of malware.

This evolving nature creates several challenges in classifying the data. Two of the most widely studied issues with data stream classification are one-pass learning and concept-drift issues. One-pass learning is required because of limited resource (memory and processing power) and continuous delivery of the data stream. Concept drift occurs in dynamic streams and is approached in

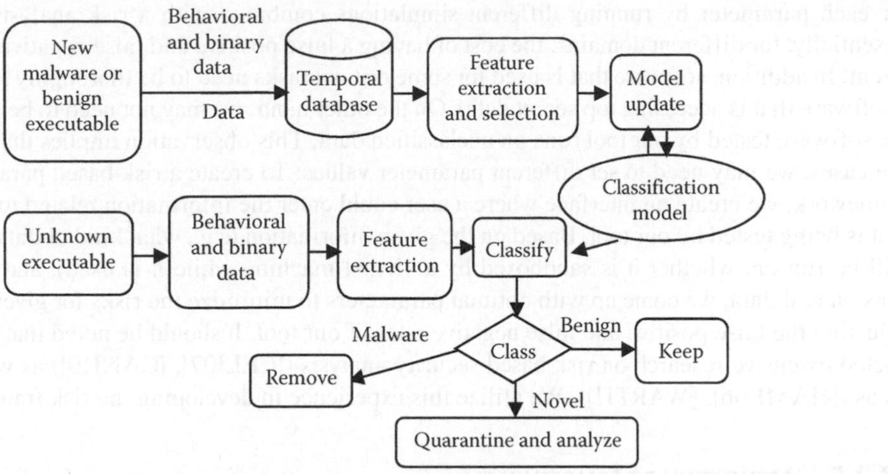

FIGURE 32.2 Classification model development.

different ways by different techniques, all of which have the same goal: to keep the classification model up-to-date with the most recent concept ([MASU11b], [MASU11b], [MASU10], [SPIN08], [HULT01]).

Data stream classifiers can be broadly divided into two categories based on how they update the classification model, namely, single model incremental approaches [HULT01], and ensemble techniques. Ensemble techniques have been more popular than their single model counterparts because of their simpler implementation and higher efficiency [MASU11a]. Most of these ensemble techniques use a chunk-based approach for learning ([MASU11b], [MASU10], [SPIN08]), in which they divide the data stream into chunks, and train a model from one chunk. We refer to these approaches as "chunk-based" approaches. In our work we investigate both techniques to update models.

32.2.3 Reverse Engineering Methods

With only the binary executable of a program, it is useful to discover the program's data structures and infer their syntactic and semantic definitions. Such knowledge is highly valuable in a variety of security and forensic applications. Although there exist efforts in program data structure inference, the existing solutions are not suitable for our targeted application scenarios. We have developed sophisticated reverse engineering techniques to automatically reveal program data structures from binaries [LIN10]. Our technique, called REWARDS, is based on dynamic analysis. More specifically, each memory location accessed by the program is tagged with a time-stamped type attribute. Following the program's runtime data flow, this attribute is propagated to other memory locations and registers that share the same type. During the propagation, a variable's type gets resolved if it is involved in a type-revealing execution point or "type sink." More importantly, besides the forward-type propagation, REWARDS involves a backward-type resolution procedure where the types of some previously accessed variables get recursively resolved starting from a type sink. This procedure is constrained by the timestamps of relevant memory locations to disambiguate variables reusing the same memory location. In addition, REWARDS is able to reconstruct in-memory data structure layout based on the type information derived. We demonstrated that REWARDS provides unique benefits to two critical applications: memory image forensics and binary fuzzing for vulnerability discovery.

32.2.4 Risk-Based Framework

Machine learning-based approaches need to be complemented by a risk framework. Certain parameters need to be set based on real-life experiments. We believe that we can find optimal values for each parameter by running different simulations combined with a risk analysis framework. Essentially, for different domains, the cost of having a false positive and false negative could be different. In addition, software that is used for some critical tasks need to be thoroughly analyzed (e.g., a software that is accessing top secret data). On the other hand, we may not need to be as stringent if the software tested by our tool runs on unclassified data. This observation implies that for different use cases, we may need to set different parameter values. To create a risk-based parameter setting framework, we create an interface where a user could enter the information related to the software that is being tested by our tool. Based on the given information (e.g., what kind of data the software will be run on, whether it is sandboxed by a virtual machine while it is used), and our previous runs on real data, we come up with optimal parameters to minimize the risks for given software by adjusting the false positive and false negative rates of our tool. It should be noted that we have conducted extensive research on risk-based security analysis ([CELI07], [CANI10]) as well as related areas ([HAML06], [WART11]). We utilize this experience in developing the risk framework.

32.2.5 Application to Smartphones

With the prevalence of smartphones with computer-like capabilities, there are more platforms and devices subject to attack by malware. According to a study from IDC [U4], smartphone manufacturers shipped 100.9 million units in the last quarter of 2010, compared to 92.1 million units of PCs shipped worldwide. It is the first time in history that smartphones are outselling personal computers. The demand for smartphones is still continuing to rise and grow exponentially. The popularity and availability of smartphones running the Android operating system is driving further growth in the smartphone market. Sales of Android phones are projected to grow 50% over the next 4 years [U2].

As an open platform, Android is especially vulnerable to attack because there is no official verification of software's trustworthiness. For example, unlike Apple's official scrutinization process, Android applications can be uploaded without any check of their trustworthiness. Developers self-sign the applications without the intervention of any certification authority. Hence, malware and Trojan horses have already been spread through the Android market, and it is even possible to install applications from outside the Android marketplace [U1]. Jupiter Networks report that Android malware increases 400% as compared to summer 2010 [U3]. "Fake Player," "Geinimi," "PJApps," and "HongToutou" are a few examples. A number of standard applications have been modified and the malware have been binded, packed, and spread through unofficial repositories. More than 50 infected Android applications were found in March of 2011 alone where all of them were infected with "DroidDream" trojan [U1] application.

Malicious applications have been spread across thousands of phones before detection. There is some work to detect those android malicious applications. Blasing et al. [BLAS10] use static analysis first and then dynamic analysis in a simulated environment. Enck et al. [ENCK10] monitor sensitive information on smartphones. Thus, they can track a suspicious third-party application that uses sensitive data as GPS location information or address book information. Portokalidis et al. [PORT10] propose a system where researchers can perform a complete malware analysis in the cloud using mobile phone replicas. Shabtai et al. [SHAB10] present a methodology to detect suspicious temporal patterns as malicious behavior, for anomaly detection on Android smartphones. This approach does not exploit behavior as features. There is a work based on behavior [BURG11]. This approach exploits clustering to detect malware. The detection algorithm is very simple and static in nature. Furthermore, none of these techniques is capable of detecting brand new malwares.

We are building on our prior research and development work [MASU12] and developing highly novel, innovative, and adaptive approaches for analyzing the Android applications. This approach allows malicious application to be detected by recognizing application anomalies based on supervised and unsupervised learning in constraint resources. In addition, we can detect brand new malware that can adapt and reinvent. Also, our goal is to collect the data generated and store them in the cloud and apply some of our BDMA techniques for malware detection and connected smartphones.

At the heart of our approach is the classification model (Figure 32.2). This model is incrementally updated with feature vector data obtained from new benign/malware applications. When a new benign executable or malware instance is chosen as a training example, it is analyzed and its behavioral and binary patterns are recorded. This recorded data will be stored in a temporal database that holds the data for a batch of *N* applications at a time. Note that the temporal database can be stored in the Android device itself in a lightweight way or at the server side. When a batch of data has been processed, it is discarded, and a new batch is stored. Each batch of data will undergo a feature extraction and selection phase. The selected features are used to compute feature vectors (one vector per executable). These vectors are used to update the existing classification model using an incremental learning technique. When an unknown application appears in the system, at first its runtime and network behavior (e.g., system call traces) are monitored and recorded. This data then undergoes a similar feature extraction phase and feature vector is created. This feature vector is classified using the classification model. Based on the class label, appropriate measures are taken.

We also complement our behavioral-based malware detection algorithms with reverse engineering techniques so that we can provide a compressive solution to the malware evolution problem.

32.2.5.1 Data Gathering

Data acquisition is responsible for obtaining data from Android applications. Collected data is composed by basic device information, installed applications list, and the result of monitoring applications with system behavior monitoring tool including both control (such as system call traces) and data (such as API/system call arguments, the return values, the sent and received messages). Next it collects, extracts, and analyzes received information from the system control and data behavior log file, and stores in a temporal database. Finally, system behavior traces are processed to produce the feature vectors that are used for classification. In addition, we may extract some static features such as request numerous permissions onto various hardware devices, certain restricted system calls, and access to other applications and possible execution paths that an application can take using a control flow graph.

32.2.5.2 Malware Detection

First, we apply the graph-based behavior analysis in a static setting with a fixed training set containing both benign and malicious applications. Then, we extend these analysis techniques to the stream environment.

32.2.5.3 Data Reverse Engineering of Smartphone Applications

While our behavior model is largely built on top of system call sequences (which is related to program control flow), the data aspect of an Android application is also crucial in our behavior model because data provides a more readable and verifiable view of a program. To this end, our framework also includes a data reverse engineering component. The basic idea for data reverse engineering is to extract the semantic information exported by an operating systems (OS) such as system call arguments and return values, and then use data flow analysis to capture the semantic data propagations. We have an earlier effort of data reverse engineering in x86 code, called REWARDS [LIN10], for the Linux platform. We believe REWARDS technique is general and can be applied to the Android platform. We are investigating the new challenges while porting it to Android, such as the program execution model has changed to Dalvik virtual machine, and in Android, it is no longer in x86 binary code and instead most applications are written in Java.

32.3 OUR EXPERIMENTAL ACTIVITIES

The purpose of the experiments is to identify which approaches are working, and to demonstrate and validate each improvement achieved. Therefore, we are performing experiments to evaluate the components developed. Furthermore, these experiments are being carried out as we complete the implementation of each component. In many cases, the experiments simply verify that we are improving the system with the new part.

We have collected the malware dataset from two sources, one is publicly available (VX Heavens—http://vx.netlux.org) and the other is a restricted access repository for malware researchers only (Project malfease—http://malfease.oarci.net/), to which we have access. VX Heavens contains close to 80,000 malware samples, and Project malfease also contains around 90,000 malware samples. Furthermore, these repositories are being enriched with new malware every day. VX Heavens also serves many malware generation engines with which we may generate a virtually infinite number of malware samples. Using these malware samples, we can easily construct a data stream such that new types of malware appear in the stream at certain (not necessarily uniform) intervals. Evaluation of the data occurs in either or both of the following ways:

1. We partition the dataset into two parallel streams (e.g., a 50–50 division), where one stream is used to train and update the existing classifier and the other stream is used to evaluate the performance of the classifier in terms of true positive, false positive, successful novel class detection rate, and so on. For example, one suitable partitioning simply separates the stream of odd-indexed members from the even-indexed ones.
2. A single, nonpartitioned stream may be used to train and evaluate as follows. The initial classification model can be trained from the first n data chunks. From the $n + 1^{st}$ chunk, we evaluate the performance of the classifier on the instances of the chunk (in terms of true positive, false positive, successful novel class detection, etc.) Then that chunk is used to update the classifier.

Below we discuss some of the systems we have developed and our initial evaluation. It should be noted that at present the evaluation is at the component stage. Our ultimate goal is to integrate the various components and carry out the evaluation of the system as a whole.

32.3.1 Covert Channel Attack in Mobile Apps

Mobile OS such as Android provide mechanisms for data protection by restricting the communication between apps within the device. However, malicious apps can still overcome such restrictions via various means such as exploiting the software vulnerability in systems or using covert channels for data transferring. In a recent paper [CHAN14], we have shown a systematic analysis of various resources available on Android for the possible use of covert channels between two malicious apps. We identified two new hardware resources, namely battery and phone call, that can also be used as covert channels. We also found new features to enrich the existing approaches for a better covert channel such as using the audio volume and screen brightness. Our experimental results show that high throughput data transmission can be achieved using these resources for covert channel attacks.

32.3.2 Detecting Location Spoofing in Mobile Apps

As the use of smartphones has increased, so has the presence of location-aware smartphone apps. Often, location data is used by service providers to personalize information and allow users to check into locations, among other uses. Therefore, it is in the best interests of app developers to determine whether reported locations are accurate. In light of this, we have designed taxonomy of location spoofing attacks, in which an attacker attempts to provide an app with fake location data. To defeat such an attack, we have designed a novel system that uses semantics analysis such as system property and velocity-based behavior analysis on a device to detect the presence of a location spoofing attack [GREE15]. Experimental results with a number of Android apps show that our approach is highly effective and has a very small overhead.

32.3.3 Large Scale, Automated Detection of SSL/TLS Man-in-the-Middle Vulnerabilities in Android Apps

Many Android apps use SSL/TLS to transmit sensitive information securely. However, developers often provide their own implementation of the standard SSL/TLS certificate validation process. Unfortunately, many such custom implementations have subtle bugs, have built-in exceptions for self-signed certificates, or blindly assert all certificates as valid, leaving many Android apps vulnerable to SSL/TLS man-in-the-middle attacks. In another recent work [SOUN14], we have implemented a system for the automatic, large-scale identification of such vulnerabilities that combines both static and dynamic analyses for identifying vulnerable apps using an active man-in-the-middle attack. We are conducting experimentation of the tools we have designed.

32.4 INFRASTRUCTURE DEVELOPMENT

We discuss two major components: (i) virtual laboratory development and (ii) curriculum development.

32.4.1 Virtual Laboratory Development

32.4.1.1 Laboratory Setup

The lab would be accessible to all of its users, around the world. A web-based interface is provided and user account is password protected. A graphical user interface (GUI) is developed using Restful API. Initially, the project is set up a virtual lab accessible to students 24/7. The students can leverage the resources and services offered by the virtual lab to undertake academic projects related to android security and forensics. For example, the students can learn how to develop secure apps capable of detecting potential malicious activities by performing static and dynamic analysis in the virtual lab's remote servers. Furthermore, the lab can facilitate mobile forensics courses by offering remote services such as forensic analysis of data acquired from the mobile hardware.

A typical scenario for using our system is as follows. A user can typically download an app onto a smartphone from an App Store, which provides numerous apps. In general, a student can either download an app or develop an app to be installed on a phone. The user then submits a request to analyze the app by logging onto our system. The APK file of the app is downloaded or submitted for analysis including static and dynamic analysis or for a data mining application, along with required information of the app. The system would perform the required operations and provide the result in terms of a report or an intractable interface, where the user can provide inputs for further analysis.

There are various challenges in developing such a system. These include requirement of high computational resources and other inherent issues of program analysis. There are two basic techniques in program analysis: static analysis and dynamic analysis. Each has its pros and cons. At a high level, static analysis is fast, scalable, complete but not precise, and dynamic analysis is precise but often very expensive. More specifically, with respect to the security analysis of Android programs, in static analysis the application is often decompiled and various heuristics are applied to determine if the application is malicious or vulnerable. Though static analysis is a powerful technique, it fails when dynamic code loading, asynchronous callbacks, or other runtime specific features are used. To tackle this problem, dynamic analysis is used. In dynamic analysis, the application is installed in a controlled environment—usually a modified version of an emulator or a device with customized OS—where the behavior of the application can be extracted at the system and at the network levels. Even though dynamic analysis promises to provide access to the applications runtime behavior, it is not without its shortcomings, especially when applied to GUI apps that are prevalent in the Android market.

The system extracts metadata from the APK file using static analysis and combines them with other information (raw data) to form a feature set, using a feature extractor. The feature is then used in a data mining algorithm based on the analysis desired by the user. The analysis is performed and a complete report is generated at the end for the user to view. This includes a rated decision to classify the app as a malware. The complete information as desired by the user can be used for further analysis or study regarding the app. This virtual lab would be then used by integrating it with cyber security courses, as shown in Figure 32.3. Our goal is to process user requests in real time or near time and support multiuser requests simultaneously. For this, we utilize our cluster (which is essentially a cloud) and utilize parallel processing (NoSQL systems). For example, Spark can be used to process requests. Spark has faster processing power than its counterpart such as Storm and Hadoop/MapReduce (see e.g., [SOLA14a], [SOLA14b], and [SOLA14c]).

As evident, the online system serves parallel analysis requests. Such a deployment would require multiple emulator-based feature extraction (using dynamic analysis) and ensemble of stochastic models to be maintained. This would involve emulator and model management system that would be developed to handle these scenarios, extending our previous work on large-scale vulnerability detection techniques.

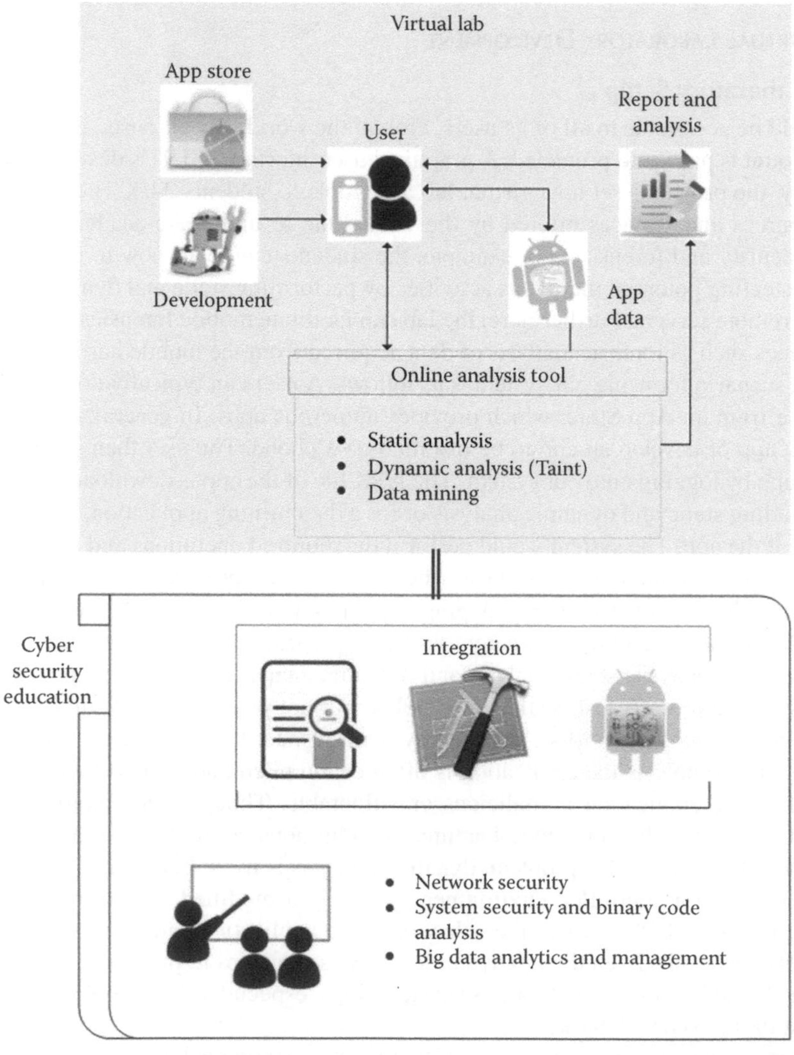

FIGURE 32.3 Architectural diagram for virtual lab and integration with cyber security courses.

32.4.1.2 Programming Projects to Support the Virtual Lab

We are devising student programming projects to support the virtual lab. We provide an overview of two sample projects and a discussion of these projects. In particular, we first describe an automatic testing tool that can be used for large-scale user-input generation. Next, we discover a tool for addressing data leaks by viewing it as a transaction over the system state.

32.4.1.3 An Intelligent Fuzzier for the Automatic Android GUI Application Testing

The recent proliferation of mobile phones has led to many software vendors shifting their services to the mobile domain. There are >700,000 Android applications in the Google Play market alone with over 500 million activated devices [WOMA12]. On the other hand, software inevitably contains bugs (because of its complexity), some of which often lead to vulnerabilities. Identifying the buggy applications (i.e., apps.) in such huge Android market calls for new efficient and scalable solutions.

32.4.1.4 Problem Statement

To get encouraging results out of dynamic analysis with Android apps, the user interface (UI) of the application has to be exercised in a way that all possible code paths are executed. An intuitive approach could work around this problem by either recording/replaying the user's actual behavior or by manually exercising the UI elements. This shortcoming cripples the ability to perform large-scale dynamic analysis. Recently novel techniques have emerged where UI enumeration is performed and input is provided to the UI elements such that automated UI traversal is possible. This advancement enables large-scale dynamic analysis. But the new UI Automation approach still uses handcrafted input to the UI input elements like text boxes.

Essentially, for Android GUI app testing, the key challenge lies in how to simulate user interactions, which requires an understanding of what is being displayed on the screen and providing intelligent input. As an example, consider the login screen of a banking application. A typical login screen contains username and password text boxes, possibly a "remember me" check box, and a login button which submits the user's credentials when clicked. The user typically provides input to these elements in this order, starting with the username and ending with tapping the login button. A useful UI automation system should be able to simulate this behavior without the need for human intervention or guidance.

After analyzing existing tools for UI automation, we have concluded we still require novel techniques. Google's Monkey tool [GOOG1] cannot accurately simulate the controlled behavior of the user because it provides randomized UI events. Another existing UI automation framework is Robotium [ROBO] which is a popular tool used widely by Android developers for testing. This framework is tightly coupled with Android's instrumentation framework which causes Robotium test scripts to be tightly coupled with the target applications. This makes the framework unsuitable as a generic UI automation solution as it requires a unique test script for each target application.

Therefore, our work aims to take the UI automation to the next level by integrating systems engineering approaches and novel data mining techniques to identify and understand the UI presented by the application and provide an appropriate input, thereby providing better coverage and usability than the existing methods. The UI automation fuzzier has two major goals: understanding the interface as it is displayed and providing an intelligent input to the application.

32.4.1.5 Understanding the Interface

The first step in automating the UI is to decompose the UI into its component elements. For each of these elements, the system extracts properties such as the coordinates that define its boundaries and what form of input (e.g., text or tap) it expects. With this information, the system crafts the appropriate input events and sends them to the application. To identify the Window's elements and extract their properties, we utilize the Android ViewServer [GUY], an internal component of the Android application tooling framework. The ViewServer provides a set of commands that can be used to query the Android WindowManager [GOOG2], which handles the display of UI elements and the dispatch of input events to the appropriate element.

32.4.1.6 Generating Input Events

Generating intelligent input for the input fields in a displaying window has always been a challenging problem in the area of UI automation. All the existing approaches have taken the route of hardcoded or handcrafted input. We solve this problem by utilizing the state-of-the-art machine learning and data mining techniques, in a data-driven manner [SAHS12]. We provide the intelligent input for input field using semisupervised clustering and label propagation [MASU12]. In general, input fields are often tagged with a text label explaining the user about the input that they have to provide. For example, in a simple application, a text label "User Name" alongside the text input box is displayed in a typical user registration screen. Furthermore, another application may have a similar screen and the developer has given the input text label as "User ID." Therefore, we expect the same input for input fields, "User Name" and "User ID." For "Zipcode" and "Postal Code" fields, we also expect the same input. Here, we treat input field ("User name") as data and input type (i.e., text pattern/integer pattern) as a class label.

To tackle this issue, (1) we need to group similar input fields together and (2) assign the same input (class label) for a group having the similar input fields. With regard to the first issue, we apply clustering algorithm (e.g., K-means) or semisupervised clustering algorithm. To measure similarity, we exploit edit distance between two input fields or external knowledge (Ontology-WordNet) [JIN03]. With respect to second issue, we apply a label propagation technique to provide input type as class label for input field.

32.4.1.7 Mitigating Data Leakage in Mobile Apps Using a Transactional Approach

To mitigate risks such as information leakage, we develop an oblivious sandbox that minimizes the leakage of sensitive input by conforming untrusted apps to predefined security policies, and also enhances usability and data security in the case of application updates. Most apps are proprietary and close-sourced (even intensively using native code) and thus arbitrarily store and transform sensitive information before sending it out. The approach works seamlessly and transparently with such apps by viewing app communication as a transactional process which coordinates access to shared resources. In particular, the vulnerability might be caused due to information leakage by an input method editor (IME) used in an app, or a bug may be introduced after an app update that may break critical functionality of the app and/or create a new vulnerability. For the case of a vulnerability based on user input, we first checkpoint the app's state before a transaction involving an user input, monitor and analyze users' input, and roll back the app's state to the most recent checkpoint if there is potential danger of leaking the user's sensitive input. In the case of app updates, a similar checkpoint and rollback functionality can be performed by checkpointing an app prior to applying an update, and rolling back if the update fails subsequent in-device testing or at the user's request. Our system is built for Android and would be tested on publicly available apps from the Google Play Market. We perform experimental validation of our techniques to mitigate the leakage of sensitive input for untrusted apps, with the goal of incurring only small runtime overhead and little impact on user experience.

An example scenario involves the use of a third-party IME typically used to enhance user experience and efficiency in providing input. A typical usage of a third-party IME may involve the editor unintentionally leaking user inputs. This can have serious consequences in the security of confidential information. For example, consider a mobile app used by an Immigration and Customs Enforcement (ICE) agent/officer to obtain and update criminal records. If the officer uses such an IME while searching criminal records or inputting a new record, an attacker may be able to obtain confidential information.

32.4.1.8 Technical Challenges

Since security is evaluated with every request instead of only at installation time, information leaks/security breaches will be challenging. With regard to the example scenario, first, commercial IME applications extensively use native code, making it very difficult to understand how they log and process user input. Second, many of them use unknown proprietary protocols, which obscure the process of collecting and transforming user input. Finally, many IME applications use encryption. Therefore, we must eventually treat most IME applications as black boxes for current privacy-preserving techniques on mobile devices. Thus, end users are faced with the choice of trusting these IME applications completely and risking leakage of sensitive input or giving up the improved user experience and instead relying only on the default IME application.

At a high level, it seems that existing techniques such as taint tracking would be an appealing approach to precisely tracking sensitive input data and preventing it from being leaked. For example, TaintDroid ([BRAD11], [ENCK14], [ENCK11], [HORN11]) has been shown to be able to track sensitive user input and detect leakage. AppFence [HORN11] extended this system to block outgoing communications when sensitive data is about to be sent out. However, there are a number of additional challenges remaining. First, IME applications tend to make extensive use of native code, but TaintDroid currently does not track tainted data through native code. Second, TaintDroid only tracks the propagation through data flows. It is a well-known problem that such data-flow-based tracking cannot capture control-based propagation. In fact, many of the keystrokes are generated through lookup tables as reported in an earlier study. Third, sensitive information is often composed of a sequence of keystrokes. It is challenging to have a well-defined policy to differentiate sensitive from nonsensitive keystrokes in TaintDroid (and AppFence).

32.4.1.9 Experimental System

Figure 32.4 shows an overview of the experimental system that the students are developing to handle transactional methods in Android. The IME/Update app is installed in the user space which intercepts communication with client apps. The daemon controls communication between a client app with other apps within the device or with an external entity via the network. The policy engine can be used to extract communication policies involving data exchange or access. In particular, we can checkpoint the state of an application before each input transaction or a range of responses. User input/responses from the application can be analyzed to detect whether it is sensitive. The

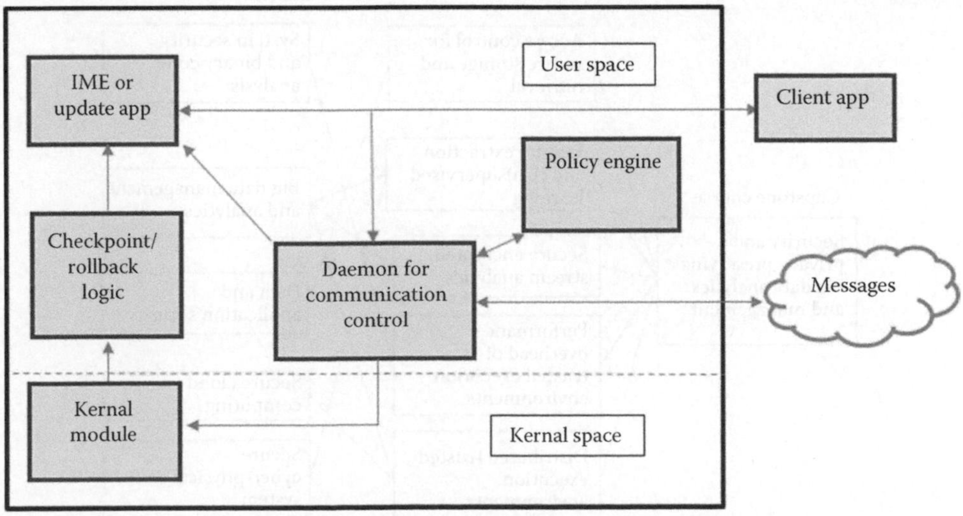

FIGURE 32.4 Overall architecture of our experimental system.

checkpoint or rollback logic is used to perform logical checks for each client application component in the case of a rollback. A kernel module installed in the kernel space is used for the checkpoint/rollback mechanism for saving and restoring the states of this app or client app as needed.

One approach is to use an oblivious IME sandbox that prevents IME applications from leaking sensitive user input. The key idea is to make an IME application oblivious to sensitive input by running the application transactionally, wiping off sensitive data from untrusted IME applications when sensitive input is detected. Specifically, we can checkpoint the state of the IME application before each input transaction. Then, user input can be analyzed by the policy engine to detect whether it is sensitive. If it is, the IME application state can be rolled back to the saved checkpoint, making it oblivious of what the user entered. Otherwise, the checkpoint can be discarded.

32.4.1.10 Policy Engine

The policy engine is used for sensitive data identification based on handcrafted and mined rules to check vulnerability. A rule may identify typical sensitive data such as social security numbers or passwords. The policy engine may be used to design specific tests. To improve efficiency and avoid degrading user experience, we can augment on-device testing with off-device testing that leverages static and dynamic analysis and data mining techniques [SOUN14] to categorize apps as benign/invulnerable, unknown, or malicious/vulnerable. As a part of the data mining process, we plan to cluster the apps into groups based on their functionality. Using this automatically learned group behavior, any app that deviates from group behavior could be singled for more examination. In addition, when off-device testing determines that an app is benign/invulnerable, we can forgo on-device testing and discard the checkpoint. When off-device testing categorizes an app as malicious/vulnerable, we can immediately initiate a rollback. Only when off-device testing is inconclusive do we fall back to on-device testing.

32.4.2 Curriculum Development

32.4.2.1 Extensions to Existing Courses

In order to integrate the virtual lab with these courses, we would design various modules that would be integrated with its existing projects. An overview is provided in Figure 32.5. These modules are

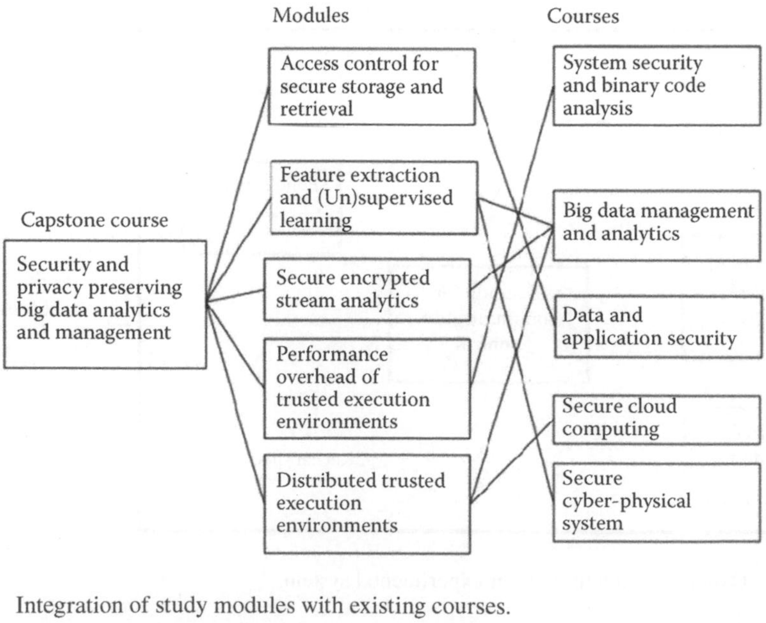

FIGURE 32.5 Integration of study modules with existing courses.

derived from our existing research and/or our virtual lab development. For example, the modules, "APK file analysis" and "taint analysis," may be integrated our regular graduate course, "digital forensic analysis" and "system security and binary code analysis." The "feature extraction" module is being integrated with our "big data management and analytics" course.

Below is a sample of our cyber security courses that are relevant to our wok in smartphones.

32.4.2.1.1 Systems Security and Binary Code Analysis

This course covers the practical aspect of computer systems, especially the low-level system details with the real system implementations. In particular, this course covers binary code analysis, OS kernel internals, Linker and Loader, and system virtualization. In support of this, this course comes with four hands-on labs. One is to design a taint analysis using dynamic binary instrumentation, the second one is to perform malware unpacking, the third one is to use library interposition to transparently harden software, and the last one is to use virtual machine introspection to monitor OS activities. These hands-on labs greatly enforce the concepts discussed in the class. This course would integrate thc study of smartphone security analysis by studying program analysis on APK files to detect malware from binary data, Android taint analysis using existing tools, or development of new tools.

32.4.2.1.2 Network Security

This course covers both theoretical and practical aspects of network security. The course includes various hands-on activities to expose students to tools and techniques that are commonly used in penetration testing and securing computer networks and related technologies. We have also created a lab manual for this course as part of our current capacity building project. Students use John the Ripper to break passwords; use nmap and nessus to scan systems for known vulnerabilities; and use metasploit to exploit vulnerabilities in a system all done in an isolated environment in our Computer Networks and Security Instructional Lab (CNSIL) facilities. In addition, we conduct an in-class cyberwar class attack and defense activity. Finally, we conduct a 48-h data science competition where students work on solving various types of data science challenges. These hands-on sessions would also involve study of various attacks and defenses of Android apps over the Internet, including study of communication protocols with Android apps.

32.4.2.1.3 Data and Applications Security

This course provides a comprehensive overview of database security, confidentiality, privacy and trust management, data security and privacy, data mining for security applications, secure social media, secure cloud computing, and web security. In addition to term papers, students also carry out a programming project that addresses any of the topics covered in class. Typical student projects have included data mining tools for malware detection as well as access control tools for social media systems. More recent versions of the course focus on more extensive data privacy topics as well as on querying encrypted data. We are introducing a module on mobile data security and privacy as well as developing programming projects such as location privacy for mobile system as well as access control for mobile data.

32.4.2.1.4 Digital Forensics

This is an undergraduate course that covers various aspects of digital forensics. Topics include digital forensics basics such as evidence collection and analysis, crime scene reconstruction as well as database forensics, network forensics, and more recently modules on cloud forensics. Students are taken on a field trip to visit the North Texas FBI lab and are exposed to state-of-the-art techniques used by the FBI for forensics. Students also have practical experience with tools such as ENCASE. While we briefly cover mobile system forensics, we are introducing more in depth material on this topic with special emphasis on Android forensics.

32.4.2.1.5 Developing and Securing the Cloud

This course covers several aspects of cloud security. Modules include basics of cloud security such as securing infrastructure, platform, and application as a service, secure cloud data management, secure cloud data storage, and cloud forensics. Student programming projects include developing access control, modules for the cloud as well as modules for secure cloud query processing. We are introducing a unit on integrating cloud, mobile, and security technologies.

32.4.2.1.6 Big Data Analytics and Management

This course focuses on data mining and machine learning algorithms for analyzing very large amounts of data or big data. MapReduce and NoSQL systems are used as tools/standards for creating parallel algorithms that can process very large amounts of data. It covers basics of Hadoop, MapReduce, NoSQL systems (Cassandra, Pig, Hive, MongoDB, Hbase, BigTable, HBASE, and SPARK), Storm, large-scale supervised machine learning, data streams, clustering, and applications including recommendation systems, web, and security. We are introducing a module on large-scale feature extraction and learning to leverage the big data platform to perform parallel and distributed analysis on Android security threats to perform large-scale behavior or stochastic analysis for security threats from malicious apps.

32.4.2.1.7 Security for Critical Infrastructure

The Critical Infrastructure Security course introduces security for infrastructures, control systems and cyber-physical systems. This course covers the security of cyber-physical systems from a multidisciplinary point of view, from computer science security research (network security and software security), to public policy (e.g., the Executive Order 13636), risk assessment, business drivers, and control-theoretic methods to reduce the cyber risk to cyber-physical critical infrastructures. There is increasing interest to integrate secure mobile computing technologies with critical infrastructures [BARR14]. Mobile interfaces are being developed for automatic control experiments. These mobile devices should be secured so that the infrastructures are not attacked. We are introducing a module into our course that addresses this integration.

32.4.2.1.8 Language-Based Security

The aim of the course is to allow each student to develop a solid understanding of at least one of the following topics, along with a more general familiarity with the range of research in the field. This course provides students with an array of powerful tools for addressing software security issues include certifying, compilers, in-lined reference monitors, software fault isolation, address space randomization, formal methods, web scripting security, and information flow control. We are introducing a module on language-based security for mobile devices in general and Android in particular.

32.4.2.2 New Capstone Course on Secure Mobile Computing

Our capstone course is motivated by (a) research and development in secure mobile computing; (b) emerging secure mobile computing research, prototypes, products, and standards; and (c) the research and experimentation on Android malware detection and the results of our virtual. The modules created for all our cyber security courses are aggregated and will be taught as part of the capstone course. The topics covered include (i) security for mobile devices and the Android operating system, (ii) secure mobile data and identity management, (iii) mobile data privacy and privacy-aware mobile computing, (iv) secure networking for mobile devices, (v) malware detection for mobile devices, (vi) mobile forensics, (vii) integrating mobile devices for secure critical infrastructures, and (viii) language-based security for mobile devices. In addition, we discuss the various secure mobile system prototypes, products, and standards. Students carry out the programming projects that contribute toward the virtual laboratory.

32.5 SUMMARY AND DIRECTIONS

This chapter has discussed malware detection in one type of IoT system, that is, connected smartphones. We discussed the security challenges for smartphones and then discussed our approach to malware detection for smartphones based on the Android operating system. Next, we discussed our virtual laboratory for experimentation. The technologies include Hadoop/MapReduce as well as Storm and Spark for designing scalable systems. We also discussed the course module we are introducing for security of smartphones. These include mobile system forensics as well as mobile data management security.

We believe that the future is in the integration of cyber security with cloud computing, mobile computing, and big data analytics. That is, scalable techniques for BDMA together with the cloud and mobile systems are essential for many applications. The challenge will be to secure such applications. The focus in this chapter is on malware detection. We need to design a comprehensive security framework for mobile systems that include access control, malicious code detection, and privacy protection.

REFERENCES

[BARR14] C. Barreto, J.A. Giraldo, A.A. Cárdenas, E. Mojica-Nava, N. Quijano, "Control Systems for the Power Grid and Their Resiliency to Attacks," *IEEE Security and Privacy*, 12 (6), 15–23, 2014.

[BLAS10] T. Blasing, A.-D. Schmidt, L. Batyuk, S.A. Camtepe, S. Albayrak, "An Android Application Sandbox System for Suspicious Software Detection," In *5th International Conference on Malicious and Unwanted Software (Malware 2010) (MALWARE'2010)*, Nancy, France, 2010.

[BRAD11] T. Bradley, DroidDream Becomes Android Market Nightmare. March 2011, http://www.pcworld.com/article/221247/droiddream_becomes_android_market_nightmare.html.

[BURG11] I. Burguera, U. Zurutuza, S. Nadjm-Tehrani, "Crowdroid: Behavior-Based Malware Detection System for Android," In *Workshop on Security and Privacy in Smartphones and Mobile Devices 2011—SPSM 2011*, ACM, Chicago, IL, pp. 15–26, October 2011.

[CANI10] M. Canim, M. Kantarcioglu, B. Hore, S. Mehrotra, "Building Disclosure Risk Aware Query Optimizers for Relational Databases," In *Proceedings of the VLDB Endowment*, Singapore, Vol. 3, No. 1, September 2010.

[CELI07] E. Celikel, M. Kantarcioglu, B.M. Thuraisingham, E. Bertino, "Managing Risks in RBAC Employed Distributed Environments," *OTM Conferences*, November 25–30, Vilamoura, Portugal, pp. 1548–1566, 2007.

[CHAN14] S. Chandra, Z. Lin, A. Kundu, L. Khan, "A Systematic Study of the Covert Channel Attacks in Smartphones," *10th International Conference on Security and Privacy in Communication Networks*, Beijing, China, 2014.

[CHUA11] S.L. Chua, S. Marsland, H.W. Guesgen, "Unsupervised Learning of Patterns in Data Streams Using Compression and Edit Distance," In *Proceedings of the 22nd International Joint Conference on Artificial Intelligence*, Barcelona, Spain, Vol. 2, pp. 1231–1236, 2011.

[EBER07] W. Eberle, L.B. Holder, "Anomaly Detection in Data Represented as Graphs," *Intell. Data Anal.*, 11 (6), 663–689, 2007.

[ENCK10] W. Enck, P. Gilbert, B.-G. Chun, L.P. Cox, J. Jung, P. McDaniel, A.N. Sheth, "Taintdroid: An Information-Flow Tracking System for Realtime Privacy Monitoring on Smartphones, In OSTI '10: *Proceedings of the 9th USENIX Conference on Operating Systems Design and Implementation*, Berkeley, CA, pp. 1–6, USENIX Association, 2010.

[ENCK11] W. Enck, D. Octeau, P. McDaniel, S. Chaudhuri, "A Study of Android Application Security," *USENIX Security Symposium*, San Francisco, CA, pp. 21–21, 2011.

[ENCK14] W. Enck, P. Gilbert, B.-G. Chun, L.P. Cox, J. Jung, P. McDaniel, A.N. Sheth, "TaintDroid: An Information Flow Tracking System for Real-Time Privacy Monitoring on Smartphones," *Communications of the ACM*, 57 (3), pp. 99–106, 2014.

[GART13] Gartner. 2013. Gartner Says Mobile App Stores Will See Annual Downloads Reach 102 Billion in 2013. September. http://www.gartner.com/newsroom/id/2592315.

[GART14a] Gartner. Gartner Says 75 Percent of Mobile Security Breaches Will Be the Result of Mobile Application Misconfiguration. May, 2014. http://www.gartner.com/newsroom/id/2753017.

[GART14b] Gartner. 2014. Gartner Says Annual Smartphone Sales Surpassed Sales of Feature Phones for the First Time in 2013. February, 2014. http://www.gartner.com/newsroom/id/2665715.

[GART14c] Gartner. 2014. Gartner Says by 2016, 25 Percent of the Top 50 Global Banks Will have Launched a Banking App Store for Customers. June. http://www.gartner.com/newsroom/id/2758617.

[GREE15] G. Greenwood, E. Bauman, Z. Lin, L. Khan, B. Thuraisingham, "*DLSMA: Detecting Location Spoofing in Mobile AppsDLSMA: Detecting Location Spoofing in Mobile Apps*," Technical Report, University of Texas at Dallas.

[GOOG1] Google. n.d. UI/Application Exerciser Monkey. http://developer.android.com/tools/help/monkey.html.

[GOOG2] Google. n.d. WindowManager. http://developer.android.com/reference/android/view/WindowManager.html.

[GUY] R. Guy. n.d. Local server for Android's HierarchyViewer. https://github.com/romainguy/ViewServer.

[HAML06] K.W. Hamlen, G. Morrisett, F.B. Schneider, "Certified In-Lined Reference Monitoring on.NET. PLAS 2006," In *Proceedings of the 2006 Workshop on Programming Languages and Analysis for Security, PLAS 2006*, Ottawa, Ontario, Canada, pp. 7–16, 2006.

[HORN11] P. Hornyack, S. Han, J. Jung, S. Schechter and D. Wetherall, "These Aren't the Droids You're Looking For, Retrofitting Android to Protect Data from Imperious Applications," In *CCS*, Chicago, IL, pp. 639–652, 2011.

[HULT01] G. Hulten, L. Spencer, P. Domingos, "Mining Time-Changing Data Streams," In *KDD '01 Proceedings of the Seventh ACM SIGKDD International Conference on Knowledge Discovery and Data Mining*, San Francisco, CA, pp. 97–106, August 26–29, 2001.

[JIN03] Y. Jin, L. Khan, L. Wang, M. Awad, "Image Annotations by Combining Multiple Evidence & Wordnet," In *MULTIMEDIA '05 Proceedings of the 13th Annual ACM International Conference on Multimedia*, Hilton, Singapore, pp. 706–715, November 6–11, 2005, ACM.

[LIN10] Z. Lin, X. Zhang, D. Xu, "Reverse Engineering Input Syntactic Structure from Program Execution and Its Applications," *IEEE Transactions on Software Engineering*, 36(5), 688–703, 2010.

[MASU10] M.M. Masud, Q. Chen, L. Khan, C. C. Aggarwal, J. Gao, J. Han, B.M. Thuraisingham, "Addressing Concept-Evolution in Concept-Drifting Data Streams," In *Proceedings of ICDM '10*, Sydney, Australia, pp. 929–934.

[MASU11a] M.M. Masud, J. Gao, L. Khan, J. Han, B. M. Thuraisingham, "Classification and Novel Class Detection in Concept-Drifting Data Streams under Time Constraints," *IEEE TKDE*, 23(1), 859–874, 2011.

[MASU11b] M.M. Masud, T.M. Al-Khateeb, L. Khan, C.C. Aggarwal, J. Gao, J. Han, B.M. Thuraisingham, "Detecting Recurring and Novel Classes in Concept-Drifting Data Streams." In *Proceedings of ICDM '11*, Vancouver, BC, pp. 1176–1181.

[MASU12] M.M. Masud, W. Clay, G. Jing, L. Khan, H. Jiawei, K.W. Hamlen, N.C. Oza, "Facing the Reality of Data Stream Classification: Coping with Scarcity of Labeled Data," *Knowledge and Information Systems*, 33 (1), 213–244, 2012.

[PARV11a] P. Parveen, J. Evans, B. Thuraisingham, K.W. Hamlen, L. Khan, "Insider Threat Detection Using Stream Mining and Graph Mining," In *Proceedings of the 3rd IEEE International Conference on Information Privacy, Security, Risk and Trust (PASSAT 2011)*, October, Boston, MA, MIT Press, 2011.

[PARV11b] P. Parveen, Z.R. Weger, B. Thuraisingham, K. Hamlen, L. Khan, "Supervised Learning for Insider Threat Detection Using Stream Mining," In *Proceedings of 23rd IEEE International Conference on Tools with Artificial Intelligence (ICTAI2011)*, November 7–9, Boca Raton, FL (Best Paper Award), 2011.

[PORT10] G. Portokalidis, P. Homburg, K. Anagnostakis, H. Bos, "Paranoid Android: Versatile Protection for Smartphones," In *Proceedings of the 26th Annual Computer Security Applications Conference (ACSAC'10)*, pp. 347–356, New York, NY, ACM, 2010.

[ROBO] Robotium. n.d. Robotium, http://robotium.com/.

[SPIN08] E.J. Spinosa, A.P. de Leon, F. de Carvalho, J. Gama, "Cluster-Based Novel Concept Detection in Data Streams Applied to Intrusion Detection in Computer Networks," In *Proceedings of ACM SAC*, pp. 976–980, 2008.

[SHAB10] A. Shabtai, U. Kanonov, Y. Elovici, "Intrusion Detection for Mobile Devices Using the Knowledge-Based, Temporal Abstraction Method," *Journal of System Software*, 83, 1524–1537, August 2010.

[SAHS12] J. Sahs and L. Khan, "A Machine Learning Approach to Android Malware Detection," *Intelligence and Security Informatics Conference (EISIC), 2012 European. IEEE*, Odense, Denmark, pp. 141–147, 2012.

[SOPH14] Sophos. "*Security Threat Report*," Sophos, 2014. http://www.sophos.com/en-us/threat-center/medialibrary/PDFs/other/sophos-security-threat-report-2014.pdf.

[SOUN14] D. Sounthiraraj, J. Sahs, G. Greenwood, Z. Lin, L. Khan, "SMV-Hunter: Large Scale, Automated Detection of ssl/tls Man-in-the-Middle Vulnerabilities in Android Apps," In *Proceedings of the 19th Network and Distributed System Security Symposium.* San Diego, CA, 2014.

[SOLA14a] M. Solaimani, L. Khan, B. Thuraisingham, "Real-Time Anomaly Detection Over VMware Performance Data Using Storm," In *The 15th IEEE International Conference on Information Reuse and Integration (IRI)*, San Francisco, CA, 2014.

[SOLA14b] M. Solaimani, M. Iftekhar, L. Khan, B. Thuraisingham, J.B. Ingram, "Spark-Based Anomaly Detection Over Multi-Source VMware Performance Data In Real-Time," In *Proceedings of the IEEE Symposium Series on Computational Intelligence (IEEE SSCI 2014)*, Orlando, FL, 2014.

[SOLA14c] M. Solaimani, M. Iftekhar, L. Khan, B. Thuraisingham, "Statistical Technique for Online Anomaly Detection Using Spark Over Heterogeneous Data from Multi-Source VMware Performance Data," In *the IEEE International Conference on Big Data 2014 (IEEE BigData 2014)*, Washington DC, 2014.

[U1] 50 Malware applications found on Android Official Market. http://m.guardian.co.uk/technology/blog/2011/mar/02/android-market-apps-malware?cat=technology&type=article.

[U2] Google Inc. Android market. https://market.android.com/.

[U3] Juniper Networks Inc, "Malicious Mobile Threats Report 2010/2011," *Technical Report*, Juniper Networks, Inc., 2011.

[U4] R.T. Llamas, W. Stofega, S.D. Drake, S.K. Crook, "Worldwide Smartphone, 2011–2015 Forecast and Analysis," *Technical Report, International Data Corporation*, 2011.

[UNUC13] R. Unuchek, The Most Sophisticated Android Trojan. June, 2013. https://securelist.com/blog/research/35929/the-most-sophisticated-android-trojan/

[WART11] R. Wartell, Y. Zhou, K.W. Hamlen, M. Kantarcioglu, B.M. Thuraisingham, "Differentiating Code from Data in x86 Binaries," *ECML/PKDD* (3), 522–536, 2011.

[WELC84] T.A. Welch, "A Technique for High-Performance Data Compression," *Computer*, 17 (6), 8–19, 1984.

[WOMA12] B. Womack, Google Says 700,000 Applications Available for Android. October, 2012. http://www.businessweek.com/news/2012-10-29/google-says-700-000-applications-available-for- android-devices.

[ZHOU12] Y. Zhou, Z. Wang, W. Zhou, X. Jiang, "Hey, You, Get Off of My Market: Detecting Malicious Apps in Official and Alternative Android Markets," NDSS, 2012.

33 Toward a Case Study in Healthcare for Big Data Analytics and Security

33.1 INTRODUCTION

While the previous two chapters focused on security issues for Internet of things (IoT) system as well as discussed a sample system which was a connected smartphone system, in this section we will discuss a planned case study that we are beginning to explore for healthcare systems which we consider to be another example of an IoT system. As the use and combination of multiple big datasets become ubiquitous and the IoT becomes a reality, we increasingly need to deal with large volumes of heterogeneous datasets. Some of these datasets are discrete data points, others are images or gridded datasets (e.g., from meteorological models or satellites). Some are observations, some are demographic or social data, and others are business transactions. Some of these datasets are available for public access; others require varying levels of access control. Some of these datasets need to be streamed in real time with low latency, others have more relaxed latency requirements. Some of these datasets are structured, others are unstructured.

The previous chapters in this book have discussed the various concepts and techniques for big data management and analytics. In addition, we have also applied our techniques for various applications such as cyber security. We have also discussed various experimental big data systems such as semantic web-based query processing and cloud-centric assured information sharing. In this chapter, we will illustrate the key points in big data analytics and security for a particular vertical domain, that is, healthcare. It should be noted that the solutions we have discussed in this chapter are yet to be developed. Our purpose is to illustrate how the concepts can be applied to design practical big data systems. In particular, we will describe a planned case study in this chapter and show how the big data analytics and security techniques can be applied in the healthcare domain where there is a need to manage and analyze massive amounts of data securely. It should be noted that while we have used the Veterans Administration (VA) application as an example in the system that we are proposing to develop, our system can be applied to any related application.

The organization of this chapter is as follows. The motivation for the planned case study is discussed in Section 33.2. Some methodologies to be used are discussed in Section 33.3. The limitations of current systems and the high-level design of future systems are discussed in Section 33.4. This chapter is summarized in Section 33.5. Figure 33.1 illustrates our system architecture.

33.2 MOTIVATION

33.2.1 The Problem

Around 3 years ago, the World Health Organization released a report stating that globally seven million premature deaths in 2012 were linked to air pollution [WHO]. To pick just one pollutant as an illustration, the many health impacts of airborne particulate matter (PM) with a diameter of 2.5 microns have been extensively studied; they depend in part on their abundance at ground level in the atmospheric boundary layer where they can be inhaled. With the increasing awareness of the health impacts of air quality, there is a growing need to characterize the spatial and temporal

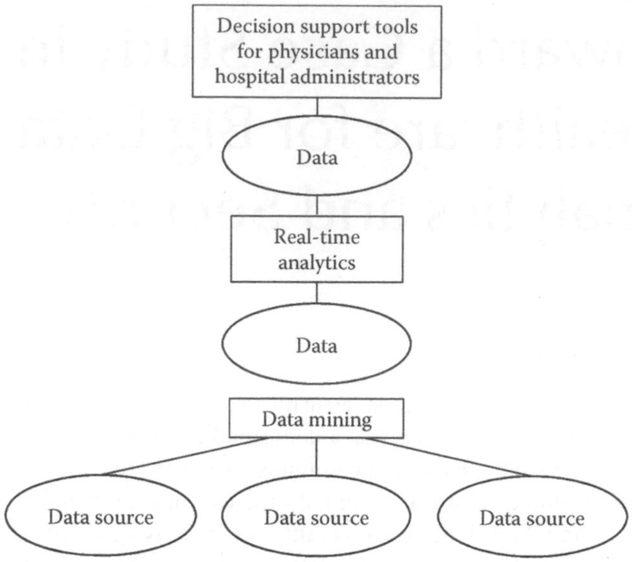

FIGURE 33.1 System architecture.

variations of the global abundance of ground-level pollution over the last two decades. Once the air quality is characterized, it is imperative that we then use this information in a proactive way to try and prevent further avoidable health issues and to improve policies. *Prevention is better than cure.* The VA is the country's largest healthcare provider, caring for seven million veterans and their families. We need enhancements to the VA decision support tools in the area of public health and air quality utilizing hourly in-situ observations from 55 countries, global population density at 10-km resolution, and multiple global NASA Satellite and Earth Science data on a daily basis from August 1997 to present. With the increasing awareness of the many health impacts of PM ranging from general mortality to specific respiratory, cardiovascular, cancer, and reproductive conditions, to name but a few, there is a growing and pressing need to have global daily estimates of the abundance of ground-level air quality.

The existing *My*Health**e**Vet Decision Support Tool is the VA's Personal Health Record system. It was designed for veterans, active duty service members, their dependents, and caregivers. *My*Health**e**Vet helps veterans partner with their healthcare team. It provides veterans opportunities and tools to make informed decisions. The four key features of the existing *My*Health**e**Vet tool for veterans are

1. Keep track of all past and upcoming visits and set preferences on how to receive appointment reminders.
2. Keep track of medications and refill prescriptions. Veterans see all the details of each medication: refill status, refill submit date, fill date, medication name, prescription number, the VA facility where veterans receive medication, and the refills remaining.
3. Secure messaging allows a two-way conversation between veterans and the VA healthcare team.
4. Health**e**living assessment. The summary report in the Health**e**living assessment shows veterans the positive effect of making changes. With graphic displays, it offers veterans the chance to see the impact of specific changes.

We believe that the current *My*Health**e**Vet system does not address the needs of the veterans. Therefore, what is needed are the following:

1. Enhance the existing *My*Health*e*Vet decision support tool to provide *timely alerts* when the current environmental conditions could trigger health incidents for an individual veteran. For example, one in 12 people (about 25 million or 8% of the U.S. population) has asthma, including many veterans. Poor air quality can trigger an asthma event. A timely reminder to carry an inhaler and avoid unnecessary strenuous activity on a day with poor air quality could preclude an asthma event and emergency room (ER) visit. Likewise, worldwide, chronic obstructive pulmonary disease (COPD) affects 329 million people or nearly 5% of the population. In 2011, it ranked as the fourth leading cause of death, killing over 3 million people. Veterans with COPD could be sent timely alerts on days with poor air quality.
2. Prepare and manage a *prototype logistical planning tool for VA ERs and walk-in clinics*. The tool will estimate the likely ERs admissions and required supplies based on the observed relationship over the last decade between air quality and the VA ERs admissions across the entire USA and supply usage. This tool has to be eventually made operational.

While we have used the air pollution monitoring domain for the planned case study, the techniques that need to be designed and developed are not only applicable to a particular domain but can span across multiple domains such as cyber security (e.g., analyzing attack data), healthcare, and geospatial applications. In particular, the framework we plan to develop will be able to accommodate geospatial data from disparate sources, preprocess them, and produce actionable insights via offline and real-time analytics.

33.2.2 Air Quality Data

Various networks of ground-based sensors routinely measure the abundance of $PM_{2.5}$. However, the spatial coverage has *many gaps*, and in some countries, there are no $PM_{2.5}$ observations altogether. This is largely due to the costs involved in operating such a sensor network. Several studies have sought to overcome the lack of direct $PM_{2.5}$ observations by using remote sensing and satellite-derived aerosol optical depth (AOD) coupled with regression and/or numerical prediction models to estimate the ground-level abundance of $PM_{2.5}$.

Many studies have shown that the relationship between $PM_{2.5}$ and AOD is a multivariate function of a *large* number of parameters (features), including humidity, temperature, boundary layer height, surface pressure, population density, topography, wind speed, surface type, surface reflectivity, season, land use, normalized variance of rainfall events, size spectrum and phase of cloud particles, cloud cover, cloud optical depth, cloud top pressure, and the proximity to particulate sources. In some cases, such as for wind speed, the relationship is highly *nonlinear*, and in many cases not well characterized. Then the picture is further complicated by the biases present in the various satellite AOD products, the difference in spatial scales of the in-situ point $PM_{2.5}$ observations and the remote sensing data (several kilometers per pixel), and finally, sharp $PM_{2.5}$ gradients that can exist in and around cities, particularly in Asia.

Taken together, these factors naturally suggest that any successful prediction techniques must be multivariate, nonlinear, nonparametric, and capable of dealing with non-Gaussian distributions. Since the aforementioned scientific data are streaming (i.e., continuous) in nature, the prediction/classification techniques need to be adaptive in nature to cope with most recent changes. Therefore, we will focus on statistical relational learning and stream mining techniques to facilitate prediction in a dynamic environment.

33.2.3 Need for Such a Case Study

We need to provide a suite of new and customized algorithms and techniques to (1) provide personalized health alerts and estimate resource needs for ERs based on machine learning/data mining, (2) deal with continuous scientific stream data, (3) deal with distributed computational methods for privacy and security-aware scientific data storing and retrieval, and (4) deal with automated/semi-automated analysis of data-enabled knowledge discovery processes.

Such tools will be beneficial to various communities including those working in public health and air quality. The technology that we need to develop will benefit VA decision support tools that need to analyze massive amounts of streaming big data with online responses. The study will further advance online stream data mining since such a technique provides an ideal platform for testing innovative stream data analysis ideas.

33.3 METHODOLOGIES

The data sources are diverse (see Figure 33.2) and produce large volumes of data which are high-dimensional, multi-DBMS due to the heavy usage of query-centric scientific workload format, sparse, and can be either structured or unstructured.

Under these constraints, the ideal choice for data storage and retrieval is array-centric and NoSQL databases due to their simplicity of design, horizontal scalability, and availability. Conventional relational database management system is a poor fit for complex analysis of scientific data and hence we must leverage specialized database systems such as SciDB. SciDB's multidimensional array data model and its ability to natively integrate complex analytics directly with data management make it an ideal candidate for complex scientific data. Cassandra and HBase are two other viable data storage platforms with optimized read–write performance for massive datasets. Since our framework needs to support random reads and writes, Hadoop/MapReduce may not be a good choice. We need to explore the right combination of these different data stores. The data collected and stored from the various sources must be correlated in such a manner that privacy of sensitive data is not breached. Therefore, explicit access control policies must be embedded in the querying and retrieval mechanisms without any substantial impact on performance. In addition, we need to support complex data analytics. Data analytics can be categorized in two ways: real time and offline. Real-time analytics must be able to process streaming data in near real time to facilitate immediate integration

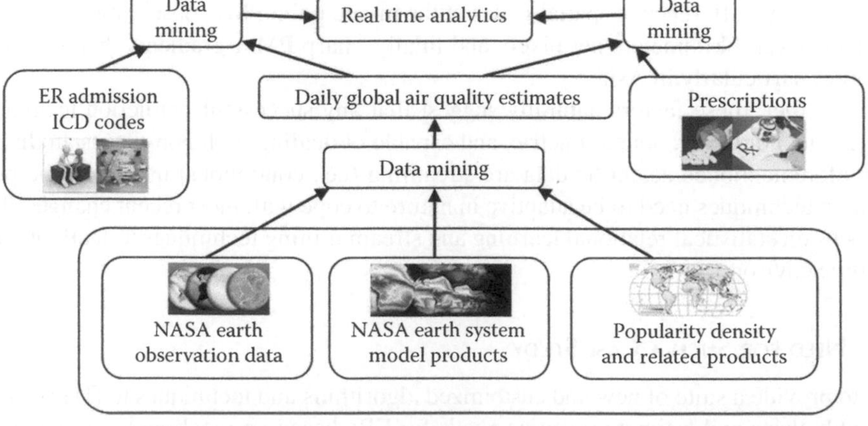

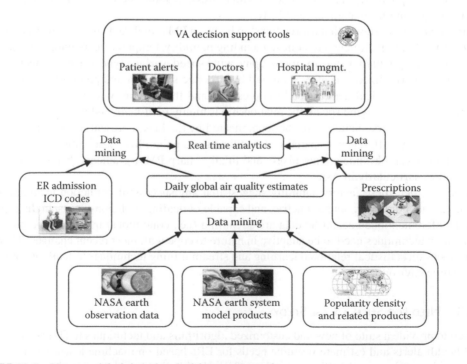

FIGURE 33.2 Veterans Administration decision support tools.

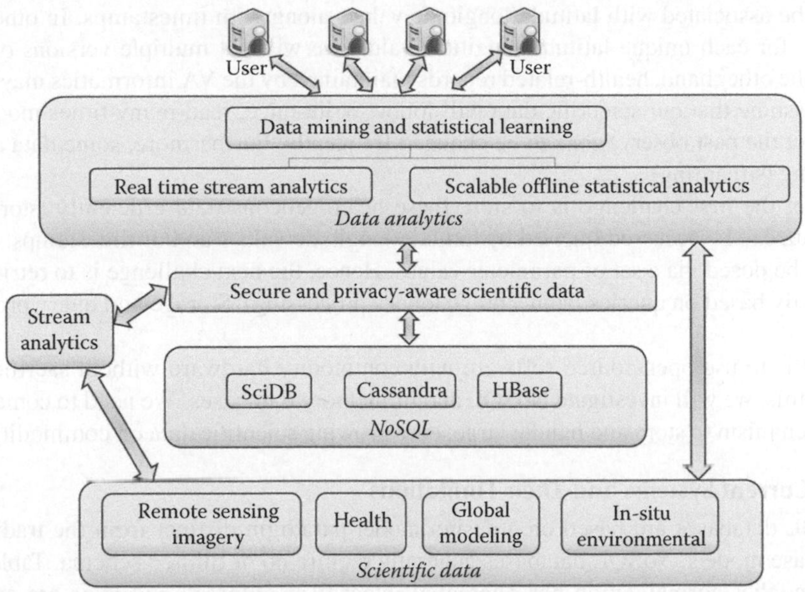

FIGURE 33.3 Architecture of the methodologies.

with decision support systems. Apache Storm is a distributed real-time computation system which can reliably process fast, large streams of data in arbitrarily complex ways. For offline analytics, SciDB offers an abstraction layer that separates data analytics from low-level data manipulation details which can be leveraged to explore new statistical and machine learning techniques that generate more actionable insights.

Figure 33.3 illustrates the architecture of the methodologies. Scientific data will be first stored into the NoSQL system as discussed above. For this, data may move from the streaming environment to the NoSQL system (i.e., persistent storage). In other words, data will move from an online to an offline environment. Second, our query processing mechanism on scientific data will interact with a middleware that enforces security and privacy policies. Finally, data analytics has to be carried out at real time and offline in a scalable manner. It would be desirable to integrate the database systems and analytics platforms with VA Informatics of the **T**imely **H**ealth **I**ndicators using **R**emote **S**ensing & **I**nnovation for the **V**itality of the **E**nvironment Medical Environment Engine and VA decision support tools. In addition, a web portal is needed to allow users to issue relevant queries. The queries will trigger the real-time analytics and generate responses that can be directly applied to decision-making, namely, whether an alert should be sent out to patients/authorities given the quality of air on the present day. The responses produced by the system will follow standard formats to support integration with standalone messaging platforms such as email servers and text-messaging systems.

33.4 THE FRAMEWORK DESIGN

Below we discuss the various challenges related to timely health indicators for big data and how we can overcome these challenges.

33.4.1 Storing and Retrieving Multiple Types of Scientific Data

33.4.1.1 The Problem and Challenges

Data may have varying degrees of structure and sparseness. For example, the relationship between $PM_{2.5}$ and AOD is a function of a large number of properties such as humidity, temperature, boundary layer height, and so on. Here, all of these parameters represent structured data. These parameter values will be associated with latitude/longitude values along with timestamps. In other words, as time passes, for each unique latitude/longitude value, we will get multiple versions of parameter values. On the other hand, health-related records maintained by the VA informatics may be unstructured. We assume that our scientific data will follow write-once, read-many-times model since we do not expect the past observations to be changed frequently. Furthermore, some data are continuously arriving (streaming).

Therefore, the first challenge is to store these heterogeneous data efficiently (storage). These scientific data can be accessed/queried by latitude/longitude values and/or timestamps. In addition, a query can be posed via a set of parameter values. Hence, the next challenge is to retrieve relevant data efficiently based on queries from storage (query processing). Storage and query processing are intertwined.

Our goal is to use open-source software with commodity hardware without sacrificing performance. For this, we will investigate NoSQL and in-memory databases. We need to come up with an efficient mechanism to store and handle large, ever-growing scientific data on commodity hardware.

33.4.1.2 Current Systems and Their Limitations

Most NoSQL databases are based on a design model paradigm distinct from the traditional relational database models. NoSQL databases generally require no or limited schema. Tables are often very wide, neither normalization nor referential integrity is enforced and joins are avoided. The databases run on commodity hardware and have been shown to scale horizontally for vast quantities of data at the expense of strong consistency [MCGL10]. Below is a list of some NoSQL systems and an investigation of each one's suitability for our purpose.

There are three most common design models in NoSQL: the distributed column store model introduced by Google's *BigTable* [CHAN08], the distributed key–value store and semiconsistent model introduced by Amazon's *Dynamo* [DECA07], and the *MapReduce* [DEAN04] programming model.

The *Google File System* [GHEM06] is a scalable distributed and fault-tolerant file system designed to utilize clusters of commodity hardware to enable data intensive applications.

Map/Reduce [DEAN04] is a programming model that enables development of parallelized, data-intensive applications on commodity hardware. A set of intermediate key–value pairs is generated by the map function and then the results are combined, organized, and reduced using the reduce function. *Hadoop/MapReduce* is an open-source software library that implements Google's MapReduce programming model. Hadoop/MapReduce is by nature suitable for batch processing and is not ideally suited to processing streams of data coming in real time. Since in Hadoop/MapReduce, schemas and declarative queries are missing, *Hive* [HIVE14] (an SQL-like query language) and *Pig* [PIG14] (a more imperative language with relational operators) have been introduced to add these features on top of Hadoop/MapReduce jobs. In our prior work, we describe a framework that we built using Hadoop to store and retrieve large numbers of sematic web data (i.e., resource description framework (RDF) triples) ([HUSA11a], [HUSA11b]). We show that our framework is scalable and efficient and can handle large amounts of RDF data, unlike traditional approaches.

HBase [CARS10] is a column-oriented data store where all data is identified by a unique row identifier (key). It is modeled after Google's BigTable design. Impala [IMPA14] provides an SQL layer above the Hadoop Distributed File Systems (HDFS) and HBase.

Cassandra [LAKS09] is a distributed database which combines the distribution design of Dynamo and the data model of HBase. Like HBase, Cassandra supports sequential row identifiers, columns, and column families.

Some NoSQL databases (such as *MongoDB* and *CouchDB*) support distributed key-document stores. A few graph databases (such asNeo4J) and XML data stores can qualify as NoSQL databases.

SciDB [STON11] is an open-source computational database with a shared-nothing, massively parallel processing distributed architecture and the ability to run on 10–1000 s of commodity hardware nodes. SciDB stores data natively in an array format which is a more natural fit for scientific data, geospatial data, sensor data, and other multifaceted complex data [ARRA14]. The array model also accelerates linear algebra operations by 10–100 times. SciDB's physical storage model is customized for both sparse and dense data which translates to faster data access. SciDB-R and SciDB-py libraries allow analysts to use the languages R and Python to leverage the native analytical power of SciDB. SciDB's all-in-one, seamlessly integrated analytics package is unmatched in other contemporary big data frameworks.

Our scientific data is multidimensional (e.g., each longitude/latitude value is associated with multiple environmental parameters and multiple versions of those parameters). SciDB uses a multidimensional array as its basic storage and processing unit. Storage of these arrays is handled by a partitioning scheme called chunking [SCID14] that distributes subsets of the array uniformly across all instances of the database where each instance is responsible for storing and updating that subset locally. Chunk assignment follows a hash-based scheme. Chunks that are frequently accessed are maintained in-memory to speed up querying and computation.

In-memory database *SAP HANA* can process queries faster and provide instant answers to complex queries; however, since it is proprietary, the total cost of ownership is high.

Apache Spark [ZAHA12] is a fast and general engine for large-scale data processing including stream data. It can run programs up to 100× faster than Hadoop/MapReduce in memory or 10× faster on a disk. However, Spark is still an Apache incubator project and at this point its machine-learning library MLlib does not cover a significant spectrum of analytical tools. In contrast, SciDB is a mature, complete, and stable product that offers much higher flexibility and richness in analytics. Furthermore, in terms of adoption by industries and stability, *Apache Storm* [STOR14] remains ahead of Spark.

33.4.1.3 The Future System

HBase/Cassandra/SciDB can be a viable option for storage and retrieval. Our scientific applications may have a variable schema where each row is slightly different. Data may be stored in collections, for example, some metadata, message data, or binary data that is all keyed on the same value. Frequent random read/write is the norm here. Therefore, HBase/Cassandra would be the suitable option.

As stated before, parameter values pertaining to $PM_{2.5}$ and AOD can be retrieved based on latitude/longitude values and/or timestamp. Our first goal is: data points close to each other in space should be close to each other on disk (storage). The second goal is to retrieve as few points as possible when responding to a query. HBase/Cassandra can fulfill these two goals via the row key mechanism. For our example, latitude and longitude values can be turned into a single value that can be used as row key/identifier. There are a number of ways to reduce multiple dimensions to a single one; geohash may be a feasible option that preserves spatial locality.

For SciDB, attribute values may be organized as a collection of three-dimensional arrays (latitude, longitude, and timestamp). Cells in a SciDB array can contain a tuple of all parameter values. Therefore, we will focus on three alternatives (HBase/Cassandra/SciDB), test various queries on each of these alternatives, and choose the one that gives the best query performance on average. Prediction of global daily estimate of $PM_{2.5}$ involves data collection from two distinct sources: (1) hourly observations of $PM_{2.5}$ sites in 55 countries from 1997 to present and (2) NASA Earth observation and Earth system model data. Given the high dimensionality and volume of the datasets, Cassandra/Hbase/SciDBare are ideal candidates as the backend database. In particular, for the same row key (location), a number of column families and content will be maintained in HBase/Cassandra. For example, a column family may represent a set of columns for International Classification of Diseases (ICD) code and a different column family may represent VA prescription-related data. To conduct predictive analytics, relevant data from multiple distinct datasets must first be retrieved based on time and location. Fetching of relevant data can be carried out from the NoSQL store or stream analytics queuing system (see Section 33.3). To handle streaming data, we plan to use Apache Storm. Next, an analytical model can be constructed that predicts an estimate of $PM_{2.5}$

abundance. These analytics can be carried out based on statistical analytics and/or real-time analytics (see Section 33.3). All analyses will be based on whatever relevant data was fetched. Hence, data are moving from one component (e.g., NoSQL store) to another component (e.g., analytics).

33.4.2 Privacy and Security Aware Data Management for Scientific Data

33.4.2.1 The Problem and Challenges

Over the years, there has been much work (including our own) toward developing privacy- and security-aware data management solutions for large data. Unfortunately, none of the existing work tries to capture the entire life cycle of the scientific data. Basically, existing works try to address the security issues that arise in different types of NoSQL systems. For example, in our past work [THUR10], we developed a system that combines the HDFS [BORT10] with Hive [HIVE14] to provide secure storage and processing solutions for very large datasets. Furthermore, we use a XACML [MOSE05] policy-based security mechanism to provide fine-grained access control over the data. As discussed before, traditional users of large scientific datasets need to use multiple data processing tools. For example, the data may be collected via a stream processing system using different types of sources with security and privacy requirements and then it may be stored on different data storage systems such as SciDB and HBase/Cassandra. Therefore, any security- and privacy-aware data management system should track the data and how it is moved and processed.

We need to create a simple yet powerful security- and privacy-aware data management layer specifically tailored for scientific data processing. Instead of trying to change each data management tool, we need to build a security middleware on top of the existing systems that can track and enforce policies across multiple data storage platforms. Unlike other existing work, including NSF SATC funded project CNS-1237235 on privacy-preserving research data sharing and our own NSF SATC funded project CNS-1228198 on distributed policy enforcement among data management systems belonging to different organizations, our focus in this project is on addressing security and privacy challenges in systems that belong to the same organization. Here, we do not consider the security and policy enforcement issues in sharing research data across multiple institutions.

Given these rich sets of tools that have different data schemas, we need to develop security and privacy management tools that can be used across multiple systems. Furthermore, we cannot afford to change each and every system to enforce the needed security and privacy policies since these systems change frequently and new data management tools continuously developed.

33.4.2.2 Current Systems and Their Limitations

Apache Accumulo [ACCU11] is a sorted, distributed key–value store based on Google's BigTable design and built on top of Apache Hadoop. Accumulo improves the BigTable design in the form of cell-based access control and a server-side programming mechanism that can modify key–value pairs at various points in the data management process. Similarly, the BigSecret [PATT13] system we developed enables secure querying of cell-level encrypted data in HBase. It also uses a heuristic approach to optimally distribute data and assign workloads over a cloud setup consisting of multiple providers (i.e., multicloud setup), under varying monetary and disclosure risk constraints. SecureMR [WEI09] is an integrity assurance framework built on top of the MapReduce model. It provides a decentralized replication-based integrity verification scheme to protect the integrity of MapReduce in open systems. Airavat [ROY10] is an application for MapReduce systems where the security and privacy are guaranteed for distributed computations on sensitive data. It employs SElinux [SELI14] for mandatory access control and information flow control. It also provides individual privacy guarantees via differentially private MapReduce computation results. Our previous work, Silver Lining [KAUT97] enforces mandatory information flow policies on the MapReduce jobs of Apache Hadoop. It achieves high modularity by implementing the security policies by means of in-lined reference monitors. Fine-grained access control policy enforcement for MapReduce systems has recently attracted attention in both industry and academia. For example, Apache Sentry

[APAC14] developed by Cloudera is intended to deliver fine-grained authorization to data stored in Apache Hadoop. Although it provides fine-grained access management for systems built atop Apache Hadoop (e.g., Hive, Impala, and Search), it assumes that the data is organized as relational tables. Vigiles [ULUS14] is a fine-grained access control system developed for MapReduce by our group, where the security policies generated via XML-based configuration files are enforced on the MapReduce jobs. The system is designed as a separate module weaved into Hadoop byte code to specify complex security policies required to process unstructured Big Data.

However, none of the aforementioned systems address the security and privacy enforcement challenges across multiple different data management systems required for scientific data. Instead, we need to capture the data mining workflow related to scientific data processing and automatically infer policies about the different components of the workflow.

33.4.2.3 The Future System

Since our goal is to create a platform that could work with different data management systems, we do not want to change the internals of any of the data management systems that we will use and make our solution specific to one system. Instead, we need to build a thin middleware on top of existing data management systems. This middleware will ensure that the results of running different data mining tasks may only be accessed by the right users. Initially, for simplicity, we assume that new data access authorizations for different resources can only be issued by users who have administrative access to the entire system. In other words, new data mining work flows can only be issued by users who are allowed to see all of the data. These admin users could then define policies to allow fine-grained access control to source data and data mining results. We need techniques to analyze the sensitivity level of the output of data mining tasks based on the input security labels.

In order to provide efficient security- and privacy-aware access control for a general scientific data mining system, we need to start by understanding the sensitivity of the data coming from different resources. We assume that each source is tagged with a sensitivity label. In practice, security labels could be represented as integers and/or strings. If an integer value is used, it may indicate a rating or relative importance compared to other resources. For example, healthcare-related datasets may have different sensitivity levels than $PM_{2.5}$ observation data.

Such security labels could be used for enforcing access control policies later on. In addition, we can also utilize special "sanitization" tasks in our data mining workflow. These tasks can process data and potentially filter out sensitive parts. For example, sanitization tasks may process "privacy-sensitive" tuples to sanitize them. The resulting sanitized tuples outputted by sanitization tasks can now be tagged as "anonymized." We would like to stress that our goal in this project is not to develop any new sanitization or anonymization algorithm. If such anonymization algorithms are relevant for the underlying scientific task, then the future system will be able to leverage them. If not, then our system could be initialized without such anonymization algorithms.

After these initial steps, we need to understand the sensitivity of the output of a data mining workflow. Although we may ask an administrator to decide the sensitivity of a given output, such a manual approach may lead to various errors especially in the case of complex workflows. Instead, we need to automate this process. In order to understand the sensitivity of a task, we need to consider various scenarios. For example, we can consider:

- Single source derivation: If a source S_i is annotated with security label "s_i" and data mining task T_j is using the output of S_i and is not a "sanitization task," then T_j output data is also annotated with security label "s_i."
- Sanitization task output derivation: If a task T_j is a sanitization task, regardless of its inputs' security labels, the output of task T_j is labeled based on the sanitization definition of the task (e.g., given a task that sanitizes patient data according to safe harbor rules of HIPAA, the output of the task may be consider not privacy-sensitive any more).

- Multisource derivation: If a task T_j uses inputs from different nodes (in this context, node could be a data source or output of a previous task) N_{i1}, N_{i2}, N_{i3}, …, and each of them respectively annotated with tags "s_{i1}," "s_{i2}," "s_{i3}," …, "s_{ik}," then task T_j is tagged with security label "s_x" where security label "s_x" is the tag with the highest priority among the list of security labels.

The above security label propagation rules could be considered conservative since we tag the output of a task with the highest security label associated with potential inputs. However, based on the application requirements the rules can be suitably modified. That is, a domain expert can restate how the security labels are propagated in domain-specific cases.

In our previous work [RACH12], we used a similar label propagation mechanism to understand how sensitive information flows in a typical workflow setting. To address similar challenges, we created an Web Ontology Language [OWL12] datatype property called tag, whose domain is class tuple and range is an integer value (xsd:integer). We used Semantic Web Rules Language [RACH12] rules for the propagation of the security labels. As a part of this work, we will explore how to efficiently capture such rules.

Using the above workflow tagging mechanisms, we plan to implement traditional mandatory control policies and basic role-based access control (RBAC) policies easily without changing the internals of the underlying systems. Basically, we use a thin wrapper to provide access control for the underlying data storage systems. We assume that each data source (e.g., array in SciDB or bolt in a streaming data system such as Storm) defined will be also associated with a security label. In addition, any sanitization tasks should be defined by the system administrator. To simplify the implementation, we assume that new tasks can only be issued by users who have administrative access to entire system. These admin users could than define basic RBAC policies to allow fine-grained access control to data mining results.

The solution discussed could be seen as a straightforward application of RBAC where the output of each task in the data mining workflow is seen as a separate object. Given the initial security labels and propagation rules, the security label of the entire workflow will be automatically inferred and policies will be automatically enforced. At the same, each user in the system is assigned to certain roles. Finally, each role is associated with different security labels that it can access by setting role to security label mappings. Clearly, such approach can be used to implement basic mandatory control policies as well as RBAC policies.

33.4.3 Offline Scalable Statistical Analytics

33.4.3.1 The Problem and Challenges

We need analyze all ER admissions and prescriptions made by the VA over the last decade in terms of the data collected from various sensors. This analysis can then be used to provide personalized health alerts and estimate resource needs for ERs.

We could use Markov logic ([DOMI09], [RICH06]), a popular statistical relational learning tool [GETO07] to achieve this. The key benefit of Markov logic is that it helps us compactly represent, learn and infer over data and knowledge that is both relational and uncertain (our sensor measurements, ICD codes, and prescriptions are noisy). Other benefits of Markov logic include the ability to easily incorporate background knowledge and the ability to quickly experiment with a large variety of models that range from simple to complex because of the easy availability of open-source software tools such as Alchemy 2.0 [GOGA13] (we are currently maintaining at UT Dallas). This allows us to explore the classic bias versus variance (simple vs. complex models) trade-off, a key problem that every application designer grapples with.

Unfortunately, in its current form, existing Markov logic learning and inference tools are not powerful enough to support such massive, heterogeneous, and mixed continuous and discrete datasets. Therefore, enhancing the power of existing Markov logic technology is a key subgoal of this project.

33.4.3.2 Current Systems and Their Limitations

Markov logic networks (MLNs) help us compactly represent and solve large, complex, uncertain real-world problems. They accomplish this by combining first-order logic (which helps manage complexity) and probability (which helps handle uncertainty). At a high level, a MLN is a collection of weighted first-order logic formulas. Unlike first-order logic in which each formula represents a hard constraint, namely if the constraint is violated then the state of the world is impossible, weighted formulas represent soft constraints, that is, if the constraint is violated then the state of the world is less probable but not impossible.

To illustrate MLNs, we consider a toy "friends-smokers" social network domain. We can represent commonsense knowledge in this domain that "smoking causes cancer" and "friends tend to have similar smoking habits" using the following two weighted formulas: (i) $\forall$x Smokes(x) $\Rightarrow$ Cancer(x); w_1 and (ii) $\forall$x,ySmokes(x) $\wedge$Friends(x,y) $\Rightarrow$ Smokes(y); w_2.

Weights in MLNs lie between $-\infty$ and $+\infty$ and reflect the strength of the constraint. The higher the weight, the stronger the constraint. Specifically, a weight of 0 represents the uniform distribution; world states satisfying the formula as well as those not satisfying the formula have the same probability. Positive (negative) weights represent that the world states satisfying the formula have higher (lower) probability than world states not satisfying the formula.

Given a set of constants that represent objects (people) in the domain (social-network), a MLN represents a Markov network, namely a compact representation of a joint probability distribution over the properties of objects in the domain. The Markov network is obtained by having a feature for each possible grounding of each first-order formula in the MLN, where a grounding of a formula is the instantiation of each logical variable in it with a constant. The weight attached to the feature (formula in propositional logic) is the weight attached to the corresponding first-order formula. For instance, given two constants Ana and Bob, the first first-order formula in the friends-smokers MLN yields the following two groundings: (i) Smokes(Ana) $\Rightarrow$ Cancer(Ana), w_1 and (ii) Smokes(Bob) $\Rightarrow$ Cancer(Bob), w_1. The second first-order formula yields the following four groundings: (i) Smokes(Ana) $\wedge$Friends(Ana,Bob) $\Rightarrow$ Smokes(Bob), w_2; (ii) Smokes(Ana) $\wedge$Friends(Ana,Ana) $\Rightarrow$ Smokes(Ana), w_2; (iii) Smokes(Bob) $\wedge$Friends(Bob,Bob) $\Rightarrow$ Smokes(Bob); w_2; and (iv) Smokes(Bob) $\wedge$Friends(Bob,Ana) $\Rightarrow$ Smokes(Ana), w_2.

Formally, given a set of weighted first-order formulas $\{f_i, w_i\}$, the probability of a state x, which is a truth-assignment to all ground atoms, is given by the following log-linear expression:

$$\Pr(x) = \frac{1}{Z}\exp\left(\sum_i w_i N_i(x)\right) \quad \text{where} \quad Z = \sum_x \exp\left(\sum_i w_i N_i(x)\right)$$

where $N_i(x)$ is the number of groundings of f_i that are true in x and Z is a normalization constant, also called the partition function, which ensures that the distribution sums to 1.

The two key tasks in Markov logic are weight learning, which is the task of learning from data the weights attached to the first-order logic formulas and inference, which is the task of answering queries posed over the learned model given observations (evidence). For instance, in the social network given above, an example inference task is computing the probability that Ana has cancer, given that she is friends with Bob who smokes (evidence) and the learning task is updating the weights attached to the two first-order formulas given data. For both these tasks, we could use and enhance the power of Alchemy 2.0 [GOVE2013], a state-of-the-art open-source software for learning and inference in Markov logic. Alchemy 2.0, which is maintained and developed (Dr. Gogate and his team at UT Dallas), has been downloaded over 1800 times and its predecessor Alchemy 1.0

[KOK08], which is maintained and developed by University of Washington, has been downloaded >15,000 times. Especially, we plan to use the weight learning approaches from data to see whether high levels of $PM_{2.5}$ correlate with certain diseases by exploring the weights of the rules of the form "high levels of $PM_{2.5}$ implies asthma attack."

Alchemy 2.0 is based on a concept called lifted probabilistic inference ([GOGA11b], [POOL03]); the idea is to perform inference at the more compact first-order or lifted level rather than at the propositional level. Propositional algorithms essentially ground the MLN yielding a Markov network and use probabilistic inference algorithms that do not take advantage of relational structure to perform inference. For instance, consider a friends-smokers social network having 1 billion ($=10^6$) people. In this case, the second first-order formula will yield 10^{12} groundings and as a result inference at the propositional (ground) level is clearly infeasible (existing inference and learning algorithms for graphical models do not scale to such levels). However, in many cases, lifted inference can take advantage of symmetries in the first-order representation and answer such queries without generating all of the 10^{12} groundings. Thus, Alchemy 2.0, which uses lifted inference, is potentially more scalable than Alchemy 1.0.

Alchemy 1.0 and 2.0 have been applied in several domains with promising results, for example, citation matching [SING06], link prediction ([GOGA11b], [RICH06]), and information extraction [POON07]. Inspired by this scientific progress, we need to integrate Alchemy 2.0 into a full-blown application which has all the characteristics of a complex machine learning system: operates online; requires personalized solutions; is rich and diverse; and so on. Thus, our approach will serve as an ideal test-bed for testing and evaluating the capabilities of Markov logic and Alchemy 2.0.

33.4.3.3 The Future System

In order to improve the accuracy, applicability, and speed of the future system, we need to solve the following problems associated with existing MLN technology (implemented in Alchemy 2.0):

1. Existing MLN inference tools perform poorly on applications involving mixed continuous and discrete datasets.
2. Learning algorithms do not scale well to massive datasets, involving billions of entries, especially when the Markov network associated with the MLN is densely connected as in our application.
3. Existing tools do not support scalable online inference, a must have for real-time analytics.

In the next three subsections, we outline an approach that addresses these three limitations.

33.4.3.4 Mixed Continuous and Discrete Domains

We could use hybrid MLNs (HMLNs) [WANG08b] as our representation framework for modeling such domains. This framework extends the weighted first-order logic representation to mixed continuous and discrete domains in a straight-forward manner; it allows numeric properties of objects as nodes, in addition to Boolean ones, and numeric terms as features, in addition to logical formulas. Since the syntax of first-order and higher order logic already includes numeric terms, no new constructs are added in HMLNs. For example, if we are interested in distances between objects as random variables, in HMLNS, we can introduce the numeric feature *Distance* (x, y). The main challenge is developing efficient approximate inference algorithms for hybrid domains. This is because existing HMLN inference algorithms do not scale well to large domains and are very inaccurate.

We need to extend sampling and local search-based approximate inference algorithms to handle numeric, continuous and hybrid domains. In particular, we need to extend the following three inference schemes for discrete MLNs to continuous domains: importance sampling ([GOGA11b], [GOGA12a]), Gibbs sampling [VENU12], and MaxWalksat [KAUT97]. In many cases, inference over continuous Gaussian variables can be carried out in closed form [LERN02] and we need to lift them by taking advantage of symmetries just as we did for propositional discrete inference

([GOGA11b], [JHA10]). For other variables and when inference is not possible in closed form, we need to explore using dynamic discretization and particle-based strategies described in [IHLE09]. In prior work, we extended advanced, Rao-Blackwellised importance sampling algorithms that combine exact inference and sampling to mixed discrete and continuous Gaussian domains ([GOGA05]). We need to lift this and other sampling algorithms by using lifted inference rules developed in our previous work ([GOGA11a], [GOGA12a], [JHA10], [VENU12]). The main idea is to replace the propositional sampling step which samples individual random variables in the Markov network by a lifted sampling step which partitions the set of variables into several groups each containing a set of indistinguishable random variables and samples each group in one go. When the number of groups, which are identified by looking at symmetries in the first-order representation without grounding the MLN, is small, this approach can be quite efficient.

33.4.3.4.1 Lifted Learning and Approximations of Pseudolikelihood

Large MLNs with dense connectivity are problematic because a single iteration of even the fastest learning algorithms such as the pseudolikelihood method [BESA75] will incur quadratic complexity in the number of ground atoms, rendering them impractical. To combat this problem, we need to develop a lifted, Rao-Blackwellised sampling-based approximation of pseudolikelihood. Formally, the pseudolikelihood approximates the likelihood using the expression: $P(x) = \prod_i P(x_i \mid x_{-i})$ where $x = (x_1, \ldots, x_n)$ is a truth-assignment to all the ground variables, x_{-i} is the projection of x on all variables except i-th variable.

To illustrate the key idea, consider the Markov logic formula $R(x) \vee T(y)$. To compute the pseudolikelihood, we have to compute the marginal probability of each atom given a truth assignment to the groundings of all other atoms in the formula, which in turn requires us to compute the number of groundings of the formula that are true given the assignment to $T(y)$. For this formula, via simple counting, it turns out that this value equals $n - I$ where n is the number of objects in the domain and I is the number of groundings of $T(y)$ that are true in the current truth-assignment. Thus, the marginal can be computed in constant time. On the other hand, existing methods will compute this value by going over n^2 groundings. The former method having constant time complexity is lifted while the latter is not.

When the formula is complicated (e.g., $R(x,y) \vee S(y,z) \vee T(x,z)$) and exact lifted computations are not possible, we can partially ground the theory ([GOGA12a], [SARK14]), sample these groundings and compute the answer. For instance, we can ground x in the formula given above, yielding a counting problem that can be solved in linear time. When the domain size of x is large, we can sample its domain to yield a Rao-Blackwellised approximation (cf. [LIU01]) of pseudolikelihood (sampling-algorithms that combine exact inference and sampling are called Rao-Blackwellised samplers and are more accurate than samplers that do not use exact inference). We need to theoretically investigate the consistency of the new estimates and experimentally evaluate them on our VA datasets.

33.4.3.4.2 Approximate Compilation for Online Inference Knowledge

This compilation is a new approach to tackle the complexity of probabilistic inference ([DARW03], [DARW02a], [DARW02b]). The key idea is to convert the MLN to a compiled structure such that inference is tractable (efficient) in the size of the compiled structure. The bulk of the computation is thus moved to the offline compilation phase while the online query answering phase is always efficient.

We need to investigate exact and approximate relational compilation techniques building on the work in [BROE11], [WANG08a]. At a high level, exact compilation techniques first run an exact inference algorithm such as probabilistic theorem proving (PTP) [GOGA11b] on the given MLN and then compress it by merging identical subtrees in the PTP execution tree. One of the problems with lifted compilation approaches is that evidence breaks symmetries and unlike propositional compilation approaches [DARW02a], inference on the lifted compiled structure may not be polynomial. We need to solve this problem by enforcing further conditions on tractability of inference. For example, one condition that we can enforce is that the size of the lifted AND/OR graph ([DECH07], [GOGA10]) after processing evidence is bounded by a constant.

Unfortunately, exact compilation techniques, such as the one described above, will not scale well to large datasets. Therefore, we need to develop approximate compilation techniques which compress and store the output of sampling-based algorithms [GOGA12b].

33.4.4 Real-Time Stream Analytics

33.4.4.1 The Problem and Challenges

Our scientific data, namely $PM_{2.5}$, Satellite AOD Data, and meteorological data are streams in nature. From these data we would like to do prediction/classification that is focused on the short term. In particular, we would like to estimate $PM_{2.5}$ (prediction) for a location based on incoming stream data. For the case of classification, we need to categorize the location based on class labels.

Data streams are continuous flows of data. Data streams demonstrate several unique properties: infinite (unbounded) length, concept drift, and limited labeled data. Concept drift occurs in data streams when the underlying characteristics of the data changes over time. Data streams also suffer from scarcity of labeled data since it is not possible to manually label all the data points in the stream. Each of these properties adds a challenge to data stream mining. We aim to handle stream classification/prediction in evolving data streams by addressing these challenges.

33.4.5 Current Systems and Their Limitations

There are a number of data stream classification techniques designed to handle concept drift ([AGGA09], [CHEN08], [FAN04], [GAO07], [HASH09], [MASU09a], [MASU11b], [SPIN08], [WANG03], [WANG07], [WENE06], [YANG05]). Two popular alternatives to handle the massive volume of data streams and concept drift are the single-model and the hybrid batch incremental approaches. In the single-model approach, a single model is dynamically updated when new data arrives. For example, [GAO07] incrementally updates a decision tree with incoming data, and [AGGA09] incrementally updates micro-clusters in the model with the new data. The batch-incremental approach builds each classification model using a batch learning technique. However, older models are replaced by newer models when the older models become obsolete ([BIFE09], [CHEN08], [HASH09], [MASU09a], [WANG03])). Some of these hybrid approaches use a single model to classify the unlabeled data (e.g., [WANG03]), whereas others use an ensemble of models (e.g., ([HASH09] and [MASU09a])). The advantage of hybrid approaches over the single-model incremental approach is that hybrid approaches use much simpler operations to update a model (such as removing a model from the ensemble).

33.4.5.1 The Future System

One possible approach is the use ensemble-based stream mining that leverages multiple classification models to achieve highly accurate classification in streams even when the stream is unbounded, evolving, and unlabeled. Here, first we list two ways we can achieve real-time analytics. One is semisupervised learning over stream data and the other one focuses on relational learning. Next, we need to address scalability issues of these predictions.

33.4.5.1.1 Semisupervised Classification/Prediction

Recent approaches in classifying evolving data streams are based on supervised learning algorithms, which can be trained with labeled data only. Manual labeling of data is both costly and time-consuming. Therefore, in a real streaming environment, where huge volumes of data appear at a high speed, labeled data may be very scarce. Thus, only a limited amount of training data may be available for building the classification models, leading to poorly trained classifiers. We apply a novel technique to overcome this problem. We build a classification model from a training set having a few labeled instances and a large number of unlabeled instances. This model is built as micro-clusters using a semisupervised clustering technique and classification is performed using k-nearest neighbor algorithms. An ensemble of these models is used to classify unlabeled data. During semisupervised clustering in our former work ([MASU11a], [MASU08]), we assigned a penalty when instances having the same class label belonged to different clusters. We need to extend the constraints beyond class labels, for example, we need to take into consideration spatial locality. We could also utilize subspace clustering instead of k-means. Since data are high dimensional, a set of points may form a cluster in a subset of dimensions instead of across all dimensions. Identification of such clusters is the goal of subspace clustering ([AHME10], [JING07]).

In addition, we need to consider efficient techniques for building traditional logistic regression models that includes $PM_{2.5}$ levels and health conditions. Using log-likelihood models, we need to explore whether high $PM_{2.5}$ levels are highly correlated with certain health conditions.

33.4.5.1. 2 Online Structure Learning Methods for Stream Classification

Data classification methods use the data distribution to evaluate a class variable, given certain evidence. Relationships between variables can be represented in terms of a network or a probabilistic graphical model [KOLL09], where each variable is represented by a node and relationships are represented by the edges in the network. An accurate representation of the data distribution in terms of network structure is necessary to provide better classification accuracy. Most data classification approaches assume the structure of this network is known; it is typically constructed manually. However, in certain cases, the network structure may not be known. Structure learning algorithms using statistical approaches such as Chow Liu trees [CHOW68] are used to evaluate the structure of a network. In the Chow Liu tree structure learning approach, a completely connected graph is initially assumed. Mutual information is then calculated using edge weight (representing a certain measure of relationship strength). A maximum likelihood tree is constructed using the maximum spanning tree over the mutual information. This is then used to evaluate the required query. With large networks, the algorithm is known to exhibit poor accuracy.

In a recent work, we developed a new tractable graphical model called Cutset networks to improve the accuracy of Chow Liu trees [RAHM14]. At a high level, Cutset networks are probabilistic decision trees or OR trees with Chow Liu trees at each leaf node of the OR tree. They model the mechanics of Pearl's Cutset conditioning method, a classic exact inference algorithm. The OR tree is constructed based on a subset of nodes, known as Cutset, which is evaluated using certain splitting and termination criteria over the variables considered. This splitting and termination condition to evaluate Cutset variables (subset of variables) improves the power of the Chow Liu algorithm because it is only run on the remaining subset of variables given an assignment to the Cutset variables. In the case of streaming data, the data instances become available at regular intervals (or continuously). The data distribution may change if the data-generating process is nonstatic. We need an online structure learning approach in the context of stream mining that uses the above described algorithm to capture concept drift. This can be done by maintaining an ensemble or a latent mixture of Cutset networks, each learned from some appropriate training data. Streaming data can be considered in chunks (sets of data instances). Each training chunk can be used for updating the network weights in the ensemble, according to certain heuristics. The goal is to capture the best possible structure that predicts the most accurate data class for a query.

Scalability issues to address scalability issues and process data in near real time, we could use a distributed framework for streaming data. In real-time systems, data comes continuously. Hadoop is not suitable to handle streams of data. However, Apache Storm, a distributed, real-time, scalable and fault-tolerant system, can guarantee data processing. Another system called Apache Spark [APAC14] can process streams as well but is less mature than Apache Storm. SAMOA [SAMO14], an open-source machine learning application program interface (API) which uses Storm and S4 [S414], lacks stability. In light of the above facts, we have decided to use Apache Storm [STOR14]. Storm supports two basic primitives for stream transformation: spout and bolt. Spout can receive stream data as tuples from several queuing systems (e.g., Kafka and RabbitMQ) and emit those tuples to bolt. In addition, raw data will be moved from online to persistent storage (NoSQL system) using bolt. In bolt for the analytics part, we need to implement our prediction and classification tasks where multiple instances of bolt will be run in parallel.

33.5 SUMMARY AND DIRECTIONS

While the previous chapters have focused on big data analytics techniques and their applications to cyber security as well as discussions of experimental systems, in this chapter we have discussed a planned case study in the healthcare domain that illustrates how the various techniques in big data management, analytics, security, and privacy could be applied. In particular, we have focused on methodologies as well as designs of a framework for the planned case study. Also, we mentioned earlier, while we have used the VA system as an example in the planned study, out system can be used for any related application. Also, the system we have proposed in this chapter could be considered to be an IoT system in the Smart Health domain.

The next step is to carry out the detailed design of the framework and the implementation. The implementation should be carried out in stages and integrated with the VA system. We also need to design appropriate evaluation approaches to ensure that the system meets the requirements. For example, for the *storage and retrieval of multiple types of data*, we need to consider various test workloads in the benchmark: read-mostly workload, read/write combination, write-mostly workload, and read–modify–write workload. These workloads need to be tested in a cluster with a varying number of nodes. For *privacy- and security-aware data management*, we need to evaluate the efficiency of our policy enforcement model under different application scenarios relevant to scientific data mining. For *statistical analysis*, models learned using statistical learning algorithms need to be evaluated against exact models on certain datasets (e.g., http://www.cs.huji.ac.il/project/PASCAL/showNet.php) [SONE07]. For *real-time stream analytics*, evaluation has to be carried out in terms of time, accuracy, receiver operating characteristic curve, and confusion matrix. We need to show that stream data can be processed without any significant delay or overhead.

REFERENCES

[WHO] World Health Organization, http://www.who.int/mediacentre/news/releases/2014/air-pollution/en/.

[ACCU11] Apache Accumulo, https://accumulo.apache.org/.

[AGGA2009] C.C. Aggarwal, "On Classification and Segmentation of MassiveAudio Data Streams," *Knowledge and Information System*, 20, 137–156, 2009.

[AHME10] M.S. Ahmed, L. Khan, M. Rajeswari, "Using Correlation Based Subspace Clustering for Multilabel Text Data Classification," *ICTAI* Arras, France, pp. 296–303, 2010.

[ARRA14] Why an array database. http://www.paradigm4.com/why-an-array-database/.

[BESA75] J. Besag, "Statistical Analysis of Non-Lattice Data, *The Statistician*, 24, 179–195, 1975.

[BIFE009] A. Bifet, G. Holmes, B. Pfahringer, R. Kirkby, R. Gavalda`, "New Ensemble Methods for Evolving Data Streams," In *Proceedings of ACMSIGKDD 15th International Conference on Knowledge Discovery and Data Mining*, Paris, France, pp. 139–148, 2009.

[BORT10] D. Borthakur, "HDFS," http://hadoop.apache.org/common/docs/current/hdfs_design.html, 2010.

[BROE11] G. Van den Broeck, N. Taghipour, W. Meert, J. Davis, L. De Raedt, "Lifted Probabilistic Inference by First-Order Knowledge Compilation," In *Proceedings of the 22nd International Joint Conference on Artificial Intelligence*, Jul. 16–22, Barcelona, Catalonia, Spain, pp. 2178–2185, 2011.

[CARS10] D. Carstoiu, A. Cernian, A. Olteanu, "Hadoop Hbase-0.20.2 Performance Evaluation," In *New Trends in Information Science and Service Science (NISS)*, Gyeongju, South Korea, pp. 84–87, 2010.

[CHAN08] F. Chang, J. Dean, S. Ghemawat, W. Hsieh, D. Wallach, M. Burrows, T. Chandra, A. Fikes, R. Gruber, "Bigtable: A Distributed Storage System for Structured Data. " *ACM Transactions on Computer Systems*, 26 (2), Article No. 4, 2008.

[CHEN08] S. Chen, H. Wang, S. Zhou, P. Yu, "Stop Chasing Trends: Discovering High Order Models in Evolving Data," In *Proceedings of IEEE 24th International Conference on Data Engineering (ICDE)*, Cancun, Mexico, pp. 923–932, 2008.

[CHOW68] C. Chow and C. Liu. "Approximating Discrete Probability Distributions with Dependence Trees." *Information Theory, IEEE Transactions* 14 (3), 462–467, 1968.

[DARW02a] A. Darwiche and P. Marquis, "A Knowledge Compilation Map." *Journal of Artificial Intelligence Research*, 17, 229–264, 2002.

[DARW02b] A. Darwiche, "A Logical Approach to Factoring Belief Networks," In *Proceedings of the 8th International Conference on Principles and Knowledge Representation and Reasoning*, Apr. 22–25, Toulouse, France, pp. 409–420, 2002.

[DARW03] A. Darwiche, "A Differential Approach to Inference in Bayesian Networks," *Journal of the ACM*, 50, 280–305, 2003.

[DEAN04] S. Dean and S. Ghemawat, "MapReduce: Simplified Data Processing on Large Clusters," In *Proceedings of the 6th Symposium on Operating Systems Design and Implementation (OSDI)*, San Francisco, CA, 2004.

[DECA07] G. DeCandia, D. Hastorun, M. Jampani, G. Kakulapati, A. Lakshman, A. Pilchin, S. Sivasubramanian, P. Vosshall, W. Vogels, "Dynamo: Amazon's Highly Available Key-Value Store," In *Proceedings of the 21st ACM Symposium on Operating System Principles (SOSP)*, Stevenson, Washington, DC, 2007.

[DECH07] R. Dechter and R. Mateescu, "AND/OR Search Spaces for Graphical Models," *Artificial Intelligence*, 171 (2–3), 73–106, 2007.

[DOMI09] P. Domingos and D. Lowd, *Markov Logic: An Interface Layer for Artificial Intelligence*, Morgan & Claypool, San Rafael, CA, 2009.

[FAN04] W. Fan, "Systematic Data Selection to Mine Concept-Drifting Data Streams," In *Proceedings of ACM SIGKDD 10th International Conference on Knowledge Discovery and Data Mining*, Seattle, WA, Aug. 22–25, pp. 128–137, 2004.

[GAO07] J. Gao, W. Fan, J. Han, "On Appropriate Assumptions to Mine Data Streams," In *Proceedings of IEEE 7th International Conference on Data Mining (ICDM)*, Omaha, NE, pp. 143–152, 2007.

[GETO07] L. Getoor and B. Taskar, editors, *Introduction to Statistical Relational Learning*, MIT Press, Cambridge, MA, 2007.

[GHEM06] S. Ghemawat, H. Gobioff, S. Leung, "The Google File System," In *Proceedings of 19th ACM Symposium on Operating Systems Principles (SOSP)*, Lake George, NY, 2003.

[GOGA05] V. Gogate and R. Dechter, "Approximate Inference Algorithms for Hybrid Bayesian Networks with Discrete Constraints," In *Proceedings of the 21st Conference on Uncertainty in Artificial Intelligence*, AUAI Press, Edinburgh, Scotland, pp. 209–216, 2005.

[GOGA10] V. Gogate and P. Domingos, "Exploiting Logical Structure in Lifted Probabilistic Inference," In *AAAI 2010 Workshop on Statistical Relational Learning*, Atlanta, GA, 2010.

[GOGA11a] V. Gogate and P. Domingos, "Approximation by Quantization," In *Proceedings of the 27th Conference on Uncertainty in Artificial Intelligence*, Barcelona, Spain, pp. 247–255, 2011.

[GOGA11b] V. Gogate and P. Domingos, "Probabilistic Theorem Proving," In *Proceedings of the 27th Conference on Uncertainty in Artificial Intelligence*, pp. 256–265, 2011.

[GOGA12a] V. Gogate, A. Jha, D. Venugopal, "Advances in Lifted Importance Sampling," In *Communications of the ACM*, 59 (7), 107–115, 2012.

[GOGA12b] V. Gogate and R. Dechter, "Importance Sampling-Based Estimation Over AND/OR Search Spaces for Graphical Models," *Artificial Intelligence*, 184–185, 38–77, 2012.

[GOGA13] V. Gogate and D. Venugopal, *"The Alchemy 2.0 System for Statistical Relational AI,"* Technical Report, Department of Computer Science, The University of Texas at Dallas, Richardson, TX, 2013. https://code.google.com/p/alchemy-2/.

[HASH09] S. Hashemi, Y. Yang, Z. Mirzamomen, M. Kangavari, "Adapted One-Versus-All Decision Trees for Data Stream Classification," *IEEE Transactions on Knowledge and Data Engineering*, 21 (5), 624–637, 2009.

[HIVE14] Apache Hive. http://wiki.apache.org/hadoop/Hive.

[HUSA11a] M.F. Husain, J.P. McGlothlin, L. Khan, B.M. Thuraisingham, "Scalable Complex Query Processing over Large Semantic Web Data Using Cloud," *IEEE CLOUD*, 187–194, 2011.

[HUSA11b] M. Husain, M.M. Masud, J. McGlothlin, L. Khan, "Greedy Based Query Processing for Large RDF Graphs Using Cloud Computing," *IEEE Transactions on Knowledge and Data Engineering*, 23(9), 1312–1327, 2011.

[IHLE09] A. Ihler, A. Frank, P. Smyth, "Particle-Based Variational Inference for Continuous Systems," In *Proceedings of NIPS 2009*, Vancouver, British Columbia, Canada, pp. 826–834, 2009.

[IMPA14] Cloudera Impala. http://en.wikipedia.org/wiki/Cloudera_Impala.

[JHA10] A. Jha, V. Gogate, A. Meliou, D. Suciu, "Lifted Inference from the Other Side: The Tractable Features," In *Proceedings of the 24th Annual Conference on Neural Information Processing Systems*, Vancouver, Canada, pp. 973–981, 2010.

[JING07] L. Jing, M.K. Ng, and J.Z. Huang, "An Entropy Weighting K-Means Algorithm for Subspace Clustering of High-Dimensional Sparse Data," *IEEE Transactions on Knowledge and Data Engineering*, 19 (8), 1026–1041, 2007.

[KOOLL09] D. Koller and N. Friedman, *Probabilistic Graphical Models: Principles and Techniques*, MIT Press, Cambridge, MA, 2009.

[KAUT97] H. Kautz, B. Selman, and Y. Jiang, "A General Stochastic Approach to Solving Problems with Hard and Soft Constraints," *The Satisfiability Problem: Theory and Applications*, D. Gu, J. Du, P. Pardalos, editors, American Mathematical Society, New York, NY, pp. 573–586, 1997.

[KOK08] S. Kok, M. Sumner, M. Richardson, P. Singla, H. Poon, D. Lowd, J. Wang, and P. Domingos, "*The Alchemy System for Statistical Relational AI," Technical Report, Department of Computer Science and Engineering*, University of Washington, Seattle, WA, 2008. http://alchemy.cs.washington.edu.

[LAKS09] A. Lakshman and P. Malik, "Cassandra: Structured Storage System on a P2P Network," In *Proceedings of 28th Annual ACM SIGACT-SIGOPS Symposium on Principles of Distributed Computing (PODC)*, Calgary, Alberta, Canada, 2009.

[LERN02] U. Lerner, Hybrid Bayesian Networks for Reasoning about Complex Systems. *PhD thesis*, Stanford University, 2002.

[LIU01] J.S. Liu, *Monte Carlo Strategies in Scientific Computing*, Springer Publishing Company, Incorporated, Springer-Verlag, New York, 2001.

[MASU08] M. Masud, J. Gao, L. Khan, J. Han, B. Thuraisingham, "A Practical Approach to Classify Evolving Data Streams: Training with Limited Amount of Labeled Data," In *Proceedings of 2008 IEEE International Conference on Data Mining (ICDM 2008)*, Pisa, Italy, pp. 929–934, December, 2008. (Acceptance Rate: 19.9%).

[MASU09a] M.M. Masud, J. Gao, L. Khan, J. Han, B.M. Thuraisingham, "Integrating Novel Class Detection with Classification for Concept-Drifting Data Streams," In *Proceedings of European Conference on Machine Learning and Knowledge Discovery in Databases (ECML PKDD)*, Bled, Slovenia, pp. 79–94, 2009.

[MASU11a] M.M. Masud, J. Gao, L. Khan, J. Han, K.W. Hamlen, N.C. Oza, Facing the Reality of Data Stream Classification: Coping with Scarcity of Labeled Data," *International Journal of Knowledge and Information Systems (KAIS)*, 33 (1), pp. 213–244, 2011, Springer, 2011.

[MASU11b] M.M. Masud, J. Gao, L. Khan, J. Han, and B.M. Thuraisingham, "Classification and Novel Class Detection in Concept-Drifting Data Streams under Time Constraints," *IEEE Transactions on Knowledge and Data Engineering*, 23 (6), 859–874, 2011.

[MCGL10] J.P. McGlothlin and L.R. Khan, *Materializing and Persisting Inferred and Uncertain Knowledge in RDF Datasets. AAAI*, Atlanta, GA, 2010.

[MOSE05] Tim Moses, "eXtensible Access Control Markup Language (XACML) Version 2.0 http://docs.oasis-open.org/xacml/2.0/access_control-xacml-2.0-core-spec-os.pdf, 2005.

[OWL12] OWL, Web Ontology Language, http://www.w3.org/TR/owl2-quick-reference/.

[PATT13] E. Pattuk, M. Kantarcioglu, V. Khadilkar, H. Ulusoy, S. Mehrotra, "Bigsecret: A Secure Data Management Framework for Key-Value Stores," In *IEEE CLOUD*, Santa Clara, CA, 2013.

[PIG14] Apache Pig. https://cwiki.apache.org/confluence/display/PIG/Index.

[POOL03] D. Poole, "First-Order Probabilistic Inference," In *Proceedings of the 18th International Joint Conference on Artificial Intelligence*, Morgan Kaufmann, Acapulco, Mexico, pp. 985–991, 2003.

[POON07] H. Poon and P. Domingos, "Joint Inference in Information Extraction," In *Proceedings of the 22nd National Conference on Artificial Intelligence*, AAAI Press, Vancouver, Canada, pp. 913–918, 2007.

[RACH12] J. Rachapalli, M. Kantarcioglu, B. Thuraisingham, "Tag-Based Information Flow Analysis for Document Classification in Provenance," In *USENIX TAPP Workshop*, Boston, MA, 2012.

[RAHM14] T. Rahman and P. Kothalkar, V. Gogate, Cutset Networks: A Simple, Tractable, and Scalable Approach for Improving the Accuracy of Chow-Liu Trees," In *Proceedings of the 31st International Conference on Machine Learning*, Beijing, China, 2014. JMLR.

[RICH06] M. Richardson and P. Domingos, "Markov Logic Networks," *Machine Learning*, 62, 107–136, 2006.

[ROY10] I. Roy, S.T.V. Setty, A. Kilzer, V. Shmatikov, E. Witchel, "Airavat: Security and Privacy for Mapreduce," In *USENIX*, San Jose, CA, pp. 20–20, 2010.

[S414] S4, Distributed Stream Processing Platform, http://incubator.apache.org/s4/.

[SAMO14] Samoa. [Online]. Available: https://github.com/yahoo/samoa.

[SARK14] S. Sarkhel, V. Venugopal, P. Singla, V. Gogate, "Lifted MAP Inference for Markov Logic Networks," In *Proceedings of the 17th International Conference on Artificial Intelligence and Statistics*, Reykjavik, Iceland, 2014.

[SCID14] SciDB chunking and scalability. http://scidb.org/HTMLmanual/13.3/scidb_ug/ch01s02s01.html.

[SELI14] Selinux. http://selinuxproject.org/. Accessed: 2014-05-11.

[SENT14b] Apache sentry. https://www.cloudera.com/products/open-source/apache-hadoop/apache-sentry.html.

[SING06] P. Singla and P. Domingos, "Memory-Efficient Inference in Relational Domains," In *Proceedings of the 21st National Conference on Artificial Intelligence*, AAAI Press, Boston, MA, 2006. This volume.

[SONE07] S. Paolo, M. Pacurar, S. Dhir, A. Kertész-Farkas, A. Kocsor, Z. Gáspári, J.A.M. Leunissen, S. Pongor, "A Protein Classification Benchmark Collection for Machine Learning," *Nucleic Acids Research*, 35, (suppl 1), D232–D236, 2007.

[SPAR14] Apache spark. [Online]. Available: http://spark.apache.org/.

[SPIN08] E.J. Spinosa, A.P. de Leon, F. de Carvalho, J. Gama, "Cluster-Based Novel Concept Detection in Data Streams Applied to Intrusion Detection in Computer Networks," In *Proceedings of ACM Symposium on Applied Computing (SAC)*, Fortaleza, Ceara, Brazil, pp. 976–980, 2008.

[STON11] M. Stonebraker, P. Brown, A. Poliakov, S. Raman, "The Architecture of SciDB," In *Proceedings of the 23rd International Conference on Scientific and Statistical Database Management (SSDBM'11)*, J.B. Cushing, J. French, S. Bowers editos, Springer-Verlag, Berlin, pp. 1–16, 2011.

[STOR14] Storm-distributed and fault-tolerant realtime computation. [Online]. Available: http://storm.incubator.apache.org/.

[THUR10] B. Thuraisingham, V. Khadilkar, A. Gupta, M. Kantarcioglu, L. Khan, "Secure Data Storage and Retrieval in the Cloud," Collaborate Comm, 2010.

[ULUS14] H. Ulusoy, M. Kantarcioglu, K. Hamlen, E. Pattuk, "Vigiles: Fine-Grained Access Control for Mapreduce Systems," In *IEEE BIGDATA*, Anchorage, AK, 2014.

[VENU12] D. Venugopal and V. Gogate, "On Lifting the Gibbs Sampling Algorithm," In *Proceedings of the 26th Annual Conference on Neural Information Processing Systems*, Lake Tahoe, NV, pp. 1664–1672, 2012.

[WANG03] H. Wang, W. Fan, P.S. Yu, J. Han, "Mining Concept-Drifting Data Streams Using Ensemble Classifiers," In *Proceedings of ACM SIGKDD 9th International Conference on Knowledge Discovery and Data Mining*, Washington, DC, pp. 226–235, 2003.

[WANG07] P. Wang, H. Wang, X. Wu, W. Wang, B. Shi, "A Low-Granularity Classifier for Data Streams with Concept Drifts and Biased Class Distribution," *IEEE Transactions on Knowledge and Data Engineering*, 19 (9), 1202–1213, 2007.

[WANG08a] C. Wang, S. Joshi, R. Khardon, "First Order Decision Diagrams for Relational MDPs," *Journal of Artificial Intelligence Research*, 31, 431–472, 2008.

[WANG08b] J. Wang and P. Domingos, "Hybrid Markov Logic Networks," In *Proceedings of the 23rd AAAI Conference on Artificial Intelligence*, Jul. 13–17, AAAI Press, Chicago, IL, pp. 1106–1111, 2008.

[WEI09] W. Wei, J. Du, T. Yu, and X. Gu, "Securemr: A Service Integrity Assurance Framework for Mapreduce," In *ACSAC. IEEE*, 2009, pp. 73–82.

[WENE06] B. Wenerstrom and C. Giraud-Carrier, "Temporal Data Mining in Dynamic Feature Spaces," In *Proceedings of 6th International Conference on Data Mining (ICDM)*, Hong Kong, pp. 1141–1145, 2006.

[YANG05] Y. Yang, X. Wu, X. Zhu, "Combining Proactive and Reactive Predictions for Data Streams," In *Proceedings of ACM SIGKDD 11th International Conference on Knowledge Discovery in Data Mining*, Chicago, IL, pp. 710–715, 2005.

[ZAHA12] M. Zaharia, M. Chowdhury, T. Das, A. Dave, J. Ma, M. McCauley, M.J. Franklin, S. Shenker, I. Stoica, "Resilient Distributed Datasets: A Fault-Tolerant Abstraction for In-Memory Cluster Computing," In *Proceedings of the 9th USENIX Conference on Networked Systems Design and Implementation (NSDI'12)*, USENIX Association, Berkeley, CA, pp. 2–2, 2012.

34 Toward an Experimental Infrastructure and Education Program for BDMA and BDSP

34.1 INTRODUCTION

While big data management and analytics (BDMA) is evolving into a field called *data science* with significant progress over the past 5 years with various courses being taught at universities, there is still a lot to be done. We find that many of the courses are more theoretical in nature and are not integrated with real-world applications. Furthermore, big data security and privacy (BDSP) is becoming a critical need and there is very little being done not only on research, but also on education programs and infrastructures for BDSP. For example, BDMA techniques on personal data could violate individual privacy. With the recent emergence of the *quantified self* (QS) movement, personal data collected by wearable devices and smartphone apps is being analyzed to guide users in improving their health or personal life habits. This data is also being shared with other service providers (e.g., retailers) using cloud-based services, offering potential benefits to users (e.g., information about health products). But such data collection and sharing are often being carried out without the users' knowledge, bringing grave danger that the personal data may be used for improper purposes. Privacy violations could easily get out of control if data collectors could aggregate financial and health-related data with tweets, Facebook activity, and purchase patterns. While some of our research is focusing on privacy protection in QS applications and controlling access to the data, education and infrastructure programs in BDSP are yet to be developed.

To address the limitations of BDMA and BDSP experimental education and infrastructure programs, we are proposing to design such programs at The University of Texas at Dallas and the purpose of this chapter is to share our plans. Our main objectives are the following: (1) to train highly qualified students to become expert professionals in big data management and analytics and data science. That is, we will be developing a course on big data management and analytics integrated with real-world applications as a capstone course. (ii) Leverage our investments in BDSP research, BDMA research and education, and cyber security education to develop a laboratory to carry out hands-on exercises for relevant courses as well as a capstone course in BDSP, including extensive experimental student projects to support the education.

To address the objectives, we are assembling an interdisciplinary team with expertise in big data management and mining, machine learning, atmospheric science, geospatial data management, and data security and privacy to develop the programs. Essentially, our team consists of computer and information scientists who will develop the fundamental aspects of the courses together with application specialists (e.g., atmospheric scientists) who will develop the experimental aspects of the courses as well as provide the data for the students to carry out experiments on. Specifically, we will be utilizing the planned case study discussed in Chapter 32 to design our education and experimental programs.

This chapter is organized in the following way. In Section 34.2, we will discuss some of our relevant current research and infrastructure development activities in BDMA and BDSP. Our new programs will be being built utilizing these efforts. In Section 34.3, we describe our plan for designing a program in BDMA. In Section 34.4, we describe our plan for designing a program in BDSP. This chapter is summarized in Section 34.5. Figure 34.1 illustrates our plan for developing a curriculum on integrated data science and cyber security.

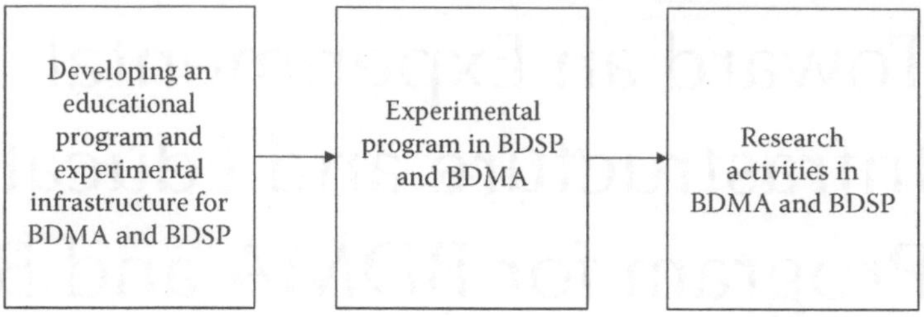

FIGURE 34.1 Developing an educational program and experimental infrastructure for big data management and analytics and big data security and privacy.

34.2 CURRENT RESEARCH AND INFRASTRUCTURE ACTIVITIES IN BDMA AND BDSP

Our experimental education program will focus mainly on developing a capacity surrounding our research on BDMA and BDSP. The topics include secure data provenance, cyber physical systems security, data analytics for insider threat detection, secure cloud, secure cyber-physical systems, and trusted execution environments (TEE). Our relevant research results will be transferred to the new infrastructures that we are designing to be discussed in this chapter. A discussion of some of our research and infrastructure activities is provided below.

34.2.1 Big Data Analytics for Insider Threat Detection

We have designed tools to determine insider threat over evolving stream activities. In particular, evidence of malicious insider activity is often buried within large data streams, such as system logs accumulated over months or years. Ensemble-based stream mining leverages multiple classification models to achieve highly accurate anomaly detection in such streams, even when the stream is unbounded, evolving, and unlabeled. This makes the approach effective for identifying insiders who attempt to conceal their activities by varying their behaviors over time. This project applies ensemble-based stream mining, supervised and unsupervised learning, and graph-based anomaly detection to the problem of insider threat detection. It demonstrates that the ensemble-based approach is significantly more effective than traditional single-model methods, supervised learning outperforms unsupervised learning, and increasing the cost of false negatives correlates to higher accuracy.

34.2.2 Secure Data Provenance

We are conducting research in collaboration with other universities on secure provenance data. In particular, we have developed a provenance management system for cyber infrastructure that includes different types of hosts, devices, and data management systems. The proof-of-concept system, referred to as Cyber-Provenance Infrastructure for Sensor-based Data-Intensive Research (CY-DIR), supports scientists throughout the lifecycle of their sensor-based data collection processes, including the continuous monitoring of sensors to ensure that provenance is collected and recorded, and the traceable use and processing of the data across different data management systems. CY-DIR provides researchers with provenance and metadata about data being collected by sensors. Provenance security will be assured by the use of efficient encryption techniques for use in sensors, secure logging techniques, and secure processors.

34.2.3 Secure Cloud Computing

We have conducted research in designing and developing a cloud. In particular, the team designed a layered framework that includes the virtualization layer, the storage layer, the data layer, and the application layer. Research was carried out on encrypted data storage in the cloud as well as on secure cloud query processing. The secure cloud was demonstrated with assured information sharing as an application.

34.2.4 Binary Code Analysis

We are working on a number of efforts on binary code analysis. For example, the team is developing techniques for extracting address-independent data reference expressions for pointers through dynamic binary analysis. This novel pointer reference expression encodes how a pointer is accessed through the combination of a base address (usually a global variable) with certain offset and further pointer dereferences. The techniques have been applied to OS kernels, and the experimental results with a number of real-world kernel malware show that we can correctly identify the hijacked kernel function pointers by locating them using the extracted pointer reference expressions when only given a memory snapshot.

34.2.5 Cyber-Physical Systems Security

We are working on an effort on tackling the security and privacy of cyber-physical systems (CPS) by integrating the theory and best practices from the information security community as well as practical approaches from the control theory community. The first part of the project focuses on security and protection of cyber-physical critical infrastructures such as the power grid, water distribution networks, and transportation networks against computer attacks in order to prevent disruptions that may cause loss of service, infrastructure damage, or even loss of life. The second part of the project focuses on privacy of CPS and proposes new algorithms to deal with the unprecedented levels of data collection granularity of physical human activity.

34.2.6 Trusted Execution Environment

We are working on an effort that investigates how to enable application developers to securely use the SGX instructions, with an open source software support including a toolchain, programming abstractions (e.g., library), and operating system support (e.g., kernel modules). In addition, this research systematically explores the systems and software defenses necessary to secure the SGX programs from the enclave itself and defeat the malicious use of SGX from the underlying OS.

34.2.7 Infrastructure Development

We have developed hardware, software and data infrastructures for our students to carry out experimental research. These include secure cloud infrastructures, mobile computing infrastructures as well as social media infrastructures. The data collected includes both geospatial data, social media data, as well as malware data. Some of these infrastructures are discussed in our previous books ([THUR14], [THUR16]).

34.3 EDUCATION AND INFRASTRUCTURE PROGRAM IN BDMA

34.3.1 Curriculum Development

We introduced our data science track in the Computer Science department for graduate students in Fall 2013 and it is the most popular track with numerous students enrolled in the program. The following courses are required for this track: statistical methods for data sciences; big data management and analytics; design and analysis of computer algorithms; and machine learning. In addition, students are required to take one of additional course such as natural language processing

(NLP) or database design. The course we are designing integrates out BDMA course with real-world applications.

Our current BDMA course focuses on data mining and machine learning algorithms for analyzing very large amounts of data. MapReduce and NoSQL system are used as tools/standards for creating parallel algorithms that can process very large amounts of data. It covers basics of Hadoop, MapReduce, NoSQL systems (e.g., key–value stores, column-oriented data stores), Cassandra, Pig, Hive, MongoDB, Hbase, BigTable, SPARK, Storm, large-scale supervised machine learning, data streams, clustering, and applications including recommendation systems. The following reference books are used to augment the material presented in lectures:

- Jimmy Lin and Chris Dyer, *Data-Intensive Text Processing with MapReduce*, Morgan & Claypool Publishers, 2010. http://lintool.github.com/MapReduceAlgorithms/
- Anand Rajaraman and Jeff Ullman, *Mining of Massive Datasets*, Cambridge Press, http://infolab.stanford.edu/~ullman/mmds/book.pdf
- Chuck Lam, *Hadoop in Action*, December, 2010|336 pages ISBN: 9781935182191.
- Spark: http://spark.apache.org/docs/latest/

Our capstone course to be designed will be titled Big Data and Machine Learning for Scientific Discovery. It will integrate several of the topics in the BDMA course as well as our course in machine learning as well as the theatrical concepts with experimental work using real-world applications such as Environmental and Remote Sensing Applications. The course will focus on the practical application of a variety of supervised and unsupervised machine learning approaches that can be used for nonlinear multivariate systems including neural networks, deep neural networks, support vector machines, random forests, and Gaussian processes. A variety of supervised and unsupervised classifiers such as self-organizing maps will be used. Many of these datasets are non-Gaussian so mutual information will be introduced. Using remote sensing from a wide variety of platforms, from satellites to aerial vehicles coupled with machine learning, multiple massive big datasets can be of great use for a wide variety of scientific, societal, and business applications. Remote sensing can provide invaluable tools for both improved understanding and making data-driven decisions and policies. This course will give an introduction to a wide range of big data applications in remote sensing of land, ocean, and atmosphere and their practical applications of major societal importance such as environmental health, drought and water issues, and fire. The experimental projects will include the processing of multiple massive datasets and machine learning. The skills developed from the big data curriculum may be used in a scenario where students can learn the practical techniques of designing algorithms using large datasets. For example, after learning NoSQL (MapReduce, Pig, Hive, SPARK) from the course, students can apply these techniques/tools to query from large datasets in a scalable manner using commodity hardware. In addition to the graduate education in BDMA, we are also planning on introducing senior design projects in collaboration with local corporations.

The Capstone BDMA course will consist of two modules. The data management part introduces various techniques and data structures to handle large data where traditional models or data structures do not efficiently scale to address the problems involving such voluminous data. The data analytics module introduces various algorithms which are widely used for analyzing the information in the large datasets. Supervised/unsupervised learning is a collection of algorithms used for classification, clustering, and pattern recognition. The module introduces generic problems, which can be ubiquitously applied to specific cases when working on a dataset in the relevant field when learning a model using the data values. For example, classification can be used for real-time anomaly detection where the anomalous data is to be classified from nonanomalous data either assuming class labels or no class labels. Relational learning is a general term used for data mining algorithms dealing with data and feature relationships. A real-world dataset may have multiple features and data items that may have specific relationships between them [CHAN14]. For example, an atmospheric dataset may have features of temperature, pressure, type of cloud, moisture content, and so on. In order to predict if a set of data indicates rain, the relationship between these features needs to be considered for a better prediction model. These relationships may be causal or noncausal in nature. A query (e.g., will it rain in the next few days?) would be better evaluated from a model that best represents the features and evidence given. Lastly, stream mining is a collection of algorithms used for handling continuously occurring data. Data streams are continuous flows of data. Examples of data streams include network traffic, sensor data, call center records, and so on. Data streams demonstrate several unique properties that together conform to the characteristics of big data (i.e., volume, velocity, variety, and veracity) and add challenges to data stream mining. Most existing data stream classification techniques ignore one important aspect of stream data: arrival of a novel class. We have addressed this issue and proposed a data stream classification technique that integrates a novel class detection mechanism into traditional classifiers, enabling automatic detection of novel classes before the true labels of the novel class instances arrive ([MASU09], [MASU11a], [MASU11b], [HAQU14], [HAQU15]). Overall, methodologies to perform such analytics from the data would be useful for students to understand the practical implications of using large datasets while designing an algorithm.

34.3.2 Experimental Program

Figure 34.2 shows an example of case studies related to the planned Capstone BDMA course. The data management part of the course includes learning about NoSQL, Hadoop, Spark, Storm, and so on. These technologies will be used while studying cases in

1. GDELT (1 and 2) Political event data which use NoSQL and Hadoop MapReduce, Spark concepts in a supervised/semisupervised settings.
2. Timely Health Indicator (3 and 5) with data management techniques using Spark while performing supervised/semisupervised learning on a stream data.
3. Scalable Inference on Graphical Models (4 and 7) studies Relational Learning using concepts of Spark with Alchemy 2.0.

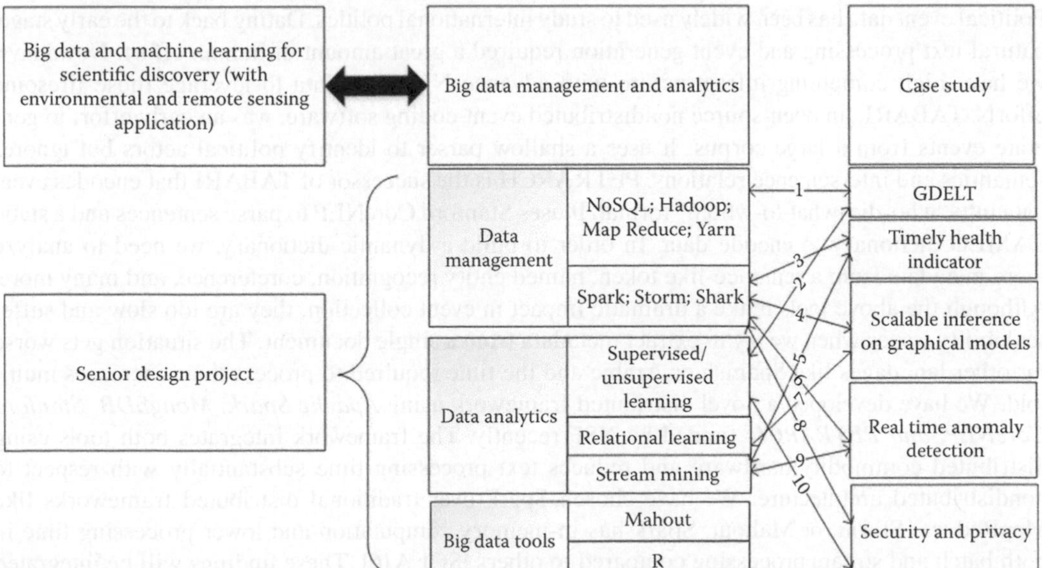

FIGURE 34.2 Association between big data management and case studies.

4. Real-Time Anomaly detection (6 and 9) using Spark to manage data while performing supervised stream mining.
5. Security and Privacy (8 and 10) issues in implementing supervised or unsupervised learning or in implementing big data management systems such as Spark or NoSQL.

These case studies, part of our research related to Big Data, will be discussed in more detail later in this Chapter. Hence, they will be integrated with the planned education module. Further, these would be supported with the knowledge in Tools such as Mahout, R, and so on depending on the application and working environment. The planned case studies discussed in Chapter 33 will also be utilized for the experimental programs.

We discuss a sample of our research projects that have contributed a great deal to our Big Data education. These projects can be integrated into the case studies of the capstone course.

34.3.2.1 Geospatial Data Processing on GDELT

Collecting observations from all international news coverage and using TABARI software to code events, the Global Database of Event, Language, and Tone (GDELT) is the only global political georeferenced event dataset with 250+million observations covering all countries in the world from January 1, 1979 to the present with daily updates. The purpose of this widely used dataset is to help understand and uncover spatial, temporal and perceptual trends of the social and international system. To query such big geospatial data, traditional relational databases can no longer be used and the need for parallel distributed solutions has become a necessity [ALNA14].

The MapReduce paradigm has proved to be a scalable platform to process and analyze big data in the cloud. Hadoop as an implementation of MapReduce is an open source application that has been widely used and accepted in academia and industry. However, when dealing with spatial data, Hadoop is not equipped well and falls short as it does not perform efficiently in terms of running time. SpatialHadoop is an extension of Hadoop with the support of spatial data. We have developed the *geographic information system querying framework* to process massive spatial data ([ALNA14], [ALNA16]).

34.3.2.2 Coding for Political Event Data

Political event data has been widely used to study international politics. Dating back to the early stage, natural text processing and event generation required a great amount of human effort. Nowadays, we have high computing infrastructure with advance NLP metadata to leverage those tiresome efforts. TABARI, an open-source nondistributed event-coding software, was an early effort to generate events from a large corpus. It uses a shallow parser to identify political actors but ignores semantics and intersentence relations. PETRARCH is the successor of TABARI that encodes event data into "who-did-what-to-whom" format. It uses Stanford CoreNLP to parse sentences and a static CAMEO dictionary to encode data. In order to build a dynamic dictionary, we need to analyze more metadata from a sentence-like token, named entity recognition, coreference, and many more. Although the above tools make a dramatic impact in event collection, they are too slow and suffer scalability issues when we try to extract metadata from a single document. The situation gets worse for other languages like Spanish or Arabic and the time required to process them increases multifold. We have developed a novel distributed framework using *Apache Spark, MongoDB, Stanford CoreNLP, and PETRARCH* funded by NSF recently. The framework integrates both tools using distributed commodity hardware and reduces text processing time substantially with respect to nondistributed architecture. We have chosen Spark over traditional distributed frameworks like MapReduce, Storm, or Mahout. Spark has in-memory computation and lower processing time in both batch and stream processing compared to others [SOLA16]. These findings will be integrated as a case study in our planned capstone course. The GDELT and political event dataset will be given to students to query using our customized framework.

34.3.2.3 Timely Health Indicator

The atmospheric scientists in our team are leading projects on timely health indicators and collaborate with the Veterans Administration. As the use and combination of multiple big datasets becomes ubiquitous and the Internet of Things becomes a reality, we increasingly need to deal with large volumes of heterogeneous datasets. These datasets may be discrete data points, images, or gridded datasets (e.g., meteorological models or satellite data). They may also be observations, demographic or social data, or business transactions. They may also be publicly available or require varying levels of access control. Further, they may need to be streamed in real time with low latency, have a relaxed latency requirement, and be structured or unstructured. In Chapter 34, we discussed a practical case study that includes not only BDMA-related topics but also data security and privacy, machine learning, and real-time anomaly detection. This case study will be used to devise various experiments for the students.

34.4 SECURITY AND PRIVACY FOR BIG DATA

34.4.1 Our Approach

Organizations own and generate humongous amounts of data that can be analyzed for understanding the customers as well as for providing various services. Computations over big data may require massive computational resources and while an organization may have its own computational resources, it may use a third-party service to outsource some computations to be cost-effective. In these cases, data may be transferred to a third-party service. The issue of trustworthiness in computation and data security arises when these data contain sensitive information. For example, consider weather data collected by the *special operations weather specialists* (SOWT) for providing intelligence on various locations to say Air Force organizations. This dataset may have information of sensitive locations that may be necessary to use in an analytical solution. Similarly, intelligence data collected from airborne systems such as drones may have sensitive information of national importance. Analytics over these data such as simulation of wartime strategies based on weather conditions and object identification in images captured by drones may require large computational resources. When a third-party server is used for computation, data inherently becomes available in untrusted environments, that is, either observed by a man-in-the-middle during data transmission or insider threat from adversaries at the third-party location where computation is performed. In these cases, data owners may need to protect their data and require cryptographic guarantees about data security and integrity of computational output from these third-party services.

Recent advancements in embedded hardware technology to support TEE (e.g., TPM [PERE06], ARM Trust Zone [SANT14], AMD SVM [DOOR06]), and Intel SGX ([ANAT13], [HOEK13], [MCKE13]) have generated exciting opportunities for research in the field of cloud computing, trusted data analytics and applied cryptography. By protecting code and data within a secure region of computation, a cloud service can ensure confidentiality and integrity of data and computations. A few studies have shown the use of TEE for data analytics ([OHIR16], [RANE15]). Despite this progress, significant challenges remain in leveraging TEE for a multitude of analytical solutions including high-dimensional data, interactive techniques, data search and retrieval, and so on. Each of these does not inherently satisfy properties of TEE architectures and has different data flows.

To establish a scientific foundation for data analytical models to leverage TEEs, evaluate their limitations, explore performance overhead, and analyze security implications such as side channels, we plan to develop a framework to support legacy systems and establish benchmark schemes for trustworthy analytics. To facilitate projects in the capstone course, we will leverage this framework. We will also enhance some of our current courses in cybersecurity (CyS) (e.g., data and applications security and privacy, secure infrastructures, secure cloud computing and BDMA) by incorporating modules in BDSP. Our laboratory, a framework to carry out hands-on activities relevant to BDSP, will be used by our students, including our SFS students, for their course projects as well as anybody in the world via open source release. Our lab together with the lab manuals as well as our courses will be made available to the researchers and educators in CyS. Our research in BDSP as well as our education program in CyS will be integrated to build a strong capacity for BDSP education program. Essentially, we aim to address the security challenges, by providing a platform accessible to Big Data users (e.g., Iota users), developers, and researchers to provide better insights for further research in BDSP.

34.4.2 Curriculum Development

34.4.2.1 Extensions to Existing Courses

In order to integrate the proposed lab with these courses, we will design various modules to be integrated with its existing projects. An overview is provided in Figure 34.3. These modules will be derived from our existing research (detailed in Section 34.3) and/or our proposed virtual lab development (detailed in Section 34.4.1). For example, the modules, "Access Control for Secure Storage and Retrieval" may be integrated with our graduate course, "Data and Applications Security and Privacy." The "Performance Overhead of Trusted Execution Environments" module will be integrated into the course "System Security and Binary Code Analysis." The "Feature Extraction & (Un) Supervised Learning," "Distributed Trusted Execution Environments," and "Secure Encrypted Stream Analytics" modules will be integrated into the "Big Data Management and Analytics" course. Below we will describe a sample of our cyber security courses that are being enhanced with BDSP models.

1. *Data and Applications Security*: This course provides a comprehensive overview of database security, confidentiality, privacy and trust management, data security and privacy, data mining for security applications, secure social media, secure cloud computing, and web security. In addition to term papers, students also carry out a programming project that addresses any of the topics covered in class. Typical student projects have included data mining tools for malware detection as well as access control tools for social media systems. We have introduced a course module in access control for secure storage and retrieval of Big Data.

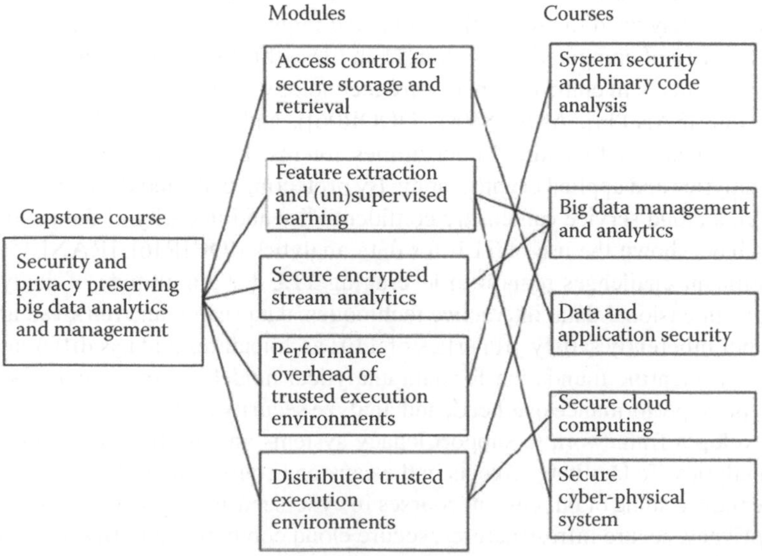

FIGURE 34.3 Integration of study modules with existing courses.

2. *System Security and Binary Code Analysis*: The goal of this course is to explain the low-level system details from compiler, linker, loader, to OS kernel and computer architectures; examine the weakest link in each system component, explore the left bits and bytes after all these transformations; and study the state-of-the-art offenses and defenses. The learning outcome is students shall be able to understand how an attack is launched (e.g., how an exploit is created) and how to do the defense (e.g., developing OS patches, analyzing the binary code, and detecting intrusions). We will introduce additional units on overhead of TEE for secure hardware extension.
3. *Big Data Analytics and Management*: As stated earlier, our current BDMA course focuses on data mining and machine learning algorithms for analyzing very large amounts of data or big data. MapReduce and NoSQL system are used as tools/standards for creating parallel algorithms that can process very large amounts of data. It covers the basics of Hadoop, MapReduce, NoSQL systems (Cassandra, Pig, Hive, MongoDB, Hbase, BigTable, HBASE, Spark), Storm, Large-scale supervised machine learning, data streams, clustering, and applications including recommendation systems, web, and security. This course focuses on large-scale feature extraction and learning to leverage the big data platform to perform parallel and distributed analysis. In addition, the course focuses on a stream analytics framework using secure hardware extension. We have also introduced a module on BDSP for this course.
4. *Secure Cloud Computing*: This course introduces the concepts of secure web services and service-oriented architecture and then describes in detail the various layers of a secure cloud. These include secure hypervisors, secure data storage, secure cloud query processing, and cloud forensics. The use of the cloud for computing intensive tasks such as malware detection is also discussed. We have introduced a module BDSP and will introduce additional modules on the set-up of TEE for secure hardware extension.
5. *Secure Cyber-Physical Systems and Critical Infrastructures*: This course introduces the security of cyber-physical systems from a multidisciplinary point of view, from computer science security research (network security and software security) to public policy (e.g., the Executive Order 13636), risk assessment, business drivers, and control-theoretic methods to reduce the cyber risk to cyber-physical critical infrastructures. We will introduce a module on feature extraction and (un/semi) supervised learning to find anomalies in cyber-physical systems.

34.4.2.2 New Capstone Course on BDSP

Our capstone course to be designed will be motivated by (a) research and development in secure storage and retrieval of big data, (b) research and development of stream data analytics over evolving continuous stream data, and (c) the research and experimentation on performance overhead of TEEs. The modules created for all our cyber security courses will be aggregated and taught as part of the capstone course in addition to some new topics. The topics covered will include (i) access control for secure storage and retrieval, (ii) feature extraction and (un) supervised learning for big data, (iii) stream mining over continuous evolving streams, (iv) secure encrypted stream analytics, and (v) performance overhead of TEE. We will also discuss the various TEE system prototypes, products, and standards. Students will carry out the programming projects based on the lab resources to conduct secure and privacy-preserving big data analytics and management research.

34.4.3 Experimental Program

34.4.3.1 Laboratory SetUp

The lab to be developed would be accessible to all of students who will enroll into relevant and capstone courses. First, we will leverage our current single Intel SGX-enabled machine and later will construct a cluster for the lab experiment. We use an Intel SGX-enabled Linux system with i7-6700

CPU (Skylake) and 64-GB RAM operating at 3.40 GHz with 8 cores, running Ubuntu 14.04. We have installed the latest Intel SGX SDK and SGX driver [SGXSDK]. While running SGX applications, the trusted hardware establishes an enclave by protecting isolated memory regions within the existing address space, called processor reserved memory (PRM), against other nonenclave memory accesses including kernel, hypervisor, and other privileged code.

Number of enclaves on single machine—A special region inside PRM called the Enclave Page Cache (EPC) stores sensitive code and data as encrypted 4 kB pages. EPC size can be configured inside BIOS setting to a maximum size of 128 MB. Hence, the number of enclaves that can be run efficiently inside a single machine is limited by EPC size.

The overhead of SGX application increases with the increase in number of enclaves run on a single machine. Typically, 5–8 enclaves can be run simultaneously on a single machine without producing significant performance overhead. SGX applications also show memory access overhead because every data read or write needs to be present inside the EPC cache. Thus, running heavy computations on large data inside the enclave can produce performance overhead. We will maintain secure enclave cluster. There are various challenges in developing such an enclave cluster. Building SGX-enabled cluster requires: (a) using SGX-enabled machine at each node and (b) securing communication between enclaves running on same machine or different machine. SGX-enabled machine protects local code and data running on a single machine. For secure communication between enclaves running on same or different machines, enclaves can first authenticate each other and establish a Diffie Hellman cryptography-based secure communication channel.

34.4.3.2 Programming Projects to Support the Lab

We will devise student programming projects to support the lab. We provide an overview of three sample projects and discuss samples of these projects. In particular, we first describe a secure data storage and retrieval mechanism for big data. Second, we describe a mechanism to estimate overhead of systematic performance study of TEE. Finally, we describe secure encrypted stream data processing using secure hardware extension.

34.4.3.2.1 Project 1: Secure Data Storage and Retrieval in the Cloud

With the advent of the World Wide Web and the emergence of e-commerce applications and social networks, organizations across the world generate a large amount of data daily. This data would be more useful to cooperating organizations if they were able to share their data. Two major obstacles to this process of data sharing are providing a common storage space and secure access to the shared data. We have addressed these issues by combining cloud computing technologies such as Hive and Hadoop with XACML policy-based security mechanisms that provide fine-grained access to resources [KHAD12]. We have further presented a web-based application that uses this combination and allows collaborating organizations to securely store and retrieve large amounts of data.

34.4.3.2.2 Project 2: Systematic Performance Study of TEE

Building trustworthy computing systems to execute trusted applications has been a grand challenge. This is simply because of the large attack surface an application could face from hardware, system management mode (SMM), BIOS, hypervisor (or virtual machine manager [VMM]), operating systems, libraries, and the application code itself. This problem becomes even worse in outsourced cloud computing since everything can be untrusted except the application code itself. While a large amount of effort has been focusing on using various layer-below security checks from hardware [MCCU07] (SMM [WANG10], BIOS [SUN12], or hypervisor ([CHEN08], [LI14], [MCCU10], [SESH07], [STEINBERG10], [ZHANG11]) to mitigate this problem, increasingly there is a growing interest of using hardware technologies (e.g., TPM [PERE06], ARM Trust Zone [SANT14], and AMD SVM [DOOR06]) to build TEE, and the most recent advancement in this direction is Intel SGX ([ANAT13], [HOEK13], [MCKE13]) which is able to reduce the trusted computing base to the smallest possible footprint, namely, just the hardware and the application code itself without trusting the hypervisor, operating systems, or the surrounding libraries.

At a high level, SGX allows an application or part of an application to run inside a secure enclave, an isolated execution environment in which code and data can execute without the fear of inspection and modification. SGX hardware, as a part of the CPU, protects the enclave against malicious software, including the operating systems, device drivers, hypervisor, or even low-level firmware code (e.g., SMM) from compromising its integrity and confidentiality. Also, physical attacks such as memory bus snooping, memory tampering, and cold boot attacks [HALD09] all will fail since the enclave secret will be only visible inside the CPUs. Coupled with remote attestation, SGX allows developers to build a root of trust even in an untrusted environment. Therefore, SGX provides an ideal platform to protect the secrets of an application in the enclave even when an attacker has full control of the entire system.

SGX is likely to make outsourced computing in data centers and the cloud practical. However, there is no study to precisely quantify the overhead of Intel SGX, partly because SGX requires programmers to use these instructions to develop the application or system software and currently there is no publicly available SGX test bed or benchmarks. To answer the question of how much overhead SGX could bring to an application, we have systematically measured the overhead of SGX programs using both macro-benchmarks and micro-benchmarks.

34.4.3.2.3 Project 3: Secure Encrypted Stream Data Processing Using Modern Secure Hardware Extensions

Data analysis involving sensitive encrypted data has been an enduring challenge in protecting data privacy and preventing misuse of information by an external adversary. While advancements in encrypted data processing have encouraged many data analytics applications, results from such mechanisms usually do not scale to very large datasets. Recent advances in trusted processor technology, such as Intel SGX, have rejuvenated the efforts of performing data analytics on sensitive encrypted data where data security and trustworthiness of computations are ensured by the hardware ([SCHU15], [DINH15] [GUPT16] [KIM15]). However, studies have shown that a powerful adversary may still be able to infer private information from side channels such as memory access, cache access, CPU usage, and other timing channels, thereby threatening data and user privacy. Though studies have proposed techniques to hide such information leaks using carefully designed data-independent access paths, these have only been shown to be applicable to traditional data analytics problems that assume a stationary environment, leaving data analytics in a nonstationary environment (e.g., data stream analytics) [MASU11c] as an open problem.

In particular, for stationary environments, studies have proposed multiple techniques to ensure data privacy and improve trustworthiness of computational results. Computations employing fully homomorphic encryption schemes [KOCH14] can be used to address these issues. In practice, however, they are known to be computationally inefficient for a wide range of operations [NAEH11]. This has encouraged developers to seek hardware solutions such as Intel SGX [ANAT13] which provides a secure region of computation to ensure data confidentiality and integrity. Applications using Intel SGX have focused on an untrusted cloud computing environment. For example, a popular big data analytics tool called Hadoop [SHVA10] is deployed over a SGX-enabled cloud service [DINH14]. While the above design can be directly applied to data streams as well, Hadoop is shown to be inefficient for data stream processing. The most relevant work to our planned efforts is the recently published data-oblivious methods for multiple machine learning algorithms [OHIR16]. This study inspired from [RANE15] details certain data-oblivious primitives to be used in a set of machine learning algorithms. However, they focused on stationary learning systems.

Data streams are a particular type of data with continuously occurring ordered instances. Sources of such streaming data include, among others, computer network traffic, social tweets, phone conversation, and so on. Data from these sources can be utilized in numerous data analytics tasks such as intrusion detection, terrorist watch list matching, and so on. With potentially unlimited data instances generated from a source, traditional learning techniques that require prior knowledge of data sizes and train once on a stationary data cannot be directly employed over a data stream.

As such, we would like to answer the following question "How can we perform computations on an encrypted dataset while remaining encrypted to an adversary?" for a large amount of continuously arriving data streams. Our goal is to keep the privacy-sensitive streaming data encrypted except while it is processed securely inside the secure enclave and perform interesting data analytics task on the encrypted data by leveraging the recent developments in secure hardware design (e.g., Intel SGX).

Therefore, we plan to develop a framework for performing data analytics over sensitive encrypted streaming data [MASU11c] using SGX to ensure data privacy. In particular, we plan to design data-oblivious mechanisms to address the two major problems of classification over continuous data streams (i.e., concept drift and concept evolution) when deployed over an Intel SGX processor. In addition, we will explore complex query processing over encrypted data streams. Using algorithmic manipulation of data access within a secure environment, we will prudently design and implement methods to perform data classification and data querying by adapting to changes in data patterns that occur over time while suppressing leakage of such information to a curious adversary via side channels. In addition to hiding data patterns during model learning or testing, we also aim to hide changes in those data patterns over time. Furthermore, we plan to support basic stream query processing on the encrypted sensitive streams in addition to building classification models. Our initial work indicates the adaptation of such algorithms perform equivalently to a data stream processing on unencrypted data, and achieve data privacy with a small overhead.

Concretely, we need to develop techniques to address the above challenges while utilizing encrypted streaming data containing sensitive and private information. As shown in Figure 34.4, encrypted data will be only decrypted inside the secure/trusted enclave protected by the hardware. Data decrypted inside the enclave cannot be accessed by the operating system or any other software running on the system. In addition, we appeal to the data obliviousness property required from an algorithm to guarantee data privacy. Here, data-obliviousness refers to the algorithmic property where memory, disk, and network accesses are performed independent of the input data. The main idea is to use appropriate data structures and introduce algorithmic "decoy" code whenever

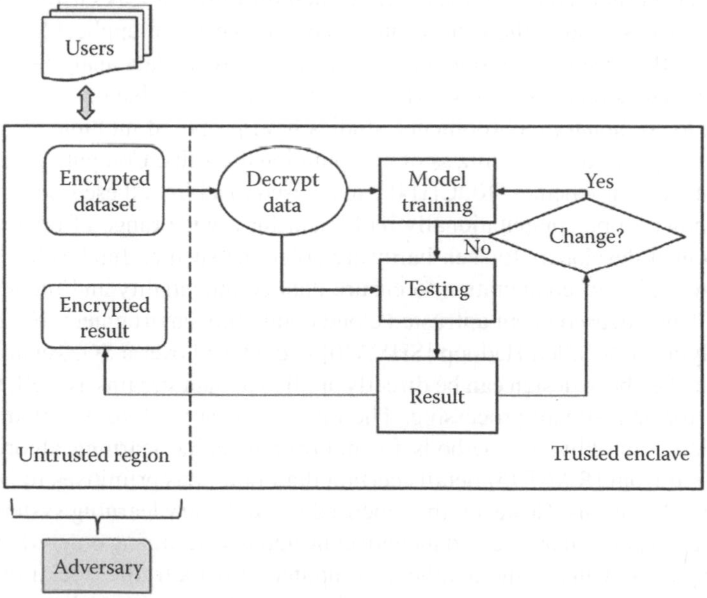

FIGURE 34.4 Overview of the proposed architecture.

necessary. In addition to using oblivious testing mechanisms for predicting class label of test data instances, we develop data-oblivious learning mechanisms which are frequently invoked during model adaptation as needed.

Furthermore, existing data stream classification techniques rely on ensemble of classifiers. These have been shown to outperform single classifiers. When developing an ensemble-based classification method over an encrypted data stream, it may be necessary to use multiple secure environments (enclaves). We plan to leverage the support of multiple enclaves by Intel SGX processors to perform such ensemble operations.

34.5 SUMMARY AND DIRECTIONS

In this chapter, we have discussed our plans for developing an education curriculum, that is, integrated with an experimental program both in BDMA and BDSP. For BDMA we will enhance our current BDMA course with experiments dealing with real-world applications including in atmospheric science. For BDSP, we will design a capstone course as well as incorporate modules into several of our current courses including in secure cloud computing as well as in data and applications security and privacy. In addition, we also plan to develop a capability in TEE and will use the infrastructure in the courses.

We will also utilize the infrastructures we have developed for secure cloud, mobile computing, and social media that we have discussed in our previous books ([THUR14], [THUR16]) and integrate them into the new infrastructure to be developed as needed. Many of our students have become experts on programming with the Hadoop/MapReduce as well as the Spark frameworks. Working with the real-world applications and learning new technologies will enable them to design scalable machine learning techniques as well as privacy-enhanced machine learning techniques that have real-world significance.

The best evaluators of our courses, experiments, and infrastructures are our students. Therefore, we will obtain detailed evaluations from our students and discuss with them how we can enhance the programs for both BDMA and BDSP. We will also get inputs from our partners (e.g., industry and academic partners in related projects) on our programs. We strongly believe that research, design, and development efforts have to be tightly integrated with the education and infrastructure efforts so that our students can be well equipped for academic, industry, and government careers.

REFERENCES

[ALNA14]. K.M. Al-Naami, S. Seker, L. Khan, "GISQF: An Efficient Spatial Query Processing System," In *7th IEEE International Conference on Cloud Computing*, June 27–July 2, 2014, Anchorage, AK.

[ALNA16]. K.M. Al-Naami, S.E. Seker, L. Khan, "GISQAF: MapReduce Guided Spatial Query Processing and Analytics System," to appear in *Journal of Software: Practice and Experience*. John Wiley & Sons, Ltd., 46 (10), 1329–1349, 2016.

[ANAT13]. I. Anati, S. Gueron, S.P. Johnson, V.R. Scarlata, "Innovative Technology for CPU Based Attestation and Sealing," In *Proceedings of the 2nd International Work Shop on Hardware and Architectural Support for Security and Privacy (HASP)*, Tel Aviv, Israel, pp. 1–8, 2013.

[CHAN14]. S. Chandra, J. Sahs, L. Khan, B. Thuraisingham, C. Aggarwal, "Stream Mining Using Statistical Relational Learning," In *IEEE International Conference on Data Mining Series (ICDM)*, December, Shenzhen, China, pp. 743–748, 2014.

[CHEN08]. X. Chen, T. Garfinkel, E.C. Lewis, P. Subrahmanyam, C.A. Waldspurger, D. Boneh, J. Dwoskin, D.R. Ports, "Overshadow: A Virtualization-Based Approach to Retrofitting Protection in Commodity Operating Systems," In *Proceedings of the 13th International Conference on Architectural Support for Programming Languages and Operating Systems, ASPLOS XIII*, ACM, Seattle, WA, USA, pp. 2–13, 2008.

[DINH14]. T.T. Anh Dinh, A. Datta, "Streamforce: Outsourcing Access Control Enforcement for Stream Data to The Clouds," *CODASPY*, 2014, 13–24, 2014.

[DINH15]. T.T. Anh Dinh, P. Saxena, E.-C. Chang, B.C. Ooi, C. Zhang, "M2R: Enabling Stronger Privacy in MapReduce Computation," *USENIX Security Symposium 2015*, Washington, DC, pp. 447–462, 2015.

[DOOR06]. L. Van Doorn, "Hardware Virtualization Trends," In *ACM/USENIX International Conference on Virtual Execution Environments: Proceedings of the 2nd International Conference on Virtual Execution Environments*, Ottawa, Ontario, Canada, vol. 14, pp. 45–45, 2006.

[GUPT16]. D. Gupta, B. Mood, J. Feigenbaum, K. Butler, P. Traynor, "Using Intel Software Guard Extensions for Efficient Two-Party Secure Function Evaluation," In *Proceedings of the 2016 FC Workshop on Encrypted Computing and Applied Homomorphic Cryptography*, Barbados, pp. 302–318, 2016.

[HALD09]. J.A. Halderman, S.D. Schoen, N. Heninger, W. Clarkson, W. Paul, J.A. Calandrino, A.J. Feldman, J. Appelbaum, E.W. Felten, "Lest We Remember: Cold-Boot Attacks on Encryption Keys," *Communications of the ACM*, 52 (5), 91–98, 2009.

[HAQU14]. A. Haque, S. Chandra, L. Khan, C. Aggarwal, "Distributed Adaptive Importance Sampling on Graphical Models Using MapReduce," In *2014 IEEE International Conference on Big Data (IEEE BigData 2014)*, Washington, DC, USA, pp. 597–602, 2014.

[HAQU15]. A. Haque, L. Khan, M. Baron, "Semi-Supervised Adaptive Framework for Classifying Evolving Data Stream," *PAKDD (2)*, Ho Chi Minh City, Vietnam, pp. 383–394, 2015.

[HOEK13]. M. Hoekstra, R. Lal, P. Pappachan, V. Phegade, J. Del Cuvillo, "Using Innovative Instructions to Create Trustworthy Software Solutions," In *Proceedings of the 2nd International Workshop on Hardware and Architectural Support for Security and Privacy (HASP)*, Tel Aviv, Israel, pp. 1–8, 2013.

[KHAD12]. V. Khadilkar, K.Y. Oktay, M. Kantarcioglu, S. Mehrotra, "Secure Data Processing over Hybrid Clouds," *IEEE Data Eng. Bull.*, 35(4), 46–54, 2012.

[KIM15]. S. Kim, Y. Shin, J. Ha, T. Kim, D. Han, "A First Step Towards Leveraging Commodity Trusted Execution Environments for Network Applications," In *Proceedings of the 14th ACM Workshop on Hot Topics in Networks (p. 7)*, November, ACM, 2015.

[KOCH14]. O. Kocabas and T. Soyata, "Medical Data Analytics in The Cloud Using Homomorphic Encryption," *Handbook of Research on Cloud Infrastructures for Big Data Analytics*, P. R. Chelliah and G. Deka (eds), IGI Global, pp. 471–488, 2014.

[LI14]. Y. Li, J. McCune, J. Newsome, A. Perrig, B. Baker, W. Drewry, "MiniBox: A Two-Way Sandbox for x86 Native Code," *USENIX 2014*, Philadelphia, PA, pp. 409–420.

[MASU09]. M.M. Masud, J. Gao, L. Khan, J. Han, B.M. Thuraisingham, "Integrating Novel Class Detection with Classification for Concept-Drifting Data Streams," In *Proceedings of European Conference on Machine Learning and Knowledge Discovery in Databases (ECML PKDD)*, Bled, Slovenia, pp. 79–94, 2009.

[MASU11a]. M.M. Masud, J. Gao, L. Khan, J. Han, K.W. Hamlen, N.C. Oza, "Facing the Reality of Data Stream Classification: Coping with Scarcity of Labeled Data," *International Journal of Knowledge and Information Systems (KAIS)*, 33 (1), 213–244, 2011, Springer, 2011.

[MASU11b]. M.M. Masud, J. Gao, L. Khan, J. Han, B.M. Thuraisingham,"Classification and Novel Class Detection in Concept-Drifting Data Streams under Time Constraints," *IEEE Transactions on Knowledge and Data Engineering*, 23 (6), 859–874, 2011.

[MASU11c]. M. Masud, J. Gao, L. Khan, J. Han, B.M. Thuraisingham, "Classification and Novel Class Detection in Concept-Drifting Data Streams Under Time Constraints," *IEEE Transactions on Knowledge and Data Engineering*, 23 (6), 859–874, 2011.

[MCCU07]. J.M. McCune, B. Parno, A. Perrig, M.K. Reiter, H. Isozaki, "*An Execution Infrastructure for TCB Minimization*," *Technical Report* CMU-CyLab-07-018, Carnegie Mellon University, Dec. 2007.

[MCCU10]. J.M. McCune, Y. Li, N. Qu, Z. Zhou, A. Datta, V. Gligor, A. Perrig, "Trustvisor: Efficient TCB Reduction and Attestation," In *Proceedings of the 2010 IEEE Symposium on Security and Privacy, IEEE Computer Society*, pp. 143–158, 2010.

[MCKE13]. F. McKeen, I. Alexandrovich, A. Berenzon, C.V. Rozas, H. Shafi, V. Shanbhogue, U.R. Savagaonkar, "Innovative Instructions and Software Model for Isolated Execution," In *Proceedings of the 2nd International Workshop on Hardware and Architectural Support for Security and Privacy (HASP)*, Tel Aviv, Israel, pp. 1–8, 2013.

[NAEH11]. M. Naehrig, K. Lauter, V. Vaikuntanathan, "Can Homomorphic Encryption be Practical?," In *Proceedings of the 3rd ACM Work Shop on Cloud Computing Security Workshop*, ACM, Chicago, IL, pp. 113–124, 2011.

[OHIR16]. O. Ohrimenko, F. Schuster, C. Fournet, A. Mehta, S. Nowozin, K. Vaswani, M. Costa, "Oblivious Multi-Party Machine Learning on Trusted Processors." *USENIX Security* Austin, TX, pp. 619–636, 2016.

[PERE06]. R. Perez, R. Sailer, L. van Doorn et al., "vTPM: Virtualizing the Trusted Platform Module," *USENIX Security Symposium*, pp. 305–320, 2006.

[RANE15]. A. Rane, C. Lin, M. Tiwari, "Raccoon: Closing Digital Side-Channels through Obfuscated Execution," In *24th USENIX Security Symposium (USENIX Security 15)*, Washington, DC, pp. 431–446, 2015.

[SANT14]. N. Santos, H. Raj, S. Saroiu, A. Wolman, "Using Arm Trustzone to Build A Trusted Language Runtime for Mobile Applications," *ACM SIGARCH Computer Architecture News*, ACM, Vol. 42(1), pp. 67–80, 2014.

[SCHU15]. F. Schuster, M. Costa, C. Fournet, C. Gkantsidis, M. Peinado, G. Mainar-Ruiz, M. Russinovich, "VC3: Trustworthy Data Analytics in the Cloud Using SGX," In *2015 IEEE Symposium on Security and Privacy*, May, IEEE, San Jose, CA, pp. 38–54, 2015.

[SESH07]. A. Seshadri, M. Luk, N. Qu, A. Perrig, "Secvisor: A Tiny Hypervisor to Provide Lifetime Kernel Code Integrity for Commodity OSes," In *Proceedings of 21st ACM SIGOPS Symposium on Operating Systems Principles, SOSP '07*, Stevenson, WA, USA, pp. 335–350, 2007.

[SGXSDK]. Intel software guard extensions (intel sgx) sdk. https://software.intel.com/en- us/sgx-sdk.

[SHVA10]. K. Shvachko, H. Kuang, S. Radia, R. Chansler, "The Hadoop Distributed File System," In *2010 IEEE 26th Symposium on Mass Storage Systems and Technologies (MSST)*, IEEE, Incline Village, NV, pp. 1–10, 2010.

[SOLA16]. M. Solaimani, R. Gopalan, L. Khan, B. Thuraisingham, "Spark-Based Political Event Coding," to appear in *the 2nd IEEE International Conference on Big Data Computing Service and Applications, IEEE BigDataService 2016*, Oxford, UK, pp. 14–23, March 29–April 1, 2016.

[STEI10]. U. Steinberg and B. Kauer. *NOVA: A Microhypervisor-Based Secure Virtualization Architecture*," ACM, Paris, France, pp. 209–222, 2010.

[SUN12]. K. Sun, J. Wang, F. Zhang, A. Stavrou. "SecureSwitch: BIOS-Assisted Isolation and Switch between Trusted and Untrusted Commodity OSes," *NDSS*, San Diego, CA, 2012.

[THUR14]. B. Thuraisingham, *Developing and Securing the Cloud*. CRC Press, Boca Raton, FL, USA, 2014.

[THUR16]. B. Thuraisingham, S. Abrol, R. Heatherly, M. Kantarcioglu, V. Khadilkar, L. Khan, *Analyzing and Securing Social Networks*. CRC Press, Boca Raton, FL, USA, 2016.

[WANG10]. J. Wang, A. Stavrou, A.K. Ghosh, "Hypercheck: A Hardware-Assisted Integrity Monitor," *Recent Advances in Intrusion Detection, 13th International Symposium, RAID 2010*, Ottawa, Ontario, Canada, September 15–17, Proceedings, pp. 158–177, 2010.

[ZHANG11]. F. Zhang, J. Chen, H. Chen, and B. Zang, "CloudVisor: Retrofitting Protection of Virtual Machines in Multi-Tenant Cloud with Nested Virtualization." In *Proceedings of the 23rd ACM Symposium on Operating Systems Principles (SOSP'11)*, Cascais, Portugal, pp. 203–216, 2011.

35 Directions for BDSP and BDMA

35.1 INTRODUCTION

While the chapters in Sections II through IV have described the experimental systems and prototypes we have developed in big data management and analytics (BDMA) and big data security and privacy (BDSP) and the previous chapters in Section V have discussed some of our exploratory work on research in BDMA and BDSP as well as our approach to developing experimental infrastructures and course in these fields, this chapter describes the direction for BDSP and BDMA. In particular, we provide a summary of the discussions of the National Science Foundation (NSF) sponsored workshop on BDSP (including applications of BDMA for BDSP) held in Dallas, Texas on September 16–17, 2014. Our goal is to build a community in BDSP to explore the challenging research problems. We also presented the results of the workshop at the National Privacy Research Strategy meeting in Washington, DC to set the directions for research and education on these topics.

Recently a few workshops and panels have been held on BDSP. Examples include the ACM CCS workshop on Big Data Security, ACM SACMAT, and IEEE Big Data Conference panels. These workshops and panels have been influenced by different communities of researchers. For example, the ACM CCS workshop series is focusing on big data for security applications while the IEEE Big Data conference is focusing on cloud security issues. Furthermore, these workshops and panels mainly address a limited number of the technical issues surrounding BDSP. For example, the ACM CCS workshop does not appear to address the privacy issues dealing with regulations or the security violations resulting from data analytics.

To address the above limitations, we organized a workshop on Big Data Security and Privacy on September 16–17, 2014 in Dallas, Texas sponsored by the NSF [NSF]. The participants of this workshop consisted of interdisciplinary researchers in the fields of higher performance computing, systems, data management and analytics, cyber security, network science, healthcare, and social sciences who came together and determined the strategic direction for BDSP. NSF has made substantial investments both in cyber security and big data. It is therefore critical that the two areas work together to determine the direction for big data security. We made a submission based on the workshop results to the National Privacy Research Strategy [NPRS]. We also gave a presentation at the NITRD (The Networking and Information Technology Research and Development) Privacy Workshop [NITRD]. This document is the workshop report that describes the issues in BDSP, presentations at the workshop, and the discussions at the workshop. We hope that this effort will help toward building a community in BDSP.

The organization of this chapter is as follows. Section 35.2 describes the issues surrounding BDSP. The workshop participants were given these issues to build upon during the workshop discussions. A summary of the workshop presentations is provided in Section 35.3. A summary of the discussions at the workshop is provided in Section 35.4. Next steps are discussed in Section 35.5. Figure 35.1 illustrates the topics discussed in this Chapter.

35.2 ISSUES IN BDSP

35.2.1 Introduction

This section describes issues in BDSP that were given to the workshop participants to motivate the discussions. These issues include both security and privacy for big data as well as BDMA for

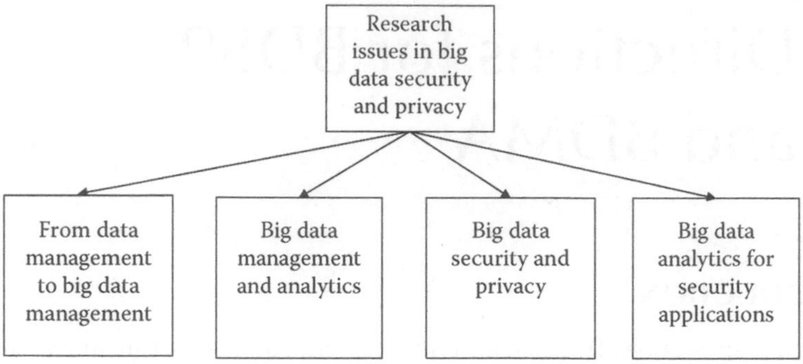

FIGURE 35.1 Research issues in big data security and privacy.

cyber security. While big data has roots in many technologies, database management is at its heart. Therefore, in this section, we will discuss how data management has evolved and will then focus on the BDSP issues.

Database systems technology has advanced a great deal during the past four decades from the legacy systems based on network and hierarchical models to relational and object database systems. Database systems can now be accessed via the web and data management services have been implemented as web services. Due to the explosion of web-based services, unstructured data management and social media and mobile computing, the amount of data to be handled has increased from terabytes to petabytes and zetabytes in just two decades. Such vast amounts of complex data have come to be known as *big data*. Not only must big data be managed efficiently, such data also has to be analyzed to extract useful nuggets to enhance businesses as well as improve society. This has come to be known as big data analytics.

Storage, management, and analysis of large quantities of data also result in security and privacy violations. Often data has to be retained for various reasons including for regulatory compliance. The data retained may have sensitive information and could violate user privacy. Furthermore, manipulating such big data, such as combining sets of different types of data could result in security and privacy violations. For example, while the raw data removes personally identifiable information, the derived data may contain private and sensitive information. For example, the raw data about a person may be combined with the person's address which may be sufficient to identify the person.

Different communities are working on the big data challenge. For example, the systems community is developing technologies for massive storage of big data. The network community is developing solutions for managing very large networked data. The data community is developing solutions for efficiently managing and analyzing large sets of data. Big data research and development is being carried out both in academia, industry, and government research labs. However, little attention has been given to security and privacy considerations for big data. Security cuts across multiple areas including systems, data, and networks. We need the multiple communities to come together to develop solutions for BDSP.

This section describes some of the issues in BDSP. An overview of BDMA is provided in Section 35.2.2. Security and privacy issues are discussed in Section 35.2.3. BDMA for cyber security are discussed in Section 32.2.4. Our goal toward building a community is discussed in Section 32.2.5.

35.2.2 Big Data Management and Analytics

BDMA research is proceeding in three directions. They are as follows:

1. Building infrastructure and high performance computing techniques for the storage of big data.

2. Data management techniques such as integrating multiple data sources (both big and small) and indexing and querying big data.
3. Data analytics techniques that manipulate and analyze big data to extract nuggets.

We will briefly review the progress made in each of the areas. With respect to building infrastructures, technologies such as Hadoop and MapReduce as well as Storm are being developed for managing large amounts of data in the cloud. In addition, main memory data management techniques have advanced so that a few terabytes of data can be managed in main memory. Furthermore, systems such as Hive and Cassandra as well as NoSQL databases have been developed for managing petabytes of data.

With respect to data management, traditional data management techniques such as query processing and optimization strategies are being examined for handling petabytes of data. Furthermore, graph data management techniques are being developed for the storage and management of very large networked data.

With respect to data analytics, the various data mining algorithms are being implemented on Hadoop- and MapReduce-based infrastructures. Additionally, data reduction techniques are being explored to reduce the massive amounts of data into manageable chunks while still maintaining the semantics of the data.

In summary, BDMA techniques include extending current data management and mining techniques to handle massive amounts of data as well as developing new approaches including graph data management and mining techniques for maintaining and analyzing large networked data.

35.2.3 Security and Privacy

The collection, storage, manipulation, and retention of massive amounts of data have resulted in serious security and privacy considerations. Various regulations are being proposed to handle big data so that the privacy of the individuals is not violated. For example, even if personally identifiable information is removed from the data, when data is combined with other data, an individual can be identified. This is essentially the inference and aggregation problem that data security researchers have been exploring for the past four decades. This problem is exacerbated with the management of big data as different sources of data now exist that are related to various individuals.

In some cases, regulations may cause privacy to be violated. For example, data that is collected (e.g., e-mail data) has to be retained for a certain period of time (usually 5 years). As long as one keeps such data, there is a potential for privacy violations. Too many regulations can also stifle innovation. For example, if there is a regulation that raw data has to be kept as is and not manipulated or models cannot be built out of the data, then corporations cannot analyze the data in innovative ways to enhance their business. This way innovation may be stifled.

Therefore, one of the main challenges for ensuring security and privacy when dealing with big data is to come up with a balanced approach toward regulations and analytics. That is, how can an organization carry out useful analytics and still ensure the privacy of individuals? Numerous techniques for privacy-preserving data mining, privacy-preserving data integration, and privacy-preserving information retrieval have been developed. The challenge is to extend these techniques for handling massive amounts of often networked data.

Another security challenge for BDMA is to secure the infrastructures. Many of the technologies that have been developed, including Hadoop, MapReduce, Hive, Cassandra, PigLatin, Mahout, and Storm, do not have adequate security protections. The question is, how can these technologies be secured and at the same time ensure high-performance computing?

Next, the big data management strategies such as access methods and indexing and query processing have to be secure. So the question is how can policies for different types of data such as structured, semistructured, unstructured, and graph data be integrated? Since big data may result from combining data from numerous sources, how can you ensure the quality of the data?

Finally, the entire area of security, privacy, integrity, data quality, and trust policies has to be examined within the context of big data security. What are the appropriate policies for big data? How can these policies be handled without affecting performance? How can these policies be made consistent and complete?

This section has listed some of the challenges with respect to security and privacy for big data. We need a comprehensive research program that will identify the challenges and develop solutions for BDSP. Security cannot be an afterthought. That is, we cannot incorporate security into each and every Big Data technology that is being developed. We need to have a comprehensive strategy so that security can be incorporated while the technology is being developed. We also need to determine the appropriate types of policies and regulations to enforce before Big Data technologies are employed by an organization. This means researchers from multiple disciplines have to come together to determine what the problems are and explore solutions. These disciplines include cyber security and privacy, high-performance computing, data management and analytics, network science, and policy management.

35.2.4 Big Data Analytics for Security Applications

While the challenges discussed in Section 32.2.3 deal with securing big data and ensuring the privacy of individuals, BDMA techniques can be used to solve security problems. For example, an organization can outsource activities such as identity management, email filtering, and intrusion detection to the cloud. This is because massive amounts of data are being collected for such applications and this data has to be analyzed. Cloud data management is just one example of big data management. The question is: how can the developments in big data management and analytic techniques be used to solve security problems? These problems include malware detection, insider threat detection, intrusion detection, and spam filtering.

35.2.5 Community Building

The various issues surrounding BDSP were discussed at the beginning of the workshop and five keynote presentations were given at the workshop that addressed many of these issues. In addition, several position papers were submitted by the workshop participants and subsequently, presentations based on these papers were given. These papers and presentations set the stage for the two breakout sessions held during the workshop. One of these sessions focused on the security and privacy issues while the other focused on the applications. The presentations and the discussions at the workshop are summarized in Sections 35.3 and 35.4 of this report. Our goal is to build a community in BDSP.

We have made some progress toward this goal over the past 2 years. In particular, we participated in the BDSP workshops organized at the Women in Cyber Security Conference series in Dallas in 2016 and in Tucson in 2017. In addition, we also organized a Women in Data Science and Engineering Workshop in San Diego as section of the *IEEE International Conference on Data Engineering* (ICDE) series. We also continue to present papers and present tutorials at various big data-related conferences.

35.3 SUMMARY OF WORKSHOP PRESENTATIONS

This section summarizes the presentations at the workshop. These presentations and the position papers can be found at http://csi.utdallas.edu/events/NSF/NSF%20papers%202014.htm.

35.3.1 Keynote Presentations

We had five keynote presentations to motivate the workshop participants. These keynote presentations discussed the various BDSP initiatives at NIST, Honeywell, and IBM as well as provided an overview of some of the research challenges. The opening keynote given by *Wo Chang* from NIST discussed the initiatives at NIST on big data and provided an overview of the big data workgroup. Later *Arnab Roy* from Fujitsu provided some details of the work by the BDSP subgroup of this workgroup. *Elisa Bertino* from Purdue discussed issues and challenges of providing security with privacy. *Raj Rajagopalan* from Honeywell discussed BDSP challenges for industrial control systems. *Sandeep Gopisetty* from IBM discussed the Big Data Enterprise efforts at IBM while *Murat Kantarcioglu* from UT Dallas provided an overview of the BDSP initiatives at UT Dallas.

There were several presentations given by the workshop participants. Below we give a summary of these presentations.

35.3.1.1 Toward Privacy Aware Big Data Analytics

Barbara Carminati from the University of Insubria Italy described a framework for privacy aware big data analytics. This framework included layers for privacy policy specifications, a unified query model, fine-grained enforcement, and a dashboard. She went on to discuss the functions of each layer.

35.3.1.2 Formal Methods for Preserving Privacy While Loading Big Data

Brian Blake from the University of Miami discussed how formal methods can be incorporated into approaches to handle privacy violations when multiple pieces of information are combined. In particular, he discussed the creation of a software life cycle and framework for big data testing.

35.3.1.3 Authenticity of Digital Images in Social Media

Balkirat Kaur from North Carolina A&T State University discussed novel solutions for detecting tampered images in social media. In particular, she discussed an approach for creating and capturing image signatures.

35.3.1.4 Business Intelligence Meets Big Data: An Overview of Security and Privacy

Claudio Ardagna from the University of Milano in Crema discussed the notions of full data and zero latency analysis within the context of BDSP.

35.3.1.5 Toward Risk-Aware Policy-Based Framework for BDSP

James Joshi from the University of Pittsburgh described a framework for BDSP that takes risk into consideration. He discussed how realizing such a framework involves the integration of policy engineering and risk management approaches.

35.3.1.6 Big Data Analytics: Privacy Protection Using Semantic Web Technologies

Csilla Farkas from the University of South Carolina discussed the use of semantic web technologies for representing policies and data and subsequently reasoning about these policies to prevent security and privacy violations.

35.3.1.7 Securing Big Data in the Cloud: Toward a More Focused and Data-Driven Approach

Ragib Hasan from the University of Alabama at Birmingham described the challenges in secure cloud computing and discussed a data-driven approach to provide some solutions. In particular, he discussed the need to look at the data life cycle and ensure trustworthy computation and attribution. He stated that provenance should be a fundamental section of clouds.

35.3.1.8 Privacy in a World of Mobile Devices

Tim Finin from the University of Maryland, Baltimore County discussed approaches to providing privacy in a mobile computing environment. He stated that our privacy is at risk due to the proliferation of mobile devices and discussed ways of ensuring privacy.

35.3.1.9 Access Control and Privacy Policy Challenges in Big Data

Ram Krishnan from the University of Texas at San Antonio stated that data is being used in unplanned ways that were unforeseen during the time of collection. He then discussed the challenges for access control and privacy policy specification and enforcement for big data applications.

35.3.1.10 Timely Health Indicators Using Remote Sensing and Innovation for the Validity of the Environment

David Lary from The University of Texas at Dallas who is a natural scientist by training discussed the big data challenges for remote sensing with applications in human health. This presentation provided an overview of an application that manages and analyzes big data and showed the need to handle data privacy.

35.3.1.11 Additional Presentations

The workshop also had additional presentations including the following. Big Noise in Big Data: Research Challenges and Opportunities in Heterogeneous Sensor Data Integration by Calton Pu from Georgia Tech and Accelerating the Performance of Private Information Retrieval Protocols using Graphical Processing Units by Gabriel Ghinita from the University of Massachusetts in Boston. Calton showed us a demonstration of integrating heterogeneous sensor data and discussed the need for data security and privacy while Gabriel discussed approaches and challenges for private information retrieval. Presentations related to BDSP were also given by Anna Squicciarini from Pennsylvania State University and Guofei Gu from Texas A&M University. Topics discussed included social media privacy and malware attacks. Finally, Andrew Greenhut from Raytheon said a few words about security and privacy needs for defense applications.

35.3.1.12 Final Thoughts on the Presentations

As can be seen, the presentations covered a wide range of topics including security and privacy issues as well as applications such as healthcare. In addition, various types of frameworks for BDSP were also discussed. Technologies discussed included social media, image processing, mobile data, and sensor information management. These presentations set the stage for the workshop discussions that took place as part of the breakout sessions. The discussions are summarized in Section 35.4.

35.4 SUMMARY OF THE WORKSHOP DISCUSSIONS

35.4.1 Introduction

This section provides a summary of the discussions on BDSP at the NSF workshop. The workshop consisted of keynote presentations, presentations by the participants, and workgroup discussions. We organized two workgroups: one on BDSP led by Dr. Elisa Bertino and the other on big data analytics for cyber security led by Dr. Murat Kantarcioglu. While the major focus of the workshop was on privacy issues due to BDMA, we also had some stimulating discussions on applying big data management analytics techniques for cyber security. Therefore, this section provides a summary of the discussions of both workgroups.

The organization of this section is as follows. The philosophy behind BDSP is discussed in Section 35.4.2. Privacy-enhanced techniques are discussed in Section 35.4.3. A framework for big data privacy is discussed in Section 35.4.4. Research challenges and interdisciplinary approaches to big data privacy are discussed in Section 35.4.5. An overview of BDMA techniques for cyber security is provided in Section 4.6.

35.4.2 Philosophy for BDSP

As discussed by Bertino [BERT14], technological advances and novel applications, such as sensors, cyber-physical systems, smart mobile devices, cloud systems, data analytics, and social networks are making it possible to capture and to quickly process and analyze huge amounts of data from which to extract information critical for security-related tasks. In the area of cyber security, such tasks include user authentication, access control, anomaly detection, user monitoring, and protection from insider threat [BERT12]. By analyzing and integrating data collected on the internet and web, one can identify connections and relationships among individuals that may in turn help with homeland protection. By collecting and mining data concerning user travels and disease outbreaks, one can predict disease spreading across geographical areas. And those are just a few examples; there are certainly many other domains where data technologies can play a major role in enhancing security.

The use of data for security tasks is however raising major privacy concerns [THUR02]. Collected data even if anonymized by removing identifiers such as names or social security numbers, when linked with other data, may lead to re-identifying the individuals to which specific data items are related to. Also, as organizations such as governmental agencies often need to collaborate on security tasks, datasets are exchanged across different organizations, resulting in these datasets being available to many different parties. Apart from the use of data for analytics, security tasks such as authentication and access control may require detailed information about users. An example is multifactor authentication that may require, in addition to a password or a certificate, user biometrics. Recently, proposed continuous authentication techniques extend user authentication to include information such as user keystroke dynamics to constantly verify the user identity. Another example is location-based access control [DAMI07] that requires users to provide to the access control system information about their current location. As a result, detailed user mobility information may be collected over time by the access control system. This information, if misused or stolen, can lead to privacy breaches.

It would then seem that in order to achieve security, we must give up privacy. However, this may not be necessarily the case. Recent advances in cryptography are making possible to work on encrypted data, for example for performing analytics on encrypted data [LIU14]. However, much more needs to be done as the specific data privacy techniques to use heavily depend on the specific use of data and the security tasks at hand. Also, current techniques are not still able to meet the efficiency requirement for use with big datasets.

In this document, we first discuss a few examples of approaches that help with reconciling security with privacy. We then discuss some aspects of a framework for data privacy. Finally, we summarize research challenges and provide an overview of the multidisciplinary research needed to address these challenges.

35.4.3 Examples of Privacy-Enhancing Techniques

Many privacy-enhancing techniques have been proposed over the last 15 years, ranging from cryptographic techniques such as oblivious data structures [WANG14] that hide data access patterns to data anonymization techniques that transform the data to make it more difficult to link specific data records to specific individuals; and we refer the reader for further references to specialized conferences, such as the privacy-enhancing symposium (PET) series (https://petsymposium.org/2014/) and journals, such as Transactions on Data Privacy (http://www.tdp.cat/). However, many such techniques either do not scale to very large datasets and/or do not specifically address the problem of reconciling security with privacy. At the same time, there are a few approaches that focus on efficiently reconciling security with privacy and we discuss them as follows:

- *Privacy-preserving data matching*: Record matching is typically performed across different data sources with the aim of identifying common information shared among these sources. An example is matching a list of passengers on a flight with a list of suspicious individuals. However, matching records from different data sources is often in contrast with privacy requirements concerning the data owned by the sources. Cryptographic approaches such as secure set intersection protocols may alleviate such concerns. However, these techniques do not scale for large datasets. Recent approaches based on data transformation and mapping into vector spaces [SCAN07] and combination of secure multiparty computation (SMC) and data sanitization approaches such as differential privacy [KUZU13] and *k*-anonymity ([INAN12], [INAN08]) have addressed scalability. However, work needs to be done concerning the development of privacy-preserving techniques suitable for complex matching techniques based, for example, on semantic matching. Security models and definitions also need to be developed supporting security analysis and proofs for solutions combining different security techniques, such as SMC and differential privacy.
- *Privacy-preserving collaborative data mining*: Conventional data mining is typically performed on big centralized data warehouses collecting all the data of interest. However, centrally collecting all data poses several privacy and confidentiality concerns when data belongs to different organizations. An approach to address such concerns is based on distributed collaborative approaches by which the organizations retain their own datasets and cooperate to learn the global data mining results without revealing the data in their own individual datasets. Fundamental work in this area includes (i) techniques allowing two parties to build a decision tree without learning anything about each other's datasets except for what can be learned by the final decision tree [LIND00] and (ii) specialized collaborative privacy-preserving techniques for association rules, clustering, k-nearest neighbor classification [VAID06]. These techniques are however still very inefficient. Novel approaches based on cloud computing and new cryptographic primitives should be investigated.
- *Privacy-preserving biometric authentication*: Conventional approaches to biometrics authentication require recording biometrics templates of enrolled users and then using these templates for matching with the templates provided by users at authentication time. Templates of user biometrics represent sensitive information that needs to be strongly protected. In distributed environments in which users have to interact with many different service providers, the protection of biometric templates becomes even more complex. A recent approach addresses such an issue by using a combination of perceptual hashing techniques, classification techniques, and zero-knowledge proof of knowledge (ZKPK) protocols [BERT14]. Under such approach, the biometric template of a user is processed to extract from it a string of bits which is then further processed by classification and some other transformation. The resulting bit string is then used, together with a random number, to generate a cryptographic commitment. This commitment represents an identification token that does not reveal anything about the original input biometrics. The commitment is then used in the ZKPK protocol to authenticate the user. This approach has been engineered for secure use on mobile phones. Much work remains, however, to be done in order to reduce the false rejection rates. Also, different approaches to authentication and identification techniques need to be investigated based on recent homomorphic encryption techniques.

35.4.4 Multiobjective Optimization Framework for Data Privacy

Although there are attempts at coming up with a privacy solution/definition that can address many different scenarios, we believe that there is no one size fits all solution for data privacy.

Instead, multiple dimensions need to be tailored for different application domains to achieve practical solutions. First of all, different domains require different definitions of data utility. For example, if we want to build privacy-preserving classification models, 0/1 loss could be a good utility measure. On the other hand, for privacy-preserving record linkage, F1 score could be a better choice. Second, we need to understand the right definitions of privacy risk. For example, in data sharing scenarios, the probability of re-identification given certain background knowledge could be considered the right measure of privacy risk. On the other hand, ε=1 could be considered an appropriate risk for differentially private data mining models. Finally, the computation, storage, and communication costs of given protocols need to be considered. These costs could be especially significant for privacy-preserving protocols that involve cryptography. Given these three dimensions, one can envisage a multiobjective framework where different dimensions could be emphasized:

- *Maximize utility, given risk and costs constraints*: This would be suited for scenarios where limiting certain privacy risks are paramount.
- *Minimize privacy risks, given the utility and cost constraints*: In some scenarios, (e.g., medical care), significant degradation of the utility may not be allowed. In this setting, the parameter values of the protocol (e.g., ε in differential privacy) are chosen in such a way that we try to do our best in terms of privacy given our utility constraints. Please note that in some scenarios, there may not be any parameter settings that can satisfy all the constraints.
- *Minimize cost, given the utility and risk constraints*: In some cases, (e.g., cryptographic protocols), you may want to find the protocol parameter settings that may allow for the least expensive protocol that can satisfy all the utility and cost constraints.

To better illustrate these dimensions, consider the privacy-preserving record matching problem addressed in [INAN12]. Existing solutions to this problem generally follow two approaches: sanitization techniques and cryptographic techniques. In [INAN12], a hybrid technique that combines these two approaches is presented. This approach enables users to make trade-offs between privacy, accuracy, and cost. This is similar to the multiobjective optimization framework discussed in this chapter. These multiobjective optimizations are achieved by using a blocking phase that operates over sanitized data to filter out pairs of records, in a privacy-preserving manner, that do not satisfy the matching condition. By disclosing more information (e.g., differentially private data statistics), the proposed method incurs considerably lower costs than those for cryptographic techniques. On the other hand, it yields matching results that are significantly more accurate when compared to the sanitization techniques, even when privacy requirements are high. The use of different privacy-parameter values allows for different cost, risk, and utility outcomes.

To enable the multiobjective optimization framework for data privacy, we believe that more research needs to be done to identify appropriate utility, risk, and cost definitions for different application domains. Especially defining correct and realistic privacy risks is paramount. Many human actions ranging from oil extraction to airline travel, involve risks and benefits. In many cases, such as trying to develop an aircraft that may never malfunction, avoiding all risks are either too costly or impossible. Similarly we believe that avoiding all privacy risks for all individuals would be too costly. In addition, assuming that an attacker may know everything is too pessimistic. Therefore, coming up with privacy risk definitions under realistic attacker scenarios are needed.

35.4.5 Research Challenges and Multidisciplinary Approaches

Comprehensive solutions to the problem of security with privacy for big data require addressing many research challenges and multidisciplinary approaches. We outline significant directions in what follows:

- *Data confidentiality*: Several data confidentiality techniques and mechanisms exist, the most notable being access control systems and encryptions. Both techniques have been widely investigated. However, for access control systems for big data we need approaches for the following:
  - *Merging large numbers of access control policies*. In many cases, big data entails integrating data originating from multiple sources; these data may be associated with their own access control policies (referred to as "sticky policies") and these policies must be enforced even when the data is integrated with other data. Therefore, policies need to be integrated and conflicts solved.
  - *Automatically administering authorizations for big data and in particular for granting permissions*. If fine-grained access control is required, manual administration on large datasets is not feasible. We need techniques by which authorization can be automatically granted, possibly based on the user digital identity, profile, and context, and on the data contents and metadata.
  - *Enforcing access control policies on heterogeneous multimedia data*. Content-based access control is an important type of access control by which authorizations are granted or denied based on the content of data. Content-based access control is critical when dealing with video surveillance applications which are important for security. As for privacy, such videos have to be protected. Supporting content-based access control requires understanding the contents of protected data and this is very challenging when dealing with multimedia large data sources.
  - *Enforcing access control policies in big data stores*. Some of the recent big data systems allow its users to submit arbitrary jobs using programming languages such as Java. For example, in Hadoop, users can submit arbitrary MapReduce jobs written in Java. This creates significant challenges to enforce fine-grained access control efficiently for different users. Although there is some existing work ([ULUS14]) that tries to inject access control policies into submitted jobs, more research needs to be done on how to efficiently enforce such policies in recently developed big data stores.
  - *Automatically designing, evolving, and managing access control policies*. When dealing with dynamic environments where sources, users, and applications as well as the data usage are continuously changing, the ability to automatically design and evolve policies is critical to make sure that data is readily available for use while at the same time assuring data confidentiality. Environments and tools for managing policies are also crucial.
- *Privacy-preserving data correlation techniques*: A major issue arising from big data is that in correlating many (big) datasets, one can extract unanticipated information. Relevant issues and research directions that need to be investigated include
  - *Techniques to control what is extracted and to check that what is extracted can be used and/or shared.*
  - *Support for both personal privacy and population privacy*. In the case of population privacy, it is important to understand what is extracted from the data as this may lead to discrimination. Also, when dealing with security with privacy, it is important to understand the trade-off of personal privacy and collective security.
  - *Efficient and scalable privacy-enhancing techniques*. Several such techniques have been developed over the years, including oblivious RAM, security multiparty computation, multi-input encryption, homomorphic encryption. However, they are not yet practically applicable to large datasets. We need to engineer these techniques, using for example parallelization, to fine tune their implementation and perhaps combine them with other techniques, such as differential privacy (like in the case of the record linkage protocols described in [SCAN07]). A possible further approach in this respect

is to first use anonymized/sanitized data, and then depending on the specific situation to get specific nonanonymized data.

- *Usability of data privacy policies.* Policies must be easily understood by users. We need tools for the average users and we need to understand user expectations in terms of privacy.
- *Approaches for data services monetization.* Instead of selling data, organizations owning datasets can sell privacy-preserving data analytic services based on these datasets. The question to be addressed then is: how would the business model around data change if privacy-preserving data analytic tools were available? Also, if data is considered as a good to be sold, are there regulations concerning contracts for buying/selling data? Can these contracts include privacy clauses be incorporated requiring for example that users to whom this data pertains to have been notified?
- *Data publication.* Perhaps we should abandon the idea of publishing data, given the privacy implications, and rather require the user of the data to utilize a controlled environment (perhaps located in a cloud) for using the data. In this way, it would be much easier to control the proper use of data. An issue would be the case of research data used in universities and the repeatability of data-based research.
- *Privacy implication on data quality.* Recent studies have shown that people lie especially in social networks because they are not sure that their privacy is preserved. This results in a decrease in data quality that then affects decisions and strategies based on these data.
- *Risk models.* Different types of relationship of risks with big data can be identified: (a) big data can increase privacy risks and (b) big data can reduce risks in many domains (e.g. national security). The development of models for these two types of risk is critical in order to identify suitable trade-off and privacy-enhancing techniques to be used.
- *Data ownership.* The question about who is the owner of a piece of data is often a difficult question. It is perhaps better to replace this concept with the concept of stakeholder. Multiple stakeholders can be associated with each data item. The concept of stakeholder ties well with risks. Each stakeholder would have different (possibly conflicting) objectives and this can be modeled according to multiobjective optimization. In some cases, a stakeholder may not be aware of the others. For example, a user about whom the data pertains to (and thus a stakeholder for the data) may not be aware that a law enforcement agency is using this data. Technology solutions need to be investigated to eliminate conflicts.
- *Human factors.* All solutions proposed for privacy and for security with privacy need to be investigated in order to determine human involvement, e.g., how would the user interact with the data and his/her specific tasks concerning the use and/or protection of the data, in order to enhance usability.
- *Data lifecycle framework.* A comprehensive approach to privacy for big data needs to be based on a systematic data lifecycle approach. Phases in the lifecycle need to be identified and their privacy requirements and implications also need to be identified. Relevant phases include

- *Data acquisition*: We need mechanisms and tools to prevent devices from acquiring data about other individuals (relevant when devices like Google glasses are used); for example, can we come up with mechanisms that automatically block devices from recording/acquiring data at certain locations (or notify a user that recording devices are around). We also need techniques by which each recorded subject may have a say about the use of the data.
- *Data sharing*: Users need to be informed about data sharing/transferred to other parties.

Addressing the above challenges requires multidisciplinary research drawing from many different areas, including computer science and engineering, information systems, statistics, risk models, economics, social sciences, political sciences, human factors, and psychology. We believe that all these perspectives are needed to develop effective solutions to the problem of privacy in the era of big data as well as to reconcile security with privacy.

35.4.6 BDMA for Cyber Security

To protect important digital assets, organizations are investing in new cyber security tools that need to analyze big data ranging from log files to e-mail attachments to prevent, detect, and recover from cyber attacks [KAR14]. As a part of this workshop, we explored the following topics:

- *What is different about big data management analytics (BDMA) for cyber security?* The workshop participants pointed out that BDMA for cyber security needs to deal with adaptive and malicious adversaries who can potentially launch attacks to avoid being detected (i.e., data poisoning attacks, denial of service, denial of information attacks, etc.). In addition, BDMA for cyber security needs to operate in high volume (e.g., data coming from multiple intrusion detection systems and sensors) and high noise environments (i.e., constantly changing normal system usage data is mixed with stealth advanced persistent threat-related data). One of the important points that came out of this discussion is that we need BDMA tools that can integrate data from hosts, networks, social networks, bug reports, mobile devices, and internet of things sensors to detect attacks.
- *What is the right BDMA architecture for cyber security*? We also discussed whether we need different types of BDMA system architectures for cyber security. Based on the use cases discussed, participants felt that existing BDMA system architectures can be adapted for cyber security needs. One issue pointed out was that real-time data analysis must be supported by a successful BDMA system for cyber security. For example, once a certain type of attack is known, the system needs to be updated to look for such attacks in real time including re-examining the history data to see whether prior attacks have occurred.
- *Data sharing for BDMA for cyber security:* It emerged quickly during our discussions that cyber security data needs to be shared both within as well as across organizations. In addition to obvious privacy, security and incentive issues in sharing cyber security data, participants felt that we need common languages and infrastructure to capture and share such cyber security data. For example, we need to represent certain low-level system information (e.g., memory, CPU states, etc.) so that it can be mapped to similar cyber security incidents.
- *BDMA for preventing cyber attacks:* There was substantial discussion on how BDMA tools could be used to prevent attacks. One idea that emerged is that BDMA systems that can easily track sensitive data using the captured provenance information can potentially detect attacks before too much sensitive information is disclosed. Based on this observation, building provenance-aware BDMA systems would be needed for cyber attack prevention. Also, BDMA tools for cyber security can potentially mine useful attacker information such as their motivations, technical capabilities, modus operandi, and so on to prevent future attacks.
- *BDMA for digital forensics:* BDMA techniques could be used for digital forensics by combining or linking different data sources. The main challenge that emerged was identifying the right data sources for digital forensics. In addition, answers to the following questions were not clear immediately: What data to capture? What to filter out (big noise in big data)? What data to link? What data to store and for how long? How to deal with machine-generated content and Internet of Things?
- *BDMA for understanding the users of the cyber systems:* Participants believe that BDMA could be used to mine human behavior to learn how to improve the systems. For example, an organization may send phishing e-mails to its users and carry out security re-training

for those who are fooled by such a phishing attack. In addition, BDMA techniques could be used to understand and build normal behavior models per user to find significant deviations from the norm.

Overall, during our workshop discussions, it became clear that all of the above topics have significant research challenges and more research needs to be done to address them. Furthermore, regardless of whether we are using BDMA for cyber security or for other applications (e.g., healthcare, finance), it is critical that we need to design scalable BDMA solutions. These include parallel BDMA techniques as well as BDMA technical implemented on cloud platforms such as Hadoop/MapReduce, Storm and Spark. In addition, we need to explore the use of BDMA systems such as HBase and CouchDB for use in various applications.

35.5 SUMMARY AND DIRECTIONS

This chapter has explored the issues surrounding BDSP as well as applying BDMA techniques for cyber security. As massive amounts of data are being collected, stored, manipulated, merged, analyzed, and expunged, security and privacy concerns will explode. We need to develop technologies to address security and privacy issues throughout the lifecycle of the data. However, technologies alone will not be sufficient. We need to understand not only the societal impact of data collection, use, and analysis, we also need to formulate appropriate laws and policies for such activities. Our workshop explored the initial directions to address some of the major challenges we are faced with today. We need an interdisciplinary approach consisting of technologists, application specialists, social scientists, policy analysts, and lawyers to work together to come up with viable and practical solutions.

This chapter has described the security and privacy issues for big data as well as discussed the issues that need to be investigated for applying BDMA techniques for cyber security. We have also provided summaries of the workshop presentations and discussions. We made a submission to the National Privacy Research Strategy on October 16, 2014 that was based on the workshop summary. We also participated in the National Privacy Research Strategy Conference in Washington, DC February 18–20, 2015 and gave a presentation of the workshop summary at this event. Our goal is to build a community in BDSP. In addition, the National Institute of Standards and Technology (NIST) has also developed a report on the security and privacy for big data [NIST1]. This report is published by NIST's BDSP Working Group which is part of NIST's [NIST2] Big Data Working Group. Furthermore, NIST is also developing a framework called NICE (National Initiative for Cyber Security Framework) for cyber security education. We need to incorporate BDSP as well as BDMA for cyber security topics into this framework. Therefore, it is important for the different agencies to continue to work together and develop strategies not only for research but also for education in BDSP as well as on applying BDMA for cyber security.

REFERENCES

[BERT12]. E. Bertino, *Data Protection from Insider Threats*, Morgan & Claypool, 2012.

[BERT14]. E. Bertino, "Security with Privacy—Opportunities and Challenges" Panel Statement, *COMPSAC* Vasteras, Sweden, pp. 436-437, 2014.

[DAMI07]. M. Damiani, E. Bertino, B. Catania, P. Perlasca, "GEO-RBAC: A Spatially Aware RBAC," *ACM Transactions on Information and System Security*, 10 (1), Article No. 2, 2007.

[HAML14]. S. Khan, K. Hamlen, M. Kantarcioglu, "Silver Lining: Enforcing Secure Information Flow at the Cloud Edge," *IC2E*, Boston, MA, pp. 37–46, 2014.

[INAN08]. A. Inan, M. Kantarcioglu, E. Bertino, M. Scannapieco, "A Hybrid Approach to Private Record Linkage," *ICDE*, Cancun, Mexico, pp. 496–505, 2008.

[INAN12]. A. Inan, M. Kantarcioglu, G. Ghinita, E. Bertino, "A Hybrid Approach to Private Record Matching," *IEEE Transactions on Dependable Secure Computing (TDSC)*, 9 (5), 684–698, 2012.

[KAR14]. S. Kar, "Gartner Report: Big Data will Revolutionize Cyber Security in the Next Two Years," cloud-times.org, Feb. 12, 2014.

[KUZU13]. M. Kuzu et al. "Efficient Privacy-Aware Record Integration," In *Proceedings of Joint 2013 EDBT/ICDT Conferences, EDBT'13*, Genoa, Italy, Mar. 18–22, ACM, 2013.

[LIND00]. Y. Lindell and B. Pinkas, "Privacy Preserving Data Mining," In *Advances in Cryptology*, Aug. 20–24, Springer-Verlag, Berlin, 2000.

[LIU14]. D. Liu, E. Bertino, X. Yi, "Privacy of Outsourced K-Means Clustering," In *Proceedings of the 9th ACM Symposium on Information, Computer and Communication Security*, Jun. 4–6, Kyoto (Japan), pp. 123-134, 2014.

[NITRD]. http://csi.utdallas.edu/events/NSF/NPRS%20Workshop%20Presentation.pdf

[NPRS]. https://www.nitrd.gov/cybersecurity/nprsrfi102014/BigData-SP.pdf

[NSF]. http://csi.utdallas.edu/events/NSF/NSF%20workshop%202014.htm

[NIST1]. https://bigdatawg.nist.gov/

[NIST2]. https://www.nist.gov/itl/applied-cybersecurity/nice

[SCAN07]. M. Scannapieco, I. Figotin, E. Bertino, A. Elmagarmid, "Privacy Preserving Schema and Data Matching," In *Proceedings of 2007 ACM SIGMOD International Conference on Management of Data*, Beijing, China, pp. 653-664, 2007.

[THUR02]. B. Thuraisingham, "Data Mining, National Security, Privacy and Civil Liberties," *SIGKDD Explorations*, 4 (2), 1–5, 2002.

[ULUS14]. H. Ulusoy et al., "Vigiles: Fine-Grained Access Control for MapReduce Systems," In *2014 IEEE International Congress on Big Data (BigData Congress)*, Anchorage, AK, pp. 40–47, 2014.

[VAID06]. J. Vaidya, Y. Zhu, C. Clifton, "Privacy Preserving Data Mining," *Advances in Information Security*, 19, Springer, New York, pp. 1–121, 2006.

[WANG14]. H.X. Wang, K. Nayak, C. Liu, E. Shi, E. Stefanov, Y. Huang, "Oblivious Data Structures," IACR Cryptology ePrint Archive, 185, 2014.

Conclusion to Part V

Part V, consisting of seven chapters, described some of our exploratory systems and plans for both big data management and analytics (BDMA) and big data security and privacy (BDSP).

Chapter 29 provided an overview of confidentiality, privacy, and trust considerations with respect to inference with an emphasis on big data systems such as social media systems. We first discussed a framework for enforcing confidentiality, privacy, and trust (CPT) for the semantic web. Next, we described our approach to confidentiality and inference control. Next, we discussed privacy for the semantic web. This was followed by a discussion of trust management as well as an integrated framework for CPT. Finally, we discussed how we can adapt the CPT framework for big data systems such as social media systems. Chapter 30 essentially integrated much of the design and implementation of the systems we have developed and described a unifying framework for big data systems. The framework includes components both for access control and inference control as well as information sharing control. We also discussed the modules of the framework as well as building the global inference controller. Chapter 31 discussed the need for IoT security and provided some use cases. Next, we described a layered architecture for secure IoT. We argued that data security and analytics are at the heart of IoT security because data is being collected from the various IoT devices. This data has to be secured. In addition, the threat/attack data has to be analyzed to determine anomalies. Chapter 32 discussed malware detection in one type of IoT system and that is connected smartphones. We discussed the security challenges for smartphones and then discussed our approach to malware detection for smartphones based on the Android operating system. Next, we discussed our virtual laboratory for experimentation. In Chapter 33, we discussed a planned case study in the healthcare domain that illustrates how the various techniques in big data management, analytics, security, and privacy could be applied. In Chapter 34, discussed our plans for developing an education curriculum that will be integrated with an experimental infrastructure both for BDMA and BDSP. Finally, in Chapter 35, we provided a summary of the discussions at the NSF workshop we organized on BDSP and BDMA for cyber security.

36 Summary and Directions

36.1 ABOUT THIS CHAPTER

This chapter brings us to a close of *Big Data Analytics with Applications in Insider Treat Detection.* We discussed several aspects including stream data analytics for insider threat detection, big data security and privacy (BDSP) as well as big data security and the cloud. The experimental systems are the ones that we have developed at The University of Texas at Dallas and include secure cloud query processing and cloud-based assured information sharing systems. We also discussed several directions for big data management, analytics, and security including secure Internet of Things (IoT) systems.

The organization of this chapter is as follows. In Section 36.2, we give a summary of this book. This summary has been taken from the summaries of each chapter. In Section 36.3, we discuss directions for big data management, analytics, and security. In Section 36.4, we give suggestions as to where to go from here.

36.2 SUMMARY OF THIS BOOK

We summarize the contents of each chapter essentially taken from the summary and directions section of each chapter. Chapter 1 provided an introduction to this book. We first provided a brief overview of the supporting technologies for big data management and analytics (BDMA) and BDSP which included data security and privacy, data mining, and cloud computing. Then, we discussed various topics addressed in this book including stream data analytics for insider threat detection and BDSP. Our framework is a five-layer framework and each layer was addressed in one section of this book. This framework was illustrated in Figure 1.7. We replicate this framework in Figure 36.1.

This book was divided into five sections. Section I, which described supporting technologies, consisted of six chapters: 2 through 7. Chapter 2 provided an overview of discretionary security policies in database systems. We started with a discussion of access control policies including authorization policies and role-based access control. Then we discussed administration policies. We briefly discussed identification and authentication. We also discussed auditing issues as well as views for security. Next, we discussed policy enforcement. The major issue in policy enforcement is policy specification, policy implementation, and policy visualization. We discussed Structured Query Language (SQL) extensions for specifying policies as well as provided an overview of query modification. We also briefly discussed how policy visualization might be used to integrate multiple policies. We focused mainly on relational databases systems. We also discussed data privacy. In Chapter 3, we first provided an overview of the various data mining tasks and techniques and then discussed some of the techniques that we utilized in this book. These included neural networks, support vector machines, and association rule mining. We have utilized a combination of these techniques together with some other techniques in the literature as well as our own techniques to develop data analytics techniques for massive data. Chapter 4 discussed data mining for security applications. We first started with a discussion of data mining for cyber security applications and then provided a brief overview of the tools we have developed. This chapter laid the foundations for the discussions in Sections II and III. Chapter 5 introduced the notion of the cloud and semantic web technologies. We first discussed concepts in cloud computing including aspects of virtualization. We also discussed the various service models and deployment models for the cloud and provided a brief overview of cloud functions such as storage management and data management. Next, we discussed technologies for the semantic web including eXtensible Markup Language (XML),

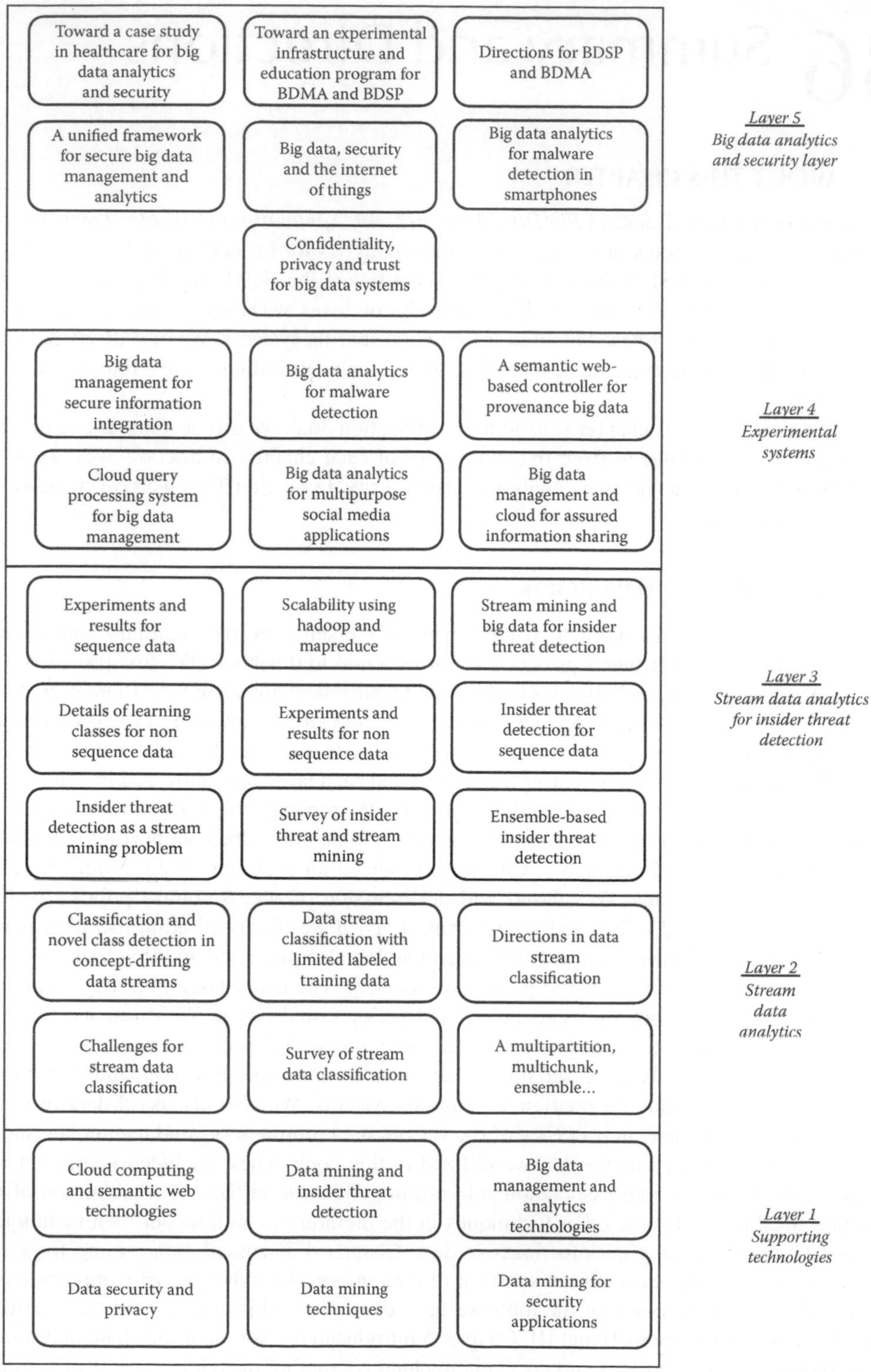

FIGURE 36.1 Layered framework for big data management and analytics and big data security and privacy.

resource description framework (RDF), Ontologies, and Web Ontology Language (OWL). This was followed by a discussion of security issues for the semantic web. Finally, we discussed cloud computing frameworks based on semantic web technologies. Chapter 6 discussed the problem of insider threat and our approach to graph mining for insider threat detection. We represent the insiders and their communication as RDF graphs and then query and mine the graphs to extract the nuggets. We also provided a comprehensive framework for insider threat detection. Much of the discussion in Section III was built on the concepts discussed in Chapter 6. Chapter 7 discussed three types of big data systems. First, we discussed frameworks for managing big data. These are essentially massive data processing platforms such as the Apache Hadoop, Spark, Storm, and Flink. Then we discussed various big data management systems. These included SQL- and NoSQL-based systems. This was followed by a discussion of big data analytics systems. Finally, we discussed cloud platforms that provide the capability for the management of massive amounts of data.

Section II, consisting of six chapters, 8 through 13, focused on stream data analytics. Chapter 8 stressed the need for mining data streams and discussed the challenges. The challenges include infinite length, concept drift, concept evolution, and limited labeled data. We also provided an overview of our approach to mining data streams. Specifically, our approach determines whether an item belongs to a pre-existing class or whether it is a novel class. Chapter 9 discussed several prior approaches that have influenced our work as well as our approach for stream analytics. For example, in the single-model classification approach, incremental learning techniques are used. The ensemble-based techniques are more efficiently built than the single-model approach. Our novel class detection approach integrates both data stream classification and novelty detection. Our data stream classification technique with limited labeled data uses a semisupervised technique. Chapter 10 introduced a multiple partition, multiple chunk (MPC) ensemble method for classifying concept-drifting data streams. Our ensemble approach is a generalization over previous ensemble approaches that train a single classifier from a single data chunk. By introducing this MPC ensemble, we have reduced the errors significantly over the single-partition, single-chunk approach. We have proved our claims theoretically, tested our approach on both synthetic data and real-world data, and obtained better classification accuracies compared to other approaches. Chapter 11 presented a novel technique to detect new classes in concept-drifting data streams. Most of the novelty detection techniques either assume that there is no concept drift, or build a model for a single "normal" class and consider all other classes as novel. But our approach is capable of detecting novel classes in the presence of concept drift and even when the model consists of multiple "existing" classes. Besides, our novel class detection technique is nonparametric, meaning, it does not assume any specific distribution of data. We also show empirically that our approach outperforms the state-of-the-art data stream-based novelty detection techniques in both classification accuracy and processing speed. It might appear to readers that in order to detect novel classes, we are in fact examining whether new clusters are being formed, and therefore, the detection process could go on without supervision. But supervision is necessary for classification. Without external supervision, two separate clusters could be regarded as two different classes, although they are not. Conversely, if more than one novel class appears in a chunk, all of them could be regarded as a single novel class if the labels of those instances are never revealed. Chapter 12 addressed a more realistic problem of stream mining: training with a limited amount of labeled data. Our technique is a more practical approach to the stream classification problem since it requires less labeled data, saving much time and cost that would be otherwise required to manually label the data. Previous approaches for stream classification did not address this vital problem. We designed and implemented a semisupervised clustering-based stream classification algorithm to solve this limited labeled data problem. We tested our technique on a synthetically generated dataset, and a real botnet dataset and received better classification accuracies than other stream classification techniques. Chapter 13 discussed our findings and provided directions for further work in stream data analytics in general and stream data classification in particular. We need to enhance the algorithms by providing greater accuracy and fewer false positives and negatives. Furthermore, we need to enhance the performance of the algorithms for handling massive amounts of stream data. Toward this end, we believe that a cloud-based implementation is a viable approach for high performance data analytics.

Section III, consisting of nine chapters, 14 through 22, discussed stream data analytics for insider threat detection. Chapter 14 defined the insider threat detection as a stream mining problem and proposed two methods (supervised and unsupervised learning) for efficiently detecting anomalies in stream data. To cope with concept evolution, our supervised approach maintains an evolving ensemble of multiple one-class support vector machine (OCSVM) models. Our unsupervised approach combines multiple graph-based anomaly detection (GBAD) models in an ensemble of classifiers. The ensemble updating process is designed in both cases to keep the ensemble current as the stream evolves. This evolutionary capability improves the classifier's survival of concept drift as the behavior of both legitimate and illegitimate agents varies over time. In the experiments, we use test data that records system call data for a large, UNIX-based, multiuser system. Chapter 15 discussed aspects of stream mining as well as applying stream mining for massive data. We argued that many of the learning techniques that have been proposed in the literature do not handle data streams. As a result, these techniques do not address the evolving nature of streams. Our goal was to adapt SVM techniques for data streams so that such techniques can be used to handle the insider threat problem. Chapter 16 discussed ensemble-based learning for insider threat detection. In particular, we described techniques for both supervised and unsupervised learning and discussed the issues involved. We believe that ensemble-based approaches are suited for data streams as they are unbounded. Chapter 17 described the different classes of learning techniques for nonsequence data. It described exactly how each method arrives at detecting insider threats and how ensemble models are built, modified, and discarded. First, we discussed supervised learning in detail and then unsupervised learning. Chapter 18 discussed our testing methodology and experimental results for mining data streams consisting of nonsequence data. In particular, the datasets used our experimental setup and results were discussed. We examined various aspects such as false positives, false negatives, and accuracy. Our results indicate that supervised learning yields better results for certain datasets. However, we need to carry out more extensive experiments for a variety of datasets. Nevertheless, our work has given guidance to experimentation for insider threat detection. Chapter 19 discussed sequenced data. We argued that insider threat detection-related sequence data is stream-based in nature. Sequence data may be gathered over time, maybe even years. We assumed a continuous data stream will be converted into a number of chunks. For example, each chunk may represent a week and contain the sequence data which arrived during that time period. We then described various techniques, both supervised and unsupervised, for mining data streams for sequence data. Chapter 20 discussed our testing methodology and experimental results for mining data streams consisting of sequence data. In particular, the datasets used our experimental setup and results were discussed. We examined various aspects such as false positives, false negatives, and accuracy. We also explained the results obtained. In Chapter 21, we discussed the scalability of our techniques and the issues in designing big data analytics techniques for insider threat detection. Finally, Chapter 22 discussed future directions for using stream data analytics for insider treat detection.

Section IV, consisting of six chapters, 23 through 28, described some of the experimental systems we have developed. These systems have also been discussed in our previous books. However, in this discussion, we also focused on the BDMA and BDSP techniques that we used to design these systems. Chapter 23 presented a framework capable of handling enormous amounts of RDF data that can be used to represent big data systems such as social networks. Since our framework is based on Hadoop, which is a distributed and highly fault-tolerant system, it inherits these two properties automatically. The framework is highly scalable. To increase the capacity of our system, all that needs to be done is to add new nodes to the Hadoop cluster. We proposed a schema to store RDF data, an algorithm to determine a query processing plan, whose worst case is bounded, to answer a SPARQL query and a simplified cost model to be used by the algorithm. Our experiments demonstrated that our system is highly scalable. Chapter 24 described the design of InXite which is a social media system. InXite will be a great asset to the analysts who have to deal with massive amounts of data streams in the form of billions of blogs and messages among others. For example, by analyzing the behavioral history of a particular group of individuals as well as details of concepts such as events, analysts will be able to predict behavioral changes in the near future and take necessary measures. We have also discussed our use of cloud computing in the implementation of InXite as well as provided an overview of the use of big data technologies to improve the performance of InXite. Chapter 25 described our design and implementation of a cloud-based information sharing system called CAISS. CAISS utilizes several of the technologies we have developed as well as open source tools. We also described the design of an ideal cloud-based assured information sharing system called CAISS++. Chapter 26 described techniques to protect data by encrypting it before storing on cloud computing servers like Amazon S3. We proposed to use two key servers to generate and store the keys. Also, we assured more security than some of the other known approaches as we do not store the actual key used to encrypt the data. We also discussed our implementation that was based on a semantic web-based framework. Chapter 27 discussed big data techniques for malware detection. We formulated both malicious code detection and botnet traffic detection as stream data analytics problems, and introduced extended MPC (EMPC), a novel ensemble learning technique for automated classification of infinite-length, concept-drifting streams. Applying EMPC to real data streams obtained from polymorphic malware and botnet traffic samples yielded better detection accuracies than other stream data classification techniques. Finally, Chapter 28 described the first of a kind inference controller that will control certain unauthorized inferences in a data management system. Our approach is powerful due to the fact that we have applied semantic web technologies for both policy representation and reasoning. Furthermore, we have described inference control for provenance data represented as RDF graphs. We also discussed the use of big data techniques for inference control.

Section V, consisting of seven chapters, 29 through 35, discussed aspects of big data analytics, security, and privacy together with a presentation of some of our exploratory systems. Chapter 29 provided an overview of security, privacy, and trust considerations with respect to inference. We first discussed a framework for enforcing confidentiality, privacy, and trust for the semantic web. Next, we described our approach to confidentiality and inference control as well as privacy for the semantic web. This was followed by a discussion of trust management as well as an integrated framework for confidentiality, privacy, and trust (CPT). Finally, we discussed how we can adapt the CPT framework for big data systems such as social media data systems. Chapter 30 essentially integrated much of the design and implementation of the various systems that we have developed and described a unifying framework for big data systems. The framework includes components both for access control and inference control and also information sharing control. Our framework can also include the modules for risk and game theoretic approaches for access and inference control as well as integrity management modules. We discussed the modules of the framework as well as developing a global inference controller. Chapter 31 discussed the need for IoT security and provided some use cases. Next, we described a layered architecture for secure IoT. We argued that data security, privacy, and analytics are at the heart of IoT security because data is being collected from the various IoT devices. This data has to be secured. In addition, the threat/attack data has to be analyzed to determine anomalies. Also, the privacy of the individuals using IoT systems has to be ensured. Chapter 32 discussed malware detection in one type of IoT system and, that is, connected smartphones. We discussed the security challenges for smartphones and then discussed our approach to malware detection for smartphones based on the Android operating system. Next, we discussed our virtual laboratory for experimentation. The technologies include Hadoop/MapReduce as well as Storm and Spark for designing scalable systems. We also discussed the course modules we are introducing for the security of smartphones. These include mobile system forensics as well as mobile data management security. Chapter 33 discussed a planned case study in the healthcare domain that illustrated how the various techniques in big data management, analytics, security, and privacy could be applied. In particular, we focused on methodologies as well as designs of a framework for the proposed case study. Finally, Chapter 34 discussed a planned education curriculum that will be integrated with an experimental infrastructure both for BDMA and BDSP. Finally, Chapter 35 provided a summary of the discussions at the National Science Foundation Workshop on BDSP. In particular, we explored the issues surrounding BDSP as well as applying BDMA techniques for cyber security. We argued that as massive amounts of data are being collected, stored, manipulated, merged, analyzed, and expunged, security and privacy concerns will explode. Therefore, we need to develop technologies to address security and privacy issues throughout the lifecycle of the data.

This book has two appendices. In Appendix A, we provide the broad picture for data management and discuss how all the books we have written fit together. In Appendix B, we discuss database management systems. Much of the work discussed in this book has evolved from the concepts and technologies discussed in Appendix B.

36.3 DIRECTIONS FOR BDMA AND BDSP

There are many directions for BDMA and BDSP. We discuss some of them for the topics addressed in this book. Figure 36.2 illustrates the directions and challenges.

As discussed in Section II, in the area of stream data mining, we need to design techniques that can scale to handle massive amounts of data. While we have discussed how cloud technologies may be applied, we need to develop experimental systems that use technologies such as Hadoop/MapReduce, Storm, and Spark. In addition, we also need to ensure that the techniques produce accurate results with very few false positive and false negatives. In Section III, we discussed how stream data analytics could be applied for insider threat detection. We need to apply the scalable techniques to real-world datasets.

In Section IV, we discussed various experimental systems that use some form of the BDMA and/or BDSP technologies. For example, we discussed our assured information sharing system that functions in the cloud, that is, based on the Hadoop/MapReduce platform. As new technologies such as Spark emerge, we need to experiment with such technologies for assured information sharing. In addition, we need to examine the various big data management systems such as HBase and CouchDB to see how they can be used to manage the massive amounts of data.

In Section V, we discussed various aspects of big data analytics, security, and privacy. A major challenge in BDMA systems is the violation of privacy. We need to develop privacy-preserving BDMA techniques. With respect to the confidentiality of the BDMA systems, we need to develop suitable access control models. The numerous access control models that have been developed in the literature need to be examined for BDMA systems and the scalability of these models have to be studied. Finally, we need to develop techniques that can detect and prevent attacks on BDMA

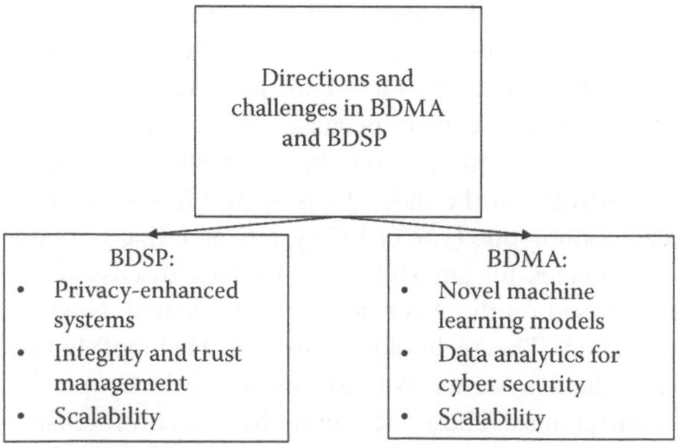

FIGURE 36.2 Directions and challenges in big data management and analytics and big data security and privacy.

systems. In addition, we also need to explore areas such as identity management, handling identity theft as well as auditing and forensics for BDMA systems.

Big data analytics technique for cyber security applications such as malware detection is an area that has emerged as a major research direction. The challenge here is to design scalable data analytics (essentially machine learning) techniques to detect the attacks to the BDMA systems. Due to the fact that BDMA systems such as Facebook have close to a billion active daily users, we need big data analytics techniques to monitor the activity and determine suspicious behavior, Furthermore, social media data which is essentially a type of big data that includes not only text but also photos, images, video, audio, and animation data has to be secure. That is, we need appropriate policies for such data. Finally, the privacy of the individuals using big data systems has to be ensured.

36.4 WHERE DO WE GO FROM HERE?

This book has focused on BDMA and BDSP in general and stream data analytics for insider threat detection in particular. We have discussed many concepts, challenges, and solutions. We also discussed experimental systems as well as exploratory systems. We need to continue with research and development efforts if we are to make progress in this very important area.

The question is where do we go from here? First of all, those who wish to work in this area must have a good knowledge of the supporting technologies including cloud, data management and analytics, semantic web, and security. For example, it is important to understand the technologies that comprise data analytics and how they scale for handling massive data.

Next, since the field is expanding rapidly and there are many developments in the field, the reader has to keep up with the developments including reading about the commercial products and prototypes as well as the emerging systems. Finally, we encourage the reader to experiment with the products and also develop analytics and security tools. This is the best way to get familiar with a particular field. That is, work on hands-on problems and provide solutions to get a better understanding. The developers should be familiar with technologies such as Hadoop, MapReduce, HBase, Storm, and Spark. The cloud will continue to have a major impact on handling massive amounts of data and processing for many big data systems including social media data systems and therefore security for the cloud will be an important aspect. Finally, big data is a broad term that includes many applications in various fields including in healthcare and finance. Therefore, it is important to examine each application and develop analytics and security solutions. The various types of attacks also have to be examined for each big data application.

We need research and development support from the federal and local government funding agencies. Agencies such as the National Science Foundation, National Security Agency, the US Army, Navy, Air Force, the Defense Advanced Research Projects Agency, the Intelligence Advanced Research Projects Activity, and the Department of Homeland Security are funding research in security and machine learning. We also need commercial corporations to invest research and development funds so that progress can be made in industrial research as well as be able to transfer the research to commercial products. We also need to collaborate with the international research community to solve problems and promote standards that are not only of national interest but also of international interest. In summary, we need public/private/academic partnerships to develop breakthrough technologies in the very important areas of BDMA and BDSP.

Appendix A: Data Management Systems: Developments and Trends

A.1 OVERVIEW

The main purpose of this appendix is to set the context of the series of books we have written in data management, data mining, and data security. Our series started back in 1997 with our book on *Data Management Systems Evolution and Interoperation* [THUR97]. Our subsequent books have evolved from this first book. We have essentially repeated Chapter 1 of our first book in Appendix A of our subsequent books. The purpose of this appendix is to provide an overview of data management systems as well as to show how the field has evolved over the years: from data to information to knowledge and now to big data. We will then discuss the relationships between the books we have written.

As stated in our series of books, the developments in information systems technologies have resulted in computerizing many applications in various business areas. Data have become a critical resource in many organizations and therefore, efficient access to data, sharing the data, extracting information from the data, and making use of the information, have become urgent needs. As a result, there have been several efforts on integrating the various data sources scattered across several sites. These data sources may be databases managed by database management systems or they could simply be files. To provide the interoperability between the multiple data sources and systems, various tools are being developed. These tools enable users of one system to access other systems in an efficient and transparent manner.

We define data management systems to be systems that manage the data, extract meaningful information from the data, and make use of the information extracted. Therefore, data management systems include database systems, data warehouses, and data mining systems. Data could be structured data such as that found in relational databases or it could be unstructured such as text, voice, imagery, and video. There have been numerous discussions in the past to distinguish between data, information, and knowledge. We do not attempt to clarify these terms. For our purposes, data could be just bits and bytes or it could convey some meaningful information to the user. We will, however, distinguish between database systems and database management systems. A database management system is that component which manages the database containing persistent data. A database system consists of both the database and the database management system.

A key component to the evolution and interoperation of data management systems is the interoperability of heterogeneous database systems. Efforts on the interoperability between database systems have been reported since the late 1970s. However, it is only recently that we are seeing commercial developments in heterogeneous database systems. Major database system vendors are now providing interoperability between their products and other systems. Furthermore, many of the database system vendors are migrating toward an architecture called the client–server architecture which facilitates distributed data management capabilities. In addition to efforts on the interoperability between different database systems and client–server environments, work is also directed toward handling autonomous and federated environments.

It should be noted technologies have evolved over the past 20 years since we published our first book in 1997. With the advent of the world wide web, the importance of data was beginning to be realized. Over the past 20 years increasingly massive amounts of data are being collected, stored, processed, and analyzed. While the challenge was to manage petabyte-sized databases which was called "the massive data problem" at that time has now evolved into zettabyte- and even exabyte-sized databases which is now called the "big data problem." Furthermore, while machine-learning techniques used to work on what was called "toy problems" at that time is now used to work on "real-world problems." This is because of the tremendous advances in hardware as well as advances in understanding data as well as more sophisticated learning techniques, especially in the field of what is called "deep learning." Therefore, as long as organizations (commercial, academic, and government) collect data and analyze data, big data analytics is here to stay. It also means we have to ensure that security and privacy policies are enforced at all stages of the data lifecycle. We have addressed some aspects of the challenges in this book.

The organization of this appendix is as follows. Since database systems are a key component of data management systems, we first provide an overview of the developments in database systems. These developments are discussed in Section A.2. Then we provide a vision for data management systems in Section A.3. Our framework for data management systems is discussed in Section A.4. Note that data mining, warehousing, as well as web data management are components of this framework. Building information systems from our framework with special instantiations is discussed in Section A.5. It should be noted that the Sections A.2 through A.5 have been taken from our first book and duplicated in each of our subsequent books. The relationship between the various texts that we have written for CRC Press is discussed in Section A.6. This appendix is summarized in Section A.7.

A.2 DEVELOPMENTS IN DATABASE SYSTEMS

Figure A.1 provides an overview of the developments in database systems technology. While the early work in the 1960s focused on developing products based on the network and hierarchical data models, much of the developments in database systems took place after the seminal paper by Codd describing the relational model [CODD70] (see also [DATE90]). Research and development work on relational database systems was carried out during the early 1970s and several prototypes were developed throughout the 1970s. Notable efforts include IBM's (International Business Machine Corporation's) System R and the University of California at Berkeley's INGRES. During the 1980s, many relational database system products were being marketed (notable among these products

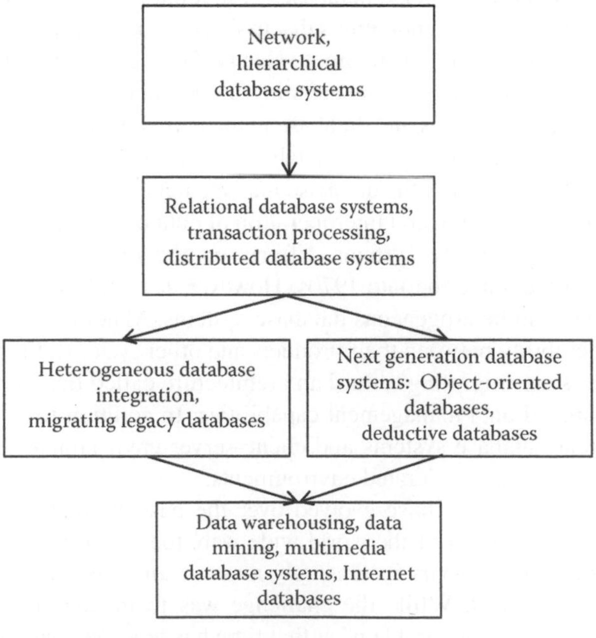

FIGURE A.1 Developments in database systems technology.

are those of Oracle Corporation, Sybase Inc., Informix Corporation, INGRES Corporation, IBM, Digital Equipment Corporation, and Hewlett Packard Company). During the 1990s, products from other vendors emerged (e.g., Microsoft Corporation). In fact, to date numerous relational database system products have been marketed. However, Codd has stated that many of the systems that are being marketed as relational systems are not really relational (see, e.g., the discussion in [DATE90]). He then discussed various criteria that a system must satisfy to be qualified as a relational database system. While the early work focused on issues such as data model, normalization theory, query processing and optimization strategies, query languages, and access strategies and indexes, later the focus shifted toward supporting a multiuser environment. In particular, concurrency control and recovery techniques were developed. Support for transaction processing was also provided.

Research on relational database systems as well as on transaction management was followed by research on distributed database systems around the mid-1970s. Several distributed database system prototype development efforts also began around the late 1970s. Notable among these efforts include IBM's System R*, DDTS (Distributed Database Testbed System) by Honeywell Inc., SDD-I and Multibase by CCA (Computer Corporation of America), and Mermaid by SDC (System Development Corporation). Furthermore, many of these systems (e.g., DDTS, Multibase, Mermaid) function in a heterogeneous environment. During the early 1990s, several database system vendors (such as Oracle Corporation, Sybase Inc., Informix Corporation) provided data distribution capabilities for their systems. Most of the distributed relational database system products are based on client–server architectures. The idea is to have the client of vendor A communicates with the server database system of vendor B. In other words, the client–server computing paradigm facilitates a heterogeneous computing environment. Interoperability between relational and nonrelational commercial database systems is also possible. The database systems community is also involved in standardization efforts. Notable among the standardization efforts are the ANSI/SPARC 3-level schema architecture, the IRDS (Information Resource Dictionary System) standard for Data Dictionary Systems, the relational query language SQL (Structured Query Language), and the RDA (Remote Database Access) protocol for remote database access.

Another significant development in database technology is the advent of object-oriented database management systems. Active work on developing such systems began in the mid-1980s and they are now commercially available (notable among them include the products of Object Design, Inc., Ontos, Inc., Gemstone Systems, Inc., and Versant Object Technology). It was felt that new generation applications such as multimedia, office information systems, CAD/CAM, process control, and software engineering have different requirements. Such applications utilize complex data structures. Tighter integration between the programming language and the data model is also desired. Object-oriented database systems satisfy most of the requirements of these new generation applications [CATT91].

According to the Lagunita report published as a result of a National Science Foundation (NSF) workshop in 1990 (see [SILB90] and [KIM90]), relational database systems, transaction processing, and distributed (relational) database systems are stated as mature technologies. Furthermore, vendors are marketing object-oriented database systems and demonstrating the interoperability between different database systems. The report goes on to state that as applications are getting increasingly complex, more sophisticated database systems are needed. Furthermore, since many organizations now use database systems, in many cases of different types, the database systems need to be integrated. Although work has begun to address these issues and commercial products are available, several issues still need to be resolved. Therefore, challenges faced by the database systems researchers in the early 1990s were in two areas. One was next-generation database systems and the other was heterogeneous database systems.

Next-generation database systems include object-oriented database systems, functional database systems, special parallel architectures to enhance the performance of database system functions, high-performance database systems, real-time database systems, scientific database systems, temporal database systems, database systems that handle incomplete and uncertain information and intelligent database systems (also sometimes called logic or deductive database systems). Ideally, a database system should provide the support for high-performance transaction processing, model complex applications, represent new kinds of data, and make intelligent deductions. While significant progress has been made during the late 1980s and early 1990s, there is much to be done before such a database system can be developed.

Heterogeneous database systems have been receiving considerable attention during the past decade [MARC90]. The major issues include handling different data models, different query processing strategies, different transaction processing algorithms, and different query languages. Should a uniform view be provided to the entire system or should the users of the individual systems maintain their own views of the entire system? These are questions that have yet to be answered satisfactorily. It is also envisaged that a complete solution to heterogeneous database management systems is a generation away. While research should be directed toward finding such a solution, work should also be carried out to handle limited forms of heterogeneity to satisfy the customer needs. Another type of database system that received some attention is a federated database system. Note that some have used the terms heterogeneous database system and federated database system interchangeably. While heterogeneous database systems can be part of a federation, a federation can also include homogeneous database systems.

The explosion of users on the web as well as developments in interface technologies has resulted in even more challenges for data management researchers. A second workshop was sponsored by NSF in 1995, and several emerging technologies were identified to be important as we entered into the twenty-first century [WIDO96]. These include digital libraries, managing very large databases, data administration issues, multimedia databases, data warehousing, data mining, data management for collaborative computing environments, and security and privacy. Another significant development in the 1990s is the development of object-relational systems. Such systems combine the advantages of both object-oriented database systems and relational database systems. Also, many corporations are now focusing on integrating their data management products with web technologies. Finally, for many organizations there is an increasing need to migrate some of the legacy databases and applications to newer architectures and systems such as client–server architectures and relational database systems. We believe there is no end to data management systems. As new technologies are developed, there are new opportunities for data management research and development.

A comprehensive view of all data management technologies is illustrated in Figure A.2. As shown, traditional technologies include database design, transaction processing, and benchmarking.

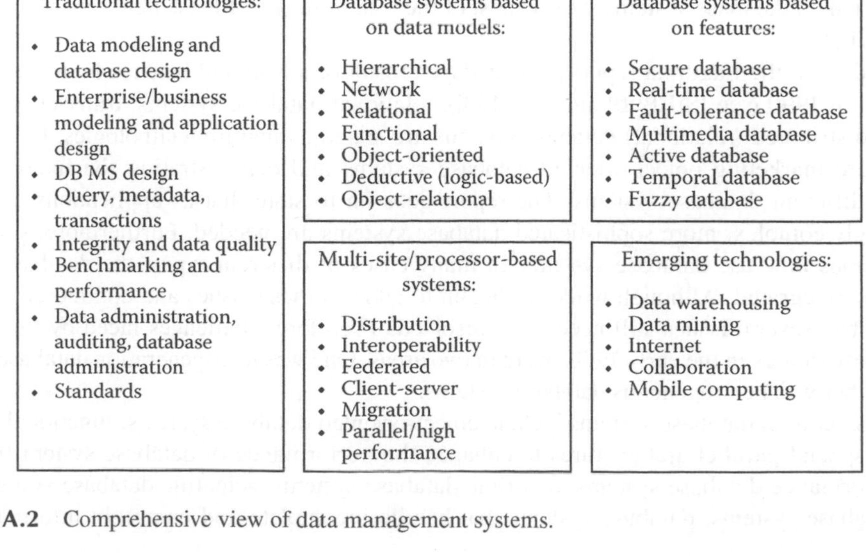

FIGURE A.2 Comprehensive view of data management systems.

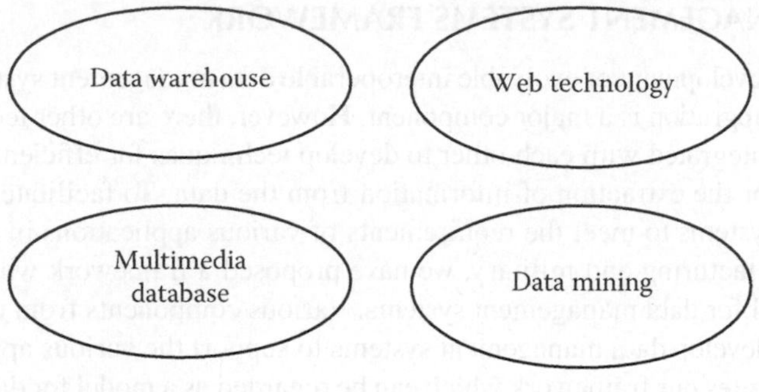

FIGURE A.3 Stand-alone systems.

Then there are database systems based on data models such as relational and object oriented. Database systems may depend on features they provide such as security and real time. These database systems may be relational or object oriented. There are also database systems based on multiple sites or processors such as distributed and heterogeneous database systems, parallel systems, and systems being migrated. Finally, there are the emerging technologies such as data warehousing and mining, collaboration, and the web. Any comprehensive text on data management systems should address all of these technologies. We have selected some of the relevant technologies and put them in a framework. This framework is described in Section A.5.

A.3 STATUS, VISION, AND ISSUES

Significant progress has been made on data management systems. However, many of the technologies are still stand-alone technologies as illustrated in Figure A.3. For example, multimedia systems are yet to be successfully integrated with warehousing and mining technologies. The ultimate goal is to integrate multiple technologies so that accurate data, as well as information, are produced at the right time and distributed to the user in a timely manner. Our vision for data and information management is illustrated in Figure A.4.

The work discussed in [THUR97] addressed many of the challenges necessary to accomplish this vision. In particular, integration of heterogeneous databases as well as the use of distributed object technology for interoperability was discussed. While much progress has been made on the system aspects of interoperability, semantic issues still remain a challenge. Different databases have different representations. Furthermore, the same data entity may be interpreted differently at different sites. Addressing these semantic differences and extracting useful information from the heterogeneous and possibly multimedia data sources are major challenges.

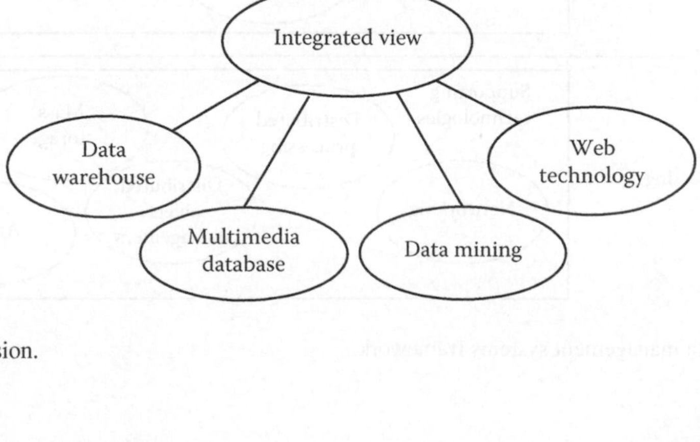

FIGURE A.4 Vision.

A.4 DATA MANAGEMENT SYSTEMS FRAMEWORK

For the successful development of evolvable interoperable data management systems, heterogeneous database systems integration is a major component. However, there are other technologies that have to be successfully integrated with each other to develop techniques for efficient access and sharing of data as well as for the extraction of information from the data. To facilitate the development of data management systems to meet the requirements of various applications in fields such as medical, financial, manufacturing and military, we have proposed a framework which can be regarded as a reference model for data management systems. Various components from this framework have to be integrated to develop data management systems to support the various applications.

Figure A.5 illustrates our framework which can be regarded as a model for data management systems. This framework consists of three layers. One can think of the component technologies which we will also refer to as components belonging to a particular layer to be more or less built upon

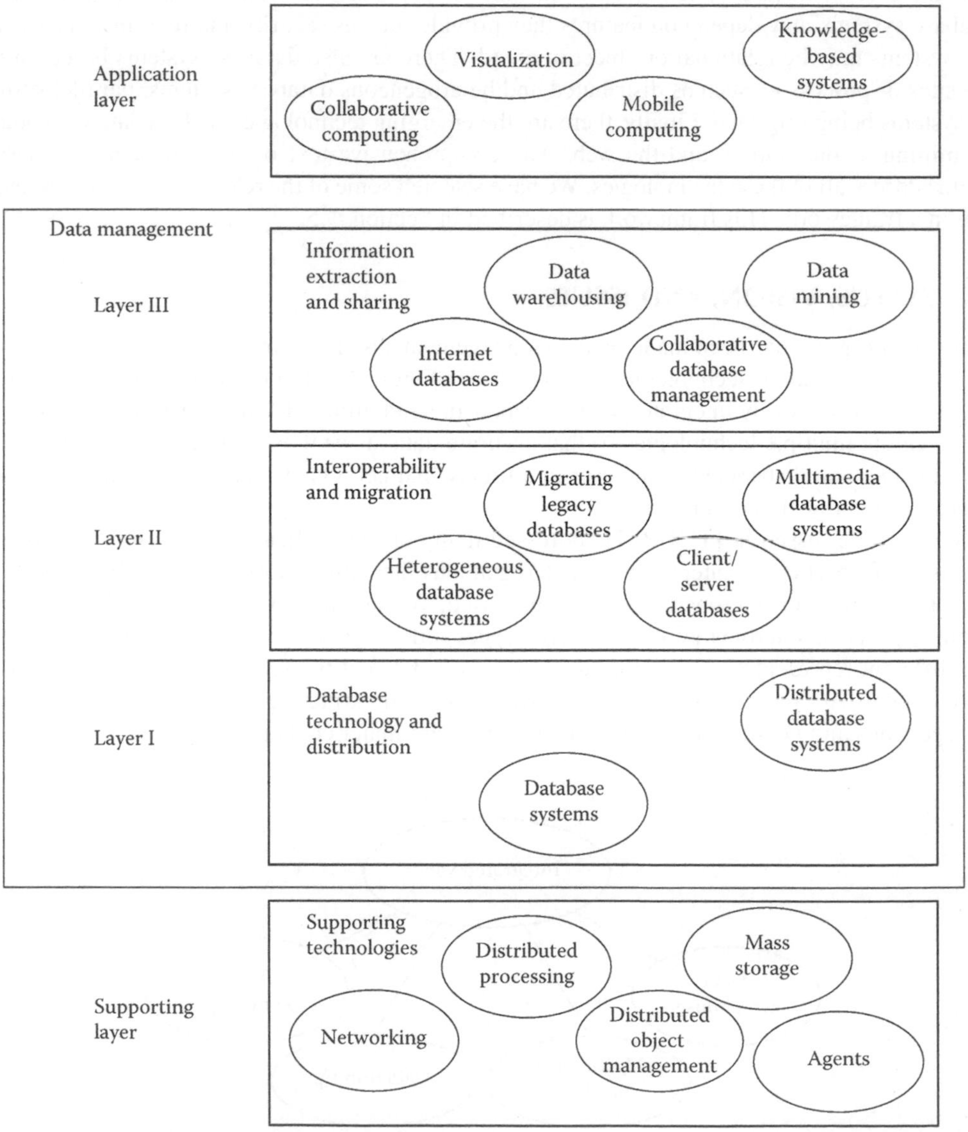

FIGURE A.5 Data management systems framework.

the technologies provided by the lower layer. Layer I is the database technology and distribution layer. This layer consists of database systems and distributed database systems technologies. Layer II is the interoperability and migration layer. This layer consists of technologies such as heterogeneous database integration, client/server databases, and multimedia database systems to handle heterogeneous data types and migrating legacy databases. Layer III is the information extraction and sharing layer. This layer essentially consists of technologies for some of the newer services supported by data management systems. These include data warehousing, data mining [THUR98], web databases, and database support for collaborative applications. Data management systems may utilize lower level technologies such as networking, distributed processing, and mass storage. We have grouped these technologies into a layer called the supporting technologies layer. This supporting layer does not belong to the data management systems framework. This supporting layer also consists of some higher-level technologies such as distributed object management and agents. Also, shown in Figure A.5 is the application technologies layer. Systems such as collaborative computing systems and knowledge-based systems which belong to this layer may utilize data management systems. Note that the application technologies layer is also outside of the data management systems framework.

The technologies that constitute the data management systems framework can be regarded to be some of the core technologies in data management. However, features like security, integrity, real-time processing, fault tolerance, and high-performance computing are needed for many applications utilizing data management technologies such as medical, financial, or military, among others. We illustrate this in Figure A.6, where a three-dimensional view relating data management technologies with features and applications is given. For example, one could develop a secure distributed database management system for medical applications or a fault-tolerant multimedia database management system for financial applications.

Integrating the components belonging to the various layers is important to developing efficient data management systems. In addition, data management technologies have to be integrated with the application technologies to develop successful information systems. However, at present, there is limited integration between these various components. Our books have addressed concepts related to the various layers of this framework.

Note that security cuts across all the layers. Security is needed for the supporting layers such as agents and distributed systems. Security is needed for all of the layers in the framework including

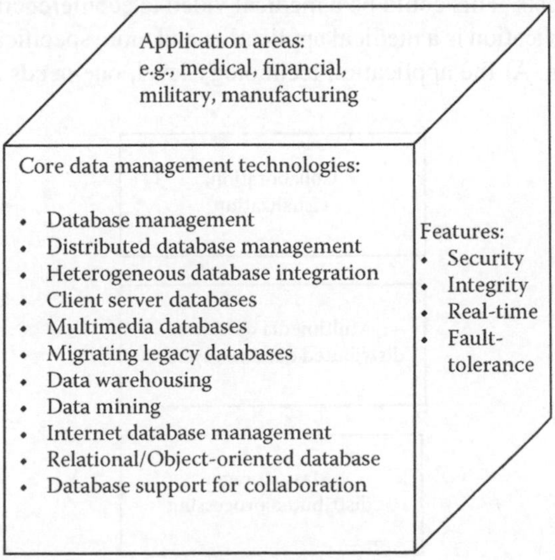

FIGURE A.6 A three-dimensional view of data management.

database security, distributed database security, warehousing security, web database security, and collaborative data management security.

A.5 BUILDING INFORMATION SYSTEMS FROM THE FRAMEWORK

Figure A.5 illustrated a framework for data management systems. As shown in the figure, the technologies for data management include database systems, distributed database systems, heterogeneous database systems, migrating legacy databases, multimedia database systems, data warehousing, data mining, web databases, and database support for collaboration. Furthermore, data management systems take advantage of supporting technologies such as distributed processing and agents. Similarly, application technologies such as collaborative computing, visualization, expert systems, and mobile computing take advantage of data management systems.

Many of us have heard of the term information systems on numerous occasions. These systems have sometimes been used interchangeably with data management systems. In our terminology, information systems are much broader than data management systems but they do include data management systems. In fact, a framework for information systems will include not only the data management system layers but also the supporting technologies layer as well as the application technologies layer. That is, information systems encompass all kinds of computing systems. It can be regarded as the finished product that can be used for various applications. That is, while hardware is at the lowest end of the spectrum, applications are at the highest end.

We can combine the technologies of Figure A.5 to put together information systems. For example, at the application technology level, one may need collaboration and visualization technologies so that analysts can collaboratively carry out some tasks. At the data management level, one may need both multimedia and distributed database technologies. At the supporting level, one may need mass storage as well as some distributed processing capability. This special framework is illustrated in Figure A.7. Another example is a special framework for interoperability. One may need some visualization technology to display the integrated information from the heterogeneous databases. At the data management level, we have heterogeneous database systems technology. At the supporting technology level, one may use distributed object management technology to encapsulate the heterogeneous databases. This special framework is illustrated in Figure A.8.

Finally, let us illustrate the concepts that we have described above by using a specific cxample. Suppose a group of physicians/surgeons wants a system where they can collaborate and make decisions about various patients. This could be a medical video teleconferencing application. That is, at the highest level, the application is a medical application and more specifically, a medical video teleconferencing application. At the application technology level, one needs a variety of technologies

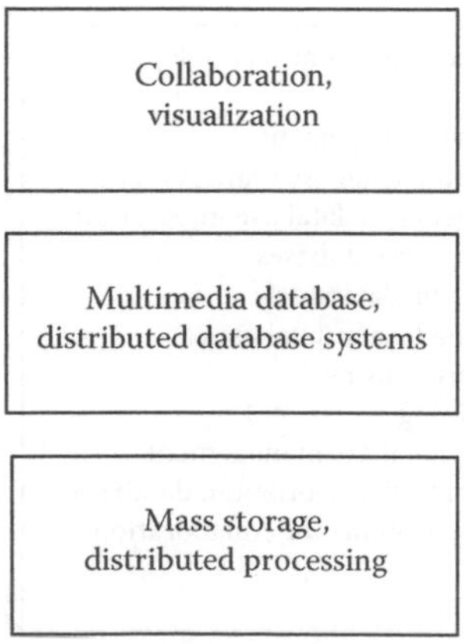

FIGURE A.7 Framework for multimedia data management for collaboration.

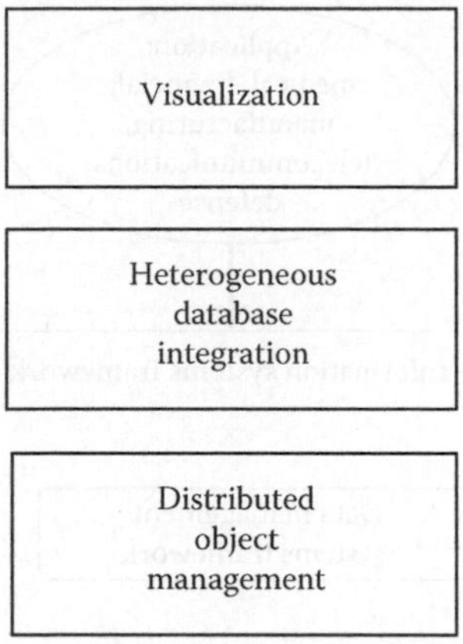

FIGURE A.8 Framework for heterogeneous database interoperability.

including collaboration and teleconferencing. These application technologies will make use of data management technologies such as distributed database systems and multimedia database systems. That is, one may need to support multimedia data such as audio and video. The data management technologies in turn draw upon lower level technologies such as distributed processing and networking. We illustrate this in Figure A.9.

In summary, information systems include data management systems as well as application layer systems such as collaborative computing systems and supporting layer systems such as distributed object management systems.

While application technologies make use of data management technologies and data management technologies make use of supporting technologies, the ultimate user of the information system is the application itself. Today numerous applications make use of information systems. These applications

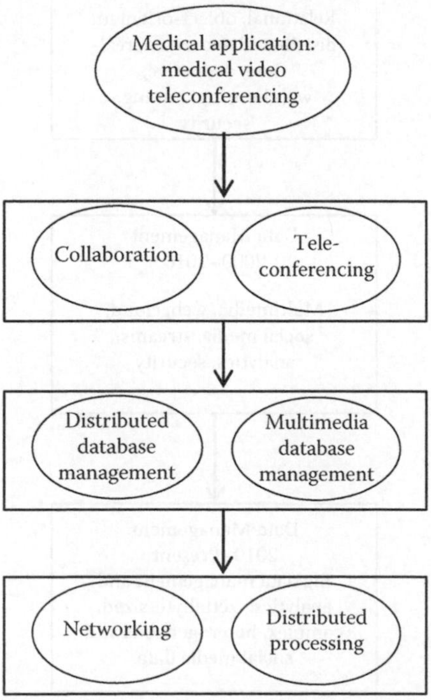

FIGURE A.9 Specific example.

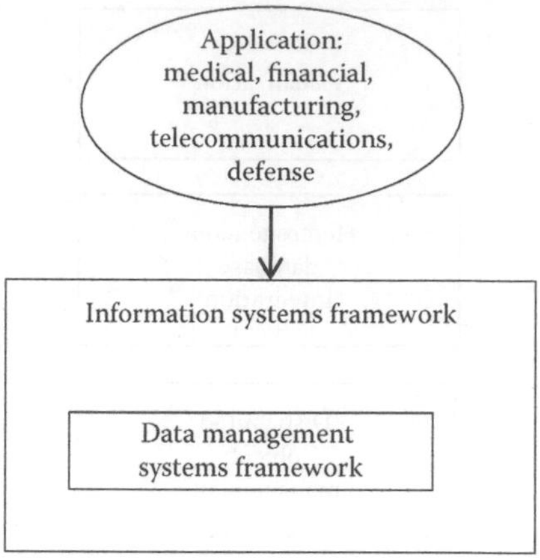

FIGURE A.10 Application framework relationship.

are from multiple domains such as medical, financial, manufacturing, telecommunications, and defense. Specific applications include signal processing, electronic commerce, patient monitoring, and situation assessment. Figure A.10 illustrates the relationship between the application and the information system. The evolution from data to big data is illustrated in Figure A.11.

A.6 RELATIONSHIP BETWEEN THE TEXTS

We have published two book series. The first series is mainly for technical managers, while the second series is for researchers and developers. The books in the first series are the following:

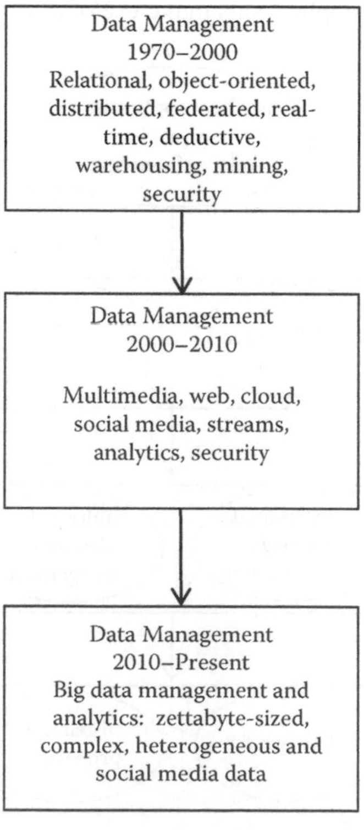

FIGURE A.11 From data to big data.

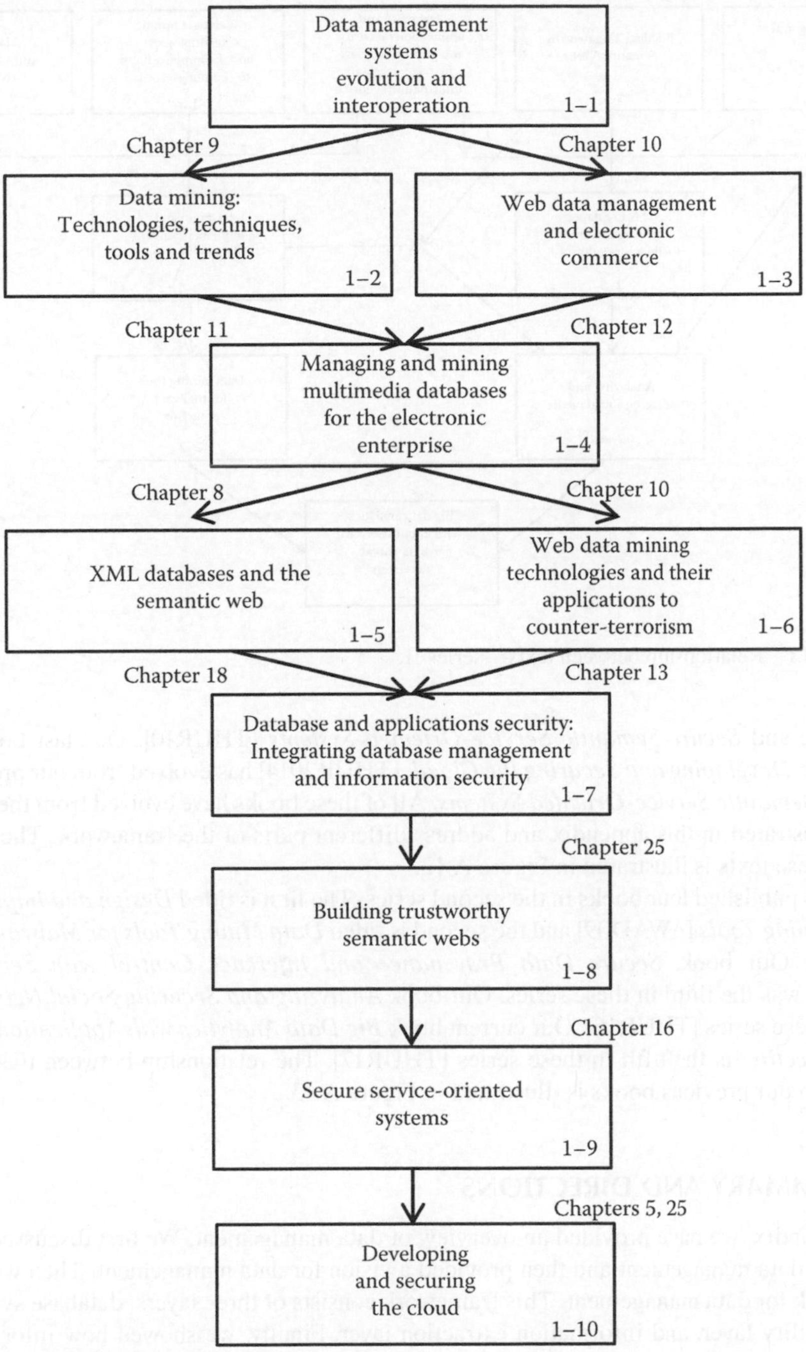

FIGURE A.12 Relationship between texts—series I.

Data Management Systems: Evolution and Interoperation [THUR97], *Data Mining: Technologies, Techniques, Tools and Trends* [THUR98], *Web Data Management and Electronic Commerce* [THUR00], *Managing and Mining Multimedia Databases for the Electronic Enterprise* [THUR01], *XML, Databases and The Semantic Web* [THUR02], *Web Data Mining and Applications in Business Intelligence and Counter-terrorism* [THUR03], *Database and Applications Security: Integrating Data Management and Information Security* [THUR05]. *Building Trustworthy Semantic Web*

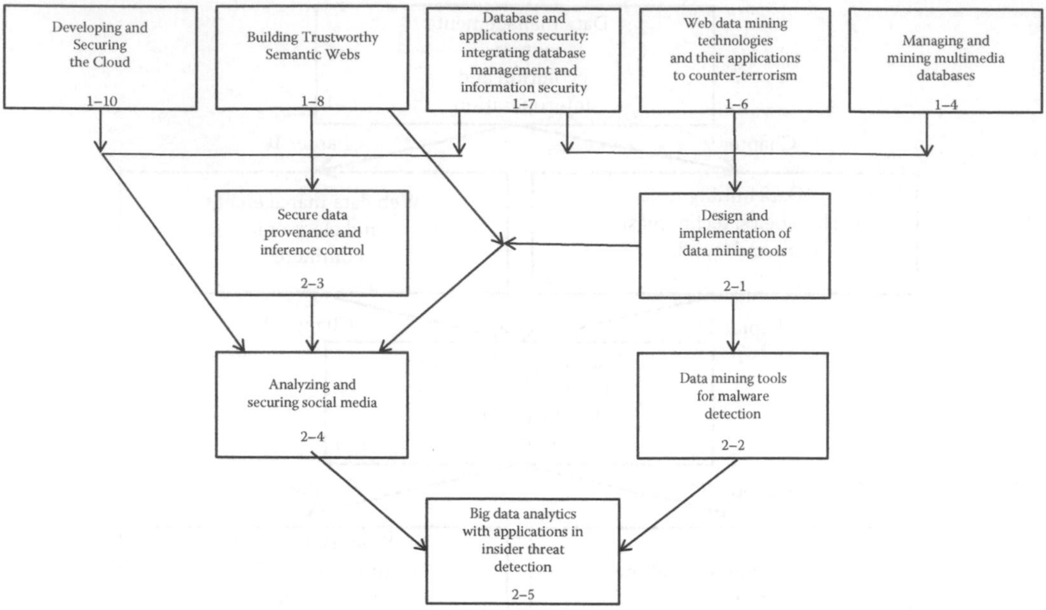

FIGURE A.13 Relationship between texts—series II.

[THUR07], and *Secure Semantic Service-Oriented Systems* [THUR10]. Our last book in these series titled: *Developing and Securing the Cloud*, [THUR2014] has evolved from our previous book on *Secure Semantic Service-Oriented Systems.* All of these books have evolved from the framework that we illustrated in this appendix and address different parts of the framework. The connection between these texts is illustrated in Figure A.12.

We have published four books in the second series. The first is titled *Design and Implementation of Data Mining Tools* [AWAD09] and the second is titled *Data Mining Tools for Malware Detection* [MASU11]. Our book, *Secure Data Provenance and Inference Control with Semantic Web* [THUR15] was the third in these series. Our book *Analyzing and Securing Social Networks* is the fourth in these series [THUR16]. Our current book *Big Data Analytics with Applications in Insider Threat Detection* is the fifth in these series [THUR17]. The relationship between these books as well as with our previous books is illustrated in Figure A.13.

A.7 SUMMARY AND DIRECTIONS

In this appendix, we have provided an overview of data management. We first discussed the developments in data management and then provided a vision for data management. Then we illustrated a framework for data management. This framework consists of three layers: database systems layer, interoperability layer, and information extraction layer. Finally, we showed how information systems could be built from the technologies of the framework.

We believe that data management is essential to many information technologies including data mining, multimedia information processing, interoperability, collaboration and knowledge management, as well as data science which integrates data management, data mining, machine learning, and statistical methods to process massive amounts of heterogeneous data. This appendix stresses on data management. Security is critical for all data management technologies and we rely on these technologies for applications such as social media and insider threat detection. While the latter part of the twentieth century was about the computer revolution, the early part of the twenty-first century is about the data revolution.

REFERENCES

[AWAD09]. M. Awad, L. Khan, B. Thuraisingham, L. Wang, *Design and Implementation of Data Mining Tools*, CRC Press, Boca Raton, FL, 2009.

[CATT91]. R. Cattell, *Object Data Management Systems*, Addison- Wesley, MA, 1991.

[CODD70]. E.F. Codd, "A Relational Model of Data for Large Shared Data Banks," *Communications of the ACM*, 13 (#6), 377–387, June 1970.

[DATE90]. C.J. Date, *An Introduction to Database Management Systems*, Addison-Wesley, MA, 1990 (6th edition published in 1995 by Addison-Wesley).

[KIM90]. W. Kim, editor, "Directions for future database research & development," *ACM SIGMOD Record*, 19 (4), December 1990.

[MARC90]. S.T. March, editors, Special Issue on Heterogeneous Database Systems, *ACM Computing Surveys*, 22 (3), September 1990.

[MASU11]. M. Masud, B. Thuraisingham, L. Khan, *Data Mining Tools for Malware Detection*, CRC Press, Boca Raton, FL, 2011.

[SILB90]. A. Silberschatz, M. Stonebraker, J.D. Ullman, (editors, "Database systems: Achievements and Opportunities," *The "Lagunita" Report of the NSF Invitational Workshop on the Future of Database Systems Research*, February 22–23, Palo Alto, CA, 1990 (TR-90-22), Department of Computer Sciences, University of Texas at Austin, Austin, TX. (also in ACM SIGMOD Record, December 1990).

[THUR97]. B. Thuraisingham, *Data Management Systems: Evolution and Interoperation*, CRC Press, Boca Raton, FL, 1997.

[THUR98]. B. Thuraisingham, *Data Mining: Technologies, Techniques, Tools and Trends*, CRC Press, Boca Raton, FL, 1998.

[THUR00]. B. Thuraisingham, *Web Data Management and Electronic Commerce*, CRC Press, Boca Raton, FL, 2000.

[THUR01]. B. Thuraisingham, *Managing and Mining Multimedia Databases for the Electronic Enterprise*, CRC Press, Boca Raton, FL, 2001.

[THUR02]. B. Thuraisingham, *XML, Databases and The Semantic Web*, CRC Press, Boca Raton, FL, 2002.

[THUR03]. B. Thuraisingham, *Web Data Mining Applications in Business Intelligence and Counter-Terrorism*, CRC Press, Boca Raton, FL, 2003.

[THUR05]. B. Thuraisingham, *Database and Applications Security: Integrating Data Management and Information Security*, CRC Press, Boca Raton, FL, 2005.

[THUR07]. B. Thuraisingham, *Building Trustworthy Semantic Webs*, CRC Press, Boca Raton, FL, 2007.

[THUR10]. B. Thuraisingham, *Secure Semantic Service-Oriented Systems*, CRC Press, Boca Raton, FL, 2010.

[THUR14]. B. Thuraisingham, *Developing and Securing the Cloud*, CRC Press, Boca Raton, FL, 2013.

[THUR15]. B. Thuraisingham, *Tyrone Cadenhead, Murat Kantarcioglu and Vaibhav Khadilkar, Secure Data Provenance and Inference Control with Semantic Web*, CRC Press, Boca Raton, FL, 2014.

[THUR16]. B. Thuraisingham, S. Abrol, R. Heatherly, M. Kantarcioglu, V. Khadilkar, L. Khan, *Analyzing and Securing Social Networks*, CRC Press, Boca Raton, FL, 2016.

[THUR17]. B. Thuraisingham et al., *Big Data Analytics with Applications in Insider Threat Detection*, CRC Press, Boca Raton, FL, 2017.

[WIDO96]. J. Widom, editor, In *Proceedings of the Database Systems Workshop*, Report published by the National Science Foundation, 1995 (also in ACM SIGMOD Record, March 1996, Vol 25 (1), Database Research: Achievements and Opportunities into the 21st Century.

Appendix B: Database Management Systems

B.1 OVERVIEW

Database systems technology has advanced a great deal during the past five decades from the legacy systems based on network and hierarchical models to relational database systems to object databases and more recently big data management systems. We consider a database system to include both the database management system (DBMS) and the database (see also the discussion in [DATE90]). The DBMS component of the database system manages the database. The database contains persistent data. That is, the data are permanent even if the application programs go away.

We have discussed database systems in this appendix as it is at the heart of big data technologies. For example, the supporting technologies discussed in Part I of this book have their roots in database systems (e.g., data mining, data security, big data management). Also, big data management systems have evolved from database query processing and transaction management that were initially developed in the 1970s. Furthermore, some of the experimental systems we have discussed in this book such as cloud-centric assured information sharing have evolved from the concepts in federated databases systems. Therefore, an understanding of database systems is essential to master the concepts discussed in this book.

The organization of this chapter is as follows. In Section B.2, relational data models, as well as entity-relationship models are discussed. In Section B.3, various types of architectures for database systems are described. These include architecture for a centralized database system, schema architecture, as well as functional architecture. Database design issues are discussed in Section B.4. Database administration issues are discussed in Section B.5. Database system functions are discussed in Section B.6. These functions include query processing, transaction management, metadata management, storage management, maintaining integrity and security, and fault tolerance. Distributed database systems are the subject of Section B.7. Heterogeneous database integration aspects are summarized in Section B.8. Object models are discussed in Section B.9. Other types of database systems and their relevance to BDMA are discussed in Section B.10. The chapter is summarized in Section B.11. More details on database systems can be found in [THUR97].

B.2 RELATIONAL AND ENTITY-RELATIONSHIP DATA MODELS

B.2.1 Overview

In general, the purpose of a data model is to capture the universe that it is representing as accurately, completely, and naturally as possible [TSIC82]. In this section, we discuss the essential points of the relational data model, as it is the most widely used model today. In addition, we discuss the entity-relationship data model, as some of the ideas have been used in object models and, furthermore, entity-relationship models are being used extensively in database design.

Many other models exist such as logic-based models, hypersemantic models, and functional models. Discussion of all of these models is beyond the scope of this book. We do however provide an overview of an object model in Section B.15 as object technology is useful for data modeling as well as for database integration.

EMP

SS#	Ename	Salary	D#
1	John	20K	10
2	Paul	30K	20
3	Mary	40K	20

DEPT

D#	Dname	Mgr
10	Math	Smith
20	Physics	Jones

FIGURE B.1 Relational database.

B.2.2 Relational Data Model

With the relational model [CODD70], the database is viewed as a collection of relations. Each relation has attributes and rows. For example, Figure B.1 illustrates a database with two relations: EMP and DEPT. EMP has four attributes: SS#, Ename, Salary, and D#. DEPT has three attributes: D#, Dname, and Mgr. EMP has three rows, also called tuples, and DEPT has two rows. Each row is uniquely identified by its primary key. For example, SS# could be the primary key for EMP and D# for DEPT. Another key feature of the relational model is that each element in the relation is an atomic value such as an integer or a string. That is, complex values such as lists are not supported.

Various operations are performed on relations. The SELECT operation selects a subset of rows satisfying certain conditions. For example, in the relation EMP, one may select tuples where the salary is more than 20K. The PROJECT operation projects the relation onto some attributes. For example, in the relation EMP, one may project onto the attributes Ename and Salary. The JOIN operation joins two relations over some common attributes. A detailed discussion of these operations is given in [DATE90] and [ULLM88].

Various languages to manipulate the relations have been proposed. Notable among these languages is the ANSI Standard SQL (Structured Query Language). This language is used to access and manipulate data in relational databases [SQL3]. There is wide acceptance of this standard among database management system vendors and users. It supports schema definition, retrieval, data manipulation, schema manipulation, transaction management, integrity and, security. Other languages include the relational calculus first proposed in the INGRES project at the University of California at Berkeley [DATE90]. Another important concept in relational databases is the notion of a view. A view is essentially a virtual relation and is formed from the relations in the database.

B.2.3 Entity-Relationship Data Model

One of the major drawbacks of the relational data model is its lack of support for capturing the semantics of an application. This resulted in the development of semantic data models. The entity-relationship (ER) data model developed by Chen [CHEN76] can be regarded to be the earliest semantic data model. In this model, the world is viewed as a collection of entities and relationships between entities. Figure B.2 illustrates two entities, EMP and DEPT. The relationship between them is WORKS.

Relationships can be either one–one, many–one, or many–many. If it is assumed that each employee works in one department and each department has one employee, then WORKS is a

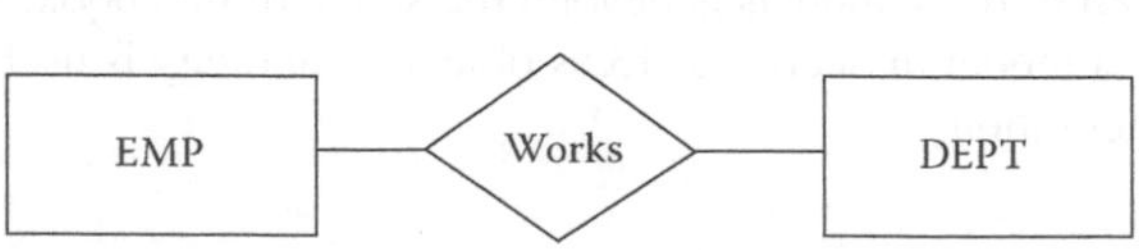

FIGURE B.2 Entity-relationship representation.

one–one relationship. If it is assumed that an employee works in one department and each department can have many employees, then WORKS is a many–one relationship. If it is assumed that an employee works in many departments, and each department has many employees, then WORKS is a many–many relationship.

Several extensions to the entity-relationship model have been proposed. One is the entity-relationship-attribute model where attributes are associated with entities as well as relationships, and another has introduced the notion of categories into the model (see, e.g., the discussion in [ELMA85]). It should be noted that ER models are used mainly to design databases. That is, many database CASE (computer-aided software engineering) tools are based on the ER model, where the application is represented using such a model and subsequently the database (possibly relational) is generated. Current database management systems are not based on the ER model. That is, unlike the relational model, ER models did not take off in the development of database management systems.

B.3 ARCHITECTURAL ISSUES

This section describes various types of architectures for a database system. First we illustrate a centralized architecture for a database system. Then we describe a functional architecture for a database system. In particular, the functions of the DBMS component of the database system are illustrated in this architecture. Then we discuss the ANSI/SPARC's (American National Standard Institute) three-schema architecture, which has been more or less accepted by the database community [DATE90]. Finally, we describe extensible architectures.

Figure B.3 is an example of a centralized architecture. Here, the DBMS is a monolithic entity and manages a database which is centralized. Functional architecture illustrates the functional modules of a DBMS. The major modules of a DBMS include the query processor, transaction manager, metadata manager, storage manager, integrity manager, and security manager. The functional architecture of the DBMS component of the centralized database system architecture (of Figure B.3) is illustrated in Figure B.4.

Schema describes the data in the database. It has also been referred to as the data dictionary or contents of the metadatabase. Three-schema architecture was proposed for a centralized database system in the 1960s. This is illustrated in Figure B.5. The levels are the external schema which provides an external view, the conceptual schema which provides a conceptual view, and the internal schema which provides an internal view. Mappings between the different schemas must be provided to transform one representation into another. For example, at the external level, one could use ER representation. At the logical or conceptual level, one could use relational representation. At the physical level, one could use a representation based on B-Trees.

There is also another aspect to architectures and that is extensible database architectures. For example, for many applications, a DBMS may have to be extended with a layer to support objects

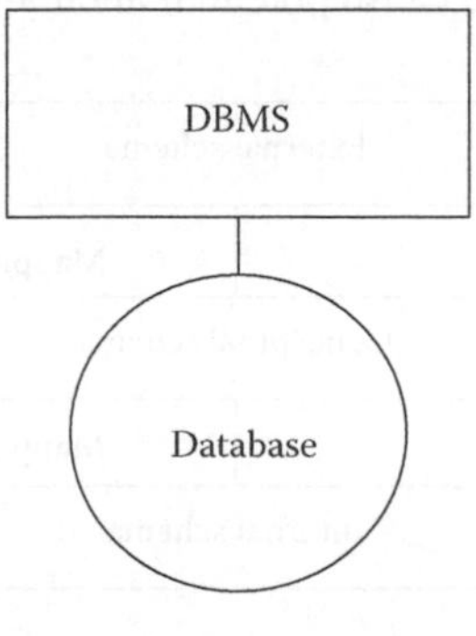

FIGURE B.3 Centralized architecture.

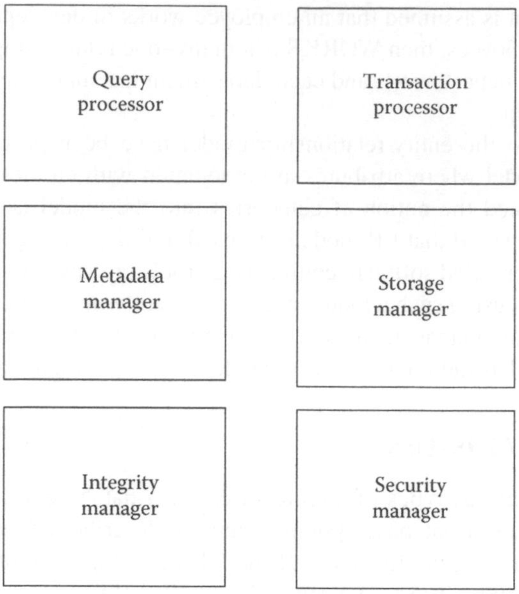

FIGURE B.4 Functional architecture for a DBMS.

or to process rules or to handle multimedia data types or even to do mining. Such an extensible architecture is illustrated in Figure B.6.

B.4 DATABASE DESIGN

Designing a database is a complex process. Much of the work has been on designing relational databases. There are three steps which are illustrated in Figure B.7. The first step is to capture the entities of the application and the relationships between the entities. One could use a model such as the entity-relationship model for this purpose. More recently, object-oriented data models which are part of object-oriented design and analysis methodologies are becoming popular to represent the application.

The second step is to generate the relations from the representations. For example, from the entity-relationship diagram of Figure B.2, one could generate the relations EMP, DEPT, and WORKS. The relation WORKS will capture the relationship between employees and departments.

The third step is to design good relations. This is the normalization process. Various normal forms have been defined in the literature (see, e.g., [MAIE83] and [DATE90]). For many applications, relations in third normal form would suffice. With this normal form, redundancies, complex values, and other situations that could cause potential anomalies are eliminated.

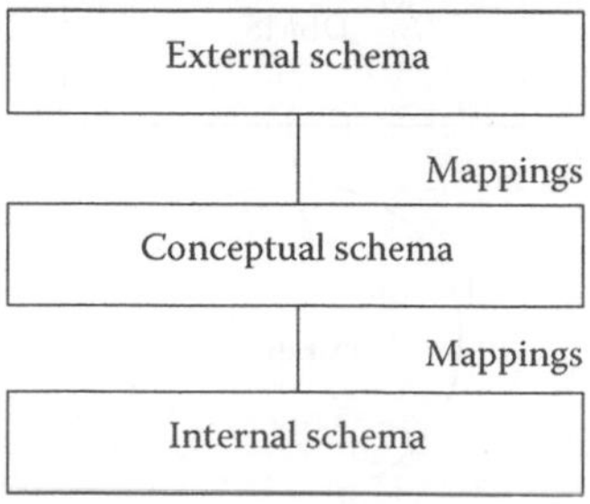

FIGURE B.5 Three-schema architecture.

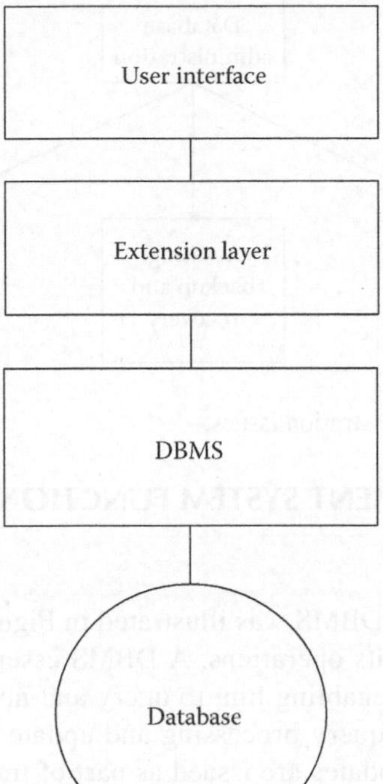

FIGURE B.6 Extensible DBMS.

B.5 DATABASE ADMINISTRATION

A database has a Database Administrator (DBA). It is the responsibility of the DBA to define the various schemas and mappings. In addition, the functions of the administrator include auditing the database as well as implementing appropriate backup and recovery procedures.

The DBA could also be responsible for maintaining the security of the system. In some cases, the System Security Officer (SSO) maintains security. The administrator should determine the granularity of the data for auditing. For example, in some cases there is tuple (or row) level auditing while in other cases there is table (or relation) level auditing. It is also the administrator's responsibility to analyze the audit data.

Note that there is a difference between database administration and data administration. Database administration assumes there is an installed database system. The DBA manages this system. Data administration functions include conducting data analysis, determining how a corporation handles its data, and enforcing appropriate policies and procedures for managing the data of a corporation. Data administration functions are carried out by the data administrator. For a discussion of data administration, we refer to [DMH96, DMH97]. Figure B.8 illustrates various database administration issues.

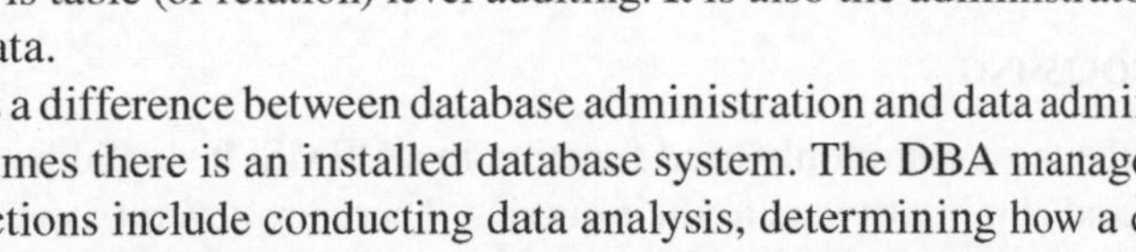

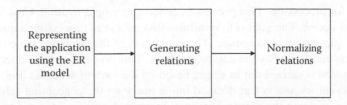

FIGURE B.7 Database design process.

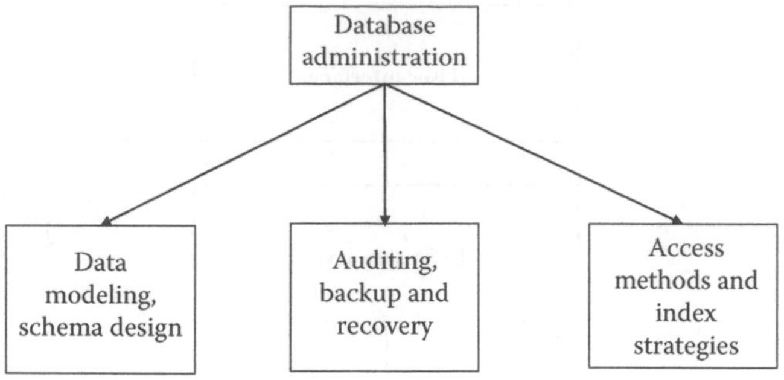

FIGURE B.8 Some database administration issues.

B.6 DATABASE MANAGEMENT SYSTEM FUNCTIONS

B.6.1 Overview

The functional architecture of a DBMS was illustrated in Figure B.4 (see also [ULLM88]). The functions of a DBMS carry out its operations. A DBMS essentially manages a database and it provides support to the user by enabling him to query and update the database. Therefore, the basic functions of a DBMS are query processing and update processing. In some applications such as banking, queries, and updates are issued as part of transactions. Therefore, transaction management is also another function of a DBMS. To carry out these functions, information about the data in the database has to be maintained. This information is called the metadata. The function that is associated with managing the metadata is metadata management. Special techniques are needed to manage the data stores that actually store the data. The function that is associated with managing these techniques is storage management. To ensure that the above functions are carried out properly and that the user gets accurate data, there are some additional functions. These include security management, integrity management, and fault management (i.e., fault tolerance).

This section focuses on some of the key functions of a DBMS. These are query processing, transaction management, metadata management, storage management, maintaining integrity, and fault tolerance. We discuss each of these functions in Sections B.6.2 to B.6.7. In Section B.6.8 we discuss some other functions.

B.6.2 Query Processing

Query operation is the most commonly used function in a DBMS. It should be possible for users to query the database and obtain answers to their queries. There are several aspects to query processing. First of all, a good query language is needed. Languages such as SQL are popular for relational databases. Such languages are being extended for other types of databases. The second aspect is techniques for query processing. Numerous algorithms have been proposed for query processing in general and for the JOIN operation in particular. Also, different strategies are possible to execute a particular query. The costs for the various strategies are computed and the one with the least cost is usually selected for processing. This process is called query optimization. Cost is generally determined by the disk access. The goal is to minimize disk access in processing a query.

Users pose a query using a language. The constructs of the language have to be transformed into the constructs understood by the database system. This process is called query transformation. Query transformation is carried out in stages based on the various schemas. For example, a query based on the external schema is transformed into a query on the conceptual schema. This is then transformed into a query on the physical schema. In general, rules used in the transformation process include the factoring of common subexpressions and pushing selections and projections down

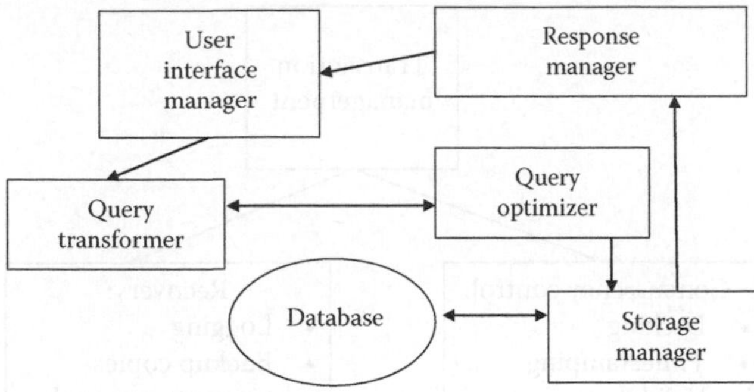

FIGURE B.9 Query processor.

in the query tree as much as possible. If selections and projections are performed before the joins, then the cost of the joins can be reduced by a considerable amount.

Figure B.9 illustrates the modules in query processing. The user-interface manager accepts queries, parses the queries, and then gives them to the query transformer. The query transformer and query optimizer communicate with each other to produce an execution strategy. The database is accessed through the storage manager. The response manager gives responses to the user.

B.6.3 Transaction Management

A transaction is a program unit that must be executed in its entirety or not executed at all. If transactions are executed serially, then there is a performance bottleneck. Therefore, transactions are executed concurrently. Appropriate techniques must ensure that the database is consistent when multiple transactions update the database. That is, transactions must satisfy the ACID (Atomicity, Consistency, Isolation, and Durability) properties. Major aspects of transaction management are serializability, concurrency control, and recovery. We discuss them briefly in this section. For a detailed discussion of transaction management, we refer to [KORT86] and [BERN87].

Serializability: A schedule is a sequence of operations performed by multiple transactions. Two schedules are equivalent if their outcomes are the same. A serial schedule is a schedule where no two transactions execute concurrently. An objective in transaction management is to ensure that any schedule is equivalent to a serial schedule. Such a schedule is called a serializable schedule. Various conditions for testing the serializability of a schedule have been formulated for a DBMS.

Concurrency Control: Concurrency control techniques ensure that the database is in a consistent state when multiple transactions update the database. Three popular concurrency control techniques which ensure the serializability of schedules are locking, time-stamping and validation (which is also called optimistic concurrency control).

Recovery: If a transaction aborts due to some failure, then the database must be brought to a consistent state. This is transaction recovery. One solution to handling transaction failure is to maintain log files. The transaction's actions are recorded in the log file. So, if a transaction aborts, then the database is brought back to a consistent state by undoing the actions of the transaction. The information for the undo operation is found in the log file. Another solution is to record the actions of a transaction but not make any changes to the database. Only if a transaction commits should the database be updated. This means that the log files have to be kept in stable storage. Various modifications to the above techniques have been proposed to handle the different situations.

When transactions are executed at multiple data sources, then a protocol called two-phase commit is used to ensure that the multiple data sources are consistent. Figure B.10 illustrates the various aspects of transaction management.

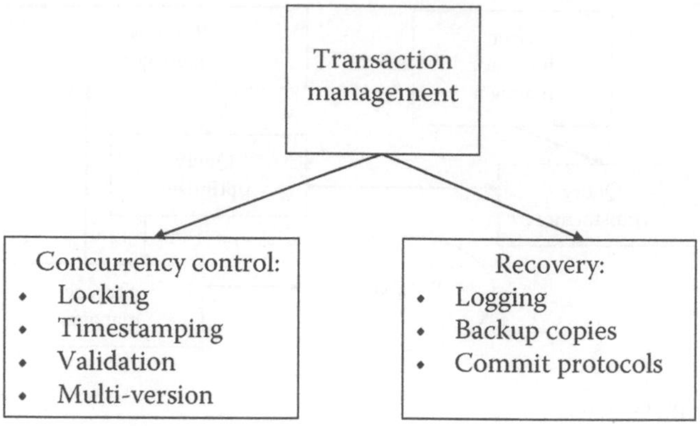

FIGURE B.10 Some aspects of transaction management.

B.6.4 Storage Management

The storage manager is responsible for accessing the database. To improve the efficiency of query and update algorithms, appropriate access methods and index strategies have to be enforced. That is, in generating strategies for executing query and update requests, the access methods and index strategies that are used need to be taken into consideration. The access methods used to access the database would depend on the indexing methods. Therefore, creating and maintaining an appropriate index file is a major issue in database management systems. By using an appropriate indexing mechanism, the query-processing algorithms may not have to search the entire database. Instead, the data to be retrieved could be accessed directly. Consequently, the retrieval algorithms are more efficient. Figure B.11 illustrates an example of an indexing strategy where the database is indexed by projects.

Much research has been carried out on developing appropriate access methods and index strategies for relational database systems. Some examples of index strategies are B-Trees and Hashing [DATE90]. Current research is focusing on developing such mechanisms for object-oriented database systems with support for multimedia data as well as for web database systems, among others.

B.6.5 Metadata Management

Metadata describes the data in the database. For example, in the case of the relational database illustrated in Figure B.1, metadata would include the following information: the database has two relations, EMP and DEPT; EMP has four attributes and DEPT has three attributes, etc. One of the main

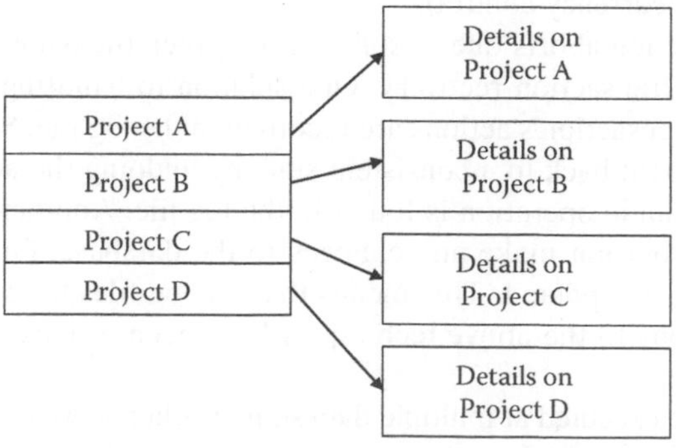

FIGURE B.11 An example index on projects.

Relation REL

Relation	Attribute
EMP	SS#
EMP	Ename
EMP	Salary
EMP	D#
DEPT	D#
DEPT	Dname
DEPT	Mgr

FIGURE B.12 Metadata relation.

issues is developing a data model for metadata. In our example, one could use a relational model to model the metadata also. The metadata relation REL shown in Figure B.12 consists of information about relations and attributes.

In addition to information about the data in the database, metadata also includes information on access methods, index strategies, security constraints, and integrity constraints. One could also include policies and procedures as part of the metadata. In other words, there is no standard definition for metadata. There are, however, efforts to standardize metadata (see, e.g., the IEEE Mass Storage Committee efforts as well as IEEE Conferences on Metadata [MASS]. Metadata continues to evolve as database systems evolve into multimedia database systems and web database systems.

Once the metadata is defined, the issues include managing the metadata. What are the techniques for querying and updating the metadata? Since all of the other DBMS components need to access the metadata for processing, what are the interfaces between the metadata manager and the other components? Metadata management is fairly well understood for relational database systems. The current challenge is in managing the metadata for more complex systems such as digital libraries and web database systems.

B.6.6 Database Integrity

Concurrency control and recovery techniques maintain the integrity of the database. In addition, there is another type of database integrity and that is enforcing integrity constraints. There are two types of integrity constraints enforced in database systems. These are application independent integrity constraints and application specific integrity constraints. Integrity mechanisms also include techniques for determining the quality of the data. For example, what is the accuracy of the data and that of the source? What are the mechanisms for maintaining the quality of the data? How accurate is the data on output? For a discussion of integrity based on data quality, we refer to [DQ]. Note that data quality is very important for mining and warehousing. If the data that is mined is not good, then one cannot rely on the results.

Application independent integrity constraints include the primary key constraint, the entity integrity rule, referential integrity constraint, and the various functional dependencies involved in the normalization process (see the discussion in [DATE90]). Application specific integrity constraints are those constraints that are specific to an application. Examples include "an employee's salary cannot decrease" and "no manager can manage more than two departments." Various techniques have been proposed to enforce application specific integrity constraints. For example, when the database is updated, these constraints are checked and the data are validated. Aspects of database integrity are illustrated in Figure B.13.

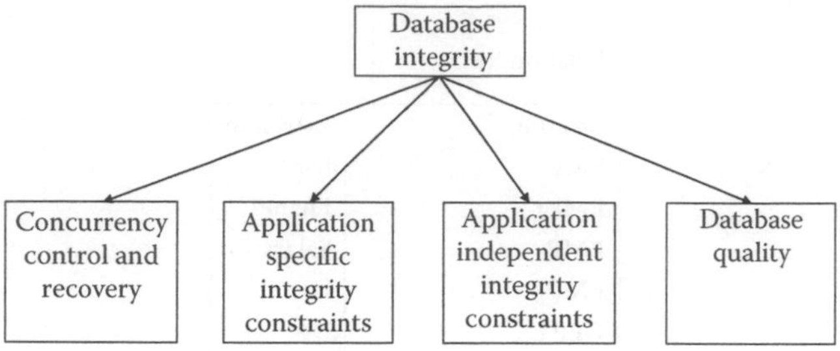

FIGURE B.13 Some aspects of database integrity.

B.6.7 Fault Tolerance

The previous two sections discussed database integrity and security. A closely related feature is fault tolerance. It is almost impossible to guarantee that the database will function as planned. In reality, various faults could occur. These could be hardware faults or software faults. As mentioned earlier, one of the major issues in transaction management is to ensure that the database is brought back to a consistent state in the presence of faults. The solutions proposed include maintaining appropriate log files to record the actions of a transaction in case its actions have to be retraced.

Another approach to handling faults is checkpointing. Various checkpoints are placed during the course of database processing. At each checkpoint it is ensured that the database is in a consistent state. Therefore, if a fault occurs during processing, then the database must be brought back to the last checkpoint. This way it can be guaranteed that the database is consistent. Closely associated with checkpointing are acceptance tests. After various processing steps, the acceptance tests are checked. If the techniques pass the tests, then they can proceed further. Some aspects of fault tolerance are illustrated in Figure B.14.

B.6.8 Other Functions

In this section we will briefly discuss some of the other functions of a database system. They are: security, real-time processing, managing heterogeneous data types, view management, and backup and recovery.

Security: Note that security is a critical function. Therefore, both discretionary security and mandatory security will be discussed throughout this book.

Real-time processing: In some situations, the database system may have to meet real-time constraints. That is, the transactions will have to meet deadlines.

```
Checkpoint A
Start processing
*
*
Acceptance test
If OK, then go to Checkpoint B
Else, roll back to Checkpoint A

Checkpoint B
Start processing
*
*
```

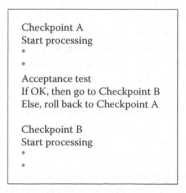

FIGURE B.14 Some aspects of fault tolerance.

Heterogeneous data types: The database system may have to manage multimedia data types such as voice, video, text, and images.

Auditing: The databases may have to be audited so that unauthorized access can be monitored.

View management: As stated earlier views are virtual relations created from base relations. There are many challenges related to view management.

Backup and Recovery: The DBA has to back-up the databases and ensure that the database is not corrupted. Some aspects were discussed under fault tolerance. More details are given in [DATE90].

B.7 DISTRIBUTED DATABASES

Although many definitions of a distributed database system have been given, there is no standard definition. Our discussion of distributed database system concepts and issues has been influenced by the discussion in [CERI84]. A distributed database system includes a distributed database management system (DDBMS), a distributed database, and a network for interconnection. The DDBMS manages the distributed database. A distributed database is data that is distributed across multiple databases. Our choice architecture for a distributed database system is a multi-database architecture which is tightly coupled. This architecture is illustrated in Figure B.15. We have chosen such an architecture that can explain the concepts for both homogeneous and heterogeneous systems based on this approach. In this architecture, the nodes are connected via a communication subsystem and local applications are handled by the local DBMS. In addition, each node is also involved in at least one global application, so there is no centralized control in this architecture. The DBMSs are connected through a component called the distributed processor (DP). In a homogeneous environment, the local DBMSs are homogeneous while in a heterogeneous environment, the local DBMSs may be heterogeneous.

Distributed database system functions include distributed query processing, distributed transaction management, distributed metadata management and enforcing security and integrity across the multiple nodes. The DP is an essential component of the DDBMS. It is this module that connects the different local DBMSs. That is, each local DBMS is augmented by a DP. The modules of the DP are illustrated in Figure B.16. The components are the Distributed Metadata Manager (DMM), the Distributed Query Processor (DQP), the Distributed Transaction Manager (DTM), the Distributed Security Manager (DSP), and the Distributed Integrity Manager (DIM). DMM manages the global metadata. The global metadata includes information on the schemas, which describe the relations in the distributed database, the way the relations are fragmented, the locations of the fragments, and the constraints enforced. DQP is responsible for distributed query processing; DTM is responsible for distributed transaction management; DSM is responsible for enforcing global security constraints;

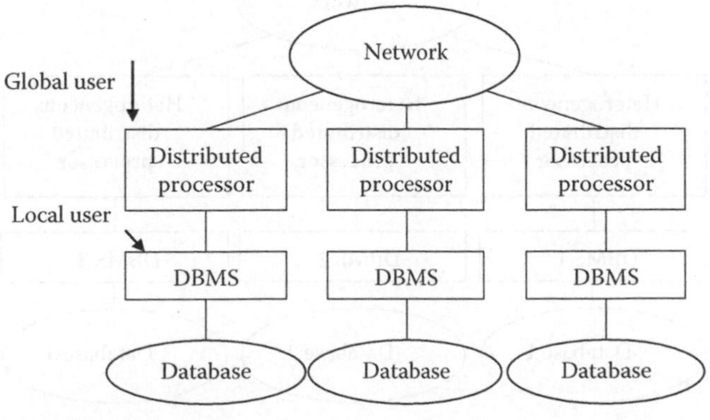

FIGURE B.15 An architecture for a DDBMS.

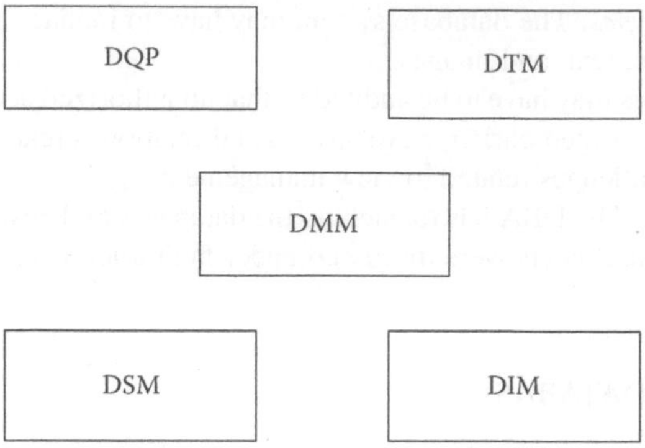

FIGURE B.16 Modules of the DP.

and DIM is responsible for maintaining integrity at the global level. Note that the modules of DP communicate with their peers at the remote nodes. For example, the DQP at node 1 communicates with the DQP at node 2 for handling distributed queries.

B.8 HETEROGENEOUS AND FEDERATED DATA MANAGEMENT

Figure B.17 illustrates an example of interoperability between heterogeneous database systems. The goal is to provide transparent access, both for users and application programs, for querying and executing transactions (see, e.g., [IEEE98 and [WIED92]). Note that in a heterogeneous environment, the local DBMSs may be heterogeneous. Furthermore, the modules of the DP have both local DBMS specific processing as well as local DBMS independent processing. We call such a DP a heterogeneous distributed processor (HDP).

There are several technical issues that need to be resolved for the successful interoperation between these diverse database systems. Note that heterogeneity could exist with respect to different data models, schemas, query processing techniques, query languages, transaction management techniques, semantics, integrity, and security. There are two approaches to interoperability. One is the federated database management approach where a collection of cooperating, autonomous and possibly heterogeneous component database systems, each belonging to one or more federations, communicates with each other. The other is the client–server approach where the goal is for multiple clients to communicate with multiple servers in a transparent manner. We discuss both federated and client–server approaches in Sections B.9 and B.10.

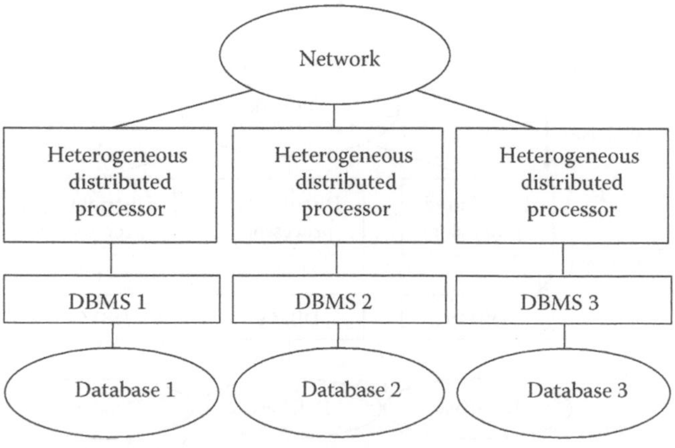

FIGURE B.17 Interoperability of heterogeneous database systems.

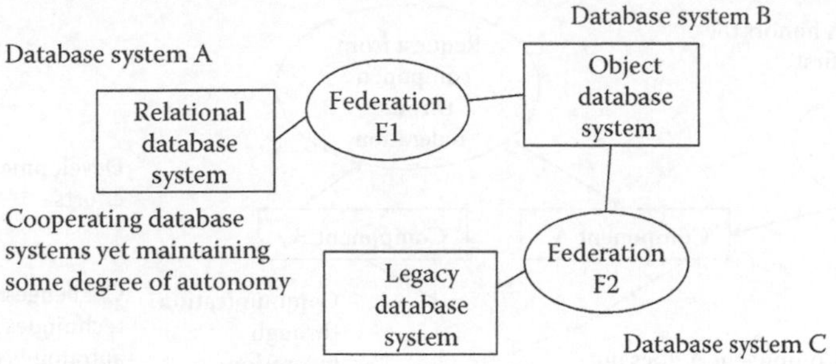

FIGURE B.18 Federated database management.

The development in heterogeneous data management was then extended into federated data management in the 1990s. As stated by Sheth and Larson [SHET90], a federated database system is a collection of cooperating but autonomous database systems belonging to a federation. That is, the goal is for the database management systems, which belong to a federation, to cooperate with one another and yet maintain some degree of autonomy. Note that to be consistent with the terminology, we distinguish between a federated database management system and a federated database system. A federated database system includes both a federated database management system, the local DBMSs, and the databases. The federated database management system is that component which manages the different databases in a federated environment.

Figures B.18 illustrates a federated database system. Database systems A and B belong to federation F1 while database systems B and C belong to federation FB. We can use the architecture illustrated in Figure B.18 for a federated database system. In addition to handling heterogeneity, the HDP also has to handle the federated environment. That is, techniques have to be adapted to handle cooperation and autonomy. We have called such an HDP an FDP (Federated Distributed Processor). An architecture for an FDS is illustrated in Figure B.19.

Figure B.20 illustrates an example of an autonomous environment. There is communication between components A and B and between B and C. Due to autonomy, it is assumed that components A and C do not wish to communicate with each other. Now, component A may get requests from its own user or from component B. In this case, it has to decide which request to honor first. Also, there is a possibility for component C to get information from component A through component B. In such a situation, component A may have to negotiate with component B before it gives a reply to component B. The developments to deal with autonomy are still in the research stages. The challenge is to handle transactions in an autonomous environment. Transitioning the research into commercial products is also a challenge.

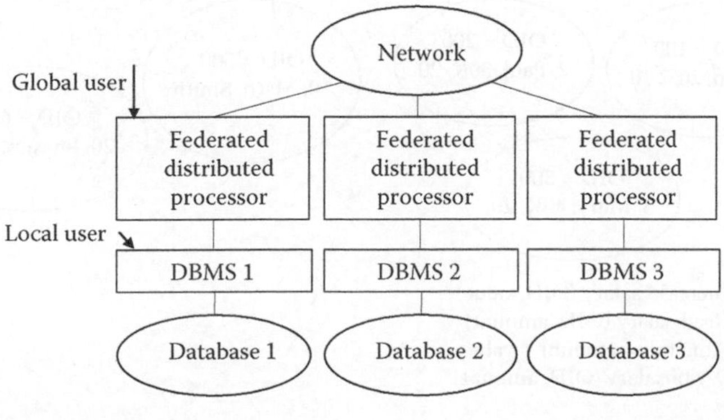

FIGURE B.19 Architecture for a federated database system.

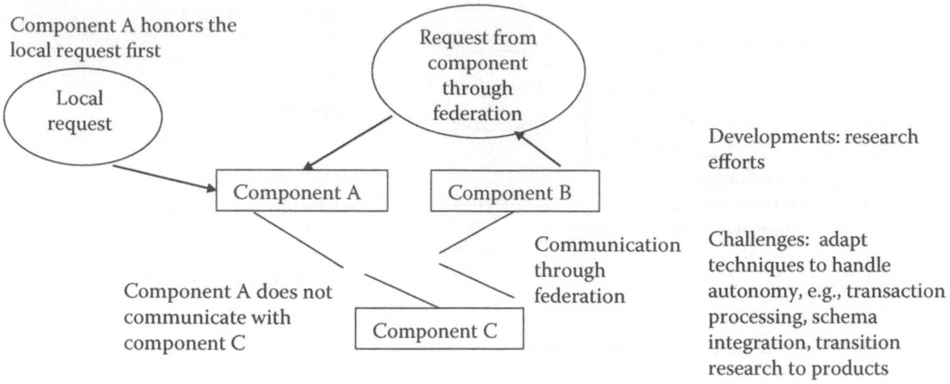

FIGURE B.20 Autonomy.

B.9 OBJECT DATA MODEL

Several object data models were proposed in the 1980s. Initially these models were to support programming languages such as Smalltalk. Later these models were enhanced to support database systems as well as other complex systems. This section provides an overview of the essential features of object models. While there are no standard object models, the Unified Modeling Language (UML) proposed by the prominent object technologists (Rumbaugh, Booch and Jacobson) has gained increasing popularity and has almost become the standard object model in recent years. Our discussion of the object model has been influenced by much of our work in object database systems as well as the one proposed by Won Kim et al. [BANE87]. We call it an object-oriented data model.

The key points in an object-oriented model are encapsulation, inheritance, and polymorphism. With an object-oriented data model, the database is viewed as a collection of objects [BANE87]. Each object has a unique identifier called the object ID. Objects with similar properties are grouped into a class. For example, employee objects are grouped into EMP class while department objects are grouped into DEPT class as shown in Figure B.21. A class has instance variables describing the properties. Instance variables of EMP are SS#, Ename, Salary, and D#, while the instance variables of DEPT are D#, Dname, and Mgr. The objects in a class are its instances. As illustrated in the figure, EMP has three instances and DEPT has two instances.

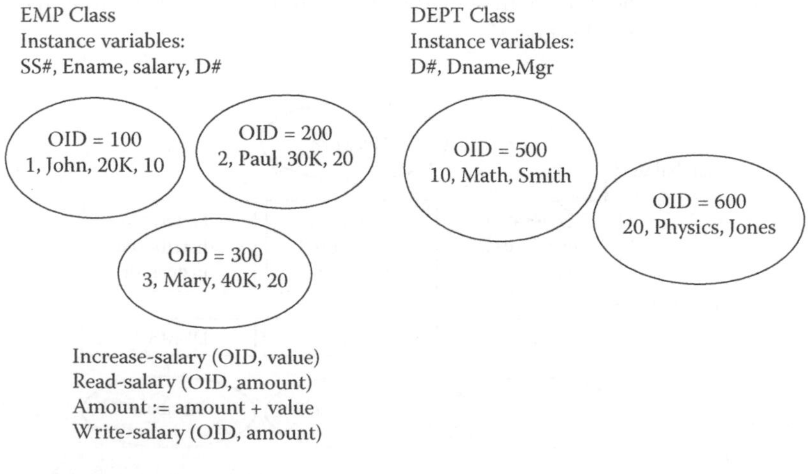

FIGURE B.21 Objects and classes.

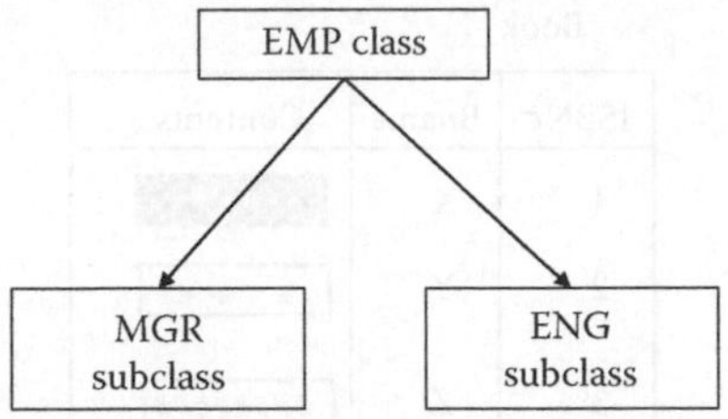

FIGURE B.22 Class/subclass hierarchy.

A key concept in object-oriented data modeling is encapsulation. That is, an object has well-defined interfaces. The state of an object can only be accessed through interface procedures called methods. For example, EMP may have a method called Increase-Salary. The code for Increase-Salary is illustrated in Figure B.22. A message, say Increase-Salary(1, 10K), may be sent to the object with object ID of 1. The object's current salary is read and updated by 10K.

A second key concept in an object model is inheritance where a subclass inherits properties from its parent class. This feature is illustrated in Figure B.22 where the EMP class has MGR (manager) and ENG (engineer) as its subclasses. Other key concepts in an object model include polymorphism and aggregation. These features are discussed in [BANE87]. Note that a second type of inheritance is when the instances of a class inherit the properties of the class.

A third concept is polymorphism. This is the situation where one can pass different types of arguments for the same function. For example, to calculate the area, one can pass a sphere or a cylinder object. Operators can be overloaded also. That is, the add operation can be used to add two integers or real numbers.

Another concept is the aggregate hierarchy also called the composite object or the is-part-of hierarchy. In this case an object has component objects. For example, a book object has component section objects. A section object has component paragraph objects. Aggregate hierarchy is illustrated in Figure B.23.

Objects also have relationships between them. For example, an employee object has an association with the department object which is the department he is working in. Also, the instance variables of an object could take integers, lists, arrays, or even other objects as values. Many of these concepts are discussed in the book by Cattell [CATT91]. Object Data Management Group has also proposed standards for object data models [ODMG93].

Relational database vendors are extending their system with support for objects. In one approach the relational model is extended with an object layer. The object layer manages objects while the relational database system manages the relations. Such systems are called extended relational database systems. In another approach, the relational model has objects as its elements. Such a model is called an object-relational data model and is illustrated in Figure B.24. A system based on the object-relational data model is called an object-relational database system.

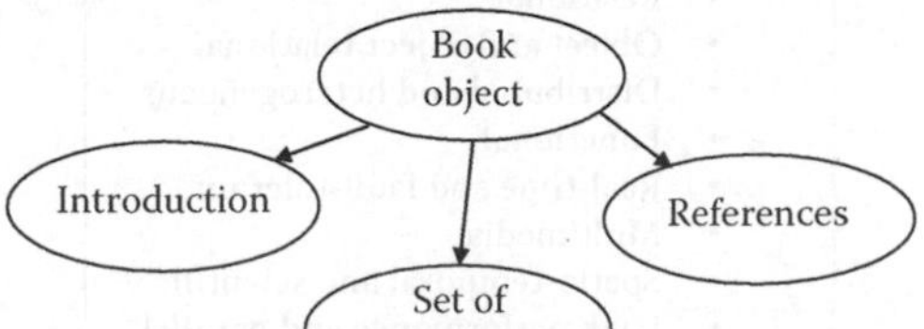

FIGURE B.23 Aggregate object.

Book

ISBN#	Bname	Contents
1	X	
2	Y	+ + + +
3	Z	########

FIGURE B.24 Object-relational data model.

B.10 OTHER DATABASE SYSYEMS

This section briefly discusses various other database systems as illustrated in Figure B.25. Some of the systems discussed in this book have evolved from such systems.

Real-time database systems: These are systems where the queries and transactions will have to meet timing constraints. Details are given in [RAMA93]. Some of our works on real-time stream-based analytics systems have evolved from real-time database systems.

Deductive database systems: These are systems that use logic as a data model. These are essentially logic programming systems that manage data. More details can be found in [FROS86] and [LLOY87]. Our work on inference control as well as cloud-based inference control has evolved from logic programming systems.

Multimedia database systems: These are database systems that manage multimedia data such as text, audio, video, and images. Details can be found in [PRAB97]. Some of our work on big data management such as managing massive amounts of data as well as social media systems has evolved from multimedia database systems.

Spatiotemporal Database Systems: For applications such as geospatial information systems and motion data management, one needs to model objects with spatial and temporal properties. Therefore, managing spatiotemporal data structures is important for such applications. Some of our work on stream data analytics as well as big data management has evolved from spatiotemporal database systems.

Parallel database systems: These systems use parallel processing techniques for executing queries and transactions so that the speed can be improved. More details can be found in [DEWI90]. Some of our work on cloud-query processing systems has evolved from parallel database systems.

Functional database systems: These systems were developed in the early 1980s. The database is viewed as a collection of functions and query evaluation amounts to function execution. Details can be found in [BUNE82]. Functional systems have impacted data warehousing systems due to the

Types of database systems:

- Network and hierarchical
- Relational
- Object and object relational
- Distributed and heterogeneous
- Functional
- Real-time and fault-tolerant
- Multimedia
- Spatio-temporal and scientific
- High performance and parallel

FIGURE B.25 Types of database systems.

OLAP (on-line analytical processing) models. OLAP models in turn have influenced data mining systems.

Data warehousing is one of the key data management technologies to support data mining and data analysis. As stated by Inmon [INMO93], data warehouses are subject oriented. Essentially data warehouses carry out analytical processing for decision-support functions of an enterprise. For example, while the data sources may have the raw data, the data warehouse may have correlated data, summary reports, and aggregate functions applied to the raw data. Big data analytics has evolved from such data warehouse systems.

We have discussed only a sample of the database systems that have been developed over the past 40 years. The challenge is to develop data models, query and transaction processing techniques as well as security and integrity for database systems that manage zettabyte- and exabyte-sized databases,

B.11 SUMMARY AND DIRECTIONS

This chapter has discussed various aspects of database systems and provided some background information to understand the various chapters in this book. We began with a discussion of various data models. We chose relational and entity-relationship models as they are more relevant to what we have addressed in this book. Then we provided an overview of various types of architectures for database systems. These include functional and schema architectures. Next we discussed database design aspects and database administration issues. We also provided an overview of the various functions of database systems. These include query processing, transaction management, storage management, metadata management, integrity, and fault tolerance. Next we discussed briefly distributed databases and interoperability. This was followed by a discussion of object models. Finally, we provided an overview of the various types of database systems that have been developed. Many of the chapters in this book have their roots in database management systems.

Various texts and articles have been published on database systems and we have referenced them throughout the book. There are also some major conferences on database systems and these include ACM SIGMOD conference series [SIGM], Very Large Database Conference series [VLDB], IEEE Data Engineering Conference series [DE], and the European Extended Database Technology Conference series [EDBT].

REFERENCES

[BANE87]. J. Banerjee et al. "A Data Model for Object-Oriented Applications," *ACM Transactions on Office Information Systems*, 5 (1), 3–26, 1987.

[BERN87]. P. Bernstein et al. *Concurrency Control and Recovery in Database Systems*. Addison-Wesley, MA, 1987.

[BUNE82]. P. Buneman et al. "An Implementation Technique for Database Query Languages," *ACM Transactions on Database Systems*, 7 (2), 1982, 164–180.

[CATT91]. R. Cattel, *Object Data Management Systems*. Addison-Wesley, MA, 1991.

[CERI84]. S. Ceri and G. Pelagatti, *Distributed Databases, Principles and Systems*. McGraw-Hill, NY, 1984.

[CHEN76]. P. Chen, "The Entity-relationship Model—Toward a Unified View of Data," *ACM Transactions on Database Systems*, 1 (1), 9–36, 1976.

[CODD70]. E.F. Codd, "A Relational Model of Data for Large Shared Data Banks," *Communications of the ACM*, 13 (6), 377–387, 1970.

[DATE90]. C. Date, *An Introduction to Database Systems*. Addison-Wesley, Reading, MA, 1990.

[DE]. *Proceedings of the IEEE Data Engineering Conference Series*, IEEE Computer Society Press, CA.

[DEWI90]. D.J. Dewitt et al. "The Gamma Database Machine Project," *IEEE Transactions on Knowledge and Data Engineering*, 2 (1), 44–62, 1990.

[DMH96]. B. Thuraisingham, editor. *Data Management Handbook Supplement*. Auerbach Publications, NY, 1996.

[DMH97]. B. Thuraisingham, editor. *Data Management Handbook*. Auerbach Publications, NY, 1997.

[DQ]. MIT Total Data Quality Management Program, http://web.mit.edu/tdqm/www/index.shtml

[EDBT]. *Proceedings of the Extended Database Technology Conference Series*, Springer Verlag, Heidelberg, Germany.

[ELMA85]. R. Elmasri et al. "The Category Concept: An Extension to the Entity-relationship Model," *Data and Knowledge Engineering Journal*, 1 (2), 75–116, 1985.

[FROS86]. R. Frost, *On Knowledge Base Management Systems*. Collins Publishers, UK, 1986.

[IEEE98]. *IEEE Data Engineering Bulletin*, 21 (2), 1998.

[INMO93]. W. Inmon, *Building the Data Warehouse*. John Wiley & Sons, NY, 1993.

[KDN]. Kdnuggets, www.kdn.com

[KORT86]. H. Korth, and A. Silberschatz, *Database System Concepts*. McGraw-Hill, NY, 1986.

[LLOY87]. J. Lloyd, *Foundations of Logic Programming*. Springer-Verlag, Heidelberg, Germany, 1987.

[MAIE83]. D. Maier, *Theory of Relational Databases*. Computer Science Press, MD, 1983.

[MASS]. IEEE Mass Storage Systems technical Committee, http://www.msstc.org/

[ODMG93]. Object Database Standard: ODMB 93, *Object Database Management Group*. Morgan Kaufmann, CA, 1993.

[PRAB97]. B. Prabhakaran, *Multimedia Database Systems*. Kluwer Publications, MA, 1997.

[RAMA93]. K. Ramaritham, "Real-Time Databases," *Journal of Distributed and Parallel Systems*, 1 (2), 199–226, 1993.

[SHET90]. A. Sheth and J. Larson, "Federated Database Systems for Managing Distributed, Heterogeneous, and Autonomous Databases," *ACM Computing Surveys*, 22 (3), 183–236, 1990.

[SIGM]. *Proceedings of the ACM Special Interest Group on Management of Data Conference Series*, ACM Press, New York, NY.

[SQL3]. SQL3, American National Standards Institute, Draft, 1992.

[THUR97]. B. Thuraisingham, *Data Management Systems Evolution and Interoperation*. CRC Press, FL, 1997.

[TSIC82]. D. Tsichritzis, and F. Lochovsky, *Data Models*. Prentice-Hall, NJ, 1982.

[ULLM88]. J. D. Ullman, *Principles of Database and Knowledge Base Management Systems*. Volumes I and II, Computer Science Press, MD 1988.

[VLDB]. *Proceedings of the Very Large Database Conference Series*, Morgan Kaufman, San Francisco, CA.

[WIED92]. G. Wiederhold, "Mediators in the Architecture of Future Information Systems," *IEEE Computer*, 25 (3), March 1992.

Index

G

H

J

K

L

M

N

T

X

Y

Z

T - #0199 - 071024 - C0 - 254/178/31 - PB - 9780367657420 - Gloss Lamination